GLENCOE
LATIN 3

# LATIN FOR AMERICANS

# LATIN FOR AMERICANS

B.L. Ullman
Albert I. Suskin

New York, New York   Columbus, Ohio   Chicago, Illinois   Peoria, Illinois   Woodland Hills, California

**Front cover:**
This photo shows Roman ruins at Volubilis, near Moulay Idriss, Morocco. The site includes a forum, a triumphal arch, a basilica, and many well-preserved mosaics. Volubilis flourished in the second and third centuries, developing a thriving trade in oil and corn.

The McGraw-Hill Companies



Send all inquiries to:
Glencoe/McGraw-Hill
8787 Orion Place
Columbus, OH 43240-4027

ISBN-13: 978-0-07-874255-2
ISBN-10: 0-07-874255-2

Printed in the United States of America.

1 2 3 4 5 6 7 8 9 027/055 12 11 10 09 08 07 06

# CONTENTS

## CICERO AGAINST CATILINE

## SALLUST'S CATILINE (SELECTIONS)

## CICERO FOR ARCHIAS (ENTIRE)

UNIT VI

## CICERO AGAINST VERRES AND ANTONY



UNIT VII

## CICERO'S LETTERS



UNIT VIII

## CICERO'S PHILOSOPHICAL WORKS

# TWO THOUSAND YEARS OF LATIN

UNIT X

# OVID

# INTRODUCTION

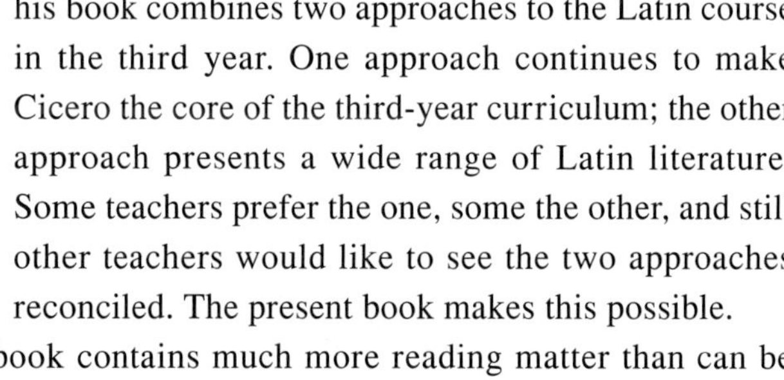

This book combines two approaches to the Latin course in the third year. One approach continues to make Cicero the core of the third-year curriculum; the other approach presents a wide range of Latin literature. Some teachers prefer the one, some the other, and still other teachers would like to see the two approaches reconciled. The present book makes this possible.

As a result, the book contains much more reading matter than can be completed in one year. Teachers will have to select what is most useful for a particular class. A survey of the contents unit by unit will be helpful for this purpose.

Unit I continues the lesson form of the Level 2 book in this series and is a review of second-year grammar and vocabulary. The stories are taken from Pliny because that author's simple style is familiar from the numerous selections in the Level 2 book and because his letters are interesting.

Unit II presents simple and interesting stories from Aulus Gellius. These may be omitted in whole or in part.

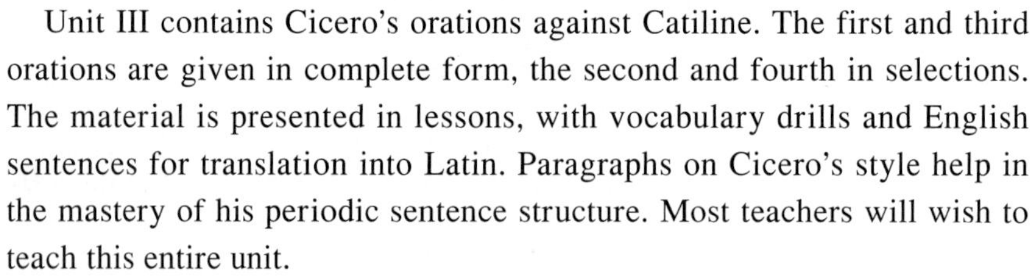

Unit III contains Cicero's orations against Catiline. The first and third orations are given in complete form, the second and fourth in selections. The material is presented in lessons, with vocabulary drills and English sentences for translation into Latin. Paragraphs on Cicero's style help in the mastery of his periodic sentence structure. Most teachers will wish to teach this entire unit.

Unit IV gives selections from Sallust's *Catiline* to supplement Cicero's version. The lesson form is kept. Some teachers may prefer to omit part of this unit.

Unit V consists of Cicero's speech for Archias. This is a universal favorite because of its praise of literature, and most teachers will wish to read it. But some chapters dealing with the technical matters of citizenship may well be omitted.

Unit VI, containing selections from the speeches against Verres, with which Cicero had his first great success, and Antony, the last of his orations, is optional. Parts may be read at sight.

Unit VII presents some of Cicero's letters. These may be read at sight. It is urged, however, that they not be omitted entirely; they are interesting and valuable for the light they throw on Cicero's personality.

Unit VIII contains selections from Cicero's philosophical works and, like Unit VI, is optional.

Unit IX, in its "Two Thousand Years of Latin," continues the popular unit of a similar name in the Level 2 book but gives a different selection from twenty-four authors. Rapid reading at sight is suggested for part of this unit.

Unit X has six stories from Ovid's *Metamorphoses* and is particularly useful in schools which do not offer a fourth year of Latin.

English sentences for translation into Latin are given in Units I–IV. This fact may cause teachers to decide to teach those units.

An attempt has been made to key the numerous illustrations to the text. They supplement the reading matter in giving a broad idea of the Roman civilization. Two special visual sections are in the text. One deals with the Forum Romanum, with photos and captions on surviving monuments that follow a path from the Arch of Titus up and onto the Capitoline Hill. The other section deals with photos of various manuscripts that show how Roman and Greek works were transmitted through the centuries up to the invention of printing. A list of these photos is found at the end of the Contents (p. IX).

Words translated in the footnotes do not appear in the end vocabulary.

The CD Audio Program for Levels 2 and 3 of ***Latin for Americans*** includes readings from various selections in the Level 3 book.

UNIT
I

# PLINY'S LETTERS

## Unit Objectives

- To read Pliny's essays and letters with understanding and appreciation
- To review impersonal verbs; indirect questions; descriptive relative clauses; future passive participle and gerund; personal pronouns; datives of reference and purpose; relative purpose clauses; **cum** clauses; genitive of description; ablative of respect; impersonal verbs; demonstrative pronouns; ablative absolute; genitive of the whole; dative with special verbs; noun clauses of result; clauses of fear; ablative of measure of difference; purpose clauses with **quō**; defective verbs and contracted verb forms; use of the reflexive pronoun; volitive noun clauses; ablative of comparison; indefinite pronouns; deponent verbs; locative case; relative purpose clauses; conditions; accusative of extent; ablative with **dignus**
- To review vocabulary from **Latin for Americans,** Level 2
- To recognize Latin root words and their English derivatives

Ronald Sheridan/Ancient Art & Architecture Collection

**In the Church of St. Mary in Cosmedin, not far from the Roman Forum and the Cloaca Maxima, is the Mouth of Truth, an ancient marble mask with a human face. Legend has it that anyone who put his hand in the mouth and swore falsely would be unable to pull his hand out.**

# PLINY'S LIFE

You may have read some of Pliny's letters in **Latin for Americans**, Level 2. You may even remember those about the eruption of Mt. Vesuvius. Pliny was born at Como, north of Milan, in A.D. 62. He was a successful lawyer and officeholder. After serving in various preliminary offices, he became consul in A.D. 100 during the reign of Nerva. He was later appointed governor of Bithynia, in Asia Minor. Among the following readings are some interesting letters he wrote to the emperor Trajan from Bithynia.

# APRIL SHOWERS BRING VERSE FLOWERS

[1] *crop* (literally, *coming forth*)
[2] *public places*
[3] *from time to time*
[4] *by Hercules*
[5] *they say*
[6] *all the idlest*
[7] *I have failed no one* (i.e., he attended everyone's readings)

Magnum prōventum[1] poētārum annus hic attulit. Tōtō mēnse Aprīlī nūllus ferē diēs quō nōn recitāret aliquis. Iuvat mē quod vigent studia, prōferunt sē ingenia hominum et ostentant, tametsī ad audiendum pigrē coitur.[1] Plērīque in statiōnibus[2] sedent tempusque audiendī fābulīs conterunt ac subinde[3] sibi nūntiārī iubent an iam recitātor intrāverit, an dīxerit praefātiōnem, an ex magnā parte ēvolverit librum. Tunc dēmum, ac tunc quoque lentē cūnctanterque veniunt; nec tamen permanent, sed ante fīnem recēdunt, aliī dissimulanter et fūrtim, aliī simpliciter et līberē. At hercule[4] memoriā parentum Claudium Caesarem[2] ferunt,[5] cum in Palātiō spatiārētur audīssetque clāmōrem, causam requīsīsse, cumque dictum esset recitāre Nōniānum, subitum recitantī vēnisse. Nunc ōtiōsissimus quisque,[6] multō ante rogātus et identidem admonitus, aut nōn venit aut, sī venit, queritur sē diem, quia nōn perdiderit, perdidisse. Sed tantō magis laudandī probandīque sunt quōs ā scrībendī recitandīque studiō haec audītōrum vel dēsidia vel superbia nōn retardat. Equidem prope nēminī dēfuī.[7] Erant sānē plērīque amīcī; neque enim est ferē quisquam quī studia, ut nōn simul et nōs amet.[3] Hīs ex causīs longius quam dēstināveram tempus in urbe cōnsūmpsī.[4] Possum iam repetere sēcessum et scrībere aliquid quod nōn recitem, nē videar, quōrum[5] recitātiōnibus adfuī, nōn audītor fuisse sed crēditor. Nam ut in cēterīs rēbus, ita in audiendī officiō perit grātia sī reposcātur. Valē. (I, 13)

---

[1] People do not want to go but feel they have to.
[2] Emperor Claudius, who ruled A.D. 41–54
[3] Supply **amet** with the **quī** clause.
[4] He went to his country home later than usual.
[5] The antecedent **eōrum** is understood.

**Questions**

1. What happened in the month of April?
2. What did Pliny do during his vacations?
3. What does one have to do to get people to attend a reading?
4. Why does Pliny criticize those who attend readings of poetry?

# GRAMMAR

## Form Review

1. Review **ferō**, including principal parts and meanings. Pay particular attention to the present tense, active and passive.
2. Review **eō**, including principal parts and meanings. Pay particular attention to the present and future tenses.
3. Review the formation and translation of deponent verbs. Remember that deponent verbs are passive in form but active in meaning.

## Syntax Review

1. Review impersonal verbs and the constructions of **licet** (*it is permitted; one may*). Remember that impersonal verbs are used only in the third person singular and the infinitive. (pp. 292, 308)
2. Review indirect questions. Remember that an indirect question is introduced by a main verb of asking, knowing, telling, or perceiving and includes an interrogative word such as *who, what,* or *where.* The subordinate verb is in the subjunctive. (p. 305)
3. Review descriptive relative clauses. Remember that a relative clause with the subjunctive may be used to describe an indefinite antecedent. This construction is especially common after **ūnus, sōlus, sunt quī** (*there are those who*), and **nēmō est quī** (*there is no one who*). (p. 304)
4. Review the gerund and gerundive. Remember that the gerund is a verbal noun and the gerundive is a verbal adjective. The gerundive is used to express obligation (what *must be* done) with a form of **sum.** The person who must do the obligation is in the dative. The gerundive may also simply modify a noun or pronoun. Finally, the gerund and gerundive may be used with **ad** + accusative or **causā** or **grātiā** + genitive to express purpose. (pp. 308–309)

### Translation

1. Ask him to what city he is going.
2. I shall complain because no one is bringing my books.
3. Those who come for the sake of hearing recitations should be praised.
4. People come *(use impersonal construction)* quickly for the sake of talking with friends.

## VOCABULARY

| | | | |
|---|---|---|---|
| **ingenium** | **aliquis** | **afferō** | **equidem** |
| **mēnsis** | **plērīque** | **dēsum** | **ferē** |
| | | **eō** | **fūrtim** |
| | | **ferō** | **identidem** |
| | | **iuvō** | **simul** |
| | | **perdō** | **tunc** |
| | | **queror** | |
| | | **requīrō** | |
| | | **sedeō** | |
| | | **volvō** | |

## WORD STUDY

From what Latin words are the following derived: **coeō, ostentō, prōventus, retardō, sēcessus, spatior, statiō?**

Explain *dissimulate, evolution, furtive, querulous, secession.*

# A PERFECT WIFE

Cum sīs pietātis exemplum frātremque optimum et amantissimum tuī[1] parī cāritāte dīlēxerīs fīliamque eius ut tuam dīligās nec tantum amitae[1] eī affectum vērum etiam patris āmissī repraesentēs, nōn dubitō maximō tibi gaudiō fore, cum cognōveris dignam patre,[2] dignam tē, dignam avō ēvādere.[2] Summum est acūmen, summa frūgālitās; amat mē. Accēdit hīs studium litterārum, quod ex meī[1] cāritāte concēpit. Meōs libellōs[3] habet, lēctitat, ēdiscit etiam. Quā illa sollicitūdine, cum videor āctūrus,[4] quantō, cum ēgī, gaudiō afficitur! Dispōnit[5] quī nūntient sibi quem assēnsum, quōs clāmōrēs excitārim, quem ēventum iūdicī tulerim. Eadem, sī quandō recitō, in proximō discrēta vēlō sedet laudēsque nostrās avidissimīs auribus excipit. Versūs quidem meōs cantat etiam fōrmatque[3] citharā, nōn artifice aliquō docente sed amōre, quī magister est optimus.

Hīs ex causīs in spem certissimam addūcor perpetuam nōbīs maiōremque in diēs futūram esse concordiam. Nōn enim aetātem meam aut corpus, quae paulātim occidunt ac senēscunt, sed glōriam dīligit. Nec aliud decet tuīs manibus ēducātam, tuīs praeceptīs īnstitūtam, quae nihil in contuberniō tuō vīderit nisi sānctum honestumque, quae dēnique amāre mē ex tuā praedicātiōne cōnsuēverit. Nam cum mātrem meam parentis locō verērēris, mē ā pueritiā statim fōrmāre, laudāre, tālemque quālis nunc uxōrī meae videor ōminārī solēbās. Certātim ergō tibi grātiās agimus, ego quod illam mihi, illa quod mē sibi dederīs, quasi in vīcem[4] ēlēgerīs. Valē. (IV, 19)

[1] *aunt*
[2] *worthy of her father*
[3] *sets to music and accompanies*
[4] *for each other*

**Questions**

1. What did Calpurnia do with Pliny's verses?
2. How did Calpurnia find out what success Pliny had had in court?
3. How does Pliny account for his wife's admirable qualities?
4. How did Calpurnia find out what sort of reception Pliny's readings had?

---

1 pronoun, not adjective
2 Supply **eam** as subject.
3 his speeches in court
4 Supply **causam:** *plead a case.*
5 Supply a word such as **hominēs.**

# GRAMMAR

### Form Review

Review personal pronouns including: **ego, nōs; tū, vōs;** and **is, ea, id.** Remember that with the ablative of accompaniment, the **cum** attaches directly to the ablative form **(mēcum,** etc.). (p. 299)

### Syntax Review

1. Review the datives of reference and purpose. Remember that the dative is sometimes used to express purpose (dative of purpose) or to show the person concerned or referred to (dative of reference). These two constructions are often used together as a double dative. (p. 296)
2. Review relative purpose clauses. Remember that **quī** may replace **ut** in a purpose clause if the antecedent is clear and definite. (p. 303)
3. Review **cum** clauses. Recall that in secondary sequence, **cum** translated as *when* is used only with the imperfect and pluperfect subjunctive. When **cum** means *since* or *although,* the verb in the subordinate clause can be in any tense of the subjunctive. (p. 304)

### Translation

1. She sends slaves to find out what I have said.
2. I must thank you because your words caused Calpurnia to love me.
3. Calpurnia sang Pliny's verses, although she never had a singing teacher.
4. It is an honor to you and to me that she likes my speeches and verses.

# VOCABULARY

| | | | |
|---|---|---|---|
| **auris** | **avidus** | **accēdō** | **paulātim** |
| **avus** | **dignus** | **concipiō** | **statim** |
| **cāritās** | **perpetuus** | **cōnsuēscō** | |
| **clāmor** | | **dubitō** | |
| **ēventus** | | **īnstituō** | |
| **gaudium** | | **occidō** | |
| **iūdicium** | | **soleō** | |
| | | **vereor** | |

# WORD STUDY

Review intensive prefixes in the Appendix. Give an example from the reading. Give an English derivative of **amita, cāritās, decet, dispōnō.**

# ORATORICAL TWINS

Librum tuum lēgī et, quam dīligentissimē potuī, adnotāvī quae commūtanda, quae eximenda arbitrārer. Nam et ego vērum dīcere assuēvī et tū libenter audīre. Neque enim ūllī patientius reprehenduntur quam quī maximē laudārī merentur. Nunc ā tē librum meum cum adnotātiōnibus tuīs exspectō. Ō iūcundās, ō pulchrās vicēs! Quam[1] mē dēlectat quod, sī qua posterīs cūra nostrī,[1] usquequāque nārrābitur quā concordiā, simplicitāte, fidē vīxerīmus! Erit rārum et īnsigne duōs hominēs aetāte, dignitāte propemodum aequālēs, nōn nūllīus in litterīs nōminis (cōgor enim dē tē quoque parcius dīcere, quia dē mē simul dīcō), alterum alterius studia fōvisse.

Equidem adulēscentulus, cum iam tū fāmā glōriāque flōrērēs, tē sequī "longō sed proximus intervāllō" et esse et haberī concupīscēbam. Et erant multa clārissima ingenia; sed tū mihi (ita similitūdō nātūrae ferēbat) maximē imitābilis, maximē imitandus vidēbāris. Quō magis gaudeō quod, sī quis dē studiīs sermō, ūnā nōmināmur, quod dē tē loquentibus statim occurrō. Nec dēsunt quī utrīque nostrum praeferantur. Sed nōs, nihil interest meā[2] quō locō, iungimur: nam mihi prīmus quī ā tē proximus. Quīn etiam in testāmentīs dēbēs adnotāsse: nisi quis forte alterutrī nostrum amīcissimus, eadem lēgāta et quidem pariter accipimus.

Quae omnia hūc spectant, ut in vicem ardentius dīligāmus, cum tot vinculīs nōs studia, mōrēs, fāma, suprēma dēnique hominum iūdicia cōnstringant. Valē. (VII, 20)

[1] *how*

[2] *it makes no difference to me* (the feminine ablative adjective is used with **interest**)

**Questions**

1. What had Pliny done for Tacitus?
2. What four things link Tacitus and Pliny?
3. What is Pliny expecting to get from Tacitus?

If you are interested in a career as an historian of Rome, you know the value of being able to read original Latin documents. Read and compare Tacitus and Caesar on the Germanic tribes. Use the library and Internet and correspond with or interview expert interpreters to research this topic for your history class. If you enjoy this process, contact organizations that hire Latinists for advice on education and employment.

---

[1] genitive plural of the pronoun

# GRAMMAR

### Form Review

Review the comparison of adjectives and adverbs. Remember that most superlatives are formed by adding **–issimus, –a, –um** to the base; but that some add **–rimus, –a, –um**; others, **–limus, –a, –um**; and some are quite irregular. There is a list of the irregular comparatives and superlatives in the Appendix.

### Syntax Review

1. Review the genitive of description. Remember that the descriptive genitive requires that an adjective be used. Generally, it is used to describe permanent qualities. (p. 294)
2. Review the ablative of respect. Remember that the ablative of respect tells in what respect a certain condition applies. There is no preposition. (p. 300)
3. Review descriptive relative clauses. These require using the subjunctive when the antecedent is negative or general. (p. 304)

### Translation

1. Pliny's friend was a man of great reputation.
2. Pliny was not inferior in oratory, but Tacitus also wrote histories.
3. A man who heard Pliny talk about his writings asked him whether he was Pliny or Tacitus.

# VOCABULARY

| **aetās** | **īnsignis** | **arbitror** | **iam** |
|---|---|---|---|
| **fidēs** | **iūcundus** | **flōreō** | **libenter** |
| **sermō** | **proximus** | **foveō** | **quīn etiam** |
| | **tot** | **gaudeō** | |
| **quis** | **ūllus** | **legō** | |
| | **uterque** | **loquor** | |
| | | **sequor** | |

# WORD STUDY

Review the diminutive suffix **–lus** and find an example in the reading.

Give an English derivative of each: **adnotō, cōnstringō, eximō, posterī, praeferō.**

Scala/Art Resource, NY

This aerial view of the Roman Forum is taken from the **Tabularium**, or Record Office. The three columns are the remains of the Temple of Castor and Pollux. The large area in front of that temple was the Basilica Julia. To the left of the three columns of Castor and Pollux is the small, round Temple of Vesta. The road leading toward the Temple of Vesta and passing by the single Column of Phocas is part of the Via Sacra. The Palatine Hill with its mansions serves as the backdrop to it all. In the distance is the Arch of Titus.

# WORKING HOURS IN VACATION

[1] *in my Tuscan (villa)*
[2] *terrace*
[3] *covered walk*
[4] *concentration*
[5] *nap*
[6] *musician* (nominative)
[7] *however long*
[8] *sometimes* (literally, *not never*)
[9] *(a thing) which*
[10] *tenant farmers*
[11] *literary activity*

Quaeris quem ad modum in Tuscīs[1] diem aestāte dispōnam. Ēvigilō cum libuit, plērumque circā hōram prīmam,$_{1}$ saepe ante, tardius rārō: clausae fenestrae manent. Mīrē enim silentiō et tenebrīs ab iīs$_{2}$ quae āvocant abductus et līber et mihi relīctus, nōn oculōs animō sed animum oculīs sequor, quī eadem quae mēns vident, quotiēns nōn vident alia. Cōgitō scrībentī ēmendantīque similis. Notārium vocō et, diē admissō, quae fōrmāveram dictō; abit rūrsusque revocātur rūrsusque dīmittitur. Ubi$_{3}$ hōra quārta vel quīnta (neque enim certum dīmēnsumque tempus), ut diēs suāsit, in xystum[2] mē vel cryptoporticum[3] cōnferō, reliqua meditor et dictō. Vehiculum ascendō. Ibi quoque idem$_{4}$ quod ambulāns aut iacēns.$_{4}$ Dūrat intentiō[4] mūtātiōne ipsā refecta. Paulum redormiō,[5] deinde ambulō, mox ōrātiōnem Graecam Latīnamve clārē et intentē, nōn tam vōcis causā quam stomachī, legō; pariter tamen et$_{5}$ illa firmātur. Iterum ambulō, ungor, exerceor,$_{6}$ lavor.$_{6}$ Cēnantī mihi, sī cum uxōre vel paucīs, liber legitur; post cēnam comoedus aut lyristēs.[6] Mox cum meīs$_{7}$ ambulō, quōrum in numerō sunt ērudītī. Ita variīs sermōnibus vespera extenditur, et quamquam[7] longissimus diēs citō conditur. Nōn numquam[8] ex hōc ōrdine aliqua mūtantur. Nam sī diū iacuī vel ambulāvī, post somnum dēmum lēctiōnemque nōn vehiculō sed (quod[9] brevius, quia vēlōcius) equō gestor. Interveniunt amīcī ex proximīs oppidīs partemque diēī ad sē trahunt interdumque lassō mihi opportūnā interpellātione subveniunt. Vēnor aliquandō, sed nōn sine pugillāribus, ut, quamvīs nihil cēperim,$_{8}$ nōn nihil referam. Datur et colōnīs,[10] ut vidētur ipsīs, nōn satis temporis, quōrum mihi agrestēs querēlae litterās[11] nostrās et haec urbāna opera commendant.$_{9}$ Valē. (IX, 36)

**Questions**

1. When does Pliny usually wake up?
2. What is the first thing he does?
3. What kind of exercise does Pliny take?
4. What does Pliny do before going to bed?

---

$_{1}$ i.e., after daybreak
$_{2}$ neuter antecedent of **quae**
$_{3}$ Supply **est.**
$_{4}$ Supply **faciō** in both places.
$_{5}$ for **etiam**
$_{6}$ used reflexively; the usage is called "middle voice"
$_{7}$ i.e., **amīcīs**
$_{8}$ **Quamvis** is used with the subjunctive.
$_{9}$ i.e., make them seem relatively more pleasant

## GRAMMAR

### Form Review

1. Review demonstrative pronouns. Remember that **hic** is translated as *this* or *the latter;* **ille** as *that* or *the former.* **Is** can be translated as *this, that,* or *he (she, it).* The demonstrative **idem** is best translated as *the same, also, likewise,* and the emphatics **ipse** by *–self, very* and **iste** by *that (of yours), such, this.* Pay particular attention to the irregular forms.
2. Review the forms and meanings of impersonal verbs, including **decet**, **libet**, **licet**, **miseret**, **oportet**, **piget**, **pudet**, and **taedet**. These occur only in the third person singular and with an infinitive. (pp. 292, 308)

### Syntax Review

1. Review the ablative absolute. Remember that the ablative absolute must be grammatically unconnected to the rest of the sentence. It exists in three combinations: noun + noun, noun + adjective, noun + participle. (p. 299)
2. Review the genitive of the whole. Also called the partitive genitive, it represents the whole to which a part belongs. The genitive of the whole is often used after such words as **nihil, satis,** and **quid;** the English word "of" is omitted. (p. 295)

### Translation

1. He decided to walk in the garden with his friends.
2. When the windows were opened, Pliny began to dictate.
3. He complained that too much time had to be given to his tenants.
4. Pliny lived in the mountains in the summer for the purpose of writing books.

## VOCABULARY

**causa**
**ōrdō**

**reliquus**

**ambulō**
**claudō**
**cōgitō**
**mē cōnferō**
**dormiō**
**iaceō**
**quaerō**
**suādeō**
**trahō**

**citō**
**iterum**
**plērumque**
**mox**
**quem ad modum**
**quotiēns**
**rūrsus**
**tamen**

## WORD STUDY

Review prefixes **dis–** and **ex–**, and explain the meaning of words in the reading that contains them.

Define *defenestration, quotient, ambulatory, mutation, dormitory.*

# FAME

Frequenter agentī$_{1}$ mihi ēvēnit ut centumvirī,$_{2}$ cum diū sē intrā iūdicum auctōritātem gravitātemque tenuissent, omnēs repente quasi victī coāctīque cōnsurgerent laudārentque; frequenter ē senātū fāmam, quālem maximē optāveram, rettulī. Numquam tamen maiōrem cēpī voluptātem quam nūper ex sermōne Cornēlī Tacitī. Nārrābat sēdisse sēcum Circēnsibus proximīs[1] equitem Rōmānum; hunc post variōs ērudītōsque sermōnēs requīsisse: "Ītalicus es an prōvinciālis?", sē respondisse: "nostī mē, et quidem ex studiīs." Ad hoc illum,$_{3}$ "Tacitus es an Plīnius?" Exprimere nōn possum quam sit iūcundum mihi quod nōmina nostra, quasi litterārum propria,[2] nōn hominum, litterīs redduntur, quod uterque nostrum hīs etiam ex studiīs nōtus quibus aliter ignōtus est.

[1] *the last Circus games*
[2] *the private property*
[3] *beyond*

Accidit aliud ante pauculōs diēs simile. Recumbēbat$_{4}$ mēcum vir ēgregius, Fabius Rūfīnus, super[3] eum mūniceps ipsīus, quī illō diē prīmum vēnerat in urbem; cui Rūfīnus, dēmōnstrāns mē, "vidēs hunc?" Multa deinde dē studiīs nostrīs. Et ille$_{5}$ "Plīnius est" inquit.

Vērum fatēbor, cupiō magnum labōris meī frūctum. An, sī Dēmosthenēs iūre laetātus est quod illum anus Attica ita nōscitāvit, ego celebritāte nōminis meī gaudēre nōn dēbeō? Ego vērō et gaudeō et gaudēre mē dīcō. Neque enim vereor nē iactantior videar, cum dē mē aliōrum iūdicium, nōn meum prōferō, praesertim apud tē, quī nec ūllīus invidēs laudibus et favēs nostrīs. Valē. (IX, 23)

**Questions**

1. What is the point of this letter?
2. What honor was shown Pliny in court?
3. What did Tacitus and the stranger talk about?

# GRAMMAR

## Form Review

Review **volō, nōlō,** and **mālō,** while paying particular attention to the present indicative and subjunctive. (pp. 291–292)

---

$_{1}$ Supply **causās.**
$_{2}$ a kind of supreme court, consisting originally of 100 men
$_{3}$ Supply **quaesīsse.**
$_{4}$ at the dinner table
$_{5}$ i.e., the man from out of town

## Syntax Review

1. Review the dative with special verbs. Remember that the dative is used with a few special verbs, including **cōnfīdō, crēdō, dēsum, faveō, ignōscō, imperō, invideō, minitor, noceō, parcō, pāreō, persuādeō, placeō, praestō, resistō, serviō,** and **studeō.** Some of these verbs become impersonal in the passive and the dative is retained. (p. 296)
2. Review noun clauses of result. Remember that after **accido** (*to happen*) and **efficio** (*to cause or effect*) you use **ut** (or **ut nōn**) plus the subjunctive to express a result clause. (p. 304)
3. Review the subjunctive after verbs of fearing. Remember that a verb of fearing is followed by a clause in the subjunctive introduced by **nē** if it is positive and **ut** if it is negative. (p. 304)
4. Review **cum** clauses and the various meanings of **cum**. (pp. 304–305)

## Translation

1. Do you think that Pliny envied Tacitus?
2. Pliny feared that he might not be recognized.
3. Pliny persuaded Tacitus to tell what the Roman knight had said.
4. It happened that all praised Pliny when he finished his speech.

## VOCABULARY

| | | | |
|---|---|---|---|
| **frūctus** | **ēveniō** | **diū** | **apud** |
| **gravitās** | **faveō** | **frequenter** | **intrā** |
| **voluptās** | **invideō** | **numquam** | |
| | **nārrō** | **praesertim** | |
| **proprius** | **reddō** | **quasi** | |
| **quidem** | **respondeō** | **repente** | |
| | **surgō** | | |

## WORD STUDY

Give an English derivative of each of the following: **ērudītus, exprimō, faveō, invideō, recumbō.**

Review the prefixes **ad–, con–, in–, re–** in the Appendix, and find three examples of each in the readings you have encountered thus far. Note the assimilated forms of each.

# PLINY'S KINDNESS TO A SERVANT

Videō quam molliter tuōs habeās;[1] quō[2] simplicius tibi cōnfitēbor quā indulgentiā meōs trāctem. Est mihi semper in animō hoc nostrum[3] "pater familiae." Quod sī essem nātūrā asperior et dūrior, frangeret mē tamen īnfirmitās lībertī meī Zōsimī, cui tantō[4] maior hūmanitās exhibenda est, quantō[4] nunc illā magis eget. Homō probus, officiōsus, litterātus; et ars quidem eius et quasi īnscrīptio[5] comoedus, in quā plūrimum facit. Nam prōnūntiat ācriter, sapienter, aptē, decenter etiam. Īdem tam commodē ōrātiōnēs et historiās et carmina legit ut hoc sōlum didicisse videātur.

Haec tibi sēdulō exposuī quō magis scīrēs quam multa ūnus mihi et quam iūcunda ministeria praestāret. Accēdit longa iam cāritās hominis, quam ipsa perīcula auxērunt. Ante aliquot annōs, dum intentē īnstanterque prōnūntiat, sanguinem reiēcit,$_1$ atque ob hoc in Aegyptum missus ā mē, post longum peregrīnātiōnem cōnfirmātus rediit nūper. Deinde dum per continuōs diēs nimis imperat[6] vōcī, veteris īnfirmitātis tussiculā[7] admonitus, rūrsus sanguinem reddidit. Quā ex causā dēstināvī eum mittere in praedia tua quae Forō Iūlī possidēs. Audīvī enim tē saepe referentem esse ibi et āera salūbrem et lac eius modī cūrātiōnibus accommodātissimum. Rogō ergō scrībās$_2$ tuīs[8] ut illī vīlla, ut domus pateat, offerant$_3$ etiam sūmptibus[9] eius sī quid opus erit; erit autem opus modicō. Est enim tam parcus et continēns ut nōn sōlum dēliciās vērum etiam necessitātēs valētūdinis frūgālitāte restringat. Ego proficīscentī$_4$ tantum viāticī dabō quantum sufficiat euntī in tua. Valē. (V, 19)

[1] *you treat your (servants)*
[2] *therefore* (literally, *by which the more frankly)*
[3] *this (phrase of) ours*
[4] *all the more* (literally, *by so much by which)*
[5] *his occupation* (literally, *his label, so to speak)*
[6] *put too much strain on*
[7] *a slight cough*
[8] i.e., *servants*
[9] *at his expense*

**Questions**

1. About whom is Pliny writing?
2. What does he ask his friend to do?
3. What duties does Zosimus perform in Pliny's home?
4. To what country had Pliny previously sent Zosimus? Why?

---

$_1$ He had tuberculosis.
$_2$ **ut** is generally used
$_3$ Supply the subject from **tuīs**; the object is the **sī** clause (*whatever;* literally, *if anything*).
$_4$ modifies **eī**, to be supplied

Scala/Art Resource, NY

**Built in A.D. 81, the Arch of Titus is a fairly simple triumphal arch with just a single archway. It was erected after his death to commemorate the conquest of Jerusalem. The inside contains two well-preserved and well-known reliefs, one of the emperor on his triumphal chariot and the other a procession of Roman soldiers carrying away the sacred furnishings of the Temple of Jerusalem during the siege of Jerusalem in A.D. 70.**

## GRAMMAR

### Form Review

Review irregular adjectives and numerals. Remember that **alius, alter, ūllus, nūllus, sōlus, tōtus, neuter,** and **uterque** are declined like **ūnus.** The plurals are regular. **Ambō** is declined like **duo.** (pp. 275–277)

### Syntax Review

1. Review the ablative of degree of difference. Remember that the ablative without a preposition is used to express the degree or measure of difference. (p. 300)
2. Review purpose clauses with **quō.** Remember that if the purpose clause contains an adjective or adverb in the comparative degree, **quō** generally replaces **ut.** (p. 303)

### Translation

1. My friend is a foot taller than I.
2. Pliny gave him as much money as sufficed for the journey.
3. I fear that the man is very ill and may not be well again.
4. He walked to the top of the hill so that he might see better.

## VOCABULARY

**carmen**
**hūmānitās**
**lībertus**
**valētūdō**

**asper**
**dūrus**
**parcus**
**vetus**

**admoneō**
**augeō**
**discō**
**expōnō**
**pateō**
**praestō**
**proficīscor**
**redeō**
**sciō**

**aptē**
**nimis**
**semper**

## WORD STUDY

Give English derivatives of the following: **asper, comoedus, discō, lac, mollis, possideō, probus, salūbris, sanguis, sēdulus.**

In the reading, find one word with suffix **–tia,** five words with suffix **–tās,** and three words with suffix **–tiō.**

# THREE STRIKES AND OUT FOR REGULUS

Assem parā[1] et accipe auream fābulam, fābulās immō. Verānia, Pīsōnis uxor, graviter iacēbat,[2] huius dīcō Pīsōnis quem Galba adoptāvit. Ad hanc Rēgulus vēnit. Prīmum impudentiam hominis quī vēnerit ad aegram, cuius marītō inimīcissimus, ipsī invīsissimus fuerat! Estō,[3] sī vēnit tantum;[4] at ille etiam proximus torō sēdit, quō diē, quā hōrā nāta esset interrogāvit.[1] Ubi audiit, compōnit vultum,[5] intendit oculōs, movet labra, agitat digitōs,[2] computat; nihil. Ut diū miseram exspectātiōne suspendit, "habēs," inquit, "clīmactēricum[6] tempus, sed ēvādēs. Quod ut tibi magis liqueat,[7] haruspicem cōnsulam quem sum frequenter expertus." Nec mora; sacrificium facit, affirmat exta[8] cum sīderum significātiōne congruere. Illa, ut in perīculō crēdula, poscit codicillōs, lēgātum Rēgulō scrībit. Mox ingravēscit, clāmat moriēns hominem nēquam,[9] perfidum, ac plūs etiam quam periūrum, quī sibi per salūtem fīliī peierāsset. Facit hoc Rēgulus nōn minus scelerātē quam frequenter, quod īram deōrum, quōs ipse cotīdiē fallit, in caput īnfēlīcis puerī dētestātur.

Velleius Blaesus, ille locuplēs cōnsulāris, novissimā[10] valētūdine cōnflīctābātur; cupiēbat mutāre testāmentum. Rēgulus, quī spērāret aliquid ex novīs tabulīs, quia nūper captāre[3] eum coeperat, medicōs hortārī, rogāre quōquō modō spīritum hominī prōrogārent. Postquam signātum est testāmentum, mūtat persōnam, vertit allocūtiōnem, īsdem medicīs,[4] "quō usque miserum cruciātis?" Moritur Blaesus, et tamquam omnia audīsset, Rēgulō nē tantulum[11] quidem.

Sufficiunt duae fābulae, an scholasticā lēge tertiam poscis? Est unde fīat. Aurēlia, ōrnāta fēmina, signātūra testāmentum sūmpserat pulcherrimās tunicās. Rēgulus cum vēnisset ad signandum, "rogō," inquit, "hās mihi lēgēs." Aurēlia lūdere hominem putābat, ille sēriō īnstābat. Nē multa,[12] coēgit mulierem aperīre tabulās ac sibi tunicās lēgāre. Observāvit scrībentem, īnspexit an scrīpsisset. Et Aurēlia quidem vīvit, ille tamen istud tamquam moritūram coēgit. (II, 20, 1–11)

[1] *get your penny ready*
[2] *lay seriously (ill)*
[3] *so be it, okay*
[4] *merely*
[5] *put on a (thoughtful) expression*
[6] *dangerous*
[7] *be clear*
[8] *entrails*
[9] *worthless* (indeclinable)
[10] *last illness*
[11] *a tiny bit*
[12] *not (to say) much, to cut the story short*

---

[1] for the purpose of making her horoscope
[2] The Romans used their fingers in a complicated system of counting.
[3] i.e., he was "buttering him up" to get something out of him
[4] Supply **inquit.**

**Questions**

1. How did Aurelia outwit Regulus?
2. Why was Verania angry with Regulus?
3. What did Velleius leave Regulus in his will?
4. What sort of questions did Regulus ask Verania?

# GRAMMAR

## Form Review

1. Review the conjugation of **fīō,** paying particular attention to the present tense. (p. 292)
2. Review defective verbs and contracted verb forms. Remember that **coepī** is used only in the perfect tenses; likewise, **meminī** and **ōdī,** although they have a present meaning. The verbs **inquam** and **aiō** are lacking several persons. Verbs whose perfect stems end in **–āv–, –ēv–,** or **–īv–** may be contracted, depending on the consonant that follows. (p. 292)

## Syntax Review

1. Review the use of the reflexive pronoun. Remember that reflexive pronouns have no nominative. Personal pronouns are used for the first and second persons; **suī** for the third person. (p. 278)
2. Review volitive noun clauses (indirect command). Remember that these are introduced by a verb such as **hortor, imperō, moneō, persuādeō, petō,** and **rogō,** plus **ut** (or **ne**) and the subjunctive. (pp. 303–304)
3. Review, if needed, descriptive relative clauses. (p. 304)

## Translation

1. Will Regulus become the heir of many Romans?
2. Regulus asked that the tunics be given to him.
3. Aurelia began to ask herself why Regulus wished the will to be opened.
4. Sacrifice is being made by Regulus in order to find out what the gods desire.

## VOCABULARY

**diēs**
**mora**

**aeger**
**aureus**
**īnfēlīx**

**aperiō**
**coepī**
**cōgō**
**experior**
**hortor**
**īnstō**
**morior**
**mūtō**
**nāscor**
**poscō**
**sūmō**
**vertō**

**nūper**
**tamquam**

**quia**

## WORD STUDY

Give English derivatives of the following words: **computō, congruō, digitus, oculus, sīdus, suspendō.**

# A HOME BY THE SEASIDE

Mīrāris cūr mē Laurentīnum[1] meum tantō opere dēlectet; dēsinēs mīrārī, cum cognōveris grātiam vīllae, opportūnitātem locī, lītoris spatium.

Decem septem mīlibus passuum ab urbe sēcessit, ut, perāctīs[2] quae agenda fuerint, salvō iam et compositō diē,[3] possīs ibi manēre. Aditur nōn ūnā viā; nam et Laurentīna et Ōstiēnsis eōdem ferunt, sed Laurentīna ā quārtō decimō lapide,[1] Ōstiēnsis ab ūndecimō relinquenda est. Utrimque excipit iter aliquā ex parte arēnōsum, iūnctīs[4] paulō gravius et longius, equo breve et molle. Varia hinc atque inde faciēs; nam modo occurrentibus silvīs via coartātur, modo lātissimīs prātīs diffunditur et patēscit; multī gregēs ovium, multa ibi equōrum, boum armenta, quae montibus hieme dēpulsa herbīs et tepōre vernō nitēscunt. Vīlla ūsibus capāx,[2] nōn sūmptuōsā tutēlā.[3] Cuius in prīmā parte ātrium frūgī[4] nec tamen sordidum, deinde porticūs in D litterae similitūdinem circumāctae, quibus parvula sed fēstīva ārea inclūditur. Ēgregium hae adversus tempestātēs receptāculum:

[1] *milestone*
[2] *big (enough) for one's needs*
[3] *upkeep not expensive*
[4] *modest* (indeclinable adjective)

---

1 villa at Laurentum
2 Supply the subject of the ablative absolute from **quae.**
3 i.e., at the end of the business day
4 i.e., a carriage with a team of horses; **equō** refers to riding on horseback

[5] = **ātrium**
[6] *African (wind)*
[7] *the last* (i.e., *ends*) *of the waves*
[8] *curve, apse,* i.e., a bay window
[9] *cold baths*
[10] *massage room and furnace*
[11] *swimming pool*
[12] *ball ground*

nam speculāribus ac multō magis imminentibus tēctīs mūniuntur. Est contrā mediās cavaedium[5] hilare, mox trīclīnium satis pulchrum, quod in lītus excurrit, ac sī quandō Āfricō[6] mare impulsum est, frāctīs iam et novissimīs[7] flūctibus leviter adluitur. Undique valvās aut fenestrās nōn minōrēs valvīs habet, atque ita ā lateribus, ā fronte quasi tria maria prōspectat.

Annectitur angulō cubiculum in apsida[8] curvātum, quod ambitum sōlis fenestrīs omnibus sequitur. Parietī eius in bibliothēcae speciem armārium īnsertum est, quod nōn legendōs librōs sed lēctitandōs capit. Adhaeret dormītōrium membrum, trānsitū interiacente, quī suspēnsus[5] et tubulātus conceptum vapōrem salūbrī temperāmentō hūc illūc dīgerit et ministrat.

Inde balneī cella frīgidāria spatiōsa et effūsa, cuius in contrāriīs parietibus duo baptistēria[9] abundē capācia, sī mare in proximō cōgitēs. Adiacet ūnctōrium,[10] hypocauston;[10] cohaeret calida piscīna[11] mīrifica, ex quā natantēs mare aspiciunt. Nec procul sphaeristērium,[12] quod calidissimō sōlī, inclīnātō iam diē, occurrit.

Iustīsne dē causīs iam tibi videor incolere, inhabitāre, dīligere sēcessum, quem tū nimis urbānus es nisi concupīscis? Atque utinam concupīscās! Ut tot tantīsque dōtibus vīllulae nostrae maxima commendātiō ex tuō contuberniō accēdat. Valē. (II, 17, 1–5, 8–9, 11–12, 29)

**Questions**

1. How far was Pliny's country place from Rome?
2. In what direction did one get a view of the sea?
3. What provisions were made for getting exercise?
4. Name three things that make it seem like a modern house.

# GRAMMAR

## Form Review

Review **possum,** paying particular attention to the present tense and the use of **–s** or **–t** in the stem. (p. 289)

---

[5] i.e., it had a double floor with pipes distributing heat

### Syntax Review

1. Review the ablative of comparison. Remember that you must omit **quam** if you use the ablative after the comparative. (p. 298)
2. Review the ablative absolute construction and methods of translating it. (p. 299)
3. Review the gerundive and gerund uses. (pp. 308–309)

### Translation

1. The facilities for swimming were excellent.
2. The chances of seeing friends were numerous.
3. In order to be able to reach Rome quickly, we had to go on horse(back).
4. After leaving Rome, Pliny proceeded on a road narrower than the Appian Way to reach his villa.

## VOCABULARY

| | | | |
|---|---|---|---|
| **bōs** | **calidus** | **adhaereō** | **hūc** |
| **faciēs** | **ēgregius** | **cognōscō** | |
| **flūctus** | **lātus** | **frangō** | |
| **hiems** | | **iungō** | |
| **lītus** | | **mīror** | |
| **passus** | | **mūniō** | |
| **tēctum** | | **occurrō** | |
| **tempestās** | | **pellō** | |

## WORD STUDY

Review suffixes **–āx, –ium, –lus, –ōsus, –tūdō** and find examples of their use in the reading.

Give an English derivative of each of the following words and show its connection in meaning with the Latin word: **bōs, capāx, flūctus, grex, hilaris, lītus, sordidus, tutēla, valva, vernus.**

# OVER SEA AND OVER LAND

Sīcut salūberrimam nāvigātiōnem, domine,[1] usque Ephesum expertus, ita inde, postquam vehiculīs iter facere coepī, gravissimīs aestibus atque etiam febriculīs vexātus Pergamī substitī. Rūrsus, cum trānsīssem in ōrāriās nāviculās, contrāriīs ventīs retentus aliquantō tardius quam spērāveram, id est XV Kal. Octōbrēs,[1] Bithyniam intrāvī. Nōn possum tamen dē morā querī, cum mihi contigerit, quod erat auspicātissimum, nātālem tuum in prōvinciā celebrāre.

Nunc reī pūblicae Prūsēnsium impendia, reditūs, dēbitōrēs excutiō; quod ex ipsō trāctātū magis ac magis necessārium intellegō.[2] Multae enim pecūniae variīs ex causīs ā prīvātīs dētinentur; praetereā quaedam minimē lēgitimīs sūmptibus ērogantur.[2] Haec tibi, domine, in ipsō ingressū meō scrīpsī.

Dispice, domine an necessārium putēs mittere hūc mēnsōrem.[3] Videntur enim nōn mediocrēs pecūniae posse revocārī ā cūrātōribus operum, sī mēnsūrae fidēliter agantur.[4] Ita certē prōspiciō ex ratiōne Prūsēnsium, quam cum maximē[5] trāctō. (X, 17)

---

Cuperem[6] sine querēlā corpusculī tuī et tuōrum pervenīre in Bithyniam potuissēs ac simile tibi iter ab Ephesō ut[7] nāvigātiōnī fuisset, quam expertus usque illō[8] erās. Quō autem diē pervēnissēs in Bithyniam cognōvī, Secunde[3] cārissime, litterīs tuīs. Prōvinciālēs, crēdō, prōspectum[4] sibi ā mē intellegent. Nam et tū dabis operam[9] ut manifēstum sit illīs[5] ēlēctum tē esse quī ad eōsdem meī locō mitterēris. Ratiōnēs autem in prīmīs tibi rērum pūblicārum excutiendae sunt; nam et esse eās vexātās satis cōnstat.

Mēnsōrēs vix etiam iīs operibus quae aut Rōmae aut in proximō fīunt sufficientēs habeō; sed in omnī prōvinciā inveniuntur quibus crēdī possit, et ideō nōn deerunt tibi, modo[10] velīs dīligenter excutere. (X, 18)

[1] *Master, Sir,* i.e., Trajan
[2] *are being paid out*
[3] *architect*
[4] *if they should be made*
[5] **cum maximē = nunc**
[6] *I could wish . . . that you might have been able*
[7] *as*
[8] *there* (adverb)
[9] *see to it*
[10] *provided that*

**Questions**

1. About when was Trajan's birthday?
2. What made the land journey in Asia difficult?
3. What request did Trajan turn down?
4. What was the first job that Pliny undertook in the province of Bithynia?

---

[1] September 17
[2] He is doing an audit of the books of the city of Prusa.
[3] Pliny's cognomen
[4] Supply **esse:** *that I have looked out for them.*
[5] with **manifēstum**

Scala/Art Resource, NY

The Basilica of Maxentius is also called the Basilica of Constantine. It was begun by the former but completed by the latter. Immense in size, it is one of the last monuments built in the memory and style of ancient Rome during the early fourth century. Its enormous vaults and arches set it apart from most other monuments. After Diocletian split the empire into two, Maxentius ruled in the west, but he was ultimately defeated by Constantine, the first Christian emperor. It is said that the Basilica of Maxentius served as the inspiration for the new St. Peter's Basilica in Rome, built in the sixteenth century.

# GRAMMAR

## Form Review

Review indefinite pronouns. Remember that the pronoun forms are **aliquis, –quid**, whereas the adjective is **aliquī, –qua, –quod;** similarly the pronoun is **quīdam, quaedam, quiddam** and the adjective has **quoddam** for **quiddam;** the pronoun **quisque, quidque** has as an adjective **quisque, quaeque, quodque.** (pp. 279–280)

## Syntax Review

1. Review the locative case. Remember that the locative is used with the names of cities, towns, small islands, **domus, humus,** and **rūs.** Otherwise, use the ablative of place where. (p. 301)
2. Study and review relative purpose clauses. A relative clause with the subjunctive, you will recall, can be used to express purpose if the antecedent is definite. (p. 303)

### Conditions

A condition consists of two clauses: a subordinate clause (the condition) introduced by **si, nisi,** or **si nōn,** and a principal clause (the conclusion). There are three main types of conditions.

A *simple* condition, or condition of fact, can have any combination of tenses, as in English.

| | |
|---|---|
| **Sī loquitur, audiō.** | *If he speaks, I listen.* |

A *contrary-to-fact* condition can have three different tense sequences.

| | |
|---|---|
| **Sī loquerētur, audīrem.** | *If he were speaking (but he isn't), I would listen.* |
| **Sī locūtus esset, audīvissem.** | *If he had spoken (but he didn't), I would have listened (then).* |
| **Sī locūtus esset, audīrem.** (mixed condition) | *If he had spoken (but he didn't), I should listen.* |

Note that in the first example, the *present* condition, the imperfect subjunctive is used in both clauses. In the second example, a *past* condition, the pluperfect subjunctive is used in both clauses. In the third example, the *mixed* condition, the condition is past but the conclusion is present.

A *future-less-vivid* (should/would) condition uses the present subjunctive in both clauses.

| | |
|---|---|
| **Sī loquātur, audiam.** | *If he should speak, I would listen.* |

### Translation

1. He stopped at Pergamum on account of the heat.
2. Trajan sent Pliny to Bithynia to examine the accounts of the cities.
3. The people of Prusa had paid too much money for their buildings.
4. If they had been more careful they would now have more money.

## VOCABULARY

| | | | |
|---|---|---|---|
| **aestus** | **contrārius** | **cōnstat** | **dīligenter** |
| **opus** | **gravis** | **contingō** | **inde** |
| **ratiō** | **mediocris** | **cupiō** | **praettereā** |
| **vehiculum** | **varius** | **dētineō** | **sīcut** |
| | | **intrō** | **usque** |
| | | **trānseō** | |
| | | **vexō** | |

## WORD STUDY

From what Latin words are the following derived: **contingō, contrārius, cūrātor, lēgitimus, mediocris, nāvicula, reditus**?

# MORE CARELESSNESS AND WASTE IN BUILDING

Theātrum, domine, Nicaeae maximā iam parte cōnstrūctum, imperfectum tamen, sēstertium,[1] ut audiō (neque enim ratiō excussa est), amplius centiēns[1] hausit; vereor nē frūstrā. Ingentibus enim rīmīs[2] dēsēdit et hiat, sīve in causā solum$_1$ ūmidum et molle, sīve lapis ipse gracilis et putris.[3] Dignum est certē dēlīberātiōne sitne faciendum an sit relinquendum an etiam dēstruendum. Nam fultūrae[4] ac substrūctiōnēs quibus subinde[5] suscipitur nōn tam firmae mihi quam sūmptuōsae videntur.

Huic theātrō ex prīvātōrum pollicitātiōnibus[6] multa dēbentur, ut basilicae circā, ut porticūs suprā caveam. Quae nunc omnia differuntur, cessante eō quod ante peragendum est.

Iīdem Nicaeēnsēs gymnasium incendiō āmissum ante adventum meum restituere coepērunt, longē numerōsius[7] laxiusque quam fuerat, et iam aliquantum$_2$ ērogāvērunt; perīculum est nē parum ūtiliter; incompositum[8] enim et sparsum est. Praettereā architectus, sānē aemulus eius ā quō opus inchoātum est, affirmat parietēs, quamquam vīgintī et duōs pedēs lātōs, imposita onera sustinēre nōn posse. Cōgor petere ā tē mittās architectum dispectūrum[9] utrum sit ūtilius post sūmptum quī factus est quōquō modō cōnsummāre opus. (X, 39, 1–4, 6)

---

Quid oporteat fierī circā[10] theātrum quod inchoātum apud Nicaeēnsēs est in rē praesentī optimē dēlīberābis et cōnstituēs. Mihi sufficiet indicārī cui sententiae accesserīs. Tunc autem ā prīvātīs exigī opera tibi cūrae sit cum theātrum, propter quod illa prōmissa sunt, factum erit.

Gymnasiīs indulgent Graeculī;$_3$ ideō forsitan Nicaeēnsēs maiōre animō cōnstrūctiōnem eius aggressī sunt. Sed oportet illōs eō contentōs esse quod possit illīs sufficere. Architectī tibi deesse nōn possunt. Nūlla prōvincia est quae nōn perītōs et ingeniōsōs hominēs habeat. (X, 40)

[1] *with* **centiēns:** *more than ten million sesterces;* literally, *one hundred times (100,000) sesterces*
[2] *cracks*
[3] *rotten*
[4] *supports*
[5] *here and there*
[6] *promises*
[7] *larger*
[8] *irregular and sprawling*
[9] *to see*
[10] *about, with reference to*

### Questions

1. What was the matter with the unfinished theater at Nicaea?
2. What was the matter with the gymnasium that had been begun?
3. What did Pliny want Trajan to do about these two projects?
4. What did Trajan tell Pliny to do about the projects at Nicaea?

---

$_1$ noun
$_2$ Supply **pecūniae.**
$_3$ The diminutive is contemptuous.

## GRAMMAR

### Form Review

Review infinitives. Remember that most verbs have six infinitives: present active and passive, perfect active and passive, and future active and passive. (pp. 309–310)

### Syntax Review

1. Review the accusative of extent. Remember that extent of time or space is expressed by the accusative without a preposition. (p. 297)
2. Review the ablative with **dignus**. Remember that both **dignus** *(worthy)* and **indignus** *(unworthy)* are followed by the ablative. (p. 300)

## VOCABULARY

| | | |
|---|---|---|
| **adventus** | **aggredior** | **enim** |
| **incendium** | **differō** | **frūstrā** |
| **lapis** | **exigō** | |
| **onus** | **hauriō** | **sīve** |
| | **oportet** | |
| **ingēns** | **restituō** | |
| **mollis** | **spargō** | |
| **perītus** | **sufficiō** | |
| | **suscipiō** | |
| | **sustineō** | |

## WORD STUDY

From what Latin words are the following derived: **cessō, imperfectus, restituō, suscipiō**?

Give English derivatives of the following: **aemulus, cōnsummō, dēstruō, frūstrā, hauriō, hiō, incendium, inchoō, spargō.**

**Excutiō** literally means *to shake out.* So *discuss* means *to shake apart* the arguments. A *concussion* is a *shaking up. Percussion* instruments are played by being *shaken thoroughly* or *struck.* What is *repercussion?*

Now that you have gained experience in translating and familiarity with Pliny's writing style, the next ten reading selections are presented with footnotes as your primary support. You might find it helpful to review the **Verba Ūtilia** before you begin each piece.

# HUNTING WITH A NOTEBOOK

**Verba Ūtilia:** contemnō, genus, licet, omnīnō, quiēs, rīdeō

Rīdēbis, et licet rīdeās. Ego ille quem nōstī[1] aprōs trēs et quidem pulcherrimōs cēpī. "Ipse?"[2] inquis. Ipse;[2] nōn tamen ut[3] omnīnō ab inertiā meā et quiēte discēderem. Ad rētia sedēbam: erat in proximō nōn vēnābulum[4] aut lancea, sed stilus et pugillārēs; meditābar[5] aliquid ēnotābamque, ut, sī manūs vacuās, plēnās tamen cērās[6] reportārem. Nōn est quod[7] contemnās hoc studiendī genus. Mīrum est ut[8] animus agitātiōne mōtūque corporis excitētur. Iam undique silvae et sōlitūdō ipsumque illud silentium quod vēnātiōnī datur magna cōgitātiōnis incitāmenta sunt. Proinde cum vēnābere, licēbit, auctōre[9] mē, ut[10] pānārium[11] et laguncular,[11] sīc[10] etiam pugillārēs ferās. Experiēris nōn Diānam magis montibus quam Minervam inerrāre. Valē. (I, 6)

[1] = **nōvisti**
[2] *(you) yourself,* followed by *(I) myself*
[3] *(with the result) that*
[4] *hunting spear*
[5] *I was composing* (either a poem or, less likely, a speech)
[6] *notebooks*
[7] *there is no reason why*
[8] *how*
[9] *on my authority*
[10] *as . . . so, i.e., not only . . . but also*
[11] *lunch basket and bottle of wine*

# BUYING A HOME IN THE COUNTRY

**Verba Ūtilia:** dēlecto, emō, magis, pretium, sollicitō

Tranquillus,[1] contubernālis meus, vult emere agellum quem vēnditāre amīcus tuus dīcitur. Rogō cūrēs quantī[2] aequum est emat:[1] ita enim dēlectābit ēmisse. Nam mala ēmptiō[3] semper ingrāta, eō maximē, quod exprobrāre stultitiam dominō vidētur. In hōc autem agellō, sī modo adrīserit pretium, Tranquillī meī stomachum[4] multa sollicitant, vīcīnitās urbis, opportūnitās viae, mediocritās vīllae, modus rūris,[5] quī āvocet magis quam distringat. Scholasticīs porrō dominīs, ut hic est, sufficit abundē tantum solī ut relevāre caput, reficere oculōs, rēptāre per līmitem ūnamque sēmitam terere omnīsque vīticulās suās nōsse et numerāre arbusculās possint.

Haec tibi exposuī quō magis scīrēs quantum esset ille mihi, ego tibi dēbitūrus, sī praediolum istud, quod commendātur hīs dōtibus, tam salūbriter[6] ēmerit ut paenitentiae locum nōn relinquat. Valē. (I, 24)

[1] Suetonius Tranquillus
[2] *for as much as*
[3] *a bad buy*
[4] *appetite, desire*
[5] *the moderate size of the land*
[6] *so cheaply* (literally, *so healthfully*)

---

[1] **ut** is omitted

Ronald Sheridan/Ancient Art & Architecture Collection

Many old Roman temples were changed or converted into churches or basilicas as Christianity spread. In Rome, the old church of Saints Cosmos and Damian was established in 527 in the older Temple of Romulus. The vestibule rises over the round Temple of Romulus and still has the bronze door with the original lock that was used in the temple.

# WHY DON'T YOU WRITE?

**Verba Ūtilia:** eximō, occāsiō, optō, valeō

Rēctēne[1] omnia, quod iam prīdem epistulae tuae cessant? An omnia rēctē, sed occupātus es tū? An tū nōn occupātus, sed occāsiō scrībendī vel rāra vel nūlla? Exime hunc mihi scrūpulum,[2] cui pār esse nōn possum, exime autem, vel[3] datā operā[4] tabellāriō missō. Ego viāticum, ego etiam praemium dabō,$_{1}$ nūntiet mihi modo[5] quod optō. Ipse valeō, sī valēre est suspēnsum et ānxium vīvere, exspectantem in hōrās$_{2}$ timentemque prō capite[6] amīcissimō quidquid accidere hominī potest. Valē. (III, 17)

[1] *all right, okay; supply* **sunt**
[2] *uneasiness*
[3] *even*
[4] *purposely, specially*
[5] *provided that*
[6] *person*

$_{1}$ Pliny will pay the special delivery fee.
$_{2}$ with **in:** *hourly*

# NEGLECT OF A GREAT MAN'S TOMB

**Verba Ūtilia:** caveō, dolor, exiguus, orbis terrārum, quondam, subeō

Cum vēnissem in socrūs[1] meae vīllam Alsiēnsem, quae aliquamdiū Rūfī Verginī fuit, ipse mihi locus optimī illīus et maximī virī dēsīderium nōn sine dolōre renovāvit. Hunc enim colere sēcessum atque etiam senectūtis suae nīdulum[2] vocāre cōnsuēverat. Quōcumque mē contulissem, illum animus, illum oculī requīrēbant. Libuit etiam monumentum eius vidēre, et vīdisse paenituit. Est enim adhūc imperfectum, nec difficultās operis in causā,$_{1}$ modicī ac potius exiguī, sed inertia eius$_{2}$ cui cūra mandāta est. Subit indignātiō cum miserātiōne post decimum mortis annum reliquiās neglēctumque cinerem sine titulō,[3] sine nōmine iacēre, cuius$_{3}$ memoriā[4] orbem terrārum glōria pervagētur. At ille mandāverat cāveratque ut dīvīnum illud et immortāle factum versibus īnscrīberētur:

Hīc situs est Rūfus, pulsō quī Vindice quondam
imperium asseruit nōn sibi sed patriae.

Tam rāra in amīcitiīs fidēs, tam parāta oblīviō mortuōrum ut ipsī nōbīs dēbeāmus etiam conditōria[5] exstruere omniaque hērēdum officia praesūmere. Nam cui nōn est verendum quod vidēmus accidisse Verginiō? Cuius[6] iniūriam, ut indigniōrem, sīc etiam nōtiōrem ipsīus clāritās facit. Valē. (VI, 10)

[1] *mother-in-law,* the mother of a previous wife
[2] *snug little nest*
[3] *inscription, epitaph*
[4] *in the memory (of men)*
[5] *tombs*
[6] *wrong to whom*

$_{1}$ We would omit **in:** *the reason.*
$_{2}$ Rufus' heir
$_{3}$ with **glōria**

# I MISS YOU

**Verba Ūtilia:** absum, careō, nox, pēs

Incrēdibile est quantō dēsīderiō tuī[1] tenear. In causā[1] amor prīmum, deinde quod nōn cōnsuēvimus abesse. Inde est quod[2] magnam noctium partem in imāgine[3] tuā vigil exigō, inde quod interdiū quibus hōrīs tē vīsere solēbam ad diaetam[4] tuam ipsī mē, ut vērissimē dīcitur, pedēs dūcunt, quod dēnique aeger et maestus ac similis exclūsō ā vacuō līmine recēdō. Ūnum tempus hīs tormentīs caret, quō in forō et amīcōrum lītibus conteror. Aestimā tū quae vīta mea sit, cui requiēs in labōre, in miseriā cūrīsque sōlācium. Valē. (VII, 5)

[1] *for you*
[2] *Hence it is that*
[3] *in picturing you*
[4] *living room*

---

[1] We would omit **in:** *the reason.*

# IS THE PRAISE OF FRIENDS A FAULT?

**Verba Ūtilia:** agnōscō, beātus, crīmen, praedicō

Ais quōsdam apud tē reprehendisse tamquam[1] amīcōs meōs ex omnī occāsiōne ultrā modum laudem. Agnōscō[2] crīmen, amplector etiam. Quid enim honestius culpā benignitātis? Quī sunt tamen istī quī amīcōs meōs melius nōrint? Sed, ut[3] nōrint, quid invident mihi fēlīcissimō errōre?[4] Ut[3] enim nōn sint tālēs quālēs ā mē praedicantur, ego tamen beātus quod mihi videntur.

Igitur ad aliōs hanc sinistram[5] dīligentiam cōnferant; nec sunt parum multī[6] quī carpere amīcōs suōs iūdicium vocant. Mihi numquam persuādēbunt ut meōs amārī ā mē nimium putem. Valē. (VII, 28)

[1] *on the ground that*
[2] *I admit the charge*
[3] *granted that*
[4] *begrudge me the delusion*
[5] *sinister, wrongheaded*
[6] **nec parum multi** = *there are not a few*

# CONGRATULATIONS

**Verba Ūtilia:** ergo, precor, suscipiō

Tua quidem pietās, imperātor sānctissime,[1] optāverat ut quam tardissimē succēderēs patrī; sed dī immortālēs festīnāvērunt virtūtēs tuās ad gubernācula reī pūblicae quam suscēperās admovēre. Precor ergō ut tibi et per tē generī hūmānō prōspera omnia, id est digna saeculō[1] tuō, contingant. Fortem tē et hilarem, imperātor optime, et prīvātim et pūblicē optō. (X, 1)

[1] *reign*

[1] Trajan, who had just become emperor

# FIRE DEPARTMENT NEEDED

**Verba Ūtilia:** dīversus, meminī, ōtiōsus, praecipiō, ūtor

Cum dīversam partem prōvinciae circumīrem, Nīcomēdiae vāstissimum incendium multās prīvātōrum domōs et duo pūblica opera, quamquam viā interiacente, absūmpsit. Est autem lātius sparsum, prīmum violentiā ventī, deinde inertiā hominum, quōs satis cōnstat ōtiōsōs et immōbilēs tantī malī spectātōrēs perstitisse; et aliōquī nūllus umquam in pūblicō sīphō,[1] nūlla hama,[2] nūllum dēnique īnstrūmentum ad incendia compescenda. Et haec quidem, ut iam praecēpī, parābuntur.

Tū, domine, dispice an īnstituendum putēs collēgium[3] fabrōrum dumtaxat[4] hominum CL. Ego attendam nē quis nisi faber recipiātur nēve iūre concessō in aliud[5] ūtātur; nec erit difficile custōdīre tam paucōs. (X, 33)

---

Tibi quidem secundum[6] exempla complūrium in mentem vēnit posse collēgium fabrōrum apud Nīcomēdēnsēs cōnstituī. Sed meminerīmus prōvinciam istam et praecipuē eās cīvitātēs[7] eius modī factiōnibus esse vexātās. Quodcumque nōmen ex quācumque causā dederimus iīs quī in idem[8] contrāctī fuerint, hetaeriae[9] brevī fīent. Satius itaque est comparārī ea quae ad coercendōs ignēs auxiliō esse possint admonērīque dominōs praediōrum ut et ipsī inhibeant, ac, sī rēs poposcerit, accursū[1] populī ad hoc ūtī. (X, 34)

[1] *fire engine* (nominative)
[2] *bucket*
[3] *company*
[4] *only*
[5] *for anything else*
[6] *following* (preposition)
[7] *cities*
[8] *for the same (purpose)*
[9] *political clubs*

[1] i.e., the spectators, those who rush to the scene

# ROMAN EFFICIENCY: A WATER SUPPLY

**Verba Ūtilia:** assequor, dēsum, modicus

Sinōpēnsēs, domine, aquā dēficiuntur;[1] quae vidētur et bona et cōpiōsa ab sextō decimō mīliāriō[2] posse perdūcī. Est tamen statim ab capite[3] paulō amplius passus mīlle[3] locus suspectus et mollis, quem ego interim explōrārī modicō impendiō iussī, an recipere et sustinēre opus$_1$ possit. Pecūnia, cūrantibus nōbīs, contrācta[4] nōn deerit, sī tū, domine, hoc genus operis et salūbritātī et amoenitātī valdē sitientis colōniae indulseris. (X, 90)

---

Ut coepistī, Secunde cārissime, explōrā dīligenter an locus ille quem suspectum habēs sustinēre opus aquaeductūs possit. Neque enim dubitandum putō quīn[5] aqua perdūcenda sit in colōniam Sinōpēnsem, sī modo ea vīribus[6] suīs assequī$_2$ potest, cum plūrimum ea rēs et salūbritātī et voluptātī eius collātūra sit. (X, 91)

[1] *are short of*

[2] *milestone*

[3] *for a little more than a mile from the source;* **amplius** does not affect the case of **passus**

[4] *collected by my efforts*

[5] *that*

[6] *resources*

---

$_1$ i.e., an aqueduct with its arches

$_2$ Supply **aquam** as object.

# WHAT SHALL WE DO ABOUT THE CHRISTIANS?

**Verba Ūtilia:** cōnsulō, fallō, interim, intersum, negō, nesciō, prōsum, pūniō, saeculum, scelus, speciēs, vetō

Sollemne est mihi, domine, omnia dē quibus dubitō ad tē referre. Quis enim potest melius vel cūnctātiōnem meam regere vel ignōrantiam īnstruere?

Cognitiōnibus dē Chrīstiānīs interfuī numquam; ideō nesciō quid et quātenus[1] aut pūnīrī soleat aut quaerī. Nec mediocriter haesitāvī sitne aliquod discrīmen aetātum an quamlibet[2] tenerī nihil ā rōbustiōribus differant, dētur paenitentiae venia an eī quī omnīnō Chrīstiānus fuit dēsīsse nōn prōsit,$_{1}$ nōmen[3] ipsum sī flāgitiīs careat, an flāgitia cohaerentia nōminī pūniantur.

Interim iīs quī ad mē tamquam Chrīstiānī dēferēbantur hunc sum secūtus modum. Interrogāvī ipsōs an essent Chrīstiānī. Cōnfitentēs iterum ac tertiō interrogāvī, supplicium minātus; persevērantēs dūcī$_{2}$ iussī. Neque enim dubitābam, quālecumque esset[4] quod fatērentur, pertināciam certē et īnflexibilem obstinātiōnem dēbēre pūnīrī. Fuērunt aliī similis āmentiae quōs, quia cīvēs Rōmānī erant, adnotāvī in urbem remittendōs. Mox ipsō trāctātū,[5] ut fierī solet, diffundente sē crīmine, plūrēs speciēs incidērunt.[6]

Prōpositus est libellus sine auctōre$_{3}$ multōrum nōmina continēns. Quī negābant esse sē Chrīstiānōs aut fuisse, cum, praeeunte mē,[7] deōs appellārent et imāginī tuae, quam propter hoc iusseram cum simulācrīs nūminum afferrī, tūre ac vīnō supplicārent, praetereā maledīcerent[8]$_{4}$ Chrīstō, quōrum nihil posse cōgī dīcuntur[9] quī sunt rē vērā Chrīstiānī, dīmittendōs$_{5}$ esse putāvī.

Aliī ab indice nōminātī esse sē Chrīstiānōs dīxērunt et mox negāvērunt: fuisse quidem, sed dēsīsse, quīdam ante triennium, quīdam ante plūrēs annōs, nōn nēmō[10] etiam ante vīgintī. Hī quoque omnēs et imāginem tuam deōrumque simulācra venerātī sunt et Chrīstō maledīxērunt.

1 *to what extent*
2 *the very young (with* **tenerī***)*
3 *the name (Christian).* Should a man be punished for being a confessed Christian or only for any crimes he might commit in the name of Christianity?
4 *whatever it was*
5 *by the handling (in the trials).* The more Pliny looked into the matter the more complex it became.
6 *more types turned up*
7 *with me speaking (the words of the oath) first*
8 *reviled*
9 *none of which things, it is said, they can be compelled (to do)* (literally, *they are said not to be able to be,* etc.)
10 *not none = some*

---

$_{1}$ The subject is **dēsīsse** (from **dēsinō**).
$_{2}$ i.e., to prison and death
$_{3}$ i.e., anonymous
$_{4}$ What was patriotism to the Romans was idolatry to the Christians.
$_{5}$ modifies the antecedent (not expressed) of **quī**

Affirmābant autem hanc fuisse summam vel culpae suae vel errōris, quod essent solitī statō diē[5] ante lūcem convenīre carmenque Chrīstō quasi deō dīcere sēcum in vicem,[11] sēque sacrāmentō nōn in scelus aliquod obstingere, sed nē fūrta, nē latrōcinia, nē adulteria committerent,[6] nē fidem fallerent, nē dēpositum appellātī[12] abnegārent; quibus perāctīs, mōrem sibi discēdendī fuisse, rūrsusque coeundī ad capiendum cibum,[7] prōmiscuum tamen et innoxium;[13] quod ipsum facere dēsīsse post ēdictum meum, quō secundum mandāta tua hetaeriās[14] esse vetueram. Quō magis necessārium crēdidī ex duābus ancillīs quae ministrae[8] dīcēbantur, quid esset vērī et[15] per tormenta quaerere. Nihil aliud invēnī quam superstitiōnem prāvam, immodicam.

Ideō, dīlātā cognitiōne, ad cōnsulendum tē dēcurrī. Vīsa est enim mihi rēs digna cōnsultātiōne, maximē propter perīclitantium numerum. Multī enim omnis aetātis, omnis ōrdinis, utrīusque sexūs etiam, vocantur in perīculum et vocābuntur. Neque cīvitātēs tantum sed vīcōs etiam atque agrōs superstitiōnis istīus contāgiō pervagāta est; quae vidētur sistī et corrigī posse. Certē satis cōnstat prope iam dēsōlāta templa coepisse celebrārī et sacra sollemnia diū intermissa repetī pāstumque vēnīre[16] victimārum, cuius adhūc rārissimus ēmptor inveniēbātur. Ex quō facile est opīnārī quae turba hominum ēmendārī possit, sī sit paenitentiae locus. (X, 96)

---

Āctum quem dēbuistī, mī Secunde, in excutiendīs causīs eōrum quī Chrīstiānī ad tē dēlātī fuerant secūtus es. Neque enim in ūniversum[17] aliquid quod quasi certam fōrmam habeat cōnstituī potest. Conquīrendī nōn sunt; sī dēferantur et arguantur, pūniendī sunt, ita tamen ut quī negāverit sē Chrīstiānum esse idque rē ipsā manifēstum fēcerit, id est supplicandō dīs nostrīs, quamvīs suspectus in praeteritum,[18] veniam ex paenitentiā impetret. Sine auctōre vērō prōpositī libellī in nūllō crīmine locum habēre dēbent. Nam et pessimī exemplī[19] nec nostrī saeculī est. (X, 97)

[11] *responsively*
[12] *when requested*
[13] *ordinary and harmless* (not the flesh of human beings, as was charged, probably through misunderstanding of Communion)
[14] *political clubs*
[15] *even*
[16] *is being sold* (from **vēneo**)
[17] *in general*
[18] *in the past*
[19] *both (a matter) of bad precedent and not*

---

[5] Sunday
[6] The clause is object of **obstringere**.
[7] the "love feast" of the early Christians
[8] Pliny so translates the Greek word **(diakonissai)**, from which comes our word "deaconess." The language of Bithynia was Greek.

UNIT
II

Scala/Art Resource, NY

# SHORT SELECTIONS FROM AULUS GELLIUS

## Unit Objectives

- To read anecdotes, history, and essays by Aulus Gellius (2nd century A.D.)
- To review future passive participle and gerund; impersonal verbs; subjunctive by attraction; **cum** clauses; indirect questions; volitive subjunctive; volitive noun clauses; anticipatory clauses; causal clauses; ablative of origin; ablative of description; descriptive relative clauses; noun clauses of result; conditions; ablative of separation, ablative of place from which; locative
- To learn the meaning of Latin prefixes and abbreviations

This Flemish tapestry depicts two great generals and their armies, Scipio Africanus and Hannibal Barca. The Romans and Carthaginians fought three long wars. The second Punic War was one of the most decisive wars in history. Hannibal, who at the age of nine was taken to Spain where he was forced to swear lifelong hostility against Rome, crossed the Alps with a train of elephants. Meanwhile, the Roman general Scipio entered Spain and drove out the remaining Carthaginian forces. Scipio continued into Africa where he defeated Hannibal at Zama in 201 B.C.

# AULUS GELLIUS

Aulus Gellius, a Roman writer of the second century (born about A.D. 130), has preserved in his only extant work, *Attic Nights* (**Noctēs Atticae**), an extremely miscellaneous but often valuable and interesting collection of literary material from earlier times.

Written during winter nights in Attica, this huge scrapbook (twenty books) contains anecdotes, bits of history and poetry, and essays on various phases of philosophy, geometry, and grammar. Of particular interest are quotations from Greek and Latin authors whose works are now wholly or in great part lost.

# A FILIBUSTER IN THE SENATE

Ante lēgem quae nunc dē senātū habendō observātur, ōrdō rogandī sententiās varius fuit. Aliās[1] prīmus rogābātur quī prīnceps ā cēnsōribus in senātum lēctus fuerat, aliās[1] quī dēsignātī cōnsulēs erant; quīdam ā cōnsulibus studiō aut necessitūdine aliquā adductī, quem īs[2] vīsum[3] erat, honōris grātiā extrā ōrdinem sententiam prīmum rogābant. Observātum[4] tamen est, cum extrā ōrdinem fieret, nē quis quemquam ex aliō quam[5] ex cōnsulārī locō sententiam prīmum rogāret. C. Caesar in cōnsulātū quem cum M. Bibulō gessit, quattuor sōlōs extrā ōrdinem rogāsse sententiam dīcitur. Ex hīs quattuor prīncipem rogābat M. Crassum; sed postquam fīliam Cn. Pompeiō dēsponderat, prīmum coeperat Pompeium rogāre.

Eius reī ratiōnem reddidisse eum₁ senātuī Tīrō Tullius, M. Cicerōnis lībertus, refert itaque sē ex patrōnō suō audīsse scrībit. Id ipsum Capitō Ateius in librō quem dē officiō senātōriō composuit scrīptum relīquit.

In eōdem librō Capitōnis id quoque scrīptum est: "C. Caesar cōnsul M. Catōnem sententiam₂ rogāvit. Catō rem quae cōnsulēbatur,[6] quoniam nōn ē[7] rē pūblicā vidēbātur, perficī nōlēbat. Eius reī dūcendae[8] grātiā longā ōrātiōne ūtēbātur eximēbatque dīcendō diem. Erat enim iūs senātōrī, ut sententiam rogātus dīceret ante quicquid vellet aliae₃ reī et quoad vellet. Caesar cōnsul viātōrem[9] vocāvit eumque, cum fīnem nōn faceret, prēndī loquentem et in carcerem dūcī iussit. Senātus cōnsurrēxit et prōsequēbātur Catōnem in carcerem. Hāc invidiā factā, Caesar dēstitit et mittī[10] Catōnem iussit." (IV, 10)

1 *at times . . . at other times*
2 = **eis**
3 *it seemed (best)*
4 *(the rule) was kept*
5 *than*
6 *was under deliberation*
7 *to the best interests of*
8 *prolonging*
9 *messenger,* though more like a sergeant-at-arms
10 *let go*

₁ Caesar
₂ Two accusatives are used with verbs of asking.
₃ for the more usual **alterius; alīus** was avoided.

**Questions**

1. Who was Caesar's colleague as consul?
2. What was the relationship of Caesar and Pompey?
3. What was the reaction of the senate to Caesar's arrest of Cato?
4. What was the order of calling upon senators for their opinions?

## GRAMMAR

### The Subjunctive by Attraction

When a verb is in a clause that is dependent on a verb in the subjunctive or infinitive, the dependent clause verb is frequently "attracted" to the subjunctive. This most often happens in a dependent clause within an indirect statement (infinitive) or indirect command or question (subjunctive).

| | |
|---|---|
| **Plīnius dicit Traiānum, quī imperātor sit, mēnsōrem mittere debēre.** | *Pliny says that Trajan, who is emperor, ought to send an architect.* |
| **Caesar petīvit ut copiae quās sociī pollicitī essent missae sint.** | *Caesar demanded that the troops that the allies had promised be sent.* |

### Syntax Review

1. Review the uses and translations of the gerundive and gerund. (pp. 308–309)
2. Review the meanings and constructions of impersonal verbs. (pp. 292, 308)
3. Find examples of these in the reading.

### Translation

1. It did not seem best to Caesar to ask Crassus.
2. He did not think that Cato should talk so much.
3. Cato was present for the sake of giving his opinion.
4. He was not ready, however, to give his opinion immediately.

## VOCABULARY

**cōnsul**
**lēx**
**prīnceps**
**senātus**
**studium**
**dēspondeō**
**nōlō**
**observō**
**rogō**
**quoad**

# SCĪPIŌ, A MAN BEYOND REPROACH

[1] *the Elder; subject of* **praestiterit** and **fuerit**
[2] *highminded*
[3] *recall* (with **memoriā**)
[4] *glorious*
[5] *we should not be*
[6] *toward* (preposition)
[7] *rascal,* i.e., Naevius
[8] *to congratulate*

Scīpiō Āfricānus antīquior[1] quantā virtūtum glōriā praestiterit et quam fuerit altus animī[2] atque magnificus, plūrimīs rēbus quae dīxit quaeque fēcit dēclārātum est. Ex quibus sunt haec duo exempla eius fīdūciae atque exsuperantiae ingentis:

Cum M. Naevius, tribūnus plēbis, accūsāret eum ad populum dīceretque accēpisse ā rēge Antiochō pecūniam ut condiciōnibus grātiōsīs et mollibus pāx cum eō populī Rōmānī nōmine fieret, et quaedam item alia crīminī[1] daret indigna tālī virō, tum Scīpiō pauca praefātus quae dignitās vītae suae atque glōria postulābat: "memoriā," inquit, "Quirītēs, repetō[3] diem esse hodiernum quō Hannibalem Poenum imperiō vestrō inimīcissimum magnō proeliō vīcī in terrā Āfricā pācemque et victōriam vōbīs peperī[2] īnspectābilem.[4] Nōn igitur sīmus[5] adversum[6] deōs ingrātī et, cēnseō, relinquāmus nebulōnem[7] hunc, eāmus hinc prōtinus Iovī optimo maximō grātulātum."[8] Id cum dīxisset, āvertit et īre ad Capitōlium coepit. Tum cōntiō ūniversa, quae ad sententiam dē Scīpiōne ferendam convēnerat, relīctō tribūnō, Scīpiōnem in Capitōlium comitāta atque inde ad aedēs eius cum laetitiā et grātulātiōne solemnī prōsecūta est. (IV, 18)

**Questions**

1. What did Naevius, the tribune, accuse Scīpiō of?
2. Whom did Scīpiō conquer?
3. What did Scīpiō do after he spoke?
4. How did the assembly **(cōntiō)** react to Scīpiō's statement?

## GRAMMAR

### Syntax Review

1. Review the hortatory and jussive subjunctives. Remember that they are essentially a command (or suggestion) in the first or third person and are generally translated using *Let*. For the negative, use **nē.** (p. 303)
2. Review **cum** clauses and indirect questions. (pp. 304–305)

### Translation

1. Everybody asked what Scīpiō had done.
2. Let us not believe that Scīpiō ever did such things.
3. When Scīpiō heard the charges, he decided to go away.
4. Do you believe that the charges were worthy of so great a man?

---

[1] dative of purpose
[2] from **pariō**

## VOCABULARY

| | | |
|---|---|---|
| **condiciō** | **hodiernus** | **āvertō** |
| **contiō** | **sollemnis** | **cēnseō** |
| **crīmen** | **ūniversus** | **pariō** |
| **dignitās** | | **postulō** |
| **fīdūcia** | | **prōsequor** |
| **laetitia** | | **relinquō** |

## WORD STUDY

Explain *exemption, fiduciary, incarcerate, incriminate, indignity, ingrate, mollify, preface.*

Explain the force of the prefix in **āvertō, exsuperantia, indignus, inimīcus, praestō, repetō.**

In the spirit of Aulus Gellius, start a class newsletter or Web page. Use Latin to report on class events, to write articles or editorials on classical culture, history, and the arts, or to explore the meaning of classical literature and its impact on various societies. Investigate careers in Latin and include the addresses or URLs for organizations that can provide more Latin career tips. Use your library and the Internet to do your research—and don't forget to include translations so you can share the concepts and skills you are acquiring with friends in other classes!

# A PROMISE MUST BE KEPT

Iūs iūrandum apud Rōmānōs inviolātē sānctēque habitum servātumque est. Id et mōribus lēgibusque multīs ostenditur, et hoc quod dīcēmus eī reī nōn tenue argumentum esse potest. Post proelium Cannēnse[1] Hannibal, Carthāginiēnsium imperātor, ex captīvīs nostrīs ēlēctōs decem Rōmam mīsit mandāvitque eīs pactusque est, ut, sī populō Rōmānō vidērētur,[2] permūtātiō fieret captīvōrum. Hoc, priusquam proficīscerentur, iūs iūrandum[1] eōs adēgit reditūrōs esse in castra Poenica, sī Rōmānī captīvōs nōn permūtārent.

Veniunt Rōmam decem captīvī. Mandātum Poenī imperātōris in senātū expōnunt. Permūtātiō senātuī nōn placita.[3] Parentēs, cognātī, affīnēsque captīvōrum amplexī eōs, dīcēbant statum eōrum integrum incolumemque esse ac nē ad hostes redīre vellent ōrābant. Tum octō ex hīs iūstum nōn esse respondērunt, quoniam dēiūriō[4] vīnctī forent,[5] statimque, utī iūrātī erant,[2] ad Hannibalem profectī sunt. Duo reliquī Rōmae mānsērunt solūtōsque esse sē ac līberātōs religiōne[3] dīcēbant, quoniam, cum ēgressī castra hostium fuissent, commentīciō[6] cōnsiliō regressī eōdem,[4] tanquam sī ob aliquam fortuitam causam, īssent atque ita, iūre iūrandō satisfactō, rūrsus iniūrātī abīssent. Haec eōrum fraudulenta calliditās tam esse turpis exīstimāta est ut contemptī vulgō sint, cēnsōrēsque eōs posteā et damnīs et ignōminiīs affēcerint, quoniam quod factūrōs dēierāverant nōn fēcissent. (VI, 18, 1–10)

[1] *the battle of Cannae*
[2] *it seemed best*
[3] *did not please* (deponent)
[4] *by an oath*
[5] = **essent**
[6] *pretended, tricky*

---

[1] subject of **adēgit**
[2] deponent
[3] i.e., the oath
[4] adverb

**Questions**

1. What was the Roman attitude toward an oath?
2. What oath did Hannibal compel the prisoners to take?
3. How did the Romans react to the two prisoners who broke their word?

# GRAMMAR

### Anticipatory Clauses

An anticipatory clause in the subjunctive occurs after **dum** *(until)*, **antequam** *(before)*, and **priusquam** *(before)* to express an action that is anticipated. To express an actual fact, the indicative is used.

| | |
|---|---|
| **Exspectābat dum cōnsul loquerētur.** | *He waited until the consul spoke.* |
| **Priusquam loquerētur, occupātus est.** | *Before he could speak, he was seized.* |
| **Antequam locūtus est, rīsit.** | *Before he spoke, he laughed.* |

### Causal Clauses

With causal *(because, since)* clauses introduced by **quod, propterеā quod**, or **quoniam**, the verb is in the indicative when it expresses the reason of the writer or speaker or is considered real. The verb is in the subjunctive when the truth of the reason given is doubtful or open to dispute.

| | |
|---|---|
| **Quod tardē erās, excēdere nōn poteram.** | *Because you were late, I was unable to leave.* |
| **Dixērunt sē irā movēre quod tardē esses.** | *They said they were angry because you were late.* |

## Syntax Review

Review volitive noun clauses (indirect commands). (pp. 303–304)

## Translation

1. We begged them not to return to Carthage.
2. Because we believe you, you will be permitted to go to Rome.
3. Before they could go to Rome, they had to swear that they would return.
4. The enemy said that they would not trust the Romans because they never told the truth.

Scala/Art Resource, NY

**The Temple of Antoninus and Faustina is one of the best preserved in the Roman Forum. Faustina was the beloved daughter of Emperor Antoninus Pius. She married Marcus Aurelius, who was the adopted son of Antoninus and who became emperor upon his father's death. The Antonines were fairly traditional builders, but when Faustina died, the emperor deified her and erected a magnificent temple in her honor. Later the temple was converted into a Christian church which, in turn, was renovated in the sixteenth century.**

## VOCABULARY

**affīnis**
**cognātus**
**ignōminia**
**iūs iūrandum**

**incolumis**
**turpis**

**amplector**
**iūrō**
**ōrō**
**ostendō**
**permūtō**
**vinciō**

**priusquam**
**quoniam**
**sānctē**

## WORD STUDY

Note the many words related to **iūs** in the preceding selection: **iūs iūrandum, iūstus, dēiūrium, iūrō, iniūrātus, dēierō.**

**Cognātus** (**co-gnātus,** *born together*) is a blood relative. **Affīnis** (**ad-fīnis,** *neighboring to*) is a relative by marriage.

# CROW EATS MAN

Dē Maximō Valeriō, quī Corvīnus appellātus est ob auxilium prōpugnātiōnemque corvī[1] ālitis, haud quisquam est nōbilium scrīptōrum quī secus[2] dīxerit. Ea rēs prōrsus mīranda sīc profectō est in librīs annālibus memorāta: Adulēscēns tālī genere ēditus,[3] L. Fūriō, Claudiō Appiō cōnsulibus,[4] fit tribūnus mīlitāris. Atque in eō tempore cōpiae Gallōrum ingentēs agrum Pomptīnum īnsēderant. Dux intereā Gallōrum vāstā et arduā prōcēritāte armīsque aurō praefulgentibus grandia ingrediēns[5] et manū tēlum reciprocāns[6] incēdēbat perque contemptum et superbiam circumspiciēns dēspiciēnsque omnia$_1$ venīre iubet et congredī, sī quis pugnāre sēcum ex omnī Rōmānō exercitū audēret. Tum Valerius tribūnus, cēterīs inter metum pudōremque ambiguīs,[7] impetrātō$_2$ prius ā cōnsulibus ut in Gallum tam arrogantem pugnāre sēsē permitterent, prōgreditur intrepidē modestēque obviam. Et congrediuntur et cōnsistunt, et cōnserēbantur iam manūs.[8] Atque ibi vīs quaedam dīvīna fit: corvus repente imprōvīsus advolat et super galeam tribūnī īnsistit atque inde in adversārī ōs atque oculōs pugnāre incipit; īnsilībat, obturbābat, et unguibus manum laniābat et prōspectum ālīs arcēbat atque, ubi satis saevierat, revolābat in galeam tribūnī. Sīc tribūnus,

1 *crow*
2 *otherwise, differently*
3 *sprung from such a family,* i.e., that of the Valerii
4 *during the consulship of L. Furius and Appius Claudius*
5 *taking big steps* (literally, *walking big*)
6 *brandishing*
7 *hesitating*
8 *they were fighting hand to hand* (literally, *hands were being joined*)

$_1$ for **omnēs;** the neuter is more inclusive and contemptuous.
$_2$ The **ut** clause is the subject of the ablative absolute.

spectante utrōque exercitū, et suā virtūte nīxus[9] et operā ālitis prōpugnātus, ducem hostium ferōcissimum vīcit interfēcitque atque ob hanc causam cognōmen habuit "Corvīnus." Id factum est annīs quadringentīs quīnque post Rōmam conditam.[10]

Statuam Corvīnō istī dīvus[11] Augustus in forō suō statuendam cūrāvit.[12] In eius statuae capite corvī simulācrum est, reī pugnaeque quam dīximus monumentum. (IX, 11)

[9] *relying on* (with ablative)
[10] *after the founding of Rome*
[11] *deified*
[12] *caused to be set up*

**Questions**

1. What does the word "annals" mean?
2. How did Augustus honor Corvinus?
3. How did Valerius get his cognomen, Corvinus?
4. What was the attitude of the leader of the Gauls toward the Romans?

## GRAMMAR

### Ablative of Origin

The ablative case with or without a preposition **(ab, ex, dē)** is used to express origin or source from which.

| | |
|---|---|
| **Ampliō genere natus est.** | *He was born of a distinguished family.* |

### Ablative of Description

The ablative, without a preposition but with an accompanying adjective, is used to describe a person or thing. It is generally used to describe temporary qualities, such as appearance.

| | |
|---|---|
| **Erat equus magnā amplitūdine.** | *He was a horse of great size.* |

## Syntax Review

Review descriptive relative clauses. (p. 304)

## Translation

1. Was there anyone who fought more bravely for freedom?
2. There is no one who has done greater things for his country.
3. Maximus, a young man of no great height, was born of a noble family.
4. A crow that fought so fiercely deserves to be rewarded with a monument.

## VOCABULARY

**adulēscēns**
**metus**
**oculus**
**ōs**
**pudor**
**superbia**

**quisquam**

**ferōx**

**arceō**
**condō**
**impetrō**
**statuō**

**intereā**
**obviam**
**prōfectō**

## WORD STUDY

Explain *ingress, congress, progress; circumspect, despise, spectator*. Give the literal meaning of **imprōvīsus, prōpugnātiō.**

# RECONCILIATION, A SIGN OF GREATNESS

P. Āfricānus superior et Tiberius Gracchus, Tiberiī et C. Gracchōrum pater, rērum gestārum magnitūdine et honōrum atque vītae dignitāte illustrēs virī, dissēnsērunt saepe dē rē pūblicā et eā[1] sīve quā aliā rē nōn amīcī fuērunt. Ea simultās cum diū mānsisset et sollemnī diē epulum Iovī lībārētur atque ob id sacrificium senātus in Capitōliō epulārētur, fors fuit ut apud eandem mēnsam duo illī iūnctim locārentur. Tum quasi diīs immortālibus arbitrīs in convīviō Iovis optimī maximī dextrās eōrum condūcentibus,[2] repente amīcissimī factī. Neque sōlum amīcitia incepta, sed affīnitās simul īnstitūta; nam P. Scīpiō fīliam virginem habēns iam virō mātūram[3] ibi tunc eōdem in locō dēspondit eam Tiberiō Gracchō.

Aemilius quoque Lepidus et Fulvius Flaccus nōbilī genere amplissimīsque honōribus ac summō locō in cīvitāte praeditī, odiō inter sēsē gravī et simultāte diūtinā cōnflīctātī sunt. Posteā populus eōs simul cēnsōrēs facit. Atque illī, ubi vōce praecōnis renūntiātī sunt, ibīdem in campō statim, nōndum dīmissā cōntiōne, ultrō uterque[4] et parī voluntāte coniūnctī complexīque sunt, exque eō diē et in ipsā cēnsurā et posteā iūgī[5] concordiā fīdissimē amīcissimēque vīxērunt. (XII, 8)

[1] *because of this or some other thing*
[2] *joining* (ablative absolute with **diis**)
[3] *old enough for a husband*
[4] *they, both of them* (with **illi**)
[5] from **iūgis,** *everlasting*

**Questions**

1. How were the enemies Africanus and Tiberius Gracchus reconciled?
2. Who was the father of Tiberius and Gaius Gracchus?
3. What office did the enemies Aemilius Lepidus and Fulvius Flaccus hold?
4. After the election, what did these two men do?

## GRAMMAR

### Two Accusatives

Certain verbs, including verbs of asking, demanding, and teaching, take two accusatives, one of the person, the other of the thing. Verbs of making, naming, choosing, showing may take two accusatives of the *same* person or thing.

| | |
|---|---|
| **Magister eōs scientiam docuit.** | *The teacher taught them science.* |
| **Populus Marcum ducem dēlēgit.** | *The people chose Marcus leader.* |

### Syntax Review

Review noun clauses of result. (p. 304)

### Translation

1. The people made them censors and they became firm friends.
2. When their enmity had lasted a long time, they met at a dinner.
3. Because they disagreed about public affairs they had become enemies.
4. It so happened that Scīpiō had a daughter whom he betrothed to Tiberius Gracchus.

## VOCABULARY

**convīvium**
**fors**
**odium**
**simultās**

**illūstris**
**praeditus**

**coniungō**
**dissentiō**

**posteā**
**ultrō**

## WORD STUDY

Explain *arbitrate, convivial, dexterity, dissension, voluntary*. What does *ibid.* stand for and what does it mean?

# HOW TO GIVE A DINNER PARTY

Lepidissimus liber est M. Varrōnis ex satirīs Menippēīs[1] quī īnscrībitur: "Nescis quid vesper sērus vehat," in quō disserit dē aptō convīvārum numerō dēque ipsīus convīviī habitū cultūque. Dīcit autem convīvārum numerum incipere oportēre ā Grātiārum numerō et prōgredī ad Mūsārum,$_1$ id est, proficīscī ā tribus et cōnsistere in novem, ut, cum paucissimī convīvae sunt, nōn pauciōrēs sint quam trēs, cum plūrimī, nōn plūrēs quam novem. "Nam multōs," inquit, "esse nōn convenit, quod turba plērumque est turbulenta. Ipsum deinde convīvium cōnstat ex rēbus quattuor et tum dēnique omnibus suīs numerīs[2] absolūtum est sī bellī$_2$ homunculī[3] collēctī sunt, sī ēlēctus locus, sī tempus lēctum, sī apparātus nōn neglēctus. Nec loquācēs autem convīvās nec mūtōs legere oportet, quia ēloquentia in forō et apud subsellia,[4] silentium vērō nōn in convīviō, sed in cubiculō esse dēbet." Sermōnēs igitur id temporis[5] habendōs cēnset nōn super rēbus ānxiīs, sed iūcundōs et cum quādam voluptāte ūtilēs, ex quibus ingenium nostrum venustius fīat et amoenius. "Quod prōfectō," inquit, "ēveniet, sī dē id genus[6] rēbus ad commūnem vītae ūsum pertinentibus cōnfābulēmur, dē quibus in forō atque in negōtiīs agendī nōn est ōtium. Dominum[7] autem convīviī esse oportet nōn tam lautum[8] quam sine sordibus.[9] In convīviō legī nōn omnia dēbent, sed ea potissimum quae simul sint βιωφελῆ[10] et dēlectent." (XIII, 11, 1–5)

1 *Menippean,* after the Greek philosopher Menippus
2 *parts*
3 diminutive of **homō,** here used affectionately: *nice people*
4 *the bench,* i.e., *the courtroom*
5 *at that time*
6 *of that kind*
7 *the host*
8 *luxurious*
9 *stinginess*
10 **biōphelē,** *helpful to life*

**Questions**

1. How many guests should there be at a dinner party?
2. What sort of conversation should there be at dinner?
3. What was the title of Varro's book of satires? What was the title of the particular book referred to here?

## GRAMMAR

1. Review conditions on page 307. Remember that simple conditions are in the indicative, whereas contrary-to-fact and future-less-vivid conditions require the subjunctive.
2. Review descriptive relative clauses. (p. 304)

---

$_1$ Supply **numerum.**
$_2$ adjective

C. M. Dixon

Located near the Temple of Vesta is the House of the Vestals. You can still see many statues and inscriptions there, including the names of some of the Vestals. One name has been erased, leaving only the letter C. It is possible that it is a reference to Claudia, who converted to Christianity in the fourth century.

## Translation

1. I prefer a dinner which is better suited to my nature.
2. If the dinner should not be good, would you tell the host?
3. If there were only four guests, it would be difficult to find places for them.

## VOCABULARY

**ēloquentia**
**habitus**
**vesper**

**amoenus**
**aptus**
**lepidus**
**paucus**

**cōnsistō**
**conveniō**
**dēlectō**
**incipiō**
**īnscrībō**
**neglegō**

**dēnique**
**potissimum**

## WORD STUDY

Explain *amenities, delectable, loquacious, negligent, sordid, turbulence, vespers.*

What does *biology* deal with?

# WHICH IS RIGHT?

[1] *study*

[2] *of no slight reputation* (with **grammaticōs**)

[3] *nominative;* literally, *upright*

Dēfessus ego quondam diūtinā commentātiōne,[1] laxandī levandīque animī grātiā in Agrippae campō deambulābam. Atque ibi duōs forte grammaticōs cōnspicātus nōn parvī in urbe Rōmā nōminis[2] certātiōnī$_1$ eōrum ācerrimae adfuī, cum alter in cāsū vocātīvō "vir ēgregī" dīcendum contenderet, alter "vir ēgregie."

Ratiō autem eius quī "ēgregī" oportēre dīcī cēnsēbat huiusce$_2$ modī fuit: "Quaecumque," inquit, "nōmina seu vocābula rēctō[3] cāsū numerō singulārī 'us' syllabā fīniuntur, in quibus ante ultimam syllabam posita est 'i' littera, ea omnia cāsū vocātīvō 'i' littera terminantur, ut 'Caelius Caelī,' 'modius modī,' 'tertius tertī,' 'Accius Accī,' 'Titius Titī,' et similia omnia; sīc igitur 'ēgregius,' quoniam 'us' syllabā in cāsū nōminandī fīnītur eamque syllabam praecēdit 'i' littera, habēre dēbēbit in cāsū vocandī 'i' litteram extrēmam, et idcircō 'ēgregī,' nōn 'ēgregie,' rēctius dīcētur."

---

$_1$ with **adfuī**

$_2$ emphatic form of **huius**

Hoc ubi ille alter audīvit: "ō," inquit, "ēgregie grammatice vel, sī id māvīs, ēgregissime, dīc, ōrō tē, 'īnscius' et 'impius' et 'sōbrius' et 'ēbrius' et 'proprius' et 'propitius' et 'ānxius' et 'contrārius,' quae 'us' syllabā fīniuntur, in quibus ante ultimam syllabam 'i' littera est, quem cāsum vocandī habent? Mē enim pudor et verēcundia tenent[4] prōnūntiāre ea secundum[5] tuam dēfīnītiōnem." Sed cum ille paulisper oppositū[6] hōrum vocābulōrum commōtus reticuisset et mox tamen sē collēgisset[7] eandemque illam quam dēfīnierat rēgulam[8] retinēret et prōpugnāret, eaque inter eōs contentiō longius dūcerētur, nōn arbitrātus ego operae pretium[9] esse eadem istaec diūtius audīre, clāmantēs compugnantēsque illōs relīquī. (XIV, 5)

[4] *keep me from*
[5] *according to* (preposition)
[6] *by the opposition*
[7] *had collected his wits*
[8] *rule*
[9] *worthwhile;* literally, *the price of the effort*

**Questions**

1. Where was Gellius walking?
2. Why had he gone there?
3. What were the grammarians discussing?
4. What was Gellius' evident opinion of the grammarians' discussion?
5. What were the grammarians doing as Gellius left them?

## Translation

1. Tell me why you prefer to say "ēgregī."
2. Give me a good reason why you prefer "ēgregie."
3. First I was wearied by my work, then I was wearied by the grammarians.

## VOCABULARY

| | | | |
|---|---|---|---|
| **cāsus** | **dēfessus** | **cōnspicor** | **forte** |
| **fīnis** | **extrēmus** | **contendō** | |
| | **ultimus** | **levō** | |
| | **verēcundus** | | |

# NEWFANGLED EDUCATION NOT WANTED

[1] = **cōnsulibus**
[2] *as*
[3] *to the best interests of, in accordance with*
[4] = **ire**

C. Fanniō Strabōne, M. Valeriō Messālā cōss.,[1] senātūs cōnsultum dē philosophīs et dē rhētoribus Latīnīs factum est: "M. Pompōnius praetor senātum cōnsuluit. Quod verba facta sunt dē philosophīs et dē rhētoribus, dē eā rē ita cēnsuērunt, ut M. Pompōnius praetor animadverteret cūrāretque, utī[2] eī ē[3] rē pūblicā fidēque suā vidērētur, utī Rōmae nē essent."

Aliquot deinde annīs post id senātūs cōnsultum Cn. Domitius Ahēnobarbus et L. Licinius Crassus cēnsōrēs dē coercendīs rhētoribus Latīnīs ita ēdīxērunt: "Renūntiātum est nōbīs esse hominēs quī novum genus disciplīnae īnstituērunt, ad quōs iuventūs in lūdum conveniat; eōs sibi nōmen imposuisse Latīnōs rhētoras;$_1$ ibi hominēs adulēscentulōs diēs tōtōs dēsidēre. Maiōrēs nostrī quae līberōs suōs discere et quōs in lūdōs itāre[4] vellent īnstituērunt. Haec nova, quae praeter cōnsuētūdinem ac mōrem maiōrum fīunt, neque placent neque rēcta videntur."

Neque illīs sōlum temporibus nimis rudibus necdum Graecā disciplīnā expolītīs philosophī ex urbe Rōmā pulsī sunt, vērum etiam, Domitiānō imperante, senātūs cōnsultō ēiectī atque urbe et Ītaliā interdictī sunt. Quā tempestāte Epictētus quoque philosophus propter id senātūs cōnsultum Nīcopolim Rōmā dēcessit. (XV, 11)

**Questions**

1. Why did Epictetus withdraw from Rome?
2. What was the decree of the Roman senate against the philosophers?
3. Who in ancient Roman times determined the education of the young?

---

$_1$ a Greek form of the masculine accusative

## GRAMMAR

1. Review the ablative of separation. Remember that most verbs use a preposition, but that **abstineō, careō, dēiciō, desistō, excēdō,** and **līberō** do not; separation from people, however, generally requires a preposition (**ab, ex, dē**). (p. 298)
2. Review the ablative of place from which. Remember that the prepositions **ab, ex,** and **dē** are used to express place from which, except with **domus** and the names of towns and cities, where the preposition is often omitted. (p. 298)
3. Review the locative case. (p. 301)

### Translation

1. They departed from Rome before they could be seized.
2. At Rome in the time of Domitian the philosophers were driven out of Rome.
3. Freed from the dangers of the new ideas (*things*), they were able to learn the right (*things*).

## VOCABULARY

| | | |
|---|---|---|
| **cēnsor** | **aliquot** | **animadvertō** |
| **cōnsuētūdō** | | **coerceō** |
| **iuventūs** | | **cūrō** |
| **praetor** | | **ēiciō** |
| | | **placeō** |

## WORD STUDY

The abbreviation **cōss**. for **cōnsulēs** indicates that in the word **cōnsul** the **n** was nasalized, as in French, and not fully pronounced. The **ss** shows that in abbreviations the last consonant of the abbreviation was doubled to indicated the plural, as in English *pp*. for *pages*.

Now that you have gained experience in translating and familiarity with the style of Aulus Gellius, the next ten reading selections are presented with glosses and footnotes as your primary support. You might find it helpful to review the **Verba Ūtilia** before you begin each piece.

# SECRET WRITING

Librī sunt epistulārum C. Caesaris ad C. Oppium et Balbum Cornēlium, quī rēbus eius absentis cūrābant.[1] In hīs epistulīs quibusdam$_1$ in locīs inveniuntur litterae singulāriae, quās tū putēs[2] positās inconditē;[3] nam verba ex hīs litterīs cōnficī nūlla possunt. Erat autem conventum$_2$ inter eōs clandestīnum de commūtandō sitū litterarum, ut in scrīptō quidem alia aliae[4] locum et nōmen tenēret, sed in legendō locus cuique suus et potestās restituerētur; quaenam vērō littera prō quā scrīberētur, ante[5] īs,[6] sīcutī dīxī, placēbat quī hanc scrībendī latebram[7] parābant. Est adeō Probī grammaticī commentārius satis cūriōsē factus dē occultā litterārum significātiōne in epistulārum C. Caesaris scrīptūrā.

Legēbāmus in vetere historiā rērum Poenicārum virum quempiam illūstrem (sīve ille Hasdrubal sīve quis alius est, nōn retineō) epistulam scrīptam super rēbus arcānīs hōc modō abscondisse: pugillāria nova nōndum etiam cērā illita accēpisse, litterās in lignum incīdisse, posteā tabulās, utī solitum est, cērā illēvisse[8] eāsque tabulās tamquam nōn scrīptās, cui$_3$ factūrum id praedīxerat mīsisse; eum deinde cēram dērāsisse litterāsque incolumēs lignō incīsās lēgisse. (XVII, 9, 1–5, 16–17)

[1] with dative: *took care of*
[2] *you would think*
[3] *in no order*
[4] = **alterius**
[5] *previously*
[6] = **eis** (with **placēbat**)
[7] *secret code*
[8] *smeared on* (from **illinō**)

**Questions**

1. Who wrote a book on Caesar's code?
2. What sort of code did Caesar use?
3. What device did Hasdrubal use for secrecy?
4. Whom did Caesar put in charge of affairs in his absence?

## Translation

1. Caesar used a new method of writing.
2. Not everyone could read what he had written.
3. Do you think that Caesar's method was a good (one)?

$_1$ with **lōcis**
$_2$ noun
$_3$ Supply **ad eum** as the antecedent.

# VOCABULARY

**cēra**
**epistula**
**significātiō**
**tabula**
**verbum**

**absēns**
**incolumis**
**occultus**

**cōnficiō**
**incīdō**

## WORD STUDY

Explain *absentia, arcanum, clandestine, curator, erasure, retentive.*

# SATURNALIA DINNER AWAY FROM HOME

Sāturnālia Athēnīs agitābāmus hilarē prōrsum ac modestē. Conveniēbāmus autem ad eandem cēnam complūsculī[1] quī Rōmānī in Graeciam vēnerāmus quīque eāsdem audītiōnēs eōsdemque doctōrēs colēbāmus. Tum quī cēnulam ōrdine[2] suō cūrābat, praemium solvendae quaestiōnis pōnēbat, librum veteris scrīptōris vel Graecum vel Latīnum et corōnam ē laurō plexam, totidemque rēs quaerēbat quot hominēs istīc erāmus; cumque eās omnīs exposuerat, rem locumque dīcendī sors dabat.[3] Quaestiō igitur solūta corōnā et praemiō dōnābātur; nōn solūta autem trāmittēbātur ad eum quī sortītō successerat. Sī nēmō dissolvēbat, corōna eius quaestiōnis deō cuius id fēstum erat dicābātur.

Tertiō in locō hoc quaesītum est, in quibus verbīs captiōnum[4] istārum fraus esset, et quō pactō distinguī resolvīque possent: "quod nōn perdidistī, habēs; cornua nōn perdidistī: habēs igitur cornua;" item altera captiō: "quod ego sum, id tū nōn es; homō ego sum: homō igitur tū nōn es." Quaesītum ibi est, quae esset huius quoque sophismatis resolūtiō: "cum mentior et mentīrī mē dīcō, mentior an vērum dīcō?" Secundum[5] ea hoc quaesītum est, verbum "vērant," [1] quod significat "vēra dīcunt," quisnam poētārum veterum dīxerit.

[1] *quite a number (of us)*
[2] *in his turn*
[3] *chance decided the subject and order*
[4] *false arguments*
[5] *following* (preposition)

---

[1] a very rare word, which Gellius has to explain for his Roman readers

Haec ubi ōrdine quō dīxī prōposita atque, singulīs sorte ductīs, disputāta explānātaque sunt, librīs corōnīsque omnēs dōnātī sumus nisi ob ūnam quaestiōnem, quae fuit dē verbō "vērant." Nēmō enim tum commeminerat dictum esse ā Q. Enniō id verbum in tertiō decimō annālium. Corōna igitur huius quaestiōnis deō fēriārum istārum Sāturnō data est. (XVIII, 2, 1–5, 9–10, 12, 15–16)

**Questions**

1. Who used the rare word **vērant?**
2. What was the prize offered at the dinner?
3. How were the guests selected for the problems?
4. What sort of problem was presented to the guests?

## Translation

1. We came to dinner not only to eat but also to win prizes.
2. Many had heard the same teachers and read the same books.
3. The questions were difficult, and we did not know what the correct answers were.

## VOCABULARY

| | | |
|---|---|---|
| **cornū** | **singulī** | **colō** |
| **corōna** | **totidem** | **mentior** |
| **nēmō** | | **solvō** |
| **pactum** | | |
| **sors** | | |

Scala/Art Resource, NY

The Temple of Vesta was one of the most sacred temples in Rome. According to tradition, the round temple was built by Numa, the second king of Rome, to safeguard the image of Minerva and other sacred objects that were carried from Troy by Aeneas. It was here that the six Vestals tended the sacred fire and kept it burning.

# TAKE IT OR LEAVE IT

[1] *whether*
[2] *at this*

**Verba Ūtilia:** deūrō, mercor, nimium, percontor, poscō, prōdō

In antīquis annālibus memoria super librīs Sibyllīnīs haec prōdita est: Anus hospita atque incognita ad Tarquinium Superbum rēgem adiit novem librōs ferēns, quōs esse dīcēbat dīvīna ōrācula; eōs velle vēndere. Tarquinius pretium percontātus est. Mulier nimium atque immēnsum poposcit; rēx, quasi anus aetāte dēsiperet, dērīsit. Tum illa trēs librōs ex novem deūrit, et ecquid[1] reliquōs sex eōdem pretiō emere vellet rēgem interrogāvit. Sed enim Tarquinius id[2] multō rīsit magis dīxitque anum iam procul dubiō dēlīrāre. Mulier ibīdem statim trēs aliōs librōs exussit atque id ipsum dēnuō placidē rogat, ut trēs reliquōs eōdem illō pretiō emat. Tarquinius ōre iam sēriō atque attentiōre animō fit, librōs trēs reliquōs mercātur nihilō minōre pretiō quam quod erat petītum prō omnibus. Librī trēs in sacrārium conditī "Sibyllīnī" appellātī; ad eōs quasi ad ōrāculum adeunt, cum dī immortālēs pūblicē cōnsulendī sunt. (I, 19)

# THE TALE OF A SNAKE

[1] *living*
[2] *hide*

**Verba Ūtilia:** cōnflīctiō, immānitās, invisitātus

Tuberō in historiīs scrīptum relīquit bellō prīmō Poenicō[1] Atīlium Rēgulum cōnsulem in Āfricā, castrīs apud Bagradam flūmen positīs, proelium grande atque ācre fēcisse adversus ūnum serpentem in illīs locīs stabulantem[1] invīsitātae immānitātis[2] eumque magnā tōtīus exercitūs cōnflīctiōne ballistīs atque catapultīs diū oppugnātum, eiusque interfecti corium[2] longum pedēs centum et vīgintī Rōmam mīsisse. (VII, 3)

---

[1] 264–241 B.C.
[2] genitive of description with **serpentem**

# THE FIRST PUBLIC LIBRARY IN ATHENS

**Verba Ūtilia:** asportō, augeō, deinceps, porrō

Librōs Athēnīs disciplīnārum līberālium pūblicē ad legendum praebendōs[1] prīmus posuisse dīcitur Pīsistratus tyrannus. Deinceps studiōsius accūrātiusque ipsī Athēniēnsēs auxērunt;$_1$ sed omnem illam posteā librōrum cōpiam Xerxēs, Athēnārum$_2$ potītus, urbe ipsā praeter arcem incēnsā, abstulit asportāvitque in Persās. Eōs porrō librōs ūniversōs multīs post tempestātibus[2] Seleucus rēx, quī Nīcānor appellātus est, referendōs Athēnās cūrāvit.[3]

Ingēns posteā numerus librōrum in Aegyptō ab Ptolemaeīs rēgibus vel conquīsītus vel cōnfectus[4] est ad mīlia fermē volūminum septingenta; sed ea omnia bellō priōre Alexandrīnō, dum dīripitur ea cīvitās, nōn sponte neque operā cōnsultā,[5] sed ā mīlitibus forte auxiliāriīs incēnsa sunt. (VII, 17)

[1] *to be offered* (modifies **librōs**)
[2] = **annis**
[3] *caused to be taken back*
[4] *made, i.e., copied*
[5] *deliberately* (literally, *by deliberate effort*)

---

$_1$ Supply **librōs.**
$_2$ genitive with **potior:** *having gained possession of*

# THE RING FINGER

**Verba Ūtilia:** ait, cor, sic, sinister, vetus

Veterēs Graecōs ānulum[1] habuisse in digitō accēpimus sinistrae manūs quī minimō est proximus. Rōmānōs quoque hominēs aiunt sīc plērumque ānulīs ūsitātōs.[2] Causam esse huius reī Āpiōn in librīs Aegyptiacīs hanc$_1$ dīcit, quod, īnsectīs apertīsque hūmānīs corporibus, ut mōs in Aegyptō fuit, quās Graecī ἀνατομάς[3] appellant, repertum est nervum quendam tenuissimum ab eō ūnō digitō dē quō dīximus ad cor hominis pergere ac pervenīre; proptereā nōn īnscītum[4] vīsum esse eum potissimum digitum tālī honōre$_2$ decorandum, quī quasi conexus esse cum prīncipātū cordis vidērētur. (X, 10)

[1] *ring*
[2] *used*
[3] **anatomas** (literally, *cutting up*)
[4] *with* **nōn:** *not stupid,* i.e., *smart*

---

$_1$ refers to **causam**
$_2$ i.e., of wearing the ring

# BOYS, YOUNG MEN, AND OLD MEN

**Verba Ūtilia:** cēnsus, idōneus, senex, suprā

Tuberō in historiārum prīmō scrīpsit Servium Tullium, rēgem populī Rōmānī, cum illās quīnque classēs seniōrum et iūniōrum cēnsūs faciendī grātiā īnstitueret, puerōs esse exīstimāsse quī minōrēs essent annīs septem decem, atque inde ab annō septimō decimō, quō[1] idōneōs iam esse reī pūblicae arbitrārētur, mīlitēs scrīpsisse,[1] eōsque ad annum quadrāgēsimum sextum "iūniōrēs" suprāque eum annum "seniōrēs" appellāsse.

Eam rem propterea notāvī, ut discrīmina quae fuerint iūdiciō mōribusque maiōrum pueritiae,[2] iuventae, senectae, ex istā cēnsiōne Servī Tullī, prūdentissimī rēgis, nōscerentur. (X, 28)

[1] *enrolled as*

[2] *those* (i.e., **discrimina**) *of boyhood*

---

1 The antecedent is **annō.**

# THE ETIQUETTE OF SWEARING

**Verba Ūtilia:** asseverō, dēiūrō, nusquam, vetus

In veteribus scrīptīs neque mulierēs Rōmānae per Herculem dēiūrant neque virī per Castorem. Sed cūr illae nōn iūrāverint Herculem,[1] nōn obscūrum est, nam Herculāneō[1] sacrificiō abstinent. Cūr autem virī Castorem iūrantēs nōn appellāverint, nōn facile dictū[2] est. Nusquam igitur scrīptum invenīre est[3] apud idōneōs quidem scrīptōrēs aut "mehercle" fēminam dīcere aut "mēcastor" virum; "edepol" autem, quod iūs iūrandum per Pollūcem est, et virō et fēminae commūne est. Sed M. Varrō asseverat antīquissimōs virōs neque per Castorem neque per Pollūcem dēiūrāre solitōs, sed id iūs iūrandum fuisse tantum fēminārum; paulātim tamen īnscitiā antīquitātis virōs dīcere "edepol" coepisse factumque esse ita dīcendī mōrem, sed "mēcastor" ā virō dīcī in nūllō vetere scrīptō invenīrī. (XI, 6)

[1] *to Hercules*

[2] *to say*

[3] *is it (possible) to find it written*

---

1 Supply **per.**

# HOW TO WRITE PLAYS

**Verba Ūtilia:** eximiē, gignō, proinde, sapiēns, sapiō

Eximiē hoc atque vērissimē Āfrānius poēta dē gignendā comparandāque Sapientiā opīnātus est, quod eam fīliam esse Ūsūs et Memoriae dīxit. Eō namque argūmentō dēmōnstrat, quī sapiēns rērum[1] esse hūmānārum velit, nōn librīs sōlīs neque disciplīnīs rhētoricīs dialecticīsque opus esse, sed oportēre eum versārī quoque exercērīque in rēbus comminus[1] nōscendīs eaque omnia ācta et ēventa firmiter meminisse et proinde sapere atque cōnsulere ex hīs quae perīcula[2] ipsa rērum docuerint, nōn quae librī tantum aut magistrī tamquam in mīmō[3] aut in somniō dēlīrāverint. Versūs Āfrānī sunt in togātā cui Sellae nōmen est:

[1] *at first hand* (adverb)
[2] *experience*
[3] *mime, play*

> Ūsus mē genuit, māter peperit Memoria,
> Sophiam vocant mē Grāī, vōs Sapientiam.
>
> (XIII, 8)

[1] genitive with **sapiēns**

# CAN YOU SPEAK TWENTY-FIVE LANGUAGES?

**Verba Ūtilia:** diciō, haud, loquor

Quīntus Ennius tria corda habēre sēsē dīcēbat, quod loquī Graecē et Oscē[1] et Latīnē scīret. Mithridātēs autem, Pontī atque Bithyniae rēx inclutus, quī ā Cn. Pompeiō bellō superātus est, quīnque et vīgintī gentium quās sub diciōne habuit linguās percalluit[1] eārumque omnium gentium virīs haud umquam per interpretem collocūtus est, sed ut[2] quemque ab eō appellārī ūsus[3] fuit, proinde linguā et ōrātiōne ipsīus nōn minus scītē quam sī gentīlis[4] eius esset locūtus est. (XVII, 17)

[1] *knew well*
[2] *when*
[3] *need*
[4] *fellow countryman*

[1] Oscan, spoken in southern Italy, was related to Latin.

UNIT
III

Robert E. Bright/Photo Researchers

# CICERO AGAINST CATILINE

## Unit Objectives

- To learn about Cicero's life and times
- To understand Cicero's public speaking style
- To read Cicero's orations against Catiline with understanding and appreciation
- To learn the meaning of new vocabulary words within the context of the Latin readings
- To recognize Latin root words and their English derivatives
- To understand how the Roman government functioned

**Cicero denounced Catiline in a series of speeches to the Roman Senate that left Catiline with no options but to run and try to hide. Frustrated by his inability to secure the consulship in 65 B.C., Catiline and his followers had conspired to murder the two consuls who were elected. Unsuccessful, they plotted anew and were caught when Cicero intercepted correspondence between the conspirators and immediately convened a meeting of the Senate. Cicero's role in suppressing the conspiracy earned him the title pater patriae.**

# CICERO'S LIFE

Marcus Tullius Cicero was intimately connected with every movement of history in the fateful period in which he lived. But although a great political figure, he is an incomparably greater literary figure, representing the combination of Greek learning and Latin culture and its practical application in Roman thought and institutions that characterized the whole of Roman literature.

Cicero was born near Arpinum (about sixty miles southeast of Rome) on January 3, 106 B.C. On December 7, 43 B.C., the year following Caesar's assassination, he was put to death. Cicero was of a well-to-do equestrian family, not of the nobility. He was sent to Rome for his education, where he studied literature, rhetoric, oratory, and philosophy under the best teachers available. In his study of law he attended the courts to hear the famous orators. He was also trained in acting to contribute to his stage presence in the making of speeches. In the Social War, Cicero completed his military service, which was a prerequisite to a public career.

Cicero made his first appearance in the courts in 81 B.C. on behalf of Publius Quinctius, who was involved in a suit for debt. The following year, in a courageous speech, he defended an anti-Sullan, Sextus Roscius, on a murder charge. After this, at the age of 26, Cicero traveled in the East (Athens, Rhodes) to pursue his studies further, particularly in philosophy and rhetoric. He returned to Rome after two years abroad and married Terentia, a wealthy woman, by whom he had two children, Tullia and Marcus.

The order of advancement in public offices, known as the **cursus honōrum**, was fixed by law and by custom. When Cicero had reached the age at which Romans were permitted to enter upon the cursus honorum, he began his official career with his election to the quaestorship (75 B.C.), in which he served with distinction in Sicily. Because of his ability and fairness, the Sicilians retained him as their counsel against their ex-governor, Verres, brought to trial for his shameless record of high-handed tyranny and rapacity. As a result of Cicero's brilliant advocacy of the Sicilian cause, Verres went into exile and Cicero supplanted Hortensius, who had defended Verres, as the leading orator of his day.

Cicero became aedile in 69 B.C. and praetor in 66, the momentous year in which he supported Pompey for an extraordinary command in the East against Mithridates, King of Pontus.

Cicero's election to the consulship in 63 B.C. resulted from a split in the opposition and from Pompey's support. Cicero, although a **novus homō,** that is, the first of his family to hold a curule office, won the election because he was considered politically safe. During his term as consul,

Cicero was confronted with the conspiracy of Catiline, crushed this attempt at revolution, and as a result was called father of his country **(pater patriae)**, the first Roman to receive this title.

The five years following Cicero's consulship marked a change in political alignments. The first triumvirate, formed in 60 B.C., consisted of Pompey, Crassus, and Caesar, who was elected consul for the year 59 B.C. This three-man consolidation of political power made various overtures to Cicero, who in his patriotism refused them all; he could not reconcile himself to what he considered the unconstitutional attitude of Caesar. In the year 58 Cicero was forced into exile on the charge, brought by Clodius, whom Cicero had offended, of having put to death Roman citizens—the conspirators associated with Catiline—without a proper trial. Cicero lived in exile from April 58 until August 57, when he was recalled with the consent of Caesar. The exile was a crushing blow to Cicero, but on his return he was enthusiastically welcomed by the people, re-entered political life, and began again to make speeches.

In 53 B.C. Cicero was elected to the College of Augurs, a religious position, and in 51 went to Cilicia in Asia Minor as governor, where he served honestly and well. On his return to Rome in 50, Cicero found Rome on the brink of the Civil War between Pompey and Caesar, which actually began in January 49. Cicero tried to effect a reconciliation between the two opponents, but he was unsuccessful. He finally left the city after Caesar crossed the Rubicon River and occupied Italy proper. Pompey fled from Italy to the Balkans, but Cicero did not follow him out of Italy. Caesar, however, pursued Pompey and defeated him at the battle of Pharsalus in 48 B.C. Subsequently Cicero was reconciled with Caesar and allowed to return to Rome, but he did not engage in political activity for some time.

In the year 46 Cicero divorced his wife Terentia and married a younger woman, Publilia, who had been his ward. In 45 Tullia, his beloved daughter, died, and he was overwhelmed with grief. It was at this time that Cicero devoted himself to writing on philosophic and literary subjects.

Cicero returned to political life after the death of Caesar (44 B.C.) because he thought he saw a chance for the restoration of the commonwealth and envisaged his duty as a fight against Antony, who was trying to seize control of the government. He wrote fourteen speeches against Antony, called the *Philippics*.

When the second triumvirate, consisting of Octavian, Antony, and Lepidus, was formed in 43 B.C., Cicero was proscribed (Octavian had reluctantly agreed) and killed by agents of Antony on December 7 of the same year.

Cicero's prose writings include speeches (over fifty still remain); treatises on political science, rhetoric, and philosophy; and approximately 800 letters. His letters, not written for publication, form one of the most interesting and valuable documents of Roman times. Cicero also wrote poetry which, although not of the highest quality, was always technically competent.

## Enrichment

The events of Cicero's life and his skill as an orator figure prominently or incidentally in numerous films and television shows. Select a few to watch in order to study the various actors' portrayals of Cicero's oratorical skills. Compare their portrayals to the oratorical styles of famous speakers from the nineteenth, twentieth, and twenty-first centuries. Do they use the same methods Cicero employed? Is the rhetoric of modern speeches as compelling as Cicero's? Consider giving a speech on Roman society to your history class; try modeling your approach on Cicero to see if it improves your public speaking.

Cicero was the greatest orator of Rome, one of its most important statesmen, and its greatest known prose writer. His influence has been incalculable, justifying Macaulay's statement, "Cicero taught Europe how to write."

# CICERO'S STYLE

Greece had long been the home of famous orators, and, in the time of Cicero especially, the Romans studied and imitated the Greek masters. Roman orators generally adopted one of three styles of Greek oratory—the Attic, which was simple, the Asiatic, characterized by ornateness, or the middle style. Cicero, who as Rome's greatest orator is often compared with Demosthenes, adopted a combination of Attic and Asiatic.

In his zeal to become a first-rate orator, Cicero studied rhetoric—the principles and rules for speaking and writing effectively—and related subjects in both Rome and Athens. His fine training, plus a natural talent and firmness of purpose, paid rich literary dividends. For generations, the perfection of Cicero's style has been an object of admiration and imitation.

What do we mean when we speak of a literary style? Style may be defined as those characteristics of a writer that exhibit his or her individuality, and distinguish him or her from other writers. Cicero's style, for example, is characterized by both terse sentences and the resounding period style, which you will study on p. 90. His style is also graceful, flowing, balanced, witty, informal, charming, and many other things, depending on the circumstances under which he was composing.

Another characteristic of Cicero's style is his frequent use of figures of speech, modes of expression that help embellish thoughts. While reading Cicero, you will meet these figures of speech, many of which are still used by writers today. These patterns, as well as other aspects of Cicero's style, will be pointed out and discussed as they occur.

Try to put yourself in the midst of Cicero's style, so that you begin to absorb it, as if by osmosis, and to feel at ease with it. From time to time the text will give you some help in this. Here are a few suggestions to get you started:

As you prepare your lesson, always read a part of the assignment aloud in Latin, pausing at the end of thought groups, often indicated by punctuation. After you have read (once or more) a paragraph or sentence, see if the notes are of any help in giving the meaning. Then attempt to translate before you look up any of the meanings in the vocabulary (the word list should be a last and not a first resort), guessing at some of the meanings. If you should find the first sentence too difficult, go on to the second sentence, which may throw light on the first.

# CATILINE'S CONSPIRACY

The revolution that resulted in the establishment of the Empire under Augustus had early origins at Rome in inequalities of representation, economic unrest, and lack of harmony among the three orders of citizens **(nōbilēs, equitēs, plēbs).** It is often said to have begun with the Gracchi brothers' attempt at reform (133–121 B.C.). In the early part of the first century B.C. there was civil war at Rome between forces led by Sulla, an autocratic dictator, and those led by Marius, a dictator supported by the people. Lucius Sergius Catiline was an active supporter of Sulla, the winner in this civil war.

Catiline was born of an old patrician family in 108 B.C. In the reaction against conservatism following the regime of Sulla (who died in 79), Catiline joined the liberals. He went through the steps of the **cursus honōrum** and was governor of Africa for two years. He returned to Rome in 66 B.C. and became a candidate for the consulship but was prevented from running by a charge, brought by the conservatives, of maladministration in Africa.

Catiline formed a conspiracy to murder the consuls of 65, but the plot was exposed and Catiline acquitted. He again ran for consul in 64 but was defeated by Cicero. Once more Catiline formed a plot to seize the government by force. Cicero learned of the secret plans of the conspirators and had enacted by the senate a **senātūs cōnsultum ultimum** that gave authority to the consuls to suppress the conspiracy. Catiline made plans to have Cicero killed on the morning of November 8, but Cicero knew about this plot immediately after the meeting at which Catiline's plans were made. On the same day Cicero called a meeting of the senate in the Temple of Jupiter Stator and made the first speech against Catiline, who was present to listen to the charges against him.

# First Oration Against Catiline

## CATILINE'S AUDACITY

**Verba Ūtilia:** audācia, caedēs, coniūrātiō, furor, iam prīdem, ignōrō, immō vērō, orbis terrae, patientia, praesidium, praetereō, studeō, timor, vigilia, vultus

[1] *How long, tell me*
[2] *still*
[3] *that madness of yours* (**Iste** is contemptuous.)
[4] *expressions on the faces*
[5] *to death, you, Catiline*

**I, 1.** Quō usque tandem[1] abūtēre,$_{1}$ Catilīna, patientiā$_{2}$ nostrā? Quam diū etiam[2] furor iste[3] tuus nōs ēlūdet? Quem ad fīnem sēsē effrēnāta iactābit audācia? Nihilne tē$_{3}$ nocturnum praesidium Palātī, nihil urbis vigiliae, nihil timor populī, nihil concursus bonōrum$_{4}$ omnium, nihil hic mūnītissimus habendī senātūs locus, nihil hōrum ōra vultūsque[4] mōvērunt? Patēre tua cōnsilia nōn sentīs, cōnstrictam iam hōrum omnium scientiā tenērī coniūrātiōnem tuam nōn vidēs? Quid$_{5}$ proximā,$_{6}$ quid superiōre nocte ēgerīs, ubi fuerīs, quōs convocāverīs, quid cōnsilī$_{7}$ cēperīs, quem nostrum$_{8}$ ignōrāre arbitrāris?

**2.** Ō tempora, ō mōrēs!$_{9}$ Senātus haec intellegit, cōnsul videt; hic tamen vīvit. Vīvit? Immō vērō etiam in senātum$_{10}$ venit, fit pūblicī cōnsilī particeps, notat et dēsignat oculīs ad caedem ūnum quemque nostrum.$_{8}$ Nōs autem, fortēs virī,$_{11}$ satis facere reī pūblicae vidēmur, sī istīus furōrem ac tēla vītāmus. Ad mortem[5] tē, Catilīna, dūcī$_{12}$ iussū cōnsulis iam prīdem oportēbat, in tē cōnferrī pestem quam tū in nōs omnīs iam diū māchināris.

---

$_{1}$ future second person singular
$_{2}$ with **abūtēre**
$_{3}$ object of **mōvērunt**
$_{4}$ The "good" people were those who supported the government.
$_{5}$ The indirect questions depend on **ignōrāre**.
$_{6}$ November 7
$_{7}$ genitive of the whole
$_{8}$ from **nōs**, not **noster**
$_{9}$ accusative of exclamation
$_{10}$ Cicero does not mean that Catiline had no right to attend a meeting of the senate (he was a member) but that he dared to after his plans were exposed.
$_{11}$ ironical
$_{12}$ The tense is indicated by **oportēbat**; in English, we show it by the translation of **dūcī**: *you ought to have been led.*

**3.** An vērō vir amplissimus, P. Scīpio, pontifex maximus, Ti. Gracchum mediocriter labefactantem statum reī pūblicae prīvātus interfēcit: Catilīnam orbem terrae caede atque incendiīs vāstāre cupientem nōs cōnsulēs perferēmus? Nam illa nimis antīqua praetereō, quod[6] C. Servīlius Ahāla Sp. Maelium[13] novīs rēbus studentem manū suā occīdit. Fuit, fuit ista quondam in hāc rē pūblicā virtūs ut virī fortēs ācriōribus suppliciīs cīvem perniciōsum quam acerbissimum hostem coercērent. Habēmus senātūs cōnsultum[14] in tē, Catilīna, vehemēns et grave, nōn deest reī pūblicae cōnsilium neque auctōritās huius ōrdinis: nōs, nōs, dīcō apertē, cōnsulēs dēsumus.

[6] *the fact that* (explains **illa**)

## Literary Style: Anaphora and Praeteritiō

One of Cicero's favorite figures of speech is anaphora, the repetition of a word at the beginning of successive phrases and clauses without the use of a connective such as **et.** A splendid example occurs at the beginning of the preceding chapter: **nihil** is used six times, and the clauses are divided into three pairs: the guards, the people, the senate.

Cicero is fond of saying that he will not talk about some point and in doing so will reveal the whole thing. This is called **praeteritiō,** from **praetereō,** *I pass over,* the word often used in saying a great deal while pretending to say nothing (see line 19).

## Translation

1. We know what you did last night.
2. I pass over the fact that Scipio killed Gracchus.
3. Catiline thought that he could kill Cicero and seize the government.
4. He ought *(imperfect)* to have been killed *(present)* before he could destroy the government.

## WORD STUDY

The word *palace* almost tells the story of the city of Rome. It is derived from **Palātium,** the hill named after Pales, the goddess of the shepherds who used to roam over that hill before Rome was founded. Because it was so convenient to the Forum, it became the most desirable district in Rome for the rich senators and other officials. Cicero owned a house on it, as did Caesar and Augustus. Gradually the emperors covered the entire hill with their buildings, and so it was that **Palātium** became *palace.*

[13] Maelius distributed grain to the poor during a famine (439 B.C.).

[14] The senate passed a resolution (called the **senātūs cōnsultum ultimum**) on October 21 delegating full powers to the consuls. It was something like a declaration of martial law today.

# WHY NOT PUT CATILINE TO DEATH?

**Verba Ūtilia:** audeō, clēmēns, condemnō, cōnfestim, crēscō, crūdēlis, dēcernō, improbus, inclūdō, maiōrēs, moenia, mōlior, nēquitia, patior, perditus

1 *should see to it*
2 *any*
3 *penalty of death*
4 *in accordance with*
5 *senators*
6 *for inaction*
7 *the mountain passes*
8 *day by day* (**Singulōs** is not really needed.)
9 *right now*
10 *I suppose I shall have to fear, not that all good citizens may say that this was done too late by me, but rather that some one person may say that it was done too cruelly.*
11 *specific, definite*
12 *no one any longer* (with **iam**)
13 *though you do not realize it* (with **tē**)

**II, 4.** Dēcrēvit quondam senātus utī L. Opīmius cōnsul vidēret[1] nē quid[2] rēs pūblica dētrīmentī$_{1}$ caperet: nox nūlla intercessit: interfectus est propter quāsdam sēditiōnum suspīciōnēs C. Gracchus,$_{2}$ clārissimō patre, avō, maiōribus, occīsus est cum līberīs M. Fulvius cōnsulāris. Similī senātūs cōnsultō C. Mariō et L. Valeriō cōnsulibus est permissa rēs pūblica: num ūnum diem posteā L. Sāturnīnum tribūnum plēbis et C. Servīlium praetōrem mors[3] ac reī pūblicae poena[3] remorāta est? At vērō nōs vīcēsimum$_{3}$ iam diem patimur hebēscere aciem hōrum auctōritātis. Habēmus enim eius modī senātūs cōnsultum, vērum inclūsum in tabulīs, tamquam in vāgīnā reconditum, quō ex[4] senātūs cōnsultō cōnfestim tē interfectum esse,$_{4}$ Catilīna, convēnit.$_{4}$ Vīvis, et vīvis nōn ad dēpōnendam sed ad cōnfirmandam audāciam. Cupiō, patrēs cōnscrīptī,[5] mē esse clēmentem, cupiō$_{5}$ in tantīs reī pūblicae perīculīs nōn dissolūtum vidērī, sed iam mē ipse inertiae[6] nēquitiaeque condemnō. **5.** Castra sunt in Italiā contrā populum Rōmānum in Etrūriae faucibus[7] collocāta, crēscit in diēs singulōs[8] hostium numerus; eōrum autem castrōrum imperātōrem ducemque hostium intrā moenia atque adeō in senātū vidētis intestīnam aliquam cotīdiē perniciem reī pūblicae mōlientem. Sī tē iam,[9] Catilīna, comprehendī, sī interficī iusserō, crēdō,$_{6}$ erit verendum mihi nē nōn hoc potius omnēs bonī sērius ā mē quam quisquam crūdēlius factum esse dīcat.[10] Vērum ego hoc quod iam prīdem factum esse oportuit certā[11] dē causā nōndum addūcor ut faciam. Tum dēnique interficiēre cum iam nēmō[12] tam improbus, tam perditus, tam tuī similis invenīrī poterit quī id nōn iūre factum esse fateātur.$_{7}$ **6.** Quam diū quisquam erit quī tē dēfendere audeat, vīvēs, et vīvēs ita ut nunc vīvis, multīs meīs et firmīs praesidiīs obsessus nē commovēre tē contrā rem pūblicam possīs. Multōrum tē etiam oculī et aurēs nōn sentientem,[13] sīcut adhūc fēcērunt, speculābuntur atque custōdient.

---

$_{1}$ genitive of the whole with **quid**
$_{2}$ younger brother of Tiberius
$_{3}$ a round number; it was actually the eighteenth day
$_{4}$ Both infinitive and main verb are in the perfect for emphasis.
$_{5}$ Emphasis is gained by position and repetition.
$_{6}$ ironical; therefore the meaning is the opposite of what is stated
$_{7}$ result clause

Scala/Art Resource, NY

The Temple of Julius Caesar was begun in 42 B.C. by Octavian to honor his uncle. After Caesar's assassination, his body was brought to this site and honored with a funeral pyre. Built on the spot where he was cremated, the temple and its altar were finally consecrated thirteen years later in 29 B.C. You can see the remains of this temple at the far left on page 9.

## Literary Style: Irony and Chiasmus

Irony consists of saying one thing but meaning the opposite. In Cicero it serves to produce a laugh at Catiline's expense. Usually an ironical statement is introduced by **crēdō,** *I suppose,* as in this reading, or **scīlicet** or **vidēlicet,** *of course.*

As a rule, series of words are arranged in parallel order, as in lines 6–7 on p. 70: **L. Sāturnīnum** (a) **tribūnum plēbis** (b) **et C. Servīlium** (a) **praetōrem** (b)**.** However, Cicero at times uses a cross order with striking effect, as in line 16: **castrōrum** (a) **imperātōrem** (b) **ducemque** (b) **hostium** (a)**.** This is called chiasmus, from the Greek letter **chī,** formed like an *X*, from two crossed lines.

## Translation

1. There will be no one who will dare speak for Catiline.
2. If any harm is done to the state, the fault will be Catiline's.
3. It is our good fortune that few men like Catiline live in Rome.
4. The senate decreed that Catiline should not be allowed to be present.

# WE KNOW YOUR PLANS, CATILINE

**Verba Ūtilia:** amplus, atrōx, coetus, cōnfīdō, domus, etenim, īnfitior, lūx, nefārius, nocturnus, oblīvīscor, pariēs, plānē, sentiō, undique

**III.** Etenim quid est, Catilīna, quod iam amplius exspectēs, sī neque nox tenebrīs obscūrāre coetūs nefāriōs nec prīvāta domus parietibus continēre vōcēs coniūrātiōnis tuae potest, sī illūstrantur, sī ērumpunt omnia? Mūtā iam istam mentem, mihi crēde, oblīvīscere caedis atque incendiōrum. Tenēris undique; lūce sunt clāriōra nōbīs tua cōnsilia omnia, quae iam mēcum licet recognōscās.[1] **7.** Meministīne mē ante diem XII Kalendās Novembrīs[1] dīcere[2] in senātū fore[3] in armīs certō diē, quī diēs futūrus esset[2] ante diem VI Kal. Novembrīs, C. Mānlium, audāciae satellitem atque administrum tuae?[4] Num mē fefellit, Catilīna, nōn modo rēs tanta, tam atrōx tamque incrēdibilis, vērum, id quod multō magis est admīrandum, diēs? Dīxī ego īdem[3] in senātū caedem tē optimātium[4] contulisse in[5] ante diem V

[1] *you may review* (literally, *it is permitted that you review*)
[2] *which was going to be*
[3] *likewise* (literally, *the same I*)
[4] *the optimates,* (the conservative party in power)

[1] October 21
[2] **Meministī** is a perfect form, though we translate it with a present.
[3] = **futūrum esse;** the subject, **Mānlium,** follows
[4] an interesting type of chiasmus; **tuae audāciae** belongs with both of the nouns
[5] The entire following phrase is the object of **in.**

Kalendās Novembrīs, tum cum multī prīncipēs cīvitātis Rōmā nōn tam suī cōnservandī[5] quam tuōrum cōnsiliōrum reprimendōrum causā profūgērunt. Num īnfitiārī potes tē illō ipsō diē meīs praesidiīs, meā dīligentiā circumclūsum commovēre tē contrā rem pūblicam nōn potuisse, cum tū discessū cēterōrum, nostrā tamen quī remānsissēmus caede contentum tē esse dīcēbās?[6] **8.** Quid?[7] Cum tē Praeneste Kalendīs ipsīs Novembribus occupātūrum nocturnō impetū esse cōnfīderēs, sēnsistīn[8] illam colōniam meō iussū meīs praesidiīs, custōdiīs, vigiliīs esse mūnītam? Nihil agis, nihil mōlīris, nihil cōgitās quod nōn ego nōn modo audiam sed etiam videam plānēque sentiam.

[5] *for the sake of saving themselves* (an illogical singular modifying **suī**, which actually is plural)

[6] *when on the departure of the others you said you were satisfied with the murder of (those of) us who remained*

[7] *Listen!*

[8] = **sēnsistine**

## Literary Style: Correlatives

All authors make some use of correlatives, that is, of conjunctions and adverbs used in pairs, to form balanced clauses. But Cicero is particularly fond of this stylistic device. Among the correlatives he uses are: **et... et, neque (nec)... neque (nec), aut... aut, vel... vel.** These should be well known to you from your previous reading. Others are:

| | |
|---|---|
| **cum (etsī)... tamen** | *although . . . nevertheless* |
| **cum(tum)... tum** | *not only . . . but also* |
| **nōn modo (sōlum)... sed (vērum)** | *not only . . . but also* |
| **sīve... sīve** | *if . . . or if* |
| **tam... quam** | *so . . . as* |
| **tot... quot** | *so many . . . as* |

Find three examples of correlatives in the preceding passage; as well as two examples of anaphora.

## Translation

1. Catiline did nothing that Cicero did not know.
2. I shall never forget the murders that you were planning.
3. Not only Catiline but also many others were plotting against the state.
4. Although you plan to kill us all, nevertheless we will be able to defend ourselves.

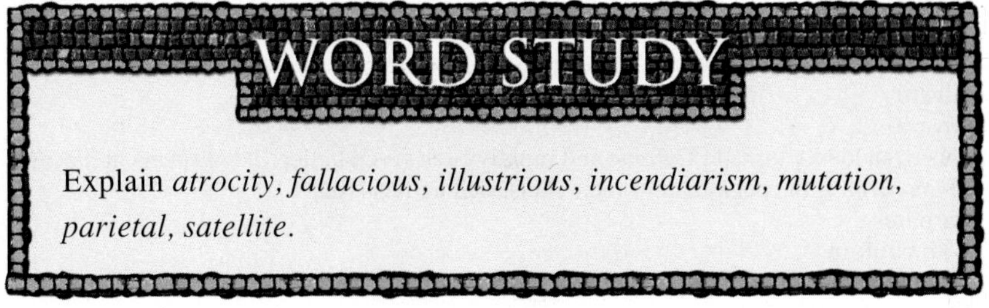


Explain *atrocity, fallacious, illustrious, incendiarism, mutation, parietal, satellite.*

# FAILURE OF THE PLOT

**Verba Ūtilia:** comperiō, distribuō, exitium, interitus, obscūrus, paulum, perniciēs, polliceor, reperiō, salūs, sānctus, taceō, tandem, vigilō, vulnerō

**IV.** Recognōsce mēcum tandem[1] noctem illam superiōrem; iam[2] intellegēs multō mē vigilāre ācrius ad salūtem quam tē ad perniciem reī pūblicae. Dīcō tē priōre nocte[3] vēnisse inter falcāriōs[4]—nōn agam obscūrē—in M. Laecae domum;$_{1}$ convēnisse eōdem$_{2}$ complūrīs eiusdem āmentiae scelerisque sociōs. Num negāre audēs? Quid[5] tacēs? Convincam, sī negās. Videō enim esse hīc in senātū quōsdam quī tēcum ūnā$_{3}$ fuērunt. **9.** Ō dī immortālēs! Ubinam gentium[6] sumus? Quam rem pūblicam habēmus? In quā urbe vīvimus? Hīc, hīc sunt in nostrō numerō, patrēs cōnscrīptī, in hōc orbis terrae sānctissimō gravissimōque cōnsiliō, quī dē nostrō omnium[7] interitū, quī dē huius urbis atque adeō dē orbis terrārum exitiō cōgitent. Hōs ego videō cōnsul et dē rē pūblicā sententiam rogō, et quōs ferrō trucīdārī oportēbat, eōs nōndum vōce vulnerō! Fuistī$_{4}$ igitur apud Laecam illā nocte, Catilīna, distribuistī partīs Italiae, statuistī quō quemque proficīscī placēret, dēlēgistī quōs Rōmae relinquerēs,$_{5}$ quōs tēcum ēdūcerēs, dīscrīpsistī urbis partīs ad incendia, cōnfirmāstī tē ipsum iam esse exitūrum, dīxistī paulum tibi esse etiam nunc morae$_{6}$ quod ego vīverem. Repertī sunt duo equitēs Rōmānī quī tē istā cūrā līberārent$_{5}$ et sē illā ipsā nocte paulō ante lūcem mē in meō lectō interfectūrōs esse pollicērentur. **10.** Haec ego omnia, vixdum[8] etiam coetū vestrō dīmissō, comperī;$_{7}$ domum meam maiōribus praesidiīs mūnīvī atque firmāvī, exclūsī eōs quōs tū ad mē salūtātum[9] māne mīserās, cum illī ipsī vēnissent quōs$_{8}$ ego iam multīs ac summīs virīs ad mē id temporis[10] ventūrōs esse praedīxeram.

[1] *I ask you*
[2] *soon* (as always with the future)
[3] *last night*
[4] *Scythemaker's Street* (Such street names used to be common: **Barbieri** *[Barbers]*, **Falegnami** *[Carpenters]*, etc., in modern Rome.)
[5] *Why?*
[6] *where in the world*
[7] *of all of us*
[8] *scarcely, almost before*
[9] *to greet* (Important people had many callers early in the morning.)
[10] *at that time* (adverbial)

### Literary Style: Twos and Threes

Cicero often uses words, phrases, and clauses in groups of two and three. For example, there are three questions in lines 7–8 of the preceding chapter. Next is a series of pairs: **hīc, hīc; in numerō, in cōnsiliō; sānctissimō, gravissimō; quī dē interitū, quī dē exitiō; urbis, orbis terrārum.** Then we find three clauses with the verbs **videō, rogō, vulnerō.** As often occurs, the last clause is longer and more complicated. Finally

---

$_{1}$ When **domus** has an adjective or genitive modifier, **in** or **ad** may be used.
$_{2}$ adverb
$_{3}$ adverb
$_{4}$ Cicero suddenly turns to Catiline and rapidly fires seven bullets, so to speak, at him; the seven verbs at the beginning of their clauses all end in **–stī.**
$_{5}$ purpose
$_{6}$ with **paulum**
$_{7}$ through Fulvia, who got the information from Curius, one of Catiline's men
$_{8}$ subject of **ventūrōs esse**

come the seven verbs mentioned in footnote 4. The first verb is introductory, setting the stage for the other six, that is, giving the meeting place of the conspirators. The others tell what was done. The first two verbs go together; they tell about dividing up Italy and assigning persons to various regions. The next pair of verbs assigns men to Rome and divides up the city for burning. Within this pair of verbs is another kind of pair, the two **quōs** clauses. The last pair indicates that Catiline is leaving Rome but is being delayed by the fact that Cicero is still alive.

### Translation

1. Where in the world were you last night?
2. There are men in this city who are preparing to burn it.
3. Catiline sent men to various parts of Italy to occupy all the cities.
4. We believe that Catiline brings too much danger and Cicero brings little protection.

# GET OUT OF ROME, CATILINE

**Verba Ūtilia:** aliquandō, calamitās, comes, concitō, cōnor, dīligentia, ēgredior, exsilium, īnfestus, mūrus, pergō, sinō, tumultus, ūtilis, versō

**V.** Quae cum ita sint,$_{1}$ Catilīna, perge quō coepistī: ēgredere aliquandō ex urbe; patent portae; proficīscere. Nimium diū tē imperātōrem tua[1] illa Mānliāna castra dēsīderant. Ēdūc tēcum etiam omnīs tuōs, sī minus,[2] quam plūrimōs; purgā urbem. Magnō mē metū līberāveris, modo[3] inter mē atque tē mūrus intersit. Nōbīscum versārī iam diūtius nōn potes; nōn feram, nōn patiar, nōn sinam.$_{2}$ **11.** Magna$_{3}$ dīs immortālibus habenda est atque[4] huic ipsī Iovī Statōrī,$_{4}$ antīquissimō custōdī huius urbis, grātia, quod hanc tam taetram, tam horribilem tamque īnfestam reī pūblicae pestem totiēns iam effūgimus. Nōn est saepius[5] in ūnō homine summa salūs perīclitanda reī pūblicae. Quam diū mihi cōnsulī dēsignātō, Catilīna, īnsidiātus es, nōn pūblicō mē praesidiō, sed prīvātā dīligentiā dēfendī. Cum proximīs comitiīs[6] cōnsulāribus mē cōnsulem in campō[7] et copetītōrēs tuōs interficere voluistī, compressī cōnātūs tuōs nefāriōs amīcōrum praesidiō et cōpiīs, nūllō tumultū pūblicē concitātō; dēnique, quotiēnscumque mē petīstī, per

[1] *of yours*
[2] *not*
[3] *provided that*
[4] *and especially*
[5] *too often*
[6] *at the last consular elections*
[7] *Campus Martius*

$_{1}$ A common form of expression, which can be translated by the one word *therefore.*
$_{2}$ anaphora and a group of three.
$_{3}$ Placing the adjective first and separating it from its noun **grātia** gives unusual emphasis, so that **magna** really means **maxima.**
$_{4}$ Cicero points to a statue of Jupiter the Stayer, who stayed the flight of the Romans when Romulus appealed to him.

mē tibi obstitī, quamquam vidēbam perniciem meam cum magnā calamitāte reī pūblicae esse coniūnctam. **12.** Nunc iam[8] apertē rem pūblicam ūniversam petis, templa deōrum immortālium, tēcta urbis, vītam[5] omnium cīvium, Italiam tōtam ad exitium et vāstitātem vocās. Quārē, quoniam id[6] quod est prīmum, et quod huius imperī[9] disciplīnaeque maiōrum proprium est, facere nōndum audeō, faciam id quod est ad[10] sevēritātem lēnius, ad commūnem salūtem ūtilius. Nam sī tē interficī iusserō, residēbit in rē pūblicā reliqua coniūrātōrum manus; sīn tū, quod tē iam dūdum hortor, exieris, exhauriētur ex urbe tuōrum comitum magna et perniciōsa sentīna[11] reī pūblicae. **13.** Quid est, Catilīna? Num dubitās id, mē imperante, facere quod iam tuā sponte faciēbās?[12] Exīre ex urbe iubet cōnsul hostem.[7] Interrogās mē, num[13] in exsilium? Nōn iubeō, sed, sī mē cōnsulis, suādeō.

[8] *even* (with **apertē**)
[9] *this power of mine*
[10] *with reference to*
[11] *the sewage (made up of) your associates*
[12] *you were trying to do*
[13] *whether*

## Literary Style: Alliteration

A familiar device in many languages, and especially in poetry, is alliteration, the repetition of the same letter at the beginning of successive words: line 11, **pūblicō mē praesidiō sed prīvātā;** lines 11–13, **comitiīs cōnsulāribus mē cōnsulem in campō et competītōrēs... compressī cōnātūs.**

Find two other examples of alliteration in the preceding reading.

You may recall reading the most striking example in all Latin, used by the poet Ennius: **Ō Tite tūte Tatī, tibi tanta, tyranne, tulistī.** In English there is the familiar *Peter Piper picked a peck of pickled peppers.* Here is another Latin example: **Sōsia in sōlāriō soleās sarciēbat suās,** *Sosia was sewing his shoes in the solarium.*

How is alliteration like anaphora? Different from anaphora? Find another example of anaphora and a group of three (besides the one in footnote 2 on page 75).

## Translation

1. Depart at once, Catiline, in order to save your life.
2. I have long been urging you to leave the city, Catiline.
3. If you were to remain in Rome, I would not be able to protect you.
4. If Catiline will not leave Rome, his life will be in the greatest danger.

## WORD STUDY

Explain *conjunction, exhaust, exhortation, insidious, intramural, nefarious, purgatory, residue.*

---

[5] We say *lives* in English; in Latin the plural means *biographies.*
[6] object of **facere**
[7] Calling Catiline a foreign enemy was a deliberate part of Cicero's plan to make it easier to get rid of him. In section 3 he calls him a dangerous citizen, worse than a bitter enemy; in 5, in connection with Manlius' camp at Faesulae, he says that the enemy is increasing in number and calls Catiline their commander, as he does again in 10.

# CATILINE'S CRIMINAL CAREER

**Verba Ūtilia:** dēdecus, dēvoveō, ēlābor, facinus, ferrum, flāgitium, haereō, necesse, ōdī, omittō, praetermittō, prīdiē, sacer, turpitūdō, vitium

**VI.** Quid est enim, Catilīna, quod tē iam in hāc urbe dēlectāre possit? In quā nēmō est extrā istam coniūrātiōnem perditōrum hominum quī tē nōn metuat, nēmō quī nōn ōderit. Quae nota domesticae turpitūdinis nōn inusta vītae tuae est? Quod prīvātārum rērum dēdecus nōn haeret in fāmā? Quae libīdō ab oculīs, quod facinus ā manibus tuīs, quod flāgitium ā tōtō corpore āfuit? Cui tū adulēscentulō$_{1}$ quem corruptēlārum illecebrīs irrētīssēs nōn aut ad audāciam ferrum aut ad libīdinem facem praetulistī? **14.** Quid vērō? Nūper cum$_{2}$ morte superiōris uxōris novīs nūptiīs locum vacuēfēcissēs, nōnne etiam aliō incrēdibilī scelere$_{3}$ hoc scelus cumulāvistī? Quod ego praetermittō et facile patior silērī, nē in hāc cīvitāte tantī facinoris immānitās[1] aut exstitisse aut nōn vindicāta esse videātur. Praetermittō ruīnās fortūnārum tuārum quās omnīs proximīs Īdibus$_{4}$ tibi impendēre sentiēs. Ad illa veniō quae nōn ad prīvātam ignōminiam vitiōrum tuōrum, nōn ad domesticam tuam difficultātem ac turpitūdinem, sed ad summam rem pūblicam[2] atque ad omnium nostrum vītam salūtemque pertinent. **15.** Potestne tibi haec lūx, Catilīna, aut huius caelī spīritus esse iūcundus, cum sciās esse hōrum nēminem quī nesciat tē prīdiē[3] Kalendās Iānuāriās, Lepidō et Tullō cōnsulibus, stetisse in comitō$_{5}$ cum tēlō, manum[4] cōnsulum et prīncipum cīvitātis interficiendōrum causā parāvisse, scelerī$_{6}$ ac furōrī tuō nōn mentem[5] aliquam aut timōrem tuum sed Fortūnam populī Rōmānī obstitisse? Ac iam illa omittō—neque enim sunt aut obscūra aut nōn multa commissa posteā—quotiēns tū mē dēsignātum, quotiēns vērō cōnsulem interficere cōnātus es! Quot ego tuās petītiōnēs[6] ita coniectās ut vītārī posse nōn vidērentur parvā quādam dēclīnātiōne et, ut aiunt, corpore[7] effūgī! Nihil agis, nihil assequeris, neque tamen cōnārī ac velle dēsistis. **16.** Quotiēns iam tibi[8] extorta est ista sīca dē manibus, quotiēns excidit cāsū aliquō et ēlāpsa est! Quae$_{7}$ quidem quibus[9]$_{8}$ abs tē initiāta sacrīs ac dēvōta sit nesciō, quod[10] eam necesse putās esse in cōnsulis corpore dēfīgere.

[1] *this savage crime*
[2] *the greatest public interests*
[3] *the day before January 1* (The allusion is to Catiline's "first conspiracy," three years earlier.)
[4] *a band (handful)* (object of **parāvisse**)
[5] *(change of) mind*
[6] *thrusts* (He is comparing Catiline to a gladiator.)
[7] *with a kind of little twist of the body*
[8] *your* (with **manibus**)
[9] *with what rites*
[10] *(seeing) that*

---

$_{1}$ with **praetulistī:** *Before what young man have you not carried the sword for bold deeds or the torch for passion?*
$_{2}$ conjunction
$_{3}$ the supposed murder of his only son, done to please his second wife, as the historian Sallust tells us
$_{4}$ Debts were payable on the Kalends (first of the month) and Ides (thirteenth or fifteenth of the month). In six days, therefore (November 13), Catiline would find himself besieged by creditors.
$_{5}$ The **comitiō** was an open space in front of the senate.
$_{6}$ with **obstitisse**
$_{7}$ i.e., **sīca**
$_{8}$ The dagger was promised to some god if it performed successfully through the god's aid.

## Literary Style: Metaphor

A metaphor is an implied comparison; it identifies one person, object, or idea with another. It is the most common figure of speech and one that is used in many different ways. For example, a metaphor is often used in naming things. The words *car, machine,* and *wagon,* which existed long before the invention of the automobile, were at first metaphorically applied to this vehicle.

The comparison in the literary metaphor usually appeals to the senses, as Cicero's many metaphors indicate. In line 3 of the preceding reading, **nota... inusta** implies a comparison with the branding of the letter *F* on the forehead of a runaway slave. But Catiline's branding is figurative, not literal. In lines 6–7 Catiline is compared metaphorically with a slave (footnote 1). Near the end of the preceding chapter is another striking metaphor: Catiline's supporters are *sewage,* which *will be drained out* of Rome.

## Translation

1. Who is it that blocked your plans?
2. I can recall no one who does not hate and fear Catiline.
3. Everybody knows that you prepared a band of men for the purpose of killing the senators.

## WORD STUDY

The calendar is so called because its chief function was to indicate the Kalends, the first of the month. In Latin the spelling with a **K** is used only in this and in a few other words before **a.** It goes back to the Etruscans, from whom the Romans borrowed the alphabet.

# YOUR COUNTRY BEGS YOU TO LEAVE

**Verba Ūtilia:** abhorreō, caedēs, careō, cōnspiciō, cōnsulāris, ēvertō, inānis, ineō, opīnor, opprimō, plācō, salūtō, socius, tacitus, vītō

**VII.** Nunc vērō quae tua est ista vīta? Sīc enim iam tēcum loquar, nōn ut odiō permōtus esse videar, quō[1] dēbeō, sed ut$_{1}$ misericordiā, quae tibi nūlla$_{2}$ dēbētur. Vēnistī paulō ante in senātum. Quis tē ex hāc tantā frequentiā, tot ex tuīs amīcīs ac necessāriīs salūtāvit? Sī hoc post hominum memoriam contigit nēminī, vōcis[2] exspectās contumēliam, cum sīs gravissimō iūdiciō taciturnitātis oppressus? Quid, quod[3] adventū tuō ista[4] subsellia vacuēfacta sunt, quod omnēs cōnsulārēs quī tibi persaepe ad caedem cōnstitūtī fuērunt, simul atque[5] assēdistī, partem istam subselliōrum nūdam atque inānem relīquērunt, quō tandem animō tibi ferendum putās? **17.** Servī mehercule meī sī mē istō pactō metuerent ut tē metuunt omnēs cīvēs tuī, domum meam relinquendam putārem; tū tibi urbem$_{3}$ nōn arbitrāris? Et sī mē meīs cīvibus iniūriā[6] suspectum tam graviter atque offēnsum vidērem, carēre mē aspectū$_{4}$ cīvium quam[7] īnfestīs omnium oculīs cōnspicī māllem; tū, cum cōnscientiā scelerum tuōrum agnōscās odium omnium iūstum et iam diū tibi dēbitum, dubitās quōrum mentīs sēnsūsque vulnerās, eōrum aspectum praesentiamque vītāre? Sī tē parentēs timērent atque ōdissent tuī neque eōs ratiōne ūllā plācāre possēs, ut opīnor, ab eōrum oculīs aliquō[8] concēderēs. Nunc tē patria, quae commūnis est parēns omnium nostrum, ōdit ac metuit et iam diū nihil tē iūdicat nisi dē parricīdiō suō cōgitāre; huius tū neque auctōritātem verēbere nec iūdicium sequēre nec vim pertimēscēs? **18.** Quae$_{5}$ tēcum, Catilīna, sīc agit et quōdam modō tacita[9] loquitur: "Nūllum iam aliquot annīs facinus exstitit nisi per tē, nūllum flāgitium sine tē; tibi ūnī multōrum cīvium necēs,$_{6}$ tibi vexātiō dīreptiōque sociōrum$_{7}$ impūnīta fuit ac lībera; tū nōn sōlum ad neglegendās lēgēs et quaestiōnēs vērum etiam ad ēvertendās perfingendāsque valuistī. Superiōra illa, quamquam ferenda nōn fuērunt, tamen ut[10] potuī, tulī; nunc vērō mē tōtam[11] esse in metū propter ūnum tē, quicquid increpuerit,[12] Catilīnam timērī, nūllum vidērī contrā mē cōnsilium inīrī posse quod ā tuō scelere abhorreat[13] nōn est ferendum.$_{8}$ Quam ob rem discēde atque hunc mihi timōrem ēripe; sī est vērus, nē opprimar, sīn falsus, ut tandem aliquandō timēre dēsinam."

[1] *with which I ought to be*
[2] *spoken* (literally, *of the voice)*
[3] *What (of the fact) that?*
[4] *those next to you* (Cicero perhaps pointed.)
[5] **simul atque,** *as soon as*
[6] *unjustly*
[7] *than*
[8] *somewhere* (adverb)
[9] *though silent*
[10] *as (best as)*
[11] *all of me* (Chiasmus, with strong emphasis, in **mē tōtam... ūnum tē**)
[12] *at the slightest noise* (literally, *whatever noise is made)*
[13] *is inconsistent with*

---

$_{1}$ Supply **permōtus esse videar.**
$_{2}$ more emphatic than **nōn**
$_{3}$ Supply **relinquendam esse.**
$_{4}$ with **carēre**
$_{5}$ i.e., **patria**
$_{6}$ Catiline had taken part in the murders of Sulla's day.
$_{7}$ Catiline was charged with graft while propraetor in Africa in 67 B.C.
$_{8}$ **Esse, timērī, vidērī** are the subjects.

### Literary Style: Personification

Personification makes a person out of a thing. In the reading, the long speech of **patria,** "though silent speaking," is a fine example.

Watch for the groups of twos and threes. In the preceding chapter (lines 1–2) we find two **ut** clauses, each containing a relative clause. Then we come to **ex... frequentiā** and **ex... amīcīs.** Note how the second phrase is expanded into a pair: **amīcīs ac necessāriīs.** Next are two **quod** clauses (lines 6–7) and two adjectives, **nūdam** and **inānem.**

Note too the chiastic arrangement of the verbs (lines 10, 12–13, 15–16): **metuerent ut tē metuunt, carēre... māllem** but **dubitās... vītāre.**

Analyze the speech of **patria** in this way.

### Translation

1. If my citizens had feared me so much, I would have left the city at once.
2. The senators left bare that section of seats in which Catiline was sitting.
3. Cicero talks in this manner to Catiline in order that he may seem to be moved by pity.

### WORD STUDY

Explain *contumely, impunity, inane, parricide, placate, vulnerable.*

The suffix **–scō** is added to the stems of verbs and adjectives to form inceptive verbs, which have in them the idea of *begin to* (from **incipiō,** *begin*): **pertimēscō,** *begin to fear.* **Hebēscō,** *begin to be dull,* occurred earlier.

# ON YOUR WAY, CATILINE

**Verba Ūtilia:** carcer, ecquis, fuga, honestus, quiēscō, sodālis, vidēlicet, vīlis, vindicō, voluntās

**VIII, 19.** Haec sī tēcum, ut dīxī, patria loquātur, nōnne impetrāre dēbeat, etiam sī vim adhibēre nōn possit? Quid, quod tū tē in custōdiam[1] dedistī, quod vītandae suspīciōnis causā ad[1] M'.[2] Lepidum tē habitāre velle dīxistī? Ā quō nōn receptus etiam ad mē venīre ausus es, atque ut domī meae tē asservārem rogāstī. Cum ā mē quoque id respōnsum tulissēs, mē nūllō modō posse īsdem parietibus[3] tūtō esse tēcum, quia magnō in perīculō essem quod īsdem moenibus[4] continērēmur, ad Q. Metellum praetōrem

[1] = **apud**
[2] = **Mānium**
[3] *within the same walls*
[4] *city walls,* contrasting with **parietibus,** *house walls*

---

[1] Catiline asked Lepidus to agree to be responsible for Catiline's appearance in court when and if Catiline was wanted.

PHOTRI/J. A. Cash

One arch and two columns are all that remain of the Basilica Aemilia, which was built by Emilius Lepidus and Fulvius Nobilior in 179 B.C. Overlooking the central square of the Forum and facing the Temple of Julius Caesar, it had at least two stories and was especially beautiful. In front of the building and toward the right in the photo is a small area marked off with a low iron fence that marks the spot where the **Cloāca Maxima**, the major sewer line that drained the marshy land of Rome, entered the Forum.

[5] = **iūdicāverit**

[6] *that it votes* (literally, *that it is pleasing to it)*

[7] *word*

[8] *at all*

[9] *violent hands*

[10] *all this* (the temple and the Forum)

vēnistī. Ā quō repudiātus ad sodālem tuum, virum optimum,[2] M. Metellum dēmigrāstī, quem tū vidēlicet et ad custōdiendum tē dīligentissimum et ad suspicandum sagācissimum et ad vindicandum fortissimum fore putāstī. Sed quam longē vidētur ā carcere atque ā vinculīs abesse dēbēre quī sē ipse iam dignum custōdiā iūdicārit?[5] **20.** Quae cum ita sint, Catilīna, dubitās, sī ēmorī aequō animō nōn potes, abīre in aliquās terrās et vītam istam multīs suppliciīs iūstīs dēbitīsque ēreptam fugae sōlitūdinīque mandāre?

"Refer," inquis, "ad senātum;"[3] id enim postulās et, sī hic ōrdō[4] placēre[6] sibi dēcrēverit tē īre in exsilium, obtemperātūrum tē esse dīcis. Nōn referam, id quod abhorret ā meīs mōribus, et tamen faciam ut intellegās quid hī dē tē sentiant. Ēgredere ex urbe, Catilīna; līberā rem pūblicam metū; in exsilium, sī hanc vōcem[7] exspectās, proficīscere.[5] Quid est? Ecquid[8] attendis, ecquid animadvertis hōrum silentium? Patiuntur, tacent. Quid exspectās auctōritātem loquentium, quōrum voluntātem tacitōrum perspicis? **21.** At sī hoc idem huic adulēscentī optimō P. Sēstiō, sī fortissimō virō M. Mārcellō dīxissem, iam mihi cōnsulī hōc ipsō in templō senātus iūre optimō vim[9] et manūs intulisset. Dē tē autem, Catilīna, cum quiēscunt, probant, cum patiuntur, dēcernunt, cum tacent, clāmant,[6] neque hī sōlum quōrum tibi auctōritās est vidēlicet cāra, vīta vīlissima, sed etiam illī equitēs Rōmānī, honestissimī atque optimī virī, cēterīque fortissimī cīvēs quī circumstant senātum, quōrum tū et frequentiam vidēre et studia perspicere et vōcēs paulō ante[7] exaudīre potuistī. Quōrum[8] ego vix abs tē iam diū manūs ac tēla contineō, eōsdem facile addūcam ut tē haec[10] quae vāstāre iam prīdem studēs relinquentem usque ad portās prōsequantur.

## Literary Style: Antithesis

Cicero often "sets" words and phrases "against" each other (that is what the Greek word **antithesis** means). In lines 25–26 **quiēscunt** and **probant** are antithetical, as are **patiuntur** and **dēcernunt, tacent** and **clāmant.** The last pair of verbs illustrates oxymoron, a figure of speech that is nothing more than an antithesis in which the words contradict each other.

Find other antitheses in the preceding reading. Find an instance of alliteration.

---

[2] **Vidēlicet** shows that this and the following adjectives are ironical.

[3] Presumably Catiline interrupted with this demand.

[4] i.e., the senate

[5] Cicero evidently paused a moment here. The senate could not exile Catiline, but Cicero cleverly maintains that it voted for exile by silence.

[6] another striking oxymoron

[7] Catiline was presumably booed when he entered the senate.

[8] The antecedent, **eōsdem,** follows.

## Translation

1. If you should flee from Rome, the whole world would rejoice.
2. He said that he could not stay in the same city because he was afraid.
3. A man who thinks he can fight against the senate should be sent into exile.
4. Do you believe that Catiline is worthy of the honor of coming into the senate?

### WORD STUDY

Explain *abhorrent, incarcerate, quiescent, sagacious, vile, vindicate.*

*Viz.* is an abbreviation of **vidēlicet.** The *z* is not really the letter *z* but a sign of abbreviation.

# CATILINE WANTS CIVIL WAR

**Verba Ūtilia:** corrigō, dexter, invidia, iussū, meditor, mōlēs, nex, pertimēscō, poena, quamquam, sēcernō, serviō, sīn, tametsī, utinam

**IX, 22.** Quamquam[1] quid loquor? Tē ut ūlla rēs frangat[2], tū ut umquam tē corrigās, tū ut ūllam fugam meditēre, tū ut ūllum exsilium cōgitēs? Utinam tibi istam mentem dī immortālēs duint!$_1$ Tametsī[3] videō, sī meā vōce perterritus īre in exsilium animum indūxeris,[4] quanta tempestās invidiae nōbīs, sī minus[5] in[6] praesēns tempus recentī memoriā scelerum tuōrum, at[7] in posteritātem impendeat. Sed est tantī,[8] dum modo tua ista sit prīvāta calamitās et ā reī pūblicae perīculīs sēiungātur. Sed tū ut vitiīs tuīs commoveāre, ut lēgum poenās pertimēscās, ut temporibus[9] reī pūblicae cēdās nōn est postulandum. Neque enim is$_2$ es, Catilīna, ut tē aut pudor ā turpitūdine aut metus ā perīculō aut ratiō ā furōre revocārit. **23.** Quam ob rem, ut saepe iam dīxī, proficīscere ac, sī mihi, inimīcō, ut praedicās, tuō, cōnflāre vīs invidiam, rēctā perge in exsilium; vix feram sermōnēs hominum, sī id fēceris, vix mōlem istīus invidiae, sī in exsilium iussū cōnsulis īveris, sustinēbō. Sīn autem servīre meae laudī$_3$ et glōriae māvīs, ēgredere$_4$ cum importūnā scelerātōrum manū, cōnfer tē ad Mānlium, concitā perditōs cīvīs, sēcerne tē ā bonīs, īnfer patriae bellum, exsultā

[1] *And yet*
[2] *How could anything crush you?*
[3] *Nonetheless*
[4] *bring yourself* (literally, *bring your mind)*
[5] *if not*
[6] *for*
[7] *at any rate*
[8] *it is worth (so) much*
[9] *critical moments*

$_1$ an early form for **dent**
$_2$ = **tālis**, followed by a result clause
$_3$ dative with **servīre**
$_4$ six imperatives, arranged in three pairs according to the thought

[10] *why should I ask you*
[11] *that famous*

impiō latrōciniō, ut ā mē nōn ēiectus ad aliēnōs, sed invītātus ad tuōs īsse videāris. **24**. Quamquam quid ego tē invītem,[10] ā quō[5] iam sciam esse praemissōs quī[6] tibi ad Forum Aurēlium praestōlārentur armātī, cui sciam pactam et cōnstitūtam cum Mānliō diem,[7] ā quō etiam aquilam illam[11] [8] argenteam, quam tibi ac tuīs omnibus cōnfīdō perniciōsam ac fūnestam futūram, cui domī tuae sacrārium scelerum cōnstitūtum fuit, sciam esse praemissam? Tū ut illā carēre diūtius possīs quam venerārī ad caedem proficīscēns solēbās, ā cuius altāribus saepe istam impiam dexteram ad necem cīvium trānstulistī?

## Literary Style: Asyndeton

Asyndeton (a Greek word meaning "not bound together") is the omission of coordinate conjunctions in a series of words or phrases. This omission of the connective gives a staccato ("detached") or sharp effect. The six unconnected imperatives in lines 15–16 are an example of asyndeton.

Find a metaphor in the preceding reading.

## Translation

1. Oh, that the gods would cause Catiline to fear!
2. Do they prefer to stay in Rome or to go to Faesulae?
3. Why should we ask you to stay in this town in which there is so much danger?

## WORD STUDY

Explain *aquiline, argentiferous, exultation, fracture, meditation, molecule.*

Explain the force of the prefix **sē–** in **sēcernō** and **sēiungō,** of **per–** in **pertimēscō,** and of **prae–** in **praemittō.**

---

[5] The antecedent is **tē;** causal relative clause.
[6] Supply the antecedent **(virōs)**.
[7] October 27
[8] So called because it once had belonged to Marius; the fact that this emblem of a Roman legion had already been sent from Rome shows that Catiline would soon follow.

# CATILINE, THE HARDENED CRIMINAL

**Verba Ūtilia:** āmentia, cōnsulātus, cupiditās, exerceō, exsultō, famēs, frīgus, iam prīdem, inopia, marītus, obeō, praeclārus, rapiō, somnus, spēs

**X, 25.** Ībis tandem aliquandō quō tē iam prīdem tua ista cupiditās effrēnāta ac furiōsa rapiēbat; neque enim tibi haec rēs$_{1}$ affert dolōrem sed quandam incrēdibilem voluptātem. Ad hanc tē āmentiam nātūra peperit, voluntās exercuit, fortūna servāvit. Numquam tū nōn modo[1] ōtium sed nē bellum quidem nisi nefārium concupīstī. Nactus es ex perditīs atque$_{2}$ ab omnī nōn modo Fortūnā$_{3}$ vērum etiam spē dērelīctīs cōnflātam$_{4}$ improbōrum manum. **26.** Hīc[2] tū quā laetitiā perfruēre, quibus gaudiīs exsultābis, quantā in voluptāte bacchābere, cum in tantō numerō tuōrum neque audiēs virum bonum quemquam neque vidēbis! Ad huius vītae studium meditātī[3] illī sunt quī feruntur[4] labōrēs tuī, iacēre$_{5}$ humī nōn sōlum ad obsidendum stuprum[5] vērum etiam ad facinus obeundum, vigilāre nōn sōlum īnsidiantem somnō marītōrum vērum etiam bonīs ōtiōsōrum. Habēs ubi[6] ostentēs tuam illam praeclāram patientiam famis, frīgoris, inopiae rērum omnium quibus tē brevī tempore cōnfectum esse sentiēs. **27.** Tantum prōfēcī, cum tē ā cōnsulātū reppulī,$_{6}$ ut exsul potius temptāre quam cōnsul vexāre rem pūblicam possēs, atque ut id quod esset ā tē scelerātē susceptum latrōcinium potius quam bellum nōminārētur.

[1] *not only have you never*
[2] *Here* (i.e., with such followers)
[3] *those hardships were practiced*
[4] *which are told about*
[5] *to practice debauchery*
[6] *(an opportunity) where*

## Literary Style: Climax and Word Play

Occasionally Cicero uses climax, a figure of speech in which ideas are arranged in the order of ascending intensity. A good example is in lines 7–8: **perfruēre,** *experience,* **exsultābis,** *exult in,* **bacchābere,** *revel in.* **Bacchābere** is a very stong word, meaning to act like a crazed follower of Bacchus, the god of wine.

Word play to us usually means punning for humorous effect. But Cicero often uses it seriously, even in the most solemn passages. In lines 15–17 the play on **exsul** and **cōnsul** is used very effectively, for Cicero had prevented Catiline from being elected **cōnsul** and now was forcing him to become an **exsul.**

---

$_{1}$ i.e., starting a civil war
$_{2}$ connects **perditīs** and **dērelīcitīs**
$_{3}$ That **Fortūnā** is personified is shown by the use of **ab.**
$_{4}$ **ex... dērelīctīs** depends on **cōnflātam** *composed of*
$_{5}$ in apposition with and explaining **labōrēs**
$_{6}$ Catiline had been a candidate for consul against Cicero.

## Translation

1. Will you enjoy your exile, Catiline?
2. By preparing a camp in Italy you have produced woe for yourself.
3. In order that Catiline might realize what he had done, Cicero told him very plainly.

### WORD STUDY

Distinguish **parō, pāreō, pariō,** and **parcō** by giving their principal parts and meanings.

Explain *adjacent, derelict, humus, somnolence.*

# WHY DON'T YOU ACT, CICERO?

**Verba Ūtilia:** ārdeō, cārus, cūnctus, dēficiō, dēprecor, gradus, inertia, iūs, penitus, quaesō

[1] *turn aside by entreaty and prayer*
[2] *should say*

**XI.** Nunc, ut ā mē, patrēs cōnscrīptī, quandam prope iūstam patriae querimōniam dētester ac dēprecer,[1] percipite, quaesō, dīligenter quae dīcam,[1] et ea penitus animīs vestrīs mentibusque mandāte. Etenim sī mēcum patria, quae mihi vītā meā multō est cārior, sī cūncta Italia, sī omnis rēs pūblica loquātur:[2][2] "M. Tullī, quid agis? Tūne[3] eum quem esse hostem comperistī, quem ducem bellī futurūm vidēs, quem exspectārī imperātōrem in castrīs hostium sentīs, auctōrem sceleris, prīncipem coniūrātiōnis, ēvocātōrem servōrum[4] et cīvium perditōrum, exīre patiēre, ut abs tē nōn ēmissus ex urbe, sed immissus in urbem esse videātur? Nōnne hunc in vincula dūcī, nōn ad mortem rapī, nōn summō suppliciō mactārī imperābis?[5] Quid tandem tē impedit? Mōsne maiōrum? **28.** At[6] persaepe etiam prīvātī in hāc rē pūblicaperniciōsōs cīvīs morte multārunt. An lēgēs quae dē cīvium Rōmānōrum suppliciō rogātae sunt? At numquam in hāc urbe quī ā rē pūblicā dēfēcērunt cīvium iūra tenuērunt.[7] An invidiam posteritātis timēs?

---

1 future
2 The long quotation caused Cicero to forget the conclusion of the condition.
3 very emphatic, not only because it comes first but because it is so far removed from its verb **(patiēre)**
4 Catiline was urged to recruit slaves but apparently did not do so. He was clever enough to realize that all Romans were opposed to this.
5 An **ut** clause is usual with **imperō**, but the infinitive may be used in its passive forms.
6 **At** is often used like quotation marks to indicate a change of speaker.
7 Here Cicero's strategy becomes clear: Catiline is no longer a citizen but a **hostis;** whether the **senātus cōnsultum ultimum** gave Cicero this right is still unsettled.

Praeclāram[8] vēro populō Rōmānō refers grātiam, quī tē, hominem per tē cognitum, nūllā commendātiōne maiōrum[9] tam mātūrē ad summum imperium[10] per omnīs honōrum gradūs extulit, sī propter invidiam aut alicuius perīculī metum salūtem cīvium tuōrum neglegis. **29.** Sed sī quis est invidiae metus, nōn est vehementius sevēritātis[3] ac fortitūdinis invidia quam inertiae ac nequitiae pertimēscenda. An, cum bellō vāstābitur Italia, vexābuntur urbēs, tēcta ārdēbunt, tum tē nōn exīstimās invidiae incendiō cōnflagrātūrum?"

[3] *resulting from severity* (with **invidia**); similarly **inertiae**

## Literary Style: Rhythm

Cicero's prose has a definite rhythm, not so pronounced as that of verse but still easily recognizable, especially at the end of sentences. Two of the favorite endings are -˘-|-˘ and -˘˘˘|-˘. An example of the latter rhythm is **esse videātur**, a phrase which occurs very frequently; of the former, **cōnflagrātūrum** at the end of the chapter.

Find six examples of a series of three in the preceding reading.

Note the word play in **ēmissus** and **immissus** (lines 8–9).

Find one metaphor in the preceding reading.

## Translation

1. The country asked Cicero what he was doing.
2. Cicero says that his country is dearer to him than life.
3. If your country should say such things to you, how would you reply?
4. Do you not think you should seize a man who is making plans for destroying the city?

Explain *defector, deprecate, emissary, gradation, mulct.*

---

[8] emphatic and ironical

[9] Cicero was a **novus homō** in politics, for no ancestor of his had held a curule office. He became consul at the minimum age of 43.

[10] the consulship

# WATCHFUL WAITING

**Verba Ūtilia:** alō, dēleō, dissimulō, exstinguō, fateor, immineō, impendeō, intendō, iūdicō, paulisper, pestis, sanguis, sēmen, stultus, vōx

**XII.** Hīs ego sānctissimīs reī pūblicae vōcibus et eōrum hominum quī hoc idem sentiunt mentibus[1] pauca respondēbō. Ego, sī hoc optimum factū iūdicārem, patrēs cōnscrīptī, Catilīnam morte multārī, ūnīus ūsūram hōrae gladiātōrī[1] istī ad vīvendum nōn dedissem. Etenim sī summī virī et clārissimī cīvēs Sāturnīnī et Gracchōrum et Flaccī et superiōrum complūrium[2] sanguine nōn modo sē nōn contāminārunt sed etiam honestārunt, certē verendum mihi nōn erat[3] nē quid,[4] hōc parricīdā[2] cīvium interfectō, invidiae mihi in posteritātem redundāret. Quod sī ea[3] mihi maximē impendēret, tamen hōc animō fuī semper ut invidiam virtūte partam[4] glōriam, nōn invidiam putārem.

**30.** Quamquam nōn nūllī sunt in hōc ōrdine quī aut ea quae imminent nōn videant aut ea quae vident dissimulent; quī spem Catilīnae mollibus sententiīs aluērunt coniūrātiōnemque nāscentem nōn crēdendō corrōborāvērunt; quōrum auctōritāte multī nōn sōlum improbī vērum etiam imperītī, sī in hunc animadvertissem, crūdēliter et rēgiē[5] factum esse dīcerent. Nunc intellegō, sī iste, quō intendit, in Mānliāna castra pervēnerit,[6] nēminem tam stultum fore quī nōn videat coniūrātiōnem esse factam, nēminem tam improbum quī nōn fateātur. Hōc autem ūnō interfectō,[7] intellegō hanc reī pūblicae pestem paulisper reprimī, nōn in perpetuum comprimī posse. Quod sī sēsē ēiecerit sēcumque suōs ēdūxerit et eōdem cēterōs undique collēctōs naufragōs[5] aggregārit, exstinguētur atque dēlēbitur nōn modo haec tam adulta reī pūblicae pestis vērum etiam stirps ac sēmen[6] malōrum omnium.

[1] *(unexpressed) thoughts*
[2] *of many men of earlier times*
[3] *I did not have to fear*
[4] *any unpopularity* (with **invidiae**)
[5] *wrecks, bums*
[6] *root and seed*

---

1 We might say *prizefighter* or *bruiser;* Cicero practically called Catiline a gladiator once before. (§15, note 6)
2 The ablative absolute has conditional force.
3 i.e., **invidia**
4 from **pariō;** two objects with **putō,** as with verbs of calling
5 To call a man a king among the Romans was something like calling an American a Communist.
6 Subjunctive in a subordinate clause in indirect discourse, but **intendit** is not subjunctive because the clause is parenthetical.
7 conditional

PHOTRI/AISA

The **Cūria** was the meeting place of the Senate, the most powerful group in Rome for several hundred years. The number of senators varied at times in history, but there were generally about six hundred members, chosen from the patrician class. They decided governmental policies and how money should be spent. During the time of the kings, the senators were mainly an advisory group, but during the Republic, they were the main governing body. The **Cūria** was rebuilt a number of times but still retained its original shape. Constantine in the early fourth century was the last emperor to refurbish it.

## Literary Style: Cicero's Periodic Sentences

Contemporary writers of English and their readers generally prefer short sentences. In older English and in Ciceronian oratory, long, complex sentences, with phrases and clauses in groups of two and three, with anaphora, with asyndeton and other rhetorical devices, with the main thought not revealed until the end, were in great favor. The sentence just finished is an example of a period. We have read many such sentences in Cicero, e.g., page 77, line 15, **Potestne;** page 79, line 11, **Et sī mē;** page 86, line 5, **M. Tullī.** In the preceding reading, line 4, we find **Etenim sī summī.**

Find an example of word play in the preceding reading.

## Translation

1. I fear that he will kill all the citizens.
2. There were men in the senate who did not believe Cicero.
3. I do not know why you wish me to do what I do not want to do.
4. If Cicero had thought it worthwhile, he would have compelled Catiline to flee.

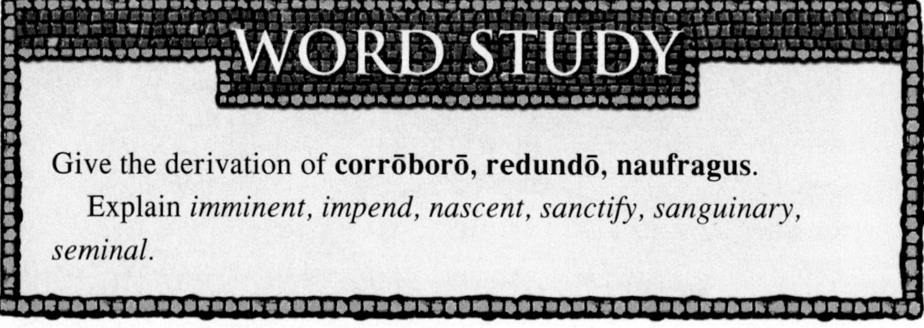

### WORD STUDY

Give the derivation of **corrōborō, redundō, naufragus.**

Explain *imminent, impend, nascent, sanctify, sanguinary, seminal.*

# OUT WITH THEM ALL!

**Verba Ūtilia:** auspicium, bibō, brevis, cūria, dēsinō, ērumpō, fax, foedus *(noun),* fortasse, frōns (–tis), latrō, morbus, ōmen, patefaciō, societās

**XIII, 31.** Etenim iam diū, patrēs cōnscrīptī, in hīs perīculīs coniūrātiōnis īnsidiīsque versāmur, sed nesciō quō pactō[1] omnium scelerum ac veteris furōris et audāciae mātūritās in nostrī cōnsulātūs tempus ērūpit. Nunc sī ex tantō latrōciniō[2] iste ūnus tollētur, vidēbimur fortasse ad breve quoddam tempus cūrā et metū esse relevātī, perīculum autem residēbit et erit inclūsumpenitus in vēnīs atque in vīsceribus reī pūblicae. Ut saepe hominēs aegrī morbō gravī, cum$_{1}$ aestū febrīque[3] iactantur, sī aquam gelidam bibērunt, prīmō relevārī videntur, deinde multō gravius vehementiusque afflīctantur, sīc hic morbus quī est in rē pūblicā relevātus$_{2}$ istīus poenā

[1] *somehow (*literally, *I do not know how)*
[2] *(band of) robbers*
[3] *heat of fever*

$_{1}$ conjunction
$_{2}$ conditional, as is the ablative absolute that follows

vehementius, reliquīs vīvīs, ingravēscet. **32.** Quārē sēcēdant improbī,[3] sēcernant sē ā bonīs, ūnum in locum congregentur, mūrō dēnique, quod[4] saepe iam dīxī, sēcernantur ā nōbīs; dēsinant īnsidiārī domī suae cōnsulī,[4] circumstāre tribūnal praetōris urbānī, obsidēre cum gladiīs cūriam, malleolōs et facēs[5] ad īnflammandam urbem comparāre; sit dēnique īnscrīptum in fronte[5] ūnīus cuiusque quid dē rē pūblicā sentiat. Polliceor hoc vōbīs, patrēs cōnscrīptī, tantam in nōbīs cōnsulibus fore dīligentiam, tantam in vōbīs auctōritātem, tantam in equitibus Rōmānīs virtūtem, tantam in omnibus bonīs cōnsēnsiōnem ut Catilīnae profectiōne omnia patefacta, illūstrāta, oppressa, vindicāta esse videātis.[6]

**33.** Hīsce[7] ōminibus, Catilīna, cum[8] summā reī pūblicae salūte, cum tuā peste ac perniciē cumque eōrum exitiō quī sē tēcum omnī scelere parricīdiōque iūnxērunt, proficīscere ad impium bellum ac nefārium. Tū,[9] Iuppiter, quī īsdem quibus haec urbs auspiciīs ā Rōmulō es cōnstitūtus,[6] quem Statōrem[10] huius urbis atque imperī vērē nōmināmus, hunc et huius sociōs ā tuīs cēterīsque templīs, ā tēctīs urbis ac moenibus, ā vītā fortūnīsque cīvium omnium arcēbis et hominēs bonōrum inimīcōs, hostīs patriae, latrōnēs Italiae scelerum foedere inter sē ac nefāriā societāte coniūnctōs aeternīs suppliciīs vīvōs mortuōsque mactābis.

[4] *as* (literally, *[a thing] which*)
[5] *forehead*
[6] *whose (worship) was established by Romulus under the same auspices as this city*

## Cicero's Style

Cicero ends his speech in a blaze of rhetorical fireworks. In line 19 we find anaphora, asyndeton, climax, and a periodic sentence ending in the favored rhythmic phrase **esse videātis.** The four clauses are arranged in two pairs: consuls and senators, knights and the rest. So are the four participles: revelation and light, crushing and punishing.

In the long periodic prayer at the end we note a series of pairs: **quī** and **quem** clauses, **urbis** and **imperī, hunc** and **sociōs.** Then comes a group of three phrases introduced by **ā,** each phrase containing a pair: **tuīs cēterīsque, tēctīs ac moenibus, vītā fortūnīsque.** These are followed by another group of three: **hominēs, hostīs, latrōnēs,** at the end of which is the pair **foedere** and **societāte,** each with an adjective. Last comes another pair, **vīvōs mortuōsque.** The speech ends with one of the favorite rhythms, **–ōsque mactābis** (-˘˘|-˘).

---

[3] It becomes clear here that **improbī,** by its contrast with **bonīs,** has a political meaning: *radicals.*
[4] dative with **īnsidiārī**
[5] from **fax**
[6] Because there is no future subjunctive, the present serves in its place.
[7] a stronger form of **Hīs**
[8] We would say *to* rather than *with.*
[9] addressed to the statue of Jupiter in the temple where the senate was meeting
[10] Cicero uses the word here in the sense of *Protector* rather than *Stayer.*

**Questions**

1. Where and when was the senate meeting held?
2. Why did Cicero make this speech?
3. Why did he not have Catiline executed?
4. Why did not the senate vote his execution?
5. What part does the word **hostis** play in Cicero's argument?
6. Who killed Tiberius Gracchus?
7. Who killed Gaius Gracchus?
8. How did Cicero learn of Catiline's plans?
9. Where was Manlius?
10. What happened on November 7?
11. What did Catiline plan for October 28?
12. Did Catiline have any supporters in the senate?

## WORD STUDY

How does the suffix **–scō** affect the meaning of **ingravēscō?**

Explain *bibulous, congregation, febrile, gelid, secession, viscera.*

# THE GOVERNMENT OF ROME

Rome developed from a small city-state, founded in the eighth century B.C., into a world empire. At the same time its constitution gradually evolved. Although the Roman constitution was never written down, a body of written legislation grew up, beginning with the Twelve Tables in the fifth century B.C.

Roman citizens came to be divided into three groups: (1) the **nōbilēs,** those who held, or had held, one of the curule offices (namely, consuls, dictators, praetors, and curule aediles) and their descendants; (2) the **equitēs,** the middle class, who were essentially an aristocracy of wealth dominating commerce and banking (the term **equitēs,** *cavalry,* recalls the early times when only the man who could afford a horse had the right of admission to this class); and (3) the **plēbs,** the lowest order of citizens. Slaves were considered property and had no rights.

In the early days of Rome the government was controlled largely by the noble oligarchy. With expansion, the **equitēs** increased their power and often aligned themselves with the aristocracy for effective control of governmental procedures. Meanwhile, there was a continuing struggle on the part of the **plēbs** for greater representation and a more equitable distribution of the functions of state, resulting ultimately (with, of course, other contributing causes) in the Civil War between Pompey and Caesar and the establishment of monarchy (though not so called) under Augustus.

The governing body of the upper classes was the senate, composed of 600 senators, all formally trained in governmental offices. All members were either former magistrates or descendants of nobles. They were called **patrēs cōnscrīptī** *(conscript fathers),* standing for **patrēs et cōnscrīptī,** a term that referred to the time when the first plebeians were admitted to the senate as "enrolled" or "added" members in distinction to the patrician members, the **patrēs.**

The popular assemblies were (1) the **comitia centūriāta,** so called because all the citizens were divided into groups of centuries, or hundreds, which elected the higher magistrates, and (2) the **comitia tribūta,** a grouping by tribes (there were thirty-five) with one vote each. In the **comitia tribūta** the **plēbs** were more influential than in the other two orders.

Every Roman official of the senatorial class was well educated and had undergone military and political training. The magistrates were elected annually (and could not immediately succeed themselves) in the **cursus honōrum.** Each official had at least one colleague and thus was prevented from monopolizing power. The officials were not salaried.

The officers in the senatorial **cursus honōrum,** all elected annually were:

| OFFICIAL | MINIMUM AGE |
|---|---|
| 1. *Quaestor*<br>Twenty in number. Served in the treasury. Two in Rome, eighteen in the provinces and the army. | 31 |
| 2. *Aedile*<br>Four in number. City officials, in charge of public entertainment and public works. | 37 |
| 3. *Praetor*<br>Eight in number. Judges in civil and criminal courts. | 40 |
| 4. *Consul*<br>Two, with equal powers. Presided over the senate; were the chief executives of the state; brought bills before the assemblies; had charge of elections. | 43 |

There were also the censors (two), usually ex-consuls, elected every five years for an eighteen-month term, who were in charge of moral standards and the eligibility of senators. During the remaining three and one-half years, the consuls performed the censors' functions. One office, that of the tribune, was in the hands of the **plēbs.** The tribunes of the plebs were ten in number, had the right of veto, and were personally sacrosanct; anyone who attacked a tribune could be put to death without trial. The veto made them very powerful.

After an official served as praetor or consul, he was usually appointed to a post as governor in a province, with the title of proconsul or propraetor.

The dictatorship at Rome was a constitutional office, resorted to in times of emergency. The dictator was appointed by the consuls at the request of the senate for a period of six months at most. Usually he retired as soon as the emergency had been handled.

# THE CICERONIAN SENTENCE

You have read about Cicero's periodic style. Here are a few other strategies to help you through one of his sentences.

You probably have realized that anaphora, groups of two and three, and other devices actually make it easier to find your way through one of Cicero's formidable periods. You will find it useful to read a sentence aloud, breaking it up into its natural parts. Often these parts are of about equal length. Take the last sentence in the first speech against Catiline:

Tū, Iuppiter, || quī īsdem quibus haec urbs auspiciīs || ā Rōmulō es cōnstitūtus, || quem Statōrem huius urbis atque imperī vērē nōmināmus, || hunc et huius sociōs || ā tuīs cēterīsque templīs, || ā tēctīs urbis ac moenibus, || ā vītā fortūnīsque cīvium omnium arcēbis || et hominēs bonōrum inimīcōs, || hostīs patriae, latrōnēs Italiae || scelerum foedere inter sē ac nefāriā societāte coniūnctōs || aeternīs suppliciīs || vīvōs mortuōsque mactābis.

In translating such a sentence as this, break it up into several short sentences.

Not only does Cicero weld his ideas into a nicely rounded period but, by various devices, he also connects the periods with one another in thought and word. The connecting relative is one such device. But besides the ordinary conjunctions such as **sed** and **et,** there are many other words and phrases used for transitions:

**age nunc,** *come now*
**age vērō,** *well then*
**at vērō,** *but*
**autem** (never first word), *however, moreover*
**dēnique,** *in short, in a word*
**enim** (never first word), *for*
**etenim,** *for really*
**hīc** (adv.), *in view of this, under these circumstances*
**iam tum,** *even then*
**iam vērō,** *moreover*
**igitur,** *then, as I was just saying*
**itaque,** *accordingly*
**nam,** *for*
**nē longum sit,** *to be brief*
**nunc,** *as it is*
**nunc vērō,** *but as it is*
**postrēmō,** *finally, at last*
**quae cum ita sint,** *and since this is so, therefore*
**quam ob rem,** *and for this reason, and therefore*
**quamquam,** *and yet, however*
**quārē,** *and for that reason, therefore*
**quid,** *tell me, again* (calling attention to a question to follow)
**quid est,** *listen*
**quid igitur,** *what then*
**quid quod,** *what of the fact that*
**quid vērō,** *look here*
**quod sī,** *but if;* occasionally, *if then*
**sīn autem,** *but if on the other hand*
**tamen** (usually not first word), *nevertheless*
**tametsī,** *and yet*
**vērō** (never first word), *in fact, but*

# Second Oration Against Catiline

The first speech was made before the senate on November 8, the second before the people on the next day. Catiline left Rome to join Manlius after the senate meeting. In the senate Cicero had a generally sympathetic audience; not so before the people, many of whom sided with Catiline. We can imagine that Cicero had rather a mixed reception. The one new thing in this speech is the detailed description of the six classes of conspirators, most valuable in explaining the background of the plot and therefore the most important part in all four speeches.

# CATILINE HAS LEFT!

**I, 1.** Tandem aliquandō, Quirītēs, L. Catilīnam, furentem audāciā, scelus anhēlantem,[1] pestem patriae nefāriē mōlientem, vōbīs$_1$ atque huic urbī ferrō flammāque minitantem ex urbe vel$_2$ ēiēcimus vel ēmīsimus[2] vel ipsum ēgredientem verbīs[3] prōsecūtī sumus. Abiit, excessit, ēvāsit, ērūpit.$_3$

[1] *breathing crime,* as we say, *breathing fire*

[2] *let go* (the original meaning of the word)

[3] *with (nice) words;* ironical

---

$_1$ with **minitantem**

$_2$ **vel,** as distinguished from **aut,** means *or, if you prefer*

$_3$ Note the rhetorical flavor of this first paragraph. Four participles are arranged in two pairs; in the first pair we have chiasmus. In **pestem patriae** and in **ferrō flammāque** there is alliteration. With the last participle there are two pairs of nouns. Then come the three verbs. The last sentence consists only of four verbs, in two pairs, reaching a climax.

# CONSPIRATORS: CLASS I

**Verba Ūtilia:** aes aliēnum, argentum, certō (–āre), errō, flamma *(in reading above),* furō *(in reading above),* locuplēs, sānō, ulcīscor, voveō

**VIII, 17.** Sed cūr tam diū dē ūnō hoste loquimur, et dē eō hoste quī iam fatētur sē esse hostem,$_1$ et quem, quia, quod$_2$ semper voluī, mūrus interest, nōn timeō; dē hīs quī dissimulant, quī Rōmae remanent, quī nōbīscum sunt, nihil dīcimus? Quōs quidem ego, sī ūllō modō fierī possit, nōn tam ulcīscī studeō quam sānāre sibi ipsōs, plācāre reī pūblicae[1] neque id quārē fierī nōn possit, sī iam mē audīre volent, intellegō. Expōnam enim vōbīs, Quirītēs, ex quibus generibus hominum istae cōpiae comparentur; deinde singulīs medicīnam cōnsilī atque ōrātiōnis$_3$ meae, sī quam[2] poterō, afferam.

**18.** Ūnum genus est eōrum quī magnō in aere aliēnō[3] maiōrēs etiam possessiōnēs habent, quārum amōre, adductī dissolvī[4] nūllō modō possunt. Hōrum hominum speciēs est honestissima, sunt enim locuplētēs; voluntās vērō et causa impudentissima. Tū$_4$ agrīs, tū aedificiīs, tū argentō, tū familiā, tū rēbus omnibus ōrnātus et cōpiōsus sīs, et dubitēs dē possessiōne dētrahere, acquīrere ad fidem?[5] Quid enim exspectās? Bellum? Quid ergō?

[1] *for (the good of) the state*

[2] *any* **(medicinam)**

[3] *(although) in great debt*

[4] *clear themselves (of debt)*

[5] *credit*

---

$_1$ Note the emphatic repetition of **hostis.**

$_2$ An excellent example of a common Latin usage that cannot be reproduced in English. The introductory words of three clauses come first; the verbs of each follow in the opposite order: **vōluī** goes with **quod, interest** with **quia, timeō** with **quem.**

$_3$ hendiadys; the two genitives explain **medicīnam**

$_4$ He addresses an imaginary member of this class.

In vāstātiōne omnium tuās possessiōnēs sacrōsānctās futūrās putās? An tabulās novās?[6] Errant quī istās ā Catilīnā exspectant; meō beneficiō tabulae novae prōferuntur, vērum auctiōnāriae;[5] neque enim istī quī possessiōnēs habent aliā ratiōne ūllā salvī esse possunt. Quod[7] sī mātūrius facere voluissent neque, id quod stultissimum est, certāre cum ūsūrīs frūctibus praediōrum,[6] et locuplētiōribus hīs et meliōribus cīvibus ūterēmur.[8] Sed hōsce hominēs minimē putō pertimēscendōs, quod aut dēdūcī dē sententiā possunt aut, sī permanēbunt, magis mihi videntur vōta factūrī contrā rem pūblicam quam arma lātūrī.

[6] *new accounts* means cancellation of debt, promised by Catiline
[7] *and this* (connecting relative)
[8] *we should find them (to be)*

## Translation

1. You hesitate to give up your fine houses?
2. I see no one who can compel Catiline to surrender.
3. Although Catiline threatened us, we let him go from Rome.
4. The men who have remained in Rome are to be feared the most.

---

[5] Cicero plans to have mortgaged property sold at auction to pay off the mortgage.
[6] Farm income was insufficient to pay off mortgage interest.

# CLASSES II AND III

**Verba Ūtilia:** adipīscor, agrestis, colōnus, concordia, furor, iactō, īnferī, potior, sūmptus, tenuis

**IX, 19.** Alterum genus est eōrum quī, quamquam premuntur aere aliēnō, dominātiōnem tamen exspectant, rērum[1] potīrī volunt, honōrēs[2] quōs, quiētā rē pūblicā, dēspērant, perturbātā,[1] sē cōnsequī posse arbitrantur. Quibus hoc praecipiendum vidētur, ūnum scīlicet et idem quod reliquīs omnibus,[2] ut dēspērent id quod cōnantur sē cōnsequī posse: prīmum omnium mē ipsum vigilāre,[3] adesse, prōvidēre reī pūblicae; deinde magnōs animōs esse in bonīs virīs, magnam concordiam ōrdinum, maximam multitūdinem, magnās praetereā mīlitum cōpiās; deōs dēnique immortālīs huic invictō populō, clārissimō imperiō, pulcherrimae urbī contrā tantam vim sceleris praesentīs[3] auxilium esse lātūrōs. Quod sī iam sint id quod summō furōre cupiunt adeptī,[4] num illī in cinere urbis et in sanguine cīvium, quae[5] mente cōnscelerātā ac nefāriā concupīvērunt, cōnsulēs sē aut dictātōrēs aut etiam rēgēs spērant futūrōs? Nōn vident id sē cupere quod, sī adeptī sint, fugitīvō alicui aut gladiātōrī concēdī sit necesse?

[1] *to acquire political control*
[2] *public offices*
[3] *in person* (with **deōs**)
[4] *but supposing they have obtained*
[5] *(things) which* (The two preceding nouns are the antecedent.)

---

[1] i.e., **rē pūblicā**
[2] Supply **praecipiendum vidētur.**
[3] The infinitives are in apposition with **hoc.**

**20.** Tertium genus est aetāte iam affectum, sed tamen exercitātiōne rōbustum; quō ex genere iste est Mānlius cui nunc Catilīna succēdit. Hī sunt hominēs ex eīs colōniīs quās Sulla cōnstituit;[4] quās ego ūniversās[6] cīvium esse optimōrum et fortissimōrum virōrum sentiō, sed tamen eī sunt colōnī quī sē in īnspērātīs ac repentīnīs pecūniīs sūmptuōsius īnsolentiusque iactārunt.[7] Hī dum aedificant tamquam beātī,[8] dum praediīs lēctīs, familiīs magnīs, convīviīs apparātīs dēlectantur, in tantum aes aliēnum incidērunt ut, sī salvī esse velint, Sulla sit eīs ab īnferīs excitandus. Quī etiam nōn nūllōs agrestīs hominēs tenuīs atque egentīs in eandem illam spem rapīnārum veterum impulērunt. Quōs ego utrōsque in eōdem genere praedātōrum dīreptōrumque pōnō, sed eōs hoc[5] moneō, dēsinant furere ac prōscrīptiōnēs et dictātūrās cōgitāre. Tantus enim illōrum temporum[6] dolor inustus est cīvitātī ut iam ista nōn modo hominēs sed nē[9] pecudēs quidem mihi passūrae esse videantur.

[6] *on the whole*
[7] *made a display of themselves*
[8] *rich* (or *blessed*)
[9] *not only not . . . but not even*

## Translation

1. This is what I urge, that you leave Rome at once.
2. Let them not remain at Rome; let them go to Manlius' camp.
3. They want to get possession of the city and all its wealth.
4. They have fallen into debt because they want to live like rich people.

---

[4] Sulla had confiscated much land in Italy in order to reward 120,000 of his veterans.
[5] **dēsinant** (with **ut** omitted) explains **hoc**
[6] the time of Sulla

# CLASSES IV, V, AND VI

**Verba Ūtilia:** dīlēctus, grex, idcircō, industria, parricīda, pereō, proprius, quam prīmum, sānē, venēnum

**X. 21.** Quārtum genus est sānē varium et mixtum et turbulentum; quī iam prīdem premuntur, quī numquam ēmergunt,[1] quī partim inertiā, partim male gerendō negōtiō, partim etiam sūmptibus in vetere aere aliēnō vacillant, quī vadimōniīs, iūdiciīs, prōscrīptiōne[2] bonōrum dēfatīgātī permultī et ex urbe et ex agrīs sē in illa castra cōnferre dīcuntur. Hōsce ego nōn tam mīlitēs ācrīs quam īnfitiātōrēs[3] lentōs esse arbitror. Quī hominēs quam prīmum, sī stāre nōn possunt, corruant, sed ita ut nōn modo cīvitās sed nē vīcīnī quidem proximī sentiant. Nam illud nōn intellegō quam ob rem, sī vīvere honestē nōn possunt, perīre turpiter velint, aut cūr minōre dolōre peritūrōs sē cum multīs quam sī sōlī pereant arbitrentur.

[1] *never get their heads above water*
[2] *summons (to court), judgment, forced sale*
[3] *slow payers*

Vanni/Art Resource, NY

The Arch of Septimius Severus was built in honor of Septimius, who ruled from 193–211, and his sons, Caracalla and Geta. With its three arched passageways, it is much more elaborate than the Arch of Titus, seen through the main entrance of the arch. Severus was a brilliant general who fought a successful campaign against the Parthians to expand the empire. After a foray into Scotland, he died at Eboracum (modern York, England).

**22.** Quīntum genus est parricīdārum, sīcāriōrum, dēnique omnium facinorōsōrum. Quōs ego ā Catilīnā nōn revocō; nam neque ab eō dīvellī possunt et pereant sānē in latrōciniō, quoniam sunt ita multī ut eōs carcer capere nōn possit.

Postrēmum autem genus est[4] nōn sōlum numerō vērum etiam genere ipsō atque vītā, quod proprium[5] Catilīnae est, dē eius dīlēctū, immō vērō dē complexū eius ac sinū; quōs pexō capillō, nitidōs, aut imberbīs[1] aut bene barbātōs vidētis, manicātīs et tālāribus tunicīs,[2] vēlīs[6] amictōs, nōn togīs; quōrum omnis industria vītae et vigilandī labor in antelūcānīs[3] cēnīs exprōmitur. **23.** In hīs gregibus[7] omnēs āleātōrēs, omnēs adulterī, omnēs impūrī impudīcīque versantur. Hī puerī tam lepidī ac dēlicātī nōn sōlum amāre et amārī neque[8] saltāre et cantāre[4] sed etiam sīcās vibrāre et spargere venēna[5] didicērunt. Quī nisi exeunt, nisi pereunt, etiam sī Catilīna perierit, scītōte[6] hoc in rē pūblicā sēminārium Catilīnārum futūrum. Vērum tamen quid sibi istī miserī volunt? Num suās sēcum mulierculās sunt in castra ductūrī? Quem ad modum autem illīs carēre poterunt, hīs praesertim iam noctibus? Quō autem pactō illī Appennīnum atque illās pruīnās ac nivīs[7] perferent? Nisi idcircō sē facilius hiemem tolerātūrōs putant, quod nūdī in convīviīs saltāre didicērunt.

[4] *is (last)*
[5] *Catiline's own*
[6] *sails* (because they contained so much cloth)
[7] *herds, gangs*
[8] *and not only*

## Translation

1. By managing business badly, they fell into debt.
2. Let them die in the snows of the highest mountains.
3. I do not understand why they want to die in disgrace.
4. I cannot tell whether they are wearing togas or sails.

---

[1] i.e., teenagers
[2] a sign of effeminacy, for most men wore sleeveless tunics, reaching to the knees
[3] i.e., they don't go home until morning from their all-night banquets
[4] Singing and dancing were not considered proper for "gentlemen."
[5] in wine, presumably
[6] future imperative plural, translated like a present: *I assure you* (literally, *know*)
[7] in contrast to Rome, where it does not snow very often

# Third Oration Against Catiline

The third speech against Catiline was made before the people on December 3, more than three weeks after the second speech, as a result of the discovery of sensational and conclusive evidence against Catiline. Before that Cicero had no real proof, and many people no doubt thought that he was just making political speeches, ones not based on fact.

After Catiline left Rome, his representatives began to deal with members of a Gallic tribe, the Allobroges, who were in Rome on an official mission. The Allobroges had complained to the senate about the dishonesty of Romans doing business in their country. The senate paid no attention to their complaints, and naturally the Allobroges were disgruntled. Catiline's men got the idea, clever at first sight, of taking advantage of this indignation. The conspirators proposed that the Allobroges send soldiers to help Catiline fight against his own country. The Allobroges, like other foreign peoples, had a Roman patron, that is, an adviser on legal matters. They consulted him about the conspirators' request, and he reported it to Cicero, who advised the Allobroges to get the request put in writing. This Catiline's representatives were stupid enough to do. Not only that—one of Catiline's men, named Lentulus, wrote Catiline, suggesting that slaves be enrolled as soldiers. His letter was sent by a messenger accompanying the Allobroges, who promised to stop and confer with Catiline at Faesulae.

Cicero arranged to have a force of soldiers intercept the group on the night of December 2. They met them at the Mulvian bridge, now within the city limits, at that time two miles north. The written request for Allobrogian assistance and Lentulus' letter to Catiline were seized and brought to Cicero. The leaders of the conspiracy were arrested and taken to the senate, where they confessed. Later in the day Cicero delivered this third oration in the Forum to tell the people what had happened.

The plan of calling on foreigners for help, of urging the use of slaves—and putting this in writing—appeared incredibly stupid to the Romans. They praised Cicero and, recalling the dangerous slave revolt a few years earlier, rejoiced at being saved by him.

# ROME IS SAVED

**Verba Ūtilia:** benevolentia, condō, coniūnx, dēlūbrum, domicilium, ergā, fātum, hodiernus, ignōrō, illūstris, manifēstus, posterus, prīncipium, sēnsus, tollō

**I, 1.** Rem pūblicam,$_{1}$ Quirītēs, vītamque$_{2}$ omnium vestrum, bona, fortūnās, coniugēs līberōsque vestrōs atque hoc domicilium clārissimī imperī, fortūnātissimam pulcherrimamque urbem, hodiernō diē deōrum immortālium summō ergā vōs amōre, labōribus, cōnsiliīs, perīculīs meīs ē flammā atque ferrō ac paene ex faucibus fātī ēreptam et vōbīs cōnservātam ac restitūtam vidētis. **2.** Et sī nōn minus nōbīs iūcundī atque illūstrēs sunt eī diēs quibus cōnservāmur quam illī quibus nāscimur, quod salūtis certa laetitia est, nāscendī incerta condiciō,[1] et quod sine sēnsū nāscimur, cum voluptāte servāmur, profectō, quoniam illum quī hanc urbem condidit ad deōs immortālīs benevolentiā fāmāque sustulimus,[2] esse apud vōs posterōsque vestrōs in honōre dēbēbit[3] is quī eandem hanc urbem conditam amplificātamque servāvit. Nam tōtī urbī,$_{3}$ templīs, dēlūbrīs, tēctīs ac moenibus subiectōs prope iam ignīs circumdatōsque restīnximus, īdemque[4] gladiōs in rem pūblicam dēstrictōs rettudimus mūcrōnēsque eōrum ā iugulīs vestrīs dēiēcimus.

**3.** Quae quoniam in senātū illūstrāta, patefacta, comperta sunt per mē, vōbīs iam expōnam breviter ut et quanta et quam manifēsta et quā ratiōne invēstīgāta et comprehēnsa sint vōs quī et ignōrātis et exspectātis scīre possītis. Prīncipiō, ut[5] Catilīna paucīs ante diēbus$_{4}$ ērūpit ex urbe, cum sceleris suī sociōs huiusce nefāriī bellī acerrimōs ducēs[6] Rōmae relīquisset, semper vigilāvī et prōvīdī, Quirītēs, quem ad modum in tantīs et tam absconditīs īnsidiīs salvī esse possēmus.

[1] *our status at birth*

[2] *we have raised to the gods with our affection and praise*

[3] *he will deserve* (**is** means Cicero)

[4] *(we) too* (literally, *the same we*)

[5] *ever since* (literally, *when)*

[6] *(as) leaders*

## Prepositional Phrases

Unlike English, Latin has few prepositional phrases depending on nouns. For example, the English phrase *a bird in the hand* would be in Latin **avis quae in manū est.** But in Latin a noun expressing feeling or attitude may have a phrase introduced by **ergā** or **in** dependent on it: **ergā vōs amōre** (line 4).

---

$_{1}$ This periodic sentence is really very simple. Its essential part is **rem pūblicam cōnservātam ac restitūtam vidētis;** the rest is elaboration. **Vītam** goes with **coniugēs līberōsque, bona** and **fortūnās** belong together; **domicilium** and **urbem,** modified by two superlatives, form a pair. **Deōrum amōre** balances in chiastic order **labōribus, cōnsiliīs, perīculīs meīs.**

$_{2}$ The plural is used in English.

$_{3}$ with **subiectōs**

$_{4}$ Time is relative: it was really over three weeks.

### Translation

1. Don't you see that the city has been saved?
2. Fires were to be applied to the entire city.
3. Cicero explained how he found out what they were planning.

## WORD STUDY

**Coniūnx** is derived from **con–** and the stem of **iungō:** *joined together.*

**Hodiernus diēs** is tautological: literally, *today's day.* We have tautologies also in the expressions *long-distance telephone* (for *telephone* means *far speaking*), *symphony concert* ("togetherness" is indicated by both Latin **con–** and its Greek synonym **syn-**), and *head of cabbage* (from **caput**).

# EVIDENCE OF TREASON

**Verba Ūtilia:** assiduus, comitātus, complūrēs, facultās, hesternus, lēgātus, pōns, restō, sollicitō, vigilia

**II.** Nam tum cum ex urbe Catilīnam ēiciēbam[1] (nōn enim iam vereor huius verbī[1] invidiam, cum illa[2] magis sit timenda, quod vīvus exierit), sed tum cum illum exterminārī[2] volēbam, aut reliquam coniūrātōrum manum simul exitūram aut eōs quī restitissent[3] īnfirmōs sine illō ac dēbilīs fore putābam. **4.** Atque ego, ut[3] vīdī, quōs maximō furōre et scelere esse īnflammātōs sciēbam, eōs nōbīscum esse et Rōmae remānsisse, in eō[4] omnīs diēs noctēsque cōnsūmpsī, ut quid agerent, quid mōlīrentur sentīrem ac vidērem, ut, quoniam auribus vestrīs propter incrēdibilem magnitūdinem sceleris minōrem fidem faceret[5] ōrātiō mea, rem ita comprehenderem ut tum dēmum animīs salūtī vestrae prōvidērētis cum oculīs maleficium ipsum vidērētis. Itaque ut comperī lēgātōs Allobrogum bellī Trānsalpīnī et tumultūs Gallicī excitandī causā ā P. Lentulō esse sollicitātōs, eōsque in Galliam ad suōs cīvīs eōdemque itinere cum litterīs mandātīsque[4] ad Catilīnam esse missōs, comitemque eīs adiūnctum esse T. Volturcium, atque huic esse ad Catilīnam datās litterās, facultātem mihi oblātam putāvī ut (quod[6] erat difficillimum quodque ego semper optābam ab dīs immortālibus) tōta rēs nōn sōlum ā mē sed etiam ā senātū et ā vōbīs manifēstō dēprēnderētur.

[1] *I was trying to drive out*
[2] *exiled* (from **terminus**, *boundary)*
[3] *would remain*
[4] *in this (task)* (explained by the following **ut** clause)
[5] *produced too little belief in you* (literally, *in your ears)*
[6] *(a thing) which,* referring to the **ut** clause

---

[1] refers to **ēiciēbam**
[2] **invidia**
[3] Watch out for **ut** in this sentence; it occurs four times; all in different uses.
[4] **litterae** were written, **mandāta** were oral

**5.** Itaque hesternō diē L. Flaccum et C. Pomptīnum praetōrēs, fortissimōs atque amantissimōs reī pūblicae virōs, ad mē vocāvī, rem exposuī, quid fierī placēret ostendī. Illī autem, quī omnia dē rē pūblicā praeclāra atque ēgregia sentīrent,[7] sine recūsātiōne ac sine ūllā morā negōtium suscēpērunt et, cum advesperāsceret, occultē ad pontem Mulvium pervēnērunt atque ibi in proximīs vīllīs ita bipertītō fuērunt ut Tiberis inter eōs et pōns interesset. Eōdem autem et[8] ipsī sine cuiusquam suspīciōne multōs fortīs virōs ēdūxerant, et ego ex praefectūrā Reātīnā complūrīs dēlēctōs adulēscentīs quōrum operā ūtor assiduē in reī pūblicae praesidiō cum gladiīs mīseram. **6.** Interim tertiā ferē vigiliā exāctā,[5] cum iam pontem Mulvium magnō comitātū lēgātī Allobrogēs ingredī inciperent ūnāque Volturcius, fit in eōs impetus; dūcuntur et ab illīs gladiī et ā nostrīs. Rēs praetōribus erat nōta sōlīs, ignōrābātur ā cēterīs.

*[7] since they had all the fine and excellent feelings about the state,* (i.e., they were anti-Catiline)

*[8] both*

## Translation

1. They proceeded toward the river with many soldiers.
2. In order to see what was happening, he went to the bridge.
3. They were sent with a letter to tell Catiline what he ought to do.
4. They said that they would not fight because they did not believe Cicero.

---

[5] The night was divided into four watches; therefore it was about 3 A.M.

# THE CONSPIRATORS UNDER ARREST

**Verba Ūtilia:** aedēs, arcessō, dīlūcēsco, integer, māne, scelus, sēdō

**III.** Tum interventū Pomptīnī atque Flaccī pugna quae erat commissa sēdātur. Litterae quaecumque erant in eō comitātū, integrīs signīs, praetōribus trāduntur; ipsī[1] comprehēnsī ad mē, cum iam dīlūcēsceret, dēdūcuntur. Atque hōrum omnium scelerum improbissimum māchinātōrem, Cimbrum Gabīnium, statim ad mē nihildum suspicantem vocāvī; deinde item arcessītus est L. Statilius et post eum Cethēgus; tardissimē autem Lentulus vēnit, crēdō quod in litterīs dandīs[2] praeter cōnsuētūdinem proximā nocte vigilārat. **7.** Cum[1] summīs et clārissimīs huius cīvitātis virīs,[3] quī, audīta

*[1] although*

---

[1] the conspirators
[2] ironical, of course: *in writing letters*
[3] with **placēret**

rē, frequentēs ad mē māne convēnerant, litterās ā mē prius aperīrī quam ad senātum dēferrī[4] placēret, nē, sī nihil esset inventum, temere ā mē tantus tumultus iniectus cīvitātī vidērētur, negāvī[2] mē esse factūrum ut dē perīculō pūblicō nōn ad cōnsilium pūblicum rem integram dēferrem. Etenim, Quirītēs, sī ea quae erant ad mē dēlāta reperta nōn essent, tamen ego nōn arbitrābar in tantīs reī pūblicae perīculīs esse mihi nimiam dīligentiam pertimēscendam. Senātum frequentem[3] celeriter, ut vīdistis, coēgī. **8.** Atque intereā statim admonitū Allobrogum C. Sulpicium praetōrem, fortem virum, mīsī quī ex aedibus Cethēgī sī quid[4] tēlōrum esset efferret; ex quibus ille maximum sīcārum numerum et gladiōrum extulit.

[2] *I said I would not so act as not to*
[3] *well attended*
[4] *whatever* (with **sī**)

### Translation

1. Before he could destroy the letter, it was seized.
2. If the letter were not found, what would Cicero do?
3. He sent a brave man to bring back any weapons he found.
4. He said he would not open the letter before the senate saw it.

---

[4] The subjunctive would be more natural, introduced by **prius quam,** but the contrast with **aperīrī** affects the construction.

### WORD STUDY

What two inceptive verbs are in the preceding reading?

Give English derivatives of **gladius, interventus, negō, sēdō, suspicor.**

# TESTIMONY IN THE SENATE

**Verba Ūtilia:** fugiō, incendō, indicō, praescrībō, praesidium, praestō, timor, ūtor, virgō, vix

**IV.** Intrōdūxī Volturcium sine Gallīs; fidem pūblicam[1] iussū senātūs dedī; hortātus sum ut ea quae scīret sine timōre indicāret. Tum ille dīxit, cum vix sē ex magnō timōre recreāsset, ā P. Lentulō sē habēre ad Catilīnam mandāta et litterās[2] ut servōrum praesidiō ūterētur, ut ad urbem quam prīmum cum exercitū accēderet; id[1] autem eō cōnsiliō ut, cum urbem ex

[1] *official promise (of immunity from prosecution)*
[2] *a letter*

---

[1] refers to the preceding **ut** clause

omnibus partibus quem ad modum dīscrīptum distribūtumque erat incendissent caedemque īnfīnītam cīvium fēcissent, praestō esset ille[2] quī et fugientīs exciperet[3] et sē cum hīs urbānīs ducibus coniungeret. **9.** Intrōductī autem Gallī iūs iūrandum sibi et litterās ā P. Lentulō, Cethēgō, Statiliō ad suam gentem datās esse dīxērunt, atque ita sibi ab hīs et ā L. Cassiō esse praescrīptum[3] ut equitātum in Italiam quam prīmum mitterent; pedestrīs sibi cōpiās nōn dēfutūrās.[4] Lentulum autem sibi cōnfirmāsse ex fātīs Sibyllīnīs haruspicumque respōnsīs sē esse tertium illum Cornēlium[5] ad quem rēgnum[6] huius urbis atque imperium pervenīre esset necesse: Cinnam ante sē et Sullam[7] fuisse. Eundemque dīxisse fātālem[4] hunc annum esse ad interitum huius urbis atque imperī, quī esset annus decimus post virginum[8] absolūtiōnem, post Capitōlī autem incēnsiōnem vīcēsimus. **10.** Hanc autem Cethēgō[5] cum cēterīs contrōversiam fuisse dīxērunt quod Lentulō et aliīs Sāturnālibus[9] caedem fierī atque urbem incendī placēret, Cethēgō nimium id longum vidērētur.

[3] *they had been directed* (impersonal)

[4] *fated*

[5] *Cethegus had had* (with **fuisse**)

## Translation

1. Did Lentulus warn Catiline not to use slaves?
2. Lentulus asked Catiline to come to Rome in order to burn the city.
3. This day was chosen for the deed since it was the first one after the holiday.

---

[2] Catiline

[3] purpose

[4] Supply *he stated that.*

[5] His whole name was P. Cornelius Lentulus Sura.

[6] Remember how hateful this word was to the Romans, as it was to Americans at the time of the Revolution.

[7] L. Cornelius Cinna and L. Cornelius Sulla

[8] We do not know what the charges against the Vestals were, but one may guess that they were blamed because the sacred fire went out.

[9] The general license and confusion of the **Sāturnālia** (beginning December 17) made it a good time for the conspirators to strike.

Scala/Art Resource, NY

A view of the **Forum Rōmānum,** looking across to the Capitoline Hill and the **Tabulārium,** which was erected in 78 B.C. The Arch of Septimius Severus is on the right and the **Rōstra,** or speaker's platform, is just to the left of the arch. The **Tabulārium,** or Record Office, is in the background and shows the foundations and original three arches of the ancient building. The top of the structure is a medieval addition that served as a palace. To the right and behind the **Tabulārium** is part of the Capitoline square, designed by Michelangelo.

# CONFESSION

**Verba Ūtilia:** argūmentum, cōnfiteor, dēbilitō, dēmēns, imāgō, intueor, recitō, superō, tabella, vultus

**V.** Ac nē longum sit,[1] Quirītēs, tabellās prōferrī iussimus quae ā quōque dīcēbantur datae.$_{1}$ Prīmō ostendimus Cēthēgō; signum cognōvit.[2] Nōs līnum incīdimus; lēgimus. Erat scrīptum ipsīus manū Allobrogum senātuī et populō sēsē quae eōrum lēgātīs cōnfirmāsset factūrum esse; ōrāre ut item illī facerent quae sibi eōrum lēgātī recēpissent.[3] Tum Cethēgus, quī paulō ante aliquid tamen dē gladiīs ac sīcīs quae apud ipsum[4] erant dēprehēnsa respondisset dīxissetque sē semper bonōrum ferrāmentōrum studiōsum[5] fuisse, recitātīs litterīs, dēbilitātus atque abiectus cōnscientiā repente conticuit. Intrōductus Statilius cognōvit et signum et manum suam. Recitātae sunt tabellae in eandem ferē sententiam;[6] cōnfessus est. Tum ostendī tabellās Lentulō et quaesīvī cognōsceretne$_{2}$ signum. Annuit. "Est vērō," inquam, "nōtum quidem signum, imāgō avī$_{3}$ tuī, clārissimī virī, quī amāvit ūnicē patriam et cīvīs suōs; quae quidem tē ā tantō scelere etiam mūta revocāre dēbuit."[7]$_{4}$ **11.** Leguntur eādem ratiōne[8] ad senātum Allobrogum populumque litterae. Sī quid dē hīs rēbus dīcere vellet,$_{5}$ fēcī potestātem. Atque ille prīmō quidem negāvit; post autem aliquantō, tōtō iam indiciō expositō atque ēditō, surrēxit, quaesīvit ā Gallīs quid sibi esset cum eīs[9] quam ob rem[10] domum suam vēnissent, itemque ā Volturciō. Quī cum illī breviter cōnstanterque respondissent per quem ad eum quotiēnsque vēnissent, quaesīssentque ab eō nihilne$_{2}$ sēcum esset dē fātīs Sibyllīnīs locūtus, tum ille subitō scelere dēmens quanta cōnscientiae vīs esset ostendit. Nam, cum id posset īnfitiārī, repente praeter opīniōnem omnium cōnfessus est. Ita eum$_{6}$ nōn modo ingenium illud[11] et dīcendī exercitātiō quā semper valuit sed etiam propter vim sceleris manifēstī atque dēprehēnsī impudentia quā superābat omnīs improbitāsque dēfēcit.$_{7}$ **12.** Volturcius vērō subitō litterās prōferrī atque aperīrī iubet quās sibi ā Lentulō ad Catilīnam datās esse dīcēbat. Atque ibi vehementissimē perturbātus Lentulus tamen et

[1] *not to be long-winded*
[2] *he acknowledged (the genuineness of) the seal*
[3] *had promised* (literally, *had taken upon themselves)*
[4] *at his house*
[5] *interested in fine weapons* (meaning that he collected them)
[6] *with about the same meaning*
[7] *ought to have recalled*
[8] *of the same nature*
[9] *what he had to do with them*
[10] *on account of which*
[11] *well-known*

---

$_{1}$ Supply **esse.**
$_{2}$ **–ne** introduces an indirect question: *whether*
$_{3}$ P. Cornelius Lentulus had been a consul.
$_{4}$ not the oxymoron in **mūta** and **revocāre**
$_{5}$ Indirect discourse is implied, and so the subordinate clause is in the subjunctive.
$_{6}$ object of **dēfēcit**
$_{7}$ singular to agree with the nearer subject **improbitās**

signum et manum suam cognōvit. Erant autem sine nōmine,[8] sed ita: "Quis sim sciēs ex eō quem ad tē mīsī. Cūrā[9] ut vir sīs et cōgitā quem in locum[12] sīs prōgressus. Vidē ecquid[13] tibi iam sit necesse et cūrā ut omnium tibi auxilia adiungās, etiam īnfīmōrum[10]." Gabīnius deinde intrōductus, cum prīmō impudenter respondēre coepisset, ad extrēmum nihil ex eīs quae Gallī īnsimulābant negāvit. **13.** Ac mihi quidem, Quirītēs, cum[14] illa certissima vīsa sunt argūmenta atque indicia sceleris, tabellae, signa, manūs, dēnique ūnīus cuiusque cōnfessiō, tum multō certiōra illa, color, oculī, vultūs, taciturnitās. Sīc enim obstupuerant, sīc terram intuēbantur, sīc fūrtim nōn numquam inter sēsē aspiciēbant ut nōn iam ab aliīs indicārī sed indicāre sē ipsī vidērentur.

[12] *how far*
[13] *whether anything*
[14] *not only* (balanced by **tum**)

## Translation

1. He begged them to do what they had promised.
2. He asked the Gauls why they had come to his house.
3. Cicero asked Lentulus whether he acknowledged the seal.
4. The seal of Lentulus' grandfather ought to have made him fear.

---

[8] i.e., unsigned
[9] verb
[10] i.e., slaves

# THE SENATE TAKES ACTION

**Verba Ūtilia:** cōnferō, coniūrātiō, custōdia, domesticus, fidēlis, interest, meritum, particeps, praetūra, togātus

**VI.** Indiciīs expositīs atque ēditīs, Quirītēs, senātum cōnsuluī dē summā rē pūblicā[1] quid fierī placēret. Dictae sunt ā prīncipibus ācerrimae ac fortissimae sententiae,[1] quās senātus sine ūllā varietāte[2] est secūtus. Et quoniam nōndum est perscrīptum senātūs cōnsultum, ex memoriā vōbīs, Quirītēs, quid senātus cēnsuerit expōnam. **14.** Prīmum mihi grātiae verbīs amplissimīs aguntur, quod virtūte, cōnsiliō, prōvidentiā meā rēs pūblica maximīs perīculīs sit līberāta.[2] Deinde L. Flaccus et C. Pomptīnus praetōrēs, quod eōrum operā fortī fidēlīque ūsus essem,[3] meritō ac iūre laudantur. Atque etiam virō fortī, collēgae[3] meō, laus impertītur, quod eōs quī huius coniūrātiōnis participēs fuissent ā suīs et ā reī pūblicae remōvisset. Atque ita cēnsuērunt ut P. Lentulus, cum sē praetūrā abdicāsset, in

[1] *the highest (welfare of the) state*
[2] i.e., *unanimously*
[3] *I had benefited by their services*

---

[1] Cicero, the presiding consul, called on the senators in a fixed order.
[2] quoted reason
[3] Antonius, Cicero's fellow consul

custōdiam trāderētur; itemque utī C. Cethēgus, L. Statilius, P. Gabīnius, quī omnēs praesentēs[4] erant, in custōdiam trāderentur; atque idem hoc dēcrētum est in L. Cassium, quī sibi prōcūrātiōnem incendendae urbis dēpoposcerat, in M. Cēpārium, cui ad sollicitandōs pāstōrēs Āpūliam attribūtam esse erat indicātum, in P. Fūrium, quī est ex eīs colōnīs quōs Faesulās L. Sulla dēdūxit, in Q. Annium Chīlōnem, quī ūnā cum hōc Fūriō semper erat in hāc Allobrogum sollicitātiōne versātus, in P. Umbrēnum, lībertīnum hominem, ā quō prīmum Gallōs ad Gabīnium perductōs esse cōnstābat. Atque eā[4] lēnitāte senātus est ūsus, Quirītēs, ut ex tantā coniūrātiōne tantāque hāc multitūdine domesticōrum hostium, novem[5] hominum perditissimōrum poenā rē pūblicā cōnservātā, reliquōrum mentīs sānārī posse arbitrārētur. **15.** Atque etiam supplicātiō dīs immortālibus prō singulārī eōrum meritō meō nōmine dēcrēta est, quod mihi prīmum post hanc urbem conditam togātō contigit,[5] et hīs dēcrēta verbīs est: "quod urbem incendiīs, caede cīvīs, Italiam bellō līberāssem." Quae supplicātiō sī cum cēterīs supplicātiōnibus cōnferātur,[6] hoc interest, quod cēterae, bene gestā, haec ūna, cōnservātā rē pūblicā, cōnstitūta est. Atque illud quod faciendum prīmum fuit factum atque trānsāctum est. Nam P. Lentulus, quamquam patefactīs indiciīs, cōnfessiōnibus suīs, iūdiciō senātūs nōn modo praetōris iūs vērum etiam cīvis āmīserat, tamen magistrātū sē abdicāvit, ut quae[7] religiō C. Mariō,[6] clārissimō virō, nōn fuerat quō minus[7] C. Glauciam, dē quō nihil nōminātim erat dēcrētum, praetōrem occīderet, eā nōs religiōne[8] in prīvātō[9] P. Lentulō pūniendō līberārēmur.

[4] *such*

[5] *(a thing) which for the first time since this city was founded happened to a civilian* **(togātō)** *(such as) me*

[6] *the scruple which Marius did not have*

[7] *(to keep him) from*

[8] *from that scruple*

[9] *private (citizen),* in contrast with **praetōrem**

## Translation

1. Nothing can prevent them from leaving the city.
2. If the senate should expel them, where would they go?
3. The task of burning the city had been assigned to Cassius.
4. I say that they should be sent into exile because they are wicked.

### WORD STUDY

What is the meaning of the phrase *particeps criminis,* used in English?

What abbreviation used in English is derived from the Latin word **cōnferō?**

A *pastor* is the "shepherd" of his *congregation* (**con–** and **grex,** *flock*).

---

[4] This word shows that the men mentioned next were not present. Only Ceparius was caught.

[5] but four escaped

[6] The condition is "mixed," i.e., the condition itself is less vivid, the conclusion is one of fact.

[7] The antecedent is **religiōne** below.

# IF CATILINE HAD BEEN IN ROME

**Verba Ūtilia:** callidus, cervīx, dēnūntiō, dum, exīstimō, fūrtum, latrōcinium, palam, temeritās, testis

**VII, 16.** Nunc quoniam, Quirītēs, cōnscelerātissimī perīculōsissimīque bellī nefāriōs ducēs captōs iam et comprehēnsōs tenētis, exīstimāre dēbētis omnīs Catilīnae cōpiās, omnīs spēs atque opēs, hīs dēpulsīs urbis perīculīs, concidisse. Quem quidem ego cum ex urbe pellēbam,[1] hoc prōvidēbam animō, Quirītēs, remōtō Catilīnā, nōn mihi esse P. Lentulī somnum nec L. Cassī adipēs nec C. Cethēgī furiōsam temeritātem pertimēscendam. Ille[1] erat ūnus timendus ex istīs[2] omnibus, sed tam diū dum urbis moenibus continēbātur. Omnia nōrat, omnium aditūs tenēbat;[3] appellāre,[4][2] temptāre, sollicitāre poterat, audēbat. Erat eī cōnsilium[5] ad facinus aptum, cōnsiliō autem neque lingua neque manus deerat. Iam ad certās rēs cōnficiendās certōs[6] hominēs dēlēctōs ac dēscrīptōs habēbat. Neque vērō, cum aliquid mandārat, cōnfectum putābat: nihil erat quod nōn ipse obīret, occurreret, vigilāret, labōrāret;[3] frīgus, sitim, famem ferre poterat. **17.** Hunc ego hominem tam ācrem, tam audācem, tam parātum, tam callidum, tam in scelere vigilantem, tam[4] in perditīs rēbus dīligentem nisi ex domesticīs īnsidiīs in castrēnse latrōcinium compulissem—dīcam id quod sentiō, Quirītēs—nōn facile hanc tantam mōlem malī ā cervīcibus vestrīs dēpulissem. Nōn ille nōbīs Sāturnālia cōnstituisset,[5] neque tantō ante[7] exitī ac fātī diem reī pūblicae dēnūntiāvisset neque commīsisset ut signum, ut litterae suae testēs manifēstī sceleris dēprehenderentur. Quae nunc, illō absente, sīc gesta sunt ut nūllum in prīvātā domō fūrtum umquam sit tam palam inventum quam haec in tōtā rē pūblicā coniūrātiō manifēstō comprehēnsa est. Quod sī Catilīna in urbe ad hanc diem remānsisset, quamquam, quoad fuit, omnibus eius cōnsiliīs occurrī atque obstitī, tamen, ut levissimē dīcam,[8] dīmicandum nōbīs cum illō fuisset, neque nōs umquam, cum ille in urbe hostis esset, tantīs perīculīs rem pūblicam tantā pāce, tantō ōtiō, tantō silentiō līberāssēmus.

[1] *trying to drive*
[2] *of all those fellows* (contemptuous)
[3] *he had (avenues of) approach to everybody*
[4] *call by name*
[5] *judgment*
[6] *particular men for particular things*
[7] *so long beforehand*
[8] *to say the least, we should have had to fight*

## Translation

1. We do not have to fear Catiline any longer.
2. I was trying to force Catiline to leave Rome.
3. But it so happened that we freed the city peacefully.
4. If Catiline had not left Rome, we should have had to fight.

---

[1] Catiline
[2] He knew everybody and knew also which of a man's three names he should use.
[3] The four verbs are in two pairs; then follow three nouns with alliteration and asyndeton.
[4] anaphora with six examples of **tam** arranged in pairs
[5] i.e., so late. That was the fault of Lentulus, objected to by Cethegus.

# THE WILL OF THE GODS

**Verba Ūtilia:** caelum, certē, cīvīlis, excelsus, flectō, forum, hūmānus, lūdus, nūmen, nūtus

**VIII, 18.** Quamquam haec omnia, Quirītēs, ita sunt ā mē administrāta ut deōrum immortālium nūtū atque cōnsiliō et gesta et prōvīsa esse videantur. Idque cum[1] coniectūrā cōnsequī possumus, quod vix vidētur hūmānī cōnsilī[2] tantārum rērum gubernātiō esse potuisse, tum vērō ita praesentēs hīs temporibus opem et auxilium nōbīs tulērunt ut eōs paene oculīs vidēre possīmus. Nam ut illa[3]$_{1}$ omittam, vīsās nocturnō tempore ab occidente facēs[4] ārdōremque caelī, ut fulminum iactūs, ut terrae mōtūs relinquam, ut omittam cētera quae tam multa, nōbīs cōnsulibus, facta sunt ut haec quae nunc fīunt canere[5] dī immortālēs vidērentur, hoc certē, Quirītēs, quod sum dictūrus neque praetermittendum neque relinquendum est. **19.** Nam profectō memoriā tenētis, Cottā et Torquātō cōnsulibus,$_{2}$ complūrīs in Capitōliō rēs dē caelō$_{3}$ esse percussās, cum et simulācra deōrum dēpulsa sunt et statuae veterum hominum dēiectae et lēgum aera[6] liquefacta et tāctus etiam ille quī hanc urbem condidit Rōmulus, quem inaurātum in Capitōliō, parvum atque lactantem, ūberibus lupīnīs inhiantem[7] fuisse meministis. Quō quidem tempore cum haruspicēs ex tōta Etrūriā$_{4}$ convēnissent, caedīs atque incendia et lēgum interitum et bellum cīvīle ac domesticum et totīus urbis atque imperī occāsum appropinquāre dīxērunt, nisi dī immortālēs omnī ratiōne plācātī suō nūmine prope fāta ipsa flexissent.[8]$_{5}$ **20.** Itaque illōrum respōnsīs tum et[9] lūdī$_{6}$ per decem diēs factī sunt neque rēs ūlla quae ad plācandōs deōs pertinēret praetermissa est. Īdemque iussērunt simulācrum Iovis facere maius et in excelsō collocāre et contrā atque[10] anteā fuerat ad orientem convertere; ac sē spērāre dīxērunt, sī illud signum quod vidētis$_{7}$ sōlis ortum et forum cūriamque cōnspiceret, fore ut[11]$_{8}$ ea cōnsilia quae clam essent inita contrā salūtem urbis atque imperī illūstrārentur ut ā senātū populōque Rōmānō$_{9}$ perspicī possent. Atque illud signum collocandum cōnsulēs illī locāvērunt;[12] sed tanta fuit operis tarditās ut neque superiōribus cōnsulibus neque nōbīs ante hodiernum diem collocārētur.

[1] *not only . . . but also* (with **tum**)
[2] *could hardly, it seems, have been (a matter) of human wisdom*
[3] *the following*
[4] *meteors in the west* (this and the following phenomena were regarded as signs of bad luck)
[5] *predict*
[6] *bronze tablets* (on which the laws were inscribed)
[7] *whose gilded (statue) as a suckling child, with open mouth* **(inhiantem)** *at the wolf's breast*
[8] *unless the gods should almost bend the fates themselves*
[9] *both . . . and not* (with **neque**)
[10] *opposite to what it was before*
[11] *(the result) would be that*
[12] *contracted to have the statue erected*

$_{1}$ a fine example of **praeteritiō**
$_{2}$ 65 B.C.
$_{3}$ i.e., they were struck by lightning
$_{4}$ examination of entrails and other forms of divination originated in Etruria
$_{5}$ **Prope** is used because not even the gods could change fate, according to the ancient view.
$_{6}$ Chariot races in the Circus Maximus. Supposedly given to appease the gods, they took the minds of the people from the omens. Holy day became holiday.
$_{7}$ He points to the statue on the Capitoline Hill, visible from the Forum.
$_{8}$ a common substitute for the rare future passive infinitive, **illūstrātum īrī**
$_{9}$ The power and glory of Rome is represented by this phrase, usually abbreviated S.P.Q.R. It is still used.

## Translation

1. I am going to say what I think.
2. They said that they would burn the city.
3. The statue of Jupiter could be seen from the Forum.
4. Everything was so carefully carried out that it seemed a miracle to all.

# JUPITER IS OUR SAVIOR

**Verba Ūtilia:** negō, nūtus, odium, pācō, patefaciō, praeceps, praesēns, restō

**IX, 21.** Hīc[1] quis potest esse tam āversus ā vērō, tam praeceps, tam mente captus[2] quī neget$_{1}$ haec omnia quae vidēmus praecipuēque hanc urbem deōrum immortālium nūtū ac potestāte administrārī? Etenim cum esset ita respōnsum, caedīs, incendia, interitum reī pūblicae comparārī, et ea[3] per cīvīs, quae tum propter magnitūdinem scelerum nōn nūllīs incrēdibilia vidēbantur, ea nōn modo cōgitāta ā nefāriīs cīvibus vērum etiam suscepta esse sēnsistis. Illud$_{2}$ vērō nōnne ita praesēns est ut nūtū Iovis Optimī Maximī factum esse videātur, ut, cum hodiernō diē māne per forum meō iussū et coniūrātī et eōrum indicēs in aedem Concordiae dūcerentur, eō ipsō tempore signum statuerētur? $_{3}$ Quō collocātō atque ad vōs senātumque conversō, omnia et senātus et vōs quae erant contrā salūtem omnium cōgitāta, illūstrāta, et patefacta vīdistis. **22.** Quō[4] etiam maiōre sunt istī odiō suppliciōque dignī quī nōn sōlum vestrīs domiciliīs atque tēctīs sed etiam deōrum templīs atque dēlūbrīs sunt fūnestōs ac nefāriōs ignīs īnferre cōnātī. Quibus ego sī mē restitisse dīcam, nimium mihi sūmam et nōn sim ferendus: ille,$_{4}$ ille Iuppiter restitit; ille Capitōlium, ille haec templa, ille cūnctam urbem, ille vōs omnīs salvōs esse voluit. Dīs ego immortālibus ducibus, hanc mentem voluntātemque suscēpī atque ad haec tanta indicia pervēnī. Iam vērō illa Allobrogum sollicitātiō,$_{5}$ iam ab Lentulō cēterīsque domesticīs hostibus tam dēmenter tantae rēs crēditae et ignōtīs et barbarīs commissaeque litterae numquam essent profectō, nisi ab dīs immortālibus huic tantae audāciae cōnsilium esset ēreptum.[5] Quid vērō? Ut hominēs Gallī ex cīvitāte male[6] pācātā, quae gēns ūna restat quae bellum populō Rōmānō facere posse et nōn nōlle videātur, spem imperī ac rērum maximārum ultrō sibi ā patriciīs hominibus oblātam neglegerent vestramque salūtem suīs opibus antepōnerent, id$_{6}$ nōn dīvīnitus esse factum putātis, praesertim quī[7] nōs nōn pugnandō sed tacendō superāre potuērunt?

[1] *in view of this* (adverb)
[2] *insane* (literally, *seized in mind*)
[3] *and those (things) by citizens (at that), (things) which*
[4] *Therefore*
[5] *unless good sense had been removed from such bold (men)*
[6] *imperfectly*
[7] *particularly since they*

---

$_{1}$ result clause
$_{2}$ explained by the **ut** clause
$_{3}$ Perhaps Cicero planned it that way.
$_{4}$ We can almost see Cicero's gestures as he points to the statue, then to the Capitoline temple, the Forum temples, the city, the people in front of him.
$_{5}$ Supply **numquam facta esset** from the following.
$_{6}$ in apposition with the preceding **ut** clause

## Translation

1. Who is so wicked that he would not thank Jupiter?
2. They are deserving of punishment who commit such crimes.
3. If they were present it would be difficult to resist them.
4. If I should say that I did this, I would not be telling the truth.

# THE GREATEST OF BLOODLESS VICTORIES

**Verba Ūtilia:** celebrō, custōs, interimō, lūctus, lūmen, partim, pertineō, quam ob rem, recordor, salvus

**X, 23.** Quam ob rem, Quirītēs, quoniam ad omnia pulvīnāria supplicātiō dēcrēta est, celebrātōte[1] illōs diēs cum coniugibus ac līberīs vestrīs. Nam multī saepe honōrēs dīs immortālibus iūstī habitī sunt ac dēbitī,[1] sed profectō iūstiōrēs numquam. Ēreptī enim estis ex crūdēlissimō ac miserrimō interitū, ēreptī sine caede, sine sanguine, sine exercitū, sine dīmicātiōne; togātī, mē ūnō togātō duce et imperātōre, vīcistis.[2] **24.** Etenim recordāminī, Quirītēs, omnīs cīvīlīs dissēnsiōnēs, nōn sōlum eās quās audīstis sed eās quās vōsmet ipsī meministis atque vīdistis. L. Sulla P. Sulpicium[3] oppressit: C. Marium,[4] custōdem huius urbis, multōsque fortīs virōs partim ēiēcit ex cīvitāte, partim interēmit. Cn. Octāvius cōnsul armīs expulit ex urbe collēgam:[5] omnis hic locus acervīs corporum et cīvium sanguine redundāvit.[6] Superāvit posteā Cinna cum Mariō: tum vērō, clārissimīs virīs interfectīs, lūmina cīvitātis exstīncta sunt. Ultus est huius victōriae crūdēlitātem posteā Sulla: nē dīcī quidem opus est quantā dēminūtiōne cīvium et quantā calamitāte reī pūblicae. Dissēnsit M. Lepidus ā clārissimō et fortissimō virō Q. Catulō: attulit nōn tam ipsīus interitus reī pūblicae lūctum quam cēterōrum.

[1] *due*

**25.** Atque illae tamen omnēs dissēnsiōnēs erant eius modī quae nōn ad dēlendam sed ad commūtandam rem pūblicam pertinērent. Nōn illī nūllam esse rem pūblicam sed in eā quae esset sē esse prīncipēs, neque hanc urbem cōnflagrāre sed sē in hāc urbe flōrēre voluērunt. Atque illae tamen

---

1 future imperative, used chiefly in legal and religious language

2 anaphora with **ēreptī**, then with **sine.** The four nouns are grouped in two pairs; **togātō** *(the man of peace)* joined with **imperātōre** constitutes an oxymoron

3 He had proposed a bill to take away from Sulla the command of the army against Mithridates and to give it to Marius.

4 He had saved the city from the Cimbri and Teutons.

5 Cinna, one of Marius' men.

6 Note the zeugma, a figure of speech we do not ordinarily tolerate in English. We would not say *overflowed with heaps of bodies and blood.*

omnēs dissēnsiōnēs, quārum nūlla exitium reī pūblicae quaesīvit, eius modī fuērunt ut nōn reconciliātiōne concordiae sed interneciōne cīvium diiūdicātae sint. In hōc autem ūnō post hominum memoriam maximō[2] crūdēlissimōque bellō, quāle bellum[3] nūlla umquam barbaria cum suā gente gessit, quō in bellō lēx[4] haec fuit ā Lentulō, Catilīnā, Cethēgō, Cassiō cōnstitūta, ut omnēs quī, salvā urbe, salvī[5] esse possent in hostium numerō dūcerentur, ita mē gessī, Quirītēs, ut salvī omnēs cōnservārēminī, et, cum hostēs vestrī tantum cīvium[6] superfutūrum putāssent quantum īnfīnītae caedī restitisset, tantum autem urbis quantum flamma obīre nōn potuisset, et urbem et cīvīs integrōs incolumīsque servāvī.

[2] *the greatest of all* (with **ūnō**)
[3] *such a war as*
[4] *principle* (explained by the **ut** clause)
[5] here *(financially) safe, solvent*
[6] *(only) so many of the citizens*

## Translation

1. If they had won, you would all be dead.
2. We have won in a war in which no one died.
3. They wanted a state in which they would be the leaders.
4. Go to the games without danger with your wives and children.

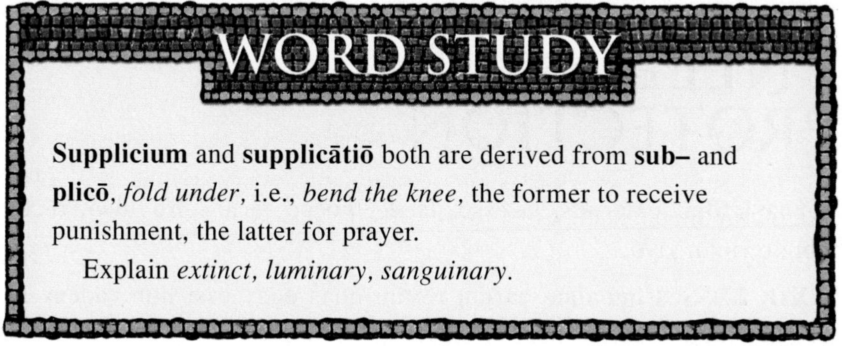

### WORD STUDY

**Supplicium** and **supplicātiō** both are derived from **sub–** and **plicō,** *fold under,* i.e., *bend the knee,* the former to receive punishment, the latter for prayer.

Explain *extinct, luminary, sanguinary.*

# ALL I ASK IS GRATITUDE

**Verba Ūtilia:** assequor, dēlectō, insignis, inveterāscō, postulō

**XI, 26.** Quibus prō tantīs rēbus[1], Quirītēs, nūllum ego ā vōbīs praemium virtūtis, nūllum īnsigne honōris, nūllum monumentum laudis postulābō praeterquam huius diēī memoriam sempiternam. In animīs ego vestrīs omnīs triumphōs meōs, omnia ōrnāmenta honōris, monumenta glōriae, laudis īnsignia condī et collocārī volō. Nihil mē mūtum[1] potest dēlectāre, nihil tacitum, nihil dēnique eius modī quod etiam minus dignī assequī

[1] *in return for these great accomplishments*

---

[1] such as a statue

[2] *my achievements will be kept alive*
[3] *literary records*
[4] *time*

possint. Memoriā vestrā, Quirītēs, nostrae rēs alentur,[2] sermōnibus crēscent, litterārum monumentīs[3] inveterāscent et corrōborābuntur; eandemque diem[4] intellegō, quam spērō aeternam fore, propagātam esse et ad salūtem urbis et ad memoriam cōnsulātūs meī, ūnōque tempore in hāc rē pūblicā duōs[2] cīvīs exstitisse, quōrum alter fīnīs vestrī imperī nōn terrae sed caelī regiōnibus termināret, alter huius imperī domicilium sēdīsque servāret.

### Translation

1. I know that you will give what I want.
2. I want none of the things which others can achieve.
3. I realize that the memory of my deeds will remain as long as Rome remains.

---

[2] Pompey, who had conquered Sertorius in the west (Spain) and Mithridates in the east, and Cicero

# I NEED YOUR PROTECTION

**Verba Ūtilia:** externus, lacessō, laedō, noceō, ōrnō, prōvideō, rēctē, subigō, violō, vīvō

[1] *the same as* (with **eadem**)
[2] *it is your (responsibility)*
[3] *if their deeds are beneficial to others (and rightly so)*
[4] *at some time*
[5] *intentions*
[6] *I, at any rate, can no longer be injured by them*
[7] **quam = et hanc:** *and those who disregard this*
[8] = **mihi**

**XII, 27.** Sed quoniam eārum rērum quās ego gessī nōn eadem est fortūna atque condiciō quae[1] illōrum quī externa bella gessērunt, quod mihi cum eīs vīvendum est quōs vīcī ac subēgī, illī hostīs aut interfectōs aut oppressōs relīquērunt, vestrum est,[2] Quirītēs, sī cēterīs facta sua rēctē prōsunt,[3] mihi mea nē quandō[4] obsint prōvidēre. Mentēs[5] enim hominum audācissimōrum scelerātae ac nefāriae nē vōbīs nocēre possent ego prōvīdī, nē mihi noceant vestrum est prōvidēre. Quamquam, Quirītēs, mihi quidem ipsī nihil ab istīs iam nocērī[6] potest. Magnum enim est in bonīs praesidium quod mihi in perpetuum comparātum est, magna in rē pūblicā dignitās quae mē semper tacita dēfendet, magna vīs conscientiae quam[7] quī neglegunt, cum mē violāre volent, sē indicābunt.[1] **28.** Est enim nōbīs[8] is animus, Quirītēs, ut nōn modo nūllīus audāciae cēdāmus sed etiam omnīs improbōs ultrō semper lacessāmus. Quod sī omnis impetus domesticōrum hostium[2] dēpulsus ā vōbīs sē in mē ūnum converterit, vōbīs erit videndum,

---

[1] But only five years later Cicero was banished, partly as a result of the Catiline affair. It almost seems as if Cicero here foresees this possibility.

[2] As **hostis** means *foreign enemy,* **domesticōrum** is a contradiction (oxymoron); but remember that Cicero justified his action against the conspirators on the grounds that they were traitors.

C. M. Dixon

The Capitoline Hill was the lowest and least inhabited of the seven hills of Rome, but for good reason. It was the center of state religion and was actually a fortified citadel and religious sanctuary. Legend has it that the sacred geese of Juno that were kept in a temple on the hill awakened and alerted the Romans to a sneak attack by the Gauls in 390 B.C., saving the city. The equestrian statue of the emperor Marcus Aurelius dates from the fourth century and was selected from the pope's antiquarian holdings by Michelangelo to be the focal point of the Capitoline square on the top of the hill.

[9] *in what situation*
[10] *in the office bestowed by you*
[11] *(acquired by) good character*
[12] *and even make more splendid*
[13] *may renown to my glory*
[14] *just as* (with **aequē**)
[15] *on that previous night*

Quirītēs, qua condiciōne[9] posthāc eōs esse velītis quī sē prō salūte vestrā obtulerint invidiae perīculīsque omnibus: mihi quidem ipsī quid est quod iam ad vītae frūctum possit acquīrī, cum praesertim neque in honōre vestrō [10] neque in glōriā virtūtis[11] quicquam videam altius quō mihi libeat ascendere? **29.** Illud[3] perficiam profectō, Quirītēs, ut ea quae gessī in cōnsulātū prīvātus tuear atque ōrnem,[12] ut, sī qua est invidia in cōnservandā rē pūblicā suscepta, laedat invidōs, mihi valeat[13] ad glōriam. Dēnique ita mē in rē pūblicā trāctābō ut meminerim semper quae gesserim, cūremque ut ea virtūte, nōn cāsū, gesta esse videantur. Vōs, Quirītēs, quoniam iam est nox, venerātī Iovem illum, custōdem huius urbis ac vestrum, in vestra tēcta discēdite et ea, quamquam iam est perīculum dēpulsum, tamen aequē ac[14] priōre[4] nocte[15] custōdiīs vigiliīsque dēfendite. Id nē vōbīs diūtius faciendum sit atque ut in perpetuā pāce esse possītis prōvidēbō, Quirītēs.

## Translation

1. Do you believe that Catiline will injure me?
2. He saw to it that they would not destroy the state.
3. I have to remain with the men who were defeated by me.
4. If you should not defend yourselves, you would suffer a great disaster.

### Questions

1. Who were the Allobroges? What were they doing in Rome?
2. What did Lentulus suggest to Catiline? How did Cicero find out about this suggestion?
3. What written evidence did Cicero have against the conspirators?
4. How many conspirators were arrested in or near Rome?
5. How many escaped?
6. Where was the evidence seized?
7. Where was Catiline?
8. Where was this speech made?
9. Before whom was it made?
10. What happened earlier in the day?
11. What did seals have to do with the evidence against the conspirators?
12. What did the conspirators plan to do to Rome?
13. How did the people react to Cicero's speech?

---

[3] explained by the **ut** clause
[4] after the second oration, in which he said to his listeners: **vestra tēcta vigiliīs custōdiīsque dēfendite**

# Fourth Oration Against Catiline

The third oration reported to the people the evidence against the conspirators that had been presented to the senate, sitting as a court of justice. The fourth oration takes us back to the senate two days later (December 5) for the debate to determine the punishment for the five men who were under arrest. The meeting was held in the Temple of Concord, at one end of the Forum, and Cicero again presided. According to regular procedure, the consul-elect, Silanus, was called upon. In his speech he voted for the death penalty. Then Caesar got up and suggested life imprisonment and confiscation of property. After further discussion Cicero summed up the two views in the present speech. In spite of an attempt to take a judicial position, not preferring one view to the other, Cicero made it clear that he favored the death penalty.

Caesar's speech, moderate in tone, had made a strong impression and it looked as if his motion would be carried. Cato then made a stirring speech in favor of the death penalty. As a result, the death penalty was voted by a large majority. Cicero promptly had the men executed in the underground prison called the Tullianum, which is still in existence. It is near one end of the Forum, at the foot of the Capitoline Hill, not far from the Temple of Concord, where the senate met.

Some weeks later Catiline was killed in battle in Etruria.

# DON'T WORRY ABOUT ME, SENATORS

**Verba Ūtilia:** acerbus, cruciātus, dēlūbrum, exitus, foedus *(adj.),* fortiter, gēns, perfugium sēdēs vacuus

**I, 1.** Videō, patrēs cōnscrīptī, in mē omnium vestrum ōra atque oculōs esse conversōs,[1] videō vōs nōn sōlum dē vestrō ac reī pūblicae, vērum etiam, sī id dēpulsum sit, dē meō perīculō esse sollicitōs. Est mihi iūcunda in malīs et grāta in dolōre vestra ergā mē voluntās, sed eam, per deōs immortālēs, dēpōnite atque oblītī salūtis meae, dē vōbīs ac dē vestrīs līberīs cōgitāte.

[1] Silanus and Caesar had made their speeches and the discussion seems to have died down. So the senators naturally turned to Cicero.

1 if the consulship were given me under these conditions

2 with a certain (amount of) pain for me and fear for you

Mihi sī haec condiciō cōnsulātūs[1] data est ut omnīs acerbitātēs, omnīs dolōrēs cruciātūsque perferrem, feram[2] nōn sōlum fortiter vērum etiam libenter, dum modo meīs labōribus vōbīs populōque Rōmānō dignitās salūsque pariātur. **2.** Ego sum ille cōnsul, patrēs cōnscrīptī, cui nōn forum, in quō omnis aequitās continētur,[3] nōn campus[4] cōnsulāribus auspiciīs cōnsecrātus, nōn cūria, summum auxilium omnium gentium, nōn domus, commūne perfugium, nōn lectus ad quiētem datus, nōn dēnique haec sēdēs honōris[5] umquam vacua mortis perīculō atque īnsidiīs fuit. Ego multa tacuī, multa pertulī, multa concessī, multa meō quōdam dolōre in vestrō timōre[2] sānāvī. Nunc sī hunc exitum cōnsulātūs meī dī immortālēs esse voluērunt, ut vōs populumque Rōmānum ex caede miserrimā, coniugēs līberōsque vestrōs virginēsque Vestālēs ex acerbissimā vexātiōne, templa atque dēlūbra, hanc pulcherrimam patriam omnium nostrum ex foedissimā flammā, tōtam Italiam ex bellō et vāstitāte ēriperem, quaecumque mihi ūnī prōpōnētur fortūna subeātur.

## Translation

1. You will be free from danger as long as I am consul.
2. This he greatly desired, that the safety of the state be preserved.
3. Provided that no harm is done to you, senators, I will endure everything.

---

2 Note the strong emphasis produced by the chiasmus. When a verb is repeated, as here, the simple form **(feram)** is often used, as the force of the prefix **per–** seems to carry over.

3 because the law courts were there

4 The campus Martius, where the elections were held. The auspices were taken to see if the omens were favorable for the election.

5 The curule chair **(sella curūlis)** was a symbol of his office.

# THE SENATE MUST DECIDE

**Verba Ūtilia:** cēnseō, concitō, coniūratiō, dubitātiō, facinus, poena, praetūra, prīdem, reus

1 in unusual language

**III, 5.** Haec omnia indicēs dētulērunt, reī[1] cōnfessī sunt, vōs multīs iam iūdiciīs iūdicāvistis, prīmum quod mihi grātiās ēgistis singulāribus verbīs[1] et meā virtūte atque dīligentiā perditōrum hominum coniūrātiōnem patefactam esse dēcrēvistis, deinde quod P. Lentulum sē abdicāre praetūra coēgistis; tum quod eum et cēterōs dē quibus iūdicāstis in custōdiam dandōs

---

1 from **reus**

cēnsuistis, maximēque quod meō nōmine supplicātiōnem dēcrēvistis, quī honōs[2] togātō habitus ante mē est nēminī;[2] postrēmō hesternō diē praemia lēgātīs Allobrogum Titōque Volturciō dedistis amplissima. Quae sunt omnia eius modī, ut eī quī in custōdiam nōminātim datī sunt sine ūllā dubitātiōne ā vōbīs damnātī esse videantur.

**6.** Sed ego īnstituī referre ad vōs, patrēs cōnscrīptī, tamquam integrum,[3] et[4] dē factō quid iūdicētis et dē poenā quid cēnseātis. Illa praedīcam quae sunt cōnsulis.[5] Ego magnum in rē pūblicā versārī furōrem et nova[6] quaedam miscērī[7] et concitārī mala iam prīdem vidēbam, sed hanc tantam, tam exitiōsam haberī coniūrātiōnem ā cīvibus numquam putāvī. Nunc quicquid est, quōcumque vestrae mentēs inclīnant atque sententiae, statuendum vōbīs ante noctem est. Quantum facinus ad vōs dēlātum sit, vidētis. Huic sī paucōs putātis affīnēs esse, vehementer errātis. Lātius opīniōne[8] dissēminātum est hoc malum; mānāvit nōn sōlum per Italiam vērum etiam trānscendit Alpēs et obscūrē serpēns[3] multās iam prōvinciās occupāvit. Id opprimī sustentandō et prōlātandō[9] nūllō pactō potest; quācumque ratiōne placet, celeriter vōbīs vindicandum est.

[2] *to no one at all*
[3] *I have begun by referring to you as if (it were) untouched*
[4] *both*
[5] *(the function) of the consul*
[6] *new (evils)*
[7] *are being stirred up*
[8] *more widely than you think*
[9] *by putting up with it and putting it off*

## Translation

1. You must punish these wicked men as soon as possible.
2. He did not want to tell the senators what they should decide.
3. It is (the duty) of the senate to decide what should be done.

---

[2] an older form of **honor**
[3] participle from **serpō**

# DEATH OR IMPRISONMENT?

**Verba Ūtilia:** adhūc, adimō, formīdō, fruor, inīquitās, mūnicipium, prīvō, recūsō, spīritus, vinculum

**IV, 7.** Videō duās adhūc esse sententiās, ūnam D. Sīlānī, quī cēnset eōs quī haec[1] dēlēre cōnātī sunt morte esse multandōs, alteram C. Caesaris, quī mortis poenam removet,[2] cēterōrum suppliciōrum omnīs acerbitātēs amplectitur.[3] Uterque et prō suā dignitāte et prō rērum magnitūdine in summā sevēritāte versātur.[4] Alter[5] eōs quī nōs omnīs, quī populum Rōmānum vītā prīvāre cōnātī sunt, quī dēlēre imperium, quī populī Rōmānī nōmen exstinguere, pūnctum temporis[6] fruī vītā et hōc commūnī spīritū nōn putat oportēre atque hoc genus poenae saepe in improbōs cīvīs in hāc rē pūblicā esse ūsūrpātum recordātur. Alter[7] intellegit mortem ā dīs

[1] *all this*
[2] *rejects*
[3] *includes*
[4] *is most stern* (literally, *is engaged in the greatest severity)*
[5] *the one* (Silanus, subject of **putat**)
[6] *for a moment of time*
[7] *the other* (Caesar)

[8] *from troubles*
[9] *for life at that* (literally, *and those perpetual)*
[10] *involve*
[11] *(those) who*
[12] *(in accordance with) their position*
[13] *be held up to*
[14] *men in the old days*
[15] *wanted (us to believe)*
[16] *what is to my interest*
[17] *perhaps* (literally, *I do not know whether)*
[18] *more trouble*
[19] *consideration*
[20] *ancestors*
[21] *guarantee* (literally, *hostage)*

immortālibus nōn esse supplicī causā cōnstitūtam, sed aut necessitātem nātūrae aut labōrum[8] ac miseriārum quiētem. Itaque eam sapientēs numquam invītī, fortēs saepe etiam libenter oppetīvērunt. Vincula vērō, et ea sempiterna,[9] certē ad singulārem poenam nefāriī sceleris inventa sunt. Mūnicipiīs dispertīrī[1] iubet. Habēre[10][2] vidētur ista rēs inīquitātem, sī imperāre velīs, difficultātem, sī rogāre. Dēcernātur tamen, sī placet. **8.** Ego enim suscipiam et, ut spērō, reperiam quī[11] id quod salūtis omnium causā statuerītis nōn putent esse suae dignitātis[12] recūsāre. Adiungit[3] gravem poenam mūnicipiīs, sī quis eōrum[4] vincula rūperit; horribilīs custōdiās circumdat et dignās scelere hominum perditōrum; sancit nē quis eōrum poenam quōs condemnat aut per senātum aut per populum levāre possit; ēripit etiam spem, quae sōla hominem in miseriīs cōnsōlārī solet. Bona praetereā pūblicārī iubet, vītam sōlam relinquit nefāriīs hominibus; quam sī ēripuisset, multās ūnō dolōre animī atque corporis miseriās et omnīs scelerum poenās adēmisset. Itaque ut aliqua in vītā formīdō improbīs esset prōposita,[13] apud īnferōs eius modī quaedam illī antīquī[14] supplicia impiīs cōnstitūta esse voluērunt,[15] quod vidēlicet intellegēbant, hīs remōtīs, nōn esse mortem ipsam pertimēscendam.

**V, 9.** Nunc, patrēs cōnscrīptī, ego meā videō quid intersit.[16] Sī eritis secūtī sententiam C. Caesaris, quoniam hanc is in rē pūblicā viam quae populāris[5] habētur secūtus est, fortasse minus erunt, hōc auctōre et cognitōre huiusce sententiae, mihi populārēs impetūs pertimēscendī; sīn illam alteram, nesciō an[17] amplius mihi negōtī[18] contrahātur. Sed tamen meōrum perīculōrum ratiōnēs[19] ūtilitās reī pūblicae vincat. Habēmus enim ā Caesare, sīcut ipsīus dignitās et maiōrum[20] eius amplitūdō postulābat, sententiam tamquam obsidem[21][6] perpetuae in rem pūblicam voluntātis. Intellēctum est,[7] quid interesset inter levitātem cōntiōnātōrum et animum vērē populārem salūtī populī cōnsulentem.

## Translation

1. A man's love of his country is shown by his actions.
2. If you approve Caesar's opinion, I shall not have to fear attack.
3. The one speaker favored the death penalty; the other, prison.
4. Let it be decided thus, if that is the action that the senate will decide upon.

---

[1] Supply **eōs** as subject.
[2] If the senate insisted on the towns' being responsible, there would be unfairness if some towns were exempted; if a mere request were made, there would be many refusals.
[3] i.e., Caesar
[4] with **vincula**
[5] Caesar was the leader of the popular, or democratic, group and was said to have been supporting Catiline.
[6] Cicero thus intimates that Caesar had no connection with Catiline's plot.
[7] i.e., when Caesar was speaking

# WHAT MIGHT HAVE HAPPENED

**Verba Ūtilia:** caedēs, cernō, concidō, dēleō, idcircō, perhorrēscō, praebeō, sīcut, trucīdō, vexātiō

**VI, 11.** Videor enim mihi vidēre hanc urbem, lūcem orbis terrārum atque arcem[1] omnium gentium, subitō ūnō incendiō concidentem. Cernō animō sepultā[2] in patriā miserōs atque īnsepultōs acervōs cīvium, versātur mihi ante oculōs aspectus Cethēgī et furor in vestrā caede bacchantis. **12.** Cum vērō mihi prōposuī rēgnantem Lentulum, sīcut ipse sē ex fātīs spērāsse cōnfessus est, purpurātum[3] esse huic Gabīnium, cum exercitū vēnisse Catilīnam, tum lāmentātiōnem mātrum familiās,$_{1}$ tum fugam virginum atque puerōrum ac vexātiōnem virginum Vestālium perhorrēscō et, quia mihi vehementer haec videntur misera atque miseranda, idcircō in eōs quī ea perficere voluērunt mē sevērum vehementemque praebēbō. Etenim quaerō, sī quis pater familiās, līberīs suīs ā servō interfectīs, uxōre occīsā, incēnsā domō, supplicium[4] dē servīs nōn quam acerbissimum sūmpserit,[4] utrum is clēmēns ac misericors an inhūmānissimus et crūdēlissimus esse videātur. Mihi vērō importūnus ac ferreus quī nōn dolōre et cruciātū nocentis suum$_{2}$ dolōrem cruciātumque lēnierit. Sīc nōs in[5] hīs hominibus, quī nōs, quī coniugēs, quī līberōs nostrōs trucīdāre voluērunt, quī singulās ūnīus cuiusque nostrum domōs et hoc ūniversum reī pūblicae domicilium dēlēre cōnātī sunt, quī id ēgērunt, ut gentem Allobrogum in vēstīgiīs[6] huius urbis atque in cinere dēflagrātī imperī collocārent, sī vehementissimī fuerimus, misericordēs habēbimur;$_{3}$ sīn remissiōrēs esse voluerimus, summae nōbīs crūdēlitātis in patriae cīviumque perniciē fāma[7] subeunda est.

[1] *bulwark*
[2] *devastated* (literally, *buried)*
[3] *dressed in royal purple* (as minister to "King" Lentulus)
[4] *inflict punishment upon*
[5] *in (the case of)*
[6] *ruins*
[7] *(bad) reputation*

## Translation

1. Tell me whether Cicero was merciful or severe.
2. Cicero saw very clearly what would have happened.
3. If Catiline had won, the fate of Rome would have been terrible.

---

$_{1}$ the old genitive form, used after **pater** and **māter**
$_{2}$ chiasmus, with special emphasis on **nocentis** and **suum**
$_{3}$ They will be regarded as merciful even if they are very severe.

# IT IS UP TO YOU, SENATORS

**Verba Ūtilia:** anima, āra, benignitās, fānum, fungor, impius, īnsidiae, obsideō, posthāc, supplex

**IX, 18.** Quae cum ita sint, patrēs cōnscrīptī, vōbīs populī Rōmānī praesidia nōn dēsunt; vōs nē populō Rōmānō dēesse videāminī, prōvidēte. Habētis cōnsulem ex plūrimīs perīculīs et īnsidiīs atque ex mediā morte nōn ad vītam suam sed ad salūtem vestram reservātum. Omnēs ōrdinēs ad cōnservandam rem pūblicam mente, voluntāte, studiō, virtūte, vōce cōnsentiunt. Obsessa facibus et tēlīs impiae coniūrātiōnis vōbīs supplex manūs tendit patria commūnis, vōbīs sē, vōbīs vītam$_1$ omnium cīvium, vōbīs arcem et Capitōlium,$_2$ vōbīs ārās Penātium,[1] vōbīs illum ignem Vestae sempiternum, vōbīs omnium deōrum templa atque dēlūbra, vōbīs mūrōs atque urbis tēcta commendat. Praetereā dē vestrā vītā, dē coniugum vestrārum atque līberōrum animā, dē fortūnīs omnium, dē sēdibus, dē focīs vestrīs hodiernō diē vōbīs iūdicandum est. **19.** Habētis ducem memorem vestrī,$_3$ oblītum suī,$_3$ quae non semper facultās[2] datur; habētis omnīs ōrdinēs, omnīs hominēs, ūniversum populum Rōmānum, id quod in cīvīlī causā[3] hodiernō diē prīmum vidēmus, ūnum atque idem sentientem. Cōgitāte quantīs labōribus fundātum imperium, quantā virtūte stabilītam lībertātem, quantā deōrum benignitāte auctās exaggerātāsque fortūnās ūna nox paene dēlērit.$_4$ Id nē umquam posthāc nōn modo nōn cōnficī sed nē cōgitārī quidem possit ā cīvibus hodiernō diē prōvidendum est. Atque haec, nōn ut vōs, quī mihi studiō paene praecurritis, excitārem, locūtus sum, sed ut mea vōx, quae dēbet esse in rē pūblicā prīnceps, officiō fūncta cōnsulārī vidērētur.

**XI, 24.** Quāpropter dē summā salūte vestrā populīque Rōmānī, dē vestrīs coniugibus ac līberīs, dē ārīs ac focīs, dē fānīs atque templīs, dē tōtīus urbis tēctīs ac sēdibus, dē imperiō ac lībertāte, dē salūte Italiae, dē ūniversā rē pūblicā dēcernite dīligenter, ut īnstituistis, ac fortiter. Habētis eum cōnsulem quī et pārēre vestrīs dēcrētīs nōn dubitet et ea quae statuerītis, quoad vīvet, dēfendere et per sē ipsum praestāre[4] possit.

[1] *the Penates*
[2] *an advantage which*
[3] *in a political matter*
[4] *carry out, perform*

---

$_1$ Use plural in English.
$_2$ The Capitoline Hill has two peaks, on one of which the **arx** was placed; on the other, the **Capitōlium,** or Temple of Jupiter.
$_3$ pronouns, not adjectives
$_4$ Two ideas are combined in this sentence: *think with what hard work the empire was founded . . .* (*and how*) *one night almost destroyed it.*

### Translation

1. Do not forget my advice, senators.
2. Cicero thought he had performed his duty.
3. Men are not lacking to (who will) defend you.

## WORD STUDY

**Sempiternus,** from **semper** and **aeternus**, is tautological, for that which is *eternal* lasts *forever*. There is an English derivative, *sempiternal*.

**Exaggerō** means *to build up a mound* (from **agger**). The higher you build it, the more you *exaggerate*.

UNIT
IV

# SALLUST'S CATILINE (SELECTIONS)

## Unit Objectives

- To compare and contrast Roman and modern politics
- To read selections from Sallust's *Catiline* with understanding and appreciation
- To learn the meaning of new vocabulary words in context
- To recognize Latin root words and their English derivatives



**The seventeenth-century French painter Claude Lorrain was especially known for his use of light in his landscapes and seascapes. From this angle, you can see the Arch of Constantine, built in A.D. 313, and the edge of the Coliseum. The Arch of Constantine was made of Carrara marble, much of which was taken from the arches of Trajan and Marcus Aurelius. The inscription reads: "To the Emperor Caesar Flavius Constantinus Maximus, the Senate and the Roman people dedicate this notable arch in honor of his triumphs, because, by Divine inspiration and greatness of mind, he freed the Republic by just wars from tyranny and from factions." This scene is a detail of the larger painting by Lorrain.**

# ROMAN POLITICS

Cicero was a clever politician, as well as a great writer, as you have seen in his speeches against Catiline. You will see his brilliance again in Sallust's account of the conspiracy.

Although Rome had no formal political parties in the modern sense, during the Republic there were generally two groups opposed to each other, conservative and liberal. Originally, it was the patricians against the plebeians, who were not allowed to hold office. But after the plebeians obtained almost all the patrician rights, the distinction between these groups vanished. Then it was the nobles, that is, the officeholders and their descendants, against the new plebeians, who included the general group of poor people and those who were not officeholders. A third group, the well-to-do or **equitēs,** became involved in politics. Cicero had belonged to this group; his family was wealthy but had not held high office. Cicero was proud of the fact that, though a **novus homō,** he had managed to get into the **cursus honōrum** and become a noble. He persuaded the **equitēs** to align themselves with the nobles or senators, and the cornerstone of his politics was the **concordia ōrdinum** between these conservative groups and against the liberal or radical **populārēs.** Cicero calls the former **bonī** or **optimātēs;** the latter, **improbī.**

The method of voting by classes made it possible for the relatively small group of nobles to retain possession of the offices. The classes in which the richer and more conservative men voted were smaller than the others. Thus the vote of a noble might be worth several times as much as that of a **populāris.**

Campaign methods in Rome bear some resemblances to those in the United States today. Our word *candidate* is derived from **candidātus,** "the man in white," because the Roman candidate wore a toga that had just come from the cleaner's. **Ambitiō** literally means "going around" looking for votes. Another word of the same derivation, **ambitus,** took on a bad sense, that of bribery, also used in going around looking for votes. **Prēnsātiō** meant "catching hold of," shaking a voter's hand or buttonholing him.

Political tours, not unlike today's political campaigns, existed even in ancient Rome. When campaigning for the consulship, Cicero wrote that he would go to northern Italy to campaign in September, when the Roman courts were closed most of the month. Ostensibly he was going on a government mission. Such a combination of government business and political campaigning certainly is not unknown today.

Fortunately, a large number of ancient election posters are preserved in Pompeii. They deal with local rather than national elections, and they took the form of appeals painted on house fronts. A typical example is: **L. Pop(idium) Secund(um) aed(īlem) d(ignum) r(ē) p(ūblicā) Tiburtīnus rogat,** "Lucius Popidius Secundus for aedile. Deserving of the state. Tiburtinus asks you (to vote for him)." The letters in parentheses represent the parts in abbreviation. Such heavy abbreviation shows that the phrases were frequently used. Often special groups made the appeal, such as barbers, cake bakers, garlic dealers, fishermen, ballplayers. One reads: **Phoebus cum ēmptōribus** *(customers)*. Another: **Sāturnīnus cum discentēs rogat.** (Can you show up Saturninus' Latin by pointing out his mistake in grammar?) **Discentēs** probably means *apprentices*. When we find support being requested by the sneakthieves **(fūrunculī)**, the late-drinkers **(sēribibī ūniversī)**, and the sleepers **(dormientēs)**, we know the opposition candidates or their supporters are at work.

One candidate's platform was: **Commūnem nummum dīvidendum cēnsiō est. Nam noster nummus magna(m) habet pecūniam**, "It is my vote that the public treasury be divided up. For our treasury has much money." The backer of another says: **Hic aerārium cōnservābit,** "He will watch the treasury," apparently running in opposition to the one who favored dividing up the public funds. Of another candidate it is said: **Pānem bonum fert,** "He delivers good bread."

No place seems to have been immune from the attentions of the eager politicians and their friends: a tombstone near Rome has carved on it the prayer that any candidate who puts a poster on it be defeated in the election. This recalls our "Post no bills." On the other hand, an election poster at Pompeii ends with this warning: **Invidiōse quī dēlēs aegrōtēs,** "May the envious person who destroys this notice become sick."

The chief political issue in the hundred years before Cicero was the land problem. Large farm owners worked their lands with cheap slave labor. The small farmers could not survive. They flocked to Rome, where they found it difficult to get work. Thus, every Roman politician had some proposal for solving the land problem. Gaius Gracchus bought wheat at reasonable prices and sold it to the poor at a low price. During his year as consul, Cicero was compelled to make four speeches on agrarian legislation. Eventually, wheat came to be sold by the government at less than cost, and finally was given free to the citizens. The result of all this is summed up in Juvenal's famous remark that all the Roman people cared about was **pānem et circēnsēs.**

Cicero's second oration against Catiline shows that most of Catiline's followers were heavily in debt. Actually, a widespread financial panic had set in, loans were called, and gold flowed out of the country, even as in modern times. Catiline's proposed solution was a simple one: cancel all debts. His proposal was nothing new. In 86 B.C., during a panic, creditors were forced to accept 25 percent of their loans as full payment. During the Civil War in 49 B.C., something similar happened.

# SALLUST'S LIFE

Gaius Sallustius Crispus was born in 86 and died in 35 B.C. He was of a plebeian family but entered the senatorial career and became quaestor in 59 B.C. The censors expelled him from the senate in 50 B.C. on a charge of improper conduct. In the Civil War he was on the side of Caesar, who reappointed him quaestor in 49 B.C. Later Sallust became praetor in Africa. After the death of Caesar, Sallust retired and lived in great luxury.

Sallust wrote historical works after his retirement from public life. *The Histories,* originally in five books, is preserved only in fragments covering the period of about ten years after the death of Sulla; and two monographs, *The War with Jugurtha* (111–106 B.C.) and *The Conspiracy of Catiline.* Sallust tried to write without partiality. His work is philosophical in concept and vividly written. You may want to compare his account of the conspiracy of Catiline with Cicero's orations.

# THE SUPERIORITY OF THE MIND

**Verba Ūtilia:** commūnis, decet, dīvitiae, fingō, nītor, ops, pecus (–oris), sileō, studeō, venter

**1.** Omnīs hominēs quī sēsē student praestāre cēterīs animālibus summā ope nītī decet, nē vītam silentiō trānseant velutī pecora, quae nātūra prōna[1] atque ventrī oboedientia fīnxit. Sed nostra omnis vīs in animō et corpore sita est: animī imperiō, corporis servitiō magis ūtimur; alterum[2] nōbīs cum dīs, alterum cum bēluīs commūne est. Quō[3] mihi rēctius vidētur ingenī quam vīrium opibus[4] glōriam quaerere, et, quoniam vīta ipsa quā fruimur brevis est, memoriam nostrī quam maximē longam efficere. Nam dīvitiārum et fōrmae glōria fluxa atque fragilis est, virtūs[5] clāra aeternaque habētur.

**2.** Multī mortālēs, dēditī ventrī atque somnō, indoctī incultīque vītam sīcutī peregrīnantēs[6] trānsiēre; quibus profectō contrā nātūram corpus voluptātī, anima onerī fuit. Eōrum ego vītam mortemque iūxtā[7] aestimō, quoniam dē utrāque silētur. Vērum[8] enim vērō[8] is dēmum mihi vīvere atque fruī animā vidētur quī aliquō negōtiō intentus praeclārī facinoris aut artis bonae fāmam quaerit. Sed in magnā cōpiā rērum$_1$ aliud aliī[9] nātūra iter ostendit. **3.** Pulchrum est bene facere reī pūblicae, etiam bene dīcere haud absurdum est; vel pāce$_2$ vel bellō clārum fierī licet;[10] et quī fēcēre et quī facta aliōrum scrīpsēre, multī[11] laudantur.

[1] *with heads bent down*
[2] *the former* **(animī imperiō)**
[3] *Therefore*
[4] *with the help of*
[5] *intellectual excellence*
[6] *like (men) going abroad*
[7] *close to (each other), alike*
[8] *But certainly*
[9] *one road to one (man), another road to another*
[10] *(one) may become famous*
[11] *many of those who* **(quī)**

$_1$ i.e., those things in which one may succeed, such as those that follow
$_2$ **in pāce** would be more usual

## Translation

1. Life is short; let us enjoy it while we may.
2. If you desire to surpass others, you must work.
3. We use the body in order to carry out the wishes of the mind.
4. Some prefer to become famous by deeds, others by their writings.

### WORD STUDY

Give Latin words related to **fragilis** and **fluxus.**

Give English derivatives of **decet, fruor, iūxtā, oboediō, onus, prōnus.**

# CATILINE'S CHARACTER

**Verba Ūtilia:** adulēscentia, avāritia, igitur, incitō, in diēs, invādō, libīdō, lūxuria, memorō, suprā

**4.** Igitur dē Catilīnae coniūrātiōne quam vērissimē poterō paucīs$_{1}$ absolvam; nam id facinus in prīmīs ego memorābile exīstimō sceleris atque perīculī novitāte. Dē cuius hominis mōribus pauca prius$_{2}$ explānanda sunt quam initium nārrandī faciam.

**5.** L. Catilīna, nōbilī genere nātus, fuit magnā vī et animī et corporis sed ingeniō malō prāvōque. Huic ab adulēscentiā bella intestīna, caedēs, rapīnae, discordia cīvīlis grāta$_{3}$ fuēre, ibique[1] iuventūtem suam exercuit. Corpus$_{4}$ patiēns[2] inediae, algōris[3], vigiliae suprā quam[4] cuiquam crēdibile est. Animus audāx, subdolus[5], varius, cuius reī libet$_{5}$ simulātor ac dissimulātor, aliēnī appetēns, suī profūsus,[6] ārdēns in cupiditātibus; satis ēloquentiae, sapientiae parum. Vāstus[7] animus immoderāta, incrēdibilia, nimis alta semper cupiēbat. Hunc post dominātiōnem L. Sullae libīdō maxima invāserat reī pūblicae capiendae, neque id quibus modīs assequerētur, dum[8] sibi rēgnum parāret, quicquam pēnsī habēbat.[9] Agitābātur magis magisque in diēs[10] animus ferōx inopiā reī familiāris et cōnscientiā scelerum, quae utraque[11] eīs artibus auxerat quās suprā memorāvī. Incitābant$_{6}$ praetereā corruptī cīvitātis mōrēs, quōs pessima ac dīversa[12] inter sē mala, lūxuria atque avāritia, vexābant.

[1] *and in them*
[2] *able to endure*
[3] *cold*
[4] *beyond what* (literally, *beyond than*)
[5] *crafty*
[6] *desirous of the property of another, extravagant with his own*
[7] *insatiable*
[8] *provided that*
[9] *have any scruple at all how* (**quibus modis**)
[10] *day by day*
[11] *both of which things*
[12] *opposite to each other*

---

$_{1}$ Supply **verbīs.**
$_{2}$ with **quam**
$_{3}$ neuter plural because it modifies nouns in varying genders and numbers
$_{4}$ Supply **erat.**
$_{5}$ for **cuiuslibet reī,** *of everything*
$_{6}$ Supply **eum** as object.

## Translation

1. I shall tell you about him as clearly as I can.
2. I must tell you about the man before I tell you about his deeds.
3. Provided that he got what he wanted, he did not care what happened to others.

# RISE AND DECLINE OF ROME

**Verba Ūtilia:** arduus, ascendō, cīvitās, cupīdō, fundō, incrēdibilis, initium, nōbilitās, properō, simul ac

[1] *(having) no permanent homes*
[2] *some living in one manner, others in another*
[3] *hard to believe how*
[4] *as soon as* (with **simul**)
[5] *able to endure war* (literally, *enduring [of] war*)
[6] *for glory* (genitive)
[7] *those (things to be) wealth*
[8] *at home and abroad* (locative)
[9] *worship*
[10] *extravagant*

**6.** Urbem Rōmam, sīcutī ego accēpī, condidēre atque habuēre initiō Troiānī, quī, Aenēā duce, profugī, sēdibus incertīs,[1] vagābantur, et cum hīs Aborīginēs$_{1}$, genus hominum agreste, sine lēgibus, sine imperiō, līberum atque solūtum. Hī postquam in ūna moenia$_{2}$ convēnēre, disparī genere, dissimilī linguā, aliī aliō mōre vīventēs,[2] incrēdibile memorātū[3] est quam facile coaluerint; ita brevī$_{3}$ multitūdō dīversa atqua vaga concordiā cīvitās facta erat. **7.** Sed cīvitās, incrēdibile memorātū est, adeptā lībertāte, quantum brevī crēverit: tanta cupīdō glōriae incesserat. Iam prīmum iuventūs, simul ac[4] bellī patiēns[5] erat, in castrīs per labōrem ūsum mīlitiae discēbat, magisque in decōrīs armīs et mīlitāribus equīs quam in convīviīs libīdinem habēbant.$_{4}$ Igitur tālibus virīs nōn labor īnsolitus, nōn locus ūllus asper aut arduus erat, nōn armātus hostis formīdulōsus; virtūs omnia domuerat. Sed glōriae[6] maximum certāmen inter ipsōs erat: sē$_{5}$ quisque hostem ferīre, mūrum ascendere, cōnspicī dum tāle facinus faceret properābat; eās[7] dīvitiās, eam bonam fāmam magnamque nōbilitātem putābant. Laudis avidī, pecūniae līberālēs erant; glōriam ingentem, dīvitiās honestās volēbant. Memorāre possum quibus in locīs maximās hostium cōpiās populus Rōmānus parvā manū fūderit, quās urbīs nātūrā mūnītās pugnandō cēperit, nī ea rēs longius nōs ab inceptō traheret. **9.** Igitur domī mīlitiaeque[8] bonī mōrēs colēbantur; concordia maxima, minima avāritia erat; iūs bonumque apud eōs nōn lēgibus magis quam nātūrā valēbat. Iūrgia, discordiās, simultātēs cum hostibus exercēbant, cīvēs cum cīvibus dē virtūte certābant. In suppliciīs[9] deōrum magnificī[10], domī parcī, in amīcōs fidēlēs erant. Duābus hīs artibus, audāciā in bellō, ubi pāx ēvēnerat, aequitāte, sēque remque pūblicam cūrābant.

---

$_{1}$ *The Aborigines* simply meant the people living at the site of Rome before the Trojans came.
$_{2}$ plural in form but singular in meaning, so that the plural **ūna** with singular meaning is used with it: *into one walled (city)*
$_{3}$ adverb
$_{4}$ Note the shift from singular (**erat, discēbat**) to plural, all with the singular subject **iuventūs.** It looks almost as if Sallust is trying to undermine your faith in the rules of grammar.
$_{5}$ subject of **ferīre** but unnecessary

**12.** Postquam dīvitiae honōrī esse coepēre et eās glōria, imperium, potentia sequēbātur,[6] hebēscere virtūs, paupertās probrō habērī, innocentia prō malivolentiā dūcī coepit. Igitur ex dīvitiīs iuventūtem lūxuria atque avāritia cum superbiā invāsēre: rapere,[7] cōnsūmere; sua parvī pendere,[11] aliēna cupere; pudōrem, pudīcitiam, dīvīna atque hūmāna prōmiscua, nihil pēnsī neque moderātī habēre.[12] Operae pretium est,[13] cum domōs atque vīllās cognōveris in urbium modum exaedificātās, vīsere templa deōrum, quae nostrī maiōrēs, religiōsissimī mortālēs, fēcēre. Vērum illī dēlūbra deōrum pietāte, domōs suās glōriā decorābant,[8] neque victīs quicquam praeter iniūriae licentiam ēripiēbant. At hī contrā[9], ignāvissimī hominēs, per summum scelus omnia ea sociīs adimere[10] quae fortissimī virī victōrēs relīquerant; proinde quasi iniūriam facere id dēmum esset imperiō ūtī.[14]

[11] *considered their own possessions of little value*

[12] *they regarded as all the same* (without distinction) *modesty and chastity, things divine and human, and showed no care for anything nor any moderation*

[13] *it is worthwhile* (literally, *it is the price of the effort*)

[14] *just as if to do wrong was (the meaning of) using power* (**Id** sums up **iniūriam facere.**)

## Translation

1. Do you know who founded that city of Rome?
2. Some responded in one way, others in another.
3. It is not permitted to take away property from the conquered.
4. The desire for glory was so great that Rome grew very quickly.

## WORD STUDY

Give English derivatives of **convīvium, crēscō, dissimulō, initium, vagor.**

Give Latin words related by derivation to **aequitās, certāmen, convīvium, cupīdō, incrēdibilis.**

---

[6] The three subjects are thought of together as a single item; **imperium** is military power, **potentia** political power.

[7] Historical infinitives; supply **iuventūs** as subject.

[8] They decorated their temples with piety, not paintings, their homes with glorious deeds, not statues and expensive furnishings.

[9] adverb

[10] historical infinitive; the governors grab what the victorious generals have left to the provincials.

# CATILINE SPEAKS TO HIS MEN

[1] *you separately*
[2] *But*
[3] *unless we ourselves make our claim to liberty*
[4] *princes*
[5] *tributary*
[6] *dependent on those*
[7] *if the state were strong*
[8] *defeat at the polls*
[9] *trials in court*
[10] *a laughingstock for the insolence of others*
[11] *on the other hand* (adverb)
[12] *events will take care of the rest*
[13] *that wealth be excessive for them*
[14] *leveling*
[15] *build a continuous row of houses*
[16] *embossed ware* (of silver)
[17] *they squander and waste*
[18] *Why don't you wake up then?*
[19] *Look!*
[20] *use me as commander-in-chief or private*

**Verba Ūtilia:** agitō, cōnsīderō, decus, nequeō, pendō, spolia, stīpendium, ūnā, vigeō, vulgus

**20.** "Sed ego quae mente agitāvī, omnēs iam anteā dīversī[1] $_{1}$ audīstis. Cēterum[2] mihi in diēs magis animus accenditur, cum cōnsīderō quae condiciō vītae futūra sit, nisi nōsmet $_{2}$ ipsī vindicāmus in lībertātem.[3] Nam postquam rēs pūblica in paucōrum potentium iūs atque diciōnem concessit, semper illīs rēgēs, tetrarchae[4] vectīgālēs[5] esse $_{3}$, populī, nātiōnēs stīpendia pendere; cēterī omnēs, strēnuī, bonī, nōbilēs atque ignōbilēs, vulgus fuimus, sine grātiā, sine auctōritāte, eīs obnoxiī[6] quibus, sī rēs pūblica valēret,[7] formīdinī essēmus. Itaque omnis grātia, potentia, honōs $_{4}$, dīvitiae apud illōs sunt aut ubi illī volunt; nōbīs relīquēre perīcula, repulsās[8], iūdicia[9], egestātem. Quae quō usque tandem patiēminī, ō fortissimī virī? Nōnne ēmorī per virtūtem praestat quam vītam miseram atque inhonestam, ubi aliēnae superbiae lūdibriō[10] fuerīs, per dēdecus āmittere? Vērum enim vērō, prō $_{5}$ deum atque hominum fidem, victōria in manū nōbīs est, viget aetās, animus valet; contrā[11] illīs annīs atque dīvitiīs omnia cōnsenuērunt. Tantum modo inceptō $_{6}$ opus est, cētera rēs expediet.[12] Etenim quis mortālium, cui virīle ingenium est, tolerāre potest illīs dīvitiās superāre,[13] quās profundant in exstruendō marī $_{7}$ et montibus coaequandīs[14], nōbīs rem familiārem etiam ad necessāria deesse? Illōs bīnās aut amplius domōs continuāre,[15] nōbīs larem familiārem nusquam ūllum esse? Cum tabulās, signa, toreumata[16] emunt, nova dīruunt, alia aedificant, postrēmō omnibus modīs pecūniam trahunt, vexant,[17] tamen summā libīdine dīvitiās suās vincere nequeunt. At nōbīs est domī inopia, forīs aes aliēnum; mala rēs, spēs multō asperior: dēnique quid reliquī habēmus praeter miseram animam?

"Quīn igitur expergīsciminī?[18] Ēn[19], illa, illa quam saepe optāstis lībertās, praetereā dīvitiae, decus, glōria in oculīs sita sunt; fortūna omnia ea victōribus praemia posuit. Rēs, tempus, perīcula, egestās, bellī spolia magnifica magis quam ōrātiō mea vōs hortantur. Vel imperātōre vel mīlite mē ūtiminī;[20] neque animus neque corpus ā vōbīs aberit. Haec ipsa, ut spērō, vōbīscum ūnā cōnsul agam, nisi forte mē animus fallit et vōs servīre magis quam imperāre parātī estis."

---

$_{1}$ The adjective is used adverbially.
$_{2}$ **–met** is an intensive particle: *we ourselves*
$_{3}$ historical infinitive with **rēgēs, tetrarchae** as subject
$_{4}$ old form of **honor**
$_{5}$ interjection: *Oh!* **deum** is genitive plural
$_{6}$ noun, ablative
$_{7}$ The Romans built concrete foundations for houses out into the sea.

Scala/Art Resource, NY

The Palatine Hill was one of the seven hills of Rome. Tradition has it that Romulus and Remus founded the town that would be Rome on the Palatine. In addition to being the nerve center of the city, it became the hill on which many famous Romans built their personal palaces. It occupied a very important position geographically, too. The Forum was located between the Palatine and the Capitoline; the Coliseum was located between the Palatine and the Esquiline. In this view, we are looking at the other side of the Palatine, not the one facing the Forum itself.

## Translation

1. It is a pleasure to me to see you.
2. There is need of help in this matter.
3. Day by day the republic is losing its liberty.
4. Use the opportunity; fight, and I will fight with you.

### WORD STUDY

Give English derivatives of **decus, optō, spolia, stīpendium, vigeō, vulgus**.

To what Latin words are the following related: **agitō, dēdecus, serviō?**

# CHERCHEZ LA FEMME

**Verba Ūtilia:** cōnfodiō, facinus, flāgitium, introeō, largior, locuplēs, polliceor, probrum, reticeō

**21.** Catilīna pollicērī[1] tabulās novās, prōscrīptiōnem locuplētium, magistrātūs, sacerdōtia, rapīnās, alia omnia quae bellum atque libīdō victōrum fert. **23.** In eā coniūrātiōne fuit Q. Cūrius, nātus haud obscūrō locō, flāgitiīs atque facinoribus coopertus, quem cēnsōrēs senātū probrī grātiā[1] mōverant. Huic hominī nōn minor vānitās inerat quam audācia; neque reticēre quae audierat neque suamet[2] ipse scelera occultāre, prōrsus[3] neque dīcere neque facere quicquam pēnsī habēbat.[4] Erat eī cum Fulviā, muliere nōbilī, vetus cōnsuētūdō.[5] Cui cum minus grātus esset, quia inopiā minus largīrī poterat, repente glōriāns maria montīsque[6] pollicērī coepit, et minārī interdum ferrō, nī sibi obnoxia[7] foret; postrēmō ferōcius agitāre quam solitus erat. At Fulvia, īnsolentiae[8] Cūrī causā cognitā, tāle perīculum reī pūblicae haud occultum habuit,[9] sed, sublātō auctōre,[10] dē Catilīnae coniūrātiōne quae quōque[11] modō audierat complūribus nārrāvit.

**28.** Igitur, perterritīs ac dubitantibus cēterīs, C. Cornēlius, eques Rōmānus, operam suam pollicitus, et cum eō L. Vargunteius senātor cōnstituēre eā nocte paulō post cum armātīs hominibus sīcutī salūtātum[12] introīre ad Cicerōnem, ac dē imprōvīsō[13] domī suae imparātum cōnfodere. Cūrius ubi intellegit quantum perīculum cōnsulī impendeat, properē per Fulviam Cicerōnī dolum quī parābātur ēnūntiat. Ita illī,[2] iānuā prohibitī, tantum facinus frūstrā suscēperant.

[1] *on account of*
[2] *his own*
[3] *in a word*
[4] *neither (what) he said or did did he regard as anything of importance*
[5] *intimacy*
[6] *mountains of money* (a proverbial expression)
[7] *submissive*
[8] *unusual behavior* (from **soleō**)
[9] *did not keep secret*
[10] *withholding her authority's (name)*
[11] *and how*
[12] *as if to pay respects*
[13] *unexpectedly* (with **dē**)

---

[1] historical infinitive
[2] Cornelius and Vargunteius

## Translation

1. The two men tried to enter in order to fight.
2. She told everyone what she knew about the conspiracy.
3. Though he was born of a noble family, he was very stupid.
4. When he realized what would happen, he quickly told Cicero.

### WORD STUDY

Explain the derivation of *frustration, occult, sacerdotal.*

Give the Latin words related to **complūrēs, imprōvīsus, rapīna, reticeō, sacerdōtium.**

# CATILINE AND MANLIUS SPEAK UP

**Verba Ūtilia:** certāmen, dēcrētum, egeō, īra, parricīda, pereō, praeceps, supplex, temere, testor

**31.** Postrēmō dissimulandī causā aut suī expūrgandī, sīcut iūrgiō lacessītus foret,[1] in senātum vēnit. Tum M. Tullius cōnsul, sīve praesentiam eius timēns sīve īrā commōtus, ōrātiōnem habuit lūculentam atque ūtilem reī pūblicae, quam posteā scrīptam ēdidit.[1] Sed ubi ille assēdit, Catilīna, ut erat parātus ad dissimulanda omnia, dēmissō vultū, vōce supplicī postulāre ā patribus coepit nē quid dē sē temere crēderent; eā[2] familiā ortum, ita sē ab adulēscentiā vītam īnstituisse ut omnia bona in spē habēret; nē exīstimārent sibi, patriciō hominī, cuius ipsīus atque maiōrum plūrima beneficia in plēbem Rōmānam essent, perditā rē pūblicā opus esse,[3] cum eam servāret M. Tullius, inquilīnus[4][2] cīvis urbis Rōmae. Ad hoc maledicta alia cum adderet, obstrepere omnēs[3], hostem atque parricīdam vocāre. Tum ille furibundus, "Quoniam quidem circumventus," inquit, "ab inimīcīs praeceps agor, incendium meum ruīnā restinguam."[4]

[1] *as if he had been provoked in a (personal) quarrel*

[2] *such*

[3] *that he had need of a ruined state* (with **sibi**)

[4] *foreign-born*

---

[1] the first oration against Catiline

[2] This is a dig at Cicero's being not a native-born Roman but a **novus homō** from Arpinum.

[3] i.e., **senātōrēs,** subject of the historical infinitives

[4] i.e., he will cause general destruction to put out the fire started against him

**33.** Dum haec Rōmae geruntur, C. Mānlius ex suō numerō lēgātōs ad Mārcium Rēgem[5] mittit cum mandātīs huiusce modī: "Deōs hominēsque testāmur, imperātor, nōs arma neque contrā patriam cēpisse neque quō[6] perīculum aliīs facerēmus, sed utī corpora nostra ab iniūriā tūta forent, quī[7] miserī, egentēs violentiā atque crūdēlitāte faenerātōrum[5] plērīque patriā[6], sed omnēs fāmā atque fortūnīs expertēs sumus. Saepe maiōrēs vestrum,[8] miseritī[7] plēbis Rōmānae, dēcrētīs suīs inopiae eius opitulātī[8] sunt, ac novissimē memoriā nostrā propter magnitūdinem aeris aliēnī, volentibus omnibus bonīs, argentum aere solūtum est.[9] Saepe ipsa plēbs, aut dominandī studiō permōta aut superbiā magistrātuum, armāta ā patribus sēcessit. At nōs nōn imperium neque dīvitiās petimus, quārum rērum causā bella atque certāmina omnia inter mortālīs sunt, sed lībertātem, quam nēmō bonus nisi cum animā simul āmittit. Tē atque senātum obtestāmur, cōnsulātis miserīs cīvibus, lēgis praesidium, quod inīquitās praetōris ēripuit, restituātis, nēve nōbīs eam necessitūdinem impōnātis, ut quaerāmus quōnam modō maximē ultī sanguinem nostrum pereāmus."[10]

[5] *moneylenders*
[6] ablative with **expertēs** *(deprived of)*
[7] *pitying* (with genitive)
[8] *relieved* (with dative)
[9] *a silver (debt) was paid in bronze* (a form of partial debt cancellation)
[10] *how we may best avenge our bloodshed (and then) perish*

## Translation

1. Cicero was so aroused that he made a fine speech.
2. Was he not a man of noble family, born in Rome?
3. If we should be freed of debt, the state would be safe.
4. Catiline asked the senators not to think that he would destroy the state.

---

5 general of the government forces opposing Manlius
6 for **ut**
7 Supply **nōs** (implied in **nostra**) as antecedent.
8 genitive of **vōs**

# THE SCUM OF THE EARTH

**Verba Ūtilia:** adeō *(adv.),* aliēnus, domō, exōrnō, fascis, īnsigne, multitūdō, occāsus, ortus, pāreō

**36.** Sed ipse paucōs diēs commorātus apud C. Flāminium in agrō Arrētīnō[1], dum vīcīnitātem anteā sollicitātam armīs exōrnat, cum fascibus atque aliīs imperī īnsignibus in castra ad Mānlium contendit. Haec[2] ubi Rōmae comperta sunt, senātus Catilīnam et Mānlium hostīs iūdicat.

[1] *at Arretium*
[2] *these facts*

Eā tempestāte[3] mihi imperium populī Rōmānī multō maximē miserābile vīsum est. Cui[1] cum ad occāsum ab ortū sōlis[4] omnia domita armīs pārērent, domī ōtium atque dīvitiae, quae prīma mortālēs putant, affluerent[5], fuēre tamen cīvēs quī sēque remque pūblicam obstinātīs animīs perditum īrent[6]. Namque duōbus senātī[2] dēcrētīs ex tantā multitūdine neque praemiō inductus[3] coniūrātiōnem patefēcerat neque ex castrīs Catilīnae quisquam omnium discesserat; tanta vīs morbī, atque utī tābēs,[7] plērōsque[4] cīvium animōs invāserat.

**37.** Neque sōlum illīs aliēna[8] mēns erat quī cōnsciī[9] coniūrātiōnis fuerant, sed omnīnō cūncta plēbēs[5] novārum rērum studiō Catilīnae incepta probābat. Id adeō mōre suō vidēbātur facere.[10] Nam semper in cīvitāte, quibus[6] opēs nūllae sunt bonīs invident, malōs extollunt, vetera ōdēre, nova exoptant, odiō suārum rērum mūtārī omnia student, turbā atque sēditiōnibus sine cūrā aluntur, quoniam egestās facile habētur sine damnō.[11] Sed urbāna plēbēs ea vērō praeceps[12] erat dē multīs causīs. Prīmum omnium quī ubīque probrō atque petulantiā maximē praestābant, item aliī per dēdecora, patrimōniīs āmissīs, postrēmō omnēs quōs flāgitium aut facinus domō expulerat, eī Rōmam sīcut in sentīnam cōnflūxerant.

[3] *time*
[4] *from sunrise to sunset, from east to west*
[5] *abounded*
[6] *would go to destroy*
[7] *like a plague*
[8] *alienated*
[9] *aware of*
[10] *The plebs seemed to do this in accordance with their custom.*
[11] *they flourish on rioting and rebellion without worry, since their poverty is easily endured without loss*
[12] *desperate*

## Translation

1. He remained a few days at the house of a friend.
2. There were no men who obeyed the decree of the senate.
3. The poor men envy the rich and are eager for revolution.

### WORD STUDY

Explain by derivation: *affluence, extol, fascism, insignia, invidious, mutation.*

What Latin words are related to **cōnfluō, cōnscius, exoptō, inceptum, miserābilis, tempestās, vīcīnitās?**

---

[1] i.e., the **imperium**
[2] old form of genitive for **senātūs:** *in spite of two decrees of the senate* (offering rewards)
[3] modifies **quisquam,** the subject
[4] We might expect the genitive, modifying **cīvium.**
[5] for **plēbs** (singular)
[6] Supply **eī** as antecedent.

# LENTULUS AND THE ALLOBROGES

**Verba Ūtilia:** adeō *(verb)*, doleō, idōneus, magistrātus, miseria, operam dō, remedium, simulō, tālis, vehementer

**39.** Īsdem temporibus Rōmae Lentulus, sīcutī Catilīna praecēperat, quōscumque mōribus aut fortūnā novīs rēbus idōneōs crēdēbat, aut per sē aut per aliōs sollicitābat, neque sōlum cīvīs, sed cuiusque modī genus hominum,[1] quod modo[2]$_1$ bellō ūsuī foret.$_2$ **40.** Igitur P. Umbrēnō cuidam negōtium dat, utī lēgātōs Allobrogum requīrat eōsque, sī possit, impellat ad societātem bellī, exīstimāns pūblicē prīvatimque aere aliēnō oppressōs,$_3$ praetereā quod nātūrā gēns Gallica bellicōsa esset, facile eōs ad tāle cōnsilium addūcī posse. Umbrēnus quod in Galliā negōtiātus erat, plērīsque prīncipibus cīvitātum nōtus erat atque eōs nōverat. Itaque sine morā, ubi prīmum lēgātōs in forō cōnspexit, percontātus pauca dē statū cīvitātis et quasi dolēns eius$_4$ cāsum requīrere coepit quem exitum tantīs malīs spērārent. Postquam illōs videt querī dē avāritiā magistrātuum, accūsāre senātum, quod in eō auxilī nihil esset, miseriīs suīs remedium mortem[3] expectāre, "At ego," inquit, "vōbīs, sī modo virī esse vultis, ratiōnem ostendam quā tanta ista mala effugiātis[4]." Haec ubi dīxit, Allobrogēs in maximam spem adductī Umbrēnum ōrāre$_5$ ut suī$_6$ miserērētur; nihil tam asperum neque tam difficile esse quod nōn cupidissimē factūrī essent, dum ea rēs cīvitātem aere aliēnō līberāret. Coniūrātiōnem aperit, nōminat sociōs, praetereā multōs cuiusque generis innoxiōs[5],$_7$ quō lēgātīs animus amplior esset. Deinde eōs pollicitōs operam suam domum dīmittit. **41.** Sed Allobrogēs diū in incertō habuēre[6] quidnam cōnsilī caperent. In alterā parte erat aes aliēnum, studium bellī, magna mercēs in spē victōriae, at in alterā maiōrēs opēs$_8$, tūta cōnsilia, prō incertā spē certa praemia. Haec illīs volventibus, tandem vīcit fortūna reī pūblicae. Itaque Q. Fabiō Sangae, cuius patrōciniō$_9$ cīvitās plūrimum ūtēbātur, rem omnem utī cognōverant aperiunt. Cicerō, per Sangam cōnsiliō cognitō, lēgātīs praecēpit ut studium coniūrātiōnis vehementer simulent, cēterōs adeant, bene polliceantur, dentque operam utī eōs quam maximē manifēstōs habeant.[7]

[1] *all sorts of men*
[2] *provided that* (literally, *which only*)
[3] *death as a remedy*
[4] *you may escape*
[5] *innocent*
[6] *were uncertain* (literally, *held (it) in uncertainty*)
[7] *that they see to it that they catch them (the conspirators) in the act, as far as possible*

---

$_1$ The antecedent of **quod** is **genus**.
$_2$ = **esset**
$_3$ modifies **eōs**
$_4$ refers to **cīvitātis**
$_5$ historical infinitive
$_6$ genitive of the reflexive, referring to **Allobrogēs**; it depends on **miserērētur**
$_7$ Perhaps he mentioned members of the popular party, even Caesar.
$_8$ i.e., the resources of the Roman state, which could crush the rebellion
$_9$ He represented them in legal matters.

## Translation

1. They begged him to free them from their troubles.
2. See to it that you find out what they are going to do.
3. Provided that you give us help, we will give you rewards.
4. If you will be men, you will persuade your friends to do this.

# DOCUMENTS SEIZED— CAESAR INVOLVED?

**Verba Ūtilia:** aliter, cōnflō, grandis, haud, index, īnfrā, mūnus, praeceptum, prex, suspicor

**44.** Sed Allobrogēs ex praeceptō Cicerōnis per Gabīnium cēterōs conveniunt. Ab Lentulō, Cethēgō, Statiliō, item Cassiō postulant iūs iūrandum,[1] quod signātum ad cīvīs perferant:$_1$ aliter haud facile eōs ad tantum negōtium impellī posse. Cēterī nihil suspicantēs dant$_2$, Cassius sēmet$_3$ eō$_4$ brevī ventūrum pollicētur ac paulō ante lēgātōs ex urbe proficīscitur. Lentulus cum eīs T. Volturcium quendam Crotōniēnsem mittit, ut Allobrogēs, prius quam domum pergerent, cum Catilīnā, datā atque acceptā fidē, societātem cōnfirmārent. Ipse Volturciō litterās ad Catilīnam dat, quārum exemplum īnfrā scrīptum est: "Quī sim, ex eō quem ad tē mīsī cognōscēs. Fac cōgitēs[2] in quantā calamitāte sīs, et meminerīs$_5$ tē virum esse. Cōnsīderēs quid tuae ratiōnēs postulent. Auxilium petās ab omnibus, etiam ab īnfimīs$_6$."

**49.** Sed īsdem temporibus Q. Catulus et C. Pīsō neque precibus neque grātiā neque pretiō Cicerōnem impellere potuēre utī per Allobrogēs aut alium indicem C. Caesar falsō nōminārētur. Nam uterque cum illō gravīs inimīcitiās exercēbant[3]. Rēs autem opportūna vidēbātur, quod is prīvātim ēgregiā līberālitāte, pūblicē maximīs mūneribus[4] grandem pecūniam dēbēbat. Sed ubi cōnsulem ad tantum facinus impellere nequeunt, ipsī singillātim circumeundō atque ēmentiendō[5] quae sē ex Volturciō aut Allobrogibus audīsse dīcerent, magnam illī invidiam cōnflāverant, usque eō[6] ut nōn nūllī equitēs Rōmānī, quī praesidī causā cum tēlīs erant circum aedem Concordiae, seu perīculī magnitūdine seu animī mōbilitāte impulsī, quō studium suum in rem pūblicam clārius esset, ēgredientī ex senātū Caesarī gladiō minitārentur.

[1] *a (written) oath*
[2] *see that you realize*
[3] *carried on*
[4] *games* (given at his own expense while aedile)
[5] *lying about*
[6] *to such an extent that*

---

$_1$ relative purpose clause
$_2$ Supply **iūs iūrandum.**
$_3$ emphatic for **sē**
$_4$ i.e., to Gaul
$_5$ The hortatory subjunctive is sometimes used instead of the imperative; this verb has no present imperative.
$_6$ He means the slaves.

## Translation

1. Many asked whether Caesar favored Catiline.
2. They tried to kill Caesar as he came out of the senate.
3. They asked for a letter that they might show to their friends.
4. In order that the matter might be more definite, Lentulus gave them a letter.

# CAESAR AND CATO

**Verba Ūtilia:** addō, beneficium, cōnstantia, dīves, ignōscō, largior, mānsuētūdō, misericordia, prope, sevēritās

**54.** Igitur eīs genus, aetās, ēloquentia prope aequālia[1] fuēre, magnitūdō animī pār, item glōria, sed alia aliī.[1] Caesar beneficiīs ac mūnificentiā magnus habēbātur, integritāte vītae Catō. Ille mānsuētūdine et misericordiā clārus factus, huic sevēritās dignitātem addiderat. Caesar dandō, sublevandō, ignōscendō, Catō nihil largiendō[2] glōriam adeptus est. In alterō miserīs perfugium erat, in alterō malīs perniciēs. Illīus facilitās, huius cōnstantia laudābātur. Postrēmō Caesar in animum indūxerat labōrāre, vigilāre; negōtiīs amīcōrum intentus, sua neglegere,[2] nihil dēnegāre quod dōnō dignum esset; sibi magnum imperium, exercitum, bellum novum exoptābat, ubi virtūs ēnitēscere posset. At Catōnī studium modestiae, decoris, sed maximē sevēritātis erat; nōn dīvitiīs cum dīvite neque factiōne cum factiōsō, sed cum strēnuō virtūte, cum modestō pudōre, cum innocente abstinentiā certābat;[3] esse quam vidērī bonus mālēbat: ita, quō minus[3] petēbat glōriam, eō magis illum assequēbātur.[4]

[1] *one (kind) to one, another to the other*
[2] *by not spending freely*
[3] *the less . . . the more*

---

[1] neuter because it modifies nouns of different genders
[2] historical infinitives
[3] He did not try to outdo a rich man in wealth, etc., but a vigorous man in courage, etc.
[4] i.e., glory

### Translation

1. What did Cato prefer to be?
2. They were equal in age and eloquence.
3. He did nothing that was unworthy of him.
4. The former was praised for his kindness, the latter for his sternness.

## WORD STUDY

In the reading find all words with suffixes in **–tās, –tia,** and **–tūdō.**

What Latin words are related to **abstinentia, ēloquentia, innocēns, mūnificentia, perfugium?**

UNIT
V

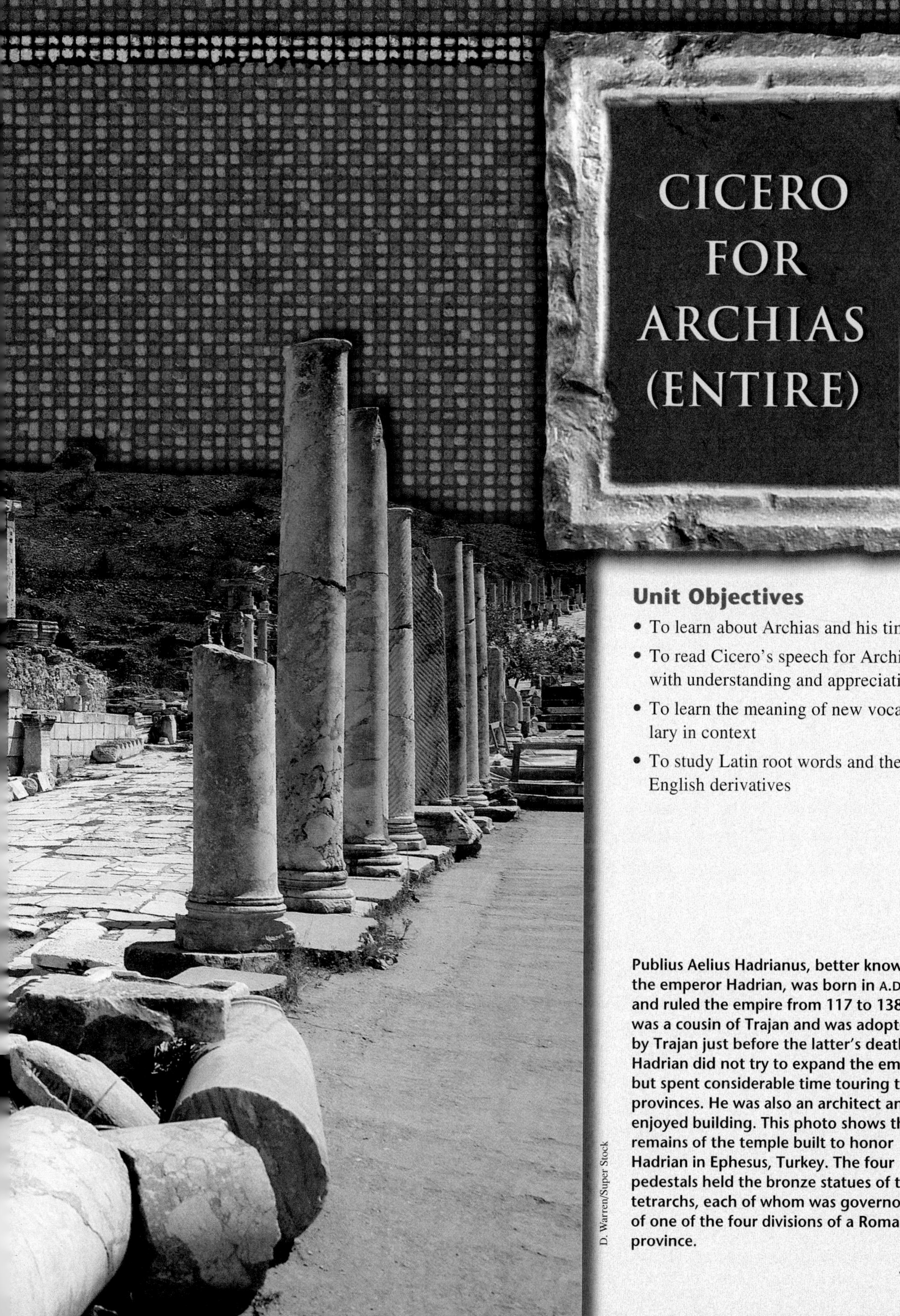

# CICERO FOR ARCHIAS (ENTIRE)

## Unit Objectives

- To learn about Archias and his times
- To read Cicero's speech for Archias with understanding and appreciation
- To learn the meaning of new vocabulary in context
- To study Latin root words and their English derivatives

**Publius Aelius Hadrianus, better known as the emperor Hadrian, was born in A.D. 76 and ruled the empire from 117 to 138. He was a cousin of Trajan and was adopted by Trajan just before the latter's death. Hadrian did not try to expand the empire, but spent considerable time touring the provinces. He was also an architect and enjoyed building. This photo shows the remains of the temple built to honor Hadrian in Ephesus, Turkey. The four pedestals held the bronze statues of the tetrarchs, each of whom was governor of one of the four divisions of a Roman province.**

D. Warren/Super Stock

# ARCHIAS

It was an ancient Greek custom, going back to Homer, for poets to wander about giving recitals of their poems, as today musicians go on concert tours. It came to be the practice for poets to make up poems on the spot using themes suggested by the audience; that is, to improvise.

One such poet was Archias, a Greek born about 120 B.C. in the city of Antioch in Syria. At a young age, Archias showed his ability to memorize and improvise. By the time he was 17, this precocious poet was traveling throughout Asia Minor and Greece to give his readings. Everywhere he met with success.

After Asia Minor and Greece, there was just one part of the Greek-speaking world to be conquered—southern Italy. Here again Archias was very successful. Where should he go next? There remained the most prominent city of Italy, Rome. It was not a Greek city, but it was becoming a thriving metropolis and was interested in Greek culture. Many prominent Romans spoke Greek well. Cato the Elder had learned Greek as an old man. Homer's *Odyssey* had been translated into Latin by Livius Andronicus and was used as a textbook in Roman schools. Greek tragedy and comedy had been translated and adapted. Greek philosophers, historians, teachers, and poets had come to Rome and settled down there. And Archias went there too, arriving in the busy city on the Tiber in 102 B.C., before he had reached the age of 18.

Before long Archias became somewhat of a sensation in Rome. The Lucullus family, in particular, took him under its wing, and his future was assured. During a trip to Sicily with M. Lucullus, Archias was made a citizen of Heraclea in southern Italy. He took the **nōmen** Licinius of his patrons the Luculli and a Roman **praenōmen**, keeping his Greek name as a **cognōmen**. He was thus known as Aulus Licinius Archias.

The Social War, so called because it was a revolt of Rome's allies **(sociī)** against the big city, broke out in 90 B.C. All the allies wanted was Roman citizenship, instead of the second-class citizenship that they had held. They lost the war but gained their demands, for a law passed the next year granted them the desired rights of Roman citizenship. So in accordance with the terms of the law of 89 B.C., Archias registered with a praetor as a Roman citizen.

Generals and governors customarily took poets with them on their expeditions, primarily to write poems about their feats. L. Lucullus took Archias with him on his expedition against Mithridates, and as Lucullus had hoped, Archias wrote a poem, now lost, about it.

In 62 B.C. Archias was brought into court on the grounds that he was not a Roman citizen, with the purpose of having him deported as an undesirable foreigner. It is certain that the charge was intended to embarrass Lucullus, and that the men behind it were political enemies of Lucullus.

Cicero undertook the defense of Archias. The presiding praetor was Cicero's brother, Quintus. The trial apparently resulted in an acquittal. In those days lawyers received no fees and generally undertook cases for personal or political reasons. Probably Cicero's chief reason for defending Archias was that the poet had promised to write about Cicero's consulship, or perhaps the orator desired to ingratiate himself with Lucullus. Still another motive may have been that the trial enabled Cicero to make a splendid and charming defense of literature.

Archias did not write the poem about Cicero's consulship; it was left to Cicero to do so himself. Ironically, Archias would have been completely forgotten had it not been for Cicero's speech on his behalf, a speech less political and more popular than any of Cicero's other speeches. Was Cicero disappointed in not getting his fee in the form of a poem? Or did he suspect that the defense of Archias gave him the opportunity of writing an oration that was to have much to do with his own immortality? We may never know.

# CICERO IS INDEBTED TO ARCHIAS

**Verba Ūtilia:** cōnfiteor, exercitātiō, exiguus, ingenium, ingredior, īus, opitulor, quoad, repetō

**I, 1.** Sī quid[1] est in mē ingenī, iūdicēs[2], quod$_1$ sentiō quam[3] sit exiguum, aut sī qua exercitātiō dīcendī, in quā mē nōn īnfitior mediocriter esse versātum, aut sī huiusce reī ratiō[4] aliqua ab optimārum artium studiīs ac disciplīnā profecta, ā quā$_2$ ego nūllum cōnfiteor aetātis meae tempus abhorruisse, eārum rērum omnium vel in prīmīs hic A. Licinius frūctum ā mē repetere prope suō iūre dēbet. Nam quoad longissimē[5] potest mēns mea respicere spatium praeteritī temporis et pueritiae memoriam recordārī ultimam, inde[6] usque repetēns,[6] hunc videō mihi prīncipem et ad suscipiendam et ad ingrediendam ratiōnem hōrum studiōrum exstitisse. Quod[7] sī haec vōx[8] huius hortātū praeceptīsque[9] cōnfōrmāta nōn nūllīs aliquandō salūtī fuit, ā quō$_3$ id accēpimus$_4$ quō cēterīs opitulārī et aliōs servāre possēmus, huic profectō ipsī, quantum est situm in nōbīs, et opem et salūtem ferre dēbēmus.

[1] *if any ability,* i.e., *whatever ability*
[2] *jurors*
[3] *how*
[4] *theoretical basis*
[5] *as far back as* (with **quoad**)
[6] *going back even to that time*
[7] *Now*
[8] *this voice (of mine)*
[9] *teaching* (in a general sense)

$_1$ = **et hoc** (connecting relative, subject of **sit**)
$_2$ The antecedent is **ratiō.**
$_3$ The antecedent is **huic;** therefore in translation **ā quō... possēmus** comes after **huic.**
$_4$ the plural of modesty, referring to himself

[10] *different*
[11] *and not*
[12] *this (of mine)*
[13] *culture*

**2.** Ac nē quis ā nōbīs hoc ita dīcī forte mīrētur,[5] quod alia[10] quaedam in hōc[6] facultās sit ingenī neque[11] haec[12] dīcendī ratiō aut disciplīna, nē nōs quidem huic ūnī studiō penitus umquam dēditī fuimus. Etenim omnēs artēs quae ad hūmānitātem[13] pertinent habent quoddam commūne vinculum et quasi cognātiōne quādam inter sē continentur.

5 Supply *let me say this* before the main verb.
6 i.e., Archias

# A NEW STYLE OF SPEAKING

[1] *a legal investigation and a state trial*
[2] *the case is being tried*
[3] *with so large an assembly*
[4] *in a character of this sort* (i.e., Archias)
[5] *the perils of the courts*

**Verba Ūtilia:** concursus, ērudītus, molestus, ōtium, quaestiō, reus, sevērus, trāctō, tribuō, venia

**II, 3.** Sed nē cui vestrum[1] mīrum esse videātur mē[2] in quaestiōne[1] lēgitimā et in iūdiciō pūblicō,[1] cum rēs agātur[2] apud praetōrem populī Rōmānī, lēctissimum virum, et apud sevērissimōs iūdicēs, tantō conventū[3] hominum ac frequentiā hōc ūtī genere dīcendī quod nōn modo ā cōnsuētūdine iūdiciōrum vērum etiam ā forēnsī sermōne abhorreat, quaesō ā vōbīs ut in hāc causā mihi dētis hanc veniam accommodātam huic reō[3], vōbīs, quem ad modum[4] spērō, nōn molestam, ut mē[5] prō summō poētā atque ērudītissimō homine dīcentem hōc concursū[3] hominum litterātissimōrum, hāc vestrā hūmānitāte, hōc dēnique praetōre exercente iūdicium, patiāminī dē studiīs hūmānitātis ac litterārum paulō loquī līberius et in eius modī persōnā,[4] quae propter ōtium ac studium minimē in iūdiciīs perīculīsque[5] trāctāta est, ūtī prope novō quōdam et inūsitātō genere dīcendī. **4.** Quod[6] sī mihi ā vōbīs tribuī concēdīque sentiam, perficiam profectō ut hunc A. Licinium nōn modo nōn sēgregandum[7], cum sit cīvis, ā numerō cīvium, vērum etiam, sī nōn esset, putētis ascīscendum fuisse.

1 genitive of **vōs**
2 subject of **ūtī** (line 4)
3 from **reus**
4 The phrase is synonymous with **ut,** *as,* avoided here because **ut** is used in a different sense just before and just after.
5 subject of **loquī**
6 connecting relative
7 Supply **fuisse** and note the tense.

## WORD STUDY

Explain by derivation: *erudition, forensic, sentient, tributary, venial.*

What Latin words are related to **concursus, ērudītus, inūsitātus, lēgitimus, quaestiō, sēgregō?**

**Persōna** is derived from the Greek word πρόσωπον, *mask* (literally, "face"), worn by actors in plays. The changes in spelling are explained by the fact that the word was first borrowed by the Etruscans, from whom the Romans got it. The masks differed and represented the different *types* or *characters.* Finally **persōna** took on the meaning *individual,* as in English *person.*

# ARCHIAS COMES TO ROME

**Verba Ūtilia:** adhibeō, antecellō, ars, celeber, cognitiō, hīc, hospitium, nancīscor, plēnus, senectūs

**III.** Nam, ut prīmum ex puerīs[1] excessit Archiās atque ab eīs artibus quibus aetās puerīlis ad hūmānitātem īnfōrmārī solet, sē ad scrībendī studium contulit, prīmum Antiochīae (nam ibi nātus est locō[2] nōbilī), celebrī[3] quondam urbe$_1$ et cōpiōsā atque ērudītissimīs hominibus līberālissimīsque studiīs affluentī, celeriter antecellere omnibus ingenī glōriā coepit. Post$_2$ in cēterīs Asiae partibus cūnctāque Graeciā sīc eius adventūs[4] celebrābantur ut fāmam ingenī expectātiō hominis, expectātiōnem ipsīus adventus admīrātiōque superāret. **5.** Erat Italia tum plēna Graecārum artium ac disciplīnārum[5], studiaque haec et in Latiō[6] vehementius tum colēbantur quam nunc īsdem in oppidīs et hic Rōmae propter tranquillitātem reī pūblicae nōn neglegēbantur. Itaque hunc et Tarentīnī et Locrēnsēs et Rēgīnī et Neāpolitānī[7] cīvitāte$_3$ cēterīsque praemiīs dōnārunt, et omnēs quī aliquid dē ingeniīs poterant iūdicāre cognitiōne atque hospitiō dignum$_4$ exīstimārunt. Hāc tantā celebritāte fāmae cum esset iam absentibus[8] nōtus, Rōmam vēnit, Mariō cōnsule et Catulō. Nactus est prīmum cōnsulēs eōs quōrum alter rēs ad scrībendum maximās, alter cum[9] rēs gestās, tum[9] etiam studium atque aurēs[10] adhibēre posset.

[1] *boyhood*
[2] *rank*
[3] *populous*
[4] *arrival (at various places)*
[5] *sciences*
[6] *Latium*
[7] *the people of Tarentum, Locri, Regium, and Naples*
[8] *to those (living) far away*
[9] *not only . . . but also*
[10] *attention* (literally, *ears*)

---

$_1$ a noun in apposition with a locative (**Antiochīae**) is in the ablative
$_2$ adverb
$_3$ i.e., honorary citizenship, as is sometimes done today
$_4$ Supply **eum**

Statim Lūcullī[5], cum praetextātus[6] etiam tum Archiās esset, eum domum suam recēpērunt. Est iam hoc nōn sōlum ingenī[11] ac litterārum vērum etiam nātūrae atque virtūtis, ut domus quae huius adulēscentiae prīma fāvit eadem esset familiārissima senectūtī. **6.** Erat temporibus illīs iūcundus[12] Q. Metellō illī Numidicō et eius Piō fīliō, audiēbātur ā M. Aemiliō, vīvēbat[13] cum Q. Catulō et patre et fīliō, ā L. Crassō colēbātur, Lūcullōs vērō et Drūsum et Octāviōs et Catōnem et tōtam Hortēnsiōrum domum dēvīnctam cōnsuētūdine[14] cum tenēret, afficiēbatur summō honōre, quod eum nōn sōlum colēbant quī aliquid percipere atque audīre studēbant vērum etiam sī quī forte simulābant.

[11] *(an indication of his) ability*
[12] *a favorite of* (literally, *agreeable to*)
[13] *was a guest of*
[14] *bound by (ties of) intimacy*

---

[5] There are two brothers, Lucius and Marcus.
[6] Literally this means *wearing the praetexta,* applied to Roman boys before they put on the **toga cīvīlis** and became citizens.

# ARCHIAS ENROLLED AS A ROMAN CITIZEN

**Verba Ūtilia:** corrumpō, dēsīderō, flāgitō, immō, immō vērō, intereō, profiteor, repudiō, satis, testimōnium

**IV.** Interim satis longō intervāllō,[1] cum esset cum M. Lūcullō in Siciliam profectus et cum ex eā prōvinciā cum eōdem Lūcullō dēcēderet, vēnit Hēraclēam. Quae cum esset cīvitās aequissimō iūre ac foedere,[2] ascrībī sē in eam cīvitātem voluit[1] idque, cum[3] ipse per sē dignus putārētur, tum[4] auctōritāte et grātiā Lūcullī ab Hērāclīēnsibus impetrāvit. **7.** Data est cīvitās[2] Silvānī lēge et Carbōnis: *Sī quī[5] foederātīs cīvitātibus ascrīptī fuissent, sī tum cum lēx ferēbātur in Ītaliā domicilium habuissent et sī sexāgintā diēbus apud praetōrem essent professī[6].*[3] Cum hic domicilium Rōmae multōs iam annōs habēret, professus est apud praetōrem Q. Metellum, familiārissimum suum. **8.** Sī nihil aliud nisi dē cīvitāte ac lēge dīcimus, nihil dīcō amplius; causa dicta est. Quid enim hōrum[4] īnfirmārī, Grattī[5], potest? Hēraclēaene esse tum ascrīptum negābis? Adest vir summā auctōritāte et religiōne[7] et fidē, M. Lūcullus; quī sē nōn opīnārī sed scīre, nōn audīvisse sed vīdisse, nōn interfuisse sed ēgisse[8] dīcit. Adsunt Hērāclīēnsēs lēgātī,

[1] *after a rather long interval*
[2] *with very favorable treaty rights* (with Rome)
[3] *although*
[4] *in addition*
[5] *whoever*
[6] *enroll*
[7] *scrupulous honesty*
[8] *acted (in the matter)*

---

[1] i.e., Archias
[2] i.e., Roman
[3] Supply *they would become citizens.*
[4] with **quid**; the three conditions mentioned in the law
[5] Grattius, of whom we know nothing, brought the charges against Archias.

nōbilissimī hominēs, huius iūdicī causā cum mandātīs et cum pūblicō testimōniō vēnerunt; quī hunc ascrīptum Hēraclēae esse dīcunt. Hīc tū tabulās dēsīderās Hēraclīēnsium pūblicās, quās Italicō bellō[6], incēnsō tabulāriō[9], interīsse scīmus omnēs? Est rīdiculum ad ea quae habēmus nihil dīcere, quaerere quae habēre nōn possumus, et dē hominum memoriā tacēre, litterārum memoriam[7] flāgitāre et, cum habeās amplissimī virī religiōnem, integerrimī[8] mūnicipī iūs iūrandum fidemque, ea quae dēprāvārī nūllō modō possunt repudiāre, tabulās quās īdem[10] dīcis solēre corrumpī[9] dēsīderāre. **9.** An[10] domicilium Rōmae nōn habuit is quī tot annīs[11] ante cīvitātem datam sēdem omnium rērum ac fortūnārum suārum Rōmae collocāvit? An nōn est professus? Immō vērō eīs tabulīs[11] professus quae sōlae ex illā professiōne collēgiōque praetōrum[12] obtinent pūblicārum tabulārum auctōritātem.

[9] *record office*
[10] *you yourself* [literally, *the same (you)*]
[11] *by means of the records*
[12] *of the registration books of the board of praetors*

## WORD STUDY

From what Latin words are the following derived: *amplification, corruption, desire, federation, incendiary, tabulation?*

What Latin words are related to the following: **ascrībō, corrumpō, domicilium, familiāris, intereō?**

[6] the Social War
[7] The *memory* of documents **(litterārum)** means that documents enable us to remember.
[8] Heraclea had a better reputation than some other towns.
[9] Grattius charges that the Roman registration records have been tampered with.
[10] This and the next sentence take up the second and third qualifications required by the law.
[11] thirteen years (102–89 B.C.)

# THE CENSUS RECORDS

**Verba Ūtilia:** ascrībō, asservō, dubitō, impertiō, irrēpō, litūra, neglegēns, scaenicus

**V.** Nam cum Appī tabulae neglegentius asservātae dīcerentur, Gabīnī[1], quam diū incolumis[1] fuit, levitās, post damnātiōnem calamitās[2] omnem tabulārum fidem resignāsset[3], Metellus, homō sānctissimus modestissimusque omnium, tantā dīligentiā fuit ut ad L. Lentulum praetōrem et ad iūdicēs vēnerit[2] et ūnīus nōminis litūrā sē commōtum esse dīxerit. Hīs igitur in

[1] *before conviction* (literally, *unharmed*)
[2] *misfortune*
[3] *destroyed* (literally, *unsealed*)

[1] with **levitās** and **calamitās;** the contrast between **Appī** and **Gabīnī** made unnecessary an **et** before the latter
[2] Metellus, in dealing with another case, said that there was only one erasure in the records, clearly then not that of Archias' name.

[4] *why is it that*

[5] *the people of Regium, Locri, Naples, Tarentum*

[6] *I suppose* (**Crēdō** is often used ironically.)

[7] *takes advantage of*

[8] *our* (Roman) *census records*

[9] *Of course* (pointing to the irony in **obscūrum**) *it is not known*

[10] *in the last censorship*

[11] *at that time quaestor* (in apposition with **eōdem**)

[12] *had conducted himself as a citizen at that time* (i.e., of the census)

[13] *both*

[14] *shared in*

[15] *rewards* (for special services)

tabulīs nūllam litūram in nōmine A. Licinī vidētis. **10.** Quae cum ita sint, quid est quod[4] dē eius cīvitāte dubitētis, praesertim cum aliīs quoque in cīvitātibus fuerit ascrīptus? Etenim cum mediocribus[3] multīs et aut nūllā aut humilī aliquā arte praeditīs grātuītō cīvitātem in Graeciā[4] hominēs impertiēbant, Rēgīnōs[5] crēdō[6] aut Locrēnsēs aut Neāpolitānōs aut Tarentīnōs, quod[5] scaenicīs[6] artificibus largīrī solēbant, id huic summā ingenī praeditō glōriā nōluisse! Quid? Cum cēterī nōn modo post cīvitātem datam sed etiam post lēgem Pāpiam[7] aliquō modō in eōrum mūnicipiōrum tabulās irrēpsērunt, hic, quī nē ūtitur[7] quidem illīs[8] in quibus est scrīptus, quod semper sē Hēraclīēnsem esse voluit, reiciētur? **11.** Cēnsūs nostrōs[8] requīris. Scīlicet, est enim obscūrum[9] proximīs cēnsōribus[10] hunc cum clārissimō imperātōre, L. Lūcullō, apud[9] exercitum fuisse, superiōribus cum eōdem quaestōre[11] fuisse in Asiā, prīmīs, Iūliō et Crassō, nūllam populī partem esse cēnsam. Sed quoniam cēnsus non iūs cīvitātis cōnfirmat ac tantum modo indicat eum quī sit cēnsus ita sē iam tum gessisse prō cīve eīs temporibus,[12] is quem tū[10] crīmināris nē ipsīus[11] quidem iūdiciō in cīvium Rōmānōrum iūre esse versātum, et[13] testāmentum saepe fēcit nostrīs lēgibus et adiit[14] hērēditātēs cīvium Rōmānōrum et in beneficiīs[15] ad aerārium dēlātus est ā L. Lūcullō prō cōnsule.

---

[3] dative, with **impertiēbant**

[4] He means **Magnā Graeciā,** a name for southern Italy.

[5] The antecedent is **id** below, referring to citizenship.

[6] At this time acting was not highly regarded by the Romans.

[7] This law called for the expulsion of all aliens, i.e., those who did not have legal residence. It was under this law that the charges were brought against Archias.

[8] Supply **tabulīs,** i.e., those of the Greek cities other than Heraclea that had granted him citizenship.

[9] He was *at* the army, not *in* it.

[10] Grattius, the plaintiff

[11] Grattius argues that Archias himself **(ipsīus)** did not consider himself a citizen because he did nothing to get himself listed.

# THE VALUE OF LITERATURE

**Verba Ūtilia:** cotīdiē, doctrīna, fōns, magnō opere, pudet, reprehendō, strepitus, tantō opere, tenebrae, vetustās

[1] *He will never be convicted either by his own judgment or that of his friends.*

[2] *(a place) where*

**VI.** Quaere argūmenta, sī quae potes; numquam enim hic neque suō neque amīcōrum iūdiciō revincētur.[1] **12.** Quaerēs ā nōbīs, Grattī, cūr tantō opere hōc homine dēlectēmur.[1] Quia suppeditat nōbīs ubi[2] et animus ex hōc

---

[1] Obviously Grattius will ask no such thing; Cicero is simply looking for an excuse to talk about the importance of literature.

Ronald Sheridan/Ancient Art & Architecture Collection

The Forum of Julius Caesar was erected in 48 B.C. It is located behind the Roman Forum and contained both temples and commercial interests. In the background is the monument to Victor Emmanuel II, begun in 1885 and inaugurated in 1911. It houses the Tomb of the Unknown Soldier and honors Italian war dead. The King was highly criticized for building such a Roman "imitation" so near the ancient monuments. Native Romans still call it the "Wedding Cake."

forēnsī strepitū reficiātur et aurēs convīciō dēfessae conquiēscant. An tū exīstimās aut suppetere nōbīs posse[3] quod cotīdiē dīcāmus in tantā varietāte rērum, nisi animōs nostrōs doctrīnā excolāmus, aut ferre animōs tantam posse contentiōnem, nisi eōs doctrīnā eādem relaxēmus? Ego vērō fateor mē hīs studiīs esse dēditum. Cēterōs pudeat,[4] sī quī ita sē litterīs[5] abdidērunt ut nihil possint ex eīs neque[6] ad commūnem afferre frūctum neque[6] in aspectum lūcemque prōferre;[7] mē autem quid pudeat[8] quī tot annōs ita vīvō, iūdicēs, ut ā nūllīus umquam mē tempore aut commodō[9] aut ōtium meum abstrāxerit aut voluptās āvocārit aut dēnique somnus retardārit? **13.** Quārē quis tandem mē reprehendat[10], aut quis mihi iūre suscēnseat, sī,[2] quantum cēterīs[3] ad suās rēs obeundās, quantum ad fēstōs diēs lūdōrum celebrandōs, quantum ad aliās voluptātēs et ad ipsam requiem animī et corporis concēditur temporum, quantum aliī[11] tribuunt tempestīvīs[12] convīviīs, quantum dēnique alveolō[13], quantum pilae, tantum mihi egomet ad haec studia recolenda sūmpserō? Atque hoc ideō mihi concēdendum est magis, quod ex hīs studiīs haec quoque crēscit ōrātiō et facultās[14], quae quantacumque est in mē, numquam amīcōrum perīculīs dēfuit. Quae[4] sī cui levior vidētur, illa[15] quidem certē quae summa sunt ex quō fonte hauriam sentiō. **14.** Nam nisi multōrum praeceptīs multīsque litterīs[16] mihi ab adulēscentiā suāsissem nihil esse in vītā magnō opere expetendum nisi laudem atque honestātem, in eā autem persequendā omnēs cruciātūs corporis, omnia perīcula mortis atque exilī parvī[17] esse dūcenda, numquam mē prō salūte vestrā in tot ac tantās dīmicātiōnēs atque in hōs prōflīgātōrum hominum cotīdiānōs impetūs obiēcissem. Sed plēnī omnēs sunt librī, plēnae sapientium vōcēs,[18] plēna exemplōrum vetustās; quae iacērent in tenebrīs omnia, nisi litterārum lūmen accēderet.[19] Quam multās nōbīs imāginēs nōn sōlum ad intuendum vērum etiam ad imitandum fortissimōrum virōrum expressās[20] scrīptōrēs et Graecī et Latīnī relīquērunt! Quās ego mihi semper in administrandā rē pūblicā prōpōnēns animum et mentem meam ipsā cōgitātiōne hominum excellentium cōnfōrmābam.

[3] *that what we talk about every day could be supplied to us*
[4] *let others be ashamed*
[5] *in literature* (ablative)
[6] *either ...or*
[7] *bringing nothing to the light (of day),* i.e., they publish nothing
[8] *why should I be ashamed*
[9] *from the critical need or advantage of any (client)*
[10] *can criticize*
[11] *some* (in contrast with **cēteris,** *all others)*
[12] *early*
[13] *gambling board*
[14] *ability in speaking*
[15] *the following (beliefs)*
[16] *much (reading of) literature*
[17] *are to be considered of little value* (not with **exsili**)
[18] *the sayings of philosophers*
[19] *if the light of literature did not shine upon them*
[20] *clear-cut portraits* (with **imāginēs**)

## WORD STUDY

Explain by derivation: *crescent, festivity, font, impudent, luminosity, reprehensible.*

Give Latin words related to **abdō, abstrahō, doctrīna, retardō, tempestīvus.**

---

[2] introduces the last word, **sūmpserō; quantum** is subject of **concēditur**
[3] dative with **concēditur**
[4] i.e., **facultās**

# NATURAL ABILITY AND TRAINING

**Verba Ūtilia:** adversus *(adj.)*, efferō, ērudiō, excellēns, eximius, gustō, prōdō, quispiam, secundus, senex

**VII, 15.** Quaeret quispiam: "Quid? Illī ipsī summī virī quōrum virtūtēs litterīs prōditae sunt, istāne doctrīnā quam tū effers laudibus ērudītī fuērunt?" Difficile est hoc dē omnibus cōnfirmāre, sed tamen est certum quid respondeam.[1] Ego multōs hominēs excellentī animō ac virtūte fuisse sine doctrīnā et nātūrae ipsīus habitū[2] prope dīvīnō per sē ipsōs et moderātōs et gravēs exstitisse[3] fateor; etiam illud adiungō, saepius ad laudem atque virtūtem nātūram sine doctrīnā quam sine nātūrā valuisse[4] doctrīnam. Atque īdem ego hoc contendō, cum ad nātūram eximiam et illūstrem accesserit ratiō quaedam cōnfōrmātiōque doctrīnae,[5] tum illud nesciō quid praeclārum ac singulāre[6] solēre exsistere. **16.** Ex hōc esse hunc numerō quem patrēs nostrī vīdērunt, dīvīnum hominem, Āfricānum$_1$, ex hōc C. Laelium, L. Fūrium, moderātissimōs hominēs et continentissimōs, ex hōc fortissimum virum et illīs temporibus doctissimum, M. Catōnem illum senem; quī profectō sī nihil ad percipiendam colendamque virtūtem litterīs adiuvārentur, numquam sē ad eārum studium contulissent. Quod sī[7] nōn hic tantus frūctus ostenderētur, et sī ex hīs studiīs dēlectātiō sōla peterētur, tamen, ut opīnor, hanc animī remissiōnem hūmānissimam ac līberālissimam iūdicārētis. Nam cēterae$_2$ neque temporum[8] sunt neque aetātum omnium neque locōrum; at haec studia adulēscentiam acuunt, senectūtem oblectant, secundās[9] rēs ōrnant, adversīs perfugium ac sōlācium praebent, dēlectant domī, nōn impediunt forīs, pernoctant nōbīscum, peregrīnantur, rūsticantur. **17.** Quodsī ipsī haec[10] neque attingere neque sēnsū nostrō gustāre possēmus, tamen ea mīrārī dēbērēmus, etiam cum in aliīs vidērēmus.

[1] *what I should say*
[2] *by the quality of their nature*
[3] *stood out as self-controlled and worthy men*
[4] *has succeeded in producing* (literally, *has had power (with regard) to* (with **ad**)
[5] *a kind of* (**quaedam**) *systematic training (resulting from) study*
[6] *something* ("I don't know what") *outstanding and unique*
[7] *But if*
[8] *are not (suitable) for*
[9] *prosperity*
[10] *can neither attain to nor enjoy with our senses these (studies)*

$_1$ Scipio the Younger (185–129 B.C.), who with Laelius and Furius encouraged the development of Greek culture in Rome. Cato (234–149 B.C.), on the other hand, opposed Greek culture and was more of a self-made man.

$_2$ i.e., **remissiōnēs**

# POETS ARE SACRED

**Verba Ūtilia:** admīror, conciliō, dīligō, immānis, īnflō, mōtus, saxum, sōlitūdō, venustās, versus

**VIII.** Quis nostrum tam animō agrestī ac dūrō fuit ut Rōscī morte nūper nōn commovērētur? Quī cum esset senex mortuus, tamen propter excellentem artem ac venustātem vidēbātur[1] omnīnō morī nōn dēbuisse. Ergō ille corporis mōtū tantum amōrem sibi conciliārat ā nōbīs omnibus; nōs animōrum incrēdibilēs mōtūs celeritātemque ingeniōrum[1] neglegēmus? **18.** Quotiēns ego hunc Archiam vīdī, iūdicēs (ūtar enim vestrā benignitāte,[2] quoniam mē in hōc novō genere dīcendī tam dīligenter attenditis), quotiēns ego hunc vīdī, cum litteram scrīpsisset nūllam,[3] magnum numerum optimōrum versuum dē eīs ipsīs rēbus quae tum agerentur, dīcere ex tempore, quotiēns, revocātum eandem rem dīcere, commūtātīs verbīs atque sententiīs! Quae vērō accūrātē cōgitātēque scrīpsisset, ea sīc vīdī probārī ut ad veterum scrīptōrum laudem pervenīret. Hunc ego nōn dīligam, nōn admīrer, nōn omnī ratiōne dēfendendum putem? Atque sīc ā summīs hominibus ērudītissimīsque accēpimus, cēterārum rērum studia ex doctrīnā et praeceptīs et arte cōnstāre[4], poētam nātūrā ipsā valēre et mentis vīribus excitārī et quasi dīvīnō quōdam spīritū inflārī. Quārē suō iūre noster ille Ennius[5] "sānctōs" appellat poētās, quod quasi deōrum aliquō dōnō atque mūnere commendātī nōbīs esse videantur. **19.** Sit igitur, iūdicēs, sānctum apud vōs, hūmānissimōs hominēs, hoc poētae nōmen, quod nūlla umquam barbaria violāvit. Saxa atque sōlitūdinēs vōcī respondent, bēstiae saepe immānēs cantū flectuntur atque cōnsistunt; nōs īnstitūtī rēbus optimīs nōn poētārum vōce moveāmur[6]? Homērum Colophōniī[7][2] cīvem esse dīcunt suum, Chiī suum vindicant, Salamīniī repetunt, Smyrnaeī vērō suum esse cōnfirmant itaque etiam dēlūbrum eius in oppidō dēdicāvērunt, permultī aliī praetereā pugnant inter sē atque contendunt.

[1] *activity of mind* (in contrast with **corporis**) and *inborn* (**ingeniōrum**) *alertness*

[2] *I avail myself of your indulgence, I beg your pardon.*

[3] *though he had not written down a single letter*

[4] *are based on*

[5] *that famous poet of ours*

[6] *should we not be moved*

[7] *the people of Colophon, Chios, Salamis, and Smyrna*

## WORD STUDY

Explain *extempore.*

Give English derivatives of **benignitās, bēstia, celeritās, conciliō.**

Name Latin words related to **admīror, cōgitātē, incrēdibilis, mōtus, sōlitūdō.**

---

[1] The subject is **quī,** but in translating it is better to make the verb impersonal: *who, it seemed.*

[2] three other places claimed him: Argos, Athens, and Rhodes

# NO FAME WITHOUT POETS

**Verba Ūtilia:** aeternus, aiō, attendō, dīmicō, faucēs, impetus, monumentum, ōlim, triumphus, vīvus

**IX.** Ergō illī aliēnum$_{1}$, quia poēta fuit, post mortem etiam expetunt; nōs hunc vīvum, quī et voluntāte et lēgibus noster est, repudiābimus, praesertim cum omne ōlim studium atque omne ingenium contulerit Archiās ad populī Rōmānī glōriam laudemque celebrandam? Nam et Cimbricās rēs$_{2}$ adulēscēns attigit et ipsī illī C. Mariō, quī dūrior[1] ad haec studia vidēbātur, iūcundus fuit. **20.** Neque enim quisquam est tam āversus ā Mūsīs[2] quī nōn mandārī versibus aeternum suōrum labōrum praecōnium facile patiātur. Themistoclem illum,[3] summum Athēnīs virum, dīxisse aiunt, cum ex eō quaererētur quod acroāma[4]$_{3}$ aut cuius vōcem libentissimē audīret: eius ā quō sua$_{4}$ virtūs optimē praedicārētur. Itaque ille Marius item eximiē L. Plōtium dīlēxit, cuius ingeniō putābat ea quae gesserat posse celebrārī. **21.** Mithridāticum vērō bellum, magnum atque difficile et in multā varietāte[5] terrā marīque versātum, tōtum ab hōc$_{5}$ expressum est; quī librī nōn modo L. Lūcullum, fortissimum et clārissimum virum, vērum etiam populī Rōmānī nōmen illūstrant. Populus enim Rōmānus aperuit, Lūcullō imperante, Pontum et rēgiīs quondam opibus et ipsā nātūrā et regiōne[6] vāllātum; populī Rōmānī exercitus, eōdem duce, nōn maximā manū innumerābilīs Armeniōrum cōpiās fūdit; populī Rōmānī laus est urbem amīcissimam Cȳzicēnōrum[7] eiusdem cōnsiliō ex omnī impetū rēgiō atque tōtīus bellī ōre ac faucibus ēreptam esse atque servātam; nostra$_{6}$ semper ferētur[8] et praedicābitur, L. Lūcullō dīmicante, cum, interfectīs ducibus, dēpressa hostium classis est, incrēdibilis apud Tenedum pugna illa nāvālis; nostra sunt tropaea, nostra monumenta, nostrī triumphī. Quae[9] quōrum ingeniīs efferuntur, ab eīs populī Rōmānī fāma celebrātur. **22.** Cārus fuit Āfricānō superiōrī$_{7}$ noster Ennius, itaque etiam in sepulcrō Scīpiōnum putātur is esse cōnstitūtus ex marmore$_{8}$; at eīs laudibus$_{9}$ certē nōn sōlum ipse quī laudātur sed etiam populī Rōmānī nōmen ōrnātur. In caelum huius$_{10}$ proavus Catō tollitur; magnus honōs populī Rōmānī rēbus adiungitur. Omnēs dēnique illī[10] Maximī, Mārcellī, Fulviī nōn sine commūnī omnium nostrum laude decorantur.

[1] *rather rough for*
[2] *so unfriendly to literature*
[3] *the famous Themistocles*
[4] *entertainment*
[5] *with many changes of fortune*
[6] *by the nature of the region*
[7] *the people of Cyzicus*
[8] *will be spoken of*
[9] *the fame of the Roman people is made known by those by whose talents these deeds* **(quae)** *are praised*
[10] *famous men such as Maximus, etc.*

---

$_{1}$ He would be a foreigner to at least six of the seven cities that claimed him.
$_{2}$ Marius' defeat of the Cimbri in 101 B.C.
$_{3}$ Greek neuter accusative singular, modified by the interrogative adjective **quod**
$_{4}$ i.e., of Themistocles
$_{5}$ Archias
$_{6}$ predicate adjective in agreement with **pugna:** *as ours*
$_{7}$ Scipio the Elder
$_{8}$ i.e., a bust of marble
$_{9}$ The praise was in the *Annales,* a poem by Ennius, of which only fragments have survived.
$_{10}$ *the present* Cato, often called Uticensis because he committed suicide at Utica, Africa. His great-grandfather was known as the Censor.

## WORD STUDY

Give English derivatives of **aeternus, attendō, celebrō, impetus, praedicō.**

What Latin words are related to the following: **ēripiō, libenter, impetus, nāvālis, vīvus?**

# POETS GIVE IMMORTALITY

**Verba Ūtilia:** expetō, fīnis, propterea, quārē, regiō, rūsticus, sānē, sonō, tumulus, vēndō

**X.** Ergō illum quī haec fēcerat,[1] Rudīnum[2] hominem, maiōrēs nostrī in cīvitātem recēpērunt; nōs hunc Hēraclīēnsem multīs cīvitātibus expetītum, in hāc$_1$ autem lēgibus cōnstitūtum dē nostrā cīvitāte ēiciēmus? **23.** Nam sī quis minōrem glōriae frūctum putat ex Graecīs versibus percipī quam ex Latīnīs, vehementer errat, propterea quod Graeca$_2$ leguntur in omnibus ferē gentibus, Latīna suīs fīnibus exiguīs sānē continentur. Quārē sī rēs eae quās gessimus orbis terrae regiōnibus dēfīniuntur, cupere dēbēmus quo[3] manuum nostrārum tēla pervēnerint, eōdem[3] glōriam fāmamque penetrāre, quod cum[4] ipsīs populīs dē quōrum rēbus scrībitur haec ampla sunt,[5] tum[4] eīs certē quī dē vītā[6] glōriae causā dīmicant, hoc maximum et perīculōrum incitāmentum est et labōrum. **24.** Quam multōs scrīptōrēs rērum suārum magnus ille Alexander sēcum habuisse dīcitur! Atque is tamen, cum in Sīgēō$_3$ ad Achillis tumulum astitisset: "Ō fortūnāte," inquit, "adulēscēns, quī[7] tuae virtūtis Homērum praecōnem invēnerīs!" Et vērē. Nam nisi Īlias illa exstitisset, īdem tumulus quī corpus eius contēxerat nōmen etiam obruisset. Quid? Noster hic Magnus[8] quī cum virtūte fortūnam adaequāvit, nōnne Theophanem Mytilēnaeum,[9] scrīptōrem rērum suārum, in cōntiōne mīlitum cīvitāte dōnāvit, et nostrī illī fortēs virī, sed[10] rūsticī ac mīlitēs, dulcēdine quādam glōriae commōtī quasi participēs eiusdem laudis magnō illud clāmōre approbāvērunt? **25.** Itaque, crēdō$_4$, sī cīvis Rōmānus Archiās lēgibus nōn esset, ut$_5$ ab aliquō imperātōre cīvitāte dōnārētur perficere nōn

[1] *who composed these (poems)*
[2] *of Rudiae*
[3] *to the same place ...where*
[4] *not only ...but also*
[5] *these poems were full of honor for the nations themselves*
[6] *for life*
[7] *since you*
[8] *Our (Pompey) the Great*
[9] *Theoph'anēs of Mytilē'ne*
[10] *though*

$_1$ i.e., Heraclea
$_2$ used as a neuter plural noun: *Greek*
$_3$ *Sigeum* (Sījē´um), a promontory near Troy
$_4$ ironical
$_5$ The clause is object of **perficere.**

potuit. Sulla cum Hispānōs et Gallōs dōnāret[6], crēdō, hunc petentem repudiāsset; quem[7] nōs in cōntiōne vīdimus, cum eī libellum malus poēta dē populō[11] subiēcisset[12],[8] quod epigramma[9] in eum fēcisset, tantum modo alternīs versibus longiusculīs,[13] statim ex eīs rēbus quās tum vēndēbat iubēre eī praemium tribuī, sed eā condiciōne, nē quid posteā scrīberet. Quī[14] sēdulitātem malī poētae dūxerit aliquō tamen praemiō dignam, huius ingenium et virtūtem in scrībendō et cōpiam nōn expetīsset? **26.** Quid? Ā Q. Metellō Piō, familiārissimō suō, quī cīvitāte multōs dōnāvit, neque per sē neque per Lūcullōs impetrāvisset? Quī praesertim usque eō[15] dē suīs rēbus scrībī cuperet ut etiam Cordubae[16] nātīs poētīs pingue quiddam sonantibus[17] atque peregrīnum tamen aurēs suās dēderet.

[11] *from among the common people*
[12] *had thrust up*
[13] *every other line being a little bit longer*
[14] *since he* (i.e., Sulla)
[15] *to such an extent*
[16] *Cordova*
[17] *having a sort of dull, foreign sound*

[6] Supply **cīvitāte.**
[7] Sulla
[8] to Sulla, who was sitting on a platform in the Forum while presiding at an auction sale of confiscated property
[9] Greek neuter accusative: *an epigram which;* in apposition with **libellum**

# THE STATESMAN'S REWARD IS IMMORTAL FAME

**Verba Ūtilia:** aditus, attingō, bellō, dēspiciō, inchōo, libellus, merx, praeter, stimulus, totiēns

**XI.** Neque est hoc dissimulandum, quod obscūrārī nōn potest sed prae nōbīs ferendum:[1] trahimur omnēs studiō laudis, et optimus quisque[2] maximē glōriā dūcitur. Ipsī illī philosophī etiam in eīs libellīs quōs dē contemnendā glōriā scrībunt nōmen suum īnscrībunt; in eō ipsō[3] in quō praedicātiōnem nōbilitātemque dēspiciunt praedicārī dē sē ac nōminārī[1] volunt.

**27.** Decimus quidem Brūtus, summus vir et imperātor, Accī, amīcissimī suī, carminibus templōrum ac monumentōrum aditūs exōrnāvit suōrum. Iam vērō ille quī cum Aetōlīs, Enniō comite, bellāvit Fulvius nōn dubitāvit Martis manubiās[4] Mūsīs cōnsecrāre. Quārē in quā urbe imperātōrēs prope armātī[5] poētārum nōmen et Mūsārum dēlūbra coluērunt, in eā nōn dēbent togātī iūdicēs ā Mūsārum honōre et ā poētārum salūte abhorrēre.

[1] *must be frankly admitted* (literally, *must be carried in front of us)*
[2] *all the best men*
[3] *in the very action*
[4] *spoils of war* (**Martis**)
[5] *almost (still) in uniform* (i.e., just after returning from war)

[1] impersonal; we would make **sē** the subject of the infinitives.

**28.** Atque ut id[2] libentius faciātis, iam mē vōbīs, iūdicēs, indicābō, et dē meō quōdam amōre glōriae, nimis ācrī fortasse, vērum tamen honestō, vōbīs cōnfitēbor. Nam quās rēs nōs[3] in cōnsulātū nostrō vōbīscum simul prō salūte huius urbis atque imperī et prō vītā cīvium prōque ūniversā rē pūblicā gessimus, attigit hic[4] versibus atque inchoāvit.[5] Quibus audītīs, quod mihi magna rēs et iūcunda vīsa est, hunc ad perficiendum adōrnāvī[6]. Nūllam enim virtūs aliam mercēdem labōrum perīculōrumque dēsīderat praeter hanc laudis et glōriae; quā quidem dētrāctā, iūdicēs, quid est quod[7] in hōc tam exiguō vītae curriculō et tam brevī tantīs nōs[6] in labōribus exerceāmus? **29.** Certē, sī nihil animus praesentīret[7] in posterum, et sī quibus regiōnibus[8] vītae spatium circumscrīptum est, eīsdem omnēs cōgitātiōnēs termināret suās, nec tantīs sē labōribus frangeret neque tot cūrīs vigiliīsque angerētur nec totiēns dē ipsā vītā dīmicāret. Nunc[9] īnsidet quaedam in optimō quōque virtūs[10], quae noctēs ac diēs animum glōriae stimulīs concitat atque admonet, nōn cum[8] vītae tempore esse dīmittendam commemorātiōnem nōminis nostrī sed cum omnī posteritāte adaequandam.

[6] *I furnished him (with the facts)*
[7] *for which*
[8] *boundaries*
[9] *as it is* (i.e., according to, not contrary to, fact)
[10] *good quality*

---

[2] i.e., see to the welfare of poets
[3] plural of modesty, for **ego**
[4] Archias
[5] The relative clause is the object.
[6] object of verb
[7] **animus** is subject of all the verbs
[8] preposition

# BE KIND TO THE POET

**Verba Ūtilia:** auctōritās, cōgitātiō, effigiēs, exprimō, orbis terrae, poliō, simpliciter, spatium, statua, tranquillus

**XII, 30.** An vērō tam parvī animī[1] videāmur[2] esse omnēs quī in rē pūblicā atque in hīs vītae perīculīs labōribusque versāmur ut, cum usque ad extrēmum spatium[1] nūllum tranquillum atque ōtiōsum spīritum dūxerīmus, nōbīscum simul moritūra omnia arbitrēmur? An[2] statuās et imāginēs, nōn animōrum simulācra sed corporum, studiōsē multī summī hominēs relīquērunt;

[1] *of such limited outlook* (literally, *so smallminded*)
[2] *are we to seem?*

---

[1] Supply **vītae.**
[2] introduces a question, but best translated by *if* or *when*

cōnsiliōrum relinquere ac virtūtum nostrārum effigiem nōnne multō mālle dēbēmus summīs ingeniīs[3] expressam et polītam? Ego vērō omnia quae gerēbam iam tum in gerendō[4] spargere$_3$ mē ac dissēmināre arbitrābar in orbis terrae memoriam sempiternam. Haec$_4$ vērō sīve ā meō sēnsū post mortem āfutūra est sīve, ut sapientissimī hominēs putāvērunt, ad aliquam animī meī partem pertinēbit[5], nunc quidem certē cōgitātiōne quādam spēque dēlector.

**31.** Quārē cōnservāte, iūdicēs, hominem pudōre eō quem amīcōrum[6] vidētis comprobārī cum dignitāte, tum etiam vetustāte, ingeniō[7] autem tantō quantum id convenit exīstimārī, quod summōrum hominum ingeniīs expetītum esse videātis, causā[8] vērō eius modī quae beneficiō lēgis$_5$, auctōritāte mūnicipī, testimōniō Lūcullī, tabulīs Metellī comprobētur. Quae cum ita sint, petimus ā vōbīs, iūdicēs, sī qua nōn modo hūmāna vērum etiam dīvīna in tantīs ingeniīs commendātiō dēbet esse, ut eum$_6$ quī vōs, quī vestrōs imperātōrēs, quī populī Rōmānī rēs gestās semper ōrnāvit, quī etiam hīs recentibus nostrīs vestrīsque domesticīs perīculīs$_7$ aeternum sē testimōnium laudis datūrum esse profitētur estque ex eō numerō quī semper apud omnēs sānctī sunt habitī itaque[9] dictī, sīc in vestram accipiātis fidem ut hūmānitāte vestrā levātus potius quam acerbitāte violātus esse videātur.

Quae dē causā prō meā cōnsuētūdine breviter simpliciterque dīxī, iūdicēs, ea cōnfīdō probāta esse omnibus: quae ā forēnsī aliēna iūdiciālīque cōnsuētūdine et dē hominis ingeniō et commūniter dē ipsō studiō locūtus sum, ea, iūdicēs, ā vōbīs spērō esse in bonam partem accepta; ab eō quī iūdicium exercet certō sciō.

[3] *by the greatest geniuses,* or *by (men of) the greatest genius*

[4] *even in doing (them)*

[5] *shall belong to,* i.e., *shall be known to*

[6] *proved not only by the high position of but also by the long acquaintance with his friends* (with **dignitāte** and **vetustāte**)

[7] *a man of so much genius as it is fitting to be judged (to be) such as you see has been sought out by men of the greatest genius*

[8] *(a man) with a case*

[9] = **et ita**

## WORD STUDY

What Latin words are related to **dissēminō, domesticus, forēnsis, mūnicipium, ōtiōsus, profiteor?**

In this reading, find five words with the suffix **–tās** and two with the suffix **–tiō.**

---

$_3$ The next infinitive explains the metaphor.

$_4$ i.e., **memoria**

$_5$ the law of 89 B.C.

$_6$ object of **accipiātis,** which is an indirect command (without **ut**), object of **petimus**

$_7$ the conspiracy of Catiline, about which Archias had promised to write

UNIT
VI

# CICERO AGAINST VERRES AND ANTONY

## Unit Objectives

- To read Cicero's speeches against Verres and Antony with understanding and appreciation
- To learn the meaning of new vocabulary in context
- To recognize Latin root words and their English derivatives

**In Segesta, Sicily, are the remains of a Roman theater. Located in northwest Sicily, ancient Segesta was traditionally a Trojan colony. It became a Carthaginian dependency sometime after 400 B.C. but thrived under later Roman domination. This exceptionally well-preserved theater is well-known for its excellent acoustics. It dates from the third century B.C. and was built on the summit of a hill. From this view, you can see the semicircular auditorium (cavea) around the smaller semicircular orchestra in front of the stage, typical of many Roman theaters.**

# VERRES AND ANTONY

Cicero's first great success as an orator was achieved with his speeches against Verres; his last success with the speeches against Antony.

In 75 B.C., Cicero was elected quaestor and served in Sicily. His fair treatment of the Sicilians won their respect and friendship, and they asked him to serve as their attorney in the prosecution of their former praetor, Verres, whose plundering of Sicilian towns seems to have broken all records. At the trial of Verres, Cicero made such a devastating attack that Verres went into voluntary exile, thus admitting his guilt. But Cicero had still more evidence against Verres, which he wrote up in five other speeches that were published but not delivered. These speeches against Verres established Cicero's fame, and he became the chief lawyer and orator in Rome.

Toward the end of his life, Cicero had outlived his great triumphs—his consulship and his defeat of Catiline. The murder of Caesar in 44 B.C. temporarily raised Cicero's hopes for a return to the senatorial form of government, but these hopes were dashed by the activities of Antony. Cicero attacked Antony in fourteen speeches, written in 44–43 B.C. These speeches were named *Philippics* because they recalled Demosthenes' well-known speeches against King Philip of Macedon. The most famous *Philippic* (Juvenal called it "divine"), the second, was not delivered but was circulated as a political document. Cicero's reward for these speeches was death—at the hands of agents of Antony.

# The Second Action Against Verres

## THE IMPORTANCE OF SICILY

**Verba Ūtilia:** antequam, benevolentia, classis, externus, laetor, parcō, ratiō, semel, subsidium, ūtilitās

**II, 2.** Atque antequam dē incommodīs Siciliae dīcō, pauca mihi videntur esse dē prōvinciae dignitāte, vetustāte, ūtilitāte dīcenda. Nam cum omnium sociōrum prōvinciārumque ratiōnem dīligenter habēre dēbētis, tum praecipuē Siciliae, iūdicēs, plūrimīs iūstissimīsque dē causīs, prīmum quod omnium nātiōnum exterārum prīnceps Sicilia sē ad amīcitiam fidemque populī Rōmānī applicāvit. Prīma omnium, id quod[1] ōrnāmentum imperī est, prōvincia est appellāta; prīma docuit maiōrēs nostrōs quam praeclārum esset exterīs gentibus imperāre; sōla fuit eā fidē benevolentiāque ergā populum Rōmānum ut cīvitātēs eius īnsulae, quae semel[2] in amīcitiam nostram vēnissent, numquam posteā dēficerent, plēraeque autem et maximē illūstrēs in amīcitiā perpetuō manērent. **3.** Itaque maiōribus nostrīs in Āfricam ex hāc prōvinciā gradus[3] imperī factus est; neque enim tam facile opēs Carthāginis tantae concidissent nisi illud et reī frūmentāriae subsidium et receptāculum classibus nostrīs patēret. Quārē P. Āfricānus, Carthāgine dēlētā,[1] Siculōrum urbīs signīs monumentīsque pulcherrimīs exōrnāvit, ut, quōs[2] victōriā populī Rōmānī maximē laetārī arbitrābātur, apud eōs monumenta victōriae plūrima collocāret. **4.** Dēnique ille ipse M. Mārcellus, cuius in Siciliā virtūtem hostēs, misericordiam victī, fidem cēterī Siculī perspexērunt, nōn sōlum sociīs in eō bellō cōnsuluit[4], vērum etiam superātīs hostibus temperāvit[5]. Urbem pulcherrimam Syrācūsās (quae cum manū[6] mūnītissima esset, tum locī nātūrā terrā ac marī clauderētur), cum vī cōnsiliōque cēpisset, nōn sōlum incolumem passus est esse, sed ita relīquit ōrnātam ut esset idem[7] monumentum victōriae, mānsuētūdinis, continentiae, cum hominēs vidērent et quid expugnāsset et quibus pepercisset et quae relīquisset: tantum ille honōrem habendum Siciliae putāvit ut nē hostium quidem urbem ex sociōrum īnsulā tollendam[8] arbitrārētur. **5.** Itaque ad omnīs rēs sīc illā prōvinciā semper ūsī sumus ut, quicquid ex sēsē posset efferre, id nōn apud nōs nāscī, sed domī nostrae conditum iam putārēmus.[9] Quandō illa frūmentum quod dēbēret nōn ad diem[10] dedit? Quandō id quod opus esse putāret nōn ultrō pollicita est? Quandō id quod imperārētur recūsāvit? Itaque ille M. Catō Sapiēns[3] cellam penāriam[11] reī pūblicae nostrae, nūtrīcem plēbis Rōmānae Siciliam nōminābat.

[1] *a thing which*
[2] *once they had* (literally, *which once*)
[3] *the step to empire*
[4] *looked out for* (with dative)
[5] *spared* (with dative)
[6] *by the hand (of man)*
[7] *at the same time* (literally, *the same memorial*)
[8] *destroyed* (literally, *removed*)
[9] *whatever she was able to produce from her own (soil) we have come to consider as not grown at home but stored there*
[10] *on the day (due)*
[11] *storehouse*

---

[1] 146 B.C.
[2] The antecedent is **eōs,** the Sicilians.
[3] Cato the Elder

# VERRES' "INTEREST" IN ART

**IV, 1.** Veniō nunc ad istīus$_1$, quem ad modum ipse appellat, studium[1], ut amīcī eius, morbum et īnsāniam, ut Siculī, latrōcinium; ego quō nōmine appellem nesciō; rem vōbīs prōpōnam, vōs eam suō, nōn nōminis, pondere penditōte.[2] Genus ipsum prius cognōscite, iūdicēs; deinde fortasse nōn magnō opere quaerētis quō id nōmine appellandum putētis. Negō in Siciliā tōtā, tam locuplētī, tam vetere prōvinciā, tot oppidīs,[3] tot familiīs tam cōpiōsīs, ūllum argenteum vās, ūllum Corinthium aut Dēliacum$_2$ fuisse, ūllam gemmam aut margarītam[4], quicquam ex aurō aut ebore factum, signum ūllum aēneum, marmoreum, eburneum, negō ūllam pictūram neque in tabulā neque in textilī[5] quīn[6] conquīsierit, īnspexerit, quod placitum sit abstulerit. **2.** Magnum videor dīcere: attendite etiam quem ad modum dīcam. Nōn enim verbī neque crīminis augendī causā complector omnia: cum dīcō nihil istum eius modī rērum in tōtā prōvinciā relīquisse, Latīnē[7] mē scītōte, nōn accūsātōriē loquī. Etiam plānius: nihil in aedibus cuiusquam, nē in hospitis$_3$ quidem, nihil in locīs commūnibus, nē in fānīs quidem, nihil apud Siculum, nihil apud cīvem Rōmānum, dēnique nihil istum, quod ad oculōs animumque acciderit, neque prīvātī neque pūblicī neque profānī neque sacrī tōtā in Siciliā relīquisse.

**3.** Unde igitur potius incipiam quam ab eā cīvitāte quae tibi ūna in amōre atque in dēliciīs fuit, aut ex quō potius numerō quam ex ipsīs laudātōribus tuīs? Facilius enim perspiciētur quālis apud eōs fuerīs quī tē ōdērunt, quī accūsant, quī persequuntur, cum apud tuōs Māmertīnōs[8] inveniāre improbissimā ratiōne esse praedātus.[9]

[1] *interest*
[2] *judge the matter by its own importance, not that of a name*
[3] *with so many towns*
[4] *pearl*
[5] *woven (cloth)*
[6] *that he did not*
[7] i.e., *the straight truth* (in the old Roman fashion)
[8] *Your (pets) the people of Messina*
[9] *to have plundered in a most wicked manner*

---

$_1$ Verres
$_2$ *Corinthian* was an alloy similar to bronze, the secret of whose manufacture had been lost, hence its value; *Delian* ware was also famous.
$_3$ Supply **aedibus.**

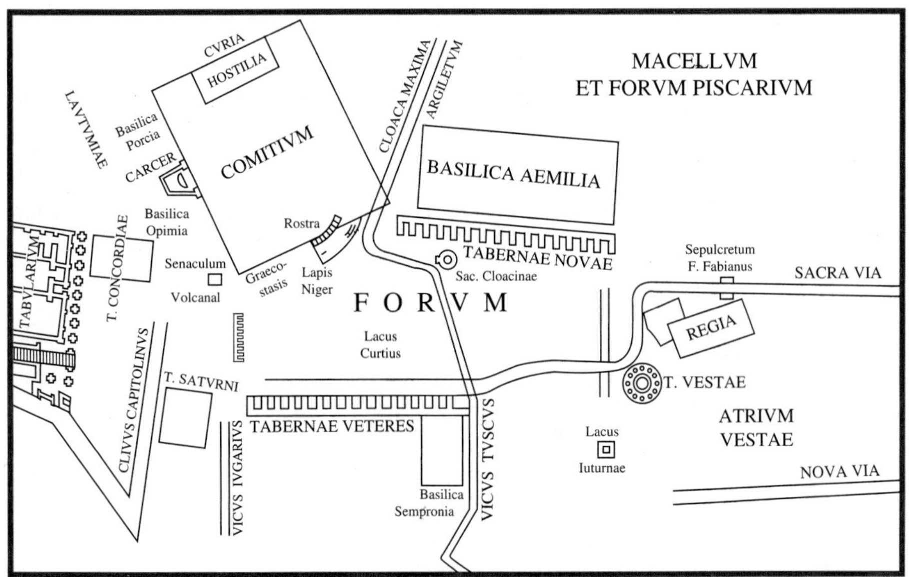


The Forum during the Republic was much simpler than during the Empire, when overcrowding became a problem. The **Tabulārium** is on the far left and from there, you would be looking toward the Palatine Hill and over the Forum itself. The **tabernae** were shops selling everything from food to cloth to lamps. Obviously, the **tabernae novae** were built after the **tabernae veterēs.**

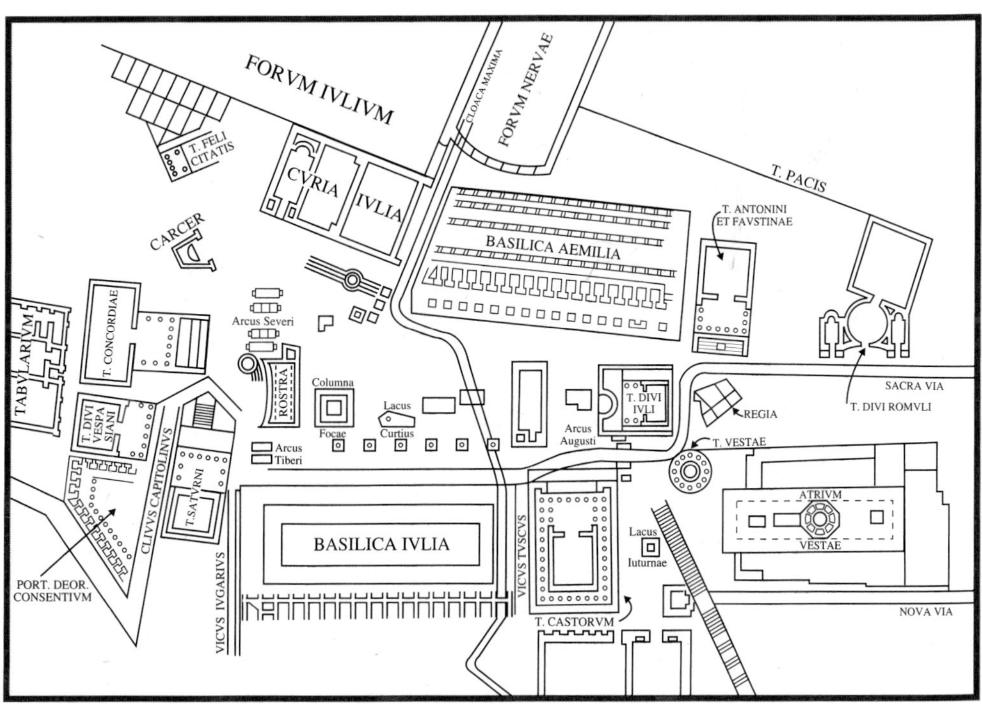


By the time of the Empire, the **tabernae veterēs** had been taken down and replaced with the Basilica Julia. The **Rōstra,** or speaker's stand, was also moved to a more central location, near the Temple of Saturn, to give the speaker a more commanding position. The **Rēgia,** near the Vestal Temple, was the house of Numa, the second king of Rome, according to tradition. The **Lapis Niger,** near the **Comitium,** is supposed to mark the place where Romulus was buried.

[1] *people run* (impersonal)
[2] *plunderer of sacred places*
[3] *that not, to keep them from*

tempore ad fānum ex urbe tōtā concurritur.[1] Ac repente Agrigentīnī concurrunt; fit magna lapidātiō; dant sēsē in fugam istīus praeclārī imperātōris nocturnī mīlitēs. Duo tamen sigilla perparvula tollunt, nē omnīnō inānēs ad istum praedōnem religiōnum[2] revertantur. Numquam tam male est Siculīs quīn[3] aliquid facētē et commodē dīcant, velut in hāc rē aiēbant in labōrēs Herculis nōn minus hunc immānissimum verrem$_{3}$ quam illum aprum Erymanthium$_{4}$ referrī oportēre.

$_{3}$ a pun on Verres' name: **verrēs** means *boar*
$_{4}$ The killing of the Erymanthian boar was one of the twelve labors of Hercules.

# CERES AND PROSERPINA

**Verba Ūtilia:** altitūdō, celeber, currus, laetus, lūcus, opīniō, perennis, subitō, vertex, vēstīgium

[1] *grain crops*
[2] *the forest of Henna*
[3] *navel*
[4] *torches*
[5] *carrying which before her* (literally, *when she carried which before her*)
[6] *steep and straight down*
[7] *so that the location itself*
[8] *carrying off* (noun)
[9] *Pluto*

**IV, 106.** Vetus est haec opīniō, iūdicēs, quae cōnstat ex antīquissimīs Graecōrum litterīs ac monumentīs, īnsulam Siciliam tōtam esse Cererī et Līberae cōnsecrātam. Nam et nātās esse hās in iīs locīs deās et frūgēs[1] in eā terrā prīmum repertās esse arbitrantur, et raptam esse Līberam, quam eandem Prōserpinam vocant, ex Hennēnsium nemore,[2] quī locus, quod in mediā est īnsulā situs, umbilīcus[3] Siciliae nōminātur. Quam$_{1}$ cum invēstīgāre et conquīrere Cerēs vellet, dīcitur īnflammāsse taedās[4] iīs ignibus quī ex Aetnae vertice ērumpunt; quās sibi cum ipsa praeferret,[5] orbem omnem peragrāsse terrārum. **107.** Henna autem, ubi ea quae dīcō gesta esse memorantur, est locō perexcelsō atque ēditō, quō in summō est aequāta agrī plānitiēs et aquae perennēs, tōta vērō ab omnī aditū circumcīsa atque dīrēcta est;[6] quam circā lacūs lūcīque sunt plūrimī atque laetissimī flōrēs omnī tempore annī, locus ut ipse[7] raptum[8] illum virginis quem iam ā puerīs accēpimus dēclārāre videātur. Etenim prope est spēlunca quaedam conversa ad aquilōnem īnfīnītā altitūdine, quā Dītem[9] patrem ferunt repente cum currū exstitisse abreptamque ex eō locō virginem sēcum asportāsse et subitō nōn longē ā Syrācūsīs penetrāsse sub terrās, lacumque in eō locō repente exstitisse, ubi usque ad hoc tempus Syrācūsānī fēstōs diēs anniversāriōs agunt celeberrimō virōrum mulierumque conventū. Propter huius opīniōnis vetustātem, quod hōrum$_{2}$ in hīs locīs vēstīgia ac prope

$_{1}$ Proserpina
$_{2}$ with **deōrum**

incūnābula reperiuntur deōrum, mīra quaedam tōtā Siciliā prīvātim ac pūblicē religiō est Cereris Hennēnsis. **109.** Hoc dīcō, hanc ipsam Cererem antīquissimam, religiōsissimam, prīncipem omnium sacrōrum quae apud omnīs gentīs nātiōnēsque fīunt, ā C. Verre ex suīs templīs ac sēdibus esse sublātam. **111.** Hic dolor erat tantus ut Verrēs alter Orcus vēnisse Hennam et nōn Prōserpinam asportāsse sed ipsam abripuisse Cererem vidērētur. Etenim urbs illa nōn urbs vidētur, sed fānum Cereris esse; habitāre apud sēsē Cererem Hennēnsēs arbitrantur, ut mihi nōn cīvēs illīus cīvitātis, sed omnēs sacerdōtēs, omnēs accolae atque antistiēs Cereris esse videantur. **112.** Hennā[10] tū simulācrum Cereris tollere audēbās, Hennā tū dē manū Cereris Victōriam ēripere et deam deae[11] dētrahere cōnātus es?

[10] *from Henna*
[11] *the goddess* (Victory) *from the goddess* (Ceres)

## WORD STUDY

The ancient grammarians felt that there must be a relationship between **lūcus** and **lūx**—but how did a grove of trees have anything to do with light? They decided that the relationship was by opposites: **lūcus ā nōn lūcendō,** *a grove of trees (is so called) from not giving light.* The idea was so far-fetched that the phrase has become the name of a type of absurd reasoning.

Give the Latin word from which the following are derived: *celebrated, excelsior, perennial, rapacious, vestige.*

# A ROMAN CITIZEN IS CRUCIFIED

**Verba Ūtilia:** anteā, assequor, barbarus, gemitus, ignōtus, impūnē, plēbs, supplicium, ūsūrpō, verber

**V, 162.** Caedēbātur virgīs[1] in mediō forō Messānae cīvis Rōmānus, iūdicēs, cum intereā nūllus gemitus, nūlla vōx alia illīus miserī inter dolōrem crepitumque plāgārum audiēbātur nisi haec, "Cīvis Rōmānus sum!" Hāc sē commemorātiōne cīvitātis omnia verbera dēpulsūrum, cruciātumque ā corpore dēiectūrum arbitrābātur. Is nōn modo hoc nōn perfēcit, ut virgārum vim dēprecārētur; sed cum implōrāret saepius ūsūrpāretque nōmen cīvitātis, crux—crux, inquam—īnfēlīcī[2] et aerumnōsō, quī numquam istam pestem[1] vīderat, comparābātur.

[1] *was beaten with rods*
[2] *for the unfortunate fellow* (with **comparābātur**)

[1] i.e., the cross—or does he mean Verres?

**163.** Ō nōmen dulce lībertātis! Ō iūs eximium nostrae cīvitātis! Ō lēx Porcia, lēgēsque Semprōniae! Ō graviter dēsīderāta, et aliquandō reddita[2] plēbī Rōmānae tribūnicia potestās! Hūcine[3] tandem haec omnia recidērunt, ut cīvis Rōmānus in prōvinciā populī Rōmānī, in oppidō foederātōrum, ab eō quī beneficiō populī Rōmānī fascīs et secūrīs habēret dēligātus in forō virgīs caederētur? Quid? Cum ignēs ārdentēsque lāminae[3] cēterīque cruciātūs admovēbantur, sī tē[4] illīus acerba implōrātiō et vōx miserābilis nōn inhibēbat, nē cīvium quidem Rōmānōrum quī tum aderant flētū et gemitū maximō commovēbāre? In crucem tū agere ausus es quemquam quī sē cīvem Rōmānum esse dīceret?

**166.** Sī tū apud Persās aut in extrēmā Indiā dēprehēnsus, Verrēs, ad supplicium dūcerēre, quid aliud clāmitārēs nisi tē cīvem esse Rōmānum? Et sī tibi ignōtō apud ignōtōs, apud barbarōs, apud hominēs in extrēmīs atque ultimīs gentibus positōs, nōbile et illūstre apud omnīs nōmen cīvitātis tuae prōfuisset, ille[5], quisquis erat, quem tū in crucem rapiēbās, quī tibi esset ignōtus, cum cīvem sē Rōmānum esse dīceret, apud tē praetōrem, sī nōn effugium, nē moram[4] quidem mortis mentiōne atque ūsūrpātiōne cīvitātis assequī potuit?

**167.** Hominēs tenuēs, obscūrō locō[5] nātī, nāvigant, adeunt ad ea loca quae numquam anteā vīdērunt, ubi neque nōtī esse eīs quō vēnērunt, neque semper cum cognitōribus[6] esse possunt. Hāc ūnā tamen fīdūciā cīvitātis nōn modo apud nostrōs magistrātūs, quī et lēgum et exīstimātiōnis[7] perīculō continentur, neque apud cīvīs sōlum Rōmānōs, quī et sermōnis[8] et iūris et multārum rērum societāte iūnctī sunt, fore sē tūtōs arbitrantur, sed, quōcumque vēnerint, hanc sibi rem praesidiō spērant futūram. Tolle hanc spem, tolle hoc praesidium cīvibus Rōmānīs, cōnstitue nihil esse opis in hāc vōce, "Cīvis Rōmānus sum," posse[9] impūne praetōrem aut alium quempiam supplicium quod velit in eum cōnstituere quī sē cīvem Rōmānum esse dīcat, quod[10] quī sit ignōret: iam omnīs prōvinciās, iam omnia rēgna, iam omnīs līberās cīvitātēs, iam omnem orbem terrārum, quī semper nostrīs hominibus maximē patuit, cīvibus Rōmānīs istā dēfēnsiōne praeclūseris.

[3] *hot plates* (of metal)

[4] *delay* (to insure trial before the people)

[5] *position*

[6] *witnesses* (who could identify them as Roman citizens)

[7] *public opinion*

[8] *language*

[9] *decide that a praetor can* (depends, like **esse**, on **cōnstitue**)

[10] *on the ground that he does not know who (the man) is*

## WORD STUDY

Define *attenuate, fascicle, impunity, nascent, pestiferous.*

To what Latin words are the following related: **assequor, cruciātus, fīdūcia, reddō, societās?**

---

[2] with **potestās;** Sulla had reduced the tribune's power to protect a citizen, but that power had just been restored

[3] = **hūcne;** the original form was **hūcene,** just as **hic** was **hice,** etc.: *have things come to this point?*

[4] Verres

[5] the man who was beaten in Messina

# THE STRUGGLES OF A *NOVUS HOMŌ*

**Verba Ūtilia:** alliciō, crīmen, dēferō, dēiciō, dīiungō, licet, occultus

**V, 180.** Quaeret aliquis fortasse, "Tantumne igitur labōrem, tantās inimīcitiās tot hominum susceptūrus es?" Nōn studiō[1] quidem hercule[2] ūllō neque voluntāte; sed nōn idem licet mihi quod iīs quī nōbilī genere nātī sunt, quibus omnia populī Rōmānī beneficia dormientibus[3] dēferuntur; longē aliā mihi lēge in hāc cīvitāte et condiciōne vīvendum est. **181.** Vidēmus quantā sit in invidiā quantōque in odiō apud quōsdam nōbilīs hominēs novōrum hominum virtūs et industria; sī tantulum[4] oculōs dēiēcerīmus, praestō[5] esse īnsidiās; sī ūllum locum aperuerīmus suspīciōnī aut crīminī, accipiendum statim vulnus esse; semper nōbīs vigilandum, semper labōrandum vidēmus. **182.** Inimīcitiae sunt, subeantur;[6] labor$_1$, suscipiātur; etenim tacitae magis et occultae inimīcitiae timendae sunt quam indictae atque apertae. Hominum nōbilium nōn ferē quisquam nostrae industriae favet; nūllīs nostrīs officiīs benevolentiam illōrum allicere possumus; quasi nātūrā et genere diiūnctī sint, ita dissident ā nōbīs animō ac voluntāte. Quārē quid habent eōrum inimīcitiae perīculī quōrum animōs iam ante habuerīs inimīcōs et invidōs quam ūllās inimīcitiās suscēperīs?

[1] *on purpose*
[2] *by Hercules*
[3] *while they are asleep* (i.e., with no effort on their part)
[4] *just a little bit*
[5] *at hand, being used*
[6] *if there are enmities, let them be endured*

---

$_1$ similarly **labor,** *trouble,* with **est** understood

# The Second Speech Against Antony

## CICERO, CAESAR, AND POMPEY

**Verba Ūtilia:** augeō, dīiungō, ēnītor, ops, opus, praetermittō, sērō

**23.** Quod vērō dīcere ausus es idque multīs verbīs, operā meā Pompeium ā Caesaris amīcitiā esse dīiūnctum ob eamque$_1$ causam culpā meā bellum cīvīle esse nātum, in eō nōn tū quidem tōtā rē sed, quod maximum est, temporibus errāstī. Ego, M. Bibulō, praestantissimō cīve, cōnsule, nihil praetermīsī, quantum facere ēnītīque potuī, quīn Pompeium ā Caesaris coniūnctiōne āvocārem.[1] In quō Caesar fēlīcior fuit. Ipse enim Pompeium ā meā familiāritāte dīiūnxit. Posteā vērō quam sē tōtum Pompeius Caesarī trādidit, quid ego illum$_2$ ab eō distrahere cōnārer?[2] Stultī erat[3] spērāre, suādēre impudentis. **24.** Duo tamen tempora incidērunt quibus aliquid contrā Caesarem Pompeiō suāserim. Ea velim reprehendās,[4] sī potes: ūnum nē quīnquennī$_3$ imperium Caesarī prōrogāret, alterum nē paterētur ferrī ut absentis eius ratiō habērētur.[5] Quōrum sī utrumvīs persuāsissem, in hās miseriās numquam incidissēmus. Atque īdem ego, cum iam opēs omnīs et suās et populī Rōmānī Pompeius ad Caesarem dētulisset, sērōque ea sentīre coepisset quae multō ante prōvīderam, īnferrīque patriae bellum vidērem nefārium, pācis, concordiae, compositiōnis auctor esse non dēstitī, meaque illa vōx est nōta multīs: "Utinam, Cn. Pompeī, cum C. Caesare societātem aut numquam coīssēs aut numquam dirēmissēs! Fuit alterum gravitātis,[6] alterum prūdentiae tuae." Haec mea, M. Antōnī, semper et dē Pompeiō et dē rē pūblicā cōnsilia fuērunt. Quae sī valuissent, rēs pūblica stāret, tū tuīs flāgitiīs, egestāte, īnfamiā concidissēs.

[1] *I have tried everything, as far as I could, to separate Pompey from Caesar* (literally, *I have omitted nothing [to prevent me] from,* etc.)

[2] *why should I have tried?*

[3] *it was (characteristic) of a foolish person*

[4] *I should like you to find fault*

[5] *that consideration be given to his absence*

[6] *(a matter of) consistency*

---

$_1$ The conjunction **–que** is not usually attached to a monosyllabic preposition.

$_2$ Pompey

$_3$ the five-year prolongation of Caesar's command in Gaul to 49 B.C.

# I AM NOT AFRAID OF YOU, ANTONY

**116.** Fuit in illō$_{1}$ ingenium, ratiō, memoria, litterae, cūra, cōgitātiō, dīligentia; rēs bellō gesserat, quamvīs reī pūblicae calamitōsās, at tamen magnās; multōs annōs rēgnāre meditātus, magnō labōre, magnīs perīculīs quod cōgitārat effēcerat; mūneribus[1], monumentīs, congiāriīs[2], epulīs multitūdinem imperītam dēlēnierat; suōs praemiīs, adversāriōs clēmentiae speciē dēvīnxerat. Quid multa? Attulerat iam līberae cīvitātī partim metū, partim patientiā cōnsuētūdinem serviendī. Cum illō ego tē dominandī cupiditāte cōnferre possum, cēterīs vērō rēbus nūllō modō comparandus es. **117.** Sed ex plūrimīs malīs quae ab illō reī pūblicae sunt inusta hoc tamen bonī est,[3] quod didicit iam populus Rōmānus quantum cuique crēderet,[4] quibus sē committeret, ā quibus cavēret. Haec nōn cōgitās, neque intellegis satis esse virīs fortibus didicisse quam sit$_{2}$ rē pulchrum,[5] beneficiō grātum, fāmā glōriōsum tyrannum occīdere? An, cum illum$_{3}$ hominēs nōn tulerint, tē ferent? **118.** Certātim posthāc, mihi crēde, ad hoc opus$_{4}$ currētur neque occāsiōnis tarditās exspectābitur.[6]

Respice, quaesō, aliquandō rem pūblicam, M. Antōnī, quibus$_{5}$ ortus sīs, nōn quibuscum vīvās cōnsīderā; mēcum,$_{6}$ ut volēs: redī cum rē pūblicā in grātiam. Sed dē tē tū vīderis;[7] ego dē mē ipse profitēbor. Dēfendī rem pūblicam adulēscēns, nōn dēseram senex; contempsī Catilīnae gladiōs, nōn pertimēscam tuōs. Quīn etiam corpus libenter obtulerim[8], sī repraesentārī[9] morte meā lībertās cīvitātis potest. **119.** Etenim sī abhinc annōs prope vīgintī hōc ipsō in templō negāvī posse mortem immātūram esse cōnsulārī, quantō vērius nunc negābō senī!$_{7}$ Mihi vērō, patrēs cōnscrīptī, iam etiam optanda mors est, perfūnctō$_{8}$ rēbus eīs quās adeptus sum quāsque gessī. Duo modo haec optō, ūnum ut moriēns populum Rōmānum līberum relinquam (hōc mihi maius ab dīs immortālibus darī nihil potest), alterum ut ita cuique ēveniat ut[10] dē rē pūblicā quisque mereātur.

[1] *shows (of gladiators)*
[2] *gifts*
[3] *there is this much good*
[4] *trust every man*
[5] *how fine it is in fact, how gratifying it is because of its good deed*
[6] *the slowness of the occasion will not be awaited* (i.e., it will happen soon)
[7] *you will see to yourself*
[8] *I would offer*
[9] *brought about at once*
[10] *as*

---

$_{1}$ Caesar
$_{2}$ The subject of **sit** is **occīdere.**
$_{3}$ Caesar
$_{4}$ killing a tyrant
$_{5}$ He was of noble ancestry; his present associates belong to the riffraff.
$_{6}$ From the following phrase, supply **redī in grātiam:** *Return to friendship with me* (*or not*).
$_{7}$ Supply **mortem immātūram esse**.
$_{8}$ modifies **mihi** and governs **rēbus**

UNIT
VII

# CICERO'S LETTERS

## Unit Objectives

- To read Cicero's letters for their insight into Roman politics, everyday life, and the Latin language
- To gain additional insight into Cicero's personality through his personal letters
- To learn new vocabulary in context

Scala/Art Resource, NY

The Capitoline She-Wolf is the symbol of Rome even today. Though the wolf itself dates from Etruscan times, probably during the early fifth century B.C., the bronzes of Romulus and Remus as babies were added later by Simone del Pollaiuolo (1457–1508). The Etruscans used bronze extensively for household furnishings and military accessories. Freestanding bronze sculpture, like this one, was an Etruscan specialty.

# INTRODUCING CICERO'S LETTERS

A number of collections of Cicero's letters were published after his death. About half of the collections have survived, notably the 16 books addressed to his best friend Atticus, who published these letters, and the 16 books published by Tiro, Cicero's secretary. In modern times, the collection published by Tiro has been given the title *Epistulae ad familiārēs,* "Letters to Friends," an inaccurate title because some of the letters are to people who are not, strictly speaking, Cicero's friends and because some of the letters are *to* Cicero, not *from* him.

Remember that Cicero's letters were not intended for publication; many of them were confidential. They are extremely interesting for the light they throw on politics, private life, language, and Cicero's character. Some put Cicero in an unfavorable light, especially some of the confidential letters to Atticus, who did his great friend no service in publishing them. Not many prominent men of the last 2000 years could afford to have *all* their personal letters published.

Nearly 900 of Cicero's letters are extant.

# THE CAMPAIGN FOR THE CONSULSHIP

Petītiōnis[1] nostrae, quam tibi summae cūrae esse sciō, huius modī ratiō est, quod[2] adhūc coniectūrā prōviderī possit. Prēnsat[3] ūnus P. Galba; sine fūcō ac fallāciīs mōre maiōrum negātur.[4] Ut opīniō est hominum, nōn aliēna ratiōnī nostrae fuit illīus haec praepropera prēnsātiō; nam illī ita negant vulgō ut mihi sē dēbēre dīcant. Ita quiddam spērō nōbīs prōficī, cum hoc percrēbrēscit, plūrimōs nostrōs amīcōs invenīrī. Nōs autem initium prēnsandī facere cōgitārāmus eō ipsō tempore quō tuum puerum[5] cum hīs litterīs proficīscī Cīncius dīcēbat, in campō[1] comitiīs tribūnīciīs a. d. XVI Kal. Sextīlēs.[2] Competītōrēs quī certī esse videantur Galba et Antōnius et Q. Cornificius. Catilīna, sī iūdicātum erit merīdiē nōn lūcēre, certus erit competītor; dē Aufidiō et dē Palicānō nōn putō tē exspectāre dum scrībam. Dē iīs quī

[1] *seeking (for office), candidacy*

[2] *as far as*

[3] *is canvassing* (literally, *is grasping hands*)

[4] *He is being turned down in the good old-fashioned way without pretense* (literally, *without pain and pretense*)

[5] *servant*

---

[1] the Campus Martius

[2] for **ante diem XVI Kalendās Sextīlēs,** *the sixteenth day before the Kalends of August,* i.e., July 17 (not July 16, for the Romans counted both ends)

nunc$_{3}$ petunt, Caesar$_{4}$ certus putātur; Thermus cum Silānō contendere exīstimātur, quī sīc inopēs et ab[6] amīcīs et exīstimātiōne sunt ut mihi videātur nōn esse ἀδύνατον$_{5}$ Cūrium obdūcere,[7] sed hoc praeter mē nēminī vidētur. Nostrīs ratiōnibus maximē condūcere vidētur Thermum fierī cum Caesare. Nēmō est enim ex iīs quī nunc petunt quī, sī in nostrum annum reciderit, firmior candidātus fore videātur, propterea quod cūrātor est viae Flāminiae, quae tum erit absolūta sānē facile; eum libenter nunc Caesarī cōnsulem accūderim.[8] Petītōrum haec est īnfōrmāta adhūc cōgitātiō. Nōs$_{6}$ in omnī mūnere candidātōriō fungendō summam adhibēbimus dīligentiam et fortasse, quoniam vidētur in suffrāgiīs multum posse[9] Gallia, cum Rōmae ā iūdiciīs forum refrīxerit,[10]$_{7}$ excurrēmus mēnse Septembrī lēgātī[11] ad Pīsōnem, ut Iānuāriō revertāmur. Cum perspexerō voluntātēs nōbilium, scrībam ad tē. (*A*. I, 1, 1–2)

[6] *from (the standpoint of)*
[7] *to run Curius* (for the consulship)
[8] *I would gladly add him to Caesar as consul*
[9] *has much influence*
[10] *has cooled off in regard to trials*
[11] *as a commissioner*

---

$_{3}$ i.e., for the consulship of 64
$_{4}$ L. (not C.) Caesar
$_{5}$ **adynaton,** *impossible*. Cicero uses many Greek words in writing to Atticus, who for many years had been living in Athens.
$_{6}$ the plural of modesty, for **ego**
$_{7}$ The **lūdī Rōmānī** kept the courts closed during much of September, and there were other interruptions until after the Saturnalia in December.

# IT'S A BOY!

L. Iūliō Caesare, C. Mārciō Figulō cōnsulibus, fīliolō mē auctum[1] scītō[2], salvā Terentiā. Abs tē tam diū nihil litterārum! Ego dē meīs ad tē ratiōnibus scrīpsī anteā dīligenter. Hōc tempore Catilīnam, competītōrem nostrum, dēfendere cōgitāmus.$_{1}$ Iūdicēs habēmus quōs voluimus, summā accūsātōris voluntāte. Spērō, sī absolūtus erit, coniūnctiōrem illum nōbīs fore in ratiōne petītiōnis; sīn aliter acciderit, hūmāniter ferēmus.

Tuō adventū nōbīs opus est mātūrō; nam prōrsus summa hominum est opīniō tuōs familiārēs, nōbilēs hominēs, adversāriōs honōrī[3] nostrō fore. Ad eōrum voluntātem mihi conciliandam maximō tē mihi ūsuī fore videō. Quārē Iānuāriō mēnse, ut cōnstituistī, cūrā ut Rōmae sīs.$_{2}$ (*A*. I, 2)

[1] *blessed*
[2] *know* (imperative)
[3] *my election*

---

$_{1}$ We say, "Politics makes strange bedfellows," and here we have an example. Nothing came of the plan.
$_{2}$ From the fact that Cicero's next letter to Atticus is not until 61 B.C., we may infer that Atticus came to Rome and presumably worked hard and well on his friend's behalf.

# THE TRIAL OF CLODIUS[1]

Quaeris ex mē quid acciderit dē iūdiciō, quod tam praeter opīniōnem omnium factum sit, et simul vīs scīre quō modō ego minus quam soleam proeliātus sim. Respondēbō tibi ὕστερον πρότερον Ὁμηρικῶς.[2] Ego enim, quam diū senātūs auctōritās mihi dēfendenda fuit, sīc ācriter et vehementer proeliātus sum ut clāmor concursusque maximā cum meā laude fierent. Quod sī tibi umquam sum vīsus in rē pūblicā fortis, certē mē in illā causā admīrātus essēs. Cum enim ille ad cōntiōnēs[1] cōnfūgisset, in iīsque meō nōmine ad invidiam ūterētur, dī immortālēs, quās ego pugnās et quantās strāgēs ēdidī, quōs impetūs in Pīsōnem, in Cūriōnem,[3] in tōtam illam manum fēcī! Quō modō sum īnsectātus levitātem senum, libīdinem iuventūtis!

Itaque, sī causam quaeris absolūtiōnis, ut iam πρὸς τὸ πρότερον[4] revertar, egestās iūdicum fuit et turpitūdō. Summō discessū[2] bonōrum, plēnō forō servōrum[5], XXV iūdicēs ita fortēs tamen fuērunt ut, summō prōpositō perīculō, vel[3] perīre māluerint quam perdere omnia;[6] XXXI fuērunt quōs famēs magis quam fāma commōverit;[7] quōrum Catulus cum vīdisset quendam, "Quid vōs?" inquit, "praesidium ā nōbīs postulābātis?[8] An nē nummī vōbīs ēriperentur timēbātis?" Habēs, ut[4] brevissimē potuī, genus iūdicī et causam absolūtiōnis.

Ut Īdibus Maiīs in senātum convēnimus, rogātus ego sententiam multa dīxī dē summā rē pūblicā. "Quō usque," inquit[9], "hunc rēgem ferēmus?" "Rēgem appellās," inquam, "cum Rēx tuī mentiōnem nūllam fēcerit?"[10] Ille autem

[1] *mass meetings*
[2] *in spite of the withdrawal*
[3] *even*
[4] *as briefly as*

---

1 To Atticus, July, 61 B.C. Cicero had appeared as a witness against Clodius, on trial for sacrilege. Bribery enabled Clodius to go free, but he never forgave Cicero, later bringing about his exile.
2 **hysteron proteron Homērikōs,** *in the Homeric fashion*
3 supporters of Clodius
4 **pros to proteron,** *to the first* (*point*)
5 Clodius' thugs, whose function it was to overawe decent citizens
6 They voted for conviction.
7 They accepted bribes to vote for acquittal, more aware of their empty stomachs than their reputations; majority vote decided cases.
8 They had asked for police protection, ostensibly against Clodius' slaves (mentioned in footnote 5).
9 Clodius. The trial is over and Cicero is making a speech. Clodius tries to defend himself.
10 Clodius had been disappointed in not being left a legacy by a man named Rex ("Mr. King"). This gives Cicero another opportunity to make a pun.

Rēgis hērēditātem spē dēvorārat.— "Domum," inquit, "ēmistī."[11] "Putēs,"[5] inquam, "dīcere: iūdicēs ēmistī."—"Iūrantī," inquit, "tibi nōn crēdidērunt." "Mihi vērō," inquam, "XXV iūdicēs crēdidērunt, XXXI, quoniam nummōs ante accēpērunt, tibi nihil crēdidērunt[12]." Magnīs clāmōribus afflīctus conticuit et concidit.

Nunc est exspectātiō comitiōrum, in quae, omnibus invītīs, trūdit noster Magnus[13] Aulī fīlium,[6] atque in eō neque auctōritāte neque grātiā pugnat, sed quibus[7] Philippus omnia castella expugnārī posse dīcēbat in quae modo[8] asellus onustus aurō posset ascendere. (*A.* I, 16, 1–2, 5, 9–10, 12)

[5] *one would think you said*
[6] *the son of Aulus* is equivalent to saying *a nobody*
[7] *with those (means) with which*
[8] *provided that into these*

[11] Cicero had bought a very expensive house on the Palatine Hill; Clodius implies, "Where did you get the money?"
[12] a pun on the two meanings of **crēdō**
[13] Pompey

# CLODIUS' THREATS

Noster Pūblius[1] mihi minitātur, inimīcus est; impendet negōtium[1], ad quod tū scīlicet advolābis. Videor mihi nostrum illum cōnsulārem exercitum[2] bonōrum omnium, etiam satis bonōrum[2] habēre firmissimum. Pompeius significat studium ergā mē nōn mediocre. Īdem affirmat verbum dē mē illum[3] nōn esse factūrum, in quō nōn mē ille fallit, sed ipse fallitur. Caesar mē sibi vult esse lēgātum. Honestior[3] haec dēclīnātiō perīculī; sed ego hoc nōn repudiō. Quid ergō est? Pugnāre mālō. Nihil tamen certī. Iterum dīcō: utinam adessēs! Sed tamen, sī erit necesse, arcessēmus. Quid aliud? Quid? Hoc opīnor: certī sumus perīsse omnia. Sed haec scrīpsī properāns et mehercule[4] timidē. Posthāc ad tē aut, sī perfidēlem habēbō cui dem,[5] scrībam plānē omnia, aut, sī obscūrē scrībam, tū tamen intellegēs. In iīs epistulīs mē Laelium, tē Fūrium faciam; cētera erunt ἐν αἰνιγμοῖς.[4] Hīc Caecilium colimus et observāmus dīligenter. Ēdicta Bibulī[5] audiō ad tē missa. Iīs[6] ārdet dolōre et īrā noster Pompeius. (*A.* II, 19, 4–5)

[1] *trouble*
[2] *somewhat conservative*
[3] *more honorable*
[4] *by Hercules*
[5] *to whom I can give* (a letter for delivery)
[6] *on account of them*

[1] Clodius
[2] not to be taken literally; he means his conservative supporters
[3] Clodius
[4] **en ainigmois,** *in enigmas,* i.e., obscure to everyone but Atticus should the letters go to the wrong person
[5] Caesar's colleague in the consulship. Ignored by Caesar, he responded by protesting his colleague's actions.

# ON THE WAY TO EXILE

Utinam illum diem videam cum tibi agam grātiās quod mē vīvere coēgistī![1] Adhūc quidem valdē mē paenitet.[2] Sed tē ōrō ut ad mē Vibōnem statim veniās, quō ego multīs dē causīs convertī iter meum. Sed eō sī vēneris, dē tōtō itinere ac fugā[1] meā cōnsilium capere poterō; sī id nōn fēceris, mīrābor, sed cōnfīdō tē esse factūrum. (*A*. III, 3)

[1] *exile*

[1] Cicero had planned to commit suicide but was dissuaded by Atticus.
[2] He regrets that he did not commit suicide.

# NOTHING TO WRITE

Nōlī putāre mē ad quemquam longiōrēs epistulās scrībere, nisi sī[1] quis ad mē plūra scrīpsit cui putō rescrībī[1] oportēre; nec enim habeō quid scrībam, nec hōc tempore quicquam difficilius faciō. Ad tē vērō et ad nostram Tulliolam[2] nōn queō sine plūrimīs lacrimīs scrībere; vōs enim videō esse miserrimās, quās ego beātissimās semper esse voluī idque praestāre dēbuī et, nisi tam timidī[3] fuissēmus, praestitissem. (*F*. XIV, 2, 1)

[1] *an answer should be sent*

[1] unnecessary; omit in translation.
[2] diminutive of affection ("my dear little Tullia")
[3] by going into exile instead of resisting Clodius in Rome

# THE SHOWS WERE POOR

Omnīnō, sī quaeris, lūdī apparātissimī, sed nōn tuī stomachī;[1] coniectūram enim faciō dē meō. Nam prīmum honōris causā in scaenam redierant iī quōs ego honōris causā$_{1}$ dē scaenā dēcesse$_{2}$ arbitrābar; dēliciae[2] vērō tuae, noster Aesōpus, eius modī fuit ut eī dēsinere per[3] omnīs hominēs licēret. Is iūrāre cum coepisset, vōx eum dēfēcit in illō locō: "Sī sciēns fallō."$_{3}$ Quid tibi ego alia nārrem? Nōstī$_{4}$ enim reliquōs lūdōs, quī nē id quidem lepōris habuērunt quod solent mediocrēs lūdī. Apparātūs enim spectātiō tollēbat omnem hilaritātem, quō quidem apparātū$_{5}$ nōn dubitō quīn animō aequissimō caruerīs. Quid enim dēlectātiōnis habent sescentī$_{6}$ mūlī in Clytaemestrā$_{7}$, aut in Equō Trōiānō$_{6}$ crēterrārum[4] tria mīlia, aut armātūra varia peditātūs et equitātūs in aliquā pugnā? Quae populārem admīrātiōnem habuērunt, dēlectātiōnem tibi nūllam attulissent.

Reliquae sunt vēnātiōnēs[5] bīnae per diēs quīnque, magnificae—nēmō negat—sed quae potest hominī esse polītō dēlectātiō, cum aut homō imbēcillus ā valentissimā bēstiā laniātur aut praeclāra bēstia vēnābulō trānsverberātur? Quae tamen, sī videnda sunt, saepe vīdistī; neque nōs quī haec spectāmus quicquam novī vīdimus. Extrēmus elephantōrum diēs fuit. In quō admīrātiō magna vulgī atque turbae, dēlectātiō nūlla exstitit; quīn etiam misericordia quaedam cōnsecūta est atque opīniō eius modī, esse quandam illī bēluae cum genere hūmānō societātem. (*F*. VII, 1, 2–3)

[1] *to your taste*
[2] *favorite*
[3] *by*
[4] *(gold) bowls* (seized as loot in the Trojan War)
[5] *hunts*

---

$_{1}$ a pun on two different meanings of the phrase: *for the sake of honoring (the occasion), for the sake of their honor*
$_{2}$ = **dēcessisse**
$_{3}$ In the play he takes an oath, saying, "If knowingly I fail,"—and just then his voice fails him.
$_{4}$ from **nōscō** (second per. sing. perf., contracted form)
$_{5}$ with **caruerīs**
$_{6}$ often used for an indefinitely large number
$_{7}$ These are the names of tragedies; we say *Clytaemnestra.*

# A TRAGEDY ABOUT BRITAIN?

Veniō nunc ad id quod nesciō an[1] prīmum esse dēbuerit. Ō iūcundās mihi tuās dē Britanniā litterās! Timēbam Ōceanum, timēbam lītus īnsulae. Reliqua nōn equidem contemnō, sed plūs habent tamen speī quam timōris, magisque sum sollicitus exspectātiōne eā quam metū. Tē vērō ὑπόθεσιν[2] scrībendī ēgregiam habēre videō. Quōs tū sitūs, quās nātūrās rērum et locōrum, quōs mōrēs, quās gentēs, quās pugnās, quem vērō ipsum imperātōrem habēs! Ego tē libenter, ut rogās,$_1$ quibus rēbus vīs adiuvābō et tibi versūs quōs rogās, hoc est "Athēnās noctuam,"[3] mittam. Sed heus tu, cēlārī[4] videor ā tē. Quōmodōnam, mi frāter, dē nostrīs versibus$_2$ Caesar? Nam prīmum librum sē lēgisse scrīpsit ad mē ante, et prīma[5] sīc ut neget sē nē Graeca quidem meliōra lēgisse; reliqua ad quendam locum ῥαθυμότερα[6]—hōc enim ūtimur verbō.$_3$ Dīc mihi vērum: num aut rēs eum aut χαρακτήρ[7] nōn dēlectat? Nihil est quod vereāre; ego enim nē pilō[8] quidem minus mē amābō. Hāc dē rē φιλαληθῶς[9] et, ut solēs scrībere, fraternē. (*Q. Fr.* II, 16, 4–5)

[1] *perhaps* (literally, *I do not know whether*)
[2] **hypothesin,** *story, outline* (for a tragedy)
[3] *an owl to Athens* (a proverbial expression)
[4] *to be kept in the dark*
[5] *the first (parts)* (of the first book)
[6] **rhathumotera,** *rather easy-going, rather careless*
[7] **charaktēr,** *style*
[8] *not a bit* (literally, *not by even a hair*)
[9] **philalēthōs,** *truthfully*

---

$_1$ Quintus evidently asked his brother to send some verses.
$_2$ the poem on Cicero's consulship
$_3$ Cicero means that this is his word, not Caesar's who was not apt to introduce Greek words.

# THE BEST LAWYER IN—SAMAROBRIVA

Quid agātis et ecquid[1] in Italiam ventūrī sītis hāc hieme fac plānē sciam.[2] Balbus mihi cōnfirmāvit tē dīvitem futūrum. Id utrum Rōmānō mōre$_1$ locutūs sit, bene nummātum[3] tē futūrum, an quō modō Stoicī dīcunt, omnēs esse dīvitēs quī caelō et terrā fruī possint, posteā vidēbō. Quī istinc veniunt superbiam tuam accūsant, quod negent tē percontantibus respondēre.$_2$ Sed tamen est quod[4] gaudeās; cōnstat enim inter omnīs nēminem tē ūnō Samarobrīvae$_3$ iūris perītiōrem esse. (*F.* VII, 16, 3)

[1] *whether*
[2] *let me know for sure*
[3] *well-heeled, with lots of coin*
[4] *there is (something for) which*

---

$_1$ i.e., literally, not figuratively
$_2$ a pun: in the literal and in the legal sense, to give legal advice
$_3$ a small town, now Amiens in northern France

# Transmission of Latin and Greek Works Before Printing: 1

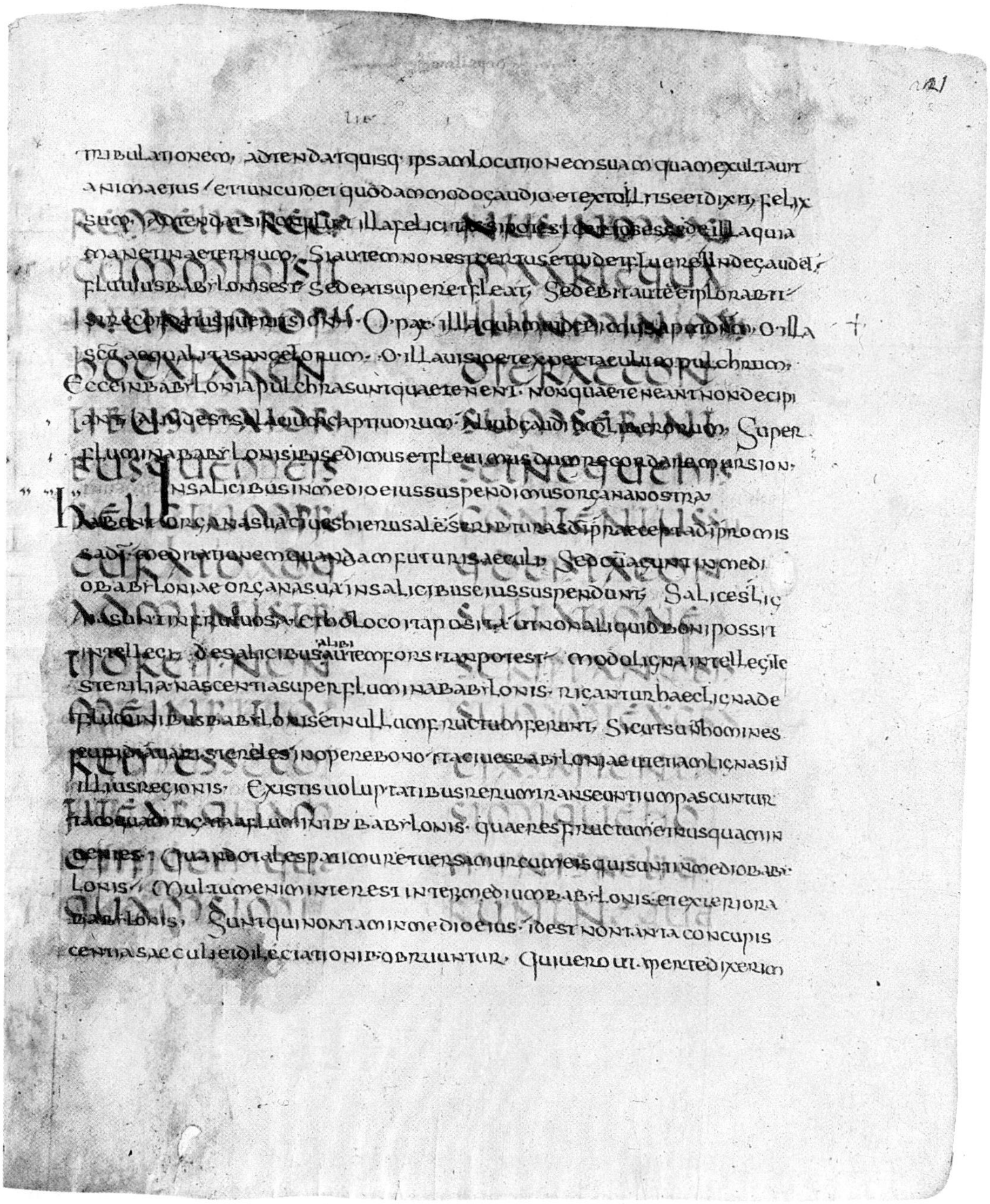

PHOTRI/AISA/Vat.

Since writing surfaces—in this case, treated sheepskin, called vellum—were expensive, the writing on older and "unimportant" vellum was scraped off to make way for "more important" works. In this way, materials were recycled. Traces of the older writing always remained faintly behind the new writing. Such manuscripts are called palimpsests. Here the larger writing in two columns is from Cicero's *De Republica,* dating from the fourth century, while the smaller writing is from a selection of St. Augustine on the Psalms, dating from the seventh century. The monks probably valued Augustine over Cicero, but in doing so preserved both! In this way, many Roman writings came down through the ages. You can probably read some of Augustine's words. Notice that there is no attempt to leave spaces between words in sentences. Larger letters are frequently used to begin new thoughts.

# TREBATIUS IS NO CHANNEL SWIMMER

[1] *an expert in the law*
[2] *where you appear to know something*
[3] = **mehercule,** *by Hercules*
[4] *chariot fighters*
[5] *blindfolded gladiator* (with **dēfraudāre**)

Lēgī tuās litterās, ex quibus intellēxī tē Caesarī nostrō valdē iūre cōnsultum[1] vidērī. Est quod gaudeās tē in ista loca vēnisse ubi aliquid sapere vidērēre.[2] Quod sī in Britanniam quoque profectus essēs,[1] profectō nēmō in illā tantā īnsulā perītior tē fuisset. Vērum tamen (rīdeāmus licet; sum enim ā tē invītātus) subinvideō[2] tibi, ultrō etiam accersītum ab eō ad quem cēterī nōn propter superbiam eius sed propter occupātiōnem aspīrāre nōn possunt. Sed tū in istā epistulā nihil mihi scrīpsistī dē tuīs rēbus, quae mercule[3] mihi nōn minōrī cūrae sunt quam meae. Valdē metuō nē frīgeās in hībernīs. Quamquam vōs nunc istīc satis calēre[3] audiō; quō quidem nūntiō valdē mercule dē tē timueram. Sed tū in rē mīlitārī multō es cautior quam in advocātiōnibus, quī neque in Ōceanō natāre voluerīs, studiōsissimus homō natandī, neque spectāre essedāriōs[4], quem anteā nē andābatā[5] quidem dēfraudāre poterāmus. Sed iam satis iocātī sumus. Ego dē tē ad Caesarem quam dīligenter scrīpserim, tūte scīs, quam saepe, ego; sed mercule iam intermīseram, nē vidērer līberālissimī hominis meīque amantissimī voluntātī ergā mē diffīdere[4]. (*F.* VII, 10, 1–3)

---

1 The contrary-to-fact condition shows that Trebatius had refused Caesar's invitation to go to Britain.
2 The prefix means *just a little bit.*
3 The Gauls are making it "hot" for the Romans.
4 with dative

# THE PANTHERS PROTEST

Dē pantherīs, per eōs quī vēnārī solent agitur mandātū meō dīligenter; sed mīra paucitās est, et eās quae sunt valdē aiunt querī quod nihil cuiquam īnsidiārum in meā prōvinciā nisi sibi fīat; itaque cōnstituisse dīcuntur in Cāriam ex nostrā prōvinciā dēcēdere. Sed tamen sēdulō fit. Quicquid erit, tibi erit, sed quid esset plānē nesciēbāmus. Mihi mercule magnae cūrae est aedīlitās tua; ipse diēs mē admonēbat, scrīpsī enim haec ipsīs Megalēnsibus[1]. Tū velim ad mē dē omnī reī pūblicae statū quam dīligentissimē perscrībās; ea enim certissima putābō quae ex tē cognōrō. (*F.* II, 11, 2)

---

1 The festival of the goddess Cybele, or Magna Mater, at which time important games were held.

# GET WELL!

Tertiam ad tē hanc epistulam scrīpsī eōdem diē, magis īnstitūtī[1] meī tenendī causā, quia nactus eram cui darem,[2] quam quō[3] habērem quid scrīberem. Igitur illa: quantum mē dīligis, tantum adhibē in tē dīligentiae; ad tua innumerābilia in mē officia adde hoc, quod mihi erit grātissimum omnium. Cum valētūdinis ratiōnem, ut spērō, habueris, habētō etiam nāvigātiōnis. In Italiam euntibus omnibus ad mē litterās dabis, ut ego euntem Patrās[4] nēminem praetermittō. Cūrā, cūrā tē, mī Tīrō. Quoniam nōn contigit ut simul nāvigārēs, nihil est[5] quod festīnēs, nec quicquam cūrēs nisi ut valeās. Etiam atque etiam valē. VII Īdūs Nov.[1] Actiō vesperī. (*F*. XVI, 6)

[1] *plan* (of writing)
[2] *to whom I could give (a letter)*
[3] *that, because*
[4] *Patrae*
[5] *there is no (reason) that*

---

[1] November 7

# PEACE OR WAR

Lippitūdinis[1] meae signum tibi sit librārī manus[2] et eadem causa brevitātis, etsī nunc quidem quod scrīberem nihil erat. Omnis exspectātiō nostra erat in nūntiīs Brundisīnīs.[3] Sī nactus hic[4] esset Gnaeum nostrum, spēs dubia pācis; sīn ille[5] ante trāmīsisset, exitiōsī bellī metus. Sed vidēsne in quem hominem[6] inciderit rēs pūblica, quam acūtum, quam vigilantem, quam parātum? Sī mehercule nēminem occīderit nec cuiquam[7][1] quicquam adēmerit, ab iīs quī eum maximē timuerant maximē dīligētur. Multum mēcum mūnicipālēs hominēs loquuntur, multum rūsticānī. Nihil prōrsus aliud cūrant nisi agrōs, nisi vīllulās, nisi nummulōs[2] suōs. Et vidē quam conversa rēs est: illum quō anteā cōnfīdēbant metuunt, hunc amant quem timēbant. Id quantīs nostrīs peccātīs vitiīsque ēvēnerit nōn possum sine molestiā cōgitāre. Quae autem impendēre putārem, scrīpseram ad tē et iam tuās litterās exspectābam. (*A*. VIII, 13)

[1] *sore eyes*
[2] *handwriting* (subject)
[3] *reports from Brundisium*
[4] Caesar
[5] Pompey
[6] Caesar
[7] *from anyone*

---

[1] Caesar's **clēmentia**, known from the war in Gaul, was being continued and was having an effect.
[2] The diminutives show contempt: *their precious farm houses and their filthy money.*

# COME BACK TO ROME[1]

Cum Furnium nostrum tantum vīdissem, neque loquī neque audīre meō commodō potuissem, properārem[2] atque essem in itinere, praemissīs iam legiōnibus, praeterīre tamen nōn potuī quīn[1] et scrīberem ad tē et illum mitterem grātiāsque agerem, etsī hoc et fēcī saepe et saepius mihi factūrus videor: ita dē mē merēris. In prīmīs ā tē petō, quoniam cōnfīdō mē celeriter ad urbem ventūrum, ut tē ibi videam, ut tuō cōnsiliō, grātiā, dignitāte, ope omnium rērum ūtī possim. Ad prōpositum revertar: festīnātiōnī meae brevitātīque litterārum ignōscēs[3]; reliqua ex Furniō cognōscēs. (*A.* IX, 6A)

[1] *without*

---

[1] a very friendly letter *from* Caesar *to* Cicero, March, 49 B.C.
[2] still with **cum**
[3] with dative

# CICERO THE PEACEMAKER

Ut lēgī tuās litterās, quās ā Furniō nostrō accēperam, quibus mēcum agēbās ut ad urbem essem, tē velle ūtī cōnsiliō et dignitāte meā minus sum admīrātus; dē grātiā et dē ope quid significārēs, mēcum ipse quaerēbam, spē tamen dēdūcēbar ad eam cōgitātiōnem, ut tē pro tuā admīrābilī ac singulārī sapientiā dē ōtiō, dē pāce, dē concordiā cīvium agī velle arbitrārer, et ad eam ratiōnem exīstimābam satis aptam esse et nātūram et persōnam meam. Quod sī ita est et sī qua[1] dē Pompeiō nostrō tuendō et tibi ac reī pūblicae reconciliandō cūra tē attingit, magis idōneum quam ego sum ad eam causam profectō reperiēs nēminem, quī et illī semper et senātuī, cum prīmum potuī, pācis auctor fuī, nec, sūmptīs armīs, bellī[2] ūllam partem attigī, iūdicāvīque eō bellō tē violārī, contrā cuius honōrem populī Rōmānī beneficiō[3] concessum inimīcī atque invidī nīterentur. Sed, ut eō tempore nōn modo ipse fautor dignitātis tuae fuī, vērum etiam cēterīs auctor ad tē adiuvandum, sīc mē nunc Pompeī dignitās vehementer movet; aliquot enim sunt annī cum vōs duo dēlēgī quōs praecipuē colerem et quibus essem, sīcut sum, amīcissimus. Quam ob rem ā tē petō vel potius omnibus tē precibus ōrō et obtestor ut in tuīs maximīs cūrīs aliquid impertiās temporis huic quoque cōgitātiōnī, ut tuō beneficiō[4] bonus[5] vir, grātus, pius[1] dēnique esse in maximī beneficī memoriā possim. (*A.* IX, 11A)

[1] *loyal* (to Pompey)

---

[1] with **cūra**
[2] Cicero had not yet joined Pompey.
[3] A law had been passed permitting Caesar to run for the consulship while still in Gaul.
[4] by not forcing Cicero to choose sides between Caesar and Pompey
[5] a conservative politically, siding with the senate

# TULLIA'S ILLNESS

In maximīs meīs dolōribus excruciat[1] mē valētūdō Tulliae nostrae, dē quā nihil est quod ad tē plūra scrībam; tibi enim aequē magnae cūrae esse certō sciō. Quod[2] mē propius vultis accēdere, videō ita esse faciendum; etiam ante fēcissem, sed mē multa impedīvērunt, quae nē nunc quidem expedīta sunt. Sed ā Pompōniō$_1$ exspectō litterās, quās ad mē quam prīmum perferendās cūrēs velim. Dā operam ut valeās. (*F*. XIV, 19)

[1] *tortures*

[2] *as to the fact that*

$_1$ Atticus, who would send his letters to Cicero at Rome, where Terentia was

# TULLIA HAS ARRIVED

S. v. b. E. v.$_1$ Tullia nostra vēnit ad mē pr.[1] Īdūs Iūn. Cuius summā virtūte et singulārī hūmānitāte graviōre etiam sum dolōre affectus nostrā factum esse neglegentiā, ut longē aliā[2] in fortūnā esset atque[2] eius pietās[3] ac dignitās postulābat. Nōbīs erat in animō Cicerōnem$_2$ ad Caesarem mittere, et cum eō Cn. Sallustium$_3$. Sī profectus erit, faciam tē certiōrem. Valētūdinem tuam cūrā dīligenter. Valē. XVII Kal. Quīnctīlīs. (*F*. XIV, 11)

[1] = **prīdiē**

[2] *different than*

[3] *devotion* (to her family)

$_1$ **Sī valēs benest** (for **bene est**). **Ego valeō.** A very formal old-fashioned formula, which confirms that he and Terentia were not getting along well. They were divorced soon after.

$_2$ Cicero's son

$_3$ not the historian Sallust

# HAVE EVERYTHING READY

In Tusculānum[1] nōs ventūrōs putāmus aut Nōnīs aut postrīdiē. Ibi ut$_1$ sint omnia parāta. Plūrēs enim fortasse nōbīscum erunt et, ut arbitror, diūtius ibi commorābimur.$_2$ Lābrum[2] sī in balineō nōn est, ut$_1$ sit; item cētera quae sunt ad vīctum et ad valētūdinem necessāria. Valē. Kal. Oct. dē Venusīnō[3]. (*F*. XIV, 20)

[1] *country home at Tusculum* (not far from Rome)

[2] *tub*

[3] *country home at Venusia*

$_1$ The **ut** clause depends on a verb such as **cūrā** to be supplied.

$_2$ This is rather casual, perhaps intended to infuriate Terentia: How many guests? How long will they stay? When will they arrive?

# MY DAY

Haec igitur est nunc vīta nostra: māne salūtāmus$_{1}$ domī et bonōs$_{2}$ virōs multōs, sed trīstīs, et hōs laetōs victōrēs, quī mē quidem perofficiōsē et peramanter observant. Ubi salūtātiō dēflūxit[1],$_{3}$ litterīs mē involvō: aut scrībō aut legō. Veniunt etiam quī mē audiunt quasi doctum hominem, quia paulō sum quam ipsī doctior. Inde corporī omne tempus datur. Patriam ēlūxī[2] iam et gravius et diūtius quam ūlla māter ūnicum fīlium. Sed cūrā, sī mē amās, ut valeās, nē ego, tē iacente,[3] bona tua comedim$_{4}$; statuī enim tibi nē aegrōtō quidem parcere. (*F*. IX, 20, 3)

[1] *is ended*
[2] *I have mourned for* (from **ēlūgeō**)
[3] *while you lie ill*

---

$_{1}$ at the morning **salūtātiō** (reception)
$_{2}$ in the usual sense of *conservatives*
$_{3}$ The metaphor is a good one, for the visitors seem to *flow away*.
$_{4}$ an old form for **comedam:** *eat up*

# ONLY SOLITUDE BRINGS COMFORT

Tē, tuīs negōtiīs relīctīs, nōlō ad mē venīre. Ego potius accēdam, sī diūtius impediēre; etsī nē discessissem quidem ē cōnspectū tuō, nisi mē plānē nihil ūlla rēs adiuvāret. Quod sī esset aliquod levāmen, id esset in tē ūnō, et cum prīmum ab aliquō poterit esse, ā tē erit. Nunc tamen ipsum[1] sine tē esse nōn possum. Sed nec tuae domī probābātur[2] nec meae poteram$_{1}$, nec, sī propius essem uspiam, tēcum tamen essem; idem enim tē impedīret quō minus mēcum essēs quod nunc etiam impedit. Mihi adhūc nihil prius[3] fuit hāc sōlitūdine, quam vereor nē Philippus$_{2}$ tollat; herī enim vesperī vēnerat.$_{3}$ Mē scrīptiō[4] et litterae[4] nōn lēniunt, sed obturbant. (*A*. XII, 16)

[1] *at this very time* (literally, *now itself*)
[2] *I did not like it* (literally, *it was not approved [by me]*)
[3] *preferable, better*
[4] *literary writing*

---

$_{1}$ Supply **esse.**
$_{2}$ a neighbor
$_{3}$ i.e., he arrived at his own villa from Rome

# MOTHER-IN-LAW TROUBLE AND A BOY IN COLLEGE

Haec ad tē meā manū.$_{1}$ Vidē, quaesō, quid agendum sit. Pūblilia ad mē scrīpsit mātrem suam—ut cum Pūbliliō loquerer$_{2}$—ad mē cum illō ventūram et sē ūnā[1], sī ego paterer. Ōrat multīs et supplicibus verbīs ut liceat et ut sibi rescrībam. Rēs quam molesta sit vidēs. Rescrīpsī mihi etiam gravius esse quam tum cum illī dīxissem mē sōlum esse velle; quārē nōlle mē hōc tempore eam ad mē venīre. Putābam, sī nihil rescrīpsissem, illam cum mātre ventūram, nunc nōn putō; appārēbat enim illās litterās nōn illīus esse.$_{3}$ Illud autem quod fore videō ipsum volō vītāre, nē illae ad mē veniant. Et ūna est vītātiō, ut aliō:[2] nōllem[3], sed necesse est. Tē hoc nunc rogō ut explōrēs ad quam diem hīc ita possim esse ut nē opprimar. Agēs, ut scrībis, temperāte.

Cicerōnī$_{4}$ velim hoc prōpōnās, ita[4] tamen sī[4] tibi nōn inīquum vidēbitur, ut sūmptūs$_{5}$ huius peregrīnātiōnis, quibus$_{6}$, sī Rōmae esset domumque condūceret, quod facere cōgitābat, facile contentus futūrus erat, accommodet ad mercēdēs Argilētī et Aventīnī et, cum eī prōposueris, ipse velim reliqua moderēre, quemadmodum ex iīs mercēdibus suppeditēmus eī quod opus sit. Praestābō nec Bibulum nec Acidīnum nec Messallam,$_{7}$ quōs Athēnīs futūrōs audiō, maiōrēs sūmptūs factūrōs quam quod ex iīs mercēdibus recipiētur. Itaque velim videās, prīmum, conductōrēs[5] quī sint et quantī[6], deinde, ut sint quī ad diem[7] solvant, et quid viāticī, quid īnstrūmentī satis sit. Iūmentō[8] certē Athēnīs nihil opus erit; quibus autem in viā ūtātur, domī sunt plūra quam opus erit, quod etiam tū animadvertis. (*A.* XII, 32)

[1] *along (with them)*
[2] *that I go elsewhere* (Supply **discēdam.**)
[3] *I could wish not*
[4] *only if*
[5] *renters* (of Cicero's apartments)
[6] *at what price*
[7] *on the day (due)*
[8] *horses* (for carrying baggage)

---

$_{1}$ This implies that many of his letters were dictated to a secretary. This one was confidential.
$_{2}$ Cicero is so excited that he is incoherent; he should have said that the mother *and brother* were coming.
$_{3}$ i.e., the letter was written by the mother in Publilia's name
$_{4}$ young Cicero
$_{5}$ object of **accommodet**
$_{6}$ The antecedent is **mercēdēs.**
$_{7}$ rich fellow students, of the best families in Rome

# WHAT A FATHER LIKES TO HEAR[1]

Athēnās vēnī a. d. XI Kal. Iūn. atque ibi, quod maximē optābam, vīdī fīlium tuum dēditum optimīs studiīs summāque modestiae fāmā.[1] Quā ex rē quantam voluptātem cēperim scīre poteris, etiam mē tacente; nōn enim nescīs quantī tē faciam[2] et quam prō[3] nostrō veterrimō vērissimōque amōre omnibus tuīs etiam minimīs commodīs, nōn modo tantō bonō[4] gaudeam. Nōlī putāre, mī Cicerō, mē hoc auribus tuīs dare;[5] nihil adulēscente[2] tuō atque adeō[6] nostrō (nihil enim mihi ā tē potest esse sēiūnctum) aut amābilius omnibus iīs[7] quī Athēnīs sunt est aut studiōsius eārum artium quās tū maximē amās, hoc est optimārum. Itaque tibi, quod vērē facere possum, libenter quoque grātulor nec minus etiam nōbīs, quod eum, quem necesse erat dīligere quāliscumque esset, tālem habēmus ut libenter quoque dīligāmus.

Quī cum mihi in sermōne iniēcisset[8] sē velle Asiam vīsere, nōn modo invītātus, sed etiam rogātus est ā mē ut id, potissimum nōbīs obtinentibus prōvinciam,[3] faceret; cui nōs et cāritāte et amōre tuum officium praestātūrōs[9] nōn dēbēs dubitāre. Illud quoque erit nōbīs cūrae, ut Cratippus[4] ūnā cum eō sit, nē putēs in Asiā fēriātum[10] illum ab iīs studiīs in quae tuā cohortātiōne incitātur futūrum; nam illum parātum, ut videō, et ingressum plēnō gradū[11] cohortārī nōn intermittēmus, quō[12] in diēs longius discendō exercendōque sē prōcēdat. (*F*. XII, 16, 1–2)

[1] *and with the highest reputation for proper behavior*
[2] *how highly I value you*
[3] *on account of*
[4] *such a blessing* (as having such a son)
[5] *that I am flattering you* (literally, *[just] giving this to your ears*)
[6] *in fact*
[7] *to those*
[8] *brought into the conversation* (i.e., *hinted*)
[9] *perform your function* (as a father)
[10] *on vacation from* (with **illum**)
[11] *at a run* (literally, *with full step*)
[12] = **ut**

---

[1] written *by* Trebonius *to* Cicero, May, 55 B.C.
[2] with **amābilius**
[3] Trebonius stopped in Athens on his way to his province in Asia Minor.
[4] The young man's philosophy teacher. Of course it was the young Cicero's suggestion that Cratippus come along.

# YOUNG CICERO PUTS ON THE CHARM[1]

**Verba Ūtilia:** amplector, cōnspectus, cotīdiānus, cumulus, dulcis, ēnītor, in diēs, praedium, rūmor, suspīciō

Cum vehementer tabellāriōs exspectārem cotīdiē, aliquandō vēnērunt post diem quadrāgēsimum et sextum quam[2] ā vōbīs discesserant. Quōrum mihi fuit adventus exoptātissimus; nam cum maximam cēpissem laetitiam ex hūmānissimī et cārissimī patris epistulā, tum vērō iūcundissimae tuae litterae cumulum mihi gaudī attulērunt.

---

[1] young Cicero to Tiro, July–October, 44 B.C.
[2] with **post**

Grātōs tibi optātōsque esse quī dē mē rūmōrēs afferuntur nōn dubitō, mī dulcissime Tīrō, praestābōque et ēnītar ut in diēs magis magisque haec nāscēns dē mē duplicētur opīniō. Quārē, quod pollicēris tē būcinātōrem[1] fore exīstimātiōnis meae, firmō id cōnstantīque animō faciās licet; tantum enim mihi dolōrem cruciātumque attulērunt errāta aetātis meae ut nōn sōlum animus ā factīs, sed aurēs quoque ā commemorātiōne abhorreant. Quoniam igitur tum ex mē doluistī, nunc ut duplicētur tuum ex mē gaudium praestābō. Cratippō mē scītō[2] nōn ut discipulum sed ut fīlium esse coniūnctissimum; nam cum audiō illum libenter, tum etiam propriam eius suāvitātem vehementer amplector. Sum tōtōs diēs cum eō noctisque saepenumerō[3] partem; exōrō enim ut mēcum quam saepissimē cēnet. Hāc intrōductā cōnsuētūdine, saepe īnscientibus nōbīs et cēnantibus obrēpit, sublātāque sevēritāte philosophiae, hūmānissimē nōbīscum iocātur. Quārē dā operam ut hunc tālem, tam iūcundum, tam excellentem virum videās quam prīmum. Nam quid ego dē Bruttiō dīcam? Huic ego locum in proximō[4] condūxī et, ut possum, ex meīs angustiīs[5] illīus sustentō tenuitātem. Praetereā dēclāmitāre Graecē apud Cassium īnstituī; Latīnē autem apud Bruttium exercērī volō.

Dē Gorgiā autem quod mihi scrībis, erat quidem ille in cotīdiānā dēclāmātiōne ūtilis, sed omnia postposuī dum modo praeceptīs patris pārērem,[3] διαρρήδην[6] enim scrīpserat ut eum dīmitterem statim. Tergiversārī[7] nōluī, nē mea nimia σπουδή[8] suspīciōnem eī[4] aliquam importāret. Deinde illud etiam mihi succurrēbat, grave esse mē dē iūdiciō patris iūdicāre. Tuum tamen studium et cōnsilium grātum acceptumque est mihi. Excūsātiōnem angustiārum[9] tuī temporis accipiō; sciō enim quam soleās esse occupātus.

Ēmisse tē praedium vehementer gaudeō, fēlīciterque tibi rem istam ēvenīre cupiō. Rūsticus Rōmānus factus es. Quō modō ego mihi nunc ante oculōs tuum iūcundissimum cōnspectum prōpōnō? Videor enim vidēre ementem tē rūsticās rēs, cum vīlicō loquentem, in laciniā[10] servantem ex mēnsā secundā[11] sēmina.

De mandātīs, quod tibi cūrae fuit, est mihi grātum; sed petō ā tē ut quam celerrimē mihi librārius[12][5] mittātur, maximē quidem Graecus; multum mihi enim ēripitur operae in exscrībendīs hypomnēmatīs.[13] (*F.* XVI, 21, 1–4, 6–8)

[1] *trumpeter* (Tiro will blow Cicero's horn for him.)
[2] *know* (imperative)
[3] = **saepe**
[4] *nearby*
[5] *slender means* (anything but true)
[6] **diarreden,** *definitely*
[7] *be evasive*
[8] **spoude,** *zeal* (for Gorgias)
[9] *restriction*
[10] *in a fold* (of your tunic)
[11] *dessert*
[12] *secretary* (to copy his notes)
[13] *notes*

---

[3] Cicero had ordered his son to dismiss Gorgias for his bad influence.
[4] the father, who might get the idea that his son really liked Gorgias
[5] "The poor boy," Tiro may have said, "has to copy his own notes."

UNIT
VIII

Scala/Art Resource, NY

# CICERO'S PHILOSOPHICAL WORKS

## Unit Objectives

- To read Cicero's philosophical writings with understanding and appreciation
- To learn new vocabulary in context

**The Acropolis of Athens sits atop the highest point in the city. Its beauty and majesty probably provided much inspiration to the early Greek philosophers. The Romans borrowed much of their philosophy from the Greeks. There were several schools of Greek philosophy, the best known of which were Stoicism and Epicureanism. Western philosophy actually began in Greece with Thales of Miletus. His two best-known students were Anaximander and Anaximenes. They sought an element or force behind things that would explain everything. Thales believed this element was water, Anaximander thought it was the infinite, and Anaximenes said it was air. Socrates of Athens was more concerned with values, morals, and how a person should act—the right way of life. Plato was a disciple of Socrates and founder of the Academy. He developed the first comprehensive philosophical system. Aristotle was a pupil of Plato but broke with him. He stressed the importance of explaining the changing world in which people live.**

Enrichment

How different do you and your class think Roman society or the history of the Western world would have been if Cicero had not written his philosophical works? What if he had not written them in an accessible style? Is there a difficult subject that you know a great deal about? See if you can write a paragraph that makes that subject easy to understand for those who know little or nothing about it. Then see if you can write it in Latin. Share your paragraphs with fellow students to see if you are achieving your aim.

# INTRODUCING CICERO'S PHILOSOPHICAL WORKS

Perhaps the word *philosophy* suggests to you something obscure and formidable. Sometimes it is just that; for example, the philosophy of the ancient Greek Zeno. But it is not frightening in the form in which Cicero offered it. He presented Greek philosophy in a popular way to his Latin-speaking audience.

It is difficult to describe the nature and boundaries of the study of philosophy, especially since philosophers themselves have not always agreed on this point. However, we can say that over the centuries many philosophers have wrestled with some of the same questions, among them: What is truth? What is beauty? How should we act to achieve happiness?

Ethics, the branch of philosophy dealing with this last type of question, was particularly attractive to the practical Romans, who were interested in such considerations as the relationship of conduct to the good life, or happiness. And so Cicero's *Dē officiīs,* "On Duties," written for his son, a student in Athens, had great appeal (but probably not for its chief target). As is apparent from letters of this period, young Cicero needed something of this sort, though there is no indication that he profited by it.

The *Dē senectūte,* "On Old Age," is put in the form of a dialogue between Cato the Elder and two young men. Cato is chosen because he is a good example of a man who remained vigorous in old age. The essay denies that old age is something undesirable and stresses its positive advantages.

The *Dē amīcitiā,* "On Friendship," is also in dialogue form. Both treatises are dedicated to Cicero's old friend Atticus; you have already read some of Cicero's letters to him.

We are indebted to Cicero the philosopher chiefly because he made the glories of Greek thought available and palatable to his fellow Romans and to later ages, and since Latin in Cicero's time had few words for Greek philosophical concepts, he had to and did create them. The influence of Cicero's Latin philosophical vocabulary is felt even in modern times.

# JUSTICE

Sed cum statuissem scrībere ad tē$_1$ aliquid hōc tempore, multa posthāc, ab eō ōrdīrī maximē voluī quod et aetātī tuae esset[1] aptissimum et auctōritātī meae. Nam cum[2] multa sint in philosophiā et gravia et ūtilia accūrātē cōpiōsēque ā philosophīs disputāta, lātissimē patēre[3] videntur ea quae dē officiīs trādita ab illīs et praecepta sunt. Nūlla enim vītae pars neque pūblicīs neque prīvātīs, neque forēnsibus neque domesticīs in rēbus, neque sī tēcum agās quid[4] neque sī cum alterō contrahās, vacāre officiō[5] potest, in eōque$_2$ et colendō sita vītae est honestās[6] omnis et neglegendō turpitūdō.

Sed iūstitiae prīmum mūnus est ut nē cui quis noceat nisi lacessītus iniūriā, deinde ut commūnibus prō[7] commūnibus ūtātur, prīvātīs ut suīs. Sunt autem prīvāta nūlla nātūrā, sed aut vetere occupātiōne, ut quī quondam in vacua[8] vēnērunt, aut victōriā, ut quī bellō potītī sunt, aut lēge$_3$, pactiōne[9], condiciōne[9], sorte[9]; ex quō fit ut ager Arpīnās Arpīnātium[10] dīcātur, Tusculānus Tusculānōrum, similisque est prīvātārum possessiōnum discrīptiō[11]. Ex quō, quia suum[12] cuiusque fit eōrum quae nātūrā fuerant commūnia,[12] quod cuique obtigit, id quisque teneat; eō plūs[13] sī quis sibi appetet, violābit iūs hūmānae societātis.

Fundāmentum autem est iūstitiae fidēs, id est dictōrum[14] conventōrumque cōnstantia et vēritās.[14]

Meminerīmus autem etiam adversus[15] īnfimōs iūstitiam esse servandam. Est autem īnfima condiciō et fortūna servōrum, quibus[16] nōn male praecipiunt quī ita iubent ūtī ut mercennāriīs[17]: operam exigendam, iūsta praebenda[18]. Cum autem duōbus modīs, id est aut vī aut fraude, fīat iniūria, fraus quasi vulpēculae[19], vīs leōnis vidētur: utrumque homine aliēnissimum$_4$, sed fraus odiō digna maiōre. Tōtīus autem iniūstitiae nūlla capitālior[20] est quam eōrum$_5$ quī tum cum maximē fallunt id agunt ut virī bonī esse videantur. Dē iūstitiā satis dictum. (*Off.* I, 4, 20, 23, 41)

[1] *would be*
[2] *although*
[3] *to have the widest practical application* (literally, *to spread most widely*)
[4] *if you are dealing with something by yourself*
[5] *be free from duty*
[6] *all that is honorable*
[7] *as*
[8] *unoccupied (lands)*
[9] *agreement, terms* (of purchase), or *allotment*
[10] *to belong to the people of Arpinum*
[11] *assignment*
[12] *of those things which had been common (property) (part) becomes the property of an individual*
[13] *more than that*
[14] *truthfully abiding by things promised and agreed upon*
[15] *toward (preposition)*
[16] *to use whom* (with **ūtī**)
[17] *hired men*
[18] *necessities to be furnished*
[19] *fox*
[20] *more deserving of capital punishment*

---

$_1$ Cicero's son
$_2$ for **inque eō**, but **–que** is not attached to monosyllabic prepositions
$_3$ such as laws giving public land to veterans
$_4$ We say *alien to* rather than *from.*
$_5$ i.e., hypocrites

# SENSE OF DUTY

Sed sī contentiō quaedam et comparātiō fīat quibus plūrimum tribuendum sit officī, prīncipēs sint patria et parentēs, quōrum beneficiīs[1] maximīs obligātī sumus, proximī līberī tōtaque domus, quae spectat[2] in nōs sōlōs neque aliud ūllum potest habēre perfugium, deinceps bene convenientēs[3] propinquī, quibuscum commūnis etiam fortūna plērumque est. (*Off.* I, 58)

[1] *services*
[2] *looks to us* (for help)
[3] *friendly*

# CIVIC COURAGE

Illud autem optimum est, in quod invādī[1] solēre ab improbīs et invidīs audiō:

Cēdant arma togae, concēdat laurea laudī.[2]

Ut enim aliōs omittam[3], nōbīs rem pūblicam gubernantibus, nōnne togae arma cessērunt? Neque enim perīculum in rē pūblicā fuit gravius umquam nec maius ōtium[4]. Ita cōnsiliīs dīligentiāque nostrā celeriter dē manibus audācissimōrum cīvium dēlāpsa arma ipsa cecidērunt. Quae rēs igitur gesta umquam in bellō tanta? Quī triumphus cōnferendus?

Licet enim mihi, M. fīlī, apud tē glōriārī, ad quem et hērēditās huius glōriae et factōrum imitātiō pertinet. Mihi quidem certē vir abundāns bellicīs laudibus, Cn. Pompeius, multīs audientibus, hoc tribuit, ut dīceret frūstrā sē triumphum tertium dēportātūrum fuisse[5] nisi meō in rem pūblicam beneficiō ubi[6] triumphāret esset habitūrus. Sunt igitur domesticae fortitūdinēs[7] nōn īnferiōrēs mīlitāribus; in quibus plūs etiam quam in hīs operae studīque pōnendum est. (*Off.* I, 77–78)

[1] *attack is made*
[2] *Let arms yield to the toga* (worn by civilians); *let the laurel wreath* (of the general) *yield to* (civilian) *glory.*
[3] *to omit*
[4] *peace*
[5] *he would have gained*
[6] *(a place) where*
[7] *civic courage*

# CHOICE OF A CAREER

Cōnstituendum est quōs nōs et quālēs esse velīmus et in quō genere[1] vītae; quae dēlīberātiō est omnium difficillima. Ineunte enim adulēscentiā,[2] cum est maxima imbecillitās cōnsilī[3], tum id sibi quisque genus aetātis dēgendae cōnstituit quod maximē adamāvit. Itaque ante[1] implicātur aliquō certō genere cursūque vīvendī quam potuit quod optimum esset iūdicāre. Plērumque autem parentium praeceptīs imbūtī ad eōrum cōnsuētūdinem mōremque[4] dēdūcimur. Aliī multitūdinis iūdiciō feruntur[5], quaeque maiōrī partī pulcherrima videntur, ea maximē exoptant; nōn nūllī tamen sīve fēlīcitāte quādam[6] sīve bonitāte nātūrae sine parentium disciplīnā rēctam vītae secūtī sunt viam. Illud autem maximē rārum genus est eōrum quī aut excellentī ingenī magnitūdine aut praeclārā ērudītiōne atque doctrīnā aut utrāque rē ōrnātī spatium etiam dēlīberandī habuērunt quem potissimum vītae cursum sequī vellent; in quā dēlīberātiōne ad suam cuiusque nātūram cōnsilium est omne revocandum.[7] (*Off.* I, 117–119)

[1] *career*
[2] *at the beginning of youth*
[3] *judgment*
[4] *their* (the parents') *customs and manners*
[5] *are carried away*
[6] *by a sort of good luck*
[7] *the judgment must be based on each person's nature* (literally, *must be called back to*)

[1] with **quam**

# PERSONAL APPEARANCE

Cum autem pulchritūdinis duo genera sint, quōrum in alterō venustās[1] sit, in alterō dignitās, venustātem muliebrem dūcere[2] dēbēmus, dignitātem virīlem. Ergō et ā fōrmā removeātur omnis virō nōn dignus ōrnātus[3] et huic simile vitium in gestū mōtūque caveātur. Nam et palaestricī mōtūs[4] sunt saepe odiōsiōrēs et histriōnum nōn nūllī gestūs[5] ineptiīs[6] nōn vacant et in utrōque genere quae sunt rēcta et simplicia laudantur. Fōrmae autem dignitās colōris[7] bonitāte tuenda est, color exercitātiōnibus corporis. Adhibenda praetereā munditia est nōn odiōsa neque exquīsīta nimis, tantum[8] quae fugiat agrestem et inhūmānam neglegentiam. Eadem ratiō est habenda vestītūs, in quō, sīcut in plērīsque rēbus, mediocritās optima est. (*Off.* I, 130)

[1] *loveliness*
[2] *consider*
[3] *every adornment not becoming to a man*
[4] *the movements (taught in the) gymnasium*
[5] *some gestures of actors*
[6] *affectation*
[7] *complexion*
[8] *only enough to avoid*

# HONORABLE CAREERS FOR GENTLEMEN

Iam dē artificiīs et quaestibus,[1] quī līberālēs habendī, quī sordidī sint, haec ferē accēpimus. Prīmum improbantur iī quaestūs quī in odia hominum incurrunt, ut portītōrum, ut faenerātōrum.[2] Illīberālēs autem et sordidī quaestūs mercennāriōrum omnium, quōrum operae[3], nōn quōrum artēs emuntur; est enim in illīs ipsa mercēs auctōrāmentum[4] servitūtis. Sordidī etiam putandī quī mercentur ā mercātōribus quod statim vēndant;$_{1}$ nihil enim prōficiant nisi admodum mentiantur, nec vērō est quicquam turpius vānitāte[5]. Opificēsque omnēs in sordidā arte versantur; nec enim quicquam ingenuum potest habēre officīna. Minimēque artēs eae probandae quae ministrae sunt voluptātum:

Cētāriī, laniī, coquī, fartōrēs, piscātōrēs,[6]$_{2}$

ut ait Terentius. Adde hūc, sī placet, unguentāriōs, saltātōrēs, tōtumque lūdum tālārium.[7] In quibus autem artibus aut prūdentia maior inest aut nōn mediocris ūtilitās quaeritur, ut medicīna, ut architectūra, ut doctrīna rērum honestārum,[8] hae sunt eīs quōrum ōrdinī conveniunt honestae.[9] Mercātūra autem, sī tenuis est, sordida putanda est; sīn magna et cōpiōsa, multa undique apportāns[10] multīsque sine vānitāte impertiēns,[11] nōn est admodum vituperanda, atque etiam sī satiāta$_{3}$ quaestū vel contenta potius, ut saepe ex altō in portum, ex ipsō portū sē in agrōs possessiōnēsque contulit,[12] vidētur iūre optimō posse laudārī. Omnium autem rērum ex quibus aliquid acquīritur, nihil est agrī cultūrā melius, nihil dulcius, nihil ūberius, nihil homine līberō dignius; dē quā quoniam in Catōne maiōre satis multa dīximus, illinc assūmēs quae ad hunc locum pertinēbunt. (*Off.* I, 150–151)

[1] *trades and gainful occupations*
[2] *tax collectors and usurers*
[3] *manual labor*
[4] *contract*
[5] *fraud*
[6] *fishsellers, butchers, cooks, sausage makers, fishermen*
[7] *burlesque show*
[8] *the teaching of worthy subjects*
[9] *these are honorable for those whose social status they suit*
[10] *importing*
[11] *distributing to many without fraud*
[12] *as they often made their way from the high seas to the harbor, so they made their way from the harbor to the possession of farms*

---

$_{1}$ i.e., retailers
$_{2}$ quoted from Terence, writer of comedy
$_{3}$ modifies **mercātūra** but actually refers to those engaged in business

# KNOWLEDGE AND COURAGE AND THEIR VALUE IN SOCIETY

Atque ut apium exāmina[1] nōn fingendōrum favōrum[2] causā congregantur, sed, cum congregābilia nātūrā sint, fingunt favōs, sīc hominēs (ac multō etiam magis nātūrā congregātī) adhibent agendī cōgitandīque$_1$ sollertiam. Itaque nisi ea virtūs$_2$ quae cōnstat ex hominibus tuendīs, id est ex societāte generis hūmānī, attingat[3] cognitiōnem rērum, sōlivaga[4] cognitiō et iēiūna videātur, itemque magnitūdō animī[5], remōtā commūnitāte coniūnctiōneque hūmānā,[6] feritās sit quaedam et immānitās. Ita fit ut vincat cognitiōnis studium cōnsociātiō hominum atque commūnitās.[7] Nec vērum est quod dīcitur ā quibusdam, propter necessitātem vītae,$_3$ quod ea quae nātūra dēsīderāret cōnsequī sine aliīs atque efficere nōn possēmus, idcircō initam esse cum hominibus commūnitātem et societātem; quod sī omnia nōbīs quae ad vīctum cultumque pertinent, quasi virgulā[8] dīvīnā, ut aiunt, suppeditārentur, tum optimō quisque ingeniō, negōtiīs omnibus omissīs, tōtum sē in cognitiōne et scientiā collocāret. Nōn est ita. Nam et sōlitūdinem fugeret et socium studī quaereret, tum docēre, tum discere vellet, tum audīre, tum dīcere. Ergō omne officium quod ad coniūnctiōnem hominum et ad societātem tuendam valet antepōnendum est illī officiō quod cognitiōne et scientiā continētur. (*Off.* I, 157–158)

[1] *swarms of bees*
[2] *honeycombs*
[3] *is attached to*
[4] *solitary*
[5] *courage*
[6] *if a social attitude is left out* (literally, *is removed*)
[7] *social needs take precedence over the pursuit of knowledge (by an individual)*
[8] *wand*

---

$_1$ i.e., together with others
$_2$ i.e., justice
$_3$ In translating, put the last part of the sentence (from **idcircō**) next, then the **quod** clause: *it is not true that social life began on account of the need of obtaining food, because* etc.

# HONOR AMONG THIEVES

Atque eīs etiam quī vēndunt, emunt, condūcunt, locant, contrahendīsque negōtiīs implicantur, iūstitia ad rem gerendam necessāria est, cuius tanta vīs est ut nē illī quidem quī maleficiō et scelere pāscuntur[1] possint sine ūllā particulā iūstitiae vīvere. Nam quī eōrum cuipiam[2] quī ūnā[3] latrōcinantur

[1] *live by crime*
[2] *from any of those who*
[3] *with him*

fūrātur aliquid aut ēripit, is sibi nē in latrōciniō quidem relinquit locum;[1] ille autem qui archipīrāta dīcitur, nisi aequābiliter praedam dispertiat, aut interficiātur ā sociīs aut relinquātur. Quīn etiam lēgēs latrōnum esse dīcuntur, quibus pāreant, quās observent. Itaque propter aequābilem praedae partītiōnem et Bardūlis Illyrius latrō, dē quō est apud Theopompum, magnās opēs habuit et multō maiōrēs Viriāthus Lūsitānus, cui quidem etiam exercitūs nostrī imperātōrēsque cessērunt, quem C. Laelius, is quī Sapiēns ūsūrpātur,[4] praetor frēgit et comminuit ferōcitātemque eius ita repressit ut facile bellum reliquīs trāderet. Cum igitur tanta vīs iūstitiae sit ut ea etiam latrōnum opēs firmet atque augeat, quantam eius vim inter lēgēs et iūdicia et in cōnstitūtā rē pūblicā fore putāmus? (*Off.* II, 40)

[4] *uses (the name of) the Wise*

[1] i.e., he loses his place in the gang of robbers (**latrōciniō**)

# THE RESPONSIBILITY OF WEALTH

Id quidem nōn dubium est, quīn[1] illa benignitās quae cōnstet ex operā[2] et industriā et honestior sit et lātius pateat[3] et possit prōdesse plūribus; nōn numquam tamen est largiendum,[4] nec hoc benignitātis genus omnīnō repudiandum est et saepe idōneīs hominibus indigentibus dē rē familiārī[5] impertiendum, sed dīligenter atque moderātē. Multī enim patrimōnia effūdērunt incōnsultē largiendō.

Atque etiam illae impēnsae meliōrēs, mūrī, nāvālia[6], portūs, aquārum ductūs omniaque quae ad ūsum reī pūblicae pertinent. Quamquam quod praesēns tamquam in manum[7] datur iūcundius est; tamen haec in posterum grātiōra. Theātra, porticūs, nova templa verēcundius[8] reprehendō propter Pompeium. Tōta igitur ratiō tālium[1] largītiōnum genere[9] vitiōsa est, temporibus[10] necessāria, et tum ipsum[11] et ad facultātēs accommodanda et mediocritāte moderanda est. In illō autem alterō genere largiendī[2], quod ā līberālitāte proficīscitur, nōn ūnō modō in disparibus causīs affectī esse dēbēmus. Alia causa est eius quī calamitāte premitur et eius quī rēs meliōrēs quaerit, nūllīs suīs rēbus adversīs.[12] Prōpēnsior benignitās esse dēbēbit in calamitōsōs, nisi forte erunt dignī calamitāte. (*Off.* II, 54, 60, 61)

[1] *that*
[2] *service*
[3] *covers more ground*
[4] *money should be given*
[5] *from one's resources*
[6] *docks*
[7] *cash in hand, so to speak* (as presents to individuals)
[8] *with more restraint*
[9] *in nature, essentially*
[10] *(but) necessary in (certain) circumstances*
[11] *even then* (literally, *then itself*)
[12] *though none of his affairs is in bad shape*

[1] i.e., of such large amounts
[2] i.e., to individuals

# Transmission of Latin and Greek Works Before Printing: 2

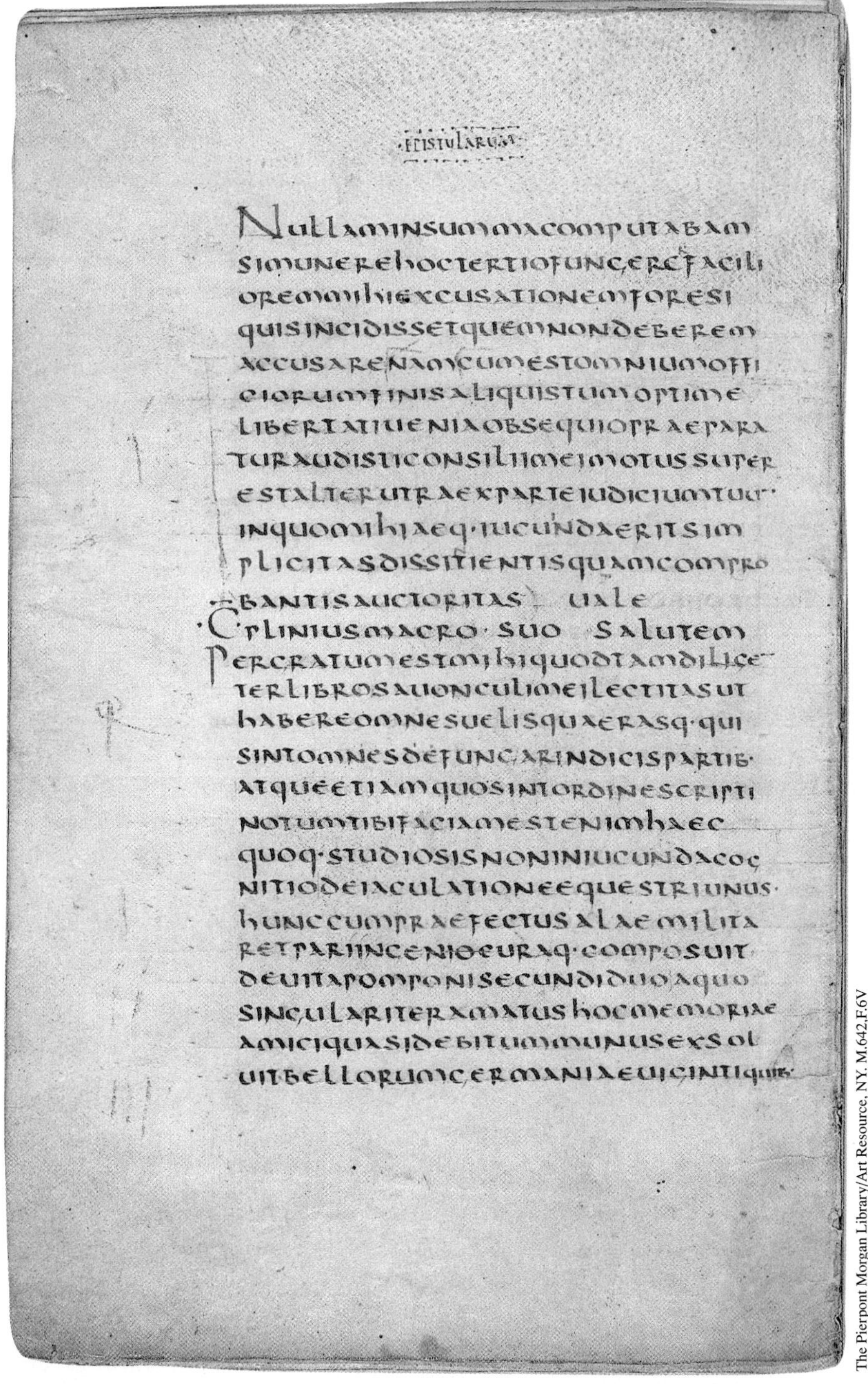
EPISTULARUM

NULLAMINSUMMACOMPUTABAM
SIMULNEREHOCTERTIOFUNGERERFACILI
OREMMIHIEXCUSATIONEMFORESI
QUISINCIDISSETQUEMNONDEBEREM
ACCUSARENAMCUMESTOMNIUMOFFI
CIORUMFINISALIQUISTUMOPTIME
LIBERTATIUENIAOBSEQUIOPRAEPARA
TURAUDISTICONSILIIMEIMOTUSSUPER
ESTALTERUTRAEXPARTEIUDICIUMTUU
INQUOMIHIAEQ·IUCUNDAERITSIM
PLICITASDISSENTIENTISQUAMCOMPRO
BANTISAUCTORITAS UALE
C·PLINIUSMACRO·SUO SALUTEM
PERGRATUMESTMIHIQUODTAMDILIGE
TERLIBROSAUONCULIMEILECTITASUT
HABEREOMNESUELISQUAERASQ·QUI
SINTOMNESDEFUNGARINDICISPARTIB·
ATQUEETIAMQUOSINTORDINESCRIPTI
NOTUMTIBIFACIAMESTENIMHAEC
QUOQ·STUDIOSISNONINIUCUNDACOG
NITIODEIACULATIONEEQUESTRIUNUS·
HUNCCUMPRAEFECTUSALAEMILITA
RETPARIINGENIOCURAQ·COMPOSUIT
DEUITAPOMPONISECUNDIDUOAQUO
SINGULARITERAMATUSHOCMEMORIAE
AMICIQUASIDEBITUMMUNUSEXSOL
UITBELLORUMGERMANIAEUIGINTIQUIB



This manuscript from the early sixth century is the oldest known copy of Pliny's letters. You can see the word **Epistulārum** at the very top. The first line reads **Nūllam in summā computābam.** What other words can you pick out? Notice that, like other ancient manuscripts, no spaces are left between words, and hyphens are not used at the end of a line. Pliny's name appears in red near the center. How can you tell—what words give you a clue—that the red line is the beginning of something new?

# CANCELLATION OF DEBTS

[1] *cancellation of debts*
[2] *what is their meaning*
[3] *a debt that would injure the state*
[4] *if there should be (a debt), (it should) not (happen) that*
[5] *profit (by) someone else's money*
[6] *holds together*
[7] *debts*
[8] *Never was there more violent agitation that (debts) be not paid than in any consulship.*
[9] *though no longer advantageous to him*

Tabulae vērō novae[1] quid habent argumentī,[2] nisi ut emās meā[1] pecūniā fundum, eum tū habeās, ego nōn habeam pecūniam? Quam ob rem nē sit aes aliēnum quod[3] reī pūblicae noceat, prōvidendum est; quod multīs ratiōnibus cavērī potest; nōn, sī fuerit, ut[4] locuplētēs suum perdant, dēbitōrēs lucrentur aliēnum.[5] Nec enim ūlla rēs vehementius rem pūblicam continet[6] quam fidēs, quae esse nūlla potest nisi erit necessāria solūtiō rērum crēditārum[7]. Numquam vehementius āctum est quam, mē cōnsule, nē solverētur.[8] Armīs et castrīs temptāta rēs est ab omnī genere hominum et ōrdine; quibus ita restitī ut hoc tōtum malum dē rē pūblicā tollerētur. Numquam nec maius aes aliēnum fuit nec melius nec[2] facilius dissolūtum est; fraudandī enim spē sublātā, solvendī necessitās cōnsecūta est. At vērō hic nunc victor, tum quidem victus, quae cōgitārat ea perfēcit, cum eius iam nihil interesset.[9] Tanta in eō peccandī libīdō fuit ut hoc ipsum eum dēlectāret, peccāre, etiam sī causa nōn esset. (*Off.* II, 84)

---

[1] i.e., that of the lender
[2] We would say *or*.

# THE ACTIVITIES OF OLD AGE

[1] *they are like (people) ... who say*
[2] *plotting evil*

Ā rēbus gerendīs senectūs abstrahit.[1] Quibus? An eīs quae iuventūte geruntur et vīribus? Nūllaene igitur rēs sunt senīlēs, quae, vel īnfirmīs corporibus, animō tamen administrentur?

Nihil igitur afferunt quī in rē gerendā versārī senectūtem negant, similēsque sunt ut sī quī gubernātōrem in nāvigandō nihil agere dīcant,[1] cum aliī mālōs scandant, aliī per forōs cursent, aliī sentīnam exhauriant, ille autem clāvum tenēns quiētus sedeat in puppī. Nōn facit ea quae iuvenēs, at vērō multō maiōra et meliōra facit. Nōn vīribus aut vēlōcitāte aut celeritāte corporum rēs magnae geruntur, sed cōnsiliō, auctōritāte, sententiā; quibus nōn modo nōn orbārī, sed etiam augērī senectūs solet. Nisi forte ego vōbīs, quī et mīles et tribūnus et lēgātus et cōnsul versātus sum in variō genere bellōrum, cessāre nunc videor cum bella nōn gerō. At senātuī quae sint gerenda praescrībō et quō modō; Carthāginī male iam diū cōgitantī[2] bellum multō ante dēnūntiō; dē quā verērī nōn ante dēsinam quam illam excīsam esse cognōverō. (*Sen.* 15, 17–18)

---

[1] This is the charge made by some people.

# A BUSY OLD AGE

Cedo[1], quī[2] vestram rem pūblicam tantam āmīsistis tam citō?

Sīc enim percontantur in Naevī poētae Lūdō; respondentur et alia et hoc in prīmīs:

Prōveniēbant ōrātōrēs novī, stultī adulēscentulī.

Temeritās est vidēlicet flōrentis aetātis, prūdentia senēscentis.

Possum nōmināre ex agrō Sabīnō rūsticōs Rōmānōs, vīcīnōs et familiārēs meōs, quibus absentibus, numquam ferē ūlla in agrō maiōra opera fīunt, nōn serendīs[3], nōn percipiendīs, nōn condendīs frūctibus. Quamquam in aliīs[4] minus hoc mīrum est; nēmō enim est tam senex quī sē annum[5] nōn putet posse vīvere; sed īdem in eīs ēlabōrant quae sciunt nihil ad sē omnīnō pertinēre:

Serīt arborēs quae alterī saeculō prōsint,
ut ait Stātius noster in Synephēbīs[6].

Vidētis ut[7] senectūs nōn modo languida atque iners nōn sit, vērum etiam sit operōsa et semper agēns aliquid et mōliēns, tāle scīlicet quāle cuiusque studium in superiōre vītā fuit. Quid quī[8] etiam addiscunt aliquid? Ut et[9] Solōnem versibus glōriantem vidēmus, quī sē cotīdiē aliquid addiscentem dīcit senem fierī, et[9] ego fēcī, quī litterās Graecās senex didicī; quās quidem sīc avidē arripuī (quasi diūturnam sitim explēre cupiēns) ut ea ipsa mihi nōta essent quibus mē nunc exemplīs[10] ūtī vidētis. Quod cum fēcisse Sōcratem in fidibus audīrem,[11] vellem[12] equidem etiam illud (discēbant enim fidibus[1] antīquī), sed in litterīs certē ēlabōrāvī. (*Sen.* 20, 24, 26)

[1] *Tell me*
[2] *how* (adverb)
[3] *at (the time of) sowing*
[4] *other things* (than the one which follows, about planting trees)
[5] *another year*
[6] *The Young Companions* (a play)
[7] *how*
[8] *What of those who*
[9] *not only . . . but also* (with the next **et**)
[10] *as examples*
[11] *when I heard that Socrates had done this* (i.e., learned in old age) *on the lyre*
[12] *I could have wished*

---

[1] Supply **canere,** *to play.*

# OCCUPATIONS IN OLD AGE

[1] *had produced a play* (literally, *he, as author, taught it [*to the actors*]*)

[2] *continued to live* (literally, *went on in life)*

[3] *account*

[4] *draft* (a demand for payment)

[5] *at times*

[6] *the natural forces of the earth*

[7] *took by surprise and put to death*

Quid in leviōribus studiīs, sed tamen acūtīs?[1] Quam gaudēbat bellō suō Pūnicō Naevius! Quam Truculentō Plautus, quam Pseudolō! Vīdī etiam senem Līvium; quī cum sex annīs ante quam ego nātus sum, fābulam docuisset,[1] Centōne Tuditānōque cōnsulibus,[2] usque ad adulēscentiam meam prōcessit aetāte.[2]

Veniō nunc ad voluptātēs agricolārum, quibus ego incrēdibiliter dēlector; quae nec ūllā impediuntur senectūte et mihi ad sapientis vītam proximē videntur accēdere. Habent enim ratiōnem[3] cum terrā, quae numquam recūsat imperium[4] nec umquam sine ūsūrā reddit quod accēpit, sed aliās[5] minōre, plērumque maiōre cum faenore. Quamquam mē quidem nōn frūctus modo, sed etiam ipsīus terrae vīs ac nātūra[6] dēlectat.

Sed veniō ad agricolās, nē ā mē ipsō recēdam. In agrīs erant[3] tum senātōrēs, id est senēs[4], siquidem arantī L. Quīnctiō Cincinnātō nūntiātum est eum dictātōrem esse factum; cuius dictātōris iussū magister equitum,[5] C. Servīlius Ahāla, Sp. Maelium rēgnum appetentem occupātum interēmit.[7] (*Sen.* 50, 51, 56)

---

[1] i.e., that demand keenness
[2] 240 B.C.
[3] i.e., they lived on farms
[4] **Senātor** is derived from **senex.**
[5] The *master of the horse* was the dictator's assistant.

# AUTHORITY, THE REWARD OF OLD AGE

[1] *that kind of old age which*

[2] *white hair* (Supply **capilli**.)

[3] *at the end* (literally, *last,* with **frūctūs**)

Sed in omnī ōrātiōne[1] mementōte eam mē senectūtem laudāre quae[1] fundāmentīs adulēscentiae cōnstitūta sit. Ex quō efficitur, id quod ego magnō quondam cum assēnsū omnium dīxī, miseram esse senectūtem quae sē ōrātiōne dēfenderet. Nōn cānī[2] nec rūgae repente auctōritātem arripere possunt, sed honestē ācta superior aetās frūctūs capit auctōritātis extrēmōs[3]. Haec enim ipsa sunt honōrābilia, quae videntur levia atque commūnia,

---

[1] Supply **meā.**

salūtārī[2], appetī, dēcēdī, assurgī, dēdūcī, redūcī,[4] cōnsulī; quae et apud nōs et in aliīs cīvitātibus, ut quaeque optimē mōrāta est,[5] ita dīligentissimē observantur. Lysandrum Lacedaemonium dīcere aiunt solitum Lacedaemonem esse honestissimum domicilium senectūtis; nusquam enim tantum tribuitur[6] aetātī, nusquam est senectūs honōrātior. Quīn etiam memoriae prōditum est, cum Athēnīs lūdīs[7] quīdam in theātrum grandis nātū[8] vēnisset, magnō consessū,[9] locum nusquam eī datum ā suīs cīvibus; cum autem ad Lacedaemoniōs accessisset, quī lēgātī cum essent,[10] certō[11] in locō cōnsēderant, cōnsurrēxisse omnēs illī dīcuntur et senem sessum[12] recēpisse. Quibus cum ā cūnctō cōnsessū plausus esset multiplex datus, dīxisse ex eīs quendam Athēniēnsēs scīre quae rēcta essent, sed facere nōlle. (*Sen.* 62–64)

[4] *that they escort us* (to the Forum) *and back* (home)
[5] *to the degree that each state has a high code of morals*
[6] *so much respect shown*
[7] *at the games*
[8] *old man* (literally, *great as to birth* [or age])
[9] *in the great crowd*
[10] *being ambassadors* (literally, *who, since they were ambassadors)*
[11] *fixed, reserved*
[12] *to sit down*

---

[2] In translating, it would be a good idea to use the active voice since two of the infinitives, **dēcēdī** and **assurgī,** are impersonal: *that people greet us,* etc.

# THE MEANING OF FRIENDSHIP

Est enim amīcitia nihil aliud nisi omnium dīvīnārum hūmānārumque rērum cum benevolentiā et cāritāte cōnsēnsiō; quā quidem haud sciō an,[1] exceptā sapientiā, nihil melius hominī sit ā dīs immortālibus datum. Dīvitiās aliī praepōnunt, bonam aliī valētūdinem, aliī potentiam, aliī honōrēs[2], multī etiam voluptātēs. Bēluārum hoc quidem extrēmum,[3] illa autem superiōra cadūca et incerta, posita[4] nōn tam in cōnsiliīs nostrīs quam in fortūnae temeritāte. Quī autem in virtūte summum bonum[5] pōnunt, praeclārē illī quidem,[1] sed haec ipsa virtūs amīcitiam et gignit et continet[6], nec sine virtūte amīcitia esse ūllō pactō potest.

Quid dulcius quam habēre quīcum[7] omnia audeās sīc loquī ut tēcum? Quī[8] esset tantus frūctus in prōsperīs rēbus, nisi habērēs quī illīs aequē ac[9] tū ipse gaudēret? Adversās[2] vērō ferre difficile esset sine eō quī illās gravius etiam quam tū ferret. (*Am.* 20, 22)

[1] **haud sciō an = nesciō an,** *perhaps* (literally, *I do not know whether)*
[2] *political offices*
[3] *this last* (i.e., **voluptātēs**) *is (characteristic) of wild beasts*
[4] *dependent on*
[5] *the highest good*
[6] *preserves*
[7] = **quōcum, cum quō**
[8] *how*
[9] *equally as*

---

[1] Supply **faciunt.**
[2] Supply **rēs;** in contrast with **prōsperīs.**

# THE ULTIMATE IN FRIENDSHIP

Quī clāmōrēs tōtā caveā[1] nūper in hospitis et amīcī meī M. Pācuvī novā fābulā, cum, ignōrante rēge uter Orestēs esset, Pyladēs Orestem sē esse dīceret, ut prō illō necārētur, Orestēs autem, ita ut erat, Orestem sē esse persevērāret. Stantēs[1] plaudēbant in rē fictā; quid arbitrāmur in vērā factūrōs fuisse? Facile indicābat ipsa nātūra vim suam, cum hominēs, quod[2] facere ipsī nōn possent, id rēctē fierī in alterō iūdicārent. (*Am.* 24)

[1] *theater*

[1] i.e., the audience in the theater
[2] i.e., die for someone else

# THE FRIENDSHIP OF LAELIUS AND SCĪPIŌ

Sed quoniam rēs hūmānae fragilēs cadūcaeque sunt, semper aliquī anquīrendī sunt quōs dīligāmus et ā quibus dīligāmur; cāritāte enim benevolentiāque sublātā, omnis est ē vītā sublāta iūcunditās. Mihi[1] quidem Scīpiō, quamquam est subitō ēreptus, vīvit tamen semperque vīvet; virtūtem[2] enim amāvī illīus virī, quae exstīncta nōn est; nec mihi sōlī versātur ante oculōs, quī illam semper in manibus habuī,[3] sed etiam posterīs erit clāra et īnsignis. Nēmō umquam animō aut spē maiōra[4] suscipiet quī sibi nōn illīus memoriam atque imāginem prōpōnendam putet.[5] Equidem ex omnibus rēbus quās mihi aut fortūna aut nātūra tribuit nihil habeō quod cum amīcitiā Scīpiōnis possim comparāre. In hāc mihi dē rē pūblicā cōnsēnsus, in hāc rērum prīvātārum cōnsilium, in eādem requiēs plēna oblectātiōnis fuit. Numquam illum nē minimā quidem rē offendī, quod[6] quidem sēnserim, nihil audīvī ex eō ipse quod nōllem; ūna domus erat, īdem vīctus isque

[1] *for me*
[2] *fine character*
[3] *For I* (**quī**) *have always had it* (**virtūtem**) *at my disposal* (literally, *in my hands*).
[4] *more (than usually) important*
[5] *without thinking* (literally, *who does not think*)
[6] *so far as I realized, at any rate*

commūnis, neque sōlum mīlitia[1] sed etiam peregrīnātiōnēs rūsticātiōnēsque commūnēs. Nam quid ego dē studiīs dīcam cognōscendī semper aliquid atque discendī? In quibus remōtī ab oculīs populī omne ōtiōsum tempus contrīvimus. Quārum rērum recordātiō et memoria sī ūnā cum illō occidisset, dēsīderium coniūnctissimī atque amantissimī virī ferre nūllō modō possem. Sed nec[2] illa[3] exstīncta sunt alunturque potius et augentur cōgitātiōne et memoriā meā, et, sī illīs plānē orbātus essem, magnum tamen affert mihi aetās[7] ipsa sōlācium. Diūtius enim iam in hōc dēsīderiō esse nōn possum. Omnia autem brevia tolerābilia esse dēbent, etiam sī magna sunt. (*Am.* 102–104).

[7] *age*

---

[1] one of the subjects of **erant,** to be supplied; **commūnēs** is predicate adjective

[2] = **et nōn,** correlative with the following **et**

[3] i.e., **recordātiō et memoria**

# UNIT IX

(167)
BALDASSARRE PERUZZI
( SIENA 1481 – ROMA 1536 )
APOLLO E LE MUSE

Alinari/Art Resource, NY

# TWO THOUSAND YEARS OF LATIN

## Unit Objectives

- To read, with understanding and appreciation, a variety of outstanding literary selections by authors spanning two thousand years
- To read condensed literary selections at sight

The nine Muses were daughters of Zeus and Mnemosyne (Memory). **Apollo,** god of music and poetry, is in the center. As the principal god of culture, he presides with the Muses over the various arts and sciences. Each Muse (from left to right) had a different realm of responsibility: **Cliō** was the Muse of history, **Euterpē** of music, **Thalia** of comedy, **Melpomenē** of tragedy, **Terpsichorē** of dance, **Erato** of love poetry, **Polyhymnia** of poetry, **Ourania** of astronomy, and **Calliopē** of eloquence. You can see their names in Greek along the bottom of this painting, entitled *Apollo and the Muses,* by Baldassarre Peruzzi (1481–1536).

# PLAUTUS

The third and second centuries B.C. were the great centuries of Roman comedy, which was an adaptation and imitation of the Greek comedy of Menander and others. The plays of two Roman comedy writers, Plautus (ca. 254–184 B.C.) and Terence (ca. 190–159 B.C.), have survived. The *Menaechmī* of Plautus is named after twin brothers who look so much alike that they are constantly confused with each other—and on the confusion hangs the humor. The Menaechmi were separated in boyhood. After Menaechmus II grows up, he travels around looking for his brother. Unaware that he has arrived at the town where his brother lives, he meets a girl who takes him for Menaechmus I and gives him an expensive dress to be altered. The dress is one that Menaechmus I had taken from his wife's wardrobe and given to the girl. The scene below shows Menaechmus II and the wife **(matrōna)** of Menaechmus I. The **matrōna** mistakes Menaechmus II for her husband and recognizes the dress.

As in other Roman comedies, the characters in the *Menaechmī* are Greek, and the scenes are laid in Greece.

## Who Is Who?

[1] *disgrace of a man*
[2] *What have I brought on myself;* i.e., *what have I done?*
[3] *curses on*
[4] *(all my) life*

Ma. Adībo atque hominem accipiam quibus dictīs meret.
Nōn tē pudet prōdīre in cōnspectum meum,
flāgitium hominis,[1] cum istōc ōrnātū? Me. Quid est?
Quae tē rēs agitat, mulier? Ma. Etiamne, impudēns,
muttīre verbum ūnum audēs aut mēcum loquī?
Me. Quid tandem admīsī in mē[2] ut loquī nōn audeam?
Ma. Rogās mē? Hominis impudentem audāciam!
Me. Nōn tū scīs, mulier, Hecubam quāpropter canem
Grāiī esse praedicābant? Ma. Nōn equidem sciō.
Me. Quia idem faciēbat Hecuba quod tū nunc facis.
Omnia mala[3] ingerēbat quemquem aspexerat.
Itaque adeō iūre coepta appellārī est canēs$_1$.
Ma. Nōn ego istaec flāgitia possum perpetī.
Nam mēd$_2$ aetātem[4] viduam esse māvelim$_3$
quam istaec flāgitia tua patī quae tū facis.
Me. Quid id ad mē, tū tē nuptam possīs$_4$ perpetī,

---

$_1$ alternate nominative form for **canis**
$_2$ old form of **mē**
$_3$ old form of **mālim**
$_4$ Supply *whether* in translation.

an sīs abitūra ā tuō virō? An mōs hīc ita est,
peregrīnō ut advenientī nārrent fābulās?
MA. Quās fābulās? Nōn, inquam, patiar praeterhāc,
quīn vidua vīvam quam[5] tuōs mōrēs perferam.
ME. Meā quidem hercle causā[6] vidua vīvitō
vel usque dum[7] rēgnum obtinēbit Iuppiter.
MA. At mihi negābās dūdum surrupuisse tē,
nunc eandem ante oculōs attinēs? Nōn tē pudet?
ME. Heu, hercle, mulier, multum et audāx et mala es.
Tūn[8] tibi hanc surruptam dīcere audēs quam mihi
dedit alia mulier, ut concinnandam darem?
MA. Nē istūc[9] mēcastor iam patrem arcessam meum
atque eī nārrābō tua flāgitia quae facis.
Ī, Deciō[5], quaere meum patrem, tēcum simul
ut veniat ad mē: ita rem esse dīcitō.
Iam ego aperiam istaec tua flāgitia. ME. Sānan[10] es?
Quae mea flāgitia? MA. Pallam atque aurum meum
domō suppīlās tuae uxōrī et tuae
dēgeris amīcae. Satin[11] haec rēctē fābulor?
ME. Quaesō hercle, mulier, sī scīs, mōnstrā quod bibam,[12]
tuam quī[13] possim perpetī petulantiam.
Quem tū hominem mēd[2] arbitrēre, nesciō;
ego tē simītū[6] nōvī cum Porthāone[7].
MA. Sī mē dērīdēs, et pol illum nōn potes,
patrem meum, quī hūc advenit. Quīn respicis?
Nōvistīn tū illum? ME. Nōvī cum Calchā[7] simul:
eōdem diē[8] illum vīdī quō tē ante hunc diem.
MA. Negās nōvisse mē? Negās patrem meum?
ME. Idem hercle dīcam sī avum vīs addūcere.
MA. Ēcastor pariter hoc atque aliās rēs solēs[9].

[5] *(rather) than*
[6] *for my part*
[7] *as long as*
[8] = **Tūne**
[9] *surely for that reason*
[10] = **Sānane**
[11] = **Satisne**
[12] *something to drink*
[13] *in order that I*

If you are studying theater, research the Roman comedy as an art form and the specific impact of Plautus and Terence on playwrights of later times. Delve further into Plautus and Terence, reading more of their work. Analyze their plots and themes; share your opinions with your theater class. With one or more partners from your Latin class, present a scene from one of the comedies to your theater class.

---

[5] a slave
[6] old form of **simul**
[7] a mythological character
[8] He had never seen either of them.
[9] Supply **agere.**

# CATULLUS

Do you remember Catullus, who wrote about the death of the pet sparrow of his sweetheart Lesbia? He wrote many other charming poems, too, of which the following are samples. C. Valerius Catullus died in 54 B.C. at about age thirty, while Caesar was conquering the Gauls.

## A Dinner Invitation

[1] *laughter*
[2] *cobwebs*

Cēnābis bene, mī Fabulle, apud mē
paucīs, sī tibi dī favent, diēbus,
sī tēcum attuleris bonam atque magnam
cēnam, nōn sine candidā puellā
et vīnō et sale et omnibus cachinnīs[1].
Haec sī, inquam, attuleris, venuste noster,
cēnābis bene; nam tuī Catullī
plēnus sacculus est—arāneārum[2].
Sed contrā accipiēs merōs amōrēs
seu quid suāvius ēlegantiusve est;
nam unguentum dabō quod meae puellae
dōnārunt Venerēs Cupīdinēsque,[1]
quod tū cum olfaciēs, deōs rogābis
tōtum ut tē faciant, Fabulle, nāsum!
(13)

---

[1] i.e., all the gods of beauty and love

## Writ in Water

Nūllī sē dīcit mulier mea nūbere[1] mālle
quam mihi, nōn sī sē Iuppiter ipse petat.
Dīcit; sed mulier cupidō quod dīcit amantī,
in ventō et rapidā scrībere oportet aquā.
(70)

---

[1] used only of women marrying; literally, *take the (marriage) veil for*

### Mixed Feelings

Ōdī et amō. Quārē id faciam fortasse requīris.
Nesciō, sed fierī sentiō et excrucior.
(85)

### At His Brother's Tomb

Multās per gentēs et multa per aequora vectus
adveniō hās miserās, frāter, ad īnferiās[1],
ut tē postrēmō dōnārem mūnere mortis
et mūtam nēquīquam alloquerer cinerem,
quandoquidem fortūna mihī tētē abstulit ipsum,
heu, miser indignē frāter adēmpte mihi.
Nunc tamen intereā haec, prīscō quae mōre parentum
trādita sunt trīstī mūnere ad īnferiās,[2]
accipe frāternō multum mānantia flētū
atque in perpetuum, frāter, avē[3] atque valē.
(101)

[1] *offerings* (as we might offer a wreath or a bunch of flowers)

[2] *for offerings*

[3] *hail and farewell*

# LIVY (XXI)

Livy (Titus Livius) was born in 59 B.C. at Padua, in northern Italy, not far from Verona.

You have read stories of early Rome based on Livy's history. His history filled 142 books, but only about a third of it has survived—Books 1–10, dealing with early history, and Books 21–45, beginning with the Second Punic War. Livy considered this war so important that he stopped to write a preface to his account of it, as if he were beginning a new work. As a matter of fact, this war had an incalculable effect on the future of the world. We can only speculate what the world would be today had the Carthaginians won; however, Rome conquered and became the dominant power. It was fitting that Livy's patriotic presentation of Rome's accomplishments should be written during the reign of Augustus, who has been called the architect of the Roman Empire.

## Hannibal

[1] *the entire work* (noun)
[2] = **rērum gestārum,** *history*
[3] *offensive and defensive strength*
[4] *Mars was impartial*
[5] *nearer*
[6] *they, the conquered, had been ruled*
[7] *coaxing*
[8] *there,* i.e., to Spain
[9] *the loss of Sicily and Sardinia* (literally, *Sicily and Sardinia lost*)
[10] *just after*
[11] *would have brought*
[12] *first choice of the soldiers*

**I.** In parte operis meī licet mihi praefārī quod in prīncipiō summae[1] tōtīus professī plērīque sunt rērum[2] scrīptōrēs, bellum maximē omnium memorābile quae umquam gesta sint mē scrīptūrum, quod, Hannibale duce, Carthāginiēnsēs cum populō Rōmānō gessēre. Nam neque validiōrēs opibus ūllae inter sē cīvitātēs gentēsque contulērunt arma neque hīs ipsīs tantum umquam vīrium[3] aut rōboris[3] fuit, et haud ignōtās bellī artēs inter sēsē sed expertās prīmō Pūnicō cōnserēbant bellō, et adeō varia fortūna bellī ancepsque Mārs[4] fuit ut propius[5] perīculum fuerint quī vīcērunt. Odiīs etiam prope maiōribus certārunt quam vīribus, Rōmānīs indignantibus quod victōribus victī ultrō īnferrent arma, Poenīs$_1$ quod superbē avārēque crēderent imperitātum[6] victīs esse. Fāma est etiam Hannibalem, annōrum fermē novem, puerīliter blandientem[7] patrī Hamilcarī ut dūcerētur in Hispāniam, cum, perfectō Āfricō bellō, exercitum eō[8] trāiectūrus sacrificāret, altāribus admōtum,$_2$ tāctīs sacrīs,$_3$ iūre iūrandō adāctum, sē cum prīmum posset hostem fore populō Rōmānō. Angēbant ingentis spīritūs virum$_4$ Sicilia Sardiniaque āmissae;[9] nam et Siciliam nimis celerī dēspērātiōne rērum concessam et Sardiniam inter mōtum Āfricae fraude Rōmānōrum, stīpendiō etiam īnsuper impositō, interceptam.

**II.** Hīs ānxius cūrīs ita sē Āfricō bellō, quod fuit sub[10] recentem Rōmānam pācem, per quīnque annōs, ita deinde novem annīs in Hispāniā augendō Pūnicō imperiō gessit ut appārēret maius eum quam quod gereret agitāre in animō bellum et, sī diūtius vīxisset, Hamilcare duce, Poenōs arma Italiae illātūrōs fuisse,[11] quī Hannibalis ductū intulērunt.

Mors Hamilcaris peropportūna$_5$ et pueritia Hannibalis distulērunt bellum. Medius Hasdrubal inter patrem ac fīlium octō fermē annōs imperium obtinuit.

**III.** In Hasdrubalis locum haud dubia rēs fuit quīn praerogātīvam mīlitārem,[12] quā extemplō iuvenis Hannibal in praetōrium dēlātus imperātorque ingentī omnium clāmōre atque assēnsū appellātus erat, favor plēbis sequerētur.

---

$_1$ i.e., **indignantibus**
$_2$ He was so small that he had to be lifted up.
$_3$ presumably some of the sacred utensils, like touching the Bible today
$_4$ Hamilcar
$_5$ from the Roman point of view

## Hannibal's Virtues and Vices

**IV.** Missus Hannibal in Hispāniam prīmō statim adventū omnem exercitum in sē convertit; Hamilcarem iuvenem redditum sibi veterēs mīlitēs crēdere; eundem vigōrem in vultū vimque in oculīs, habitum ōris līneāmentaque intuērī. Dein brevī$_{1}$ effēcit ut pater in sē[1] minimum mōmentum[2] ad favōrem conciliandum esse. Numquam ingenium idem ad rēs dīversissimās, pārendum[3] atque imperandum, habilius[4] fuit. Itaque haud facile discernerēs[5] utrum imperātōrī an exercituī cārior esset; neque Hasdrubal alium quemquam praeficere mālle ubi quid fortiter ac strēnuē agendum esset, neque mīlitēs aliō duce plūs cōnfīdere aut audēre. Plūrimum audāciae ad perīcula capessenda, plūrimum cōnsiliī inter ipsa perīcula erat. Nūllō labōre aut corpus fatīgārī aut animus vincī poterat. Calōris ac frīgoris patientia pār; cibī potiōnisque dēsīderiō nātūralī, nōn voluptāte modus fīnītus; vigiliārum somnīque nec diē nec nocte discrīmināta tempora: id quod gerendīs rēbus[6] superesset quiētī datum; ea neque mollī strātō neque silentiō accersita; multī saepe mīlitārī sagulō opertum humī iacentem inter custōdiās statiōnēsque mīlitum cōnspexērunt. Vestītus nihil[7] inter aequālēs excellēns, arma atque equī cōnspiciēbantur. Equitum peditumque īdem longē prīmus erat; prīnceps in proelium ībat, ultimus, cōnsertō proeliō, excēdēbat. Hās tantās virī virtūtēs ingentia vitia aequābant: inhūmāna crūdēlitās, perfidia plūs quam Pūnica,$_{2}$ nihil vērī, nihil sānctī, nūllus deum metus, nūllum iūs iūrandum, nūlla religiō. Cum hāc indole virtūtum atque vitiōrum trienniō sub Hasdrubale imperātōre meruit, nūllā rē quae agenda videndaque magnō futūrō ducī$_{3}$ esset praetermissā.

[1] *the father in him,* i.e., *his likeness to his father*
[2] *impulse*
[3] *obeying and commanding*
[4] *more suitable*
[5] *could you distinguish*
[6] *from doing things*
[7] *not at all*

---

$_{1}$ Supply **tempore.**
$_{2}$ **Pūnica fidēs** was proverbial in the sense of **perfidia.** The Romans said the same of the Greeks.
$_{3}$ dative of agent with **videnda**

# HORACE

The Augustan Age was the greatest in Roman literature, producing such writers as Vergil, Horace, Ovid, Livy, Tibullus, and Propertius. It was to Roman literature what the Age of Pericles was to Athens and the Elizabethan Age to England. Horace (Q. Horatius Flaccus) was one of the glories of the Augustan Age. He is famous for his *Odes, Satires,* and *Epistles.* The charm of his writing, described in antiquity as **cūriōsa fēlīcitās,** "happy turns of expression worked out with great care," is a notable characteristic. In the following poem we have an ode in which he draws a moral lesson from an adventure. Remember that this is poetry, not history, that the lesson he draws is not based on fact but is true only in a poetic sense. The other selection, part of a longer poem, is a fable to be applied to human beings: the simple life of the country is preferred over the elaborate luxury of city life.

## Integer Vītae

[1] *upright in* (literally, *of*) *life and free from crime*

Integer vītae scelerisque pūrus[1]
nōn eget Maurīs iaculīs neque arcū
nec venēnātīs gravidā sagittīs,
Fusce, pharetrā,

sīve per Syrtīs iter aestuōsās,
sīve factūrus per inhospitālem
Caucasum vel quae loca fābulōsus
lambit Hydaspēs.

Namque mē silvā lupus in Sabīnā,
dum meam cantō Lalagēn$_1$ et ultrā
terminum cūrīs vagor expedītīs,
fūgit inermem,

quāle portentum neque mīlitāris
Dauniās$_2$ lātīs alit aesculētīs
nec Iubae tellūs generat, leōnum
ārida nūtrīx.

---

$_1$ accusative, name of his sweetheart, Lalage
$_2$ Apulia, where Horace was born

Pōne mē pigrīs[2] ubi nūlla campīs
arbor aestīvā recreātur aurā,
quod latus mundī[3] nebulae malusque
Iuppiter[3] urget.

Pōne sub currū nimium propinquī
sōlis in terrā domibus[4] negātā:
dulce rīdentem Lalagēn amābō,
dulce loquentem.
(*Od.* I, 22)

[2] *frozen* (literally, *sluggish* [from cold])
[3] = **latus mundī quod**
[4] *denied to (human) habitation* (on account of the heat)

[3] Jupiter is god of the sky; therefore this means a dark, cloudy sky.

## The City Mouse and His Country Cousin

Rūsticus urbānum mūrem mūs paupere fertur
accēpisse cavō, veterem vetus hospes amīcum,
asper et attentus quaesītīs, ut tamen artum
solveret hospitiīs animum.[1] Quid multa? Neque ille
sēpositī ciceris nec longae invīdit[1] avēnae,
āridum et ōre ferēns acinum sēmēsaque lardī
frūsta dedit, cupiēns variā fastīdia cēnā
vincere tangentis male[2] singula dente superbō;
cum pater ipse[3] domūs paleā porrēctus in hōrnā[4]
ēsset[2] ador loliumque,[5] dapis meliōra relinquēns.
Tandem urbānus ad hunc, "quid tē iuvat," inquit, "amīce,
praeruptī[6] nemoris patientem vīvere dorsō[7]?
Vīs[8] tū hominēs urbemque ferīs praepōnere silvīs?
Carpe viam, mihi crēde, comes; terrestria quandō
mortālīs animās vīvunt sortīta, neque ūlla est
aut magnō aut parvō lētī fuga: quō, bone, circā[3],
dum licet, in rēbus iūcundīs vīve beātus,
vīve memor quam sīs aevī brevis." Haec ubi dicta
agrestem pepulēre[9], domō levis exsilit; inde
ambō prōpositum peragunt iter, urbis aventēs
moenia nocturnī subrēpere. Iamque tenēbat
nox medium caelī spatium, cum pōnit uterque

[1] *begrudge*
[2] *hardly touching the items*
[3] *the host,* i.e., the country mouse
[4] *this year's straw*
[5] *spelt* (an old-fashioned wheat) *and darnel* (a weed)
[6] *steep*
[7] *ridge*
[8] *Won't you*
[9] *affected, influenced*

[1] He was "tight" (**artum**) and attentive to gain, but he did not stint hospitality.
[2] from **edō**, *eat*
[3] with **quō** = *therefore*

[10] *courses*
[11] *to one side*
[12] *of the evening before*
[13] *acts, plays*
[14] *as soon as, when*

in locuplēte domō vēstīgia, rubrō ubi coccō
tīncta super lectōs candēret vestis eburnōs,
multaque dē magnā superessent fercula[10] cēnā,
quae procul[11] exstrūctīs inerant hesterna[12] canistrīs.
Ergō ubi purpureā porrēctum in veste locāvit
agrestem, velutī succīnctus[4] cursitat hospes
continuatque dapēs, nec nōn vernīliter ipsīs
fungitur officiīs, praelambēns omne quod affert.
Ille cubāns gaudet mūtātā sorte bonīsque
rēbus agit[13] laetum convīvam, cum subitō ingēns
valvārum strepitus lectīs excussit utrumque.
Currere per tōtum pavidī conclāve, magisque
exanimēs trepidāre, simul[14] domus alta Molossīs[5]
personuit canibus. Tum rūsticus, "haud mihi vītā
est opus hāc," ait et "valeās; me silva cavusque
tūtus ab īnsidiīs tenuī sōlābitur ervō."
(*Sat.* II, 6, 80–117)

---

[4] *(his tunic) pulled up,* like a servant (**vernīliter**). He even stuck his fingers in everything and then licked them (**praelambēns**).
[5] large, fierce dogs

# SULPICIA

Sulpicia is the only known Latin woman poet. She was of aristocratic birth and was the niece of Messalla, a prominent citizen and supporter of the arts. She was welcome in Tibullus' literary circle and probably wrote around 30 B.C. Her contributions indicate the more prominent role women were beginning to play in fashionable society. Only six of her love poems, written to Cerinthus, have survived.

[1] *exhausted*
[2] *fever*
[3] *otherwise*

Estne tibī, Cērinthe, tuae pia cura puellae,
   quod mea nunc vexat corpora fessa[1] calor[2]?
at ego nōn aliter[3] tristēs ēvincere morbōs
   optārim, quam tē sī quoque velle putem.
at mihi quid prōsit morbōs ēvincere, sī tū
   nostra potes lentō pectore ferre mala?

# Transmission of Latin and Greek Works Before Printing: 3

Many ancient and medieval manuscripts are beautifully scripted and decorated. This page comes from the beginning of the Gospel according to John. It begins, **In prīncipiō erat verbum.** (In English, the next words are: "And the word was with God and the Word was God." Can you translate this part into Latin?) Notice that the **In** is so integrated into the design that it is hardly visible. If you compare this manuscript to the ones in Units VII and VIII, you can clearly see the increased sophistication and beauty that was added to manuscripts. Dating from the ninth century, the script used in this piece is Carolingian (French).

# PHAEDRUS

Fables, which are part of folklore, were passed on by word of mouth. The Greek writer Aesop wrote some of them down; his fables are still famous and have been translated into many languages. The Roman Phaedrus translated them into Latin verse during the Age of Augustus. For a long time, fables of Phaedrus and versions of them were the ones generally known, until in modern times Aesop was again translated.

## Mūlī Duo et Raptōrēs (Two Mules and Thieves)

Mūlī gravātī sarcinīs ībant duo:
ūnus ferēbat fiscōs[1] cum pecūniā,
alter tumentēs multō saccōs hordeō[2].
Ille onere dīves celsā cervīce ēminet
clārumque collō iactat tintinnābulum;
comes quiētō sequitur et placidō gradū.
Subitō latrōnēs ex īnsidiīs advolant
interque caedem ferrō mūlum sauciant,
dīripiunt nummōs, neglegunt vīle hordeum.
Spoliātus igitur cāsūs cum flēret suōs:
"Equidem," inquit alter, "mē contemptum gaudeō,
nam nīl āmīsī nec sum laesus vulnere."
Hōc argumentō tūta est hominum tenuitās[3];
Magnae perīclō[4] sunt opēs obnoxiae[5].
(II, 7)

[1] *money bags*
[2] *barley*
[3] *poverty*
[4] = **periculō**
[5] *subject to*

## Lupus ad Canem (The Wolf to the Dog)

Quam dulcis sit lībertās breviter prōloquar.
Canī perpāstō[1] maciē cōnfectus lupus
forte occucurrit. Dein salūtātum[2] invicem
ut[3] restitērunt: "Unde sīc, quaesō, nitēs?
Aut quō cibō fēcistī tantum corporis?
Ego, quī sum longē fortior, pereō fame."
Canis simpliciter: "Eadem est condiciō tibi,
Praestāre dominō sī pār officium potes."
"Quod?" inquit ille. "Custōs ut sīs līminis,
ā fūribus tueāris et noctū domum."
"Ego vērō sum parātus; nunc patior nivēs
imbrēsque in silvīs asperam vītam trahēns.
Quantō est facilius mihi sub tēctō vīvere,

[1] *well fed*
[2] *to greet each other*
[3] *when*

et ōtiōsum largō satiārī cibō!"
"Venī ergō mēcum." Dum prōcēdunt, aspicit
lupus ā catēnā collum dētrītum canī[4].
"Unde hoc, amīce?" "Nihil est." "Dīc, quaesō, tamen."
"Quia videor ācer, alligant mē interdiū,
lūce ut quiēscam, et vigilem nox cum vēnerit;
crepusculō[5] solūtus, quā vīsum est[6] vagor.
Affertur ultrō pānis; dē mēnsā suā
dat ossa dominus; frūsta iactant familia
et quod fastīdit quisque pulmentārium.[7]
Sīc sine labōre venter implētur meus."
"Age, abīre sī quō est animus, est licentia?"
"Nōn plānē est," inquit. "Fruere quae laudās, canis;
rēgnāre nōlō, līber ut[8] nōn sim mihi."
(III, 7)

[4] *for the dog* (we would say *of*)
[5] *at twilight*
[6] *wherever I like*
[7] *whatever food anyone doesn't like*
[8] *on condition that*

## Soror et Frāter (Sister and Brother)

Praeceptō monitus saepe tē cōnsīderā.[1]
Habēbat quīdam fīliam turpissimam
īdemque īnsignem pulchrā faciē fīlium.
Hī, speculum in cathedrā mātris ut positum fuit,
puerīliter lūdentēs forte īnspexērunt.
Hic sē formōsum iactat; illa īrāscitur
nec glōriantis[2] sustinet frātris iocōs,
accipiēns quippe cūncta in contumēliam.[3]
Ergō ad patrem dēcurrit laesūra[4] invicem
magnāque invidiā crīminātur fīlium,
vir nātus quod rem fēminārum tetigerit.[5]
Amplexus ille utrumque et carpēns ōscula
dulcemque in ambōs cāritātem partiēns;
"cotīdiē," inquit, "speculō vōs ūtī volō;
tū fōrmam nē corrumpās nēquitiae malīs;
tū faciem ut istam mōribus vincās bonīs."
(III, 8)

[1] *look at yourself*
[2] *boasting*
[3] *as an insult* (to herself)
[4] *to hurt* (her brother)
[5] *because, though born a man, he touched women's things* (i.e., mirrors)

## Dē Vitiīs Hominum (The Imperfections of Men)

Pērās[1] imposuit Iuppiter nōbīs duās:
propriīs replētam vitiīs post tergum dedit,
aliēnīs[1] ante pectus suspendit gravem.
Hāc rē vidēre nostra mala nōn possumus;
aliī simul[2] dēlinquunt, cēnsōrēs sumus.
(IV, 10)

[1] *sacks*
[2] *as soon as*

[1] Supply **vitiīs.**

# SENECA

Seneca the Younger wrote verse tragedies that had a great influence on Shakespeare and other Elizabethan writers and philosophical works in prose, in which he preached Stoic doctrines. These too had a wide influence.

Seneca was Nero's tutor and later became his adviser, in effect his prime minister during the first five "golden years," as they were called, of Nero's reign. Then Nero forced Seneca to commit suicide and started on his mad course.

The following selections are from Seneca's letters to his friend Lucilius. They are not really letters but essays.

## Read Intensively, Not Extensively

Illud autem vidē, nē ista lēctiō auctōrum multōrum et omnis generis volūminum habeat aliquid vagum et īnstabile. Certīs ingeniīs$_1$ immorārī et innūtrīrī oportet, sī velīs aliquid trahere quod in animō fidēliter sedeat. Nusquam est quī ubīque est. Vītam in peregrīnātiōne exigentibus hoc ēvenit, ut multa hospitia habeant, nūllās amīcitiās. Idem accidat necesse est hīs quī nūllīus sē ingeniō familiāriter applicant, sed omnia cursim et properantēs trānsmittunt. Nōn prōdest cibus nec corporī accēdit quī statim sūmptus ēmittitur. Nihil aequē sānitātem impedit quam remediōrum crēbra mūtātiō. Nōn venit vulnus ad cicātrīcem in quō medicāmenta temptantur. Nōn convalēscit planta quae saepe trānsfertur. Nihil tam ūtile est ut in trānsitū[1] prōsit: distringit librōrum multitūdō. Itaque cum legere nōn possīs quantum habuerīs, satis est habēre quantum legās. "Sed modo," inquis, "hunc librum ēvolvere volō, modo illum." Fastīdientis stomachī est multa dēgustāre, quae ubi varia sunt et dīversa, inquinant, nōn alunt. Probātōs itaque semper lege, et sī quandō ad aliōs dīvertī libuerit, ad priōrēs redī; aliquid cotīdiē adversus paupertātem, aliquid adversus mortem auxiliī comparā, nec minus adversus cēterās pestēs. Et cum multa percurrerīs, ūnum excerpe quod illō diē concoquās[2]. Hoc ipse quoque faciō: ex plūribus quae lēgī aliquid apprehendō. Hodiernum hoc est quod apud Epicūrum nānctus sum (soleō enim et in aliēna castra trānsīre, nōn tamquam trānsfuga, sed tamquam explōrātor): "Honesta," inquit, "rēs est laeta paupertās." Illa vērō nōn est paupertās, sī laeta est; cui cum paupertāte bene convenit,[3] dīves est. Nōn quī parum habet, sed quī plūs cupit, pauper est. (*Epist.* 2, 2–6)

[1] *in transit,* i.e., when used only in passing
[2] *can digest*
[3] *he who is on good terms with poverty*

$_1$ i.e., books written by geniuses

## The Proper Treatment of Slaves

Libenter ex hīs quī ā tē veniunt cognōvī familiāriter tē cum servīs tuīs vīvere. Hoc prūdentiam tuam, hoc ērudītiōnem decet. "Servī sunt." Immō hominēs. "Servī sunt." Immō contubernālēs. "Servī sunt." Immō humilēs amīcī. "Servī sunt." Immō cōnservī. Itaque rīdeō istōs quī turpe exīstimant cum servō suō cēnāre. Quārē? Nisi quia superbissima cōnsuētūdō cēnantī dominō stantium servōrum turbam circumdedit. Deinde eiusdem arrogantiae prōverbium iactātur: *totidem hostēs esse quot servōs.* Nōn habēmus illōs hostēs sed facimus. Alius pretiōsās avēs scindit:$_1$ per pectus et clūnēs certīs ductibus circumferēns ērudītam manum frūsta excutit. Īnfēlīx quī huic ūnī reī vīvit, ut altilia decenter secet; nisi quod miserior est quī hoc voluptātis causā docet quam quī necessitātis$_2$ discit. Adice obsōnātōrēs[1], quibus dominicī palātī nōtitia subtilis est, quī sciunt cuius illum reī sapor excitet,[2] cuius dēlectet aspectus, cuius novitāte nausiābundus ērigī possit, quid iam ipsā satietāte fastīdiat, quid illō diē ēsuriat.[3] Cum hīs cēnāre nōn sustinet et maiestātis suae dīminūtiōnem putat ad eandem mēnsam cum servō suō accēdere. Vīs tū[4] cōgitāre istum quem servum tuum vocās, ex iīsdem sēminibus ortum, eōdem fruī caelō, aequē spīrāre, aequē vīvere, aequē morī? Nōlō in ingentem mē locum immittere et dē ūsū servōrum disputāre, in quōs superbissimī, crūdēlissimī, contumēliōsissimī sumus. Haec tamen praeceptī meī summa est: sīc cum īnferiōre vīvās quemadmodum tēcum superiōrem[5] velīs vīvere. Quotiēns in mentem venerit quantum tibi in servum liceat, veniat in mentem tantundem in tē dominō tuō licēre. Vīve cum servō clēmenter, comiter quoque, et in sermōnem illum admitte et in cōnsilium et in convīctum. Nē illud quidem vidētis quam[6] omnem invidiam maiōrēs nostrī dominīs, omnem contumēliam servīs dētrāxerint? Dominum patrem familiae appellavērunt, servōs, familiārēs. Īnstituērunt diem fēstum, nōn quō sōlō cum servīs dominī vēscerentur, sed quō utique honōrēs illīs in domō gerere, iūs dīcere permīsērunt et domum pusillam rem pūblicam esse iūdicāvērunt. Quid ergō? Omnēs servōs admovēbō mēnsae meae? Nōn magis quam omnēs līberōs. Errās sī exīstimās mē quōsdam quasi sordidiōris operae reiectūrum, ut putā[7] illum mūliōnem et illum bubulcum: nōn ministeriīs illōs aestimābō, sed mōribus. Sibi quisque dat mōrēs: ministeria cāsus assignat.[8] Nōn est, mī Lūcilī, quod amīcum tantum in forō et in cūriā quaerās; sī dīligenter attenderis, et domī inveniēs. "Servus est." Sed fortasse līber animō. "Servus est." Hoc illī nocēbit? Ostende quis nōn sit: alius libīdinī servit, alius avāritiae, alius ambitiōnī, omnēs timōrī. (*Epist.* 47, 1–2, 5–6, 8, 10–11, 13–17)

[1] *The ones who go to market*
[2] *the taste of what thing will tempt the master*
[3] *what he is hungry for*
[4] *Won't you*
[5] *your master*
[6] *how*
[7] *for example*
[8] *chance assigns their jobs*

$_1$ the expert carver
$_2$ Supply **causā.**

# PETRONIUS

Petronius, who lived in the age of Nero, wrote a novel telling of the adventures of three rascals as they wandered about southern Italy, constantly getting into difficulties through cheating, stealing, and similar activities. Unfortunately much of the novel has been lost, but we do have the description of a dinner party given by an extremely rich self-made man whose education left much to be desired. In the following selection the host, Trimalchio, boasts of his collection of antiques.

## Trimalchio's Dinner

Quam[1] cum Agamemnōn$_1$ propius cōnsīderāret, ait Trimalchiō: "Sōlus sum quī vēra Corinthia habeam." Exspectābam ut prō[2] reliquā īnsolentiā dīceret sibi vāsa Corinthō[3] afferrī. Sed ille melius et "forsitan," inquit, "quaeris quārē sōlus Corinthia vēra possideam. Quia scīlicet aerārius[4] ā quō emō Corinthus vocātur. Quid est autem Corinthium nisi quis Corinthum[5] habeat? Et nē mē putētis nesapium[6] esse, valdē bene sciō unde prīmum Corinthia nāta sint. Cum Īlium captum est, Hannibal, homō vafer et magnus stēliō[7], omnēs statuās aēneās et aureās et argenteās in ūnum rogum congessit et eās incendit. Factae sunt in ūnum aera miscellānea.[8] Ita ex hāc māssā fabrī sustulērunt et fēcērunt catilla[9] et parapsidēs[9] et statuncula. Sīc Corinthia nāta sunt, ex omnibus in ūnum, nec hoc nec illud." (50, 2–6)

[1] *it* (referring to a plate)
[2] *in accordance with*
[3] *from Corinth*
[4] *worker in bronze*
[5] *has a Corinthus (to make it)*
[6] *nit-wit*
[7] *rascal*
[8] *into one miscellaneous mass*
[9] *dishes*

$_1$ one of the guests

# QUINTILIAN

The schoolteacher M. Fabius Quintilianus (ca. 35–96 A.D.) has left us a famous textbook on teaching, called *Institutio Oratoria, Introduction to Public Speaking*. How could a textbook on public speaking be a textbook on teaching? Most teaching, especially at the higher levels, prepared for law and a public career, and therefore involved public speaking. This passage deals with the education of the young.

Mihi ille dētur puer quem laus excitet, quem glōria iuvet, quī victus fleat. Hic erit alendus ambitū, hunc mordēbit obiūrgātiō, hunc honor excitābit, in hōc dēsidiam numquam verēbor. Danda est tamen omnibus aliqua remissiō[1], nōn sōlum quia nūlla rēs est quae perferre possit continuum labōrem, atque ea quoque quae sēnsū et animā carent, ut servāre vim suam possint, velut quiēte alternā retenduntur,[2] sed quod studium discendī voluntāte, quae cōgī nōn potest, cōnstat.[3] Itaque et vīrium plūs afferunt ad discendum renovātī ac recentēs et ācriōrem animum, quī ferē necessitātibus repugnat.[4] Nec me offenderit lūsus in puerīs (est et hoc signum alacritātis). Modus tamen sit remissiōnibus, nē aut odium studiōrum faciant negātae[5] aut ōtiī cōnsuētūdinem nimiae.[5] Sunt etiam nōnnūllī acuendīs puerōrum ingeniīs nōn inūtilēs lūsūs, cum positīs invicem cuiusque generis quaestiunculīs aemulantur. Mōrēs quoque sē inter lūdendum simplicius dētegunt. (I, 3, 7–12)

[1] *relaxation*
[2] *are relaxed by alternating rest periods, so to speak*
[3] *is based on willingness*
[4] *fights against requirements*
[5] *if denied . . . if excessive*

# MARTIAL

The first century A.D. was the Spanish century of Latin literature. As at an earlier date Catullus, Vergil, Livy, and others had come from Cisalpine Gaul (northern Italy), so now we have the two Senecas, Lucan, Martial, and Quintilian from Hispania (Spain). Martial is famous for his epigrams; in fact, it was he who gave the word *epigram* its present meaning—a short poem with a clever point, sometimes not revealed until the last word.

**1.** Petit Gemellus nūptiās Marōnillae
et cupit et īnstat et precātur et dōnat.
Adeōne pulchra est? Immō foedius nīl est.
Quid ergō in illā petitur et placet? Tussit.
(I, 10)

**2.** Nōn amo tē, Sabidī, nec possum dīcere quārē;
hoc tantum possum dīcere, nōn amo tē.
(I, 32)

**3.** Nūper erat medicus, nunc est vispillo[1] Diaulus;
quod vispillo facit, fēcerat et medicus.
(I, 47)

[1] *undertaker*

**4.** Vērōna doctī syllabās amat vātis$_1$,
Marōne$_2$ fēlīx Mantua est,
cēnsētur Aponī$_3$ Līviō suō tellus
Stēllaque$_4$ nec Flaccō$_4$ minus,
Apollodōrō$_5$ plaudit imbrifer Nīlus,
Nāsōne Paelignī$_6$ sonant,
duōs Senecās ūnicumque Lūcānum
fācunda loquitur[2] Corduba,
gaudent iocōsae Caniō suō Gādēs,
Ēmerita$_7$ Deciānō meō:
tē, Liciniāne, glōriābitur nostra
nec mē tacēbit Bilbilis.
(I, 61)

[2] *speaks of*

**5.** "Rīdē, sī sapis, Ō puella, rīdē,"
Paelignus, putō, dīxerat poēta$_8$;
sed nōn dīxerat omnibus puellīs.
Vērum ut[3] dīxerit omnibus puellīs,
nōn dīxit tibi; tū puella nōn es,
et trēs[4] sunt tibi, Maximīna, dentēs,
sed plānē piceīque buxeīque.[5]
Quārē sī speculō mihīque crēdis,
dēbēs nōn aliter timēre rīsum
quam ventum Spanius manumque Prīscus,$_9$
quam crētāta[6] timet Fabulla nimbum,
cērussāta[7] timet Sabella sōlem.
Vultūs indue tū magis sevērōs
quam coniūnx Priamī nurusque maior.
Mīmōs rīdiculī Philistiōnis
et convīvia nequiōra vītā$_{10}$
et quicquid lepidā procācitāte
laxat perspicuō labella rīsū.

[3] *grant that*
[4] *(only) three*
[5] *black and brown* (literally, *like fir and boxwood*)
[6] *powdered* (literally, *chalked*)
[7] *painted with white lead*

---

$_1$ Catullus
$_2$ Vergil
$_3$ Aponus was a spring near Padua, Livy's birthplace.
$_4$ unknown contemporary writer from Padua
$_5$ another unknown
$_6$ Ovid's birthplace was Sulmo, in the country of the Paeligni.
$_7$ Merida
$_8$ Ovid
$_9$ Spanius fears that the wind might disarrange his carefully combed hair; Priscus did not want to have his toga disturbed.
$_{10}$ verb

# Transmission of Latin and Greek Works Before Printing: 4

Ronald Sheridan/Ancient Art & Architecture Collection

From the twelfth century, we have a fine example of a page from a medical text describing the uses of herbs. The illustrations not only make the text more beautiful to look at but also more informative to the reader. Many monasteries grew herbs for both culinary and medicinal purposes. Hildegard von Bingen (see page 235) was especially well-known for her knowledge of the uses of herbs and medicines.

tē maestae decet assidēre mātrī
lūgentīque virum piumve frātrem,
et tantum tragicīs vacāre Mūsīs.
at tū iūdicium secūta nostrum
plōrā, sī sapis, Ō puella, plōrā.
(II, 41)

**6.** Hanc tibi, Fronto pater, genetrīx Flācilla, puellam[11]
ōscula[12] commendō dēliciāsque meās,
parvula nē nigrās horrēscat Erōtion umbrās
ōraque Tartareī[8] prōdigiōsa canis.
Implētūra fuit sextae modo frīgora brūmae,
vīxisset totidem[13] nī minus illa diēs.
Inter tam veterēs lūdat lascīva patrōnōs
et nōmen blaesō garriat ōre meum.
Mollia nōn rigidus caespes tegat ossa nec illī,
terra, gravis fuerīs:[14] nōn fuit illa tibi.
(V, 34)

**7.** Vītam quae faciant beātiōrem,
iūcundissime Martiālis[15], haec sunt:
rēs[9] nōn parta labōre sed relīcta,
nōn ingrātus ager, focus perennis,
līs numquam, toga rāra, mēns quiēta,
vīrēs ingenuae,[16] salūbre corpus,
prūdēns simplicitās, parēs amīcī,
convīctus facilis, sine arte[10] mēnsa,
nox nōn ēbria sed solūta cūrīs,
nōn trīstis torus et tamen pudīcus,
somnus quī faciat brevēs tenebrās,
quod sīs esse velīs[11] nihilque mālīs,
summum nec metuās diem nec optēs.
(X, 47)

[8] *of Tartarus*
[9] *property*
[10] *plain, not fancy*
[11] *wish to be what you are and prefer nothing else*

---

[11] Unlike most of the epigrams of Martial, this one accords with the early Greek sense of an epitaph; it is about a little girl named Erotion, *Lovey,* similar to *Mabel,* from *Amabilis.* He asks his father and mother, now in the Lower World, to take care of the girl.
[12] in apposition with **puellam,** *sweetheart*
[13] i.e., six
[14] a variant of the formula found on hundreds of Roman tombstones: **sit tibi terra levis**
[15] not the poet but a friend by the same name
[16] suitable for a "gentleman," not an athlete or a working man

# APULEIUS

Apuleius was born in northern Africa about A.D. 125. His greatest work was the *Metamorphoses,* in which he tells, among others, the charming story of Cupid and Psyche. Psyche was so beautiful that, human though she was, she made the goddess Venus jealous. So Venus told her son Cupid to marry her off to some impossible man. However, Cupid fell in love with her and married her, though remaining invisible. With the aid of a lamp, Psyche discovered that her husband was very handsome. But then her troubles began, for she was punished by Venus. Finally Cupid appealed to Jupiter, and everything ended happily with a marriage in heaven.

Nec mora,[1] cum cēna nūptiālis affluēns exhibētur. Accumbēbat summum torum marītus, Psȳchēn gremiō suō complexus. Sīc et cum suā Iūnōne Iuppiter ac deinde per ōrdinem tōtī[2] deī. Tunc, dum pōculum nectaris, quod vīnum deōrum est, Iovī quidem suus pōcillātor[3], ille rūsticus puer, cēterīs vērō Līber[1] ministrābat, Vulcānus cēnam coquēbat, Hōrae rosīs et cēterīs flōribus purpurābant omnia, Grātiae spargēbant balsama, Apollō cantābat ad citharam, Mūsae quoque canōra personābant, Venus suāvī mūsicae superingressa[4] fōrmōsa saltāvit, scaenā sibi sīc concinnātā ut Mūsae quidem chorum canerent et tībiās īnflārent, Satyrus et Pāniscus ad fistulam dīcerent. Sīc rītē Psȳchē convenit in manum Cupīdinis et nāscitur illīs mātūrō partū fīlia, quam Voluptātem nōmināmus. (*Met.* VI, 23)

[1] *without delay* (literally, *(there is) no delay when*)
[2] = **omnēs**
[3] *cupbearer*
[4] *coming in to the music*

---

[1] Bacchus

# HADRIAN

The historian Spartianus, in the collection of biographies of emperors called *Scriptores Historiae Augustae,* tells us that on his deathbed the emperor Hadrian, who died in A.D. 138, composed these verses about his soul.

Animula[1] vagula, blandula,
hospes comesque corporis,
quae nunc abībis in loca[2]
pallidula, rigida, nūdula,
nec, ut solēs, dabis iocōs.
(25)

---

[1] **Anima** is not merely *soul* in our sense, but *life, the breath of life.*
[2] The Lower World is pictured as dark, cold, and bare.

# MACROBIUS

About the year A.D. 400 Macrobius wrote a book called *Saturnalia,* somewhat similar to the *Attic Nights* of Aulus Gellius. A group of cultured men meet on the Saturnalia and discuss literary and historical subjects. They get to talking about Cicero's jokes. Macrobius found these in a Cicero jokebook prepared by Cicero's secretary Tiro. The purpose of the book was to supply material for public speakers.

[1] *have kept silent about the jokes*
[2] *It doesn't show its age*
[3] *miracle*
[4] *Cicero had been reluctant*
[5] *those saying* (dative)

Sed mīror omnēs vōs ioca tacuisse[1] Cicerōnis, in quibus fācundissimus, ut in omnibus, fuit. Cicerō, cum apud Damasippum cēnāret, et ille, mediocrī vīnō positō, dīceret: "Bibite Falernum$_1$ hoc; annōrum quadrāgintā est," "Bene," inquit, "aetātem fert."[2]

Īdem cum Lentulum, generum suum, exiguae statūrae hominem, longō gladiō accīnctum vīdisset, "Quis," inquit, "generum meum ad gladium alligāvit?"

Nec Q. Cicerōnī frātrī pepercit. Nam cum in eā prōvinciā quam ille$_2$ rēxerat vīdisset imāginem eius$_3$ ingentibus līneāmentīs usque ad pectus ex mōre pictam (erat autem Quīntus ipse statūrae parvae), ait: "Frāter meus dīmidius$_4$ maior est quam tōtus."

In cōnsulātū Vatīniī, quem paucīs diēbus gessit, notābilis Cicerōnis urbānitās circumferēbātur. "Magnum ostentum[3]," inquit, "annō Vatīniī factum est, quod, illō cōnsule, nec brūma nec vēr nec aestās nec autumnus fuit."

Querentī deinde Vatīniō, quod gravātus esset[4] ad sē īnfirmum venīre, respondit: "Voluī in cōnsulātū tuō venīre, sed nox mē comprehendit."

Pompeius Cicerōnis facētiārum impatiēns fuit. Cum Cicerō ad Pompeium vēnisset, dīcentibus[5] sērō eum vēnisse respondit: "Minimē sērō vēnī: nam nihil hīc parātum videō." Deinde interrogantī Pompeiō ubi gener eius Dolābella$_5$ esset, Cicerō respondit: "Cum socerō tuō." (II, 3)

---

$_1$ an excellent brand of wine
$_2$ Marcus Cicero
$_3$ Quintus
$_4$ The painting showed the bust but was larger than the whole of the real Quintus.
$_5$ Pompey, knowing that Dolabella had joined Caesar, reproaches Cicero for having a relative on the other side. Cicero neatly reminds Pompey that he (Pompey) was the son-in-law of Caesar.

# THE VULGATE

The Vulgate is the Latin translation of the Bible made by Jerome (Hieronymus) before and after the year 400. He translated the Old Testament from the Hebrew and the New Testament from the Greek. Jerome's translation is still an accepted version used in the Catholic Church. The following selection is from the first chapter of Genesis.

In prīncipiō creāvit Deus caelum et terram.

Terra autem erat inānis et vacua, et tenebrae erant super faciem abyssī; et Spīritus Deī ferēbātur super aquās.

Dīxitque Deus: "Fīat lūx." Et facta est lūx.

Et vīdit Deus lūcem quod[1] esset bona, et dīvīsit lūcem ā tenebrīs.

Appellāvitque lūcem diem, et tenebrās noctem; factumque est vespere et māne, diēs ūnus.

Dīxit quoque Deus: "Fīat firmāmentum in mediō aquārum; et dīvidat aquās ab aquīs."

Et fēcit Deus firmāmentum dīvīsitque aquās quae erant sub firmāmentō ab hīs quae erant super firmāmentum. Et factum est ita.

Vocāvitque Deus firmāmentum caelum; et factum est vespere et māne, diēs secundus.

Dīxit vērō Deus: "Congregentur aquae quae sub caelō sunt in locum ūnum, et appāreat ārida." Et factum est ita.

Et vocāvit Deus āridam terram, congregātiōnēsque aquārum appellāvit maria. Et vīdit Deus quod esset bonum.

Et ait: "Germinet terra herbam virentem et facientem sēmen, et lignum pōmiferum faciēns frūctum iūxtā genus suum, cuius sēmen in sēmetipsō[2] sit super terram." Et factum est ita.

Et prōtulit terra herbam virentem et facientem sēmen iūxtā genus suum, lignumque faciēns frūctum et habēns ūnumquodque[3] sēmentem secundum speciem suam. Et vīdit Deus quod esset bonum.

Et factum est vespere et māne, diēs tertius.

Dīxit autem Deus: "Fīant lūmināria in firmāmentō caelī, et dīvidant diem ac noctem, et sint in[4] signa et tempora et diēs et annōs.

Ut lūceant in firmāmentō caelī et illūminent terram." Et factum est ita.

Fēcitque Deus duo lūmināria magna: lūmināre maius ut praeesset[5] diēī, et lūmināre minus ut praeesset noctī, et stēllās.

Et posuit eās in firmāmentō caelī ut lūcērent super terram.

(I, 1–17)

[1] *that*
[2] *in itself*
[3] *each one*
[4] *for*
[5] *rule*

# BEDE

Bede was an Englishman who lived in the seventh century. The best of his writings is the *Historia ecclēsiastica gentis Anglōrum,* for which he has been called the father of English history. The selection that follows tells about the conversion of Britain to Christianity.

[1] *story*
[2] *placed* (there for sale as slaves)
[3] *O grief!*
[4] *the author of darkness*
[5] *such beauty of an exterior*
[6] *the word (of God)*

Nec silentiō praetereunda opīniō[1] quae dē beātō Gregoriō trāditiōne maiōrum ad nōs usque perlāta est; quā vidēlicet ex causā admonitus tam sēdulam ergā salūtem nostrae gentis cūram gesserit. Dīcunt quia diē quādam cum, advenientibus nūper mercātōribus, multa vēnālia in forum fuissent collāta, multī ad emendum cōnflūxissent, et ipsum Gregorium inter aliōs advēnisse ac vīdisse inter alia puerōs vēnālēs positōs[2] candidī corporis ac venustī vultūs, capillōrum quoque fōrmā ēgregiā. Quōs cum aspiceret, interrogāvit, ut aiunt, dē quā regiōne vel terrā essent allātī. Dictumque est quia dē Britanniā īnsulā, cuius incolae tālis essent aspectūs. Rūrsus interrogāvit utrum īdem īnsulānī Chrīstiānī an pāgānīs adhūc errōribus essent implicātī. Dictum est quod essent pāgānī. At ille, intimō ex corde longa trahēns suspīria: "Heu, prō dolor!"[3] inquit, "quod tam lūcidī vultūs hominēs tenebrārum auctor[4] possidet, tantaque grātia frontispiciī[5] mentem ab internā grātiā$_1$ vacuam gestat!" Rūrsus ergō interrogāvit quod esset vocābulum gentis illīus. Respōnsum est quod Anglī vocārentur. At ille: "Bene," inquit; "nam et angelicam habent faciem, et tālēs angelōrum in caelīs decet esse cohērēdēs. Quod habet nōmen ipsa prōvincia dē quā istī sunt allātī?" Respōnsum est quod Deīrī vocārentur īdem prōvinciālēs. At ille: "Bene," inquit, "Deīrī; dē īrā ērutī, et ad misericordiam Chrīstī vocātī. Rēx prōvinciae illīus quōmodō appellātur?" Respōnsum est quod Aellī dīcerētur. At ille allūdēns ad nōmen ait: "Allēlūia, laudem Deī Creātōris, illīs in partibus oportet cantārī."

Accēdēnsque ad pontificem Rōmānae et apostolicae sēdis (nōndum enim erat ipse pontifex factus), rogāvit ut gentī Anglōrum in Britanniam aliquōs verbī[6] ministrōs per quōs ad Chrīstum converterētur mitteret; sē ipsum parātum esse in hoc opus, Dominō cooperante, perficiendum, sī tamen apostolicō papae hoc ut fieret placēret. Quod dum perficere nōn posset, quia, etsī pontifex concēdere illī quod petierat voluit, nōn tamen cīvēs Rōmānī ut tam longē ab urbe sēcēderet potuēre permittere; mox ut ipse pontificātūs officiō fūnctus est,$_2$ perfēcit opus diū dēsīderātum. (II, 1)

$_1$ in the Christian sense of *grace*
$_2$ A.D. 590–604

# PAULUS DIACONUS

Paul the Deacon was a Lombard from northern Italy who lived in the eighth century. He was a Benedictine monk of the famous monastery of Monte Cassino. The following selection is from his history of the Lombards.

Haud ab rē esse arbitror paulisper nārrandī ōrdinem postpōnere, et quia adhūc stilus in Germāniā vertitur,[1] mīrāculum quod illīc apud omnēs celebre habētur, seu[1] et quaedam alia breviter intimāre. In extrēmīs circium versus[2] Germāniae fīnibus, in ipsō ōceanī lītore, antrum sub ēminentī rūpe cōnspicitur, ubi septem virī, incertum ex quō tempore, longō sōpitī sopōre quiēscunt, ita illaesīs nōn sōlum corporibus sed etiam vestīmentīs, ut ex hōc ipsō, quod sine ūllā per tot annōrum curricula corruptiōne perdūrant, apud indocilēs eāsdem et barbarās nātiōnēs venerātiōne habeantur. Hī dēnique, quantum ad habitum spectat, Rōmānī esse cernuntur. Ē quibus dum ūnum quīdam cupiditāte stimulātus vellet exuere[3], mox eius, ut dīcitur, bracchia āruērunt[4], poenaque sua[5] cēterōs perterruit nē quis eōs ulterius contingere audēret. (I, 4)

[1] *and also* (with **et**)
[2] *toward the northwest*
[3] *strip, take off his clothes*
[4] *dried up, withered*
[5] = **eius**

---

[1] **Stilus vertitur** literally means *my stilus is turned* (for erasure) but here means *my pen is engaged.*

# HILDEGARD VON BINGEN

Hildegard von Bingen (1098–1179) was the first German female physician, the mother of German botany, and one of the most accomplished abbesses of the Middle Ages. She also wrote numerous songs and at least one play, all embracing good virtues and showing the constant battle between good and evil. The following are excerpts from her play *The Virtues.*

Ecce quadrāgēsimō tertiō temporālis cursus meī annō,
cum cēlestī magnō timōre,
tremulā intentiōne inhērerem[1],
vīdī maximum splendōrem,
in quō facta est vōx dē cēlō[2] ad mē dicēns:
ō homō fragilis,
et cinis cineris
et pūtrēdō pūtrēdinis
dīc et scrībe quē vidēs et audīs.
***

[1] *I lived*
[2] = **caelō**

[3] *all creation was verdant*
[4] *greenness*
[5] *champion*
[6] *to grow dry*
[7] *are exposed to mockery*
[8] *reach*

In principiō omnēs creāturē viruērunt[3]
in mediō flōrēs flōruērunt;
posteā viriditās[4] dēscendit.
Et istud vir prēliātor[5] vīdit et dīxit:
Hic sciō, sed aureus numerus nōndum est plēnus.
Tū ergō, paternum speculum aspice:
in corpore meō fatīgātiōnem sustineō,
parvulī etiam meī dēficiunt.
Nunc memor estō, quod plēnitūdō quē[1] in prīmō facta est
ārēscere[6] nōn dēbuit,
et tunc in tē habuistī
quod oculus tuus numquam cēderet
usque dum corpus meum vidērēs plēnum gemmārum.
Nam mē fatīgat quod omnia membra mea in irrisiōnem vādunt.[7]
Pater, vidē, vulnera mea tibi ostendō.
Ergō nunc, omnēs hominēs,
genua vestra ad patrem vestrum flectite,
ut vōbīs manum suam porrigat[8].

[1] quae

# CAESAR OF HEISTERBACH

Caesar was a monk in the monastery of Heisterbach, near Bonn, in the thirteenth century. He wrote a book of miracles, of which the following is one.

[1] *of Treves*
[2] *subject, theme*
[3] *homage*
[4] *yes*

In ecclēsiā sānctī Simeōnis diōcēsis Trēverēnsis[1] scholāris parvulus erat. Hic cum diē quādam, datā eī māteriā[2] ā magistrō suō, versūs ex eā compōnere nequīret trīstisque sedēret, sōlī sīc sedentī diabolus in speciē hominis appāruit. Cui cum dīceret: "Quid dolēs, puer, quid sīc trīstis sedēs?" respondit puer: "Magistrum meum timeō, quia de themate quod ab eō recēpī versūs compōnere nequeō." Et ille: "Vīs mihi facere hominium[3] et ego versūs tibi compōnam?" Puerō vērō nōn intelligente quod inimīcus omnium diabolus tenderet ad malum suum, respondit: "Etiam[4], domine, parātus sum facere quicquid iusseris, dum modo versūs habeam et nōn vāpulem." Nesciēbat enim quis esset. Porrēxit eī manum, hominium eī faciēns. Ā quō continuō versūs dictātōs in tabulīs accipiēns, dictātōrem amplius nōn vīdit.

Quōs[1] cum tempore congruō magistrō suō redderet, ille versuum excellentiam mīrātus expāvit, dīvīnam, nōn hominis, in illīs cōnsīderāns scientiam. Quī ait: "Dīc mihi, quis tibi dictāvit hōs versūs?" Dīcente puerō, "Ego,

[1] i.e., the verses

## Transmission of Latin and Greek Works Before Printing: 5

Giraudon/Art Resource, NY

Cicero's rhetorical work, *Dē Ōrātōre,* dealt with the history and theory of oratory, as well as the education and characteristics of the ideal orator. This manuscript page from the late thirteenth century is a translation into French of Cicero's work. Richly decorated, it even includes a drawing, complete with a caption, of a professor lecturing to six students and two adults. The upheld book represents the work he is lecturing on. Notice that, at least in the French version, small spaces are left between the words.

magister," et ille omnīnō, dum nōn crēderet, immō puerum dīligentius īnstāret interrogātiōnis verbum saepius repetēns, cōnfessus est puer omnia secundum ōrdinem quae gesserat. Tunc ait magister: "Fīlī, malus ille versificātor fuit, scīlicet diabolus," et adiēcit: "Cārissime, paeniteat tē sēductōrī illī hominium fēcisse?" Respondente puerō: "Etiam, magister," ait ille: "Modo abrenūntiā diabolō et hominiō eius et omnibus pompīs eius et omnibus eius operibus." Et fēcit sīc. Magister autem superpellicī eius manicās abscīdēns[5] diabolō iactāvit dīcēns: "Hae manicae tuae sunt, hominum sēductor, nīl aliud in hāc deī creātūrā possidēbis." Statimque raptae sunt manicae cōram[6] omnibus et fulminātae sunt,[7] corpore tamen puerī incorruptō. Haec mihi dicta sunt ā quōdam priōre Trēverēnsis ecclēsiae. (II, 14)

[5] *cutting off the sleeves from the surplice* (an outer garment)
[6] *in the presence of*
[7] *were struck by lightning*

# PETRARCH

Petrarch (1304–1374) was born at Arezzo, Italy, but early in life he moved to southern France. He is most famous for his Italian poems but he wrote far more in Latin, including his letters. He had a great enthusiasm for the ancient classics and awakened other people's interest in them. Cicero was one of his favorite authors.

Petrarch searched far and wide for copies of the classics. He played a very important part in starting the movement called the Renaissance, a revival of interest in the classics.

## The Craving for Books

Ūna inexplēbilis cupiditās mē tenet, quam frēnāre hāctenus nec potuī certē nec voluī; mihi enim interblandior[1] honestārum rērum nōn inhonestam esse cupīdinem. Exspectās audīre morbī genus? Librīs satiārī nequeō. Et habeō plūrēs forte quam oportet; sed sīcut in cēterīs rēbus, sīc et in librīs accidit: quaerendī successus avāritiae calcar est. Quīn immō, singulāre quiddam in librīs est: aurum, argentum, gemmae, purpurea vestis, marmorea domus, cultus ager, pictae tabulae, cēteraque id genus,[2] mūtam habent et superficiāriam voluptātem; librī medullitus[3] dēlectant, colloquuntur, cōnsulunt et vīvā quādam nōbīs atque argūtā familiāritāte iunguntur, neque sōlum sēsē lēctōribus quisque suīs īnsinuat, sed et aliōrum nōmen ingerit et alter alterius dēsīderium facit. Ac nē rēs egeat exemplō, Mārcum mihi Varrōnem

[1] *I flatter myself*
[2] *other things of this sort*
[3] *to the heart, deep within* (adverb)

cārum et amābilem Cicerōnis *Acadēmicus*$_{1}$ fēcit; Enniī nōmen in *Officiōrum* librīs audīvī; prīmum Terentiī amōrem ex *Tusculānārum quaestiōnum* lēctiōne concēpī.

Sunt quī librōs, ut cētera, nōn ūtendī studiō cumulent, sed habendī libīdine, neque tam ut ingeniī praesidium, quam ut thalamī ōrnāmentum. Ammōnicus Serēnus bibliothēcam habuisse memorātur sexāgintā duo librōrum mīlia continentem, quōs omnēs Gordiānō minōrī, quī tunc erat imperātor, amantissimō discipulō suō, moriēns relīquit; quae rēs nōn minus illum quōdam modō quam imperium honestāvit. Haec prō excūsātiōne vitiī meī prōque sōlāciō tantōrum comitum dicta sint. Tū vērō, sī tibi cārus sum, aliquibus fīdīs et litterātīs virīs hanc cūram impōnitō: Etrūriam perquīrant, religiōsōrum[4] armāria[5] ēvolvant cēterōrumque studiōsōrum hominum, sī quid usquam ēmergeret lēniendae dīcam an[6] irrītandae sitī meae idōneum. Quōque vigilantior fīās, scītō mē eāsdem precēs amīcīs aliīs in Britanniam Galliāsque et Hispāniās dēstināsse. (*Fam.* III, 18)

[4] *of the monks*
[5] *shelves*
[6] *or shall I say*

---

$_{1}$ title of a book by Cicero

## To Marcus Tullius Cicero

Ō Rōmānī ēloquiī summe parēns, nec sōlus ego sed omnēs tibi grātiās agimus, quīcumque Latīnae linguae flōribus ōrnāmur; tuīs enim prāta dē fontibus irrigāmus, tuō ducātū dīrēctōs,$_{1}$ tuīs suffrāgiīs adiūtōs,$_{1}$ tuō nōs lūmine illūstrātōs ingenuē profitēmur; tuīs dēnique, ut ita dīcam, auspiciīs ad hanc, quantulacumque est, scrībendī facultātem ac prōpositum pervēnisse.

Quid dē vītā, quid dē ingeniō tuō sentiam, audīstī. Exspectās audīre dē librīs tuīs, quaenam illōs excēperit fortūna, quam seu vulgō seu doctiōribus probentur?[1] Exstant equidem praeclāra volūmina, quae nē dīcam[2] perlegere, sed nec[3] ēnumerāre sufficimus. Fāma rērum tuārum celeberrima atque ingēns et sonōrum nōmen; perrārī autem studiōsī$_{2}$, seu temporum adversitās seu ingeniōrum hebetūdō ac sēgnitiēs seu, quod magis arbitror, aliō[4] cōgēns animōs cupiditās causa est. Itaque librōrum aliquī, nesciō quidem an irreparābiliter, nōbīs tamen quī nunc vīvimus, nisi fallor, periēre; magnus dolor meus, magnus saeculī nostrī pudor, magna posteritātis iniūria.

Reliquum est ut urbis Rōmae ac Rōmānae reī pūblicae statum audīre velīs, quae patriae faciēs, quae cīvium concordia, ad quōs rērum summa pervēnerit, quibus manibus quantōque cōnsiliō frēna trāctentur imperiī; Histerne[5] et Gangēs, Hibērus, Nīlus et Tanais līmitēs nostrī sint, an vērō quisquam surrēxerit "Imperium Ōceanō, fāmam quī terminet astrīs." Vērum enimvērō tacēre melius fuerit; crēde enim mihi, Cicerō, sī quō in statū rēs nostrae sint audieris, excident tibi lacrimae, quamlibet[6] vel caelī vel Erebī partem tenēs. Aeternum valē. (*Fam.* XXIV, 4)

[1] *how they are regarded by the common people and the more learned*
[2] *not to say*
[3] *not even*
[4] *in other directions*
[5] *whether the Danube*
[6] *whatever*

---

$_{1}$ with **nōs**
$_{2}$ Supply **sunt.**

# COLUCCIO SALUTATI

Coluccio Salutati (1331–1406) was a busy man as chancellor of Florence for more than thirty years, but he still had time to follow in Petrarch's footsteps, becoming an eager reader of the ancient classics and interesting a large number of young men in them. Thus he founded the group of humanists who made Florence the center of the new learning and developed the great movement called the Renaissance. He was chiefly responsible for bringing the Greek teacher Manuel Chrysoloras to Florence in 1396, thus starting the study of Greek, largely unknown in the West before that time.

## To Manuel Chrysoloras

[1] *that . . . I have arranged that*
[2] *from so far away*

. . . Nunc autem scītō mē tibi quod[1] in hāc urbe rēgiā Graecās doceās litterās salāriō pūblicō prōcūrāsse;[1] nec pigēbit, ut arbitror, mūtāsse caelum,[1] cum hīc et honorābilem vītam et plūrimōs quī tē colent invēneris. Quid tē deceat quī tam ā longē[2] vocāris, Graecus in Italiam, Thrācius in Tusciam et Byzantius Flōrentiam, tū vidēbis.

[1] i.e., changed your home

## The Defense of Poetry

[1] *to put it more correctly*
[2] *that's up to you* (literally, *you see to it*)

Vīdī nūper et rīsī, venerābilis in Chrīstō pater, litterās tuās quās mittis ad ēgregium virum Angelum Corbinellum, dīlēctissimum fīlium[1] meum, quibus eum mōre tuō cōnāris ā poēticīs et saeculāribus studiīs revocāre, vel, quō rēctius dīxerim,[1] dēterrēre. Quod an rēctē faciās tū vīderīs.[2] Vērum tē videō nōndum quaestiōnis terminōs intellegere versārīque in illō tuae simplicitātis errōre, quō reputās ista nostra poētica grave et inexpiābile nefās esse et perniciōsa mendācia. Quod sī vērum est, nec potest sub verbōrum cortice mendācium latēre pūritās et integritās vēritātis, dīc, obsecrō, quō modō vērum est: "spīritus Dominī ferēbātur super aquās"; et illud: "dīxit Deus: 'fīat lūx'";[2] et sescenta[3] tālia? Quō modō fertur enim, quod corporālium est, "spīritus Dominī super aquās," quī prōrsus incorporeus est? Quō modō: "dīxit Deus: 'fīat lūx'"; cum Deus nec ōs habeat nec linguam,

[1] not literally
[2] Coluccio's point is that these two passages from the Bible cannot be understood literally, that therefore poetry need not be so understood.
[3] We would say *thousand.*

quae sunt necessāria membra īnstrūmentaque dīcentis? Vērum haec aliās. Nunc autem, quō vidēre possīs liquidius vēritātem, ostendam prius quid per poēticam intellegere dēbeāmus; cōnsequenter clārum efficiam sacrās litterās dīvīnamque Scrīptūram nēdum[3] habēre cum istā[4] commercium, sed vērē nihil esse nisi poēticam; tertiō vērō quantum oportet annītar ostendere etiam fidēlibus Chrīstiānīs nōn esse prohibendam gentīlium poētarum lēctiōnem; tandemque cōnābor ad illa quae dīxerīs respondēre.

[3] *not only*

Quid inter istōs est cūr dēbeant prohibērī? Sciō legōque cotīdiē apud Hieronymum, Ambrosium, et Augustīnum ēgregia philosophōrum et ōrātōrum dicta carminaque poētarum, quae velut sīdus aliquod inter trāctātūs illōs sānctissimōs ēminent et resplendent; quae quidem tē nōn arbitror quasi crīmen aliquod condemnāre. Sī vēra, sī sāncta, sī decōra pulchraque sunt apud istōs doctōrēs inventa et ibi sine peccātō leguntur, cūr apud auctōrēs suōs dīcī dēbent nefāria vel profāna? Cūr nōbīs prohibita, sī sacrīs doctōribus concessa sunt?

---

[4] i.e., poetry

# LEONARDO BRUNI

Leonardo Bruni was a disciple of Coluccio. In this letter he writes to Poggio, another of Coluccio's disciples, about Poggio's discoveries of manuscripts of previously unknown authors and better manuscripts of other authors.

Sī valēs, bene est; ego quidem valeō. Lēgī apud Nīcolāum[1] nostrum litterās quās dē hāc ultimā profectiōne ac dē inventiōne quōrundam librōrum scrīpsistī. Nec tantum dē iīs sed dē optimā spē quam prō cēterōrum adeptiōne suscēpisse tē videō laetandum exīstimō. Erit profectō haec tua glōria, ut āmissa iam ac perdita excellentium virōrum scrīpta tuō labōre ac dīligentiā saeculō nostrō restituās. Nec ea rēs sōlum nōbīs grāta erit sed et posterīs nostrīs, id est studiōrum nostrōrum successōribus. Neque enim silēbuntur ista nec oblitterābuntur sed exstābit memoriā haec[2] dūdum longō intervāllō perdita et iam plānē dēplōrāta per tuam industriam recuperāta ac restitūta nōbīs fuisse. Utque Camillus secundus ā Rōmulō conditor[1] dictus est, quod ille[3] statuit urbem, hic āmissam restituit, sīc tū omnium quae iam āmissa tuā virtūte ac dīligentiā nōbīs restitūta fuerint secundus auctor meritō nuncupābere.

[1] *second founder (of Rome) after Romulus*

---

[1] Niccolò Niccoli was another disciple of Coluccio.
[2] i.e., **scrīpta**
[3] Romulus

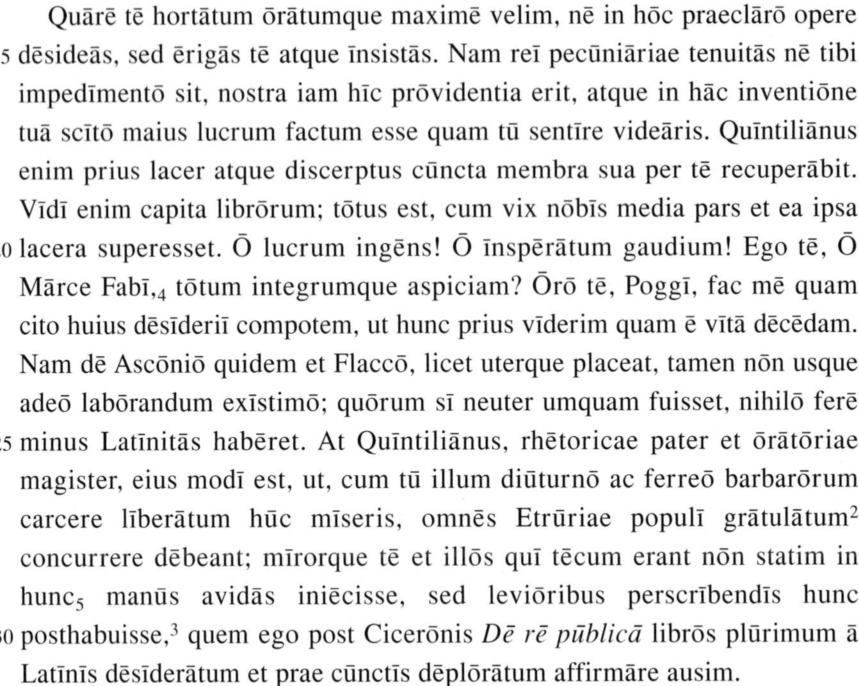

Quārē tē hortātum ōrātumque maximē velim, nē in hōc praeclārō opere dēsideās, sed ērigās tē atque īnsistās. Nam reī pecūniāriae tenuitās nē tibi impedīmentō sit, nostra iam hīc prōvidentia erit, atque in hāc inventiōne tuā scītō maius lucrum factum esse quam tū sentīre videāris. Quīntiliānus enim prius lacer atque discerptus cūncta membra sua per tē recuperābit. Vīdī enim capita librōrum; tōtus est, cum vix nōbīs media pars et ea ipsa lacera superesset. Ō lucrum ingēns! Ō īnspērātum gaudium! Ego tē, Ō Mārce Fabī,[4] tōtum integrumque aspiciam? Ōrō tē, Poggī, fac mē quam cito huius dēsīderiī compotem, ut hunc prius vīderim quam ē vītā dēcēdam. Nam dē Asconiō quidem et Flaccō, licet uterque placeat, tamen nōn usque adeō labōrandum exīstimō; quōrum sī neuter umquam fuisset, nihilō ferē minus Latīnitās habēret. At Quīntiliānus, rhētoricae pater et ōrātōriae magister, eius modī est, ut, cum tū illum diūturnō ac ferreō barbarōrum carcere līberātum hūc mīseris, omnēs Etrūriae populī grātulātum[2] concurrere dēbeant; mīrorque tē et illōs quī tēcum erant nōn statim in hunc[5] manūs avidās iniēcisse, sed leviōribus perscrībendīs hunc posthabuisse,[3] quem ego post Cicerōnis *Dē rē pūblicā* librōs plūrimum ā Latīnīs dēsīderātum et prae cūnctīs dēplōrātum affirmāre ausim.

Proximum est, ut tē moneam, nē in iīs quae hīc habēmus tempus terās, sed quae nōn habēmus conquīrās, quōrum maximē Varrōnis et Cicerōnis opera tibi prōposita sint. Valē et mē amā. Flōrentiae, Īdibus Septembr. MCCCCXVI.

² *to congratulate*

³ *postponed this in favor of copying less important books*

---

[4] Quintilian

[5] the Quintilian manuscript

## Enrichment

Visit a museum to see Roman coins, statues, scrolls, and other ancient objects. Ask or write to museum curators about differing translations of ancient inscriptions, scrolls, and manuscripts. See if curators can put you in touch with fluent Latin speakers and writers with whom you can converse and correspond. Discover the value of mastering Latin for an archaeological or curatorial career. Ask museum staff for specific career tips.

# POGGIO BRACCIOLINI

Poggio was Coluccio's most important disciple, particularly famous for discovering manuscripts, especially at the monastery of St. Gall in Switzerland, which he visited while attending a church council at Constance, Germany. He spent several years in England and helped spread the new gospel of humanism (the reading of the classics) there. He was a papal secretary and, like Bruni, chancellor of Florence.

## Great Discoveries

Sed quam temere persaepe ēveniunt quae nōn audeās optāre! ut inquit Terentius noster. Fortūna quaedam fuit cum sua tum maximē nostra[1] ut, cum essēmus Cōnstantiae ōtiōsī, cupīdō incesseret videndī eius locī quō ille$_1$ reclūsus tenēbātur. Est autem monastērium Sānctī Gallī prope urbem hanc. Itaque nōnnūllī[2] animī$_2$ laxandī et simul perquīrendōrum librōrum, quōrum magnus numerus esse dīcēbātur, grātiā eō perrēximus. Ibi inter cōnfertissimam librōrum cōpiam, quōs longum esset recēnsēre, Quīntiliānum comperimus adhūc salvum et incolumem, plēnum tamen sitū et pulvere squālentem. Erant enim nōn in bibliothēcā librī illī, ut eōrum dignitās postulābat, sed in taeterrimō quōdam et obscūrō carcere, fundō scīlicet ūnīus turris, quō nē capitālis quidem reī damnātī[3] retrūderentur. Atquī ego prō certō exīstimō, sī essent quī haec barbarōrum ergastula, quibus hōs dētinent virōs$_3$, rīmārentur ac recognōscerent mōre maiōrum, similem fortūnam expertūrōs in multīs.

[1] *not only his* (Quintilian's) *but especially mine, with* **fortūna**
[2] *several (of us)*
[3] *not even those convicted of a capital crime*

$_1$ Quintilian
$_2$ with **grātiā**
$_3$ i.e., their writings

## The Ruins of Rome

Nūper, cum pontifex Martīnus, paulō antequam diem suum obīret,[1] ab urbe in agrum Tusculānum$_1$ sēcessisset valētūdinis grātiā, nōs autem essēmus negōtiīs cūrīsque pūblicīs vacuī, vīsēbāmus saepe dēserta urbis, Antōnius Luscus,$_2$ vir clārissimus, egoque, admīrantēs animō tum ob veterem collāpsōrum aedificiōrum magnitūdinem et vāstās urbis antīquae ruīnās, tum ob tantī imperiī ingentem strāgem stupendam profectō ac dēplōrandam fortūnae varietātem. Cum autem cōnscendissēmus aliquandō Capitōlīnum collem, Antōnius obequitandō paulum fessus cum quiētem appeteret, dēscendentēs ex equīs cōnsēdimus in ipsīs Tarpeiae arcis$_3$ ruīnīs pōne[2] ingēns portae cuiusdam, ut putō, templī marmoreum līmen plūrimāsque passim cōnfrāctās columnās, unde magnā ex parte prōspectus urbis patet.

Hīc Antōnius, cum aliquantum hūc illūc oculōs circumtulisset, suspīrāns stupentīque similis,[3] "Ō quantum," inquit, "Poggī, haec Capitōlia ab illīs distant quae noster Marō cecinit,

Aurea nunc, ōlim silvestribus horrida dūmīs!

[1] *met his day,* i.e., *died*
[2] *behind* (preposition)
[3] *like one who was stupefied*

$_1$ Tusculum was in the hills southeast of Rome.
$_2$ Antonio Loschi was still another of Coluccio's disciples.
$_3$ the Capitoline Hill, where the Tarpeian rock was

[4] *though*

Ēvolvās licet[4] historiās omnēs, omnia scrīptōrum monumenta pertrāctēs, omnēs gestārum rērum annālēs scrūtēris, nūlla umquam exempla mūtātionis suae maiōra fortūna prōtulit quam urbem Rōmam, pulcherrimam ōlim ac magnificentissimam omnium quae aut fuēre aut futūrae sunt.

Id vērō gravissimum et haud parvā cum admīrātiōne recēnsendum, hunc Capitōliī collem, caput quondam Rōmānī imperiī atque orbis terrārum arcem, quem omnēs rēgēs ac prīncipēs tremēbant, in quem triumphantēs tot imperātōrēs ascendērunt, dōnīs ac spoliīs tot tantārumque gentium ōrnātum flōrentemque ac ūniversō orbī spectandum, adeō dēsōlātum atque ēversum et ā priōre illō statū immūtātum ut vīneae in senātorum subsellia successerint.

# LORENZO VALLA

Lorenzo Valla (1407–1457) wrote a book on the Latin language and was one of the most prominent humanists in the Italy of his time.

[1] *sacred nature*
[2] *by us Romans*

Magnum Latīnī sermōnis sacrāmentum[1] est, magnum profectō nūmen, quod apud peregrīnōs, apud barbarōs, apud hostēs sānctē ac religiōsē per tot saecula custōdītur, ut nōn tam dolendum nōbīs Rōmānīs[2] quam gaudendum sit atque, ipsō etiam terrārum orbe exaudiente, glōriandum. Āmīsimus Rōmam, āmīsimus rēgnum, āmīsimus dominātum, tametsī nōn nostrā sed temporum culpā, vērum tamen per hunc splendidiōrem dominātum$_1$ in magnā adhūc orbis parte rēgnāmus. Nostra est Italia, nostra Gallia, nostra Hispānia, Germānia, Pannonia, Dalmatia, Illyricum, multaeque aliae nātiōnēs. Ibi namque Rōmānum imperium est ubicumque Rōmāna lingua dominātur.

---

$_1$ i.e., of the Latin language

# PIUS II *(ENEA SILVIO PICCOLOMINI)*

Pope Pius II (1405–1464), a Sienese poet in his youth and a famous pope in his later years (1458–1464), was a great supporter of the Roman classics. Here he gives advice to his nephew.

Rettulit mihi Nannēs, pater tuus, tē, dum puer adhūc forēs, mīrō litterārum amōre fuisse incēnsum, postquam vērō ex ephēbīs[1] excessistī, nēminem esse quī tibi amplius ut studeās queat persuādēre; quae rēs nōn mīra tantum mihi sed stupenda fuit. Cēterī enim pueritiam simul et stultitiam dēpōnunt, virīlem togam et prūdentiam induentēs. Tū contrā sapiēns puer, stultus vir cupis vidērī et barbam quasi umbrāculum[2] virtūtis recipis. Doleō certē tuī causā nec quid dē tē futūrum sit sciō. Iubet Cicerō ut quīlibet in adulēscentiā viam ēligat et genus vītae honestum quō ūtī dēbeat. Idem Herculēs factitāvit. Nam cum per quiētem[3] duae sibi mulierēs suprā hūmānam fōrmam venustae appārērent et altera sibi voluptātem, labōrem altera prōmitteret, hanc secūtus est sciēns quod post labōrem praemium certāminis datur. Nec corōnātur, ut inquit apostolus, nisi quī lēgitimē certāverit. Tū vērō, ut audiō, vagārī vīs semper nec aliquod genus vītae honestum amplectī studēs. Litterās, quās puer amāstī, iam vir odiō habēs. Pudet mē tuī causā. Nesciō enim quid esse possīs absque[4] litterīs, nisi asinus bipēs. Quid enim homō est absque doctrīnā quantumvīs[5] dīves, quantumvīs potēns? Quid inter hominem illitterātum et marmoream statuam interest? Nōn dux, nōn rēx, nōn imperātor alicuius pretiī est litterārum ignārus.

[1] *from boyhood*
[2] *umbrella*
[3] *in sleep*
[4] *without*
[5] *no matter how*

UNIT
X

# OVID

## Unit Objectives

- To read stories from Ovid's *Metamorphōsēs* with understanding and appreciation
- To read condensed literary selections at sight
- To understand word order in Latin poetry
- To read Latin verse properly

Apelles was a very famous Greek artist who lived in the fourth century B.C. Pliny the Elder thought him the greatest painter who ever lived. He was a friend of Alexander the Great and was court painter to Philip of Macedon. His style was characterized by graceful figures, spatial depth, fine line quality, and attention to detail. He was conscious of showing realism and only used four colors, which he considered basic earth colors: black, white, red, and yellow. Unfortunately, all of his works are lost, but in the fifteenth century, Sandro Botticelli, the great Italian Renaissance painter, tried to recreate two of them based on descriptions in Pliny and Lucan. This one is called *The Calumny of Apelles* and shows King Midas, with donkey's ears, sitting in judgment on "Ignorance" and "Suspicion," as "Calumny" is brought in as a witness.

# OVID'S LIFE

Pūblius Ovidius Nāsō was born on March 20, 43 B.C., in Sulmo, about 90 miles southeast of Rome. After studying law, Ovid began a career in public life but soon turned away to give his full attention to the writing of poetry. He said of himself that he was unable to write prose, that every statement came out as poetry. He became the most cherished poet of the smart set, brilliant and witty and popular. At the age of 50 he was removed from his position as a poet of pleasure in cosmopolitan Rome by exile to Tomis on the Black Sea, where he died in A.D. 17. The reasons for his exile, resulting from the displeasure of the emperor Augustus, are still a mystery; the allusions Ovid makes to those reasons are couched in veiled terms.

In his earlier years Ovid was acclaimed for his love poems *(Amōrēs, Ars Amatōria, Heroidēs),* but his greatest work was the *Metamorphōsēs,* 15 books of stories of transformation of animals, human beings, and inanimate objects into other forms. A work on the calendar, the *Fastī,* was left unfinished (six books, one for each month of the first half of the year), interrupted by exile. At Tomis, Ovid wrote the *Trīstia* and *Epistulae ex Pontō,* elegies with some pleas for recall.

The *Metamorphōsēs,* comprising 250 stories of changes, from the creation of the world out of chaos down to the transformation of Julius Caesar into a star, constitutes our main storehouse of Greek and Roman mythology. Ovid was an excellent poet technically, writing with grace, humor, and charm. He is one of the great poets of Rome.

To appreciate the construction of poetry in Latin, you might want to try writing several lines of your own. Explore your own thoughts on Ovid's theme of transformation. Try to incorporate an idiomatic expression. See if your classmates would enjoy conducting a poetry reading and discussing their thoughts regarding each other's poems and the poetic form of artistic expression.

### Poetic Word Order

The order of words in Latin poetry is even freer than in prose. Words that belong together are often widely separated. This is especially true of adjectives and their nouns. Note particularly the following points, illustrated by references to lines in the first selection, "Pyramus and Thisbe":

1. The order adjective–preposition–noun is common. Often a number of other words come between the adjective and the preposition. In such cases preposition and noun are likely to be at the end of the line. Cf. lines 100, 166.
2. An interlocking order, in which two or more phrases are involved, occurs frequently. A particular favorite is the use of two nouns and two adjectives in all possible combinations. Cf. lines 57–58, 69–70, 81, 100, 104.

3. A verb or participle is particularly likely to come between adjective and noun. Cf. lines 57, 62, 81, 82, 83, 87.
4. Subjects and other words often precede the introductory word of the subordinate clauses to which they belong. Cf. lines 111, 147.
5. Coordinating conjunctions (**et, sed,** etc.) sometimes come second instead of first in their clauses.
6. Other remarkable characteristics are illustrated in the following lines: 64 (**magis tegitur, tēctus magis**); 71 (**hinc Thisbē, Pȳramus illinc**); 91–92 (**lūx... praecipitātur aquīs et aquīs nox exit**); 117 (**dedit nōtae lacrimās, dedit ōscula vestī**).

## Reading Latin Verse

The rhythm of Latin verse does not depend on word accent as does that of English but on the length of syllables. The rules for determining the length of syllables are:

1. A syllable is long by nature if it contains a long vowel or a diphthong.
2. A syllable is long by position if it contains a short vowel followed by two or more consonants or the consonant **x (= cs).**

In poetry a long syllable is treated as twice the length of a short syllable. Since a line of poetry is considered one long word, in a case like **is facit** the first word is a long syllable because the (short) vowel is followed by two consonants (**s, f**).

Several syllables are combined to form a foot. The dactyl is a foot consisting of a long syllable followed by two short syllables, written – ⏑ ⏑.

The spondee consists of two long syllables, – –. When a line contains six feet, it is called a hexameter. The *Metamorphōsēs* is written in the dactylic hexameter. A spondee may be substituted for a dactyl in every foot except the fifth, though occasionally a spondee is used even here. The sixth foot is always a spondee.[1] The beat is on the first syllable of each foot.

A stop (**p, b, t, d, c, g**) followed by a liquid (**l, r**) does not make a syllable long, although there are occasional exceptions. **H** is disregarded entirely. The combinations **qu** and **gu** (before a vowel) constitute one consonant; the **u** is disregarded.

[1] The last syllable is often short, but the "rest" at the end of the line fills out the foot

### Elision

If a word ends in a vowel or a vowel plus **m** and the next word begins with a vowel or **h**, the first vowel disappears entirely. This is called *elision;* the vowel is said to be "elided."

> **foribusqu(e) excēdere** is pronounced **foribusquexcēdere.**

Before **es** or **est,** *prodelision* occurs—that is, the first vowel of the following word disappears.

> **nimium est** is pronounced **nimiumst.**

### Scansion

The first five lines of *Pyramus and Thisbe* are scanned (marked) to show the meter, as follows:

Pȳramus | et This|bē, iuve|num pul|cherrimus | alter, |
altera, | quās Ori|ēns habu|it, prae|lāta pu|ellīs, |
contigu|ās tenu|ēre do|mōs, ubi | dīcitur | altam |
coctili|bus mū|rīs cīn|xisse Se|mīramis | urbem. |
Nōtiti|am prī|mōsque gra|dūs vī|cīnia | fēcit |

# PYRAMUS AND THISBE

This is the famous story of two lovers living in adjacent homes in ancient Babylonia who were forbidden by their parents to see each other. Conversing through a crack in the common wall between the two houses, they arranged a secret meeting at night outside the city. Their trysting place was under a mulberry tree. The metamorphosis in this story is the change in the color of the fruit of the mulberry from white to red, from the blood of the young people.

Pȳramus et Thisbē, iuvenum pulcherrimus alter,
altera, quās[1] Oriēns habuit, praelāta puellīs,
contiguās tenuēre domōs, ubi dīcitur altam
coctilibus[1] mūrīs cīnxisse Semīramis urbem.
Nōtitiam prīmōsque gradūs[2] vīcīnia fēcit,
tempore crēvit amor; taedae quoque iūre[3] coīssent,

[1] *of brick* (literally, *baked*)
[2] i.e., *of love*
[3] *in lawful wedlock* (literally, *by the law of the torch*)

---

[1] The relative clause precedes the antecedent, **puellīs.**

sed vetuēre patrēs. Quod nōn potuēre vetāre,
ex aequō captīs ārdēbant mentibus ambō.
Cōnscius omnis abest; nūtū signīsque loquuntur,
quōque magis[4] tegitur, tēctus magis aestuat ignis.
Fissus erat$_{2}$ tenuī rīmā, quam dūxerat[5] ōlim
cum fieret, pariēs domuī commūnis utrīque.
Id vitium nūllī per saecula longa notātum
(quid nōn sentit amor?) prīmī vīdistis amantēs
et vōcis fēcistis iter;[6] tūtaeque per illud
murmure blanditiae minimō trānsīre solēbant.
Saepe, ubi cōnstiterant, hinc Thisbē, Pȳramus illinc,
inque vicēs fuerat captātus anhēlitus ōris,[7]
"Invide," dīcēbant, "pariēs, quid amantibus obstās?
Quantum erat[8] ut sinerēs tōtō nōs corpore iungī,
aut, hoc sī nimium est, vel ad ōscula danda patērēs$_{3}$!
Nec sumus ingrātī; tibi nōs dēbēre fatēmur
quod[9] datus est verbīs ad amīcās trānsitus aurēs."
Tālia dīversā nēquīquam sēde locūtī
sub noctem[10] dīxēre, "Valē," partīque dedēre
ōscula quisque[11] suae nōn pervenientia contrā.
Postera nocturnōs Aurōra remōverat ignēs,
sōlque pruīnōsās radiīs siccāverat herbās;
ad solitum coiēre locum. Tum murmure parvō
multa prius questī$_{4}$, statuunt ut nocte silentī
fallere custōdēs foribusque excēdere temptent,$_{5}$
cumque domō exierint, urbis quoque tēcta relinquant,$_{5}$
nēve sit errandum lātō spatiantibus$_{6}$ arvō,
conveniant$_{5}$ ad busta Ninī$_{7}$ lateantque$_{5}$ sub umbrā
arboris: arbor ibī niveīs ūberrima pōmīs,
ardua mōrus[12], erat gelidō contermina fontī.
Pācta placent; et lūx[13] tardē discēdere vīsa
praecipitātur aquīs et aquīs nox exit ab īsdem.
Callida per tenebrās, versātō cardine,[14] Thisbē
ēgreditur fallitque suōs adopertaque vultum
pervenit ad tumulum distāque sub arbore sēdit.
Audācem$_{8}$ faciēbat amor. Venit ecce recentī
caede leaena boum$_{9}$ spūmantēs oblita[15] rictūs[16]

[4] *the more*
[5] *it had acquired*
[6] *a passage for the voice*
[7] *and each had heard the other's breathing*
[8] *how small a thing it would be*
[9] *the fact that*
[10] *at nightfall*
[11] *each*
[12] *mulberry tree* (feminine)
[13] *daylight*
[14] *opening the door* (literally, *turning the hinge*)
[15] *smeared* (from **oblinō**)
[16] *jaws*

---

$_{2}$ The subject is **pariēs.**
$_{3}$ i.e., wide enough (from **pateō**)
$_{4}$ from **queror**
$_{5}$ volitive clause, object of **statuunt**
$_{6}$ modifies **eīs** understood, dative of agent: *that they need not wander at random*
$_{7}$ Semiramis' husband
$_{8}$ Supply **eam.**
$_{9}$ from **bōs;** genitive with **caede**

dēpositūra[17] sitim vīcīnī fontis in undā.
Quam procul ad lūnae radiōs Babylōnia Thisbē
vīdit et obscūrum timidō pede fūgit in antrum;
dumque fugit tergō [18] vēlāmina lāpsa relīquit.
Ut lea saeva sitim multā compescuit undā,
dum redit in silvās, inventōs forte sine ipsā [10]
ōre cruentātō tenuēs laniāvit amictūs.
Sērius ēgressus vēstīgia vīdit in altō
pulvere certa ferae tōtōque expalluit ōre
Pȳramus. Ut vērō vestem quoque sanguine tīnctam
repperit, "Ūna duōs," inquit, "nox perdet amantēs,
ē quibus illa fuit longā dignissima vītā;
nostra nocēns anima est. Ego tē, miseranda, perēmī,
in loca plēna metūs quī iussī nocte venīrēs
nec prior hūc vēnī. Nostrum dīvellite corpus
et scelerāta ferō cōnsūmite vīscera morsū,
Ō quīcumque sub hāc habitātis rūpe, leōnēs!
Sed timidī [19] est optāre necem!" Vēlāmina Thisbēs[11]
tollit et ad pāctae sēcum fert arboris umbram.
Utque dedit nōtae[12] lacrimās, dedit ōscula vestī,
"Accipe nunc," inquit, "nostrī quoque sanguinis haustūs."
Quōque[13] erat accīnctus dēmīsit in īlia ferrum,
nec mora,[14] ferventī moriēns ē vulnere trāxit[15]
et iacuit resupīnus humō[16]. Cruor ēmicat altē,
nōn aliter quam cum vitiātō fistula plumbō
scinditur et tenuī strīdente forāmine longās
ēiaculātur aquās atque ictibus āera rumpit.[20]
Arboreī fētūs aspergine[21] caedis in ātram
vertuntur faciem, madefactaque sanguine rādīx
purpureō tingit pendentia mōra colōre.
Ecce metū nōndum positō, nē fallat amantem,
illa redit iuvenemque oculīs animōque requīrit,
quantaque vītārit nārrare perīcula gestit[22].
Utque[23] locum et vīsā [24] cognōscit in arbore fōrmam,
sīc[23] facit incertam pōmī color: haeret an haec sit.

[17] *to quench*
[18] *from her back* (with **lāpsa**)
[19] *it is (the part of) a coward*
[20] *just as when a faulty lead water pipe splits and sends long (streams of) water through the small, hissing hole and bursts through the air with its jets*
[21] *spray*
[22] *is anxious*
[23] *and although . . . yet*
[24] *seen (before)* (with **arbore**)

[10] i.e., Thisbe
[11] genitive
[12] modifies **vestī**
[13] = **quō** and **–que; ferrum** is the antecedent
[14] Supply **est.**
[15] Supply **ferrum.**
[16] ablative (instead of locative **humī**): *on the ground*

Dum dubitat, tremebunda videt pulsāre cruentum
membra solum[25] retrōque pedem tulit ōraque buxō[26]
pallidiōra gerēns exhorruit aequoris īnstar[27]
quod tremit exiguā cum summum[28] stringitur aurā.
Sed postquam remorāta suōs cognōvit amōrēs,[29]
percutit indignōs[17] clārō plangōre lacertōs
et laniāta comās amplexaque corpus amātum
vulnera supplēvit lacrimīs flētumque cruōrī
miscuit et gelidīs in vultibus ōscula fīgēns
"Pȳrame," clāmāvit,"quis tē mihi cāsus adēmit?
Pȳrame, respondē! Tua tē cārissima Thisbē
nōminat; exaudī vultūsque attolle iacentēs!"
Ad nōmen Thisbēs oculōs ā morte gravātōs
Pȳramus ērēxit vīsāque recondidit illā.
Quae postquam vestemque suam cognōvit et ēnse[18]
vīdit ebur[30] vacuum, "Tua tē manus," inquit, "amorque
perdidit, īnfēlīx. Est et mihi fortis in ūnum
hoc[31] manus; est et amor; dabit hic in vulnera vīrēs.
Persequar exstīnctum[19] lētīque miserrima dīcar
causa comesque tuī; quīque ā mē morte revellī
heu sōlā poterās, poteris nec[32] morte revellī.
Hoc[20] tamen ambōrum verbīs estōte rogātī[33],
Ō multum miserī meus illīusque parentēs,
ut quōs certus amor, quōs hōra novissima iūnxit,
compōnī tumulō nōn invideātis eōdem.
At tū quae rāmīs arbor[21] miserābile corpus
nunc tegis ūnīus, mox es tēctūra duōrum,
signa tenē caedis pullōsque et lūctibus aptōs
semper habē fētūs, geminī monumenta cruōris."
Dīxit et aptātō pectus mūcrōne sub īmum
incubuit ferrō, quod adhūc ā caede tepēbat.
Vōta tamen tetigēre deōs, tetigēre parentēs;
nam color in pōmō est, ubi permātūruit, āter,
quodque rogīs superest,[34] ūnā requiēscit in urnā.
(IV, 55–166)

[25] *ground*
[26] *paler than boxwood*
[27] *like the sea*
[28] *surface*
[29] *lover*
[30] *sheath* (literally, *ivory*)
[31] *for this one act*
[32] *not even*
[33] *let me make this request* (literally, *be asked*)
[34] *and what remains from the pyres* (i.e., *the ashes*)

---

[17] i.e., they did not deserve a beating
[18] ablative of separation with **vacuum**
[19] Supply **tē.**
[20] object of **rogātī**
[21] prose order: **tū, arbor, quae**

# MIDAS

Midas, king of Phrygia, helped restore to Bacchus his companion and attendant, the satyr (half goat, half man) Silenus. In return for this service Bacchus offered Midas anything he desired.

Quī$_{1}$ simul agnōvit$_{2}$ socium comitemque sacrōrum$_{3}$,
hospitis adventū fēstum geniāliter ēgit
per bis quīnque diēs et iūnctās ōrdine noctēs.
Et iam stellārum sublīme coēgerat agmen
Lūcifer[1] ūndecimus, Lȳdōs cum laetus in agrōs
rēx venit et iuvenī Sīlēnum reddit alumnō[2].
Huic deus optandī grātum sed inūtile fēcit
mūneris arbitrium[3], gaudēns altōre[4] receptō.
Ille$_{4}$ male ūsūrus dōnīs ait, "Effice quicquid
corpore contigerō fulvum vertātur$_{5}$ in aurum."
Annuit optātis$_{6}$ nocitūraque mūnera solvit
Līber$_{7}$ et indoluit quod nōn meliōra petīsset.
Laetus abit gaudetque malō Berecyntius hērōs$_{8}$
pollicitīque fidem tangendō singula temptat.
Vixque sibī crēdēns, nōn altā$_{9}$ fronde virentem
īlice dētrāxit virgam: virga aurea facta est.
Tollit humō saxum: saxum quoque palluit aurō.
Contigit et glaebam: contāctū glaeba potentī
māssa fit. Ārentēs Cereris[5] dēcerpsit aristās:
aurea messis erat. Dēmptum tenet arbore pōmum:
Hesperidās dōnāsse putēs[6]. Sī postibus altīs
admōvit digitōs, postēs radiāre videntur.
***
Vix spēs ipse suās animō capit[7], aurea fingēns
omnia. Gaudentī$_{10}$ mēnsās posuēre ministrī
exstrūctās dapibus nec tostae frūgis egentēs.[8]

[1] *day*
[2] *foster son,* i.e., Bacchus
[3] *free choice*
[4] *foster father*
[5] *of Ceres (grain)*
[6] *you would think*
[7] *grasps*
[8] *and not without bread* (literally, *not lacking baked grain*)

---

$_{1}$ Bacchus
$_{2}$ The subject is Midas.
$_{3}$ Midas was celebrating a festival.
$_{4}$ Midas
$_{5}$ Supply **ut.**
$_{6}$ Supply **rēbus:** *his choice of gift.*
$_{7}$ Bacchus
$_{8}$ Midas
$_{9}$ modifies **īlice**
$_{10}$ Supply **eī.**

# Transmission of Latin and Greek Works Before Printing: 6

Ovid's mythological subject matter was obviously a joy to illustrate (see the small pictures). This fourteenth-century manuscript is from an early part of the ***Metamorphōsēs.*** You can just read the words **Liber prīmus** at the top. The rest of the manuscript is in French. Annotations made are in the margins among the birds and vines. The really popular works of Latin authors were translated into many languages. This work of Ovid was among the most popular. The manuscript itself was written and illustrated for a French nobleman.

Tum vērō, sīve ille suā Cereālia dextrā
mūnera contigerat, Cereālia dōna rigēbant;
sīve dapēs avidō convellere dente parābat,
lāmina fulva dapēs,[9] admōtō dente, premēbat;
miscuerat pūrīs auctōrem mūneris[10] undīs:
fūsile per rictūs aurum fluitāre vidērēs.[11]
Attonitus novitāte malī dīvēsque miserque
effugere optat opēs et quae modo vōverat ōdit.
Cōpia nūlla famem relevat; sitis ārida guttur
ūrit, et invīsō meritus torquētur ab aurō,
ad caelumque manūs et splendida bracchia tollēns,
"Dā veniam, Lēnaee[12] pater! Peccāvimus," inquit,
"sed miserēre, precor, speciōsōque ēripe[11] damnō."
Mīte deum[13] nūmen: Bacchus peccāsse fatentem
restituit factīque fidē [14] data mūnera solvit.[15]
"Nēve male optātō maneās circumlitus[16] aurō,
vāde," ait, "ad magnīs vīcīnum Sardibus amnem
perque iugum Lȳdum lābentibus obvius undīs[17]
carpe viam, dōnec veniās ad flūminis ortūs.
Spūmigerōque tuum fontī, quā plūrimus exit,
subde caput corpusque simul, simul ēlue crīmen."
Rēx iussae succēdit aquae: vīs aurea tīnxit
flūmen et hūmānō dē corpore cessit in amnem.
Nunc quoque, iam veteris perceptō sēmine vēnae,[18]
arva rigent aurō[12] madidīs pallentia glaebīs.
Ille perōsus opēs silvās et rūra colēbat
Pānaque[13] montānīs habitantem semper in antrīs.
Pingue[19] sed ingenium mānsit, nocitūraque, ut ante,
rūrsus erant dominō stultae praecordia mentis.[14]
Nam freta prōspiciēns lātē riget arduus altō
Tmōlus[15] in ascēnsū clīvōque extēnsus utrōque
Sardibus hinc, illinc parvīs fīnītur Hypaepīs.
Pān ibi dum tenerīs iactat sua carmina nymphīs
et leve cērātā modulātur harundine carmen,[20]
ausus Apollineōs prae[21] sē contemnere cantūs,
iūdice sub Tmōlō certāmen vēnit ad impār.

[9] *a golden layer covered the food*
[10] *the author (giver) of the gift* (Bacchus), i.e., *wine*
[11] *You might have seen liquid gold flowing over his jaws.*
[12] *Bacchus*
[13] = **deōrum**
[14] *a proof*
[15] *removed the gift*
[16] *smeared*
[17] *meeting the waters,* i.e., *going upstream*
[18] *having received the seed of ancient vein*
[19] *fat,* i.e., *stupid*
[20] *plays a song*
[21] *compared to himself*

---

[11] Supply **mē** as object.
[12] with **madidīs**
[13] accusative singular
[14] **stultae praecordia mentis = stulta mēns**
[15] here the god of the mountain

Monte suō senior iūdex cōnsēdit et aurēs
līberat arboribus. Quercū coma caerula tantum
cingitur, et pendent circum cava tempora glandēs.
Isque deum[16] pecoris spectāns, "In iūdice," dīxit,
"nūlla mora est." Calamīs agrestibus īnsonat ille
barbaricōque Midān (aderat nam forte canentī)
carmine dēlēnit. Post hunc sacer ōra retorsit
Tmōlus ad ōs Phoebī; vultum sua silva secūta est.
Ille caput flāvum laurō Parnāside vīnctus
verrit humum Tyriō saturātā mūrice pallā,
īnstrictamque fidem[22] gemmīs et dentibus Indīs
sustinet ā laevā,[23] tenuit manus altera plēctrum;
artificis status ipse fuit. Tum stāmina[24] doctō
pollice sollicitat, quōrum dulcēdine captus
Pāna iubet Tmōlus citharae[17] summittere cannās.
Iūdicium sānctīque placet sententia montis
omnibus; arguitur[25] tamen atque iniūsta vocātur
ūnīus sermōne Midae. Nec Dēlius[18] aurēs
hūmānam stolidās patitur retinēre figūram,
sed trahit in spatium[26] vīllīsque albentibus implet
īnstabilēsque īmās[27] facit et dat[28] posse movērī.
Cētera sunt hominis; partem damnātur in ūnam[29]
induiturque aurēs lentē gradientis asellī.
Ille quidem cēlāre cupit turpīque pudōre
tempora purpureīs temptat vēlāre tiārīs;
sed solitus longōs ferrō resecāre capillōs
vīderat hoc famulus;[19] quī cum nec prōdere vīsum
dēdecus audēret, cupiēns efferre sub aurās,[30]
nec posset reticēre tamen, sēcēdit humumque
effodit et, dominī quālēs aspexerit aurēs,
vōce refert parvā terraeque immurmurat haustae[31]
indiciumque suae vōcis, tellūre regestā,
obruit et scrobibus[32] tacitus discēdit opertīs.
Crēber harundinibus tremulīs ibi surgere lūcus
coepit et, ut prīmum plēnō mātūruit annō
prōdidit agricolam[20]: lēnī nam mōtus ab austrō
obruta verba refert dominīque coarguit aurēs.
(XI, 94–193)

[22] *lyre*
[23] *on the left (side)*
[24] *strings*
[25] *(the judgment) is challenged*
[26] *lengthens them* (literally, *draws them into space*)
[27] *loose at the bottom*
[28] *causes them*
[29] *in respect to one part*
[30] *in the open*
[31] *dug out*
[32] *hole*

---

[16] Pan
[17] dative
[18] Apollo
[19] i.e., his servant saw it while cutting his hair
[20] i.e., the **famulus** (barber)

# DAEDALUS

Daedalus was a famous Greek sculptor, architect, and inventor. He went to Crete to build the labyrinth to house the Minotaur, a beast half-man, half-bull that was the son of King Minos. Later imprisoned with his son Icarus by King Minos, Daedalus made an escape plan.

Daedalus intereā, Crētēn longumque perōsus
exsilium, tāctusque locī nātālis[1] amōre,
clausus erat pelagō. "Terrās licet[1]," inquit, "et undās
obstruat,[2] at[2] caelum certē patet; ībimus illāc.
Omnia possideat,[3] nōn possidet āera Mīnōs."
Dīxit, et ignōtās animum dīmittit[4] in artīs
nātūramque novat,[5] nam pōnit in ōrdine pennās,
ā minimā coeptās,[6] longam breviōre sequente,
ut clīvō crēvisse putēs;[7] sīc rūstica quondam
fistula[8] disparibus paulātim surgit avēnīs.
Tum līnō mediās et cērīs alligat īmās,
atque ita compositās parvō curvāmine flectit
ut vērās imitētur avīs. Puer Īcarus ūnā
stābat et, ignārus sua sē trāctāre perīcla,[9]
ōre renīdentī modo quās vaga mōverat aura
captābat plūmās, flāvam modo pollice cēram
mollībat[10], lūsūque suō mīrābile patris
impediēbat opus. Postquam manus ultima[11] coeptō [12]
imposita est, geminās opifex lībrāvit[13] in ālās
ipse suum corpus, mōtāque pependit in aurā.
Īnstruit et nātum, "Mediō" que "ut līmite currās,
Īcare," ait, "moneō, nē, sī dēmissior[14] ībis,
unda gravet pennās, sī celsior, ignis adūrat.
Inter utrumque volā. Nec tē spectāre Boōtēn[3]
aut Helicēn[3] iubeō strictumque Ōrīonis[3] ēnsem:
mē duce, carpe viam." Pariter praecepta volandī
trādit et ignōtās umerīs accommodat ālās.

[1] *though*
[2] *at least*
[3] *although Minos possesses all things*
[4] *directs*
[5] *changes (the laws of) nature*
[6] *beginning with the smallest*
[7] *so that you would think they grew on a slope*
[8] *a (shepherd's) pipe,* (made of reeds)
[9] = **pericula:** *not knowing that he was handling (things that were) dangerous to him*
[10] = **molliēbat**
[11] *final touch*
[12] *(his) work*
[13] *balanced*
[14] *too low*

---

[1] Athens
[2] Supply **Mīnōs** as subject.
[3] constellations; **Helicē** = Ursa Major, the constellation containing the Big Dipper

Inter opus monitūsque genae[15] maduēre senīlēs,
et patriae tremuēre manūs; dedit ōscula nātō—
nōn iterum repetenda!—suō, pennīsque levātus
ante volat comitīque timet, velut āles, ab altō
quae teneram prōlem prōdūxit in āera nīdō,
hortāturque sequī [16] damnōsāsque ērudit artīs,
et movet ipse suās et nātī respicit ālās.
Hōs aliquis, tremulā dum captat arundine piscīs,
aut pāstor baculō[17], stīvāve[17] innīxus arātor,
vīdit et obstupuit, quīque aethera carpere[18] possent
crēdidit esse deōs. Et iam Iūnōnia laevā
parte Samos (fuerant Dēlosque Parosque relīctae),
dextra Lebinthus erat fēcundaque melle Calymnē,
cum puer audācī coepit gaudēre volātū
dēseruitque ducem caelīque cupīdine tāctus
altius ēgit iter; rapidī vīcīnia sōlis
mollit odōrātās, pennārum vincula, cērās.
Tābuerant cērae: nūdōs quatit ille lacertōs,
rēmigiōque[19] carēns nōn ūllās percipit aurās,[20]
ōraque caeruleā patrium clāmantia nōmen
excipiuntur aquā,[21] quae nōmen trāxit ab illō[4].
At pater īnfēlīx, nec iam pater, "Īcare," dīxit,
"Īcare," dīxit, "ubi es? Quā tē regiōne requīram?"
"Īcare," dīcēbat: pennās aspexit in undīs,
dēvōvitque suās artīs, corpusque sepulchrō
condidit. Et tellūs[5] ā nōmine dicta sepultī.
(VIII, 183–235)

[15] *cheeks*
[16] *encourages him to follow*
[17] *staff, plow*
[18] *fly*
[19] *wings* (literally, *rowing*)
[20] *does not take hold of the air*
[21] *his mouth* (i.e., *voice*) *is drowned by the water*

[4] the Icarian Sea
[5] Icaria, an island near Samos

# NIOBE

Niobe, queen of Thebes and beautiful mother of seven sons and seven daughters, feels that she is more worthy of honor and worship than Latona, the goddess mother of Apollo and Diana.

[1] *surrounded by a throng*
[2] *tossing, along with her head, her hair flowing down on*
[3] *tall, standing erect*
[4] *to prefer gods (merely) heard of to those (you have) seen*
[5] *incense* (used in worship)
[6] *father*
[7] *royal palace*
[8] *put together by the lyre*
[9] *there is in addition*
[10] *some Coeus or other*
[11] *a Titan's daughter, born of Coeus*
[12] *to whom about to give birth* (with **cui**)
[13] *offspring* (literally, *womb*)
[14] *I am too great for Fortune to harm*
[15] *grant that*
[16] *my wealth* (i.e., my children) *has gone beyond fear*
[17] *even if I am robbed*
[18] *Latona's crowd* (in apposition with **duōrum**)

Ecce venit comitum Niobē crēberrima turbā,[1]
vestibus intextō Phrygiīs spectābilis aurō
et, quantum īra sinit, fōrmōsa movēnsque decōrō
cum capite immissōs umerum per utrumque capillōs.[2]
Cōnstitit, utque oculōs circumtulit alta[3] superbōs,
"Quis furor$_1$ audītōs," inquit, "praepōnere vīsīs
caelestēs?[4] Aut cūr colitur Lātōna per ārās,
nūmen adhūc sine tūre[5] meum est? Mihi Tantalus auctor[6],
cui licuit sōlī superōrum tangere mēnsās;
Plēiadum soror est genetrīx mea; maximus Atlās
est avus, aetherium quī fert cervīcibus axem;
Iuppiter alter avus; socerō quoque glōrior illō.
Mē gentēs metuunt Phrygiae, mē rēgia[7] Cadmī
sub dominā$_2$ est, fidibusque meī commissa[8] marītī
moenia cum populīs ā mēque virōque reguntur.
In quamcumque domūs advertī lūmina partem
immēnsae spectantur opēs. Accēdit eōdem[9]
digna deā faciēs; hūc nātās adice septem
et totidem iuvenēs et mox generōsque nurūsque.
Quaerite nunc, habeat quam nostra superbia causam;
nesciō$_3$ quōque[10] audēte satam Tītānida Cōeō[11]
Lātōnam praeferre mihī, cui maxima quondam
exiguam sēdem paritūrae[12] terra negāvit.
Nec caelō nec humō nec aquīs dea vestra recepta est;
exsul erat mundī, dōnec miserāta$_4$ vagantem,
'Hospita tū terrīs errās, ego,' dīxit, 'in undīs,'
īnstabilemque$_5$ locum Dēlos dedit. Illa duōrum
facta parēns; uterī [13] pars haec est septima nostrī.
Sum fēlīx (quis enim neget hoc?) fēlīxque manēbō
(hoc quoque quis dubitet?) tūtam mē cōpia fēcit.
Maior sum quam cui possit Fortūna nocēre,[14]
multaque ut [15] ēripiat, multō mihi plūra relinquet.
Excessēre metum mea iam bona.[16] Fingite dēmī
huic aliquid populō nātōrum posse meōrum,$_6$
nōn tamen ad numerum redigar spoliāta[17] duōrum,
Lātōnae turbae:[18] quae quantum distat ab orbā?

---

$_1$ Supply **est.**
$_2$ with **mē**
$_3$ **nesciō** here = two long syllables
$_4$ modifies **Dēlos**
$_5$ Delos was then a floating island.
$_6$ *suppose that something could be taken from this nation* (*that*) *my children constitute,* i.e., her children are so numerous that they form a nation

Īte satis properē sacrīs[19] laurumque capillīs
pōnite[20]." Dēpōnunt et sacra īnfecta[21] relinquunt,
quodque[7] licet, tacitō venerantur murmure nūmen.
Indignāta dea est summōque in vertice Cynthī
tālibus est dictīs geminā cum prōle locūta:
"Ēn ego vestra parēns, vōbīs animōsa creātīs,[22]
et nisi Iūnōnī nūllī cessūra deārum,
an dea sim dubitor,[23] perque omnia saecula cultīs[8]
arceor, Ō nātī, nisi vōs succurritis, ārīs.
Nec dolor hic sōlus: dīrō convīcia factō
Tantalis[24] adiēcit vōsque est postpōnere nātīs
ausa suīs et mē (quod in ipsam reccidat)[25] orbam
dīxit et exhibuit linguam scelerāta paternam."
Adiectūra precēs erat hīs Lātōna relātīs:
"Dēsine," Phoebus ait, "poenae mora longa querēla est."
Dīxit idem Phoebē celerīque per āera lāpsū
contigerant tēctī Cadmēida[26] nūbibus arcem.
Plānus erat lātēque patēns prope moenia campus,
assiduīs pulsātus equīs, ubi turba rotārum
dūraque mollierat subiectās ungula glaebās.
Pars ibi dē septem genitīs Amphīone fortēs
cōnscendunt in equōs Tyriōque rubentia sūcō[27]
terga premunt aurōque gravēs moderantur habēnās.
Ē quibus Ismēnus, quī mātrī sarcina[28] quondam
prīma suae fuerat, dum certum flectit in orbem
quadrupedis cursūs spūmantiaque ōra coercet,
"Ei mihi!"[29] conclāmat mediōque in pectore fīxa
tēla gerit, frēnīsque manū moriente remissīs,
in latus[9] ā dextrō paulātim dēfluit armō[30].
Proximus, audītō sonitū per ināne[10] pharetrae,
frēna dabat Sipylus, velutī cum praescius imbris
nūbe fugit vīsā, pendentiaque undique rēctor[31]
carbasa dēdūcit,[32] nē quā[33] levis effluat aura;
frēna tamen dantem nōn ēvītābile tēlum
cōnsequitur, summāque tremēns cervīce sagitta
haesit, et exstābat nūdum dē gutture ferrum.
Ille, ut erat prōnus, per colla admissa iubāsque[34]
volvitur et calidō tellūrem sanguine foedat.

[19] *go away from the rites quickly*
[20] = **dēpōnite**
[21] *unfinished*
[22] *proud of you (whom I have) borne*
[23] *my divinity is being questioned*
[24] *daughter of Tantalus,* i.e., Niobe
[25] *may this fall to her lot*
[26] *of Cadmus* (with **arcem**)
[27] *dye* (used on the saddlecloth)
[28] *burden,* i.e., *child*
[29] *Oh!* **Mihi** *is dative of reference.*
[30] *shoulder (of the horse)*
[31] *pilot (of a ship)*
[32] *unfurls the sails*
[33] *anywhere*
[34] *the swift neck and the mane (of the horse)*

[7] The antecedent is the clause that follows.
[8] with **ārīs**
[9] accusative of the noun **latus,** *side*
[10] noun

Phaedimus īnfēlīx et avītī nōminis hērēs,
Tantalus, ut solitō fīnem imposuēre labōrī,
trānsierant ad opus nitidae iuvenāle palaestrae,[35]
et iam contulerant artō luctantia nexū
pectora pectoribus: contentō concita nervō,[36]
sīcut erant iūnctī, trāiēcit utrumque sagitta.
Ingemuēre simul, simul incurvāta[37] dolōre
membra solō[38] posuēre, simul suprēma iacentēs
lūmina versārunt,[39] animam simul exhālārunt[40].
Aspicit Alphēnor laniātaque pectora plangēns[41]
ēvolat, ut gelidōs complexibus allevet artūs,
inque piō cadit officiō; nam Dēlius illī
intima fātiferō rūpit praecordia ferrō.
Quod simul[42] ēductum est, pars et pulmōnis in hāmīs
ēruta[43] cumque animā cruor est effūsus in aurās.
At nōn[11] intōnsum simplex Damasichthona[12] vulnus
afficit: ictus erat quā crūs esse incipit et quā
mollia nervōsus facit internōdia poples.
Dumque manū temptat trahere exitiābile tēlum,
altera per iugulum pennīs tenus[44] ācta sagitta est.
Expulit hanc sanguis sēque ēiaculātus in altum
ēmicat et longē terebrātā prōsilit aurā.
Ultimus Īlioneus nōn prōfectūra[45] precandō
bracchia sustulerat "dī" que "Ō commūniter omnēs,"
dīxerat, ignārus nōn omnēs[13] esse rogandōs,
"parcite!" Mōtus erat, cum iam revocābile tēlum
nōn fuit, Arcitenēns. Minimō tamen occidit ille
vulnere, nōn altē percussō corde sagittā.
Fāma malī populīque dolor lacrimaeque suōrum
tam subitae mātrem certam fēcēre ruīnae,[46]
mīrantem potuisse,[47] īrāscentemque quod ausī
hōc essent superī, quod tantum iūris habērent.
Nam[14] pater Amphīōn, ferrō per pectus adāctō,
fīnierat moriēns pariter cum lūce dolōrem.
Heu quantum haec Niobē Niobē distābat ab illā
quae modo Lātōīs populum summōverat ārīs
et mediam tulerat[48] gressūs resupīna per urbem,[48]
invidiōsa suīs, at nunc miseranda vel hostī!

[35] *of the glistening (with oil) wrestling places*

[36] *an arrow sent from the taut string (of the bow)* (with **sagitta**)

[37] *writhing*

[38] *on the ground*

[39] *they moved their eyes (for the) last (time)* (with **lūmina**)

[40] *expired*

[41] *beating his torn breast* (but of course it was not torn until he beat it)

[42] = **simul ac**

[43] *part of his lungs was torn out (and stuck to) the barbs (of the arrow)*

[44] *up to the feathers*

[45] i.e., *in vain*

[46] *informed the mother of the sudden disaster*

[47] *wondering (that the gods) could (do this)*

[48] *had walked proudly through the city*

---

[11] with **simplex**
[12] accusative (Greek form)
[13] A prayer to Apollo would have been preferable.
[14] This line and the next explain why Niobe was not joined in grief by her husband.

# Transmission of Latin and Greek Works Before Printing: 7

Erich Lessing/Art Resource, NY

This magnificent French manuscript from the fifteenth century is richly illustrated throughout in true Renaissance style, including detailed scenes, a fancy initial capital letter, and marginal flora and fauna. The text tells the story of the landing in England by Julius Caesar. It was written by the historian Jean Mansel. You can read Caesar's name in French *(Cesar)* in the second line of column 1 and the fifth line of column 2. By the fifteenth century, the making of manuscripts was a fairly large industry and not all confined to monasteries. Soon printing on paper (1450 onward) would supplant manuscripts and provide many copies of the same work to an increasingly expanded reading public. From then on, the Roman and Greek classics were safely preserved!

Corporibus gelidīs incumbit et ōrdine nūllō
ōscula dispēnsat nātōs suprēma per omnēs.
Ā quibus ad caelum līventia[15] bracchia tollēns,
"Pāscere, crūdēlis, nostrō, Lātōna, dolōre;
pāscere," ait, "satiāque meō tua pectora lūctū
corque ferum satiā," dīxit. "Per fūnera septem
efferor.[49] Exsultā victrīxque inimīca triumphā!
Cūr autem victrīx? Miserae mihi plūra supersunt
quam tibi fēlīcī; post tot quoque fūnera vincō."
Dīxerat, et sonuit contentō nervus ab arcū[16],
quī praeter Niobēn ūnam conterruit omnēs;
illa malō[50] est audāx. Stābant cum vestibus ātrīs
ante torōs[51] frātrum, dēmissō crīne, sorōrēs.
Ē quibus ūna trahēns haerentia vīscere tēla[52]
impositō[53] frātrī moribunda relanguit ōre.
Altera sōlārī miserum cōnāta parentem
conticuit subitō duplicātaque[54] vulnere caecō est,
ōraque compressit, nisi postquam spīritus ībat.[55]
Haec frūstrā fugiēns collābitur; illa sorōrī
immoritur; latet haec; illam trepidāre vidērēs.
Sexque datīs lētō dīversaque vulnera passīs,
ultima restābat. Quam tōtō corpore māter,
tōtā veste tegēns, "Ūnam minimamque[56] relinque!
Dē multīs minimam poscō," clāmāvit, "et ūnam."
Dumque rogat, prō quā [17] rogat occidit. Orba resēdit
exanimēs inter nātōs nātāsque virumque
dēriguitque malīs; nūllōs movet aura capillōs,
in vultū color est sine sanguine, lūmina maestīs
stant immōta genīs, nihil est in imāgine vīvum.
Ipsa quoque interius cum dūrō lingua palātō
congelat, et vēnae dēsistunt posse movērī;
nec flectī cervīx nec bracchia reddere mōtūs
nec pēs īre potest; intrā quoque vīscera saxum est.
Flet tamen et validī circumdata turbine ventī[57]
in patriam[18] rapta est. Ibi fīxa cacūmine montis
līquitur, et lacrimās etiam nunc marmora mānant.[19]
(VI, 165–312)

[49] *I am carried out (i.e., to the grave)*
[50] *because of her misfortune*
[51] *biers*
[52] *the weapon fixed in (her brother's) heart*
[53] *her face placed upon her brother*
[54] *was bent double*
[55] *after her breath left her,* i.e., when she died, her mouth opened
[56] *the youngest*
[57] *a strong gust of wind*

---

[15] as a result of beating herself in grief
[16] of Diana, who will kill the daughters
[17] Supply **ea** as antecedent of **quā** and subject of **occidit.**
[18] Phrygia
[19] The rock on Mt. Sipylus was called Niobe and resembled a female form. The tears are explained by the spring trickling down the face of the figure.

# PHILEMON AND BAUCIS

A kind aged couple of Phrygia entertain to the best of their resources Jupiter and Mercury who, disguised as wanderers, have been refused hospitality in other homes. The gods reward Philemon and Baucis for their purity with many blessings in life and in death.

Iuppiter hūc$_1$ speciē mortālī, cumque parente
vēnit Atlantiadēs positīs cādūcifer[1] ālīs.
Mīlle domōs adiēre locum requiemque petentēs,
mīlle domōs clausēre serae[2]. Tamen ūna recēpit,
parva quidem stipulīs et cannā tēcta palūstrī,[3]
sed pia Baucis anus[4] parilīque aetāte Philēmōn
illā$_2$ sunt annīs iūnctī iuvenālibus, illā$_2$
cōnsenuēre casā paupertātemque fatendō
effēcēre levem nec inīquā mente ferendō.
Nec rēfert[5] dominōs illīc famulōsne requīrās;
tōta domus duo sunt, īdem pārentque iubentque.
Ergō ubi caelicolae parvōs tetigēre Penātēs[6]
submissōque humilēs intrārunt vertice[7] postēs,
membra senex positō iussit relevāre sedīlī,
quō superiniēcit textum rude sēdula Baucis;
inque focō tepidum cinerem dīmōvit et ignēs
suscitat hesternōs foliīsque et cortice siccō
nūtrit et ad flammās animā prōdūcit anīlī,
multifidāsque facēs[8] rāmāliaque[9] ārida tēctō[10]
dētulit et minuit[11] parvōque admōvit aēnō[12].
Quodque suus coniūnx riguō collēgerat hortō,
truncat holus foliīs. Furcā levat ille bicornī
sordida terga suis$_3$ nigrō pendentia tignō
servātōque diū resecat dē tergore partem
exiguam sectamque domat[13] ferventibus undīs.
Intereā mediās fallunt[14] sermōnibus hōrās,
concutiuntque torum[15] dē mollī flūminis ulvā[16]
impositum lectō spondā[17] pedibusque salignīs.[17]

[1] *the bearer of the caduceus* (a wand), i.e., Mercury
[2] *locks*
[3] *covered with straw and marsh reeds*
[4] *old woman*
[5] *It does not matter whether . . . or* (–**ne**)
[6] *household gods,* i.e., *house*
[7] *head(s)*
[8] *fine-split kindling*
[9] *branches*
[10] *from (under the) roof*
[11] *broke into pieces*
[12] *bronze (kettle)*
[13] *makes tender*
[14] *they pass the time*
[15] *mattress*
[16] *sedge-grass*
[17] *with willow frame and feet*

$_1$ the home of Philemon and Baucis
$_2$ with **casā**
$_3$ **suis** from **sūs,** *pork blackened* (by smoke)

Vestibus hunc vēlant quās nōn nisi tempore fēstō
sternere cōnsuerant, sed et [18] haec vīlisque vetusque
vestis erat lectō nōn indignanda salignō.
Accubuēre[19] deī. Mēnsam succīncta[20] tremēnsque
pōnit anus, mēnsae sed erat pēs tertius impār:[4]
testa parem fēcit; quae postquam subdita clīvum
sustulit, aequātam mentae tersēre virentēs.[21]
Pōnitur hīc bicolor[5] sincērae bāca Minervae,[5]
conditaque in liquidā corna autumnālia faece[22]
intibaque[23] et rādīx et lactis[24] māssa coāctī,[24]
ōvaque nōn ācrī leviter versāta favīllā,
omnia fictilibus[25], Post haec caelātus eōdem
sistitur argentō [26][6] crāter fabricātaque fāgō
pōcula, quā cava sunt, flāventibus illita cērīs.[27]
Parva mora est, epulāsque focī mīsēre calentēs,
nec longae rūrsus referuntur vīna senectae,
dantque locum mēnsīs paulum sēducta secundīs[28].
Hīc nux, hīc mixta est rūgōsīs cārica[29] palmīs
prūnaque et in patulīs redolentia māla canistrīs
et dē purpureīs collēctae vītibus ūvae.
Candidus in mediō favus est; super omnia vultūs
accessēre bonī nec iners pauperque voluntās.
Intereā totiēns haustum crātēra[7] replērī
sponte suā per sēque vident succrēscere vīna.
Attonitī novitāte pavent manibusque supīnīs
concipiunt Baucisque precēs timidusque Philēmōn
et veniam dapibus nūllīsque parātibus[8] ōrant.
Ūnicus ānser erat, minimae custōdia vīllae,
quem dīs hospitibus dominī mactāre parābant.
Ille celer pennā tardōs aetāte fatīgat
ēlūditque diū, tandemque est vīsus ad ipsōs
cōnfūgisse deōs; superī vetuēre necārī
"Di" que "sumus, meritāsque luet vīcīnia poenās
impia," dīxērunt; "vōbīs immūnibus huius
esse malī dabitur.[30] Modo vestra relinquite tēcta
ac nostrōs comitāte gradūs et in ardua montis
īte simul." Pārent ambō baculīsque levātī
nītuntur longō vēstīgia pōnere clīvō.

[18] = **etiam**

[19] *reclined at the table*

[20] *with tucked up skirts* (literally, *girded up*)

[21] *green mint wiped the balanced (table)*

[22] *autumn cornel berries preserved in the lees of wine*

[23] *endive*

[24] *cheese*

[25] *earthenware dishes*

[26] *the same silver*

[27] *coated on the inside* (literally, *where they are hollow*) *with yellow wax* (to prevent leaks)

[28] *the second course,* i.e., dessert

[29] *figs*

[30] *you will be exempt from this misfortune*

---

[4] The table had three legs.

[5] i.e., green and black (ripe) olives

[6] a humorous reference to **fictilibus**

[7] accusative singular (Greek form)

[8] i.e., poor entertainment; literally, *for no preparation*

Tantum aberant summō[31] quantum semel īre sagitta
missa potest; flexēre oculōs et mersa palūdē
cētera prōspiciunt, tantum sua tēcta manēre.
Dumque ea mīrantur, dum dēflent fāta suōrum,
illa vetus dominīs etiam casa parva duōbus
vertitur in templum. Furcās subiēre columnae,[32]
strāmina flāvēscunt, adopertaque marmore tellūs
caelātaeque forēs aurātaque tēcta videntur.
Tālia tum placidō Sāturnius[9] ēdidit ōre:
"Dīcite, iūste senex et fēmina coniuge iūstō
digna, quid optētis." Cum Baucide pauca locūtus
iūdicium superīs aperit commūne Philēmōn:
"Esse sacerdōtēs dēlūbraque vestra tuērī
poscimus, et quoniam concordēs ēgimus annōs,
auferat hōra duōs eadem, nec coniugis umquam
busta meae videam neu sim tumulandus[33] ab illā."
Vōta fidēs sequitur;[10] templī tutēla fuēre,
dōnec vīta data est. Annīs aevōque solūtī[34]
ante gradūs sacrōs cum stārent forte locīque
nārrārent cāsūs, frondēre Philēmona Baucis,
Baucida cōnspexit senior frondēre Philēmōn.
Iamque super geminōs crēscente cacūmine vultūs,
mūtua, dum licuit, reddēbant dicta "Valē" que
"Ō coniūnx"[35] dīxēre simul, simul abdita tēxit
ōra frutex.[36] Ostendit adhūc Thynēius[37] illīc
incola dē geminō vīcīnōs corpore truncōs.
Haec mihi nōn vānī (neque erat cūr fallere vellent)
nārrāvēre senēs. Equidem pendentia vīdī
serta super rāmōs pōnēnsque recentia dīxī
"Cūra deum dī sint, et quī coluēre colantur."
(VIII, 626–724)

[31] *the top*
[32] *columns took the place of the (wooden) supports (forks)*
[33] *buried*
[34] *weakened*
[35] *dear mate*
[36] *foliage*
[37] *Bithynian*

[9] Jupiter
[10] i.e., their prayer was answered

# DAPHNE AND APOLLO

Apollo, the god of archery, falls in love with Daphne, the daughter of the river god Peneus. Cupid, out of envy and revenge, inspired Apollo with his passion for Daphne, a passion made hopeless by her resistance, also caused by Cupid. She turned into a laurel tree.

[1] *bow*
[2] *equipment*
[3] *some love or other* (with **amōrēs**)
[4] *do not lay claim to my honors*
[5] *as much as all living things yield to (you), a god*
[6] *striking the air by beating his wings*
[7] *of opposite effects*
[8] *the (arrow) which*
[9] *is tipped with lead* (literally, *has lead under the shaft*)
[10] *struck the heart of Apollo, piercing the bones and marrow*
[11] *the rival of the maiden Diana*

Prīmus amor Phoebī Daphnē Pēnēia, quem nōn
fors ignāra dedit sed saeva Cupīdinis īra.
Dēlius$_{1}$ hunc, nūper victō serpente superbus,
vīderat adductō flectentem$_{2}$ cornua[1] nervō
"Quid" que$_{3}$ "tibī$_{4}$, lascīve puer, cum fortibus armīs?"
dīxerat; "ista decent umerōs gestāmina[2] nostrōs,
quī dare certa ferae, dare vulnera possumus hostī,
quī modo pestiferō tot iūgera ventre prementem
strāvimus innumerīs tumidum Pȳthōna$_{5}$ sagittīs.
Tū face nesciō quōs[3] estō contentus amōrēs
irrītāre tuā$_{6}$, nec laudēs assere nostrās." [4]
Fīlius huic Veneris, "Fīgat tuus omnia, Phoebe,
tē meus arcus," ait, "quantōque animālia cēdunt
cūncta deō,[5] tantō minor est tua glōria nostrā."
Dīxit et, ēlīsō percussīs āere pennīs,[6]
impiger umbrōsā Parnāsī cōnstitit arce
ēque sagittiferā prōmpsit duo tēla pharetrā
dīversōrum operum:[7] fugat hoc$_{8}$, facit illud$_{8}$ amōrem.
Quod[8] facit, aurātum est et cuspide fulget acūtā;
quod fugat, obtūsum est et habet sub harundine plumbum.[9]
Hoc deus in nymphā Pēnēide$_{9}$ fīxit; at illō
laesit Apollineās trāiecta per ossa medullās.[10]
Prōtinus alter amat, fugit altera nōmen amantis
silvārum latebrīs captīvārumque ferārum
exuviīs gaudēns innuptaeque aemula Phoebēs.[11]

---

$_{1}$ Apollo
$_{2}$ Supply **eum,** Cupid.
$_{3}$ connects the two verbs **vīderat** and **dīxerat**
$_{4}$ Originally the second *i* of **tibi** was long; supply **est**.
$_{5}$ accusative (Greek form)
$_{6}$ modifies **face**
$_{7}$ = **ē** and **-que**
$_{8}$ Supply **tēlum.**
$_{9}$ ablative of **Pēnēis,** daughter of Peneus, i.e., Daphne

Vitta coercēbat positōs sine lēge capillōs.
Multī illam petiēre, illa āversāta petentēs[12]
impatiēns expersque virī nemora āvia lūstrat,
nec quid Hymēn, quid Amor, quid sint cōnūbia cūrat.
Saepe pater dīxit, "Generum mihi, fīlia, dēbēs";
saepe pater dīxit, "Dēbēs mihi, nāta, nepōtēs."
Illa, velut crīmen taedās exōsa iugālēs
pulchra verēcundō suffūderat ōra rubōre
inque patris blandīs haerēns cervīce lacertīs,
"Dā mihi perpetuā, genitor cārissime," dīxit,
"virginitāte fruī.[13] Dedit hoc pater ante[10] Diānae."
Ille quidem obsequitur. Sed tē decor iste quod optās
esse vetat,[14] vōtōque tuō tua fōrma repugnat.
Phoebus amat vīsaeque[11] cupit cōnūbia Daphnēs,
quodque cupit, spērat, suaque illum ōrācula[12] fallunt.
Utque levēs stipulae dēmptīs[15] adolentur aristīs,[15]
ut facibus saepēs ārdent quās forte viātor
vel nimis admōvit vel iam sub lūce relīquit,
sīc deus in flammās abiit,[16] sīc pectore tōtō
ūritur et sterilem spērandō nūtrit amōrem.
Spectat inōrnātōs collō pendēre capillōs,
et "Quid sī cōmantur?" ait; videt igne micantēs
sīderibus similēs oculōs, videt ōscula[17], quae nōn
est vīdisse satis; laudat digitōsque manūsque
bracchiaque et nūdōs mediā plūs parte lacertōs;[18]
sī qua latent meliōra putat.[19] Fugit ōcior aurā
illa levī neque ad haec revocantis verba resistit:
"Nympha, precor, Pēnēi, manē! Nōn īnsequor hostis;[20]
nympha, manē! Sīc agna lupum, sīc cerva leōnem,
sīc aquilam pennā fugiunt trepidante columbae,
hostēs quaeque suōs: amor est mihi causa sequendī.
Mē miserum! [21] Nē [22] prōna cadās, indignave[23] laedī
crūra notent sentēs[24], et sim tibi causa dolōris.
Aspera quā properās loca sunt. Moderātius, ōrō,
curre fugamque inhibē, moderātius īnsequar ipse.

[12] *rejecting* (object of **āversāta**)
[13] *grant me . . . to enjoy*
[14] *forbids you to be what you desire* (i.e., remain unmarried)
[15] *when the grain has been harvested*
[16] *went up in flames* (of love)
[17] *mouth,* which then came to mean *kiss*
[18] *arms more than half bare*
[19] *he believes her hidden features lovelier*
[20] *as an enemy* (nominative)
[21] *How wretched I am!*
[22] *for fear that*
[23] *that do not deserve it* (with **crūra**)
[24] *thorns*

[10] adverb
[11] with **Daphnēs,** genitive (Greek form): *at first sight*
[12] i.e., gifts of prophecy

Cui placeās,[25] inquīre tamen: nōn incola montis,
nōn ego sum pāstor, nōn hīc armenta gregēsque
horridus observō. Nescīs, temerāria, nescīs
quem fugiās, ideōque fugis. Mihi Delphica tellūs
et Claros et Tenedos Patarēaque rēgia servit;
Iuppiter est genitor; per mē quod eritque fuitque
estque patet; per mē concordant carmina nervīs.[26]
Certa quidem nostra est,[27] nostrā tamen ūna sagitta
certior, in vacuō quae vulnera pectore fēcit.
Inventum medicīna meum est,[28] opiferque per orbem
dīcor, et herbārum subiecta potentia nōbīs.
Ei mihi, quod nūllīs amor est sānābilis herbīs,
nec prōsunt dominō quae prōsunt omnibus artēs!"
Plūra locūtūrum timidō Pēnēia cursū
fūgit cumque ipsō verba imperfecta relīquit.[29]
Tum quoque vīsa decēns; nūdābant corpora ventī,
obviaque adversās vibrābant flāmina vestēs,
et levis impulsōs retrō dabat aura capillōs,
auctaque fōrma fugā est. Sed enim nōn sustinet ultrā
perdere blanditiās iuvenis deus,[30] utque movēbat
ipse amor, admissō [31] sequitur vēstīgia passū.[31]
Ut canis in vacuō leporem cum Gallicus arvō
vīdit, et hic[13] praedam pedibus petit, ille salūtem;
alter inhaesūrō similis[32] iam iamque tenēre
spērat et extentō stringit vēstigia rōstrō;[33]
alter in ambiguō est an sit comprēnsus et ipsīs
morsibus ēripitur [34] tangentiaque ōra relinquit,
sīc deus et virgō; est hic spē celer, illa timōre.
Quī tamen īnsequitur, pennīs adiūtus amōris
ōcior est requiemque negat tergōque fugācis
imminet et crīnem sparsum cervīcibus afflat.[35]

[25] *who your suitor is*
[26] *songs harmonize with the strings (of the lyre)*
[27] *my arrow is unerring, to be sure*
[28] *medicine is my invention*
[29] *left him and his unfinished words*
[30] *The youthful god cannot bear to waste his persuasive words further.*
[31] *at quickened pace*
[32] *like one about to pounce*
[33] *grazes the heels (of the hare) with outstretched muzzle*
[34] *escapes from*
[35] *breathes upon her hair streaming down her neck*

---

13 i.e., the dog

Vīribus absūmptīs, expalluit illa citaeque
victa labōre fugae spectāns Pēnēidas undās,
"Fer, pater," inquit, "opem, sī flūmina nūmen habētis!
Quā nimium placuī, mūtandō perde figūram!"[36]
Vix prece fīnītā, torpor gravis occupat artūs,
mollia cinguntur tenuī praecordia librō[37],
in frondem crīnēs, in rāmōs bracchia crēscunt;
pēs[38] modo tam vēlōx pigrīs rādīcibus haeret,
ōra cacūmen habet.[39] Remanet nitor ūnus in illā.[40]
Hanc[14] quoque Phoebus amat, positāque in stīpite dextrā,
sentit adhūc trepidāre novō sub cortice pectus,
complexusque suīs rāmōs, ut membra,[41] lacertīs
ōscula dat lignō: refugit tamen ōscula lignum.
Cui deus, "At quoniam coniūnx mea nōn potes esse,
arbor eris certē," dīxit, "mea. Semper habēbunt
tē coma[15], tē citharae, tē nostrae, laure, pharetrae.
Tū ducibus Latiīs aderis, cum laeta Triumphum
vōx canet et vīsent longās Capitōlia pompās.[16]
Postibus Augustīs eadem fīdissima custōs
ante forēs stābis[17] mediamque tuēbere quercum[18],
utque meum intōnsīs caput est iuvenāle capillīs,
tū quoque perpetuōs semper gere frondis honōrēs."
Fīnierat Paeān[19]. Factīs modo laurea rāmīs[42]
annuit utque caput[43] vīsa est agitāsse cacūmen.
(I, 452–567)

547 [36] *destroy by changing (this) form by which I pleased too much*
[37] *bark*
[38] = **pedēs**
550 [39] *a treetop has (is) her face*
[40] *her beauty alone remains*
[41] *as though (they were human) limbs*
[42] *with its newly made branches*
[43] *like a head*

[14] i.e., Daphne changed into a tree
[15] Apollo's long hair
[16] The triumphal processions of Roman generals are referred to here.
[17] Two laurels stood at the entrance of Augustus' palace on the Palatine.
[18] A wreath of oak leaves was over the door of the palace.
[19] Apollo

# APPENDIX

## Important Dates, Events, and People

| | |
|---|---|
| **B.C.** | |
| **753** | Rome founded (traditional date) |
| **753–509** | Legendary kings |
| **509** | Republic established |
| **494** | Secession of the plebs |
| **451–450** | Laws of the Twelve Tables |
| **390** | Gauls capture Rome |
| **280–275** | War with Pyrrhus |
| **264–241** | First Punic War |
| **254–184** | Plautus, comic writer |
| **218–201** | Second Punic War |
| **149–146** | Third Punic War |
| **146** | Capture of Corinth |
| **111–106** | War with Jugurtha |
| **106–48** | Pompey, general |
| **106–43** | Cicero, orator, statesman |
| **100–44** | Caesar, general, statesman |
| **99?–24?** | Cornelius Nepos |
| **96?–55** | Lucretius, poet |
| **90–88** | Social War |
| **87?–54?** | Catullus, poet |
| **86–34** | Sallust, historian |
| **70** | Cicero against Verres |
| **70–19** | Vergil, poet |
| **65–8** | Horace, poet |
| **63–A.D. 14** | Augustus |
| **62** | Cicero defends Archias |
| **60** | First triumvirate (Caesar, Crassus, Pompey) |
| **59–A.D. 17** | Livy, historian |
| **58–50** | Caesar in Gaul |
| **51** | Cicero governor of Cilicia |
| **49** | Caesar crosses the Rubicon, precipitating the Civil War |
| **48** | Battle of Pharsalus, Pompey defeated |
| **46** | Caesar reforms calendar |
| **44** | Caesar assassinated, March 15; Cicero against Antony |
| **43** | Cicero's death |
| **43–A.D. 17** | Ovid, poet |
| **31–A.D. 14** | Reign of Augustus |
| **15?–A.D. 50?** | Phaedrus, fabulist |
| **4?–A.D. 65** | Seneca, philosopher |
| **?–A.D. 66?** | Petronius |
| **A.D.** | |
| **8** | Ovid banished |
| **14–37** | Reign of Tiberius |
| **35–96?** | Quintilian, teacher |
| **37–41** | Reign of Caligula |
| **40?–104** | Martial, epigrammatist |
| **41–54** | Reign of Claudius |
| **54–68** | Reign of Nero |
| **62–114?** | Pliny the Younger |
| **68–69** | Reigns of Galba, Otho, Vitellius |
| **69–79** | Reign of Vespasian |
| **79–81** | Reign of Titus |
| **81–96** | Reign of Domitian |
| **96–98** | Reign of Nerva |
| **98–117** | Reign of Trajan |
| **117–138** | Reign of Hadrian |
| **125?–?** | Apuleius, philosopher |
| **138–161** | Reign of Antonius Pius |
| **161–180** | Reign of Marcus Aurelius |

## Basic Forms

### *Nouns*

| | **First Declension** | | **Second Declension** | |
|---|---|---|---|---|
| | SINGULAR | PLURAL | SINGULAR | PLURAL |
| NOM. | vi**a** | vi**ae** | serv**us** | serv**ī** |
| GEN. | vi**ae** | vi**ārum** | serv**ī** | serv**ōrum** |
| DAT. | vi**ae** | vi**īs** | serv**ō** | serv**īs** |
| ACC. | vi**am** | vi**ās** | serv**um** | serv**ōs** |
| ABL. | vi**ā** | vi**īs** | serv**ō** | serv**īs** |
| VOC. | | | serv**e** | |

Nouns in **–ius** often have –**ī** in the genitive and vocative singular: **fīlī, Cornēlī.** The accent does not change.[1]

**Second Declension**

| | SING. | PLUR. | SING. | PLUR. | SING. | PLUR. |
|---|---|---|---|---|---|---|
| NOM. | ager | agr**ī** | puer | puer**ī** | sign**um** | sign**a** |
| GEN. | agr**ī** | agr**ōrum** | puer**ī** | puer**ōrum** | sign**ī** | sign**ōrum** |
| DAT. | agr**ō** | agr**īs** | puer**ō** | puer**īs** | sign**ō** | sign**īs** |
| ACC. | agr**um** | agr**ōs** | puer**um** | puer**ōs** | sign**um** | sign**a** |
| ABL. | agr**ō** | agr**īs** | puer**ō** | puer**īs** | sign**ō** | sign**īs** |

Nouns in **–ium** often have **–ī** in the genitive singular: **cōnsilī.** The accent does not change.[1]

**Third Declension**

| | SING. | PLUR. | SING. | PLUR. | SING. | PLUR. |
|---|---|---|---|---|---|---|
| NOM. | mīles | mīlit**ēs** | lēx | lēg**ēs** | corpus | corpor**a** |
| GEN. | mīlit**is** | mīlit**um** | lēg**is** | lēg**um** | corpor**is** | corpor**um** |
| DAT. | mīlit**ī** | mīlit**ibus** | lēg**ī** | lēg**ibus** | corpor**ī** | corpor**ibus** |
| ACC. | mīlit**em** | mīlit**ēs** | lēg**em** | lēg**ēs** | corpus | corpor**a** |
| ABL. | mīlit**e** | mīlit**ibus** | lēg**e** | lēg**ibus** | corpor**e** | corpor**ibus** |

**Third Declension I–Stems**

| | SINGULAR | PLURAL | SINGULAR | PLURAL |
|---|---|---|---|---|
| NOM. | cīv**is** | cīv**ēs** | mar**e** | mar**ia** |
| GEN. | cīv**is** | cīv**ium** | mar**is** | mar**ium** |
| DAT. | cīv**ī** | cīv**ibus** | mar**ī** | mar**ibus** |
| ACC. | cīv**em** | cīv**ēs (–īs)** | mar**e** | mar**ia** |
| ABL. | cīv**e** | cīv**ibus** | mar**ī** | mar**ibus** |

**Turris** and a few proper nouns have **–im** in the accusative singular. **Turris, ignis, nāvis,** and a few proper nouns sometimes have **–ī** in the ablative singular.

The rules for determining whether or not a noun is an ī–stem are:

*(a)* The class of masculine and feminine ī–stem nouns are:

1. Nouns ending in **–is** and **–ēs** in the nominative with the same numbers of syllables in the genitive: **cīvis, nūbēs.**
2. Nouns of one syllable whose base ends in two consonants: **pars** (gen. **part–is**), **nox** (gen. **noct–is**).
3. Nouns whose nominative ends in **–ns** or **–rs: cliēns, adulescēns.**

*(b)* Neuter nouns whose nominative ends in **–e, –al,** or **–ar: mare, animal, calcar.**

---

[1] From the time of Augustus, the form in **–iī** becomes common.

### Fourth Declension

| | SINGULAR | PLURAL | SINGULAR | PLURAL |
|---|---|---|---|---|
| NOM. | cās**us** | cās**ūs** | corn**ū** | corn**ua** |
| GEN. | cās**ūs** | cās**uum** | corn**ūs** | corn**uum** |
| DAT. | cās**uī** | cās**ibus** | corn**ū** | corn**ibus** |
| ACC. | cās**um** | cās**ūs** | corn**ū** | corn**ua** |
| ABL. | cās**ū** | cās**ibus** | corn**ū** | corn**ibus** |

### Fifth Declension

| | SINGULAR | PLURAL | SINGULAR | PLURAL |
|---|---|---|---|---|
| NOM. | di**ēs** | di**ēs** | r**ēs** | r**ēs** |
| GEN. | di**ēī** | di**ērum** | r**eī** | r**ērum** |
| DAT. | di**ēī** | di**ēbus** | r**eī** | r**ēbus** |
| ACC. | di**em** | di**ēs** | r**em** | r**ēs** |
| ABL. | di**ē** | di**ēbus** | r**ē** | r**ēbus** |

### Irregular Nouns

| | SING. | PLUR. | SING. | SING. | PLUR. |
|---|---|---|---|---|---|
| NOM. | v**īs** | vīr**ēs** | nēm**ō** | dom**us** | dom**ūs** |
| GEN. | ——— | vīr**ium** | (nūll**īus**) | dom**ūs** (**–ī**) | dom**uum** (**–ōrum**) |
| DAT. | ——— | vīr**ibus** | nēmin**ī** | dom**uī** (**–ō**) | dom**ibus** |
| ACC. | v**im** | vīr**ēs** (**–īs**) | nēmin**em** | dom**um** | dom**ōs** (**–ūs**) |
| ABL. | v**ī** | vīr**ibus** | (nūll**ō**) | dom**ō** (**–ū**) | dom**ibus** |
| LOC. | | | | dom**ī** | |

## *Adjectives and Adverbs*

### First and Second Declensions

| | SINGULAR | | | PLURAL | | |
|---|---|---|---|---|---|---|
| | M | F | N | M | F | N |
| NOM. | magn**us** | magn**a** | magn**um** | magn**ī** | magn**ae** | magn**a** |
| GEN. | magn**ī** | magn**ae** | magn**ī** | magn**ōrum** | magn**ārum** | magn**ōrum** |
| DAT. | magn**ō** | magn**ae** | magn**ō** | magn**īs** | magn**īs** | magn**īs** |
| ACC. | magn**um** | magn**am** | magn**um** | magn**ōs** | magn**ās** | magn**a** |
| ABL. | magn**ō** | magn**ā** | magn**ō** | magn**īs** | magn**īs** | magn**īs** |
| VOC. | magn**e** | | | | | |

| | SINGULAR | | | SINGULAR | | |
|---|---|---|---|---|---|---|
| | M | F | N | M | F | N |
| NOM. | līber | līber**a** | līber**um** | noster | nostr**a** | nostr**um** |
| GEN. | līber**ī** | līber**ae** | līber**ī** | nostr**ī** | nostr**ae** | nostr**ī** |
| DAT. | līber**ō** | līber**ae** | līber**ō** | nostr**ō** | nostr**ae** | nostr**ō** |
| ACC. | līber**um** | līber**am** | līber**um** | nostr**um** | nostr**am** | nostr**um** |
| ABL. | līber**ō** | līber**ā** | līber**ō** | nostr**ō** | nostr**ā** | nostr**ō** |

Plural, **līberī, līberae, lībera,** etc.

Plural, **nostrī, –ae, –a,** etc.

## Third Declension

*(a)* THREE ENDINGS

| | SINGULAR | | | PLURAL | | |
|---|---|---|---|---|---|---|
| | M | F | N | M | F | N |
| NOM. | ācer | ācr**is** | ācr**e** | ācr**ēs** | ācr**ēs** | ācr**ia** |
| GEN. | ācr**is** | ācr**is** | ācr**is** | ācr**ium** | ācr**ium** | ācr**ium** |
| DAT. | ācr**ī** | ācr**ī** | ācr**ī** | ācr**ibus** | ācr**ibus** | ācr**ibus** |
| ACC. | ācr**em** | ācr**em** | ācr**e** | ācr**ēs (–īs)** | ācr**ēs (–īs)** | ācr**ia** |
| ABL. | ācr**ī** | ācr**ī** | ācr**ī** | ācr**ibus** | ācr**ibus** | ācr**ibus** |

*(b)* TWO ENDINGS

| | SINGULAR | | PLURAL | |
|---|---|---|---|---|
| | M F | N | M F | N |
| NOM. | fort**is** | fort**e** | fort**ēs** | fort**ia** |
| GEN. | fort**is** | fort**is** | fort**ium** | fort**ium** |
| DAT. | fort**ī** | fort**ī** | fort**ibus** | fort**ibus** |
| ACC. | fort**em** | fort**e** | fort**ēs (–īs)** | fort**ia** |
| ABL. | fort**ī** | fort**ī** | fort**ibus** | fort**ibus** |

*(c)* ONE ENDING[1]

| | SINGULAR | | PLURAL | |
|---|---|---|---|---|
| | M F | N | M F | N |
| NOM. | pār | pār | par**ēs** | par**ia** |
| GEN. | par**is** | par**is** | par**ium** | par**ium** |
| DAT. | par**ī** | par**ī** | par**ibus** | par**ibus** |
| ACC. | par**em** | pār | par**ēs (–īs)** | par**ia** |
| ABL. | par**ī** | par**ī** | par**ibus** | par**ibus** |

PRESENT PARTICIPLE

| | SINGULAR | | PLURAL | |
|---|---|---|---|---|
| | M F | N | M F | N |
| NOM. | portāns | portāns | portant**ēs** | portant**ia** |
| GEN. | portant**is** | portant**is** | portant**ium** | portan**ium** |
| DAT. | portant**ī** | portant**ī** | portant**ibus** | portant**ibus** |
| ACC. | portant**em** | portāns | portant**ēs (–īs)** | portant**ia** |
| ABL. | portant**e (–ī)** | portant**e (–ī)** | portant**ibus** | portant**ibus** |

The ablative singular regularly ends in **–e**, but **–ī** is used wherever the participle is used simply as an adjective.

IRREGULAR ADJECTIVES AND NUMERALS

| | M | F | N | M F | N |
|---|---|---|---|---|---|
| NOM. | ūn**us** | ūn**a** | ūn**um** | tr**ēs** | tr**ia** |
| GEN. | ūn**īus** | ūn**īus** | ūn**īus** | tr**ium** | tr**ium** |
| DAT. | ūn**ī** | ūn**ī** | ūn**ī** | tr**ibus** | tr**ibus** |
| ACC. | ūn**um** | ūn**am** | ūn**um** | tr**ēs** | tr**ia** |
| ABL. | ūn**ō** | ūn**ā** | ūn**ō** | tr**ibus** | tr**ibus** |

| | M | F | N | M F N *(adj.)* | N *(noun)* |
|---|---|---|---|---|---|
| NOM. | du**o** | du**ae** | du**o** | mīlle | mīl**ia** |
| GEN. | du**ōrum** | du**ārum** | du**ōrum** | mīlle | mīl**ium** |
| DAT. | du**ōbus** | du**ābus** | du**ōbus** | mīlle | mīl**ibus** |
| ACC. | du**ōs** | du**ās** | du**o** | mīlle | mīl**ia** |
| ABL. | du**ōbus** | du**ābus** | du**ōbus** | mīlle | mīl**ibus** |

[1] **Vetus** has **vetere** in the ablative singular and **veterum** in the genitive plural.

Declined like **ūnus** are **alius, alter, ūllus, nūllus, sōlus, tōtus, uter, neuter, uterque;** the plurals are regular. The nominative and accusative singular neuter of **alius** is **aliud;** for the genitive singular, **alterius** is generally used. **Ambō** is declined like **duo.**

### Comparison of Regular Adjectives and Adverbs

| POSITIVE | | COMPARATIVE | | SUPERLATIVE | |
|---|---|---|---|---|---|
| ADJ. | ADV. | ADJ. | ADV. | ADJ. | ADV. |
| alt**us** | alt**ē** | alt**ior** | alt**ius** | alt**issimus** | alt**issimē** |
| fort**is** | fort**iter** | fort**ior** | fort**ius** | fort**issimus** | fort**issimē** |
| līber | līber**ē** | līber**ior** | līber**ius** | līber**rimus** | līber**rimē** |
| ācer | ācr**iter** | ācr**ior** | ācr**ius** | ācer**rimus** | ācer**rimē** |
| facil**is** | facil**e** | facil**ior** | facil**ius** | facil**limus** | facil**limē** |

Like **facilis** are **difficilis, similis, dissimilis, gracilis, humilis,** but their adverbs (not used in this book) vary in the positive degree. Adjectives in **–er** are like **līber** or **ācer.**

### Comparison of Irregular Adjectives

| POSITIVE | COMPARATIVE | SUPERLATIVE |
|---|---|---|
| bon**us** | mel**ior** | opt**imus** |
| mal**us** | pe**ior** | pess**imus** |
| magn**us** | ma**ior** | max**imus** |
| parv**us** | min**or** | min**imus** |
| mult**us** | ——, plūs | plūr**imus** |
| īnfer**us** | īnfer**ior** | īnf**imus** *or* **īmus** |
| super**us** | super**ior** | supr**ēmus** *or* summ**us** |
| —— | pr**ior** | pr**īmus** |
| —— | prop**ior** | prox**imus** |
| —— | ulter**ior** | ult**imus** |

### Comparison of Irregular Adverbs

| | | |
|---|---|---|
| ben**e** | mel**ius** | opt**imē** |
| mal**e** | pe**ius** | pess**imē** |
| (magnopere) | mag**is** | max**imē** |
| —— | min**us** | min**imē** |
| mult**um** | plūs | plūr**imum** |
| diū | diū**tius** | diū**tissimē** |
| prop**e** | prop**ius** | prox**imē** |

### Declension of Comparatives

| | SINGULAR | | PLURAL | | SINGULAR | PLURAL | |
|---|---|---|---|---|---|---|---|
| | M F | N | M F | N | N | M F | N |
| NOM. | altior | altius | altiōr**ēs** | altiōr**a** | plūs[1] | plūr**ēs** | plūr**a** |
| GEN. | altiōr**is** | altiōr**is** | altiōr**um** | altiōr**um** | plūr**is** | plūr**ium** | plūr**ium** |
| DAT. | altiōr**ī** | altiōr**ī** | altiōr**ibus** | altiōr**ibus** | —— | plūr**ibus** | plūr**ibus** |
| ACC. | altiōr**em** | altius | altiōr**ēs** | altiōr**a** | plūs | plūr**ēs** | plūr**a** |
| ABL. | altiōr**e** | altiōr**e** | altiōr**ibus** | altiōr**ibus** | plūr**e** | plūr**ibus** | plūr**ibus** |

[1] Masculine and feminine are lacking in the singular.

## Numerals

| | ROMAN | CARDINAL | ORDINAL |
|---|---|---|---|
| 1 | **I** | **ūnus, –a, –um** | **prīmus, –a, –um** |
| 2 | **II** | **duo, duae, duo** | **secundus (alter)** |
| 3 | **III** | **trēs, tria** | **tertius** |
| 4 | **IIII** *or* **IV** | **quattuor** | **quārtus** |
| 5 | **V** | **quīnque** | **quīntus** |
| 6 | **VI** | **sex** | **sextus** |
| 7 | **VII** | **septem** | **septimus** |
| 8 | **VIII** | **octō** | **octāvus** |
| 9 | **VIIII** *or* **IX** | **novem** | **nōnus** |
| 10 | **X** | **decem** | **decimus** |
| 11 | **XI** | **ūndecim** | **ūndecimus** |
| 12 | **XII** | **duodecim** | **duodecimus** |
| 13 | **XIII** | **tredecim** | **tertius decimus** |
| 14 | **XIIII** *or* **XIV** | **quattuordecim** | **quārtus decimus** |
| 15 | **XV** | **quīndecim** | **quīntus decimus** |
| 16 | **XVI** | **sēdecim** | **sextus decimus** |
| 17 | **XVII** | **septendecim** | **septimus decimus** |
| 18 | **XVIII** | **duodēvīgintī** | **duodēvīcēsimus**[1] |
| 19 | **XVIIII** *or* **XIX** | **ūndēvīgintī** | **ūndēvīcēsimus** |
| 20 | **XX** | **vīgintī** | **vīcēsimus** |
| 21 | **XXI** | **vīgintī ūnus** *or* **ūnus et vīgintī** | **vīcēsimus prīmus** *or* **ūnus et vīcēsimus** |
| 30 | **XXX** | **trīgintā** | **trīcēsimus** |
| 40 | **XXXX** *or* **XL** | **quadrāgintā** | **quadrāgēsimus** |
| 50 | **L** | **quīnquāgintā** | **quīnquāgēsimus** |
| 60 | **LX** | **sexāgintā** | **sexāgēsimus** |
| 70 | **LXX** | **septuāgintā** | **septuāgēsimus** |
| 80 | **LXXX** | **octōgintā** | **octōgēsimus** |
| 90 | **LXXXX** *or* **XC** | **nōnāgintā** | **nōnāgēsimus** |
| 100 | **C** | **centum** | **centēsimus** |
| 101 | **CI** | **centum (et) ūnus** | **centēsimus (et) prīmus** |
| 200 | **CC** | **ducentī, –ae, –a** | **ducentēsimus** |
| 300 | **CCC** | **trecentī, –ae, –a** | **trecentēsimus** |
| 400 | **CCCC** | **quadringentī, –ae, –a** | **quadringentēsimus** |
| 500 | **D** | **quīngentī, –ae, –a** | **quīngentēsimus** |
| 600 | **DC** | **sescentī, –ae, –a** | **sescentēsimus** |
| 700 | **DCC** | **septingentī, –ae, –a** | **septingentēsimus** |
| 800 | **DCCC** | **octingentī, –ae, –a** | **octingentēsimus** |
| 900 | **DCCCC** | **nōngentī, –ae, –a** | **nōngentēsimus** |
| 1000 | **M** | **mīlle** | **mīllēsimus** |
| 2000 | **MM** | **duo mīlia** | **bis mīllēsimus** |

[1] The forms in **–ēsimus** are sometimes spelled **–ēnsimus.**

*Pronouns*

**Personal**

| | SING. | PLUR. | SING. | PLUR. | M | F | N |
|---|---|---|---|---|---|---|---|
| NOM. | **ego** | **nōs** | **tū** | **vōs** | **is** | **ea** | **id** |
| GEN. | **meī** | **nostrum (nostrī)** | **tuī** | **vestrum (–trī)** | (For the full declension, | | |
| DAT. | **mihi** | **nōbīs** | **tibi** | **vōbīs** | see the demonstrative | | |
| ACC. | **mē** | **nōs** | **tē** | **vōs** | **is** chart.) | | |
| ABL. | **mē** | **nōbīs** | **tē** | **vōbīs** | | | |

**Reflexive**

Not used in the nominative, reflexives have no nominative form.

| | FIRST PERSON | | SECOND PERSON | | THIRD PERSON | |
|---|---|---|---|---|---|---|
| | SINGULAR | PLURAL | SINGULAR | PLURAL | SINGULAR | PLURAL |
| GEN. | **meī** | **nostrī** | **tuī** | **vestrī** | **suī** | **suī** |
| DAT. | **mihi** | **nōbīs** | **tibi** | **vōbīs** | **sibi** | **sibi** |
| ACC. | **mē** | **nōs** | **tē** | **vōs** | **sē (sēsē)** | **sē (sēsē)** |
| ABL. | **mē** | **nōbīs** | **tē** | **vōbīs** | **sē (sēsē)** | **sē (sēsē)** |

**Demonstrative**

| | SINGULAR | | | PLURAL | | |
|---|---|---|---|---|---|---|
| | M | F | N | M | F | N |
| NOM. | **hic** | **haec** | **hoc** | **hī** | **hae** | **haec** |
| GEN. | **huius** | **huius** | **huius** | **hōrum** | **hārum** | **hōrum** |
| DAT. | **huic** | **huic** | **huic** | **hīs** | **hīs** | **hīs** |
| ACC. | **hunc** | **hanc** | **hoc** | **hōs** | **hās** | **haec** |
| ABL. | **hōc** | **hāc** | **hōc** | **hīs** | **hīs** | **hīs** |
| NOM. | **is** | **ea** | **id** | **eī (iī)** | **eae** | **ea** |
| GEN. | **eius** | **eius** | **eius** | **eōrum** | **eārum** | **eōrum** |
| DAT. | **eī** | **eī** | **eī** | **eīs (iīs)** | **eīs (iīs)** | **eīs (iīs)** |
| ACC. | **eum** | **eam** | **id** | **eōs** | **eās** | **ea** |
| ABL. | **eō** | **eā** | **eō** | **eīs (iīs)** | **eīs (iīs)** | **eīs (iīs)** |

| | SINGULAR | | | PLURAL | | |
|---|---|---|---|---|---|---|
| | M | F | N | M | F | N |
| NOM. | **īdem** | **eadem** | **idem** | **eīdem (īdem)** | **eaedem** | **eadem** |
| GEN. | **eiusdem** | **eiusdem** | **eiusdem** | **eōrundem** | **eārundem** | **eōrundem** |
| DAT. | **eīdem** | **eīdem** | **eīdem** | **eīsdem (īsdem)** | **eīsdem (īsdem)** | **eīsdem (īsdem)** |
| ACC. | **eundem** | **eandem** | **idem** | **eōsdem** | **eāsdem** | **eadem** |
| ABL. | **eōdem** | **eādem** | **eōdem** | **eīsdem (īsdem)** | **eīsdem (īsdem)** | **eīsdem (īsdem)** |

| | SINGULAR | | | SINGULAR | | |
|---|---|---|---|---|---|---|
| | M | F | N | M | F | N |
| NOM. | **ille** | **illa** | **illud** | **ipse** | **ipsa** | **ipsum** |
| GEN. | **illīus** | **illīus** | **illīus** | **ipsīus** | **ipsīus** | **ipsīus** |
| DAT. | **illī** | **illī** | **illī** | **ipsī** | **ipsī** | **ipsī** |
| ACC. | **illum** | **illam** | **illud** | **ipsum** | **ipsam** | **ipsum** |
| ABL. | **illō** | **illā** | **illō** | **ipsō** | **ipsā** | **ipsō** |

(The plural is regular like **magnus.**)    (The plural is regular.)

**Iste** is declined like **ille.**

### Relative / Interrogative

| | SINGULAR | | | PLURAL | | | SINGULAR (Interrogative) | |
|---|---|---|---|---|---|---|---|---|
| | M | F | N | M | F | N | M F | N |
| NOM. | **quī** | **quae** | **quod** | **quī** | **quae** | **quae** | **quis** | **quid** |
| GEN. | **cuius** | **cuius** | **cuius** | **quōrum** | **quārum** | **quōrum** | **cuius** | **cuius** |
| DAT. | **cui** | **cui** | **cui** | **quibus** | **quibus** | **quibus** | **cui** | **cui** |
| ACC. | **quem** | **quam** | **quod** | **quōs** | **quās** | **quae** | **quem** | **quid** |
| ABL. | **quō** | **quā** | **quō** | **quibus** | **quibus** | **quibus** | **quō** | **quō** |

The plural of **quis** is like **quī.** The interrogative adjective **quī** is like the relative **quī**.
Both parts of **quisquis** are declined like **quis,** except that the neuter is usually **quicquid.**

### Indefinite

| | SINGULAR | | PLURAL | | |
|---|---|---|---|---|---|
| | M F | N | M | F | N |
| NOM. | **aliquis** | **aliquid** | **aliquī** | **aliquae** | **aliqua** |
| GEN. | **alicuius** | **alicuius** | **aliquōrum** | **aliquārum** | **aliquōrum** |
| DAT. | **alicui** | **alicui** | **aliquibus** | **aliquibus** | **aliquibus** |
| ACC. | **aliquem** | **aliquid** | **aliquōs** | **aliquās** | **aliqua** |
| ABL. | **aliquō** | **aliquō** | **aliquibus** | **aliquibus** | **aliquibus** |

The adjective form is **aliquī, –qua, –quod,** etc.

| | SINGULAR | | |
|---|---|---|---|
| | M | F | N |
| NOM. | **quīdam** | **quaedam** | **quiddam** |
| GEN. | **cuiusdam** | **cuiusdam** | **cuiusdam** |
| DAT. | **cuidam** | **cuidam** | **cuidam** |
| ACC. | **quendam** | **quandam** | **quiddam** |
| ABL. | **quōdam** | **quādam** | **quōdam** |
| | PLURAL | | |
| NOM. | **quīdam** | **quaedam** | **quaedam** |
| GEN. | **quōrundam** | **quārundam** | **quōrundam** |
| DAT. | **quibusdam** | **quibusdam** | **quibusdam** |
| ACC. | **quōsdam** | **quāsdam** | **quaedam** |
| ABL. | **quibusdam** | **quibusdam** | **quibusdam** |

The adjective has **quoddam** for **quiddam.**

| | SINGULAR | | SINGULAR | |
|---|---|---|---|---|
| | M F | N | M F | N |
| NOM. | **quisquam** | **quicquam (quidquam)** | **quisque** | **quidque** |
| GEN. | **cuiusquam** | **cuiusquam** | **cuiusque** | **cuiusque** |
| DAT. | **cuiquam** | **cuiquam** | **cuique** | **cuique** |
| ACC. | **quemquam** | **quicquam (quidquam)** | **quemque** | **quidque** |
| ABL. | **quōquam** | **quōquam** | **quōque** | **quōque** |
| | (The plural is lacking.) | | (The plural is rare.) | |

The adjective form of **quisque** is **quisque, quaeque, quodque,** etc.

The indefinite pronoun **quis** (declined like the interrogative) and adjective **quī** (declined like the relative, but in the nominative feminime singular and the nominative and accusative neuter plural **qua** may be used for **quae**) are used chiefly after **sī, nisi, num,** and **nē.**

### *Verbs*

#### First Conjugation

PRINCIPAL PARTS: **portō, portāre, portāvī, portātus**

| | ACTIVE | | PASSIVE | |
|---|---|---|---|---|
| | INDICATIVE | | | |
| PRESENT | *I carry,* etc. | | *I am carried,* etc. | |
| | port**ō** | portā**mus** | port**or** | portā**mur** |
| | portā**s** | portā**tis** | portā**ris (–re)** | portā**minī** |
| | porta**t** | porta**nt** | portā**tur** | porta**ntur** |
| IMPERFECT | *I was carrying,* etc. | | *I was (being) carried,* etc. | |
| | portā**bam** | portā**bāmus** | portā**bar** | portā**bāmur** |
| | portā**bās** | portā**bātis** | portā**bāris (–re)** | portā**bāminī** |
| | portā**bat** | portā**bant** | portā**bātur** | portā**bantur** |
| FUTURE | *I shall carry,* etc. | | *I shall be carried,* etc. | |
| | portā**bō** | portā**bimus** | portā**bor** | portā**bimur** |
| | portā**bis** | portā**bitis** | portā**beris (–re)** | portā**biminī** |
| | portā**bit** | portā**bunt** | portā**bitur** | porta**buntur** |
| PERFECT | *I carried, have carried,* etc. | | *I was carried, have been carried,* etc. | |
| | portāv**ī** | portāv**imus** | portāt**us** (–a, –um) { **sum** | portāt**ī** (–ae, –a) { **sumus** |
| | portāv**istī** | portāv**istis** | **es** | **estis** |
| | portāv**it** | portāv**ērunt (–ēre)** | **est** | **sunt** |
| PLUPERFECT | *I had carried,* etc. | | *I had been carried,* etc. | |
| | portāv**eram** | portāv**erāmus** | portāt**us** (–a, –um) { **eram** | portāt**ī** (–ae, –a) { **erāmus** |
| | portāv**erās** | portāv**erātis** | **erās** | **erātis** |
| | portāv**erat** | portāv**erant** | **erat** | **erant** |

| | ACTIVE | | PASSIVE | |
|---|---|---|---|---|
| FUTURE PERFECT | *I shall have carried,* etc. | | *I shall have been carried,* etc. | |
| | portā**verō** | portā**verimus** | portā**tus** (**–a, –um**) { **erō** | portā**tī** (**–ae, –a**) { **erimus** |
| | portā**veris** | portā**veritis** | { **eris** | { **eritis** |
| | portā**verit** | portā**verint** | { **erit** | { **erunt** |

SUBJUNCTIVE

| | | | | |
|---|---|---|---|---|
| PRESENT | port**em** | port**ēmus** | port**er** | port**ēmur** |
| | port**ēs** | port**ētis** | port**ēris (–re)** | port**ēminī** |
| | port**et** | port**ent** | port**ētur** | port**entur** |
| IMPERFECT | portā**rem** | portā**rēmus** | portā**rer** | portā**rēmur** |
| | portā**rēs** | portā**rētis** | portā**rēris (–re)** | portā**rēminī** |
| | portā**ret** | portā**rent** | portā**rētur** | portā**rentur** |
| PERFECT | portā**verim** | portā**verīmus** | portā**tus** (**–a, –um**) { **sim** | portā**tī** (**–ae, –a**) { **sīmus** |
| | portā**verīs** | portā**verītis** | { **sīs** | { **sītis** |
| | portā**verit** | portā**verint** | { **sit** | { **sint** |
| PLUPERFECT | portā**vissem** | portā**vissēmus** | portā**tus** (**–a, –um**) { **essem** | portā**tī** (**–ae, –a**) { **essēmus** |
| | portā**vissēs** | portā**vissētis** | { **essēs** | { **essētis** |
| | portā**visset** | portā**vissent** | { **esset** | { **essent** |

PRESENT IMPERATIVE

| | | |
|---|---|---|
| 2D SING. | portā, *carry* | portā**re**, *be carried* |
| 2D PLUR. | portā**te**, *carry* | portā**minī**, *be carried* |

FUTURE IMPERATIVE

| | | |
|---|---|---|
| 2D SING. | portā**tō**, *carry* | portā**tor**, *be carried* |
| 3D SING. | portā**tō**, *he shall carry* | portā**tor**, *he shall be carried* |
| 2D PLUR. | portā**tōte**, *carry* | |
| 3D PLUR. | port**antō**, *they shall carry* | port**antor**, *they shall be carried* |

INFINITIVE

| | | |
|---|---|---|
| PRESENT | portā**re**, *to carry* | portā**rī**, *to be carried* |
| PERFECT | portā**visse**, *to have carried* | portā**tus esse**, *to have been carried* |
| FUTURE | portā**tūrus esse**, *to be going to carry* | (portā**tum īrī**, *to be going to be carried*) |

PARTICIPLE

| | | |
|---|---|---|
| PRESENT | portā**ns**, *carrying* | |
| PERFECT | | portā**tus** (*having been*) *carried* |
| FUTURE | portā**tūrus**, *going to carry* | port**andus**, (*necessary*) *to be carried* |

GERUND

GEN. port**andī**, *of carrying,* etc. DAT. port**andō** ACC. port**andum** ABL. port**andō**

SUPINE

ACC. portā**tum**, *in order to carry* ABL. portā**tū**, *in carrying*

## Second, Third, and Fourth Conjugations

| | *2d Conj.* | *3d Conj.* | *4th Conj.* | *3d Conj.* ***(–iō)*** |
|---|---|---|---|---|
| | | PRINCIPAL PARTS | | |
| | **doceō** | **pōnō** | **mūniō** | **capiō** |
| | **docēre** | **pōnere** | **mūnīre** | **capere** |
| | **docuī** | **posuī** | **mūnīvī** | **cēpī** |
| | **doctus** | **positus** | **mūnītus** | **captus** |
| | | INDICATIVE ACTIVE | | |
| PRESENT | doce**ō** | pōn**ō** | mūni**ō** | capi**ō** |
| | docē**s** | pōn**is** | mūnī**s** | cap**is** |
| | doce**t** | pōn**it** | mūn**it** | cap**it** |
| | docē**mus** | pōni**mus** | mūnī**mus** | capi**mus** |
| | docē**tis** | pōni**tis** | mūnī**tis** | capi**tis** |
| | doce**nt** | ponu**nt** | mūni**unt** | capi**unt** |
| IMPERFECT | docē**bam** | pōnē**bam** | mūni**ēbam** | capi**ēbam** |
| | docē**bās** | pōnē**bās** | mūni**ēbās** | capi**ēbās** |
| | docē**bat** | pōnē**bat** | mūni**ēbat** | capi**ēbat** |
| | docē**bāmus** | pōnē**bāmus** | mūni**ēbāmus** | capi**ēbāmus** |
| | docē**bātis** | pōnē**bātis** | mūni**ēbātis** | capi**ēbātis** |
| | docē**bant** | pōnē**bant** | mūni**ēbant** | capi**ēbant** |
| FUTURE | docē**bō** | pōn**am** | mūni**am** | capi**am** |
| | docē**bis** | pōn**ēs** | mūni**ēs** | capi**ēs** |
| | docē**bit** | pōn**et** | mūni**et** | capi**et** |
| | docē**bimus** | pōn**ēmus** | mūni**ēmus** | capi**ēmus** |
| | docē**bitis** | pōn**ētis** | mūni**ētis** | capi**ētis** |
| | docē**bunt** | pōn**ent** | mūni**ent** | capi**ent** |
| PERFECT | docu**ī** | posu**ī** | mūnīv**ī** | cēp**ī** |
| | docu**istī** | posu**istī** | mūnīv**istī** | cēp**istī** |
| | docu**it** | posu**it** | mūnīv**it** | cēp**it** |
| | docu**imus** | posu**imus** | mūnīv**imus** | cēp**imus** |
| | docu**istis** | posu**istis** | mūnīv**istis** | cēp**istis** |
| | docu**ērunt** | posu**ērunt** | mūnīv**ērunt** | cēp**ērunt** |
| | (**–ēre**) | (**–ēre**) | (**–ēre**) | (**–ēre**) |
| PLUPERFECT | docu**eram** | posu**eram** | mūnīv**eram** | cēp**eram** |
| | docu**erās** | posu**erās** | mūnīv**erās** | cēp**erās** |
| | docu**erat** | posu**erat** | mūnīv**erat** | cēp**erat** |
| | docu**erāmus** | posu**erāmus** | mūnīv**erāmus** | cēp**erāmus** |
| | docu**erātis** | posu**erātis** | mūnīv**erātis** | cēp**erātis** |
| | docu**erant** | posu**erant** | mūnīv**erant** | cēp**erant** |

| | *2d Conj.* | *3d Conj.* | *4th Conj.* | *3d Conj.* ***(–iō)*** |
|---|---|---|---|---|
| FUTURE PERFECT | docu**erō** | posu**erō** | mūnīv**erō** | cēp**erō** |
| | docu**eris** | posu**eris** | mūnīv**eris** | cēp**eris** |
| | docu**erit** | posu**erit** | mūnīv**erit** | cēp**erit** |
| | docu**erimus** | posu**erimus** | mūnīv**erimus** | cēp**erimus** |
| | docu**eritis** | posu**eritis** | mūnīv**eritis** | cēp**eritis** |
| | docu**erint** | posu**erint** | mūnīv**erint** | cēp**erint** |

SUBJUNCTIVE ACTIVE

| | | | | |
|---|---|---|---|---|
| PRESENT | doce**am** | pōn**am** | mūni**am** | capi**am** |
| | doce**ās** | pōn**ās** | mūni**ās** | capi**ās** |
| | doce**at** | pōn**at** | mūni**at** | capi**at** |
| | doce**āmus** | pōn**āmus** | mūni**āmus** | capi**āmus** |
| | doce**ātis** | pōn**ātis** | mūni**ātis** | capi**ātis** |
| | doce**ant** | pōn**ant** | mūni**ant** | capi**ant** |
| IMPERFECT | docē**rem** | pōne**rem** | mūnī**rem** | cape**rem** |
| | docē**rēs** | pōne**rēs** | mūnī**rēs** | cape**rēs** |
| | docē**ret** | pōne**ret** | mūnī**ret** | cape**ret** |
| | docē**rēmus** | pōne**rēmus** | mūnī**rēmus** | cape**rēmus** |
| | docē**rētis** | pōne**rētis** | mūnī**rētis** | cape**rētis** |
| | docē**rent** | pōne**rent** | mūnī**rent** | cape**rent** |
| PERFECT | docu**erim** | posu**erim** | mūnīv**erim** | cēp**erim** |
| | docu**erīs** | posu**erīs** | mūnīv**erīs** | cēp**erīs** |
| | docu**erit** | posu**erit** | mūnīv**erit** | cēp**erit** |
| | docu**erīmus** | posu**erīmus** | mūnīv**erīmus** | cēp**erīmus** |
| | docu**erītis** | posu**erītis** | mūnīv**erītis** | cēp**erītis** |
| | docu**erint** | posu**erint** | mūnīv**erint** | cēp**erint** |
| PLUPERFECT | docu**issem** | posu**issem** | mūnīv**issem** | cēp**issem** |
| | docu**issēs** | posu**issēs** | mūnīv**issēs** | cēp**issēs** |
| | docu**isset** | posu**isset** | mūnīv**isset** | cēp**isset** |
| | docu**issēmus** | posu**issēmus** | mūnīv**issēmus** | cēp**issēmus** |
| | docu**issētis** | posu**issētis** | mūnīv**issētis** | cēp**issētis** |
| | docu**issent** | posu**issent** | mūnīv**issent** | cēp**issent** |

PRESENT IMPERATIVE ACTIVE

| | | | | |
|---|---|---|---|---|
| 2D SING. | docē | pōne[1] | mūnī | cape[1] |
| 2D PLUR. | docē**te** | pōni**te** | mūnī**te** | capi**te** |

[1] **Dīcō, dūcō,** and **faciō** have **dīc, dūc, fac** in the imperative singular.

| | *2d Conj.* | *3d Conj.* | *4th Conj.* | *3d Conj.* ***(–iō)*** |
|---|---|---|---|---|
| | | FUTURE IMPERATIVE ACTIVE | | |
| 2D SING. | docē**tō** | pōni**tō** | mūnī**tō** | capi**tō** |
| 3D SING. | docē**tō** | pōni**tō** | mūnī**tō** | capi**tō** |
| 2D PLUR. | docē**tōte** | pōni**tōte** | mūnī**tōte** | capi**tōte** |
| 3D PLUR. | docen**tō** | pōnu**ntō** | mūni**untō** | capi**untō** |
| | | INFINITIVE ACTIVE | | |
| PRESENT | docē**re** | pōne**re** | mūnī**re** | cape**re** |
| PERFECT | docu**isse** | posu**isse** | mūnīv**isse** | cēp**isse** |
| FUTURE | doct**ūrus esse** | posit**ūrus esse** | mūnīt**ūrus esse** | capt**ūrus esse** |
| | | PARTICIPLE ACTIVE | | |
| PRESENT | docē**ns** | pōnē**ns** | mūniē**ns** | capiē**ns** |
| FUTURE | doct**ūrus** | posit**ūrus** | mūnīt**ūrus** | capt**ūrus** |
| | | GERUND | | |
| GEN. | docen**dī** | pōne**ndī** | mūni**endī** | capi**endī** |
| DAT. | docen**dō** | pōne**ndō** | mūni**endō** | capi**endō** |
| ACC. | doce**ndum** | pōne**ndum** | mūni**endum** | capi**endum** |
| ABL. | docen**dō** | pōne**ndō** | mūni**endō** | capi**endō** |
| | | SUPINE | | |
| ACC. | doct**um** | posit**um** | mūnīt**um** | capt**um** |
| ABL. | doct**ū** | posit**ū** | mūnīt**ū** | capt**ū** |
| | | INDICATIVE PASSIVE | | |
| PRESENT | doce**or**<br>docē**ris (–re)**<br>docē**tur** | pōn**or**<br>pōne**ris (–re)**<br>pōni**tur** | mūni**or**<br>mūnī**ris (–re)**<br>mūnī**tur** | capi**or**<br>cape**ris (–re)**<br>capi**tur** |
| | docē**mur**<br>docē**minī**<br>docen**tur** | pōni**mur**<br>pōni**minī**<br>pōnu**ntur** | mūnī**mur**<br>mūnī**minī**<br>mūni**untur** | capi**mur**<br>capi**minī**<br>capi**untur** |
| IMPERFECT | docē**bar**<br>docē**bāris (–re)**<br>docē**bātur** | pōnē**bar**<br>pōnē**bāris (–re)**<br>pōnē**bātur** | mūni**ēbar**<br>mūni**ēbāris (–re)**<br>mūni**ēbātur** | capi**ēbar**<br>capi**ēbāris (–re)**<br>capi**ēbātur** |
| | docē**bāmur**<br>docē**bāminī**<br>docē**bantur** | pōnē**bāmur**<br>pōnē**bāminī**<br>pōnē**bantur** | mūni**ēbāmur**<br>mūni**ēbāminī**<br>mūni**ēbantur** | capi**ēbāmur**<br>capi**ēbāminī**<br>capi**ēbantur** |

| | *2d Conj.* | *3d Conj.* | *4th Conj.* | *3d Conj.* ***(–iō)*** |
|---|---|---|---|---|
| FUTURE | docē**bor** | pōn**ar** | mūni**ar** | capi**ar** |
| | docē**beris (–re)** | pōn**ēris (–re)** | mūni**ēris (–re)** | capi**ēris (–re)** |
| | docē**bitur** | pōn**ētur** | mūni**ētur** | capi**ētur** |
| | docē**bimur** | pōn**ēmur** | mūni**ēmur** | capi**ēmur** |
| | docē**biminī** | pōn**ēminī** | mūni**ēminī** | capi**ēminī** |
| | docē**buntur** | pōn**entur** | mūni**entur** | capi**entur** |
| PERFECT | doct**us sum** | posit**us sum** | mūnīt**us sum** | capt**us sum** |
| | doct**us es** | posit**us es** | mūnīt**us es** | capt**us es** |
| | doct**us est** | posit**us est** | mūnīt**us est** | capt**us est** |
| | doct**ī sumus** | posit**ī sumus** | mūnīt**ī sumus** | capt**ī sumus** |
| | doct**ī estis** | posit**ī estis** | mūnīt**ī estis** | capt**ī estis** |
| | doct**ī sunt** | posit**ī sunt** | mūnīt**ī sunt** | capt**ī sunt** |
| PLUPERFECT | doct**us eram** | posit**us eram** | mūnīt**us eram** | capt**us eram** |
| | doct**us erās** | posit**us erās** | mūnīt**us erās** | capt**us erās** |
| | doct**us erat** | posit**us erat** | mūnīt**us erat** | capt**us erat** |
| | doct**ī erāmus** | posit**ī erāmus** | mūnīt**ī erāmus** | capt**ī erāmus** |
| | doct**ī erātis** | posit**ī erātis** | mūnit**ī erātis** | capt**ī erātis** |
| | doct**ī erant** | posit**ī erant** | mūnīt**ī erant** | capt**ī erant** |
| FUTURE PERFECT | doct**us erō** | posit**us erō** | mūnīt**us erō** | capt**us erō** |
| | doct**us eris** | posit**us eris** | mūnīt**us eris** | capt**us eris** |
| | doct**us erit** | posit**us erit** | mūnīt**us erit** | capt**us erit** |
| | doct**ī erimus** | posit**ī erimus** | mūnīt**ī erimus** | capt**ī erimus** |
| | doct**ī eritis** | posit**ī eritis** | mūnīt**ī eritis** | capt**ī eritis** |
| | doct**ī erunt** | posit**ī erunt** | mūnīt**ī erunt** | capt**ī erunt** |
| | | SUBJUNCTIVE PASSIVE | | |
| PRESENT | doce**ar** | pōn**ar** | mūni**ar** | capi**ar** |
| | doce**āris (–re)** | pōn**āris (–re)** | mūni**āris (–re)** | capi**āris (–re)** |
| | doce**ātur** | pōn**ātur** | mūni**ātur** | capi**ātur** |
| | doce**āmur** | pōn**āmur** | mūni**āmur** | capi**āmur** |
| | doce**āminī** | pōn**āminī** | mūni**āminī** | capi**āminī** |
| | doce**antur** | pōn**antur** | mūni**antur** | capi**antur** |
| IMPERFECT | docē**rer** | pōne**rer** | mūnī**rer** | cape**rer** |
| | docē**rēris (–re)** | pōne**rēris (–re)** | mūnī**rēris (–re)** | cape**rēris (–re)** |
| | docē**rētur** | pōne**rētur** | mūnī**rētur** | cape**rētur** |
| | docē**rēmur** | pōne**rēmur** | mūnī**rēmur** | cape**rēmur** |
| | docē**rēminī** | pōne**rēminī** | mūnī**rēminī** | cape**rēminī** |
| | docē**rentur** | pōne**rentur** | mūnī**rentur** | cape**rentur** |

| | *2d Conj.* | *3d Conj.* | *4th Conj.* | *3d Conj. (–iō)* |
|---|---|---|---|---|
| PERFECT | doct**us sim** | posit**us sim** | mūnīt**us sim** | capt**us sim** |
| | doct**us sīs** | posit**us sīs** | mūnīt**us sīs** | capt**us sīs** |
| | doct**us sit** | posit**us sit** | mūnīt**us sit** | capt**us sit** |
| | doct**ī sīmus** | posit**ī sīmus** | mūnīt**ī sīmus** | capt**ī sīmus** |
| | doct**ī sītis** | posit**ī sītis** | mūnīt**ī sītis** | capt**ī sītis** |
| | doct**ī sint** | posit**ī sint** | mūnīt**ī sint** | capt**ī sint** |
| PLUPERFECT | doct**us essem** | posit**us essem** | mūnīt**us essem** | capt**us essem** |
| | doct**us essēs** | posit**us essēs** | mūnīt**us essēs** | capt**us essēs** |
| | doct**us esset** | posit**us esset** | mūnīt**us esset** | capt**us esset** |
| | doct**ī essēmus** | posit**ī essēmus** | mūnīt**ī essēmus** | capt**ī essēmus** |
| | doct**ī essētis** | posit**ī essētis** | mūnīt**ī essētis** | capt**ī essētis** |
| | doct**ī essent** | posit**ī essent** | mūnīt**ī essent** | capt**ī essent** |
| | | PRESENT IMPERATIVE PASSIVE | | |
| 2D SING. | docē**re** | pōne**re** | mūnī**re** | cape**re** |
| 2D PLUR. | docē**minī** | pōni**minī** | mūnī**minī** | capi**minī** |
| | | FUTURE IMPERATIVE PASSIVE | | |
| 2D SING. | docē**tor** | pōni**tor** | mūnī**tor** | capi**tor** |
| 3D SING. | docē**tor** | pōni**tor** | mūnī**tor** | capi**tor** |
| 3D PLUR. | doc**entor** | pōn**untor** | mūnī**untor** | capi**untor** |
| | | INFINITIVE PASSIVE | | |
| PRESENT | docē**rī** | pōn**ī** | mūnī**rī** | cap**ī** |
| PERFECT | doct**us esse** | posit**us esse** | mūnīt**us esse** | capt**us esse** |
| FUTURE | doct**um īrī** | posit**um īrī** | mūnīt**um īrī** | capt**um īrī** |
| | | PARTICIPLE PASSIVE | | |
| PERFECT | doct**us** | posit**us** | mūnīt**us** | capt**us** |
| FUTURE | doc**endus** | pōn**endus** | mūni**endus** | capi**endus** |

## Deponent Verbs

Deponent verbs are active in meaning but passive in form, conjugated like the passive forms of the conjugations to which they belong: **arbitror,** *I think*. But the present and future participles and the future infinitive are active in both form and meaning. The perfect participle, though passive in form, is active in meaning.

| *1st Conj.* | *2d Conj.* | *3d Conj.* | *4th Conj.* | *3d Conj. (–iō)* |
|---|---|---|---|---|
| | | PRINCIPAL PARTS | | |
| **arbitror** | **vereōr** | **loquor** | **orior** | **gradior** |
| **arbitrārī** | **verērī** | **loquī** | **orīrī** | **gradī** |
| **arbitrātus** | **veritus** | **locūtus** | **ortus** | **gressus** |

| | *1st Conj.* | *2d Conj.* | *3d Conj.* | *4th Conj.* | *3d Conj.* **(–iō)** |
|---|---|---|---|---|---|
| | | | INDICATIVE | | |
| PRESENT | arbitr**or**, *I think* | vere**or**, *I fear* | loqu**or**, *I talk* | ori**or**, *I rise* | gradi**or**, *I walk* |
| IMPERFECT | arbitrā**bar** | verē**bar** | loquē**bar** | oriē**bar** | gradiē**bar** |
| FUTURE | arbitrā**bor** | verē**bor** | loqu**ar** | ori**ar** | gradi**ar** |
| PERFECT | arbitrāt**us** **sum** | verit**us** **sum** | locūt**us** **sum** | ort**us** **sum** | gress**us** **sum** |
| PLUPERFECT | arbitrāt**us** **eram** | verit**us** **eram** | locūt**us** **eram** | ort**us** **eram** | gress**us** **eram** |
| FUTURE PERFECT | arbitrāt**us** **erō** | verit**us** **erō** | locūt**us** **erō** | ort**us** **erō** | gress**us** **erō** |
| | | | SUBJUNCTIVE | | |
| PRESENT | arbitr**er** | vere**ar** | loqu**ar** | ori**ar** | gradi**ar** |
| IMPERFECT | arbitrā**rer** | verē**rer** | loque**rer** | orī**rer** | grade**rer** |
| PERFECT | arbitrāt**us** **sim** | verit**us** **sim** | locūt**us** **sim** | ort**us** **sim** | gress**us** **sim** |
| PLUPERFECT | arbitrāt**us** **essem** | verit**us** **essem** | locūt**us** **essem** | ort**us** **essem** | gress**us** **essem** |
| | | | IMPERATIVE | | |
| PRESENT | arbitrā**re** | verē**re** | loque**re** | orī**re** | grade**re** |
| FUTURE | arbitrā**tor** | verē**tor** | loqui**tor** | orī**tor** | gradi**tor** |
| | | | INFINITIVE | | |
| PRESENT | arbitrā**rī** | verē**rī** | loqu**ī** | orī**rī** | grad**ī** |
| PERFECT | arbitrāt**us** **esse** | verit**us** **esse** | locūt**us** **esse** | ort**us** **esse** | gress**us** **esse** |
| FUTURE | arbitrāt**ūrus** **esse** | verit**ūrus** **esse** | locūt**ūrus** **esse** | ort**ūrus** **esse** | gress**ūrus** **esse** |
| | | | PARTICIPLE | | |
| PRESENT | arbitrā**ns** | verē**ns** | loquē**ns** | oriē**ns** | gradiē**ns** |
| PERFECT | arbitrāt**us** | verit**us** | locūt**us** | ort**us** | gress**us** |
| FUTURE ACTIVE | arbitrāt**ūrus** | verit**ūrus** | locūt**ūrus** | ort**ūrus** | gress**ūrus** |
| FUTURE PASSIVE | arbitra**ndus** | vere**ndus** | loque**ndus** | orie**ndus** | gradie**ndus** |

| | 1st Conj. | 2d Conj. | 3d Conj. | 4th Conj. | 3d Conj. (–iō) |
|---|---|---|---|---|---|
| | | | GERUND | | |
| GEN. | arbitra**ndī,** etc. | ver**endī,** etc. | loqu**endī,** etc. | ori**endī,** etc. | gradi**endī,** etc. |
| | | | SUPINE | | |
| ACC. | arbitrāt**um** | verit**um** | locūt**um** | ort**um** | gress**um** |
| ABL. | arbitrāt**ū** | verit**ū** | locūt**ū** | ort**ū** | gress**ū** |

A few verbs (called "semideponent") are active in the present system and deponent in the perfect system, as **audeō, audēre, ausus.**

## Irregular Verbs

PRINCIPAL PARTS: **sum, esse, fuī, futūrus**

| | INDICATIVE | | | SUBJUNCTIVE | |
|---|---|---|---|---|---|
| PRESENT | su**m,** *I am* | su**mus,** *we are* | PRESENT | si**m** | sī**mus** |
| | es, *you are* | es**tis,** *you are* | | sī**s** | sī**tis** |
| | es**t,** *he is* | su**nt,** *they are* | | si**t** | si**nt** |
| IMPERFECT | *I was,* etc. | | | | |
| | er**am** | er**āmus** | IMPERFECT | ess**em** (for**em**) | ess**ēmus** |
| | er**ās** | er**ātis** | | ess**ēs** (for**ēs**) | ess**ētis** |
| | er**at** | er**ant** | | ess**et** (for**et**) | ess**ent** (for**ent**) |
| FUTURE | *I shall be,* etc. | | | | |
| | er**ō** | er**imus** | | | |
| | er**is** | er**itis** | | | |
| | er**it** | er**unt** | | | |
| PERFECT | *I was,* etc. | | | | |
| | fu**ī** | fu**imus** | PERFECT | fu**erim** | fu**erīmus** |
| | fu**istī** | fu**istis** | | fu**erīs** | fu**erītis** |
| | fu**it** | fu**ērunt (–ēre)** | | fu**erit** | fu**erint** |
| PLUPERFECT | *I had been,* etc. | | | | |
| | fu**eram** | fu**erāmus** | PLUPERFECT | fu**issem** | fu**issēmus** |
| | fu**erās** | fu**erātis** | | fu**issēs** | fu**issētis** |
| | fu**erat** | fu**erant** | | fu**isset** | fu**issent** |
| FUTURE PERFECT | *I shall have been,* etc. | | | | |
| | fu**erō** | fu**erimus** | | | |
| | fu**eris** | fu**eritis** | | | |
| | fu**erit** | fu**erint** | | | |

| | INFINITIVE | PRESENT IMPERATIVE | | | |
|---|---|---|---|---|---|
| PRESENT | es**se**, *to be* | 2D SING. | es, *be* | 2D PLUR. | es**te**, *be* |
| PERFECT | fu**isse**, *to have been* | | | | |
| | | FUTURE IMPERATIVE | | | |
| FUTURE | fut**ūrus esse** (for**e**), *to be going to be* | 2D SING. | es**tō** | 2D PLUR. | es**tōte** |
| | | 3D SING. | es**tō** | 3D PLUR. | su**ntō** |

| | PARTICIPLE |
|---|---|
| FUTURE | fut**ūrus**, *going to be* |

PRINCIPAL PARTS: **possum, posse, potuī, ——**

| | INDICATIVE | | SUBJUNCTIVE | | |
|---|---|---|---|---|---|
| PRESENT | *I am able, I can,* etc. | | | | |
| | pos**sum** | pos**sumus** | PRESENT | pos**sim** | pos**sīmus** |
| | pot**es** | pot**estis** | | pos**sīs** | pos**sītis** |
| | pot**est** | pos**sunt** | | pos**sit** | pos**sint** |
| IMPERFECT | *I was able, I could,* etc. | | | | |
| | pot**eram**, etc. | | IMPERFECT | pos**sem**, etc. | |
| FUTURE | *I shall be able,* etc. | | | | |
| | pot**erō**, etc. | | | | |
| PERFECT | *I was able, I could,* etc. | | | | |
| | potu**ī**, etc. | | PERFECT | potu**erim**, etc. | |
| PLUPERFECT | *I had been able,* etc. | | | | |
| | potu**eram**, etc. | | PLUPERFECT | potu**issem**, etc. | |
| FUTURE PERFECT | *I shall have been able,* etc. | | | | |
| | potu**erō**, etc. | | | | |

| | INFINITIVE | | PARTICIPLE |
|---|---|---|---|
| PRESENT | pos**se**, *to be able* | PRESENT | pot**ēns** (*adj.*), *powerful* |
| PERFECT | potu**isse**, *to have been able* | | |

PRINCIPAL PARTS: **ferō, ferre, tulī, lātus**

| | ACTIVE | | PASSIVE | |
|---|---|---|---|---|
| | INDICATIVE | | | |
| PRESENT | **ferō** | **ferimus** | **feror** | **ferimur** |
| | **fers** | **fertis** | **ferris (–re)** | **feriminī** |
| | **fert** | **ferunt** | **fertur** | **feruntur** |
| IMPERFECT | **ferēbam**, etc. | | **ferēbar**, etc. | |
| FUTURE | **feram**, **ferēs**, etc. | | **ferar**, **ferēris**, etc. | |
| PERFECT | **tulī**, etc. | | **lātus sum**, etc. | |
| PLUPERFECT | **tuleram**, etc. | | **lātus eram**, etc. | |
| FUTURE PERFECT | **tulerō**, etc. | | **lātus erō**, etc. | |

| | ACTIVE | | PASSIVE | |
|---|---|---|---|---|
| | | SUBJUNCTIVE | | |
| PRESENT | **feram, ferās,** etc. | | **ferar, ferāris,** etc. | |
| IMPERFECT | **ferrem,** etc. | | **ferrer,** etc. | |
| PERFECT | **tulerim,** etc. | | **lātus sim,** etc. | |
| PLUPERFECT | **tulissem,** etc. | | **lātus essem,** etc. | |
| | | PRESENT IMPERATIVE | | |
| 2D PERS. | **fer** | **ferte** | **ferre** | **feriminī** |
| | | FUTURE IMPERATIVE | | |
| 2D PERS. | **fertō** | **fertōte** | **fertor** | |
| 3D PERS. | **fertō** | **feruntō** | **fertor** | **feruntor** |
| | | INFINITIVE | | |
| PRESENT | **ferre** | | **ferrī** | |
| PERFECT | **tulisse** | | **lātus esse** | |
| FUTURE | **lātūrus esse** | | **(lātum īrī)** | |
| | | PARTICIPLE | | |
| PRESENT | **ferēns** | | | |
| PERFECT | | | **lātus** | |
| FUTURE | **lātūrus** | | **ferendus** | |

GERUND

GEN. **ferendī** DAT. **ferendō** ACC. **ferendum** ABL. **ferendō**

SUPINE

ACC. **lātum** ABL. **lātū**

PRINCIPAL PARTS: **eō, īre, iī, itūrus**

| | INDICATIVE | | SUBJUNCTIVE | INFINITIVE |
|---|---|---|---|---|
| PRESENT | **eō** | **īmus** | **eam,** etc. | **īre** |
| | **īs** | **ītis** | | |
| | **it** | **eunt** | | |
| IMPERFECT | **ībam,** etc. | | **īrem,** etc. | |
| FUTURE | **ībō** | **ībimus** | | **itūrus esse** |
| | **ībis** | **ībitis** | | |
| | **ībit** | **ībunt** | | |
| PERFECT | **iī** | **iimus** | **ierim,** etc. | **īsse** |
| | **īstī** | **īstis** | | |
| | **iit** | **iērunt (–ēre)** | | |
| PLUPERFECT | **ieram,** etc. | | **īssem,** etc. | |
| FUTURE PERFECT | **ierō,** etc. | | | |

| | PARTICIPLE | IMPERATIVE | |
|---|---|---|---|
| PRESENT | **iēns**, GEN. **euntis** | **ī** | **īte** |
| FUTURE | **itūrus** (PASSIVE **eundus**) | **ītō** | **ītōte** |
| | | **ītō** | **euntō** |

| | GERUND | SUPINE |
|---|---|---|
| GEN. | **eundī** | |
| DAT. | **eundō** | |
| ACC. | **eundum** | **itum** |
| ABL. | **eundō** | **itū** |

PRINCIPAL PARTS

| | | |
|---|---|---|
| **volō** | **nōlō** | **mālō** |
| **velle** | **nōlle** | **mālle** |
| **voluī** | **nōluī** | **māluī** |

| | | | | | | |
|---|---|---|---|---|---|---|
| | | | INDICATIVE | | | |
| PRESENT | **volō** | **volumus** | **nōlō** | **nōlumus** | **mālō** | **mālumus** |
| | **vīs** | **vultis** | **nōn vīs** | **nōn vultis** | **māvīs** | **māvultis** |
| | **vult** | **volunt** | **nōn vult** | **nōlunt** | **māvult** | **mālunt** |
| IMPERFECT | **volēbam**, etc. | | **nōlēbam**, etc. | | **mālēbam**, etc. | |
| FUTURE | **volam**, **volēs**, etc. | | **nōlam**, **nōlēs**, etc. | | **mālam**, **mālēs**, etc. | |
| PERFECT | **voluī**, etc. | | **nōluī**, etc. | | **māluī**, etc. | |
| PLUPERFECT | **volueram**, etc. | | **nōlueram**, etc. | | **mālueram**, etc. | |
| FUTURE PERFECT | **voluerō**, etc. | | **nōluerō**, etc. | | **māluerō**, etc. | |
| | | | SUBJUNCTIVE | | | |
| PRESENT | **velim** | **velīmus** | **nōlim** | **nōlīmus** | **mālim** | **mālīmus** |
| | **velīs** | **velītis** | **nōlīs** | **nōlītis** | **mālīs** | **mālītis** |
| | **velit** | **velint** | **nōlit** | **nōlint** | **mālit** | **mālint** |
| IMPERFECT | **vellem**, etc. | | **nōllem**, etc. | | **māllem**, etc. | |
| PERFECT | **voluerim**, etc. | | **nōluerim**, etc. | | **māluerim**, etc. | |
| PLUPERFECT | **voluissem**, etc. | | **nōluissem**, etc. | | **māluissem**, etc. | |
| | | | PRESENT AND FUTURE IMPERATIVE | | | |
| 2D PERS. | —— | —— | **nōlī** | **nōlīte** | —— | —— |
| 2D PERS. | —— | —— | **nōlītō** | **nōlītōte** | —— | —— |
| | | | INFINITIVE | | | |
| PRESENT | **velle** | | **nōlle** | | **mālle** | |
| PERFECT | **voluisse** | | **nōluisse** | | **māluisse** | |

| | | PARTICIPLE | | | | |
|---|---|---|---|---|---|---|
| PRESENT | **volēns** | | **nōlēns** | | —— | |

PRINCIPAL PARTS: **fīō, fierī, (factus)**

| | INDICATIVE | | SUBJUNCTIVE | IMPERATIVE | | INFINITIVE |
|---|---|---|---|---|---|---|
| PRESENT | **fīō** | **fīmus** | **fīam**, etc. | | | **fierī** |
| | **fīs** | **fītis** | | **fī** | **fīte** | |
| | **fit** | **fīunt** | | | | |
| IMPERFECT | **fīēbam**, etc. | | **fierem**, etc. | | | |
| FUTURE | **fīam, fīēs**, etc. | | | | | |

## Defective Verbs

**Coepī** is used only in the perfect system. For the present system **incipiō** is used. With a passive infinitive the passive of **coepī** is used: **Lapidēs iacī coeptī sunt,** *Stones began to be thrown.* **Meminī** and **ōdī** likewise are used only in the perfect system but with present meaning. The former has an imperative **mementō, mementōte.**

The only forms of **inquam** in common use are in the present indicative: **inquam, inquis, inquit, inquiunt.** Similarly **aiō, ais, ait, aiunt** and the imperfect: **aiēbam,** etc.

Impersonal verbs are used only in the third personal singular and the infinitive: **decet, libet, licet, miseret, oportet, piget, pudet, taedet.**

## Contracted Forms

Verbs having perfect stems ending in **–āv–** or **–ēv–** are sometimes contracted by dropping **–ve–** before **–r–** and **–vi–** before **–s–: amārunt, cōnsuēsse.** Verbs having perfect stems ending in **–īv–** drop **–vi–** before **–s–** but only **–v–** before **–r–: audīsset, audierat.**

## Syntax[1]

### *Questions*

Information questions are introduced by interrogative pronouns or adverbs (**quis, ubi,** etc.) Other questions are introduced as follows:

1. In questions the answer to which might be either *yes* or *no,* the particle **–ne** is attached to the first word.

   **Frāterne venit?** *Is your brother coming?*

2. In questions that expect a *yes* answer, the introductory word is **nōnne** (i.e., **nōn** + **ne;** cf. English).

   **Nōnne frāter venit?** *Isn't your brother coming? Your brother is coming, isn't he?*

3. In questions that expect a *no* answer, the introductory word is **num.**

   **Num frāter venit?** *Your brother is not coming, is he?*

4. Double questions are introduced by **utrum, –ne** or nothing at all and are connected by **an.**

   **Frāterne bonus an malus est?** *Is your brother good or bad?*

For *or not* in a double question Latin uses **annōn** or **necne.**

### *Reflexive Pronouns and Adjectives*

The personal pronouns of the first and second persons and the possessive adjectives derived from them may be used reflexively. It is only in the third person that the Latin uses a distinct reflexive pronoun, **suī** (adjective **suus**).

*a.* Both **suī** and **suus** commonly refer to the subject of the clause in which they stand (direct reflexive).

**Sē suaque omnia dēdidērunt.** *They surrendered themselves and all their possessions.*

*b.* Sometimes **suī** or **suus,** occurring in a subordinate clause, refers not to the subject of its own clause, but to the subject of the main verb (indirect reflexive).

**Petēbant utī Caesar sibi potestātem faceret.** *They begged that Caesar give them a chance.*

In order to avoid ambiguity, if it ever becomes necessary to refer to the subjects of both clauses, **ipse** is used as the indirect reflexive, and **suī** (or **suus**) as the direct reflexive.

### *Agreement*

1. *Adjectives.* Adjectives and participles agree in number, gender, and case with the nouns they modify. When an adjective modifies several nouns of different numbers or genders, it either agrees with the last or is put in the neuter plural.
2. *Adjectives as Nouns (substantives).* Sometimes adjectives are used as nouns: **nostrī,** *our (men);* **malum,** *evil.*

---

[1] In this summary only those constructions that are relatively more important and that occur repeatedly in the text or are referred to in the book are included.

A plural verb may be used with a singular subject that is plural in thought.

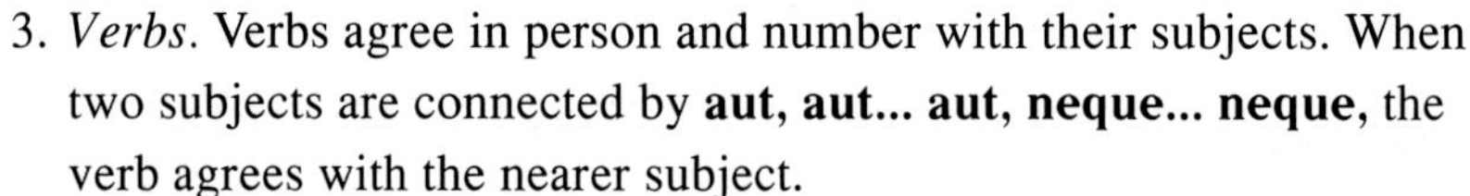

3. *Verbs.* Verbs agree in person and number with their subjects. When two subjects are connected by **aut, aut... aut, neque... neque,** the verb agrees with the nearer subject.
4. *Relative Pronoun.* The relative pronoun agrees in gender and number with its antecedent, but its case depends upon its use in its own clause.
   *a.* The antecedent of the relative pronoun is sometimes omitted.
   *b.* Sometimes the antecedent is represented by an entire clause, in which case the pronoun is best translated *a thing that.*
   *c.* In Latin a relative pronoun is often used at the beginning of a sentence to refer to the entire thought of the preceding sentence. The English idiom calls for a demonstrative or personal pronoun.

| | |
|---|---|
| **quā de cāusā** | *for this reason* |

5. *Appositives.* Appositives agree in case. It is often best to supply *as* in translating the appositive.

| | |
|---|---|
| **eōdem homine magistrō ūtī** | *to use the same man as teacher* |

### *Noun Syntax*

### Nominative

1. *Subject.* The subject of a finite verb is in the nominative case.
2. *Predicate.*
   *a.* A noun or adjective used in the predicate with a linking verb (*is, are, seem,* etc.) is in the nominative.

| | |
|---|---|
| **Īnsula est magna.** | *The island is large.* |
| **Sicilia est īnsula.** | *Sicily is an island.* |

With the active voice of these verbs, two accusatives are used.

   *b.* Predicate nouns and adjectives are used not only with **sum** but also with **fīō** and the passive voice of verbs meaning *call, choose, appoint, elect,* and the like.

| | |
|---|---|
| **Caesar dux factus est.** | *Caesar was made leader.* |
| **Cicerō Pater Patriae appellātus est.** | *Cicero was called the Father of his Country.* |

### Genitive

1. *Of Possession.* Possession is expressed by the genitive.

| | |
|---|---|
| **viae īnsulae** | *the roads of the island* |

2. *Predicate.* The possessive genitive may be used in the predicate with **sum** (or **faciō**), often translated *it is the part of, the duty of,* etc.

| | |
|---|---|
| **Sapientiae est vidēre.** | *It is the part of wisdom to see.* |

The descriptive genitive is largely confined to permanent qualities such as measure and number.

3. *Of Description.* The genitive, if modified by an adjective, may be used to describe a person or thing.

| | |
|---|---|
| **virī magnae virtūtis** | *men of great courage* |
| **spatium decem pedum** | *a space of ten feet* |

4. *Of the Whole.* The genitive of the whole (also called partitive genitive) represents the whole to which the part belongs.

| | |
|---|---|
| **hōrum omnium fortissimī** | *the bravest of all these* |
| **nihil praesidī** | *no guard* |

*a.* This is similar to the English idiom except when the genitive is used with such words as **nihil, satis, quid.**

*b.* Instead of the genitive of the whole, the ablative with **ex** or **dē** is regularly used with cardinal numerals (except **mīlia**) and **quīdam,** often also with other words, such as **paucī** and **complūrēs.**

| | |
|---|---|
| **quīnque ex nostrīs** | *five of our men* |
| **quīdam ex mīlitibus** | *certain of the soldiers* |

5. *Subjective.* The subjective genitive expresses the subject of the verbal idea of the noun on which it depends. If this noun is turned into a verb, the genitive becomes subject.

| | |
|---|---|
| **timor populī** | *the fear of the people* (i.e., *the people feared*) |

6. *Objective.* The objective genitive expresses the object of the verbal idea of the noun or adjective on which it depends. If this noun or adjective is turned into a verb, the genitive becomes object.

| | |
|---|---|
| **amantissimōs reī pūblicae virōs** | *patriotic men* (i.e., *they loved the state*) |

7. *Of the Charge and Penalty.* With verbs of *accusing, condemning,* or *acquitting* the genitive is used to indicate either the charge or the penalty.

| | |
|---|---|
| **capitis damnātum** | *condemned to death* (lit., *of the head*) |
| **Accūsō tē inertiae.** | *I accuse you of inaction.* |

8. *Of Indefinite Value.* The genitive is used with **sum** and other verbs to express indefinite value.

| | |
|---|---|
| **Est tantī.** | *It is worth that much.* |
| **parvī esse dūcenda** | *to be considered of little value* |

9. *With Special Verbs.* With **oblīvīscor** *(forget),* **meminī, reminīscor** *(remember),* **misereor** *(pity),* and occasionally **potior** *(get possession of),* the genitive is used.

| | |
|---|---|
| **Oblīvīscere caedis atque incendiōrum.** | *Forget bloodshed and burning.* |

Sometimes the accusative is used with **meminī** and **reminīscor;** regularly so with **recordor** *(remember).*

10. *With Adjectives.* The genitive is used with certain adjectives. In many cases the English idiom is the same; in others, it is not.

| | |
|---|---|
| **bellandī cupidus** | *desirous of waging war* |
| **reī mīlitāris perītus** | *skilled in warfare* |
| **tuī similis** | *like you* |

The ablative is sometimes used with these words (except **expers**).

The dative of reference is often used with the dative of purpose to show the person or thing affected (double dative).

11. *Of Plenty and Want.* With certain adjectives and verbs having the idea of plenty or want, the genitive is regularly used: **plēnus** and **refertus,** *full of;* **inānis, inops,** and **expers,** *empty, without, devoid of.*

**Dative**

1. *Of Indirect Object.* The indirect object of a verb is in the dative. It is used with verbs of giving, reporting, telling, etc.

| | |
|---|---|
| **Nautae pecūniam dōnō.** | *I give money to the sailor.* |

2. *Of Purpose.* The dative is sometimes used to express purpose.

| | |
|---|---|
| **Locum castrīs dēlēgit.** | *He chose a place for a camp.* |

3. *Of Reference.* The dative of reference shows the person concerned or referred to.

| | |
|---|---|
| **sī mihi dignī esse vultis** | *if you wish to be worthy in my sight* (literally, *for me*) |
| **Haec castra erunt praesidiō oppidō.** | *This camp will be (for) a protection to the town.* |

4. *Of Separation.* The dative of separation (really reference) is usually confined to persons and occurs chiefly with verbs compounded with **ab, dē,** and **ex.**

| | |
|---|---|
| **scūtō ūnī mīlitī dētrāctō** | *having seized a shield from a soldier* |

5. *With Adjectives.* The dative is used with certain adjectives, as **amīcus, idōneus, pār, proximus, similis, ūtilis,** and their opposites. In many cases the English idiom is the same.

| | |
|---|---|
| **Hic liber est similis illī.** | *This book is similar to that.* |

6. *With Special Verbs.* The dative is used with a few intransitive verbs, such as **cōnfīdō, crēdō, dēsum, faveō, ignōscō, imperō, invideō, minitor, noceō, parcō, pāreō, persuādeō, placeō, praestō, resistō, serviō,** and **studeō.**

| | |
|---|---|
| **Tibi pāret sed mihi resistit.** | *He obeys you but resists me.* |

*a.* Some of these verbs become impersonal in the passive and the dative is retained. The perfect passive participle of such verbs is used only in the neuter.

| | |
|---|---|
| **Eī persuāsum est.** | *He was persuaded.* |

*b.* A neuter pronoun or adjective or an **ut** clause may be used as a direct object with **imperō** and **persuādeō.**

| | |
|---|---|
| **Hoc mihi persuāsit.** | *He persuaded me of this.* |

7. *With Compounds.* The dative is often used with certain compound verbs, especially when the noun goes closely with the prefix of the verb. No general rule can be given. Sometimes both an accusative and a dative are used when the main part of the verb is transitive.

**Gallīs bellum intulit.** — *He made war against the Gauls.*

8. *Possession.* The possessor may be expressed by the dative with **sum.**

**Liber mihi est.** — *I have a book.*

9. *Agent.* The dative of agent is used with the gerundive (future passive participle) to indicate the person upon whom the obligation rests. Occasionally it is used with the perfect participle.

**Hoc opus vōbīs faciendum est.** — *This work is to be done by you,* i.e., *This work must be done by you.*

**Accusative**

1. *Of Direct Object.* The direct object of a transitive verb is in the accusative.

**Viam parāmus.** — *We are preparing a way.*

2. *Of Extent of Space* and *Duration of Time.* Extent of time or space is expressed by the accusative without a preposition.

**Duōs annōs remānsit.** — *He remained two years.*
**Flūmen decem pedēs altum est.** — *The river is ten feet deep.*

3. *Of Place to Which.* The accusative with **ad** *(to)* or **in** *(into)* expresses *place to which.* These prepositions, however, are omitted before **domum** and names of towns and cities.

**Lēgātōs ad eum mittunt.** — *They send envoys to him.*
**Rōmam eunt.** — *They go to Rome.*

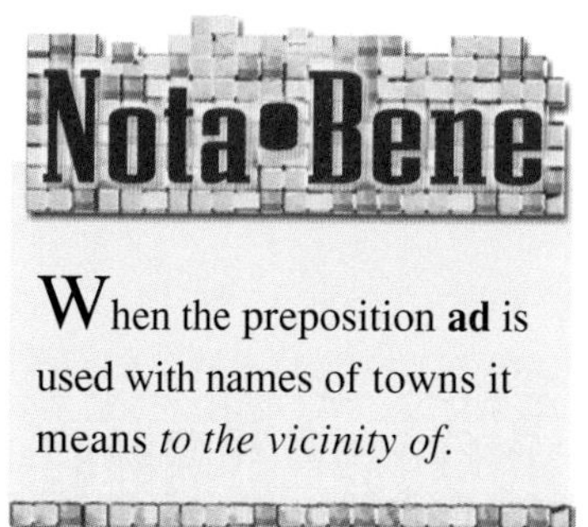


When the preposition **ad** is used with names of towns it means *to the vicinity of.*

4. *Subject of Infinitive.* The subject of an infinitive is in the accusative.

**Puerōs esse bonōs volumus.** — *We want the boys to be good.*

5. *Two Accusatives.* With **trādūcō** and **trānsportō** two accusatives are used. In the passive the word closely connected with the prefix **(trāns)** remains in the accusative.

**Cōpiās *Rhēnum* trādūcit.** — *He leads his forces across the Rhine.*
**Cōpiae *Rhēnum* trādūcuntur.** — *The forces are led across the Rhine.*

6. *With Prepositions.* The accusative is used with prepositions (except those listed in **Ablative,** 19, page 300). When **in** and **sub** show the direction toward which a thing moves, the accusative is used.

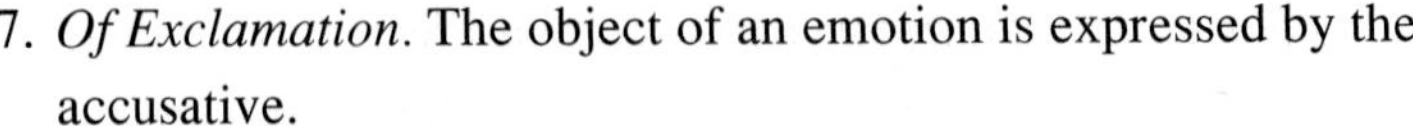

Some examples are classed as direct objects of the passive verb used in a middle (reflexive) sense.

7. *Of Exclamation.* The object of an emotion is expressed by the accusative.

| | |
|---|---|
| **Ō fortūnātam rem pūblicam!** | *O fortunate republic!* |
| **Ō tempora, Ō mōrēs!** | *O what a time, what a state of affairs!* |

8. *Of Respect.* In poetry the accusative of respect is used with verbs and adjectives to indicate the part affected.

| | |
|---|---|
| **hirsūta capillōs** | *with shaggy hair* (lit., *shaggy as to the hair*) |

**Ablative**

*Summary.* The uses of the ablative may be grouped under three heads:

I. The *true* or *"from"* ablative (**ab,** *from,* and **lātus,** *carried*), used with the prepositions **ab, dē,** and **ex**—if any preposition is used.

II. The *associative* or *"with" ablative,* used with the preposition **cum**—if any preposition is used.

III. The *place* or *"in" ablative,* used with the prepositions **in** and **sub**—if any preposition is used.

1. *Of Separation.* Separation may be expressed by the ablative without a preposition, always so with **careō** and **līberō,** often also with **abstineō, dēsistō, excēdō,** and other verbs; also adjectives such as **līber** and **vacuus.**

   *a.* **Prohibeō,** *keep from,* is generally used without a preposition but occasionally with it.

   | | |
   |---|---|
   | **Suīs fīnibus eōs prohibent.** | *They keep them from their own territory.* |

   *b.* Other verbs expressing separation regularly require the prepositions **ab, dē,** or **ex.**

The preposition is regularly omitted before **domō** as well as before names of towns and cities. When it is used with such names, it means *from the vicinity of.*

2. *Of Place from Which.* The ablative with **ab, dē,** or **ex** expresses *place from which.*

| | |
|---|---|
| **ex agrīs** | *out of the fields* |

3. *Of Origin.* The ablative without or with a preposition (**ab, dē, ex**) expresses origin.

| | |
|---|---|
| **amplissimō genere nātus** | *born of most illustrious family* |

4. *Of Agent.* The ablative with **ā** or **ab** is used with a passive verb to show the person (or animal) by whom something is done.

| | |
|---|---|
| **Amāmur ab amīcīs.** | *We are loved by our friends.* |

5. *Of Comparison.* After a comparative the ablative is used when **quam** *(than)* is omitted.

| | |
|---|---|
| **amplius pedibus decem** | *more than ten feet* |
| **Nec locus tibi ūllus dulcior esse dēbet patriā.** | *No spot ought to be dearer to you than your native land.* |

6. *Of Accompaniment.* The ablative with **cum** expresses accompaniment.

| | |
|---|---|
| **Cum servō venit.** | *He is coming with the slave.* |

*a.* When **cum** is used with a personal, reflexive, or relative pronoun, it is attached to it as an enclitic: **vōbīscum,** *with you;* **sēcum,** *with himself;* **quibuscum,** *with whom.*

*b.* **Cum** may be omitted in military phrases indicating accompaniment, if modified by an adjective other than a numeral.

| | |
|---|---|
| **omnibus suīs cōpiīs** | *with all his forces* |
| **cum tribus legiōnibus** | *with three legions* |

7. *Of Manner.* The ablative of manner with **cum** describes how something is done. **Cum** is sometimes omitted if an adjective modifies the noun.

| | |
|---|---|
| **(Cum) magnō studiō labōrat.** | *He labors with great eagerness (very eagerly).* |

8. *Absolute.* A noun in the ablative used with a participle, adjective, or other noun and having no grammatical connection with any other word in its clause is called an ablative absolute. In translating, an ablative absolute should, as a rule, be changed to a clause expressing time, cause, condition, means, or concession, according to the context. At times it may best be rendered by a coordinate clause.

| | |
|---|---|
| **Servō accūsātō, dominus discessit.** | *After accusing the slave* (lit., *the slave having been accused*), *the master departed.* |
| **Oppidīs notrīs captīs, bellum gerēmus.** | *If our towns are captured* (lit., *our towns captured*), *we shall wage war.* |

9. *Of Means.* The means by which a thing is done is expressed by the ablative without a preposition.

| | |
|---|---|
| **Ratibus trānsībant.** | *They were trying to cross by means of rafts.* |

10. *With Special Verbs.* The ablative is used with a few verbs, notably **fruor, fungor, potior,** and **ūtor,** whose English equivalents generally govern a direct object.

| | |
|---|---|
| **Castrīs potītī sunt.** | *They got possession of the camp.* |

11. *Of Cause.* The ablative of cause is used chiefly with verbs and adjectives expressing feeling.

| | |
|---|---|
| **labōrāre iniūriā** | *to suffer because of the wrong* |
| **vīribus cōnfīsī** | *relying on their strength* |

12. *Of Degree of Difference.* The ablative without a preposition expresses the measure of difference.

| | |
|---|---|
| **tribus annīs ante** | *three years ago* (lit., *before by three years*) |
| **multō maior** | *much larger* (lit., *larger by much*) |

13. *Of Description.* The ablative, like the genitive, is used with an adjective to describe a noun. It is regularly used of temporary qualities, such as personal appearance.

| | |
|---|---|
| **hominēs inimīcā faciē** | *men with an unfriendly appearance* |

14. *Of Place Where.* The ablative with **in** or **sub** expresses *place where.* The preposition may be omitted, however, with certain words like **locō, locīs,** and **parte** and also in certain fixed expressions like **tōtō orbe terrārum,** *in the whole world.* In poetry the omission of the preposition is more frequent. See also **Locative.**

15. *Of Time When. Time when* or *time within which* is expressed by the ablative without a preposition.

| | |
|---|---|
| **aestāte** | *in summer* |
| **paucīs diēbus** | *within a few days* |

16. *Of Respect.* The ablative tells in what respect the statement applies.

| | |
|---|---|
| **Nōs superant numerō.** | *They surpass us in number.* |

17. *Of Accordance.* The ablative is used with a few words to express the idea *in accordance with.*

| | |
|---|---|
| **mōre suō** | *in accordance with his custom* |

18. *With* ***Dignus.*** The ablative is used with **dignus** and **indignus.**

| | |
|---|---|
| **dignus patre** | *worthy of his father* |

19. *With Prepositions.* The ablative is used with the prepositions **ab, cum, dē, ex, prae, prō, sine;** sometimes with **in** and **sub.**

20. *With* ***Opus Est*** *and* ***Egeō.*** **Opus est,** meaning *there is need,* and **egeō,** *need,* may be followed by the ablative.

| | |
|---|---|
| **Pecūniā opus est.** | *There is need of money.* |

21. *With* ***Cōnfīdō.*** With **fīdō** and **cōnfīdō** *(trust)* the ablative may be used. Regularly the dative (of persons) is used.

| | |
|---|---|
| **cum affīnitāte Pompeī cōnfīderet** | *since he trusted in his relationship with Pompey* |

22. *With* **Rēfert** *and* **Interest.** With **rēfert** and **interest,** *it concerns, it is for the interest of,* if a noun, the genitive of the person or thing concerned is used; otherwise the feminine ablative singular of the possessive is used.

| | |
|---|---|
| **Rēgis rēfert**. | *It concerns the king.* |
| **Meā videō quid intersit**. | *I see what is to my interest.* |

The construction originated in such expressions as **Quid meā rē fert?** *What does it bear on my affair?*

**Locative**

**Domus, rūs,** and the names of towns, cities, and large islands require a separate case, called the locative, to express *place where*. The locative has the same ending as the genitive in the singular of nouns of the first and second declensions; it has the same ending as the ablative in the plural of these declensions and in the third declension, singular and plural.

| | |
|---|---|
| **domī** | *at home* |
| **Rōmae** | *at Rome* |
| **Athēnīs** | *at Athens* |

**Vocative**

The vocative is used in addressing a person. Unless emphatic, it never stands first.

| | |
|---|---|
| **Quid facis, amīce?** | *What are you doing, my friend?* |

***Verb Syntax***

**Tenses**

The tenses of the indicative in Latin are in general used like those in English, but the following points should be noted.

1. *Present.* The Latin present has the force of the English simple present and of the progressive present.

| | |
|---|---|
| **vocat** | *he calls, he is calling, he does call* |

2. *Historical Present.* The historical present is used for vivid effect instead of a past tense in Latin as in English.

| | |
|---|---|
| **Rōmam proficīscuntur**. | *They depart(ed) for Rome.* |

*a.* In clauses introduced by **dum,** meaning *while,* the historical present is always used. In translating use the English past. For **dum** meaning *as long as* or *until* see **Indicative Mood**, 2; **Subjunctive Mood**, 12.

| | |
|---|---|
| **dum haec geruntur** | *while these things were going on* |

3. *Imperfect.* The Latin imperfect expresses repeated, customary, or continuous action in the past and is usually best translated by the English progressive past, sometimes by the auxiliary *would,* or by a phrase, such as *used to* or *kept on.*

| | |
|---|---|
| **Pugnābant**. | *They were fighting.* |

Sometimes the imperfect expresses attempted action *(trying to).*

4. *Perfect.* The Latin perfect is generally equivalent to the English past, occasionally to the present perfect.

| | |
|---|---|
| **Vīcī.** | *I conquered. I have conquered.* |

5. *Sequence of Tenses.* The subjunctive mood is used chiefly in subordinate clauses whose tenses are determined by the principle of "sequence of tenses," as shown in the following summary and examples:

| | |
|---|---|
| *a.* PRIMARY TENSES | (referring to the present or future) |
| *Indicative:* | present, future, future perfect |
| *Subjunctive:* | present, perfect |
| 1. **Venit ut mē videat.** | *He is coming to see me (that he may see me).* |
| 2. **Veniet ut mē videat.** | *He will come to see me (that he may see me).* |
| 3. **Excesserō priusquam veniat.** | *I shall have departed before he comes.* |
| 4. **Rogō quid crās faciās** (*or* **factūrus sīs**). | *I ask what you will do tomorrow.* |
| 5. **Rogō quid herī fēcerīs.** | *I ask what you did yesterday.* |
| *b.* SECONDARY TENSES | (referring to the past) |
| *Indicative:* | imperfect, perfect, pluperfect |
| *Subjunctive:* | imperfect, pluperfect |
| 1. **Vēnit ut mē vidēret.** | *He came to see me (that he might see me).* |
| 2. **Rogābam quid facerēs.** | *I kept asking what you were doing.* |
| 3. **Rogābam quid anteā fecissēs.** | *I kept asking what you had done before.* |
| 4. **Excesseram priusquam venīret.** | *I had departed before he came.* |

*a.* The historical present, used for vivid effect in describing a past action, is often followed by a secondary tense.
*b.* In result clauses, the perfect subjunctive sometimes follows a secondary tense.

Primary indicative tenses are followed by primary subjunctive tenses; secondary, by secondary.

6. *Epistolary Tenses.* In writing letters the Roman determined the tense from the standpoint of the reader, not the writer. Therefore he or she used a past tense for events going on when he or she wrote. Such tense usage is known as *epistolary*.

| | |
|---|---|
| **Hanc epistulam scrīpsī.** | *I am writing this letter.* |

### Indicative Mood

The indicative mood is generally used in Latin as in English. The following points should be noted.

1. *Relative Clauses.* Most relative clauses are in the indicative, as in English. But see **Subjunctive Mood**, 3, 10, 14.

2. *Adverbial Clauses.* Clauses introduced by **postquam, posteāquam** *(after),* **ubi, ut** *(when),* **cum prīmum, simul ac** *(as soon as),* **dum** *(while, as long as),* **quamquam, etsī** *(although)* are in the indicative.

| | |
|---|---|
| **Postquam id cōnspexit, signum dedit.** | *After he noticed this, he gave the signal.* |

3. *Noun Clauses.* A clause introduced by **quod** *(the fact that, that)* is in the indicative and may be used as subject or object of the main verb or in apposition with a demonstrative.

| | |
|---|---|
| **Grātum est quod mē requīris.** | *It is gratifying that you miss me.* |

**Subjunctive Mood**

1. *Volitive.* The volitive **(volō)** subjunctive represents an act as willed and is translated by *let.* The negative is **nē.** When the volitive is used in the first person *(let us),* it is often called the hortatory subjunctive. When used in the third person (singular or plural), it is called the jussive subjunctive *(let him, let them).*

| | |
|---|---|
| **Patriam dēfendāmus.** | *Let us defend our country.* |
| **Nē id videat.** | *Let him not see it.* |

2. *Purpose Clauses.* The subjunctive is used in a subordinate clause with **ut** or **utī** (negative **nē**) to express the purpose of the act expressed by the principal clause.

| | |
|---|---|
| **Venīmus ut videāmus.** | *We come that we may see.*<br>*We come to see.* |
| **Fugit nē videātur.** | *He flees that he may not be seen.* |

3. *Relative Purpose Clauses.* If the principal clause contains (or implies) a definite antecedent, the purpose clause may be introduced by the relative pronoun **quī** (= **ut is** or **ut eī**) instead of **ut.**

| | |
|---|---|
| **Mīlitēs mīsit quī hostem impedīrent.** | *He sent soldiers to hinder the enemy.* |

4. ***Quō*** *Purpose Clauses.* If the purpose clause contains an adjective or adverb in the comparative degree, **quō** is generally used instead of **ut.**

| | |
|---|---|
| **Accēdit quō facilius audiat.** | *He approaches in order that he may hear more easily.* |

For other ways to express purpose see **Dative, Gerundive, Gerund.**

5. *Volitive Noun Clauses.* Clauses in the subjunctive with **ut** (negative **nē**) are used as the objects of such verbs as **moneō, rogō, petō, hortor, persuādeō,** and **imperō.**

| | |
|---|---|
| **Mīlitēs hortātus est ut fortēs essent.** | *He urged the soldiers to be brave.* |
| **Helvētiīs persuāsit ut exīrent.** | *He persuaded the Helvetians to leave.* |

The infinitive is often used with **prohibeō** (*prevent*) and with **dubitō** when it means *hesitate*.

**Caesar prohibuit eōs trānsīre.**
*Caesar prevented them from crossing.*

*a.* With **iubeō** *(order),* unlike **imperō,** the infinitive is generally used. The subject of the infinitive is in the accusative.

| | |
|---|---|
| **Iussit eōs venīre.** | *He ordered them to come.* |
| **Imperāvit eīs ut venīrent.** | *He ordered them to come.* |

*b.* **Vetō** *(forbid)* and **cupiō** *(desire)* are used like **iubeō.**

6. *Clauses with Verbs of Hindering.* With verbs of hindering, preventing, and doubting, as **impediō, dēterreō,** and **dubitō,** the subjunctive introduced by **nē** or **quō minus** is used if the main clause is affirmative, by **quīn** if negative.

| | |
|---|---|
| **Tū dēterrēre potes nē maior multitūdō trādūcātur.** | *You can prevent a greater number from being brought over.* |

7. *Clauses of Fear.* With verbs of fearing, clauses in the subjunctive introduced by **nē** *(that)* and **ut** *(that not)* are used.

| | |
|---|---|
| **Verēbātur nē tū aeger essēs.** | *He feared that you were sick.* |
| **Timuī ut venīrent.** | *I was afraid that they would not come.* |

Result clauses are usually anticipated by some word in the main clause meaning *so* or *such* (**ita, tantus, tot, tam,** etc.).

8. *Result Clauses.* The result of the action or state of the principal verb is expressed by a subordinate clause with **ut (utī),** negative **ut nōn (utī nōn),** and the subjunctive.

| | |
|---|---|
| **Tantum est perīculum ut paucī veniant.** | *So great is the danger that few are coming.* |
| **Ita bene erant castra mūnīta ut nōn capī possent.** | *So well had the camp been fortified that it could not be taken.* |

9. *Noun Clauses of Result.* Verbs meaning *to happen* (**accidō**) or *to cause* or *effect* (**efficiō**) require clauses of result in the subjunctive with **ut (utī)** or **ut (utī) nōn,** used as subject or object of the main verb:

| | |
|---|---|
| **Accidit ut mē nōn vidēret.** | *It happened that he did not see me.* |
| **Efficiam ut veniat.** | *I shall cause him to come.* |

Sometimes a descriptive clause expresses cause, concession, or result. After a negative, **quīn** may be used to introduce the clause.

10. *Descriptive Relative Clauses.* A relative clause with the subjunctive may be used to describe an indefinite antecedent. Such clauses are called relative clauses of description (characteristic) and are especially common after such expressions as **ūnus** and **sōlus, sunt quī** *(there are those who),* and **nēmō est quī** *(there is no one who).*

11. ***Cum*** *Clauses.* In secondary sequence, **cum** *(when)* is used with the imperfect or the pluperfect subjunctive to describe the circumstances under which the action of the main verb occurred.

| | |
|---|---|
| **Cum mīlitēs redīssent, Caesar ōrātiōnem habuit.** | *When the soldiers had returned, Caesar made a speech.* |

*a.* In some clauses **cum** with the subjunctive is best translated *since.*

| | |
|---|---|
| **Quae cum ita sint, nōn ībō.** | *Since this is so, I shall not go* (lit., *When this is so*). |

*b.* In some clauses **cum** with the subjunctive is best translated *although.*

| | |
|---|---|
| **Cum ea ita sint, tamen nōn ībō.** | *Although this is so, yet I shall not go* (lit., *When,* etc.). |

When **ut** means *although, granted that,* its clause is in the subjunctive.

12. *Anticipatory Clauses.* **Dum** *(until),* **antequam,** and **priusquam** (*before*) introduce clauses (*a*) in the indicative to indicate *an actual fact,* (*b*) in the subjunctive to indicate an act as *anticipated.*

| | |
|---|---|
| **Silentium fuit dum tū vēnistī.** | *There was silence until you came.* |
| **Caesar exspectāvit dum nāvēs convenīrent.** | *Caesar waited until the ships should assemble.* |
| **Priusquam tēlum adigī posset, omnēs fūgērunt.** | *Before a weapon could be thrown, all fled.* |

13. *Indirect Questions.* In a question indirectly quoted or expressed after some introductory verb such as *ask, doubt, learn, know, tell, hear,* etc., the verb is in the subjunctive.

| | |
|---|---|
| **Rogant quis sit.** | *They ask who he is.* |

14. *Subordinate Clauses in Indirect Discourse.* An indicative in a subordinate clause becomes subjunctive in indirect discourse. If the clause is not regarded as an essential part of the quotation but is merely explanatory or parenthetical, its verb may be in the indicative.

| | |
|---|---|
| **Dīxit sē pecūniam invēnisse quam āmīsisset.** | *He said that he found the money which he had lost.* |

15. *By Attraction.* A verb in a clause dependent upon a subjunctive or an infinitive, is frequently "attracted" to the subjunctive, especially if its clause is an essential part of the statement.

| | |
|---|---|
| **Dat negōtium hīs utī ea quae apud Belgās gerantur cognōscant.** | *He directs them to learn what is going on among the Belgians.* |

16. ***Quod*** *Causal Clauses.* Causal clauses introduced by **quod** (or **propterea quod**) and **quoniam** *(since, because)* are in the indicative when they give the writer's or speaker's reason, the subjunctive when the reason is presented as that of another person.

| | |
|---|---|
| **Amīcō grātiās ēgī quod mihi pecūniam dederat.** | *I thanked my friend because he had given me money.* |
| **Rōmānīs bellum intulit quod agrōs suōs vāstāvissent.** | *He made war against the Romans because (as he alleged) they had laid waste his lands.* |

The first member of a double indirect question is introduced by **utrum** or **–ne,** the second by **an.**

**Quaerō utrum vērum an falsum sit.**

*I ask whether it is true or false.*

17. *Proviso Clauses.* The subjunctive with **dum, dum modo, modo,** meaning *provided that,* is used to express a proviso (negative **nē**).

| | |
|---|---|
| **modo inter mē atque tē mūrus intersit** | *provided that a wall is between you and me* |

18. *Deliberative.* In questions of doubt and perplexity where the speaker asks himself or someone else for advice or in questions or exclamations expressing surprise or indignation, the subjunctive is used, sometimes with **ut.** The negative is **nōn.** The deliberative subjunctive is commonly used in questions that expect a *no* answer and is therefore purely rhetorical.

| | |
|---|---|
| **Quid fīat?** | *What shall be done?* |
| **Cūr ego nōn laeter?** | *Why should I not rejoice?* |
| **Tū ut umquam tē corrigās?** | *Do you ever reform?* |

19. *Optative.* The optative **(optō)** subjunctive represents a wish. It frequently is preceded by **utinam** *(would that).* The negative is **nē.**
    *a.* The present (rarely the perfect) is used when the wish can come true:

| | |
|---|---|
| **Vīvās fēlīciter!** | *May you live happily!* |

*b.* The imperfect expresses a wish contrary to fact in present time:

| | |
|---|---|
| **Utinam venīret!** | *How I wish that he were coming* (but he is not)! |

*c.* The pluperfect expresses a wish contrary to fact in past time:

| | |
|---|---|
| **Utinam nē vēnisset!** | *How I wish that he had not come* (but he did)! |

20. *Potential.* The potential subjunctive expresses the possibility or capability of something being done. The negative is **nōn.** The present and perfect refer to present or future time, the imperfect to past time. It is variously translated by *may, might, can, could.*

| | |
|---|---|
| **Aliquis mihi dīcat.** | *Someone may say to me.* |
| **Aurum fluitāre vidērēs.** | *You might have seen the gold flowing.* |

21. *Of Obligation.* The negative is **nōn.** It is translated by *should* or *ought.*

| | |
|---|---|
| **Quid ego cōnārer?** | *Why should I have tried?* |

22. *Of Comparison.* With words meaning *as if* (**quasi, velut,** etc.) the subjunctive is used.

| | |
|---|---|
| **quasi nātūrā dīiūnctī sint** | *as if they were naturally separated* |

23. *Second Singular Indefinite.* When the second person singular is not applied to an individual but generally (where we use *one* in English), the subjunctive may be used.

| | |
|---|---|
| **Putēs dīcere.** | *One might think you are saying.* |

**Conditions**

*a.* Subordinate clause (condition) introduced by **sī, nisi,** or **sī nōn.**

*b.* Principal clause (conclusion).

1. *Simple* (nothing implied as to truth). Any possible combination of tenses of the indicative, as in English.

| | |
|---|---|
| **Sī mē laudat, laetus sum.** | *If he praises me, I am glad.* |

2. *Contrary-to-Fact.*

*a. Present:* imperfect subjunctive in both clauses.

| | |
|---|---|
| **Sī mē laudāret, laetus essem.** | *If he were praising me* (but he isn't), *I would be glad* (now). |

*b. Past:* past perfect subjunctive in both clauses.

| | |
|---|---|
| **Sī mē laudāvisset, laetus fuissem.** | *If he had praised me* (but he didn't) *I would have been glad* (then). |

*c. Mixed:* past condition and present conclusion.

| | |
|---|---|
| **Sī mē laudāvisset, laetus essem.** | *If he had praised me* (but he didn't) *I would be glad* (now). |

3. *Future-Less-Vivid* (should/would). Present subjunctive in both clauses.

| | |
|---|---|
| **Sī mē laudet, laetus sim.** | *If he should (were to) praise me, I would be glad.* |

Sometimes the indicative is used in the conclusion for greater vividness or to emphasize the certainty of the result if the condition were or had been true.

**Imperative Mood**

Affirmative commands are expressed by the imperative, negative commands by the present imperative of **nōlō (nōlī, nōlīte)** and the infinitive. The imperative with **nē** is used in poetry.

| | |
|---|---|
| **Amā inimīcōs tuōs.** | *Love your enemies.* |
| **Nōlīte īre.** | *Do not go* (lit., *Be unwilling to go*). |

*a.* The future imperative is rare, found chiefly in religious and legal language.

*b.* Exhortations (volitive subjunctive) and commands, though main clauses, become subjunctive in indirect discourse.

| | |
|---|---|
| (Direct) **Īte!** | *Go!* |
| (Indirect) **Dīxit īrent.** | *He said that they should go.* |

*c.* Occasionally the subjunctive is used instead of the imperative.

| | |
|---|---|
| **Mihi hās lēgēs.** | *Will these to me.* |

**Impersonal Verbs**

*a.* Some verbs are used only impersonally and therefore have no forms in the first and second persons.

*b.* The various constructions with **licet** are as follows:

| | |
|---|---|
| **Licet** {**tibi** / **tē**} **īre.** | *You may go.* |
| **Licet (ut) eās.** | *You may go.* |

*c.* Other verbs may at times be used impersonally, i.e., without a personal subject.

*d.* Intransitive verbs are used only impersonally in the passive.

| | |
|---|---|
| **Ventum erat.** | *He* (or *they*) *had come.* |

See also **Dative,** 6, *a.*

**Reflexive Use of the Passive**

Occasionally the passive form of a verb or participle is used in a "middle" or reflexive sense.

| | |
|---|---|
| **armārī** | *to arm themselves* |

**Participle**

1. The tenses of the participles (present, perfect, future) indicate time present, past, or future from the standpoint of the main verb.
2. *a.* Perfect participles are often used simply as adjectives: **nōtus,** *known.*

   *b.* Participles, like adjectives, may be used as nouns: **factum,** *having been done, deed.*
3. The Latin participle is often a one-word substitute for a subordinate clause in English introduced by *who* or *which, when* or *after, since* or *because, although,* and *if.*

**Gerundive (Future Passive Participle)**

The gerundive (future passive participle) is a verbal adjective, having thirty forms. It has two distinct uses:

1. As a predicate adjective with forms of **sum,**[1] when it naturally indicates, as in English, what must be done. The person upon whom the obligation rests is in the dative.

| | |
|---|---|
| **Caesarī omnia erant agenda.** | *Caesar had to do all things* (lit., *all things were to be done by Caesar*). |

2. As modifier of a noun or pronoun in various constructions, with no idea of obligation:

| | |
|---|---|
| **dē Rōmā cōnstituendā** | *about founding Rome* (lit., *about Rome to be founded*) |

---

[1] the so-called passive periphrastic, a term not used in this book; the term should be avoided because it is not only useless but troublesome.

3. With phrases introduced by **ad** and the accusative or by **causā** (or **grātiā**) and the genitive, it expresses purpose. **Causā** and **grātiā** are always placed after the participle.

| | |
|---|---|
| **Ad eās rēs cōnficiendās Mārcus dēligitur.** | *Marcus is chosen to accomplish these things* (lit., *for these things to be accomplished*). |
| **Caesaris videndī causā** (or **grātiā**) **vēnit.** | *He came for the sake of seeing Caesar* (lit., *for the sake of Caesar to be seen*). |

4. It is used in agreement with the object of **cūrō, locō, dō,** *etc.*

| | |
|---|---|
| **Pontem faciendum cūrat.** | *He attends to having a bridge built.* |

The gerund usually does not have an object. Instead the gerundive is used, modifying the noun.

**Gerund**

The gerund is a verbal noun of the second declension with only four forms—genitive, dative, accusative, and ablative singular.

The uses of the gerund are similar to some of those of the gerundive.

| | |
|---|---|
| **cupidus bellandī** | *desirous of waging war* |
| **Ad discendum vēnī.** | *I came for learning* (i.e., *to learn*). |
| **Discendī causā** (or **grātiā**) **vēnī.** | *I came for the sake of learning.* |

With the passive third singular (impersonal) of these verbs the infinitive is the subject.

**Caesarī nūntiātur eōs trānsīre.**
*It is reported to Caesar that they are crossing.*

**Infinitive**

1. The infinitive is an indeclinable neuter verbal noun, and as such it may be used as the subject of a verb.

| | |
|---|---|
| **Errāre hūmānum est.** | *To err is human.* |
| **Vidēre est crēdere.** | *To see is to believe.* |

2. With many verbs the infinitive, like other nouns, may be used as a direct object.

| | |
|---|---|
| **Cōpiās movēre parat.** | *He prepares to move the troops.* |

3. The infinitive object of some verbs, such as **iubeō, volō, nōlō,** and **doceō,** often has a noun or pronoun subject in the accusative.

4. Statements that give indirectly the thoughts or words of another, used as the objects of verbs of saying, thinking, knowing, hearing, perceiving, etc., have verbs in the infinitive with their subjects in the accusative.

| | |
|---|---|
| (Direct) **Dīcit, "Puerī veniunt."** | *He says, "The boys are coming."* |
| (Indirect) **Dīcit puerōs venīre.** | *He says that the boys are coming.* |

5. *a.* The present infinitive represents time or action as going on at the same time, from the standpoint of the introductory verb:

**Dīcit / Dīxit eōs pugnāre.** *He {says / said} (that) they {are / were} fighting.*

*b.* The future infinitive represents time or action as subsequent to or after that of the introductory verb:

**Dīcit / Dīxit eōs pugnā-tūrōs esse.** *He {says / said} (that) they {will / would} fight.*

*c.* The perfect infinitive represents time or action as completed before that of the introductory verb:

**Dīcit / Dīxit eōs pugnāvisse.** *He {says / said} (that) they {have / had} fought.*

6. *Historical Infinitive.* The historical infinitive with its subject in the nominative has the force of the indicative imperfect or perfect. It is used for vividness, as in English we use the present indicative instead of the past. Usually two or more such infinitives are used together.

| | |
|---|---|
| **Omnēs obstrepere, hostem atque parricīdam vocāre.** | *All cried out against him, called him an enemy and traitor.* |

**Supine**

The supine, like the gerund, is a verbal noun. It has only two cases.

*a.* The accusative in **–um,** used with the verbs of motion to express purpose:

| | |
|---|---|
| **Pācem petītum vēnērunt.** | *They came to seek peace.* |

*b.* The ablative in **–ū,** used to express respect. It is used only with certain adjectives, e.g., **facilis, difficilis, mirabile,** and **optimus.**

| | |
|---|---|
| **difficile factū** | *hard to do* (lit., *hard in the doing*) |

## Summary of Prefixes and Suffixes

### *Prefixes*

Many Latin words are formed by joining prefixes (**prae,** *in front;* **fīxus,** *attached*) to root words. These same prefixes, most of which are prepositions, are those chiefly used in English, and by using them many new words can be formed.

Some prefixes change their final consonants to make them like the initial consonants of the words to which they are attached. This change is called assimilation (**ad,** *to;* **similis,** *like*).

Many prefixes in Latin and English have intensive force, especially **con-, ex-, ob-, per-.** They are then best translated either by an English intensive, such as *up* or *out,* or by an adverb, such as *completely, thoroughly, deeply.* Thus **commoveō** means *move greatly,* **permagnus,** *very great,* **obtineō,** *hold on to,* **concitō,** *rouse up,* **excipiō,** *catch, receive.*

1. **ab (abs, ā),** *from:* **abs-tineō;** *ab-undance, abs-tain, a-vocation.*
2. **ad,** *to, toward:* **ad-iciō;** *ac-curate, an-nounce, ap-paratus, ad-vocate.*
3. **ante,** *before:* **ante-cēdō;** *ante-cedent.*
4. **bene,** *well:* **bene-dīcō;** *bene-factor.*
5. **bi-, bis-,** *twice, two:* **bi-ennium;** *bi-ennial.*
6. **circum,** *around:* **circum-eō;** *circum-ference.*
7. **con-,** *with, together:* **con-vocō;** *con-voke, col-lect, com-motion, cor-rect.*
8. **contrā,** *against: contra-dict.*
9. **dē,** *from, down from, not:* **dē-ferō;** *de-ter.*
10. **dis-,** *apart, not:* **dis-cēdō;** *dis-locate, dif-fuse, di-vert.*
11. **ex (ē),** *out of, from:* **ex-eō;** *ex-port, e-dit, ef-fect.*
12. **extrā,** *outside: extra-legal.*
13. **in,** *in, into, against:* **in-dūcō;** *in-habit, im-migrant, il-lusion, en-chant.*
14. **in-,** *not, un-:* **im-mēnsus;** *il-legal, im-moral, ir-regular.*
15. **inter,** *between, among:* **inter-clūdō;** *inter-class.*
16. **intrā,** *within, inside: intra-collegiate.*
17. **intro-,** *within: intro-duce.*
18. **male,** *ill: male-factor, mal-formation.*
19. **multi-,** *much, many: multi-graph.*
20. **nōn,** *not: non-sense.*
21. **ob,** *against, toward:* **ob-tineō;** *oc-cur, of-fer, o-mit, op-pose, ob-tain.*
22. **per,** *through, thoroughly:* **per-moveō;** *per-fect.*
23. **post,** *after: post-pone.*
24. **prae,** *before, in front of:* **prae-ficiō;** *pre-cede.*
25. **prō,** *for, forward:* **prō-dūcō;** *pro-mote.*
26. **re- (red-),** *back, again:* **re-dūcō, red-igō;** *re-fer.*
27. **sē-,** *apart from:* **sē-cēdō;** *se-parate.*
28. **sēmi-,** *half, partly:* **sēmi-barbarus;** *semi-annual.*
29. **sub,** *under, up from under:* **suc-cēdō;** *suf-fer, sug-gest, sup-port, sub-let.*
30. **super (sur-),** *over, above:* **super-sum;** *super-fluous, sur-mount.*
31. **trāns (trā-),** *through, across:* **trā-dūcō;** *trans-fer.*
32. **ultrā,** *extremely: ultra-fashionable.*
33. **ūn- (ūni-),** *one: uni-form.*

### *Suffixes*

Participles that are attached to the ends of words are called suffixes (**sub,** *under, after;* **fīxus,** *attached*). Like the Latin prefixes, the Latin suffixes play a very important part in the formation of English words.

The meaning of suffixes is often far less definite than that of prefixes. In many cases they merely indicate the part of speech.

Suffixes are often added to words that already have suffixes. Thus, *functionalistically* has six suffixes, all of Latin or Greco-Latin origin except the last. A suffix often combines with a preceding letter or letters to form a new suffix. This is especially true of suffixes added to perfect participles whose base ends in **-s-** or **-t-.** In the following list no account is taken of such English suffixes as *-ant,* derived from the ending of the Latin present participle.

1. **-ālis** *(-al), pertaining to:* **līber-ālis;** *annu-al.*
2. **-ānus** *(-an, -ane, -ain), pertaining to:* **Rōm-ānus;** *capt-ain, hum-ane.*
3. **-āris** *(-ar), pertaining to:* **famili-āris;** *singul-ar.*
4. **-ārium** *(-arium, -ary), place where: aqu-arium, gran-ary.*
5. **-ārius** *(-ary), pertaining to:* **frūment-ārius;** *ordin-ary.*
6. **-āticum** *(-age): bagg-age.*
7. **-āx** *(-acious), tending to:* **aud-āx;** *rap-acious.*
8. **-faciō, -ficō** *(-fy), make:* **signi-ficō;** *satis-fy.*
9. **-ia** *(-y),* **-cia, -tia** *(-ce),* **-antia** *(-ance, -ancy),* **-entia** *(-ence, -ency), condition of:* **memor-ia, grā-tia, cōnst-antia, sent-entia;** *memor-y, provin-ce, gra-ce, const-ancy, sent-ence.*
10. **-icus** *(-ic), pertaining to:* **pūbl-icus;** *civ-ic.*
11. **-idus** *(-id), having the quality of:* **rap-idus;** *flu-id.*
12. **-ilis** *(-ile, -il),* **-bilis** *(-ble, -able, -ible), able to be:* **fac-ilis, laudā-bilis;** *fert-ile, no-ble, compar-able, terr-ible.*
13. **-īlis** *(-ile, -il), pertaining to:* **cīv-īlis;** *serv-ile.*
14. **-īnus** *(-ine), pertaining to:* **mar-īnus;** *div-ine.*
15. **-iō** *(-ion),* **-siō** *(-sion),* **-tiō** *(-tion), act* or *state of:* **reg-iō, mān-siō, ōrā-tiō;** *commun-ion, ten-sion, rela-tion.*
16. **-ium** *(-y),* **-cium, -tium** *(-ce):* **remed-ium, sōlā-cium, pre-tium;** *stud-y, edifi-ce.*
17. **-īvus** *(-ive), pertaining to:* **capt-īvus;** *nat-ive.*
18. **-lus, -ellus, -ulus** *(-lus, -le) little* ("diminutive"): **parvu-lus, castel-lum;** *gladio-lus, parti-cle.*
19. **-men** *(-men, -min, -me):* **lū-men;** *cri-min-al, cri-me.*
20. **-mentum** *(-ment), means of:* **im-pedī-mentum;** *comple-ment.*
21. **-or** *(-or), state of:* **tim-or;** *terr-or.*
22. **-or, -sor, -tor** *(-sor, -tor), one who:* **scrīp-tor;** *inven-tor.*
23. **-ōrium** *(-orium, -ory, -or), place where: audit-orium, fact-ory, mirr-or.*
24. **-ōsus** *(-ous, -ose), full of:* **ōti-ōsus;** *copi-ous.*
25. **-tās** *(-ty), state of:* **līber-tās;** *integri-ty.*
26. **-tō, -sō, -itō,** *keep on* ("frequentative"): **dic-tō, prēn-sō, vent-itō.**
27. **-tūdō** *(-tude), state of:* **magni-tūdō;** *multi-tude.*
28. **-tūs** *(-tue), state of:* **vir-tūs;** *vir-tue.*
29. **-ūra, -sūra, -tūra** *(-ure, -sure, -ture):* **fig-ūra, mēn-sūra, agricul-tūra;** *proced-ure, pres-sure, na-ture.*

## Latin–English

Verbs of the first conjugation whose parts are regular (i.e., like **portō,** p. 280) are indicated by the number 1. Proper names are not included unless they are spelled differently in English or are difficult to pronounce in English. Their English pronunciation is indicated by a simple system. The vowels are as follows: ā as in *hate,* ă as in *hat,* ē as in *feed,* ĕ as in *fed,* ī as in *bite,* ĭ as in *bit,* ō as in *hope,* ŏ as in *hop,* ū as in *cute,* ŭ as in *cut.* In the ending *ēs* the *s* is soft as in *rose.* When the accented syllable ends in a consonant, the vowel is short; otherwise it is long.

### A

**A.,** *abbreviation for* **Aulus, –ī,** *m.,* Aulus

**ā, ab, abs,** *prep. w. abl.,* from, away from, by

**abdicō,** 1, disown; *w.* **sē,** resign

**abditus, –a, –um,** hidden

**abdō, –ere, abdidī, abditus,** put away, bury

**abdūcō, –ere, abdūxī, abductus,** lead *or* take away, withdraw

**abeō, –īre, abiī, abitus,** go away *or* off, depart

**abhinc,** *adv.,* ago

**abhorreō, –ēre, uī, —,** shrink from, be inconsistent with

**abiectus, –a, –um,** cast down

**abnegō,** 1, refuse, deny

**abrenūntiō,** 1, renounce

**abripiō, –ere, abripuī, abreptus,** snatch away

**abscīdō, –ere, –cīdī, –cīsus,** cut off, separate, divide

**abscondō, –ere, –condī, –conditus,** hide, conceal

**absēns,** *gen.* **–entis,** absent

**absolūtiō, –ōnis,** *f.,* acquittal

**absolvō, –ere, absolvī, absolūtus,** acquit; finish

**abstinentia, –ae,** *f.,* abstinence

**abstineō, –ēre, –uī, –tentus,** abstain from

**abstrahō, –ere, –trāxī, –trāctus,** draw away

**absum, abesse, āfuī, āfutūrus,** be away, be distant; be absent; *w.* **ab,** fail

**absūmō, –ere, absūmpsī, absūmptus,** consume, destroy

**absurdus, –a, –um,** harsh, absurd, stupid

**abundē,** *adv.,* enough

**abūtor, abūtī, abūsus,** abuse, take advantage of

**abyssus, –ī,** *m.,* a bottomless pit, abyss, Hades

**ac,** *see* **atque**

**Acadēmicus, –a, –um,** of the Academy *(where Plato taught); as noun, m.,* an Academic philosopher

**accēdō, –ere, accessī, accessus,** come to, approach; be added

**accendō, –ere, accendī, accēnsus,** inflame, excite

**accersō,** *see* **arcessō**

**accidō, –ere, accidī, —,** fall (to), befall, happen (*w. dat.*)

**accingō, –ere, accīnxī, accīnctus,** gird on, equip, arm

**accipiō, –ere, accēpī, acceptus,** receive, accept; hear

**Accius, –cī,** *m.,* Accius

**accola, –ae,** *m. or f.,* neighbor

**accommodō,** 1, adapt, adjust, suit

**accumbō, –ere, accubuī, accubitus,** lie down, recline at table

**accūrātē,** *adv.,* carefully

**accursus, –ūs,** *m.,* gathering

**accūsātor, –ōris,** *m.,* accuser

**accūsātōriē,** *adv.,* as a prosecutor, in an accusing manner

**accūsō,** 1, blame, censure

**ācer, ācris, ācre,** sharp, keen, fierce, bitter, severe, active
**acerbitās, –tātis,** *f.,* severity
**acerbus, –a, –um,** bitter, harsh
**acervus, –ī,** *m.,* heap, multitude
**Achillēs, –is,** *m.,* Achilles
**Acidīnus, –ī,** *m.,* Acidinus
**aciēs, aciēī,** *f.,* (keen) edge, battle line
**acinus, –ī,** *m.,* small berry, grape, wine, vinegar
**acquīrō, –ere, acquīsīvī, acquīsītus,** add to
**ācriter,** *adv.,* vigorously, sharply
**Actium, –tī,** *n.,* Actium
**āctum, –ī,** *n.,* deed, transaction, decree, law
**āctus, –ūs,** *m.,* driving impulse
**acūmen, –inis,** *n.,* acuteness, keenness, sharpness
**acuō, –ere, acuī, acūtus,** sharpen
**acūtus, –a, –um,** sharp, keen
**ad,** *prep. w. acc.,* to, toward, near, for, until, according to
**adaequō,** 1, make equal (to)
**adamō,** 1, love
**addiscō, –ere, addidicī, —,** learn in addition, gain knowledge of
**addō, –ere, addidī, additus,** add
**addūcō, –ere, addūxī, adductus,** lead to, bring, influence, move
**adeō, adīre, adiī, aditus,** go to, approach
**adeō,** *adv.,* so, so much, to such a degree; in fact
**adeptiō, –ōnis,** *f.,* obtaining, attainment
**adhaereō, –ēre, adhaesī, adhaesus,** stick (to), trail after
**adhibeō, –ēre, adhibuī, adhibitus,** hold toward, admit, summon; use, furnish
**adhūc,** *adv.,* up to this time, thus far, still
**adiaceō, –ēre, —, —,** be adjacent
**adiciō, –ere, adiēcī, adiectus,** throw (to), add
**adigō, –ere, adēgī, adāctus,** drive (to), hurl (to)
**adimō, –ere, adēmī, adēmptus,** take away
**adipēs, –ium,** *m. and f. pl.,* fat; corpulence
**adipīscor, –ī, adeptus,** obtain
**aditus, –ūs,** *m.,* approach
**adiungō, –ere, adiūnxī, adiūnctus,** join to, add, attach, win over
**adiuvō, –āre, adiūvī, adiūtus,** help
**adluō, –ere, adluī, —,** flow near to, wash against
**administer, –trī,** *m.,* assistant, servant, tool
**administrō,** 1, conduct, carry on, govern
**admīrābilis, –e,** admirable
**admīrātiō, –ōnis,** *f.,* admiration
**admīror,** 1, wonder (at), admire
**admittō, –ere, admīsī, admissus,** let in, admit
**admodum,** *adv.,* very (much)
**admoneō, –ēre, admonuī, admonitus,** remind, warn
**admonitus, –ūs,** *m.,* suggestion
**admoveō, –ēre, admōvī, admōtus,** (move to), place near, apply
**adnotātiō, –ōnis,** *f.,* noting down, remark
**adnotō,** 1, direct
**adoleō, –ēre, adoluī, —,** destroy by fire
**adoperiō, –īre, adoperuī, adopertus,** cover, close
**adoptō,** 1, select, choose, adopt
**adōrō,** 1, worship
**adrīdeō, –ēre, adrīsī, adrīsus,** laugh, smile at
**adsum, adesse, adfuī, adfutūrus,** be near, be on hand, be present; assist
**adulēscēns, –entis,** *m. and f.,* young person
**adulēscentia, –ae,** *f.,* youth
**adulescentulus, -ī,** *m.,* mere lad, young man
**adulter, –erī,** *m.,* adulterer
**adulterium, –rī,** *n.,* adultery
**adultus, –a, –um,** full grown
**adūrō, –ere, adussī, adustus,** set fire to, scorch
**adveniō, –īre, advēnī, adventus,** arrive
**adventus, –ūs,** *m.,* approach, arrival
**adversārius, –a, –um,** opposed; *as noun, m.,* enemy
**adversitās, –tātis,** *f.,* opposition
**adversus, –a, –um,** adverse
**adversus,** *prep. w. acc.,* toward, against
**advertō, –ere, advertī, adversus,** turn to, direct
**advesperāscit, –āre, –avit, —,** *(impers.),* approaches evening, is twilight
**advocātiō, –ōnis,** *f.,* legal case
**advolō,** 1, fly to, hasten to
**aedēs, –is,** *f.,* building, temple; *pl.,* house
**aedificium, –cī,** *n.,* building
**aedificō,** 1, build
**aedīlitās, –tātis,** *f.,* aedileship
**aeger, aegra, aegrum,** sick, ill, suffering

**aegrōtō**, 1, be ill, be sick
**aegrōtus, –a, –um**, ill
**Aegyptiacus, –a, –um**, Egyptian
**Aegyptiī, –ōrum**, *m. pl.*, the Egyptians
**Aegyptus, –ī**, *f.*, Egypt
**Aellius, –lī**, *m.*, Aellius
**Aemilius, –lī**, *m.*, Aemilius
**aemulor**, 1, rival
**aemulus, –a, –um**, rivalling; comparable, similar (*of things*)
**Aenēās, –ae**, *m.*, Aeneas
**aēneus, –a, –um**, of copper, of bronze
**Aeolus, –ī**, *m.*, Aeolus
**aequābilis, –e**, equal
**aequābiliter**, *adv.*, equally
**aequālis, –e**, equal
**aequē**, *adv.*, justly
**aequitās, –tātis**, *f.*, equality, justice
**aequō**, 1, make even *or* level
**aequor, –oris**, *n.*, surface of the sea, ocean
**aequus, –a, –um**, even, equal, just, calm, right; **aequō animō**, calmly, with resignation; **ex aequō**, equally
**āēr, āēris**, *m.*, air (*acc.* **āera**)
**aerārium, –rī**, *n.*, treasury
**aerumnōsus, –a, –um**, wretched
**aes, aeris**, *n.*, copper, bronze, money; **aes aliēnum**, debt
**aesculētum, –ī**, *n.*, forest of oaks
**aestās, -tātis**, *f.*, summer
**aestimō**, 1, estimate, value
**aestīvus, –a, –um**, of summer
**aestuō**, 1, be hot, be excited; burn
**aestuōsus, –a, –um**, burning, hot
**aestus, –ūs**, *m.*, heat
**aetās, -tātis**, *f.*, age, life
**aeternus, –a, –um**, everlasting, endless
**aethēr, –eris**, *m.*, upper air, sky
**aetherius, –a, –um**, of heaven
**Aetna, –ae**, *f.*, (Mt.) Etna
**Aetōlī, –ōrum**, *m. pl.*, the Aetolians
**aevum, –ī**, *n.*, time, age
**affectus, –ūs**, *m.*, affection
**afferō, afferre, attulī, allātus**, bring (to), apply, cause, present, produce
**afficiō, –ere, affēcī, affectus**, affect, afflict with, wound
**affīnis, –is**, *m.*, relative (*by marriage*)
**affīnitās, –tātis**, *f.*, relationship by marriage
**affirmō**, 1, assert
**afflīctō**, 1, afflict
**afflīgō, –ere, afflīxī, afflictus**, discourage
**afflō**, 1, blow on, breathe on; inspire
**affluēns**, *gen.* **–entis**, abounding in
**Āfrānius, –nī**, *m.*, Afrānius
**Āfrica, –ae**, *f.*, Africa
**Āfricānus, –a, –um**, African; **Africānus, –ī**, *m.*, Africānus
**Āfricus, –a, –um**, African; *i.e., from the southwest; as noun, m.*, the southwest wind
**Agamemnon, –onis**, *m.*, Agamemnon, *king of Mycenae*
**agellus, –ī**, *m.*, little field, small estate
**ager, agrī**, *m.*, field, farm, land, country; **agrī cultūra, –ae**, *f.*, agriculture
**aggredior, aggredī, aggressus**, attack
**aggregō**, 1, gather
**agitō**, 1, plan, act; stir, excite; express, spend
**agmen, agminis**, *n.*, line of march, column
**agna, –ae**, *f.*, ewe lamb
**agnōscō, –ere, agnōvī, agnitus**, recognize, acknowledge
**agō, –ere, ēgī, āctus**, drive, act, do; treat, discuss, speak, plead with *or* for; make; live *or* spend (*of time*); *pass.*, be at stake; **grātiās agō**, thank; **iter agō**, pursue a course; **vītam agō**, lead a life
**agrestis, –e**, rustic, boorish
**agricola, –ae**, *m.*, farmer, planter
**agricultūra, –ae**, *f.*, agriculture
**Ahāla, –ae**, *m.*, Ahala
**Ahēnobarbus, –ī**, Ahenobarbus
**ait**, he/she says, asserts
**āla, –ae**, *f.*, wing
**alacritās, –tātis**, *f.*, eagerness, delight
**albēns**, *gen.* **–entis**, white
**albus, –a, –um**, white
**āleātor, –ōris**, *m.*, gambler
**āles**, *gen.* **–itis**, winged; *as noun, m. and f.*, bird
**Alexander, –drī**, *m.*, Alexander, *king of Macedonia*

**Alexandrīnus, –a, –um,** Alexandrian
**algor, –ōris,** *m.,* coldness
**aliēnus, –a, –um,** of another, another's, foreign; unfavorable; *as noun, m.,* stranger
**aliōquī,** *adv.,* besides, moreover
**aliquamdiū,** *adv.,* a while, for some time
**aliquandō,** *adv.,* some time, at last
**aliquantō,** *adv.,* a little
**aliquantum, –ī,** *n.,* for some time
**aliquis, aliquid,** someone, anyone; some, any; something, anything
**aliquot,** *indecl. adj.,* some, several, few
**aliter,** *adv.,* otherwise
**alius, alia, aliud,** other, another; different, else; **alius... alius,** one . . . another; **aliī... aliī,** some . . . others
**Allēlūia,** *interj.,* praise ye Jehovah
**allevō,** 1, raise
**alliciō, –ere, allexī, allectus,** attract
**alligō,** 1, tie (to), fasten
**Allobrogēs, –um,** *m. pl.,* the Allobroges, *a Gallic tribe*
**allocūtiō, –ōnis,** *f.,* address, comforting
**alloquor, alloquī, allocūtus,** speak to, address
**allūdō, –ere, allūsī, allūsus,** play, joke, pun
**alō, –ere, aluī, altus (alitus),** feed, nourish, sustain
**Alpēs, –ium,** *f. pl.,* the Alps
**Alphēnōr, –oris,** *m.,* Alphē´nor, *one of Niobe's sons*
**altāria, –ium,** *n. pl.,* altar
**altē,** *adv.,* high, deeply, far
**alter, altera, alterum,** the other (*of two*), another, second; **alter... alter,** the one . . . the other
**alternus, –a, –um,** alternating
**alteruter, –utra, –utrum,** one or the other, either this or that, one of two
**altilis, –is,** fattened, fat; *as noun, f.,* a fattened bird
**altitūdō, –dinis,** *f.,* height, depth
**altus, –a, –um,** high, tall, deep
**amābilis, –e,** lovely, attractive
**amāns,** *gen.* **amantis,** fond, loving; *as noun, m.,* lover
**ambiguum, ī,** *n.,* doubt
**ambiguus, –a, –um,** uncertain, wavering; obscure
**ambiō, ambīre, ambiī, ambitus,** go round, encircle, canvass for votes, solicit
**ambitiō, –ōnis,** *f.,* courting, flattery; desire for honor
**ambitus, –ūs,** *m.,* circuit; suing for office
**ambō, -ae, -o,** both
**Ambrosius, –sī,** *m.,* Ambrose
**ambulō,** 1, walk
**āmentia, –ae,** *f.,* madness, folly
**Americānus, –a, –um,** American; **Americānus, –ī,** *m.,* an American
**amīca, –ae,** *f.,* friend
**amīcitia, –ae,** *f.,* friendship
**amictus, –a, –um,** clothed
**amictus, –ūs,** *m.,* mantle
**amīcus, –a, –um,** friendly; **amīcus, –ī,** *m.,* friend **amīca, –ae,** *f.,* friend
**āmittō, –ere, āmīsī, āmissus,** lose, let go, send away
**Ammōnicus,** Ammonicus Serenus
**amnis, –is,** *m.,* stream, river
**amō,** 1, love, like
**amoenitās, –tātis,** *f.,* delightfulness, charm
**amoenus, –a, –um,** pleasant
**amor, –ōris,** *m.,* love, affection
**Amphīōn, –ōnis,** *m.,* Amphī´on, *husband of Niobe*
**amphitheātrum, –ī,** *n.,* amphitheater
**amplector, –ī, amplexus,** embrace
**amplificō,** 1, enlarge, increase
**amplitūdō, –dinis,** *f.,* greatness
**amplius,** *adv.,* more, further
**amplus, –a, –um,** great, ample, generous, distinguished
**an,** *conj.,* or, *introducing the second part of a double question;* **utrum... an,** (whether) . . . or; *w. indir. question,* whether; *w.* **vērō,** or indeed
**anceps, ancipitis,** double, two-headed; doubtful; dangerous
**angelicus, –a, –um,** like an angel, angelic
**angelus, –ī,** *m.,* angel
**Angelus,** Angelo (Corbinelli)
**Anglī, –ōrum,** *m. pl.,* the Angles
**Anglicus, –a, –um,** English

**angō, –ere, —, —,** trouble
**angulus, –ī,** *m.,* angle, corner
**anhēlitus, –ūs,** *m.,* panting
**anīlis, –e,** old woman's, feeble
**anima, –ae,** *f.,* breath, soul; existence
**animadvertō, –ere, –vertī, –versus,** give attention to, notice, punish
**animal, –ālis,** *n.,* animal
**animālis, –e,** of life, living
**animula, –ae,** *f.,* little soul
**animus, –ī,** *m.,* soul, spirit, heart, mind, feeling, courage, desire
**annālis, –e,** relating to a year; *as noun, m.,* a record of events, annals
**annectō, –ere, annexuī, annexus,** tie to, fasten on, annex
**annītor, ī, annixus,** lean upon; strive
**anniversārius, –a, –um,** annual, yearly
**annuō, –ere, annui, —,** nod (to), assent to
**annus, –ī,** *m.,* year
**anquīrō, –ere, –sīvī, –sītus,** look about, search after; inquire diligently
**ānser, –eris,** *m.,* goose
**ante,** *adv. and prep. w. acc.,* before (*of time or place*), beforehand, ago
**anteā,** *adv.,* before
**antecēdō, –ere, –cessī, –cessus,** go before, take the lead
**antecellō, –ere, —, —,** excel
**anteeō, –īre, –iī, –itus,** precede; surpass; anticipate
**antelūcānus, –a, –um,** before dawn
**antepōnō, –ere, –posuī, –positus,** place before, prefer
**antequam (ante quam),** *conj.,* before
**Antiochia, –ae,** *f.,* Antioch, *chief city of Syria*
**Antiochus, –ī,** *m.,* Antiochus, *king of Syria*
**antīquitās, –tātis,** *f.,* antiquity
**antīquus, –a, –um,** old, ancient
**antistes, –itis,** *m., and f.,* priest
**Antōnius, –nī,** *m.,* Antonius, Antony
**antrum, –ī,** *n.,* cave
**anus, –ūs,** *f.,* old woman
**ānxius, –a, –um,** troubled, causing anxiety; cautious
**aper, aprī,** *m.,* wild boar
**aperiō, –īre, aperuī, apertus,** open, uncover
**apertē,** *adv.,* openly, frankly
**apertus, –a, –um,** open, unprotected
**Apollineus, –a, –um,** of Apollo
**Apollō, –inis,** *m.,* Apollo, *god of prophecy*
**Apollodorus, –ī,** *m.,* Apollodorus
**Aponius, –nī,** *m.,* Aponius
**apostolicus, –a, –um,** apostolic
**apostolus, –ī,** *m.,* apostle
**apparātus, –a, –um,** well prepared
**apparātus, –ūs,** *m.,* preparation, splendor
**appāreō, –ēre, –uī, –itus,** appear
**appellō,** 1, call, speak to, name, address
**Appennīnus, –ī,** *m.,* Appennines, *mountain range in Italy*
**appetō, –ere, appetīvī, appetītus,** seek for
**Appius, –a, –um,** *adj.,* of Appius, Appian; **Appius, –pī,** *m.,* Appius
**applicō,** 1, apply, direct (to); drive to
**apprehendō, –ere, –dī, –sus,** seize
**approbō,** 1, approve
**appropinquō,** 1, draw near
**Aprīlis, –e,** (of) April
**aptō,** 1, fit, place carefully
**aptus, –a, –um,** fit, suited, suitable (*w. dat.*)
**apud,** *prep. w. acc.,* at, among, near, with, before, in the presence of, at the house of
**aqua, –ae,** *f.,* water
**aquaeductus, –ūs,** *m.,* aqueduct
**aquila, –ae,** *f.,* eagle; legionary standard
**aquilō, –ōnis,** *m.,* north wind, north
**Aquītānus, –ī,** *m.,* an Aquitanian
**āra, –ae,** *f.,* altar
**arātor, –ōris,** *m.,* ploughman
**arbiter, –trī,** *m.,* witness, judge
**arbitrium, –rī,** *n.,* judgment, opinion, choice
**arbitror,** 1, think
**arbor, –oris,** *f.,* tree
**arboreus, –a, –um,** of a tree
**arbuscula, –ae,** *f.,* small tree
**arcānus, –a, –um,** secret; shut, closed
**arceō, –ere, –uī, —,** keep away, ward off, prevent

**arcessō, –ere, arcessīvī, arcessītus,** summon, invite, accuse

**Archiās, –ae,** *m.,* Archias, *a Greek poet*

**archipīrāta, –ae,** *m.,* pirate captain

**architectūra, –ae,** *f.,* architecture

**architectus, –ī,** *m.,* architect

**Arcitenēns, –entis,** *m.,* (bow-bearing) Apollo

**arcus, –ūs,** *m.,* bow, arch

**ārdeō, –ēre, ārsī, ārsus,** be on fire, burn; be aroused

**arduus, –a, –um,** steep, lofty; *as noun, n. pl.,* heights

**ārea, –ae,** *f.,* flat surface; threshing-floor

**arēna, –ae,** *f.,* arena, sand, desert, seashore

**arēnōsus, –a, –um,** full of sand

**āreō, –ēre, –uī, —,** be parched

**argenteus, –a, –um,** of silver, silvery

**argentum, –ī,** *n.,* silver, money

**argumentum, –ī,** *n.,* proof, argument, subject

**arguō, –ere, –uī, –ūtus,** make known, accuse

**argūtus, –a, –um,** bright

**āridus, –a, –um,** dry, arid

**arista, –ae,** *f.,* head of grain

**arma, –ōrum,** *n. pl.,* arms, weapons

**armārium, –rī,** *n.,* closet, chest, safe

**armātūra, –ae,** *f.,* equipment

**armātus, –a, –um,** armed

**armentum, –ī,** *n.,* cattle, herd

**arō,** 1, plow

**Arpīnās,** *gen.,* **–ātis,** of Arpinum

**arripiō, –ere, arripuī, arreptus,** grasp

**arrogantia, –ae,** *f.,* arrogance, insolence

**arrogō,** 1, associate with, claim

**ars, artis,** *f.,* skill, art, profession, practice

**artifex, –ficis,** *m.,* artist; *w.* **scaenicus,** actor

**artificium, –cī,** *n.,* profession, trade; theory; art, craft

**artus, –a, –um,** tight

**artus, –ūs,** *m.,* joint, limb

**ārula, –ae,** *f.,* small altar

**arundō, –inis,** *f.,* reed, fishing rod, shepherd's pipe, flute

**arvum, –ī,** *n.,* field

**arx, arcis,** *f.,* citadel

**as, assis,** *m.,* whole; penny

**ascendō, –ere, ascendī, ascēnsus,** climb (up), mount, ascend

**ascēnsus, –ūs,** *m.,* ascent

**ascīscō, –ere, ascīvī, ascītus,** admit

**Ascōnius, –nī,** *m.,* Asconius

**ascrībō, –ere, ascrīpsī, ascrīptus,** enroll

**asellus, –ī,** *m.,* donkey

**Asia, –ae,** *f.,* Asia

**asinus, –ī,** *m.,* ass, fool

**aspectus, –ūs,** *m.,* appearance, sight

**asper, –era, –erum,** rough, harsh, cruel

**aspiciō, –ere, aspexī, aspectus,** look at, behold, see

**aspīrō,** 1, aspire, reach

**asportō,** 1, carry off

**assēnsus, –ūs,** *m.,* agreement, approval

**assentiō, –īre, assēnsī, assēnsus,** agree with, approve

**assequor, assequī, assecūtus,** accomplish, obtain

**asserō, –ere, asseruī, assertus,** claim, appropriate

**asservō,** 1, watch over, keep

**assevērō,** 1, assert

**assīdō, –ere, assēdī, assessus,** sit near, sit at the side of, be seated

**assiduus, –a, –um,** continual, incessant

**assignō,** 1, allot, assign; entrust; ascribe

**assuēscō, –ere, assuēvī, assuētus,** become accustomed

**assūmō, –ere, assūmpsī, assūmptus,** take

**assurgō, –ere, assurrēxī, assurrēctus,** rise up, stand up

**astrum, –ī,** *n.,* star, constellation

**at,** *conj.,* but, on the other hand

**Ateius, –eī,** *m.,* Ateius

**āter, ātra, ātrum,** black, dark

**Athēna,** *f., a Greek goddess* = Minerva

**Athēnae, –ārum,** *f. pl.,* Athens

**Athēniēnsēs, –ium,** *m., pl.,* the Athenians

**Atlantiadēs, –ae,** *m.,* Mercury

**Atlās, –antis,** *m.,* Atlas, *a giant*

**atque (ac),** *conj.,* and, and especially; than

**ātrium, ātrī,** *n.,* atrium, entry hall, house

**atrōx,** *gen.* **–ōcis,** cruel, inhuman

**attendō, –ere, attendī, attentus,** (stretch toward), direct, give heed (to), listen

**attentus, –a, –um,** attentive

**atterō, –ere, attrīvī, attrītus,** rub or wear away

**attineō, –ēre, attinuī, —,** detain, delay; reach; concern

**attingō, –ere, attigī, attāctus,** assign

**attollō, –ere, —, —,** lift

**attonitus, –a, –um,** astounded

**attribuō, –ere, attribuī, attribūtus,** assign

**attrītus, –a, –um,** worn

**auctor, –ōris,** *m.,* maker, author, authority, writer, voucher

**auctōritās, –tātis,** *f.,* authority, influence, opinion

**audācia, –ae,** *f.,* boldness

**audāx,** *gen.* **audācis,** bold, daring, courageous

**audeō, –ēre, ausus,** *semideponent,* dare

**audiō, –īre, –īvī (–iī), –ītus,** hear, hear of, listen (to)

**audītiō, –ōnis,** *f.,* lecture

**audītor, –ōris,** *m.,* hearer, auditor

**auferō, auferre, abstulī, ablātus,** take away, remove

**Aufidius, –dī,** *m.,* Aufidius

**augeō, –ēre, auxī, auctus,** increase

**Augustīnus, –ī,** *m.,* Augustine

**Augustus, –a, –um,** of Augustus; *as noun, m.,* Augustus, *the emperor*

**aura, –ae,** *f.,* breeze, air

**aurātus, –a, –um,** covered with gold

**Aurēlia, –ae,** *f.,* Aurelia

**aureus, –a, –um,** golden, made of gold; *as noun, m.,* gold piece

**aurīga, –ae,** *m.,* charioteer

**auris, –is,** *f.,* ear

**Aurōra, –ae,** *f.,* morning, dawn

**aurum, –ī,** *n.,* gold

**auspicātus, –a, –um,** auspicious

**auspicia, –ōrum,** *n. pl.,* auspices

**auspicor,** 1, take the auspices

**auster, –trī,** *m.,* south wind

**aut,** or; **aut... aut,** either . . . or

**autem,** *conj.* (*never first word*), however, but, moreover

**autumnālis, –e,** of autumn

**autumus, –ī,** *m.* autumn, fall

**auxiliārius, –a, –um,** auxiliary

**auxilium, –lī,** *n.,* aid, help, assistance; *pl.* reinforcements

**avārē,** *adv.,* greedily

**avāritia, –ae,** *f.,* greed, avarice

**avēna, –ae,** *f.,* reed

**aveō, –ēre, —, —,** long for, crave

**aversor,** 1, repulse, avoid

**avertō, –ere, avertī, aversus,** turn from, turn away, turn off, remove

**āvia, –ōrum,** *n. pl.,* pathless regions

**avidus, –a, –um,** eager

**avis, avis,** *f.,* bird

**avītus, –a, –um,** of a grandfather

**āvocō,** 1, call away *or* aside

**avus, –ī,** *m.,* grandfather, ancestor

**axis, –is,** *f.,* axle, chariot; globe

## B

**Babylōnius, –a, –um,** Babylonian

**bāca, –ae,** *f.,* fruit, berry

**bacchor,** 1, revel

**Bacchus, –ī,** *m.,* Bacchus, *god of wine*

**baculum, –ī,** *n.,* staff

**Bagrada, –ae,** *m.,* Bagrada

**Balbus, –ī,** *m.,* Balbus

**balineum (balneum), –ī,** *n.,* bath

**ballista, –ae,** *f.,* ballista

**balsamum, –ī,** *n.,* fragrant gum, balsam

**barba, –ae,** *f.,* beard

**barbaria, –ae,** *f.,* savage people

**barbaricus, –a, –um,** barbaric

**barbarus, –a, –um,** foreign; savage, uncivilized, barbarous; *as noun, m.,* foreigner, barbarian

**barbātus, –a, –um,** bearded

**Bardulis, –is,** *m.,* Bardulis, *king of Illyria*

**basilica, –ae,** *f.,* basilica

**Baucis, –idis** (*acc.* **–ida**), *f.,* Baucis (Bausis), *wife of Philemon*

**beātus, –a, –um,** happy, blessed, rich

**Belgae, –ārum,** *m. pl.,* the Belgians; the Belgian people

**bellicōsus, –a, –um,** warlike

**bellō,** 1, wage war

**bellum, –ī,** *n.,* war
**bellus, –a, –um,** nice, charming, pretty
**bēlua, –ae,** *f.,* (wild) beast
**bene,** *adv.,* well, well done, successfully; *comp.* **melius,** better; *superl.* **optimē,** best, very good
**beneficium, –cī,** *n.,* kindness, favor; honor, benefit
**benevolentia, –ae,** *f.,* good will, kindness
**benignē,** thank you
**benignitās, –tātis,** *f.,* kindness
**benignus, –a, –um,** kind
**Berecyntius, –a, –um,** Berecyntian
**bēstia, –ae,** *f.,* beast
**bibliothēca, –ae,** *f.,* library
**bibō, –ere, bibī, —,** drink
**Bibulus, –ī,** *m.,* Bibulus
**bicolor, –ōris,** two-colored
**bicornis, –e,** two-pronged
**Bilbilis, –is,** *f.,* Bilbilis, *a town in Spain*
**bīnī, –ae, –a,** two each, two
**bipertītō,** *adv.,* in two divisions
**bipēs, bipedis,** two-footed
**bis,** *adv.,* twice
**Bithynia, –ae,** *f.,* Bithynia, *a province in Asia Minor*
**blaesus, –a, –um,** lisping
**blanditiae, –ārum,** *f.,* fond words
**blandulus, –a, –um,** pleasing, charming
**blandus, –a, –um,** coaxing, caressing
**bonitās, –tātis,** *f.,* goodness
**bonus, –a, –um,** good; *comp.* **melior, melius,** better; *superl.* **optimus, –a, –um,** best; **bona, –ōrum,** *n.,* goods, property
**Boōtes, –ae,** *m.,* Bo-o´tēs, *a constellation*
**bos, bovis,** *m. and f.,* ox, cow; *pl.* cattle (*gen. pl.,* **boum** *or* **bovum)**
**bracchium, –chī,** *n.,* arm
**brevī,** *adv.,* in a short time, soon
**brevis, –e,** short
**brevitās, –tātis,** *f.,* brevity
**breviter,** *adv.,* briefly
**Britannia, –ae,** *f.,* Britain
**Britannus, –ī,** *m.,* a Briton
**brūma, –ae,** *f.,* winter
**Brūtus, –ī,** *m.,* Brutus
**bubulcus, –ī,** *m.,* ploughman
**bustum, –ī,** *n.,* pyre; tomb
**Byzantius, –a, –um,** Byzantine, of Byzantium *(Constantinople)*

# C

C., *abbreviation for* **Gāius**
**cacūmen, –minis,** *n.,* peak; tree top
**Cadmus, –ī,** *m.,* Cadmus, *founder of Thebes*
**cadō, –ere, cecidī, cāsus,** fall, die, be slain
**cadūcus, –a, –um,** falling, frail, perishable
**Caecilius, –lī,** *m.,* Caecilius
**caedēs, –is,** *f.,* slaughter, murder, bloodshed
**caedō, –ere, cecīdī, caesus,** cut, beat
**caelestis, –is,** *m. and f.,* heavenly being
**caelicola, –ae,** *m.,* god
**Caelius, –lī,** m., Caelius
**caelō,** 1, carve, emboss
**caelum, –ī,** *n.,* sky; weather
**caerulus (-eus), –a, –um,** blue
**Caesar, –aris,** *m.,* Caesar; emperor
**caespes, –itis,** *m.,* sod, earth
**calamitās, –tātis,** *f.,* loss, misfortune, defeat, ruin
**calamitōsus, –a, –um,** unfortunate, disastrous
**calamus, –ī,** *m.,* reed, reed pipe
**calcar, –āris,** *n.,* stimulus, goad
**Calchas, –antis,** *m.,* Calchas, *a mythological seer*
**calcō,** 1, tread
**caleō, –ēre, –uī, –itus,** be warm *or* hot
**calidus, –a, –um,** warm
**calliditās, –tātis,** *f.,* shrewdness, cunning
**callidus, –a, –um,** cunning
**calor, –ōris,** *m.,* heat
**Calymnē, –ēs,** *f.,* Calym´ne, *an island in the Aegean*
**Camillus, –ī,** *m.,* Camillus
**campus, –ī,** *m.,* field, plain; the Campus Martius, *a park and place of assembly at Rome*
**candeō, –ēre, –uī, —,** shine, be brilliant, glitter
**candidātōrius, –a, –um,** of a candidate
**candidātus, –ī,** *m.,* candidate
**candidus, –a, –um,** white, clear
**Canīnius, –nī,** *m.,* Caninius
**canis, –is,** *m. and f.,* dog
**canistrum, –ī,** *n.,* reed basket

**Canius, –nī,** *m.,* Canius
**canna, –ae,** *f.,* reed
**Cannēnsis, –e,** of Cannae
**canō, –ere, cecinī, cantus,** sing, predict, play
**canōrus, –a, –um,** melodious, harmonious
**cantō,** 1, sing
**cantus, –ūs,** *m.,* song
**cānus, –a, –um,** white, hoary
**capāx,** *gen.* **capācis,** spacious; capable of
**caper, caprī,** *m.,* goat
**capessō, –ere, –īvī, –ītus,** strive to reach, undertake
**capillus, –ī,** *m.,* hair; *pl.,* locks, hair
**capiō, –ere, cēpī, captus,** take, seize, hold, captivate, capture; **cōnsilium capiō,** adopt a plan
**Capitō, –ōnis,** *m.,* Capito
**Capitōlium, –lī,** *n.,* the Capitol, *temple of Jupiter at Rome;* the Capitoline Hill
**captiō, –ōnis,** *f.,* deception; sophism; injury, loss
**captīvus, –a, –um,** captive; captured; *as noun, m.,* prisoner
**captīvus, –ī,** *m.;* **captīva, –ae,** *f.,* prisoner
**captō,** 1, capture, grasp, seize
**caput, capitis,** *n.,* head
**Carbō, –ōnis,** *m.,* Carbo
**carcer, –eris,** *m.,* prison
**cardō, –dinis,** *m.,* hinge
**careō, –ēre, caruī, caritus,** be without, lack, be deprived of
**Cāria, –ae,** *f.,* Caria, *a province in Asia Minor*
**cāritās, –tātis,** *f.,* high price; affection
**carmen, –minis,** *n.,* song, poem
**carpō, –ere, carpsī, carptus,** pick, seize; *of a road,* pursue, traverse
**carrus, –ī,** *m.,* cart, wagon
**Carthāginiēnsēs, –ium,** *m. pl.,* the Carthaginians
**Carthāgō, –ginis,** *f.,* Carthage, *a city in Africa;* **Carthāgō Nova,** New Carthage, *in Spain*
**cārus, –a, –um,** dear
**casa, –ae,** *f.,* house, cottage
**Cassius, –sī,** *m.,* Cassius
**castellum, –ī,** *n.,* fort
**Castor, –oris,** *m.,* Castor, *one of the twins, with* Pollux
**castra, –ōrum,** *n. pl.,* camp
**castrēnsis, –e,** of the camp, open
**cāsus, –ūs,** *m.,* fall, chance, event, misfortune, accident; case
**catapulta, –ae,** *f.,* catapult
**catēna, –ae,** *f.,* chain; constraint
**cathedra, –ae,** *f.,* chair, litter; professor's chair
**Catilīna, –ae,** *m.,* Catiline, *the conspirator of 63 B.C.*
**Catō, –ōnis,** *m.,* Cato, *a Roman senator*
**Catulus, –ī,** *m.,* Catulus
**Caucasus, –ī,** *m.,* Caucasus, *a chain of mountains in Asia*
**causa, –ae,** *f.,* cause, reason; case, pretext; position; **causā,** for the sake of, for the purpose of
**cautus, –a, –um,** cautious
**cavea, –ae,** *f.,* cage, den; *(in a theater)* auditorium, spectators' seats
**caveō, –ēre, cāvī, cautus,** beware (of), take care
**cavus, –a, –um,** hollow
**–ce,** *(enclitic),* here, this, that
**cēdō, –ere, cessī, cessus,** go away, retreat, retire, yield
**celeber, –bris, –bre,** populous, crowded
**celebritās, –tātis,** *f.,* throng; renown
**celebrō,** 1, throng, celebrate, attend, honor
**celer, celeris, celere,** swift
**celeritās, –tātis,** *f.,* speed, swiftness, quickness
**celeriter,** *adv.,* quickly, swiftly
**cella, –ae,** *f.,* storeroom; closet
**cēlō,** 1, hide, keep secret
**celsus, –a, –um,** high
**Celtae, –ārum,** *m. pl.,* Celts, *a people of Gaul*
**cēna, –ae,** *f.,* dinner
**cēnō,** 1, dine
**cēnseō, –ēre, cēnsuī, cēnsus,** enroll; think; decree
**cēnsiō, –ōnis,** *f.,* census
**cēnsor, –ōris,** *m.,* censor
**cēnsūra, –ae,** *f.,* censorship
**cēnsus, –ūs,** *m.,* census
**centum,** hundred
**centumvirī, –ōrum,** *m. pl.,* the hundred men, *a special jury for important civil suits*

**cēnula, –ae,** *f.,* little dinner

**Cēpārius, –rī,** *m.,* Ceparius

**cēra, –ae,** *f.,* wax

**cērātus, –a, –um,** waxed

**Cereālis, –e,** of Ceres; **Cereālia, –ium,** *n. pl.,* the festival of Ceres

**Cerēs, Cereris,** *f.,* Ceres, *goddess of agriculture*

**cernō, –ere, crēvī, crētus,** separate, discern, see

**certāmen, –minis,** *n.,* contest

**certātim,** *adv.* earnestly, eagerly

**certātiō, –ōnis,** *f.,* strife, dispute

**certē,** *adv.,* certainly

**certō,** 1, struggle

**certus, –a, –um,** fixed, certain, sure; **certiōrem facere,** inform (him); **certior fierī,** be informed

**cerva, –ae,** *f.,* deer

**cervīx, –īcis,** *f.,* neck; *pl.,* shoulders

**cessō,** 1, delay, stop, be idle

**cēterī, –ae, –a,** the other(s), the rest; everything else

**Cethēgus, –ī,** *m.,* Cethegus

**chorus, –ī,** *m.,* choral dance; choir

**Chrīstiānus, –a, –um,** *adj. and n.,* Christian

**Chrīstus, –ī,** *m.,* Christ

**cibus, –ī,** *m.,* food

**cicātrix, –īcis,** *m.,* scar

**cicer, –eris,** *n.,* chickpea

**Cicerō, –ōnis,** *m.,* Cicero (Marcus Tullius, the *orator;* Quintus, *his brother;* Marcus, *his son*)

**cingō, –ere, cīnxī, cīnctus,** surround; crown

**cinis, cineris,** *m.,* ashes

**circā,** *adv. and prep. w. acc.,* around, about

**Circē, –ae,** *f.,* Circe, *a sorceress*

**circum,** *prep. w. acc.,* about, around

**circumagō, –ere, –ēgī, –āctus,** drive *or* turn around

**circumcīsus, –a, –um,** cut off, steep, inaccessible

**circumclūdō, –ere, –clūsī, –clūsus,** surround

**circumdō, –dare, –dedī, –datus,** put around, surround (with)

**circumeō, –īre, –iī, –itus,** go around

**circumferō, –ferre, –tulī, –lātus,** bear *or* spread around, cast about

**circumscrībō, –ere, –scrīpsī, –scrīptus,** bound, circumscribe

**circumspiciō, –ere, –spexī, –spectus,** look around

**circumstō, –āre, –stetī, —,** stand around

**circumveniō, –īre, –vēnī, –ventus,** surround

**circus, –ī,** *m.,* circle, circus, *esp. the Circus Maximus at Rome*

**cithara, –ae,** *f.,* cithara, lyre

**citus, –a, –um,** swift; **cito,** quickly, speedily

**cīvīlis, –e,** civil

**cīvis, cīvis,** *m. and f.,* citizen

**cīvitās, –tātis,** *f.,* citizenship, state; city

**clam,** *adv.,* secretly

**clāmitō,** 1, keep shouting

**clāmō,** 1, noise, shout, cry out

**clāmor, –ōris,** *m.,* shout(ing), noise, uproar; applause

**clandestīnus, –a, –um,** secret

**clārē,** *adv.,* clearly

**clāritās, –tātis,** *f.,* fame

**Claros, –ī,** *f.,* Claros

**clārus, –a, –um,** clear, brilliant, illustrious, loud, famous

**classis, –is,** *f.,* class, fleet

**Claudius, –dī,** *m.,* Claudius, *Roman emperor*

**claudō, –ere, clausī, clausus,** close, shut, cut off, bar

**clāva, –ae,** *f.,* rough stick, club

**clāvus, –ī,** *m.,* nail; rudder, helm

**clēmēns,** *gen.* **–entis,** mild, gentle, merciful

**clēmenter,** *adv.,* gently, with forbearance

**clēmentia, –ae,** *f.,* mercy

**clīvus, –ī,** *m.,* slope, hillside

**clūnis, –is,** *m. and f.,* buttock, haunch

**Cn.,** *abbreviation for* **Gnaeus, –ī,** *m.,* Gnaeus (Nē´us)

**coalēscō, –ere, –aluī, –alitus,** grow together

**coarguō, –ere, –uī, —,** make known, betray

**coartō,** 1, compress, confine; abridge, shorten

**coccum, –ī,** n., berry *(yielding a scarlet dye)*

**codicillī, –ōrum,** *m. pl.,* writing tablet, petition, will

**coeō, –īre, –iī, –itus,** come together, assemble, unite

**coepī, coepisse, coeptus** *(used only in perfect tenses),* have begun, began

**coerceō, –ēre, –uī, –itus,** check, repress

**coetus, –ūs,** *m.,* meeting
**cōgitātē,** *adv.,* thoughtfully
**cōgitātiō, –ōnis,** *f.,* thought, meditation
**cōgitō,** 1, think (of), consider, plan
**cognātiō, –ōnis,** *f.,* kinship
**cognātus, –ī,** *m.,* kinsman
**cognitiō, –ōnis,** *f.,* (learning to know), trial, acquaintance
**cognitor, –ōris,** *m.,* supporter
**cognōmen, –minis,** *n.,* nickname, surname
**cognōscō, –ere, cognōvī, cognitus,** become acquainted with, learn; recognize, note; *perf.,* have learned, know, understand
**cōgō, –ere, coēgī, coactus,** drive together, assemble; force, compel, collect
**cohaereō, –ēre, cohaesī, cohaesus,** cling together, be connected with
**cohērēs, –ēdis,** *m. and f.,* fellow heir
**cohors, cohortis,** *f.,* cohort
**cohortātiō, –ōnis,** *f.,* encouragement
**cohortor,** 1, urge
**collābor, –lābī, –lāpsus,** fall in ruin, sink down
**collēga, –ae,** *m.,* colleague
**collēgium, –gī,** *n.,* company
**colligō, –ere, –lēgī, –lēctus,** collect, infer
**collis, –is,** *m.,* hill
**collocō,** 1, put, establish, set up
**colloquor, –loquī, –locūtus,** talk (with), hold a conference
**collum, –ī,** *n.,* neck
**colō, –ere, coluī, cultus,** worship, cultivate, till, inhabit, attend, cherish, honor
**colōnia, –ae,** *f.,* colony
**colōnus, –ī,** *m.,* settler, colonist
**color, –ōris,** *m.,* color
**Colossēum, –ī,** *n.,* the Colosseum, *an amphitheater at Rome*
**columba, –ae,** *f.,* dove, pigeon
**columna, –ae,** *f.,* pillar, column
**coma, –ae,** *f.,* hair
**comes, –itis,** *m. and f.,* companion
**cōmitās, –tātis,** *f.,* courtesy, kindness, friendliness
**comitātus, –ūs,** *m.,* escort, company
**cōmiter,** *adv.,* affably
**comitium, –tī,** n., comitium, *an assembly place in Rome; pl.,* election, assembly
**comitō, comitor,** 1, accompany
**commeminī, –isse,** remember
**commemorātiō, –ōnis,** *f.,* remembrance, mention
**commendātiō, –ōnis,** *f.,* recommendation
**commendō,** 1, entrust, commend, approve
**commercium, –cī,** *n.,* trade, commerce; fellowship
**comminuō, –ere, –uī, –ūtus,** weaken
**committō, –ere, –mīsī, –missus,** join together, commit, start, entrust; **proelium committō,** begin battle
**commodē,** *adv.,* suitably
**commodus, –a, –um,** fit, suitable, favorable, convenient; *as noun, n.,* advantage
**commoror,** 1, linger, remain
**commoveō, –ēre, –mōvī, –mōtus,** disturb, move
**commūnis, –e,** common
**commūnitās, –tātis,** *f.,* fellowship
**commūniter,** *adv.,* in general
**commūtō,** 1, change, alter
**cōmō, –ere, compsī, comptus,** comb, adorn
**comoedus, –ī,** *m.,* comedian, comic actor
**comparātiō, –ōnis,** *f.,* comparison
**comparō,** 1, get ready, prepare; collect, provide; constitute; compare
**comperiō, –īre, –perī, –pertus,** find out, discover
**compescō, –ere, –pescuī, —,** check, restrain
**competītor, –ōris,** *m.,* rival, competitor
**complector, –plectī, –plexus,** embrace, include
**complexus, –ūs,** *m.,* embrace
**complūrēs, –a (–ia),** several, many
**compōnō, –ere, –posuī, –positus,** put together, compose, settle, arrange; bury
**compos, –potis,** master of, possessing
**compositiō, –ōnis,** *f.,* agreement
**comprehendō (comprēndō), –ere, –hendī, –hēnsus,** seize, catch, detect, understand; arrest
**comprimō, –ere, –pressī, –pressus,** press together, restrain, repress
**comprobō,** 1, approve
**compugnō,** 1, fight together
**computō,** 1, sum up, compute; count
**cōnātus, –ūs,** *m.,* attempt
**concēdō, –ere, –cessī, –cessus,** give way, retire, grant

**concidō, –ere, –cidī, —,** fall (together), collapse
**conciliō,** 1, win (over)
**concilium, –lī,** *n.,* meeting, council
**concinnō,** 1, cause, produce, make fit
**concipiō, –ere, –cēpī, –ceptus,** take up, receive, utter
**concitō,** 1, arouse
**conclāmō,** 1, cry out, exclaim, shout
**conclāve, –is,** *n.,* room, chamber
**concordia, –ae,** *f.,* harmony, concord
**concordō,** 1, agree, be consistent
**concors,** *gen.* **–cordis,** in harmony
**concupīscō, –ere, –cupīvī, –ītus,** long (for), desire, covet
**concurrō, –ere, –currī, –cursus,** run, gather
**concursus, –ūs,** *m.,* running together, gathering, throng
**concutiō, –ere, –cussī, –cussus,** strike together, shake (up)
**condemnō,** 1, condemn
**cōndestim,** *adv.,* at once
**condiciō, –ōnis,** *f.,* condition, terms
**condītus, –a, –um,** seasoned; ornamented
**condō, –ere, –didī, –ditus,** found, establish; bring to an end; bury
**condūco, –ere, –duxī, –ductus,** hire, rent, be of help
**conexus, –a, –um,** adjoining
**cōnfābulor,** 1, talk
**conferō, conferre, contulī, collātus,** bring together, join, compare, collect; postpone; **mē conferō,** go, proceed
**cōnfertus, –a, –um,** crowded, compact, full
**cōnfessiō, –ōnis,** *f.,* confession
**cōnficiō, –ere, –fēcī, –fectus,** do up, complete, exhaust, destroy
**cōnfīdō, –ere, cōnfīsus,** *semideponent,* trust, be confident, rely on, have confidence (in)
**cōnfirmō,** 1, strengthen, assure, establish, declare, encourage, make firm
**cōnfiteor, –ērī, confessus,** confess, admit
**cōnflagrō,** 1, be consumed *(by fire)*
**cōnflīctiō, –ōnis,** *f.,* combat
**cōnflīctor,** 1, struggle, conflict, contend
**cōnflō,** 1, blow up, kindle, excite; compose
**cōnfluō, –ere, –flūxī, –flūxus,** flock (together)
**cōnfodiō, –ere, –fōdī, –fossus,** stab
**cōnfōrmō,** 1, mold, train
**cōnfringō, –ere, –frēgī, –frāctus,** shatter, destroy
**cōnfugiō, –ere, –fūgī, –fugitus,** flee for refuge
**congelō,** 1, freeze; stiffen
**congerō, –ere, –gessī, –gestus,** bring together, collect
**congredior, –ī, –gressus,** meet
**congregābilis, –e,** easily brought together, social
**congregātiō, –ōnis,** *f.,* union, society, association
**congregō,** 1, collect; *pass.,* assemble
**congruō, –ere, –uī, —,** coincide, agree, suit, accord
**congruus, –a, –um,** suitable
**coniciō, –ere, –iēcī, –iectus,** throw, aim
**coniectūra, –ae,** *f.,* guess
**coniūnctiō, –ōnis,** *f.,* association
**coniungō, –ere, –iūnxī, –iūnctus,** join with, connect
**coniūnx, –iugis,** *m. and f.,* husband, wife
**coniūrātī, –ōrum,** *m. pl.,* conspirators
**coniūratiō, –ōnis,** *f.,* conspiracy
**cōnor,** 1, attempt, try, endeavor
**conquiēscō, –ere, –quiēvī, –quiētus,** find rest
**conquīrō, –ere, –quīsīvī, –quīsītus,** seek out, hunt up, collect
**cōnscelerātus, –a, –um,** wicked
**cōnscendō, –ere, –scendī, –scēnsus,** climb, mount, scale, embark
**cōnscientia, –ae,** *f.,* consciousness, conscience
**cōnscius, –cī,** *m.,* witness
**cōnscrīptī, patrēs cōnscrīptī,** senators
**cōnsecrō,** 1, dedicate
**cōnsenēscō, –ere, –senuī, —,** grow old together
**cōnsēnsiō, –ōnis,** *f.,* agreement
**cōnsēnsus, –ūs,** *m.,* agreement
**cōnsentiō, –īre, –sēnsī, –sēnsus,** agree
**cōnsequenter,** *adv.,* then
**cōnsequor, –ī, cōnsecūtus,** follow (up), pursue; result; obtain, accomplish
**cōnserō, –ere, –sēvī, –situs,** plant
**cōnserō, –ere, –seruī, –sertus,** bind, join, connect
**cōnservō,** 1, keep, save, maintain, preserve

**cōnservus, –ī,** *m.,* fellow slave
**cōnsīderō,** 1, consider
**cōnsīdō, –ere, –sēdī, –sessus,** sit down, encamp, sink
**cōnsilium, –lī,** *n.,* plan, purpose, prudence, advice, wisdom; council, counsel
**consistō, –ere, constitī, constitus,** stop, stand still
**cōnsociātiō, –ōnis,** *f.,* union, association
**cōnsōlātiō, –ōnis,** *f.,* consolation, comfort
**cōnsōlor,** 1, comfort
**cōnspectus, –ūs,** *m.,* sight
**cōnspiciō, –ere, –spexī, –spectus,** catch sight of, look upon, see
**cōnspicor,** 1, catch sight of
**cōnstāns,** *gen.* **–antis,** firm
**cōnstanter,** *adv.,* firmly, consistently
**cōnstantia, –ae,** *f.,* firmness
**Cōnstantia, –ae,** *f.,* Constance
**constituō, –ere, –stituī, –stitūtus,** put, establish, settle; appoint, create; determine, decide, agree upon
**cōnstō, –stāre, –stitī, –stātus,** stand together, agree; **cōnstat,** it is evident, it is agreed
**cōnstringō, –ere, –strīnxī, –strictus,** bind, hold in check
**cōnstrūctiō, –ōnis,** *f.,* construction
**cōnstruō, –ere, –strūxī, –strūctus,** heap together; pile up; erect
**cōnsuēscō, –ere, –suēvī, –suētus,** become accustomed; *perfect,* be accustomed
**cōnsuētūdō, –dinis,** *f.,* custom, habit, practice; intimacy
**cōnsul, –ulis,** *m.,* consul, *the highest Roman official*
**cōnsulāris, –e,** consular, of consular rank; *as noun, m.,* ex-consul, man of consular rank
**cōnsulātus, –ūs,** *m.,* consulship
**cōnsulō, –ere, –suluī, –sultus,** consider, consult, put the question; look out for
**cōnsultātiō, –ōnis,** *f.,* consultation
**cōnsultum, –ī,** *n.,* decree
**cōnsummō,** 1, complete
**cōnsūmō, –ere, –sūmpsī, –sūmptus,** take (wholly), spend; destroy, consume
**cōnsurgō, –ere, –surrēxī, –surrēctus,** rise together
**contāctus, –ūs,** *m.,* touch
**contāgiō, –ōnis,** *f.,* touch, infection
**contāminō,** 1, stain, defile
**contegō, –ere, –tēxī, –tēctus,** cover
**contemnō, –ere, –tempsī, –temptus,** despise, disregard
**contemptus, –ūs,** *m.,* contempt, scorn, disgrace
**contendō, –ere, –tendī, –tentus,** contend, struggle, hasten, stretch
**contineō, –ēre, –uī, –tentus,** hold (together), contain
**contentiō, –ōnis,** *f.,* struggle, dispute
**contentus, –a, –um,** satisfied, content
**conterminus, –a, –um,** adjoining, neighboring
**conterō, –ere, –trīvī, –trītus,** waste
**conterreō, –ēre, –uī, –itus,** terrify
**conticēscō, –ere, –uī, —,** be silent, be still
**contiguus, –a, –um,** adjoining
**continēns,** *gen.* **–entis,** temperate, self-restrained; *as noun, f.,* the mainland
**continentia, –ae,** *f.,* self-control
**contineō, –ēre, –tinuī, –tentus,** bound; hold fast; restrain; comprise
**contingō, –ere, –tigī, –tāctus,** touch, reach; happen
**continuō,** 1, prolong
**continuō,** *adv.,* continuously
**continuus, –a, –um,** successive
**cōntiō, –ōnis,** *f.,* assembly, meeting
**cōntiōnātor, –ōris,** *m.,* demagogue
**contrā,** *adv. and prep. w. acc.,* against, contrary to, opposite; to the other side
**contrahō, –ere, –trāxī, –trāctus,** draw together; contract
**contrārius, –a, –um,** opposite, opposed
**contrōversia, –ae,** *f.,* dispute
**contubernālis, –is,** *m. and f.,* companion, mate
**contubernium, –nī,** *n.,* dwelling together; household
**contumēlia, –ae,** *f.,* insult, abuse; outrage
**contumēliōsus, –a, –um,** abusive, insulting
**cōnūbium, –bī,** *n.,* marriage
**convalēscō, –ere, –valuī, —,** recover from an illness, regain health
**convellō, –ere, –vellī, –vulsus,** tear away

**conveniō, –īre, –vēnī, –ventus,** come together, assemble, meet; be suited to; *impers.*, it is fitting or agreed
**conventum, –ī,** *n.,* agreement
**conventus, –ūs,** *m.,* assembly
**convertō, –ere, –vertī, –versus,** turn, change
**convīcium, –cī,** *n.,* violent reproach, wrangling
**convīctus, –ūs,** *m.,* living together, intimacy
**convīva, –ae,** *m. and f.,* table companion, guest
**convīvium, –vī,** *n.,* feast, banquet
**convocō, –āre, –āvī, –ātus,** 1, call together
**cooperiō, –īre, cooperuī, coopertus,** overwhelm
**cooperor,** 1, work with or together, unite
**cōpia, –ae,** *f.,* supply, abundance; fluency; *pl.,* resources, troops, forces
**cōpiōsus, –a, –um,** well supplied, plentiful, rich
**coquō, –ere, coxī, coctus,** cook, burn
**cor, cordis,** *n.,* heart
**Corduba, –ae,** *f.,* Cor´dova, *a city in Spain*
**Corinthius, –a, –um,** Corinthian
**Corinthus, –ī,** *f.,* Corinth, *a city in Greece*
**Cornēlius, –lī,** *m.,* Cornelius
**cornū, –ūs,** *n.,* horn; wing *(of an army),* flank, tip *(of the moon)*
**corōna, –ae,** *f.,* wreath, crown
**corōnō,** 1, crown
**corporālis, –e,** corporeal
**corpus, –poris,** *n.,* body
**corpusculum, –ī,** *n.,* a little body, dear person
**corrigō, –ere, –rēxī, –rēctus,** correct
**corrōborō,** 1, strengthen
**corrumpō, –ere, –rūpī, –ruptus,** corrupt, falsify; waste
**corruō, –ere, –ruī, —,** fall together
**corruptēla, –ae,** *f.,* corruption
**corruptiō, –ōnis,** *f.,* bribery, illness
**cortex, –ticis,** *m. and f.,* bark, shell, hull
**Corvīnus, –ī,** *m.,* Corvinus
**cotīdiānus, –a, –um,** daily
**cotīdiē,** *adv.,* daily
**crās,** tomorrow
**Crassus, –ī,** *m.,* Crassus
**crātēr, –is,** *m.,* large bowl
**Cratippus, –ī,** *m.,* Cratippus
**Creātor, –oris,** *m.,* the Creator
**creātūra, –ae,** *f.,* creation, act of creation
**crēber, –bra, –brum,** thick, frequent, numerous
**crēdibilis, –e,** credible
**crēditor, –ōris,** *m.,* creditor
**crēdō, –ere, –didī, –ditus,** believe, suppose; entrust (*w. dat.*)
**crēdulus, –a, –um,** credulous, unsuspecting, trustful
**creō,** 1, make, create
**crepitus, –ūs,** *m.,* sound
**crēscō, –ere, crēvī, crētus,** grow, increase
**Crēta, –ae,** *f.,* (*acc.* **Crētan**), Crete, *an island south of Greece*
**crīmen, –minis,** *n.,* accusation, charge, crime
**crīminor,** 1, charge
**crīnis, –is,** *m.,* hair
**Crotōniēnsis, –e,** Crotonian, of Croton *(a city in southern Italy)*
**cruciātus, –ūs,** *m.,* torture
**cruciō,** 1, torture; afflict
**crūdēlis, –e,** cruel
**crūdēliter,** *adv.,* cruelly
**crūdēlitās, –tātis,** *f.,* cruelty
**cruentus, –a, –um,** bloody
**cruentātus, –a, –um,** bloody
**cruor, cruōris,** *m.,* blood
**crūs, crūris,** *n.,* leg
**crux, crucis,** *f.,* cross
**cubiculum, –ī,** *n.,* bedroom, lounging room
**cubō, –āre, –uī, –itus,** lie down; sleep
**culpa, –ae,** *f.,* fault, guilt
**cultūra, –ae,** *f.,* cultivation; **agrī cultūra,** agriculture
**cultus, –ūs,** *m.,* culture
**cum,** *prep. w. abl.,* with
**cum,** *conj.,* when, while, since, although; **cum... tum,** not only . . . but also
**cumulō,** 1, heap up, crown
**cumulus, –ī,** *m.,* heap, increase
**cūnctanter,** *adv.,* reluctantly
**cūnctātiō, –ōnis,** *f.,* hesitancy, uncertainty
**cūnctus, –a, –um,** all together, all
**cupiditās, –tātis,** *f.,* desire, greed
**cupīdō, –dinis,** *f.,* desire, longing; love
**cupidus, –a, –um,** eager

**cupiō, –ere, cupīvī, cupītus,** desire, be eager, wish, want

**cūr,** *adv.,* why

**cūra, –ae,** *f.,* care, concern, anxiety; **(cum) magnā cūrā,** very carefully

**cūrātiō, –ōnis,** *f.,* care; cure

**cūrātor, –ōris,** *m.,* manager, commissioner, guardian

**cūria, –ae,** *f.,* curia, senate house

**cūriōsē,** *adv.,* carefully

**Cūrius, –rī,** *m.,* Curius

**cūrō,** 1, care for, look after; take care, arrange, cause *(to be done),* cure

**curriculum, –ī,** *n.,* course

**currō, –ere, cucurrī, cursus,** run; fly

**currus, –ūs,** *m.,* chariot

**cursim,** *adv.,* quickly, speedily

**cursitō, –āre, —, —,** run constantly

**cursō,** 1, run around

**cursus, -ūs,** *m.* running; race, way, voyage, course, career

**curvāmen, –minis,** *n.,* curve

**curvō,** 1, curve

**cuspis, –idis,** *f.,* point; sting

**custōdia, –ae,** *f.,* guard, custody, protection, prison

**custōdiō, –īre, –īvī, –ītus,** guard, watch

**custōs, –ōdis,** *m.,* guard, custodian, parent

**Cynthus, –ī,** *m.,* Cynthus, *a mountain on Delos*

## D

**Dalmatia, –ae,** *f.,* Dalmatia, *a region on the eastern shore of the Adriatic*

**Damasichthōn, –onis,** *m.,* Damasich´thon, *one of Niobe's sons*

**Damasippus, –ī,** *m.,* Damasip´pus

**damnātiō, –ōnis,** *f.,* conviction

**damnō,** 1, condemn

**damnōsus, –a, –um,** harmful

**damnum, –ī,** *n.,* loss; fine, penalty; curse

**Daphnē, – ēs,** *f.,* Daphne, *daughter of the river-god Peneus*

**daps, dapis,** *f.,* meal, feast; food

**Daunius, –a, –um,** Daunian, Apulian

**dē,** *prep. w. abl.,* from, down from, concerning, about, for, during

**dea, –ae,** *f.,* goddess

**deambulō, –āre, —, —,** take a walk

**dēbeō, –ēre, dēbuī, dēbitus,** ought, owe, should, must; *pass.,* be due

**dēbilis, –e,** weak, helpless

**dēbilitō,** 1, weaken

**dēbitor, –ōris,** *m.* debtor

**dēcēdō, –ere, –cessī, –cessus,** depart

**decem,** ten

**decenter,** *adv.,* becomingly, properly

**dēcernō, –ere, –crēvī, –cretus,** decide, decree, vote (for)

**dēcerpō, –ere, –cerpsī, –cerptus,** pluck

**decet, –ēre, decuit,** *impers.,* becomes, befits

**Deciānus, –ī,** *m.,* Decianus

**decimus, –a, –um,** tenth; **Decimus, –ī,** *m.,* Decimus

**Decius, –ci,** *m.,* Decius

**dēclamatiō, –ōnis,** *f.,* oratorical exercise, declamation

**dēclāmitō,** 1, declaim

**dēclārō,** 1, show, declare

**dēclīnatiō, –ōnis,** *f.,* bending aside, avoidance

**decor, –ōris,** *m.,* charm, beauty

**decorō,** 1, adorn, honor, embellish

**decōrus, –a, –um,** handsome, proper

**dēcrētum, –ī,** *n.,* decree

**decurrō, –ere, –cucurrī (–currī), –cursus,** run (down), hasten

**decus, decoris,** *n.,* honor

**dēdecus, –coris,** *n.,* disgrace, vice

**dēdicō,** 1, dedicate

**dēdō, –ere, dēdidī, dēditus,** hand over, surrender, devote

**dēdūcō, –ere, –dūxī, –ductus,** lead (away)

**dēfatīgō,** 1, wear out

**dēfendō, –ere, dēfendī, dēfēnsus,** defend

**dēfēnsiō, –ōnis,** *f.,* defense

**dēferō, dēferre, dētulī, dēlātus,** bring, report

**dēfessus, –a, –um,** wearied

**dēficiō, –ere, dēfēcī, dēfectus,** fail, revolt

**dēfīgō, –ere, dēfīxī, dēfīxus,** fix, plunge

**dēfīniō, –īre, dēfīnīvī, dēfīnītus,** limit, fix, appoint, define

**dēfīnītiō, –ōnis,** *f.,* definition

**dēflagrō**, 1, burn down
**dēfleō, –ēre, dēflēvī, dēflētus**, weep over
**dēfluō, –ere, dēflūxī, dēflūxus**, flow *or* sink down
**dēfraudō**, 1, cheat out of
**dēgerō, –ere, —, —**, carry off
**dēgō, –ere, dēgī, —**, spend, pass
**dēgustō**, 1, taste
**dēiciō, –ere, dēiēcī, dēiectus**, throw *or* cast down, push aside
**dēierō, dēiūrō**, 1, swear
**dein, deinde**, *adv.*, then, next
**deinceps**, *adv.*, next
**Deīrī, –ōrum**, *a tribe of the Angles*
**dēlabor, –ī, dēlāpsus**, fall, sink
**delectātiō, –ōnis**, *f.*, delight
**dēlecto**, 1, please, charm, delight in
**dēlēniō, –īre, dēlēnīvī, dēlēnītus**, allay, charm
**dēleō, –ēre, dēlēvī, dēlētus**, blot out, destroy
**dēlīberātiō, –ōnis**, *f.*, deliberation, question
**dēlīberō**, 1, think about, consider
**dēlicātus, –a, –um**, effeminate
**dēliciae, –ārum**, *f. pl.*, delight, pleasure
**dēligō**, 1, tie up
**dēligō, –ere, dēlēgī, dēlēctus**, select, choose
**dēlinquō, –ere, dēlīquī, dēlictus**, fail, do wrong
**dēlīrō**, 1, be crazy, rave
**Dēlius, –a, –um**, Delian, of Delos
**Dēlos, –ī**, *f.*, Delos, *an island in the Aegean*
**Delphicus, –a, –um**, Delphic, of Delphi, *a famous Greek oracle*
**dēlūbrum, –ī**, *n.*, shrine
**dēmēns**, *gen.* **–entis**, mad
**dēmenter**, *adv.*, foolishly
**dēmigro**, 1, go off, depart
**dēminūtiō, –ōnis**, *f.*, sacrifice, loss
**dēmissus, –a, –um**, downcast; *w.* **crīne**, disheveled
**dēmittō, –ere, dēmīsī, dēmissus**, let down
**dēmō, –ere, dēmpsī, dēmptus**, take away
**dēmōnstrō**, 1, point out, show
**dēmum**, *adv.*, at length, at last
**dēnegō**, 1, deny
**dēnique**, *adv.*, finally, after all, in short
**dēns, dentis**, *m.*, tooth
**dēnūntiō**, 1, threaten
**dēnuō**, *adv.*, once more, again
**dēpellō, –ere, dēpulī, depulsus**, drive from, avert, remove, overthrow
**dēplōrō**, 1, lament, deplore
**dēpōnō, –ere, dēposuī, dēpositus**, put down, lay aside, put aside; quench
**dēpositum, –ī**, *n.*, deposit, loan
**dēprāvō**, 1, corrupt, tamper with
**dēprecor**, 1, avert by prayer
**dēprēndō, –ere, dēprēndī, dēprēnsus**, seize, catch; perceive
**dēprimō, –ere, dēpressī, dēpressus**, press down, sink
**dērādō, –ere, dērāsī, dērāsus**, scrape off
**dērelinquō, –ere, dērelīquī, dērelictus**, abandon, forsake
**dērīdeō, –ēre, dērīsī, dērīsus**, laugh at, mock
**dērigēscō, –ere, dēriguī, —**, become rigid
**dēscendō, –ere, dēscendī, dēscēnsus**, descend, resort
**dēserō, –ere, dēseruī, dēsertus**, desert
**dēsertus, –a, –um**, lonely
**dēsideō, –ēre, dēsēdī, dēsessus**, be idle
**dēsīderium, –rī**, *n.*, longing, desire
**dēsīderō**, 1, desire, miss
**dēsidia, –ae**, *f.*, idleness
**dēsignō**, 1, mark out, elect, choose
**dēsiliō, –īre, dēsiluī, dēsultus**, jump down, dismount
**dēsinō, –ere, dēsiī, dēsitus**, cease
**dēsipiō, –ere, dēsipuī, —**, be silly *or* foolish
**dēsistō, –ere, dēstitī, dēstitus**, stand away, cease
**dēsōlō**, 1, leave alone, desert
**dēspērātiō, –ōnis**, *f.*, hopelessness, despair
**dēspērō**, 1, despair (of)
**dēspiciō, –ere, dēspexī, dēspectus**, look down on, despise
**dēspondeō, –ēre, dēspondī, dēspōnsus**, promise, betroth
**dēstinō**, 1, bind; intend, determine
**dēstringō, –ere, dēstrīnxī, dēstrictus**, unsheath
**dēstruō, –ere, destrūxī, dēstrūctus**, tear down, destroy
**dēsum, dēesse, dēfuī, dēfutūrus**, fail, be lacking
**dētegō, –ere, dētēxī, dētēctus**, uncover

**dēterō, –ere, dētrīvī, dētrītus,** wear away, weaken

**dēterreō, –ēre, dēterruī, dēterritus,** deter

**dētestor,** 1, curse, denounce, deprecate

**dētineō, –ēre, dētinuī, dētentus,** hold

**dētrahō, –ere, dētrāxī, dētrāctus,** draw *or* take from, pull off, remove, withdraw

**dētrimentum, –ī,** *n.,* loss, defeat

**deūrō, –ere, deussī, deustus,** burn up

**deus, –ī,** *m.,* god; *nom. pl.,* **diī** *or* **dī**

**dēvinciō, –īre, dēvinxī, dēvinctus,** bind, unite

**dēvorō,** 1, devour, swallow

**dēvoveō, –ēre, dēvōvī, dēvōtus,** vow, dedicate; curse

**dexter, –tra (–tera), –trum (–terum),** right; *comp.* **dexterior, –ius,** right; *as noun, f.,* right hand

**diabolus, –ī,** *m.,* devil

**dialecticus, –a, –um,** dialectic; *as noun, m.,* logician

**Diāna, –ae,** *f.,* Diana, *goddess of hunting*

**Diaulus, –ī,** Diaulus

**diciō, –ōnis,** *f.,* power

**dīcō, –ere, dīxī, dictus,** say, speak, tell, call

**dictātor, –ōris,** *m.,* dictator

**dictātūra, –ae,** *f.,* dictatorship

**dictō,** 1, dictate

**dictum, –ī,** *n.,* word

**diēs, diēī,** *m. and f.,* day

**differō, diferre, distulī, dīlātus,** postpone; differ

**difficilis, –e,** difficult, hard

**difficultās, –tātis,** *f.,* difficulty, trouble

**diffīdō, –ere, –fīsus,** *semideponent,* mistrust

**diffundō, –ere, –fūdī, –fūsus,** spread out

**dīgerō, –ere, dīgessī, dīgestus,** force apart, separate

**digitus, –ī,** *m.,* finger

**dignitās, –tātis,** *f.,* dignity

**dignus, –a, –um,** worthy

**dīiūdicō,** 1, decide, settle

**dīiungō, –ere, dīiūnxī, dīiūnctus,** separate

**dīlēctus, –ūs,** *m.,* choice

**dīligēns,** *gen.* **–entis,** careful, scrupulous

**dīligenter,** *adv.,* carefully

**dīligentia, –ae,** *f.,* care, diligence

**dīligō, –ere, dīlexī, dīlectus,** single out, esteem, love

**dīlūcēscō, –ere, dīlūxī, —,** grow light

**dīmētior, –īrī, dīmēnsus,** measure, lay out

**dīmicātiō, –ōnis,** *f.,* struggle

**dīmicō,** 1, fight, contend, struggle

**dīmidius, –a, –um,** half, halved

**dīminūtiō, –ōnis,** *f.,* decrease

**dīmittō, –ere, dīmīsī, dīmissus,** let go, lose, abandon, send away, dismiss

**dīmoveō, –ēre, dīmōvī, dīmōtus,** move apart, stir

**diocēsis, –is,** *f.,* diocese *(district ruled by a bishop)*

**dīrēctus, –a, –um,** straight

**dīreptiō, –ōnis,** *f.,* plundering, loot

**dīreptor, –ōris,** *m.,* plunderer

**dirimō, –ere, dirēmī, dirēmptus,** break off

**dīripiō, –ere, dīripuī, dīrēptus,** plunder

**dīruō, –ere, dīruī, dīrutus,** tear down

**dīrus, –a, –um,** awful

**discēdō, –ere, –cessī, –cessus,** go away, depart

**discernō, –ere, –crēvī, crētus,** set apart, distinguish, discern

**discerpō, –ere, –cerpsī, –cerptus,** tear in pieces, dismember

**discessus, –ūs,** *m.,* departure

**disciplīna, –ae,** *f.,* training, instruction, discipline

**discipulus, –ī,** *m.,* **discipula, –ae,** *f.,* student learner, pupil, disciple, follower

**discō, –ere, didicī, —,** learn

**discordia, –ae,** *f.,* discord

**discrībō, –ere, discrīpsī, discrīptus,** assign

**discrīmen, –minis,** *n.,* difference, decision, danger, crisis

**discrīminō,** 1, divide, separate

**dispār,** *gen.* **–paris,** unequal

**dispēnso,** 1, distribute

**dispertiō, –īre, –īvī, –ītus,** distribute

**dispiciō, –ere, dispexī, dispectus,** consider

**dispōnō, –ere, –posuī, –positus,** place here and there, arrange, dispose

**disputō,** 1, discuss, argue

**disseminō,** 1, spread abroad

**dissēnsiō, –ōnis,** *f.,* quarrel

**dissentiō, –īre, –sēnsī, –sēnsus,** disagree, differ

**disserō, –ēre, disseruī, disertus,** examine, discuss, discourse

**dissideō, –ēre, –sēdī, –sessus,** disagree

**dissimilis, –e,** unlike
**dissimulanter,** *adv.,* secretly
**dissimulātor, –ōris,** *m.,* dissembler
**dissimulō,** 1, conceal (the truth), deny
**dissolūtus, –a, –um,** lax, remiss
**dissolvō, –ere, –solvī, –solūtus,** solve
**distinguō, –ere, –tīnxī, –tīnctus,** distinguish
**distō, –āre, —, —,** stand apart, be distant, be different
**distrahō, –ere, –trāxī, –trāctus,** draw away
**distribuō, –ere, –tribuī, –tribūtus,** distribute, assign
**distringō, –ere, –distrīnxī, districtus,** distract the attention
**diū,** *adv.,* for a long time, long; *comp.* **diūtius;** *superl.* **diūtissimē**
**diūtinus, –a, –um,** long, of long duration
**diūturnus, –a, –um,** long lasting
**dīvello, –ere, dīvellī, dīvulsus,** tear away, rend, separate
**dīversus, –a, –um,** opposite, different, widely separated
**dīves,** *gen.* **dīvitis,** rich
**dīvidō, –ere, dīvīsī, dīvīsus,** divide, extend
**dīvīnitus,** *adv.,* providentially
**dīvīnus, –a, –um,** divine, godlike
**dīvitiae, –ārum,** *f. pl.,* riches
**dīvus, –a, –um,** divine; *as noun, m.,* god, deity
**dō, dare, dedī, datus,** give, put; **poenam dō,** pay the penalty
**doceō, –ēre, docuī, doctus,** teach, show
**doctor, –ōris,** *m.,* teacher
**doctrīna, –ae,** *f.,* teaching, learning
**doctus, –a, –um,** learned, skilled
**Dolābella, –ae,** *m.,* Dolabella
**doleō, –ēre, doluī, dolitus,** suffer, grieve, deplore
**dolor, –ōris,** *m.,* pain, grief, grievance
**dolus, –ī,** *m.,* trick, snare
**domesticus, –a, –um,** private, domestic
**domicilium, –lī,** *n.,* home, residence
**domina, –ae,** *f.,* mistress
**dominātiō, –ōnis,** *f.,* mastery, rule
**dominātus, –ūs,** *m.,* mastery
**dominicus, –a, –um,** of a lord *or* master; the Lord's
**dominor,** 1, rule, be master
**dominus, –ī,** *m.,* master, owner; *voc.,* Sir; **Dominus,** the Lord
**Domitiānus, –ī,** *m.* Domitian, *a Roman emperor*
**Domitius, –tī,** *m.,* Domitius
**domō, –āre, –uī, –itus,** tame
**domus, –ūs,** *f.,* house, home; household; *loc.* **domī,** at home
**dōnec,** *conj.,* until, as long as
**dōnō,** 1, give, present
**dōnum, –ī,** *n.,* gift
**dormiō, –īre, –īvī, –ītus,** sleep
**dormītōrius, –a, –um,** for sleeping
**dōs, dōtis,** *f.,* dowry, endowment, talent
**Drūsus, –ī,** *m.,* Drusus
**dubitātiō, –ōnis,** *f.,* doubt
**dubitō,** 1, hesitate, doubt, be in doubt
**dubius, –a, –um,** doubtful, uncertain
**ducātus, –ūs,** *m.,* military leadership, command
**dūcō, –ere, dūxī, ductus,** lead, draw, attract, construct, draw out, consider
**ductus, –ūs,** *m.,* command, motion
**dūdum,** *adv.,* for a long time
**dulcēdō, –dinis,** *f.,* sweetness, charm
**dulcis, –e,** sweet
**dum,** *conj.,* while, as long as; provided that (*often w.* **modo**)
**dūmus, –ī,** *m.,* thorn; bush
**duo, –ae, –o,** two
**duodecim,** twelve
**dupliciter,** *adv.,* doubly
**duplicō,** 1, double
**dūrē,** *adv.,* harshly
**dūrō,** 1, last, remain
**dūrus, –a, –um,** hard, cruel, insensible, harsh
**dux, ducis,** *m.,* leader, general

## E

**ē, ex,** *prep. w. abl.,* from, out of, of, after, out from, in accordance with
**ea,** she *(nom.)*
**ebrius, –a, –um,** full, drunk
**ebur, –oris,** *n.,* ivory
**eburneus, –a, –um; eburnus, –a, –um,** of ivory
**ecastor!** *interj.,* by Castor! *(used by women)*

**ecce!** *interj.,* look here!
**ecclesia, –ae,** *f.,* church
**edepol!** *interj.,* by Pollux! Indeed!
**ēdīcō, –ere, ēdīxī, ēdictus,** declare
**ēdictum, –ī,** *n.,* edict
**ēdiscō, –ere, ēdidicī, —,** learn (thoroughly)
**ēditus, –a, –um,** lofty
**ēdō, –ere, ēdidī, ēditus,** publish, utter
**ēducō,** 1, bring up
**ēdūcō, –ere, ēdūxī, ēductus,** lead out *or* forth, draw out
**efferō, efferre, extulī, ēlātus,** carry out; bring; exalt, extol
**efficiō, –ere, effēcī, effectus,** make (out), cause, accomplish, produce, bring about, complete
**effigiēs, –ēī,** *f.,* copy; likeness
**effluō, –ere, efflūxī, —,** flow out; escape
**effodiō, –ere, effōdī, effossus,** dig up
**effrēnātus, –a, –um,** unbridled, unrestrained
**effugiō, –ere, effūgī, effugitus,** escape
**effugium, –gī,** *n.,* escape
**effundō, –ere, effūdī, effusus,** pour out
**egeō, egēre, eguī, —,** need, be in need of, lack
**egestās, –tātis,** *f.,* poverty
**ego, meī,** I; **egomet,** I myself
**ēgredior, ēgredī, ēgressus,** go *or* march out, go, leave
**ēgregius, –a, –um,** excellent, distinguished
**ei!** *interj.,* Oh!
**ēiaculor,** 1, shoot *or* spurt out
**ēiciō, –ere, ēiēcī, ēiectus,** throw out
**eius,** his, her
**ēlābor, ēlābī, ēlāpsus,** slip away, escape
**ēlabōrō,** 1, work hard
**ēlegāns,** *gen.* **–antis,** choice
**ēleganter,** *adv.,* tastefully, finely, elegantly
**elephantus, –ī,** *m.,* elephant
**ēlīdō, –ere, ēlīsī, ēlīsus,** tear out; shatter, destroy
**ēligō, –ere, ēlēgī, ēlectus,** pick out, select
**ēloquentia, –ae,** *f.,* eloquence
**ēloquium, –ī,** *n.,* speech, utterance, eloquence
**ēlūdō, –ere, ēlūsī, ēlūsus,** escape; mock, make sport of
**ēluō, –ere, ēluī, ēlūtus,** wash (off); remove
**ēmendō,** 1, correct, improve
**ēmentior, –īrī, ēmentītus,** feign, fabricate
**ēmergō, –ere, ēmersī, ēmersus,** rise, emerge
**ēmicō, –āre, –uī, –ātus,** dart forth, spurt
**ēmineō, –ēre, –uī, —,** stand out, be prominent
**ēmittō, –ere, ēmīsī, ēmissus,** let go
**emō, –ere, ēmī, ēmptus,** take, buy
**ēmorior, ēmorī, ēmortuus,** die
**ēmptiō, –ōnis,** *f.,* purchase
**ēmptor, –ōris,** *m.,* buyer
**ēn,** *interj.,* behold! see! there!
**enim,** *conj., (never first word),* for; *w.* **at,** but you say
**enimvērō,** *adv.,* yes, indeed; assuredly
**ēnitēscō, –ere, ēnituī, —,** shine forth
**ēnītor, –ī, ēnīxus (ēnīsus),** make one's way
**Ennius, –nī,** *m.,* Ennius, *a Roman poet*
**ēnotō,** 1, mark out, note down
**ēnsis, –is,** *m.,* sword
**ēnumerō,** 1, count out; recount, describe
**ēnūntiō,** 1, report
**eō, īre, iī, itus,** go
**Ephesus, –ī,** *m.,* Ephesus, *a famous city in Asia*
**Epicūrus, –ī,** *m.,* Epicurus, *a Greek philosopher*
**Ēpīrus, –ī,** *f.,* Epirus, *a province in Greece*
**epistula, –ae,** *f.,* letter
**epulae, –ārum,** *f.,* food, banquet
**epulor,** 1, hold a banquet
**epulum, –ī,** *n.,* feast
**eques, equitis,** *m.,* horseman, knight; *pl.,* cavalry
**equidem,** *adv., (w. 1st person),* for my part, at any rate
**equitātus, –ūs,** *m.,* cavalry
**equus, –ī,** *m.,* horse
**Erebus, –ī,** *m.,* Erebus, *the lower world*
**ergā,** *prep. w. acc.,* toward
**ergastulum, –ī,** *n.,* prison
**ergō,** *adv.,* accordingly, therefore, then
**ērigō, –ere, ērēxī, ērēctus,** raise, set up, erect, encourage
**ēripiō, –ere, ēripuī, ēreptus,** snatch *or* take away, rescue from, remove
**ērogō,** 1, appropriate, pay
**errātum, –ī,** *n.,* error
**errō,** 1, wander, be mistaken

**error, –ōris,** *m.,* error
**ērudiō, –īre, –īvī, –ītus,** teach
**ērudītiō, –ōnis,** *f.,* instruction
**ērudītus, –a, –um,** educated, learned
**ērumpō, –ere, ērūpī, ēruptus,** break out, burst forth
**ēruō, ēruere, ēruī, ērutus,** tear out
**ervum, –ī,** *n.,* bitter vetch *(a plant)*
**et,** *conj.,* and, even, also, too; **et... et,** both . . . and
**etenim,** *conj.,* for truly, and indeed
**etiam,** *adv.,* even, also, too, still; **nōn sōlum... sed etiam,** not only . . . but also; **etiam atque etiam,** again and again
**Etrūria, –ae,** *f.,* Etruria, *a district of Italy*
**Etrūscī, –ōrum,** *m. pl.,* the Etruscans
**Eumaeus, –ī,** *m.,* Eumaeus (Ūmē´us)
**Eurōpa, –ae,** *f.,* Europe
**ēvādō, –ere, ēvāsī, ēvāsus,** go out, escape
**ēveniō, –īre, ēvēnī, ēventus,** (come out), turn out, happen
**ēventus, –ūs,** *m.,* occurrence; fate
**ēvertō, –ere, ēvertī, ēversus,** overthrow, destroy, ruin
**ēvigilō,** 1, awake
**ēvītābilis, –e,** avoidable
**ēvocātor, –ōris,** *m.,* a caller to arms
**ēvocō,** 1, summon, call out
**ēvolō,** 1, fly *or* rush forth
**ēvolvō, –ere, ēvolvī, evolūtus,** unroll (and read)
**ex,** *see* **ē**
**exaedificō,** 1, finish building, erect
**exaggerō,** 1, increase
**exanimis, –e,** lifeless, dead
**exaudiō, –īre, –īvī, –ītus,** hear (plainly)
**excēdō, –ere, –cessī, –cessus,** go forth, withdraw, depart
**excellens,** *gen.* **–entis,** superior, remarkable
**excellentia, –ae,** *f.,* superiority, excellence
**excelsus, –a, –um,** elevated, high
**excerpō, –ere, –cerpsī, –cerptus,** choose, select
**excīdō, –ere, –cidī, —,** fall (out), disappear
**excīdō, –ere, –cīdī, –cīsus,** destroy
**excipiō, –ere, –cēpī, –ceptus,** take out *or* up, receive, catch, intercept; follow; except
**excitō,** 1, arouse; raise
**exclamo,** 1, shout
**exclūdō, –ere, –clūsī, –clūsus,** shut out
**excolō, –ere, –uī, excultus,** cultivate
**excruciō,** 1, torment, torture, harass
**excurrō, –ere, –cucurrī, –cursus,** run out *or* up
**excūsātiō, –ōnis,** *f.,* excuse
**excutiō, –ere, –cussī, –cussus,** shake off, force away; search, examine
**exemplum, –ī,** *n.,* example, copy, precedent
**exeō, –īre, –iī, –itus,** go *or* come forth, depart
**exerceō, –ēre, exercuī, exercitus,** train, exercise; keep busy; conduct
**exercitātiō, –ōnis,** *f.,* training, exercise
**exercitus, –ūs,** *m.,* (trained) army
**exhauriō, –īre, exhausī, exhaustus,** drain
**exhibeō, –ēre, –uī, –itus,** show
**exhorreō, –ēre, uī, —,** shudder at, dread
**exigō, –ere, exēgī, exāctus,** drive out, demand; *of time,* spend, pass
**exiguus, –a, –um,** small, slight, narrow
**exilis, –e,** thin, meager, poor; worthless
**eximiē,** *adv.,* exceedingly
**eximius, –a, –um,** extraordinary
**eximō, –ere, exēmī, exemptus,** take away, consume
**exīstimātiō, –ōnis,** *f.,* reputation
**exīstimō,** 1, think, suppose, consider
**exitiābilis, –e,** fatal
**exitiōsus, –a, –um,** deadly; destructive
**exitium, –tī,** *n.,* ruin, destruction, death
**exitus, –ūs,** *m.,* end
**exoptātus, –a, –um,** earnestly desired, longed for
**exoptō,** 1, desire
**exōrnō,** 1, adorn
**exōrō,** 1, beg
**exōsus, –a, –um,** hating, detesting
**espallēscō, –ere, expalluī, —,** turn pale
**expavēscō, –ere, expāvī, —,** be terrified, dread
**expectātiō, –ōnis,** *f.,* awaiting, expectation, longing
**expediō, –īre, –iī, –ītus,** set free, procure
**expellō, –ere, expulī, expulsus,** drive out, expel; deprive of
**experior, –īrī, expertus,** try, test; find
**expers, expertis,** having no share in

**expertus, –a, –um,** tried, proved; experienced in
**expetō, –ere, –īvī, –ītus,** seek
**explānō,** 1, explain
**expleō, –ēre, explēvī, explētus,** fill, satisfy
**explicō,** 1, unfold, explain
**explōrātor, –ōris,** *m.,* spy, scout
**explōrō,** 1, investigate, explore
**expoliō, –īre, –īvī, ītus,** smooth, polish, adorn, refine
**expōnō, –ere, exposuī, expositus,** put out, expose, explain
**exprimō, –ere, expressī, espressus,** press out, portray, describe
**exprobrō,** 1, accuse of, charge
**exprōmō, –ere, exprōmpsī, exprōmptus,** display; disclose
**expugnō,** 1, take by storm, capture, capture by assault
**expūrgō,** 1, clear
**exquīsītus, –a, –um,** exquisite, excessive
**exscrībō, –ere, exscrīpsī, exscrīptus,** copy
**exsiliō, –īre, exsiluī, —,** leap up
**exsilium, –lī,** *n.,* exile, banishment
**exsistō, –ere, exstitī, —,** stand forth, appear
**exspectātiō, –ōnis,** *f.,* waiting, anticipation
**exspectō,** 1, look out for, expect, await, wait (for)
**exstinguō, –ere, exstīnxī, exstīnctus,** extinguish, destroy
**exstō, –āre, —, —,** stand out, protrude; exist
**exstruō, –ere, exstrūxī, exstrūctus,** heap up, build
**exsul, –ulis,** *m. and f.,* exile
**exsultō,** 1, (leap up), exult
**exsuperantia, –ae,** *f.,* superiority
**extemplō,** *adv.,* immediately
**extendō, –ere, –tendī, –tentus (–tensus),** stretch out, prolong
**externus, –a, –um,** foreign
**exterus, –a, –um,** outside, foreign
**extollō, –ere, —, —,** raise up
**extorqueō, –ēre, extorsī, extortus,** wrest
**extrā,** *(prep. w. acc.),* outside (of), beyond
**extrēmus, –a, –um,** farthest, last, end of
**exūrō, –ere, exussī, exustus,** burn (up)
**exuviae, –ārum,** *f.,* spoils

# F

**faber, –brī,** *m.,* mechanic, fireman
**fabricō,** 1, build, construct
**fābula, –ae,** *f.,* story, play
**Fabulla, –ae,** *f.,* Fabulla
**Fabullus, –ī,** *m.,* Fabullus
**fābulor,** 1, speak, say, utter
**fābulōsus, –a, –um,** storied, fabulous
**facētē,** *adv.,* wittily
**facētiae, –ārum,** *f. pl.,* jest, wit
**faciēs, –ēī,** *f.,* appearance, face
**facile,** *adv.,* easily, readily
**facilis, –e,** easy
**facilitās, –tātis,** *f.,* friendliness
**facinorōsus, –ī,** *m.,* criminal
**facinus, –noris,** *n.,* deed, crime
**faciō, –ere, fēcī, factus,** do, make, form, cause; **proelium faciō,** fight a battle; **verba faciō,** speak, make a speech
**factiō, –ōnis,** *f.,* faction
**factiōsus, –a, –um,** seditious
**factitō,** 1, make *or* do frequently
**factum, –ī,** *n.,* deed
**facultās, –tātis,** *f.,* ability, means, opportunity
**fācundus, –a, –um,** eloquent
**faenerātor, –ōris,** *m.,* moneylender
**faenus, faenoris,** *n.,* interest
**Faesulae, –ārum,** *f.,* Faesulae, Fiesole, *a town in Etruria*
**fāgus, –ī,** *f.,* beech tree, beechwood
**Falernum, –ī,** *n.,* Falernian wine
**fallō, –ere, fefellī, falsus,** deceive, elude, escape the notice of; disappoint; *w.* **fidem,** break one's word
**falsus, –a, –um,** false
**fāma, –ae,** *f.,* report, story; fame, reputation; *w.* **est,** it is said
**famēs, –is,** *f.,* hunger
**familia, –ae,** *f.,* household, family; slaves
**familiāris, –e,** belonging to the family, friendly, private, intimate; *as noun, m.,* intimate friend
**familiāritās, –tātis,** *f.,* friendship
**familiāriter,** *adv.,* intimately
**famulus, –ī,** *m.,* servant
**fāmōsus, –a, –um,** famous, notorious

**Fannius, –nī,** *m.,* Fannius
**fānum, –ī,** *n.,* shrine
**fās,** *indeclinable, n.,* right
**fascis, –is,** *m.,* bundle; *pl.,* **fascēs**
**fastīdiō, –īre, fastīdīvī, fastīdītus,** feel disgust, disdain
**fastīdium, –dī,** *n.,* loathing, aversion
**fatālis, –e,** fated, deadly
**fateor, –ērī, fassus,** confess, admit
**fātifer, –era, –erum,** deathbringing, fatal
**fatīgō,** 1, weary
**fātum, –ī,** *n.,* fate; *often personified,* the Fates
**faucēs, –ium,** *f. pl.,* throat, jaws; pass
**fautor, –ōris,** *m.,* promoter
**faveō, –ēre, fāvī, fautus,** be favorable to, favor
**favilla, –ae,** *f.,* embers
**favor, –ōris,** *m.,* favor; cheering
**favus, –ī,** *m.,* honeycomb
**fax, facis,** *f.,* torch
**febricula, –ae,** *f.,* fever, slight fever
**fēcundus, –a, –um,** fruitful, rich
**fēlīx,** *gen.* **fēlīcis,** happy, fortunate, productive
**fēmina, -ae,** *f.,* woman, wife
**fenestra, –ae,** *f.,* window
**fera, –ae,** *f.,* wild beast
**ferē, fermē,** *adv.,* almost, about; *w. neg.,* hardly
**feriae, -ārum,** *f. pl.,* holidays
**ferio, -īre, -īvī, -ītus,** hit, strike, knock
**feritās, –tātis,** *f.,* wildness
**fermē,** see **ferē**
**ferō, ferre, tulī, lātus,** bear, carry, bring, direct, produce, obtain; say; *w.* **lēgem,** propose, pass; *w.* **pedem retrō,** start back
**ferōcitās, –tātis,** *f.,* fierceness
**ferōciter,** *adv.,* fiercely
**ferōx, –ōcis,** fierce
**ferrāmentum, –ī,** *n.,* sword, dagger
**ferreus, –a, –um,** of iron, hard
**ferrum, –ī,** *n.,* iron; sword, point
**ferus, –a, –um,** savage, cruel
**fervēns,** *gen.* **–entis,** hot, burning
**fessus, –a, –um,** wearied, worn out
**festīnātiō, –ōnis,** *f.,* haste, despatch, speed
**festīnō,** 1, hasten, hurry
**fēstīvus, –a, –um,** merry, pleasant, kind
**fēstum, –ī,** *n.,* holiday
**fēstus, –a, –um,** festive
**fētus, –ūs,** *m.,* offspring, fruit
**fidēlis, –e,** faithful
**fidēliter,** *adv.,* faithfully, loyally
**fidēs, –ēī,** *f.,* trust, belief; credit, honor, loyalty, pledge
**fīdūcia, –ae,** *f.,* trust, confidence
**fīdus, –a, –um,** trusty, faithful, reliable, loyal
**fīgō, –ere, fīxī, fīxus,** fix, set
**Figulus, –ī,** *m.,* Figulus
**figūra, –ae,** *f.,* shape, figure
**fīlia, –ae,** *f.,* daughter
**fīliolus, –ī,** *m.,* little son
**fīlius, –lī,** *m.,* son
**fingō, ere, fīnxī, fictus,** form, imagine, suppose
**fīniō, –īre, –īvī, –ītus,** end, finish, bound
**fīnis, –is,** *m.,* end, limit; *pl.,* borders, territory
**fīnitimus, –a, –um,** neighboring, near; *as noun,* neighbor
**fīō, fierī, —, factus,** become, be made, be done, happen
**firmāmentum, –ī,** *n.,* foundation, firmament
**firmiter,** *adv.,* firmly
**firmō,** 1, strengthen
**firmus, –a, –um,** strong, firm
**fissus, –a, –um,** split
**fistula, –ae,** *f.,* (shepherd's) pipe
**fixus,** *see* **fīgō**
**Flaccus, –ī,** *m.,* Flaccus
**Flacilla, –ae,** *f.,* Flacilla
**flagellum, –ī,** *n.,* whip
**flāgitium, –tī,** *n.,* disgraceful act, crime
**flāgitō,** 1, demand, insist upon
**flāmen, –inis,** *n.,* breeze
**Flāminius, –nī,** Flaminius
**Flāminius, –a, –um,** Flaminian
**flamma, –ae,** *f.,* flame, fire
**flāvēscō, –ere, —, —,** become golden
**flāvus, –a, –um,** yellow, golden
**flectō, –ere, flexī, flexus,** turn, bend, influence
**fleō, flēre, flēvī, flētus,** weep
**flētus, –ūs,** *m.,* weeping

**Flōrentia, –ae,** *f.,* Florence, *a city in Italy*
**flōreō, –ēre, –uī, —,** bloom, flourish
**flōs, flōris,** *m.,* flower
**fluctus, -ūs,** *m.,* wave
**flūmen, flūminis,** *n.,* river
**fluō, –ere, flūxī, flūxus,** flow
**flūxus, –a, –um,** fleeting
**focus, –ī,** *m.,* hearth
**foederātus, –a, –um,** allied
**foedō,** 1, stain
**foedus, –a, –um,** vile, shameful
**foedus, –deris,** *n.,* league, alliance, compact
**folium, –lī,** *n.,* leaf
**fōns, fontis,** *m.,* spring, fountain, source
**forēnsis, –e,** of the Forum, public
**foris, –is,** *f.,* door
**forīs,** *adv.,* out of doors, abroad
**fōrma, –ae,** *f.,* shape, image, form, beauty, plan
**formīdō, –dinis,** *f.,* fear, dread
**formīdolōsus, –a, –um,** alarming, formidable
**fōrmō,** 1, form, compose
**fōrmōsus, –a, –um,** handsome, beautiful
**fors, fortis,** *f.,* chance
**forsitan,** *adv.,* perhaps
**fortasse,** *adv.,* perhaps
**forte,** *adv.,* by chance
**fortis, –e,** strong, brave
**fortiter,** *adv.,* bravely
**fortitūdō, –dinis,** *f.,* strength
**fortuitus, –a, –um,** accidental
**fortūna, –ae,** *f.,* fortune, luck
**fortūnātus, –a, –um,** happy, fortunate
**forum, –ī,** *n.,* forum, market place; **Forum Aurēlium,** *n., a town in Etruria,* Forum (*at Rome*)
**forus, –ī,** *m.,* gangway
**foveō, –ēre, fōvī, fōtus,** warm, cherish, support
**fragilis, –e,** fragile, weak
**frangō, –ere, frēgī, frāctus,** break, shatter, crush, overcome
**frāter, frātris,** *m.,* brother
**frāternus, –a, –um,** of one's brother
**fraudulentus, –a, –um,** deceitful
**fraus, fraudis,** *f.,* fraud, deceit
**frēnō,** 1, bridle, curb
**frenum, –ī; frēna (–ī), –ōrum;** also **frenī, –ōrum,** *n. or m.,* bridle, rein
**frequēns,** *gen.* **–entis,** in crowds
**frequenter,** *adv.,* often, in great numbers
**frequentia, –ae,** *f.,* throng, large number
**fretum, –ī,** *n.,* strait, sea, water
**frētus, –a, –um,** relying on
**frīgeō, –ēre, —, —,** be cold, freeze
**frīgidārius, –a, –um,** cooling
**frīgidus, –a, –um,** cold
**frīgus, –goris,** *n.,* cold, coolness
**frondeō, –ēre, —, —,** put forth leaves
**frōns, frondis,** *f.,* leaf
**frōns, frontis,** *f.,* front, forehead
**Frontō, –ōnis,** *m.,* Fronto, *a Roman writer*
**frūctus, –ūs,** *m.,* enjoyment, fruit, income, benefit, products
**frugālitās, –tātis,** *f.,* thrift
**frūmentārius, –a, –um,** of grain; *w.* **auxilium,** granary; *w.* **rēs,** grain supply
**frūmentum, –ī,** *n.,* grain
**fruor, fruī, frūctus** *(+ abl.),* enjoy
**frūstrā,** *adv.,* in vain
**frūstum, –ī,** *n.,* bit
**fūcus, –ī,** *m.,* red dye; pretense
**fuga, –ae,** *f.,* flight; **in fugam dō,** put to flight
**fugāx,** *gen.* **–ācis,** fleeing
**fugiō, –ere, fūgī, fugitus,** run away, flee, avoid, escape
**fugitīvus, –ī,** *m.,* runaway slave
**fugō,** 1, put to flight, repel
**fulgeō, –ēre, fulsī, —,** gleam
**fulmen, –minis,** *n.,* lightning, thunderbolt
**Fulvia, –ae,** *f.,* Fulvia
**Fulvius, –vī,** *m.,* Fulvius
**fulvus, –a, –um,** yellow
**fundāmentum, –ī,** *n.,* foundation, basis, beginning
**fundō,** 1, found
**fundō, –ere, fūdī, fūsus,** pour; rout
**fundus, –ī,** *m.,* estate, bottom
**funestus, –a, –um,** fatal
**fungor, –ī, functus,** perform

**fūnus, fūneris,** *n.,* funeral, death; ruin
**fūr, fūris,** *m. and f.,* thief, robber
**furca, –ae,** *f.,* forked pole
**furibundus, –a, –um,** full of rage
**furiōsus, –a, –um,** insane, furious
**Fūrius, –rī,** *m.,* Furius
**Furnius, –nī,** *m.,* Furnius
**furō, –ere, –uī, —,** rage, be mad
**furor, –ōris,** *m.,* madness, fury
**fūrtim,** *adv.,* secretly
**fūrtum, –ī,** *n.,* theft
**Fuscus, –ī,** *m.,* Fuscus
**fūstis, –is,** *m.,* staff, club
**futūrus,** *see* **sum**

## G

**Gadēs, –ium,** *f. pl.,* Cadiz, *a city in Spain*
**Gāius, –ī,** *m.,* Gaius
**Galba, –ae,** *m.,* Galba, *a Roman emperor*
**galea, –ae,** *f.,* helmet
**Gallia, –ae,** *f.,* Gaul, *ancient France*
**Gallicus, –a, –um,** Gallic, of Gaul
**Gallus, –a, -um,** Gallic *(from Gaul); as noun, m.,* a Gaul
**Gangēs, –is,** *m.,* Ganges, *a river in India*
**garriō, īre, –īvī, –ītus,** chatter
**gaudeō, –ēre, gāvīsus,** *semideponent,* rejoice
**gaudium, –dī,** *n.,* joy, gladness, delight
**gelidus, –a, –um,** cold
**Gemellus, –ī,** *m.,* Gemellus
**geminus, –a, –um,** twin, two, both
**gemitus, –ūs,** *m.,* groan, lamentation
**gemma, –ae,** *f.,* precious stone
**gena, –ae,** *f.,* cheek
**gener, –erī,** *m.,* son-in-law
**genetrīx, –īcis,** *f.,* mother
**geniāliter,** *adv.,* merrily
**genitor, –ōris,** *m.,* father
**gēns, gentis,** *f.,* tribe, people, nation, family, class
**gentīlis, –e,** belonging to the same clan *or* race; pagan
**genus, generis,** *n.,* birth, race; kind, class, family, sort
**Germānia, –ae,** *f.,* Germany
**Germānus, –ī,** *m.,* a German
**germinō,** 1, bud, germinate, sprout
**gerō, –ere, gessī, gestus,** bear, carry on, manage, do, accomplish, wear; hold; **mē gerō,** act
**gestāmen, –inis,** *n.,* load; *pl.,* arms
**gestō,** 1, carry, bear; *pass.,* ride
**gestus, –ūs,** *m.,* gesture
**gignō, –ere, genuī, genitus,** bring forth, produce; *pass.,* be born
**gladiātor, –ōris,** *m.,* gladiator
**gladius, –dī,** *m.,* sword
**glaeba, –ae,** *f.,* clod
**glāns, glandis,** *f.,* acorn
**glōria, –ae,** *f.,* glory, fame
**glorior,** 1, boast
**glōriōsus, –a, –um,** glorious
**Gnaeus, –ī,** *m.,* Gnaeus (Nē´us)
**Gordiānus, –ī,** *m.,* Gordianus
**Gorgiās, –ae,** *m.,* Gorgias
**Gracchus, –ī,** *m.,* Gracchus
**gracilis, –e,** thin, slender
**gradior, –ī, gressus,** step, walk
**gradus, –ūs,** *m.,* step, grade
**Graecia, –ae,** *f.,* Greece
**Graecus, –a, –um,** Greek; **Graecus, –ī,** *m.,* a Greek; *as noun, m. pl.,* the Greeks
**Graiī, –ōrum,** *m.,* the Greeks
**grammaticus, –ī,** *m.,* school teacher, grammarian
**grandis, –e,** large; **grandis nātū,** old man
**grātē,** *adv.,* gratefully
**grātia, –ae,** *f.,* gratitude, favor, influence; **grātiās agō,** thank; **grātiam referō,** show one's gratitude; **grātiam habeō,** feel grateful; **grātiā,** for the sake of; **Grātiae, –ārum,** *f. pl.,* the Graces
**grātiōsus, –a, –um,** popular, acceptable, agreeable
**Grattius, –tī,** *m.,* Grattius
**grātuītō,** *adv.,* without pay, freely
**grātulātiō, –ōnis,** *f.,* congratulation
**grātulor,** 1, congratulate
**grātus, –a, –um,** pleasing, grateful; **grātum faciō,** do a favor
**gravidus, –a, –um,** heavy
**gravis, –e,** heavy, difficult, important, severe
**gravitās, –tātis,** *f.,* weight, dignity, seriousness

**graviter,** *adv.,* heavily, seriously, strongly
**gravō,** 1, make heavy, weigh down; *pass.,* be reluctant
**Gregorius, –rī,** *m.,* Gregory
**gremium, –mī,** *n.,* bosom
**grex, gregis,** *m.,* herd
**gubernāculum, –ī,** *n.,* rudder; guidance, government
**gubernātiō, –ōnis,** *f.,* control
**gubernātor, –ōris,** *m.,* pilot
**gubernō,** 1, steer, navigate
**gustō,** 1, taste, enjoy
**guttur, –uris,** *n.,* throat
**gymnasium, –sī,** *n.,* gymnasium; lecture room

## H

**habēna, –ae,** *f.,* rein
**habeō, –ēre, habuī, habitus,** have, hold, regard, consider; **grātiam habeō,** feel grateful (*w. dat.*); **ōrātiōnem habeō,** deliver an oration
**habitō,** 1, live, dwell
**habitus, –ūs,** *m.,* nature
**hāctenus,** *adv.,* so far
**haereō, –ēre, haesī, haesus,** stick, cling; be in doubt
**haesitō,** 1, stick fast, be undecided, be at a loss
**Hamilcar, –aris,** *m.,* Hamilcar, *the father of Hannibal*
**Hannibal, –alis,** *m.,* Hannibal, *a Carthaginian general*
**haruspex, –picis,** *m.,* soothsayer, fortune teller
**Hasdrubal, –alis,** *m.,* Hasdrubal, *a brother and an uncle of Hannibal*
**haud,** *adv.,* not, by no means
**hauriō, –īre, hausī, haustus,** draw; empty
**haustus, –ūs,** *m.,* drawing, shedding
**hebēscō, –ere, —, —,** grow dull
**hebētūdō, –inis,** *f.,* bluntness, dullness
**Hecuba, –ae,** *f.,* Hecuba, *wife of Priam, king of Troy*
**Heius, –ī,** *m.,* Heius
**Helicē, –ēs,** *f.,* Helice (Hel´isē), *a constellation*
**Hēraclēa, –ae,** *f.,* Heraclea, *a Greek city in southern Italy*
**Hēracliēnsis, –e,** of Heraclea; *as noun, m.,* a Heraclean
**herba, –ae,** *f.,* herb, plant; *pl.* grass
**hercle!** by Hercules! *(used by men)*
**Herculāneum, –eī,** *n.,* Herculaneum, *a town of Campania*
**Herculēs, –is,** *m.,* Hercules, *a Greek hero*
**hērēditās, –tātis,** *f.,* inheritance
**hērēs, –ēdis,** *m. and f.,* heir, heiress
**herī,** *adv.,* yesterday
**hērōs, –ōis,** *m.,* hero
**Hesperidēs, –um,** *f. pl.,* Hesperides, *daughters of Atlas*
**hesternus, –a, –um,** of yesterday; *w.* **diēs,** yesterday
**heu!** *interj.,* alas!
**hīberna, –ōrum,** *n.,* winter quarters
**Hibernia, –ae,** *f.,* Ireland
**Hibērus, –ī,** *m.,* the Ebro, *a river in Spain*
**hic, haec, hoc,** *dem. pron.,* this, the latter; he, she, it *(enclitic* **–ce** *added for emphasis)*
**hīc,** *adv.,* here, hereupon, in view of this
**hiems, hiemis,** *f.,* winter
**Hieronymus, –ī,** *m.,* Jerome, *a Father of the Church*
**hilaris, –e,** cheerful, glad
**hilaritās, –tātis,** *f.,* gaiety
**hilum, –ī,** *n.,* shred, trifle
**hinc,** *adv.,* from this place; **hinc... illinc,** on this side . . . on that
**hiō,** 1, gape; be amazed; long for
**Hispānia, –ae,** *f.,* Spain
**Hispānus, –ī,** *m.,* Spaniard
**Hister, –trī,** *m.,* Danube River
**historia, –ae,** *f.,* history, account
**hodiē,** *adv.,* today
**hodiernus diēs,** this day, today
**holus, –leris,** *n.,* vegetables
**Homērus, –i,** *m.,* Homer
**hominium, –nī,** *m.,* homage
**homō, hominis,** *m.,* man, person, human being; *pl.,* people
**honestās, –tātis,** *f.,* honor, honesty
**honestō,** 1, honor, distinguish
**honestus, –a, –um,** honorable
**honor, –ōris,** *m.,* honor, office
**honōrābilis, –e,** honorable

**honōrātus, –a, –um,** honored
**hōra, –ae,** *f.,* hour
**hordeum, –ī,** *n.,* barley
**hornus, –a, –um,** of this year
**horrēscō, –ere, horruī, —,** grow rough; tremble
**horribilis, –e,** dreadful
**horridus, –a, –um,** rough, crude, wild
**hortātus, –ūs,** *m.,* urging
**Hortēnsius, –sī,** *m.,* Hortensius
**hortor,** 1, urge, encourage
**hortus, –ī,** *m.,* garden
**hospes, –pitis,** *m. and f.,* stranger, guest; host
**hospita, –ae,** *f.,* guest, stranger
**hospitālis, –e,** of a guest, of a host, hospitable
**hospitium, –tī,** *n.,* hospitality
**hostis,** *m.,* enemy (*usually pl.*)
**hūc,** *adv.,* to this place, here
**hūmānitās, –tātis,** *f.,* kindness, sympathy, culture
**hūmānus, –a, –um,** human, cultured, refining
**humilis, –e,** low, humble
**humus, –ī,** *f.,* ground, earth
**Hydaspēs, –is,** *m., a river in India*
**Hymēn, –enis,** *m.,* Hymen, *the god of marriage*
**Hypaepa, –ōrum,** *n. pl.,* Hypaepa (Hype´pa), *a town at the base of Mt. Tmolus*

## I

**iaceō, –ēre, iacuī, —,** lie, be prostrate
**iaciō, –ere, iēcī, iactus,** throw, hurl
**iactō,** 1, throw, toss; boast of; *w.* **mē,** display myself
**iactus, –ūs,** *m.,* throwing; stroke
**iaculum, –ī,** *n.,* dart, javelin
**iam,** *adv.,* already, now; *w. neg.,* no longer; *of future time,* soon, presently; *w.* **diū dūdum,** *or* **prīdem,** long ago; *w.* **vērō,** furthermore
**iānua, –ae,** *f.,* door
**Iānuārius, –a, –um,** January
**ibi,** *adv.,* there, then
**ibīdem,** *adv.,* in the same place
**Īcarus, –ī,** *m.,* Icarus, *son of Daedalus*
**īcō, (–ere), īcī, ictus,** strike
**idcircō,** *adv.,* for this (that) reason, therefore
**īdem, eadem, idem,** *dem. pron.,* same; also, likewise
**identidem,** *adv.,* again and again
**ideō,** *adv.,* for this reason, therefore
**idōneus, –a, –um,** suitable
**Īdūs, –uum,** *f. pl.,* the Ides *(15th of March, May, July, and October; 13th of the other months)*
**iēiūnus, –a, –um,** poor
**igitur,** *adv.,* therefore
**ignārus, –a, –um,** not knowing, ignorant
**ignāvus, –a, –um,** lazy; cowardly
**ignis, –is,** *m.,* fire
**ignōbilis, –e,** not noble
**ignōminia, –ae,** *f.,* disgrace
**ignōrantia, –ae,** *f.,* want of knowledge, ignorance
**ignōrō,** 1, be ignorant of, not know
**ignōscō, –ere, ignōvī, ignōtus,** overlook; forgive
**ignōtus, –a, –um,** unknown
**īlex, īlicis,** *f.,* oak
**īlia, –ōrum,** *n. pl.,* abdomen, groin
**Ilias, Iliadis,** *f.,* the Iliad
**Ilioneus, –ī,** *m.,* Ilī´oneus, *one of Niobe's sons*
**Ilium, –lī,** *n.,* Troy, *a city in Asia Minor*
**illāc,** *adv.,* that way
**illaesus, –a, –um,** unharmed, unhurt
**ille, illa, illud,** *dem. pron.,* that, the former; he, she, it
**illecebra, –ae,** *f.* enticement
**illīberālis, –e,** ignoble, sordid, mean
**illīc,** *adv.,* in that place, there
**illinc,** *adv.,* from that side
**illinō, –ere, illēvī, illitus,** smear, cover
**illitterātus, –a, –um,** unlettered, illiterate
**illūc,** *adv.,* there
**illūminō,** 1, illuminate, make conspicuous
**illūstris, –e,** brilliant, noble, glorious
**illūstrō,** 1, bring to light, reveal, glorify
**Īllyricus, –a, –um; Illyrius, –a, –um,** Illyrian, *of Illyria, a country on the Adriatic Sea*
**imāgō, –ginis,** *f.,* likeness, image, statue; appearance
**imbecillitās, –tātis,** *f.,* weakness
**imbecillus, –a, –um,** weak
**imber, imbris,** *m.,* rain, storm
**imberbis, –e,** beardless
**imbrifer, –era, –erum,** rain-bringing

**imbuō, –ere, –uī, –ūtus,** wet, soak
**imitābilis, –e,** imitable
**imitātiō, –ōnis,** *f.,* imitation
**imitor,** 1, imitate
**immānis, –e,** vast; savage
**immānitās, –tātis,** *f.,* enormity; fierceness, barbarism
**immātūrus, –a, –um,** untimely
**immēnsus, –a, –um,** immeasurable, boundless
**immineō, –ēre, —, —,** threaten
**immittō, –ere, immīsī, immissus,** let loose, send in *or* against
**immō,** *adv.,* on the contrary; *w.* **vērō,** rather
**immōbilis, –e,** immovable
**immoderātus, –a, –um,** immoderate
**immodicus, –a, –um,** beyond measure, excessive
**immorior, –morī, –mortuus,** die upon
**immoror,** 1, remain in, linger near
**immortālis, –e,** immortal
**immōtus, –a, –um,** unmoved; fixed
**immurmurō,** 1, murmur into
**immūtātus, –a, –um,** changed
**impār,** *gen.* **imparis,** unequal; short
**imparātus, –a, –um,** unprepared
**impatiēns,** *gen.* **–entis,** not bearing, impatient
**impedīmentum, –ī,** *n.,* hindrance, impediment; *pl.,* baggage
**impediō, –īre, –īvī, –ītus,** hinder, prevent
**impellō, –ere, impulī, impulsus,** urge on, prevail upon, induce
**impendeō, –ēre, —, —,** overhang, threaten
**impendium, –dī,** *n.,* outlay, expense
**impēnsa, –ae,** *f.,* expense
**imperātor, –ōris,** *m.,* commander-in-chief, general; emperor
**imperfectus, –a, –um,** unfinished
**imperītus, –a, –um,** inexperienced, ignorant
**imperium, –rī (rīi),** *n.,* command, control, military power, government, empire
**imperō,** 1, command, govern, command (*w. dat.*)
**impertiō, –īre, –īvī, –ītus,** share with, bestow
**impetrō,** 1, gain (a request), obtain
**impetus, –ūs,** *m.,* attack, fury, force; **impetum faciō in** *(w. acc.),* make an attack against
**impiger, –gra, –grum,** diligent, quick
**impius, –a, –um,** undutiful, wicked
**impleō, –ēre, implēvī, implētus,** fill, fulfill
**implicō, –āre, implicuī, implicitus,** enfold, involve, unite
**implōrātiō, –ōnis,** *f.,* entreaty
**implōrō,** 1, implore
**impōnō, –ere, imposuī, impositus,** place upon, put
**importō,** 1, bring
**importūnus, –a, –um,** cruel
**improbitās, –tātis,** *f.,* wickedness, dishonesty
**improbō,** 1, disapprove
**improbus, –a, –um,** wicked
**imprōvīsus, –a, –um,** unexpected
**impudēns,** *gen.* **–entis,** shameless, presumptuous
**impudenter,** *adv.,* impudently
**impudentia, –ae,** *f.,* shamelessness, effrontery
**impudīcus, –a, –um,** shameless
**impūnē,** *adv.,* without punishment
**impūnītus, –a, –um,** unpunished
**impūrus, –a, –um,** vile, impure
**īmus, –a, –um,** *see* **īnferus**
**in,** *prep. w. acc.,* into, to, toward, against, for; *w. abl.,* in, on, upon
**inānis, –e,** empty
**inaurō,** 1, overlay with gold
**incēdo, –ere, incessī, incessus,** advance, proceed
**incēnātus, –a, –um,** without dinner
**incendium, –dī,** *n.,* fire, burning, conflagration
**incendō, –ere, incendī, incēnsus,** set on fire, burn
**incēnsiō, –ōnis,** *f.,* burning
**inceptum, –ī,** *n.,* beginning, undertaking
**incertus, –a, –um,** uncertain
**inchoō,** 1, begin
**incidō, –ere, incidī, —,** fall, happen
**incīdō, –ere, incīdī, incīsus,** cut into
**incipiō, –ere, incēpī, inceptus,** take to, begin
**incitāmentum, –ī,** *n.,* incentive, stimulus
**incitō,** 1, urge on, arouse
**inclinō,** 1, lean, sink
**inclūdō, –ere, inclūsī, inclūsus,** shut up, confine
**inclutus, –a, –um,** famous
**incognitus, –a, –um,** unknown

**incola, –ae,** *m. and f.,* inhabitant
**incolō, –ere, incoluī, incultus,** live, inhabit
**incolumis, –e,** unharmed, safe; undefeated
**incommodum, –ī,** *n.,* inconvenience; loss, defeat
**inconditē,** *adv.,* without order
**incōnsultē,** *adv.,* thoughtlessly
**incorporeus, –a, –um,** incorporeal, without body
**incorruptus, –a, –um,** unspoiled, uninjured
**incrēdibilis, –e,** extraordinary, incredible
**incrēdibiliter,** *adv.,* incredibly
**incultus, –a, –um,** untilled; rude
**incumbō, –ere, incubuī, incubitus,** bend to, devote oneself, press on
**incūnābula, –ōrum,** *n. pl.,* cradle, birthplace, beginnings
**incurrō, –ere, –currī, –cursus,** run into *or* up against
**inde,** *adv.,* then, from there
**index, –dicis,** *m.,* informer, witness
**indicium, –cī,** *n.,* testimony, proof
**indicō,** 1, point out, prove
**indictus, –a, –um,** declared
**indigēns,** *gen.* **–entis,** in need of, wanting
**indignātiō, –ōnis,** *f.,* indignation
**indignē,** *adv.,* unworthily
**indignor,** 1, regard as unworthy; be angry
**indignus, –a, –um,** unworthy
**indocilis, –e,** unteachable, ignorant
**indoctus, –a, –um,** ignorant; unskilled
**indolēs, –is,** *f.,* native quality, nature
**indolēscō, –ere, indoluī, —,** be grieved
**indūcō, –ere, indūxī, inductus,** bring in, influence
**indulgentia, –ae,** *f.,* kindness
**indulgeō, –ēre, indulsī, indultus,** yield to, favor
**induō, –ere, induī, indūtus,** put on, assume
**Indus, –a, –um,** Indian
**industria, –ae,** *f.,* diligence, care
**industrius, –a, –um,** enterprising
**inedia, –ae,** *f.,* fasting
**ineō, inīre, iniī, initus,** enter upon
**inermis, –e,** unarmed
**inerrō,** 1, wander, roam upon
**iners,** *gen.* **inertis,** unskilled; sluggish
**inertia, –ae,** *f.,* lack of skill, inactivity, laziness
**inexpiābilis, –e,** irreconcilable, implacable
**inexplēbilis, –e,** insatiable
**infāmia, –ae,** *f.,* disgrace
**īnfēlīx,** *gen.* **īnfēlīcis,** unhappy, unfortunate
**īnferī, –ōrum,** *m.,* inhabitants of the Underworld
**īnferō, īnferre, intulī, illātus,** apply, bring
**īnferus, –a, –um,** below; *as noun, m. pl.,* the dead; *comp.* **īnferior, -ius,** lower; *superl.,* **īnfimus, īmus,** lowest
**īnfēstus, –a, –um,** hostile, dangerous
**īnfimus,** *see* **īnferus**
**īnfīnītus, –a, –um,** endless
**īnfirmitās, –tātis,** *f.,* sickness, weakness
**īnfirmō,** 1, weaken, refute
**īnfirmus, –a, –um,** weak, sick
**īnfitior,** 1, deny
**īnflammō,** 1, set on fire, burn; inflame
**inflexibilis, –e,** unbending, inflexible
**īnflō,** 1, blow into; inspire
**īnfōrmō,** 1, mold, train
**īnfrā,** *adv.,* below
**ingemēscō, –ere, –uī, —,** groan, sigh (over)
**ingeniōsus, –a, –um,** clever
**ingenium, –nī,** *n.,* ability, nature, spirit, genius
**ingēns,** *gen.* **ingentis,** huge
**ingenuē,** *adv.,* nobly
**ingenuus, –a, –um,** noble
**ingerō, –ere, ingessī, ingestus,** press upon
**ingrātus, –a, –um,** ungrateful
**ingravēscō, –ere, —, —,** become heavier, grow worse
**ingredior, ingredī, ingressus,** step into, enter (upon)
**ingressus, –ūs,** *m.,* entrance
**inhabitō,** 1, dwell in
**inhaereō, –ēre, inhaesī, inhaesus,** cling, stick to
**inhibeō, –ēre, –uī, –itus,** restrain
**inhiō,** 1, gape
**inhonestus, –a, –um,** dishonorable
**inhospitālis, –e,** inhospitable
**inhūmānus, –a, –um,** inhuman; rude
**iniciō, –ere, iniēcī, iniectus,** throw into, cause, inspire
**inimīcitia, –ae,** *f.,* enmity

**inimīcus, –a, –um,** unfriendly, hostile; *as noun, m.,* enemy

**inīquitās, –tātis,** *f.,* unfairness, injustice

**inīquus, –a, –um,** unequal, sloping; unfavorable, discontented

**initiō,** 1, initiate, consecrate

**initium, –tī,** *n.,* beginning

**iniūrātus, –a, –um,** not having sworn

**iniūria, –ae,** *f.,* injustice, wrong, injury

**iniūriōsus, –a, –um,** harmful

**iniūrus, –a, –um,** unjust

**iniūstus, –a, –um,** unjust

**innītor, innītī, innīxus,** lean upon

**innocēns,** *gen.* **–entis,** harmless

**innocentia, –ae,** *f.,* innocence

**innumerābilis, –e,** countless

**innumerus, –a, –um,** countless

**innuptus, –a, –um,** unmarried; *as noun, f.,* virgin

**innūtriō, –īre, –īvī, –ītus,** nourish

**inopia, –ae,** *f.,* lack (of funds), poverty, need

**inops,** *gen.* **inopis,** poor

**inōrnātus, –a, –um,** unadorned

**inprīmīs,** *adv.,* especially

**inquam, inquis, inquit,** *defective,* say; **inquit,** he/she says

**inquinō,** 1, stain, defile

**inquīrō, –ere, inquīsīvī, inquīsītus,** inquire (into)

**īnsānia, –ae,** *f.,* madness

**insānus, –a, –um,** insane

**īnsciēns,** *gen.* **–entis,** not knowing

**īnscitia, –ae,** *f.,* ignorance

**īnscius, –a, –um,** not knowing; ignorant

**īnscrībō, –ere, īnscrīpsī, īnscrīptus,** inscribe, entitle

**īnscrīptiō, –ōnis,** *f.,* inscription

**īnsecō, –āre, īnsecuī, īnsectus,** cut into

**īnsector,** 1, attack

**īnsepultus, –a, –um,** unburied

**īnsequor, īnsequī, īnsecūtus,** follow up, pursue

**īnserō, –ere, īnseruī, īnsertus,** thrust into

**īnsideō, –ēre, īnsēdī, īnsessus,** (sit upon), take possession of; dwell, be fixed

**īnsidiae, –ārum,** *f. pl.,* plot, danger

**īnsidior,** 1, plot against

**īnsigne, –is,** *n.,* mark

**īnsignis, –e,** remarkable, notable

**īnsiliō, –īre, –uī, —,** leap upon

**īnsinuō,** 1, ingratiate oneself

**īnsistō, –ere, īnstitī, —,** pursue

**īnsolēns,** *gen.* **–entis,** unaccustomed; haughty

**īnsolentia, –ae,** *f.,* insolence

**īnsolitus, –a, –um,** unusual

**īnsonō, –āre, –uī, —,** play on

**īnspērātus, –a, –um,** unexpected

**īnspiciō, –ere, īnspexī, īnspectus,** look at, inspect, examine

**īnstabilis, –e,** unstable

**īnstanter,** *adv.,* earnestly

**instituō, –ere, instituī, institūtus,** establish, decide (upon), begin; train

**instō, –āre, institī, —,** threaten, press on, pursue

**īnstringō, –ere, īnstrīnxī, īnstrictus,** fasten; set

**instruō, –ere, īnstrūxī, instrūctus,** arrange, provide, draw up, instruct

**īnsula, –ae,** *f.,* island

**īnsulānus, –ī,** *m.,* islander

**īnsum, inesse, īnfuī —,** be in

**integer, –gra, –grum,** untouched, fresh

**intellegō, –ere, –lexī, –lectus,** understand

**intempestus, –a, –um,** timeless; unhealthy

**intendō, –ere, intendī, intentus,** stretch, intend

**inter,** *prep. w. acc.,* between, among

**intereā,** *adv.,* meanwhile

**intercipiō, –ere, –cēpī, –ceptus,** intercept, cut off, steal

**interclūdō, –ere, –clūsī, –clūsus,** cut off

**interdiū,** *adv.,* for awhile

**interficiō, –ere, –fēcī, –fectus,** kill

**interiaceō, –ēre, –uī, —,** lie between

**interim,** *adv.,* meanwhile

**interimō –ere, –ēmī, ēmptus,** kill

**interitus, –ūs,** *m.,* destruction, death

**interius,** *adv.,* within

**intermittō, –ere, –mīsī, –missus,** let go, stop, interrupt, neglect

**interneciō, –ōnis,** *f.,* massacre

**internōdium, –dī,** *n.,* space between two joints

**internus, –a, –um,** inward, internal

**interpellātiō, –ōnis,** *f.,* interruption

**interpres, –pretis,** *m.,* interpreter
**interrogātiō, –ōnis,** *f.,* inquiry, examination
**interrogō,** 1, ask
**intersum, –esse, –fuī, –futūrus,** be between, be present, be different
**intervāllum, –ī,** *n.,* interval, distance
**interveniō, –īre, –vēnī, –ventus,** come in (between), interrupt
**interventus, –ūs,** *m.,* intervention
**intestīnus, –a, –um,** internal, civil
**intexō, –ere, –texuī, –textus,** interweave, envelop
**intimō,** 1, intimate
**intimus, –a, –um,** inmost
**intōnsus, –a, –um,** unshorn, long-haired
**intrā,** *prep. w. acc.,* within
**intrepidus, –a, –um,** unshaken, undaunted
**intrō,** 1, enter
**intrōdūcō, –ere, –dūxī, –ductus,** bring in, introduce
**introeō, –īre, –iī, –itus,** enter
**intueor, –ērī, –itus,** look at *or* upon
**inūrō, –ere, inussī, inustus,** burn in, brand
**inūsitātus, –a, –um,** unusual
**inūtilis, –e,** useless
**invādō, –ere, invāsī, invāsus,** rush upon, seize
**inveniō, –īre, invēnī, inventus,** find, come upon, invent
**inventiō, –ōnis,** *f.,* invention
**invēstīgō,** 1, track, discover
**inveterāscō, –ere, –āvī, —,** become established
**invicem,** *adv.,* in turn, alternately
**invictus, –a, –um,** unconquered, invincible
**invideō, –ēre, invīdī, invīsus,** envy
**invidia, –ae,** *f.,* envy, unpopularity
**invidiōsus, –a, –um,** hateful
**invidus, –a, –um,** envious
**inviolātē,** *adv.,* inviolably
**invīsitātus, –a, –um,** uncommon
**invīsus, –a, –um,** hated, displeasing
**invītō,** 1, invite
**invītus, –a, –um,** unwilling
**involvō, –ere, involvī, involūtus,** wrap up in, bury
**iō,** *interj.,* hurrah!
**iocor,** 1, joke
**iocōsus, –a, –um,** humorous
**iocus, –ī,** *m. (pl.* **ioca,** *n.),* joke
**Iovis, Iovī,** *see* **Iuppiter**
**ipse, ipsa, ipsum,** –self, the very
**īra, –ae,** *f.,* anger
**īrāscor, –ī, īrātus,** be angry at
**irreparābiliter,** *adv.,* irreparably
**irrēpō, –ere, irrēpsī, —,** creep in
**irrētiō, –īre, –īvī, –ītus,** ensnare
**irrigō,** 1, water, irrigate
**irritō,** 1, excite, stir up
**is, ea, id,** *dem. pron.,* this, that; *as pron.,* he, she, it
**Ismēnus, –ī,** *m.,* Ismenus, *one of Niobe's sons*
**iste, ista, istud,** *dem. pron.,* that (of yours), such this; that fellow
**istīc,** *adv.,* there
**istōc,** *adv.,* that way
**ita,** *adv.,* so, in this way, thus; as follows; *w.* **ut,** just as
**Italia, –ae,** *f.,* Italy
**Italicus, –a, –um,** Italian
**itaque,** *adv.,* and so, therefore, accordingly, and as a result
**item,** *adv.,* also
**iter, itineris,** *n.,* journey, road, march, route
**iterum,** *adv.,* again, a second time
**itō, itāre, —, —,** go
**iubeō, –ēre, iussī, iussus,** order, command
**iūcunditās, –tātis,** *f.,* pleasantness, delight
**iūcundus, –a, –um,** pleasant, agreeable
**iūdex, iūdicis,** *m.,* judge, juror
**iūdiciālis, –e,** judicial
**iūdicium, –cī,** *n.,* judgment, opinion, trial; court
**iūdicō,** 1, judge
**iugālis, –e,** yoked, together
**iūgerum, –ī,** *n.,* acre
**iugulum, –ī,** *n.,* throat
**iugum, –ī,** *n.,* yoke; ridge
**Iūlius, –lī,** *m.,* Julius; **Iūlia, –ae,** *f.,* Julia
**iūnctim,** *adv.,* jointly, together
**iungō, –ere, iūnxī, iūnctus,** join (to), harness
**iūnior, –ius,** younger, junior
**Iūnius, –a, –um,** of June
**Iūnō, –ōnis,** *f.,* Juno, *a goddess, sister and wife of Jupiter*

**Iūnōnius, –a, –um,** sacred to Juno
**Iuppiter, Iovis,** *m.,* Jupiter, *king of the gods*
**iūrgium, –gī,** *n.,* quarrel
**iūrō,** 1, take an oath, swear
**iūs, iūris,** *n.,* right, justice, law, authority; **iūs iūrandum, iūris, –ī,** *n.,* oath
**iussū,** *abl.,* by order
**iussum, –ī,** *n.,* order
**iūstē,** *adv.,* justly
**iūstitia, –ae,** *f.,* justice
**iūstus, –a, –um,** just, proper
**iuvenālis, –e,** youthful
**iuvenis, –is,** *m. and f.,* youth
**iuventa, –ae,** *f.,* **iuventūs, –tūtis,** *f.,* youth
**iuvō, –āre, iūvī, iūtus,** help, aid; please
**iūxtā,** *adv. and prep. w. acc.,* near, close to

## L

**L.,** *abbreviation for* **Lūcius**
**labefactō,** 1, cause to fall, weaken, destroy
**labellum, –ī,** *n.,* little lip
**labor, –ōris,** *m.,* work, trouble, effort, hardship
**lābor, –ī, lāpsus,** slip, glide; err
**labōrō,** 1, work
**labrum, –ī,** *n.,* lip; edge, tub
**lac, lactis,** *n.,* milk
**Lacedaemonius, –a, –um,** Spartan
**lacer, –era, –erum,** shattered
**lacertus, –ī,** *m.,* arm
**lacessō, –ere, lacessīvī, lacessītus,** provoke, attack
**lacrima, –ae,** *f.,* tear
**lacrimō,** 1, weep
**lactō,** 1, suck milk
**lacus, –ūs,** *m.,* lake
**Laeca, –ae,** *m.,* Laeca (Le´ka)
**laedō, –ere, laesī, laesus,** hurt
**Laelius, –lī,** *m.,* Laelius
**laetitia, –ae,** *f.,* joy
**laetor,** 1, be glad, rejoice
**laetus, –a, –um,** joyous, glad
**laevus, –a, –um,** left
**Lalagē, –ēs,** *f.,* Lalage (Lal´ajē), *a girl's name*
**lambō, –ere, lambī, lambitus,** lick
**lāmentātiō, –ōnis,** *f.,* lamentation
**lancea, –ae,** *f.,* lance
**languidus, –a, –um,** weak
**laniō,** 1, tear (in pieces)
**lanterna, –ae,** *f.,* lantern
**lapidātiō, –ōnis,** *f.,* stoning
**lapis, lapidis,** *m.,* stone
**lāpsus, –ūs,** *m.,* gliding, flight
**Lar, Laris,** *m.,* Lar, hearth; *a household god; w.* **familiāris,** home
**lardum, –ī,** *n.,* lard
**largior, –īrī, ītus,** be lavish, bestow
**largītiō, –ōnis,** *f.,* gift
**largus, –a, –um,** plentiful, large
**lascīvē,** *adv.,* wantonly, licentiously
**lascīvus, –a, –um,** wanton, playful
**lassitūdō, –tūdinis,** *f.,* weariness
**lassus, –a, –um,** tired
**lātē,** *adv.,* widely, far and wide
**latebra, –ae,** *f.,* secret code; *pl.,* hiding place
**lateō, –ēre, latuī, —,** lie hidden, hide, escape notice
**Latīnē,** *adv.,* in Latin
**Latīnus, –a, –um,** Latin, belonging to Latium; **Latīni, –ōrum,** *m.,* the Latins
**Latīnus, –ī,** *m.,* Latinus
**Latium, –tī,** *n.,* Latium (Lā´shium), *a district of central Italy*
**Latius, –a, –um,** of Latium
**Lātōna, –ae,** *f.,* Latona, *mother of Apollo and Diana*
**Lātōus, –a, –um,** of Latona
**latrō, –ōnis,** *m.,* bandit, robber
**latrōcinium, –nī,** *n.,* robbery, brigandage
**latrōcinor,** 1, plunder
**latus, lateris,** *n.,* side, flank
**lātus, –a, –um,** wide, broad
**laudātor, –ōris,** *m.,* praiser
**laudō,** 1, praise
**Laurentīnus, –a, –um,** of Laurentum
**laurus, –ī,** *f.,* laurel
**laus, laudis,** *f.,* praise
**lavō, –āre, lāvī, lautus,** wash, bathe
**laxō,** 1, relax
**laxus, –a, –um,** open, relaxed
**lea, –ae; leaena, –ae,** *f.,* lioness

**Lebinthus, –ī,** *f.,* Lebinthus, *an island in the Aegean*
**lēctiō, –ōnis,** *f.,* reading
**lēctitō,** 1, read eagerly
**lēctor, –ōris,** *m.,* reader
**lēctus, –a, –um,** choice, excellent
**lectus, –ī,** *m.,* couch, bed
**lēgātus, –ī,** *m.,* envoy; legate, lieutenant general
**legiō, –ōnis,** *f.,* legion
**lēgitimē,** *adv.,* lawfully
**lēgitimus, –a, –um,** lawful
**lēgō,** 1, appoint, bequeath
**legō, –ere, lēgī, lectus,** collect, gather, choose, pick; read
**lēniō, –īre, –īvī, –ītus,** soften, conciliate
**lēnis, –e,** gentle, mild
**lēnitās, –tātis,** *f.,* leniency
**lentē,** *adv.,* slowly
**Lentulus, –ī,** *m.,* Lentulus
**lentus, –a, –um,** flexible; slow, lazy
**leō, –ōnis,** *m.,* lion
**lepidus, –a, –um,** charming
**Lepidus, –ī,** *m.,* Lepidus
**lepōs, –ōris,** *m.,* charm
**lētum, –ī,** *n.,* death
**levāmen, –minis,** *n.,* relief
**levis, –e,** light (*in weight*); trivial
**levitās, –tātis,** *f.,* lack of principle
**leviter,** *adv.,* lightly, gently
**levō,** 1, lift, lighten, relieve
**lēx, lēgis,** *f.,* law, condition, bill
**libellus, –ī,** *m.,* (little) book, manuscript; indictment
**libenter,** *adv.,* gladly, with pleasure
**līber, –era, –erum,** free, unrestricted
**Līber, –erī,** *m.,* Bacchus
**liber, librī,** *m.,* book
**Lībera, –ae,** *f.,* Proserpina
**līberālis, –e,** liberal
**līberē,** *adv.,* freely; boldly
**līberī, –ōrum,** *m. pl.,* children
**līberō,** 1, free, set free
**lībertās, –tātis,** *f.,* freedom, liberty
**lībertīnus, –ī,** *m.,* freedman
**lībertus, –ī,** *m.,* freedman
**libet, –ēre, libuit** *or* **libitum,** it pleases
**libīdo, –dinis,** *f.,* longing, pleasure, lust
**lībō,** 1, sip, offer; skim
**librārius, –rī,** *m.,* secretary
**librō,** 1, balance
**licentia, –ae,** *f.,* liberty, freedom
**licet, –ēre, licuit** *or* **licitum,** it is permitted, one may
**Liciniānus, –ī,** *m.,* Licinianus
**Licinius, –nī,** *m.,* Licinius (Lisin´ius)
**ligneus, –a, –um,** wooden
**lignum, –ī,** *n.,* piece of wood; *n. pl.,* firewood
**ligō,** 1, bind, tie
**līmen, līminis,** *n.,* threshold, door
**līmes, līmitis,** *m.,* path
**līneāmentum, –ī,** *n.,* line, feature
**lingua, –ae,** *f.,* tongue, language
**līnum, –ī,** *n.,* string, thread
**liquefaciō, –ere, –fēcī, –factus,** melt
**liquidus, –a, –um,** flowing, clear
**līquor, –ī, —, —,** flow, melt
**līs, lītis,** *f.,* lawsuit
**littera, –ae,** *f.,* letter (*of the alphabet*), *pl.,* a letter (*epistle*), letters (*if modified by an adjective such as* **multae**), literature; learning
**litterātus, –a, –um,** lettered, well educated
**litūra, –ae,** *f.,* erasure
**lītus, –ōris,** *n.,* shore
**līvēns,** *gen.* **–entis,** black and blue, bruised
**Līvius, –vī,** *m.,* Livy, *a Roman historian*
**locō,** 1, place
**locuplēs,** *gen.* **–ētis,** rich
**locuplētō,** 1, enrich
**locus, –ī,** *m.,* (*pl.* **loca, –ōrum,** *n.*), place, room, rank, occasion
**longē,** *adv.,* far, far away, by far; long
**longus, –a, –um,** long; distant
**loquāx,** *gen.* **–ācis,** talkative, chattering
**loquor, loquī, locūtus,** speak, talk
**Lūcānus, –ī,** *m.,* Lucan, *a Roman poet*
**lūceō, –ēre, lūxī, —,** be light, shine
**lūcidus, –a, –um,** bright, shining
**Lūcilius, –lī,** *m.,* Lucilius
**Lūcius, –cī,** *m.,* Lucius
**lucrum, –ī,** *n.,* gain, profit

**luctāns**, *gen.* **–antis**, struggling, reluctant
**lūctus, –ūs**, *m.*, sorrow, affliction
**lūculentus, –a, –um**, brilliant
**Lūcullus, –ī**, *m.*, Lucullus
**lūcus, –ī**, *m.*, grove
**lūdō, –ere, lūsī, lūsus**, play
**lūdus, ī**, *m.*, game, sport; school; *pl.*, public games
**lūgeō, –ēre, lūxī, lūctus**, mourn
**lūmen, lūminis**, *n.*, light; eye
**lūmināre, –āris**, *n.*, lamp
**lūna, –ae**, *f.*, moon
**luō, –ere, luī, —**, loose; suffer
**lupus, –ī**, *m.*, wolf
**Lūsitānia, –ae**, *f.*, Portugal
**Lūsitānus, –a, –um**, Lusitanian, Portuguese
**lūstrō**, 1, light up, survey
**lūsus, –ūs**, *m.*, playing
**lūx, lūcis**, *f.*, light, daylight; life
**lūxuria, –ae**, *f.*, extravagance
**Lydus, –a, –um**, Lydian

## M

**M.**, *abbreviation for* **Mārcus, –ī**, *m.*, Marcus; **M'** *for* **Mānius, –nī**, *m.*, Manius
**māchinātor, –ōris**, *m.*, plotter
**māchinor**, 1, devise, plot
**maciēs, –ēī**, *f.*, thinness
**mactē**, *interj.*, well done!
**mactō**, 1, sacrifice, put to death, afflict
**madefaciō, –ere, –fēcī, –factus**, soak
**mādēscō, –ere, maduī, —**, become moist
**madidus, –a, –um**, drenched, dripping
**maestus, –a, –um**, sad
**magis**, *adv.*, more, rather; *superl.* **maximē**, most, especially
**magister, –trī**, *m.*, teacher
**magistra, –ae**, *f.*, teacher
**magistrātus, –ūs**, *m.*, (public) office; magistrate
**magnificēns**, *gen.* **–entis**, magnifying, glorifying
**magnificus, –a, –um**, splendid
**magnitūdō, –dinis**, *f.*, greatness, size, importance
**magnus, –a, –um**, large, great; *comp.* **maior, maius**, greater; **maiōrēs (nātū)**, older men, ancestors, forefathers; *superl.* **maximus, –a, –um**, greatest, very great; **magnō opere** *or* **magnopere**, greatly
**maiestās, –tātis**, *f.*, majesty
**maior**, *see* **magnus**
**Maius, –a, –um**, of May
**male**, *adv.*, badly, unsuccessfully; *comp.*, **peius**, worse; *superl.* **pessimē**, worst
**maledīcō, –ere, –dīxī, –dictus**, curse
**maledictum, –ī**, *n.*, insult
**maleficium, –cī**, *n.*, evil deed, wrong
**malivolentia, –ae**, *f.*, hatred, envy
**malleolus, –ī**, *m.*, firebrand
**mālō, mālle, māluī, —**, prefer
**malum, –ī**, *n.*, evil, trouble
**mālum, –ī**, *n.*, apple
**malus, –a, –um**, bad; *comp.* **peior, peius**, worse; *superl.* **pessimus, –a, –um**, very bad, worst
**Mamertīnus, –a, –um**, of Messina
**mandātum, –ī**, *n.*, order, instruction, command
**mandātū**, by order
**mandō**, 1, commit, instruct, entrust
**māne**, *adv.*, early in the morning
**maneō, –ēre, mānsī, mānsus**, remain, last
**manicae, –ārum**, *f. pl.*, handcuffs
**manifēstus, –a, –um**, clear, plain
**Mānius, –nī**, *m.*, Manius
**Mānliānus, –a, –um**, of Manlius
**Mānlius, –lī**, *m.*, Manlius
**mānō**, 1, flow, drip
**mānsuētūdō, –dinis**, *f.*, gentleness
**Mantua, –ae**, *f.*, Mantua, *a town of northern Italy*
**manus, –ūs**, *f.*, hand, handwriting; force, band
**Mārcius, –cī**, *m.*, Marcius (Mar´shus)
**Mārcus, –ī**, *m.*, Marcus
**mare, maris**, *n.*, sea
**marītus, –ī**, *m.*, husband
**Marius, –rī**, *m.*, Marius, *a Roman general*
**marmor, –oris**, *n.*, marble
**marmoreus, –a, –um**, made of marble, marble
**Marō, –ōnis**, *m.*, Maro (Vergil)
**Maronilla, –ae**, *f.*, Maronilla
**Mārs, Mārtis**, *m.*, Mars, *god of war*
**Martiālis, –is**, *m.*, Martial
**Martīnus, –ī**, *m.*, Martin
**massa, –ae**, *f.*, mass; mound, lump (of gold)
**māter, mātris**, *f.*, mother
**māteria, –ae**, *f.*, matter, timber

**mātrimōnium, –nī,** *n.,* marriage
**mātūrēscō, –ere, mātūruī, —,** come to maturity
**mātūritās, –tātis,** *f.,* ripeness, maturity
**mātūrō,** 1, hasten
**mātūrus, –a, –um,** ripe, mature; early
**Maurī, –ōrum,** *m. pl.,* the Moors, Mauritanians
**maximē,** *adv.,* very greatly, especially; *see* **magis**
**Maximīna, –ae,** *f.,* Maximina
**maximus,** *see* **magnus**
**Maximus, –ī,** *m.,* Maximus
**mēcastor!** *interj.,* by Castor!
**medicāmentum, –ī,** *n.,* medicine
**medicīna, –ae,** *f.,* medicine
**medicus, –ī,** *m.,* doctor, physician
**mediocris, –cre,** moderate, ordinary
**mediocritās, –tātis,** *f.,* mean, moderation; mediocrity
**mediocriter,** *adv.,* slightly, moderately
**Mediterrāneum (Mare),** Mediterranean Sea
**meditor,** 1, plan, compose
**medius, –a, –um,** middle; midst (of); intervening; *as noun, n.,* middle
**medulla, –ae,** *f.,* marrow
**mehercule, meherculēs!** *interj.,* by Hercules!
**mel, mellis,** *n.,* honey
**melior,** *see* **bonus**
**membrum, –ī,** *n.,* limb, member
**meminī, meminisse,** *(perf. translated as pres.),* remember
**memor, –oris,** mindful of
**memorābilis, –e,** memorable
**memoria, –ae,** *f.,* memory; **memoriā teneō,** remember
**memorō,** 1, call to mind, relate
**mendācium, –cī,** *n.,* lie
**mendāx,** *gen.* **–ācis,** lying
**mēns, mentis,** *f.,* mind, intention, feeling, heart
**mēnsa, –ae,** *f.,* table, banquet
**mēnsis, –is,** *m.,* month
**mēnsūra, –ae,** *f.,* measurement, extent
**mentiō, –ōnis,** *f.,* mention
**mentior, –īrī, –ītus,** lie, deceive; invent
**mentum, –ī,** *n.,* chin
**mercātor, –ōris,** *m.,* merchant
**mercātūra, –ae,** *f.,* trade
**mercennārius, –rī,** *m.,* hired man
**mercēs, –ēdis,** *f.,* pay, reward
**mercor,** 1, trade
**Mercurius, –rī,** *m.,* Mercury
**mereō, –ēre, meruī, meritus,** deserve, earn
**mergō, –ere, mersī, mersus,** sink
**merīdiēs, –ēī,** *m.,* noon
**Messāla, –ae,** *m.,* Messala
**–met,** *enclitic,* -self
**mēta, –ae,** *f.,* goal, turning post (*in the Circus*)
**metuō, –ere, –uī, —,** fear
**metus, –ūs,** *m.,* fear
**meus, –a, –um,** my, mine
**micō,** 1, flash
**migrō,** 1, depart
**mīles, mīlitis,** *m.,* soldier
**mīlitia, –ae,** *f.,* warfare
**mīlle,** *pl.,* **mīlia,** thousand
**Minerva, –ae,** *f.,* Minerva, *a goddess*
**minister, –trī,** *m.,* **ministra, –ae,** *f.,* servant
**minimē,** *adv.,* not at all; *interj.,* no
**minimus, minor,** *see* **parvus**
**minor,** 1, jut out, threaten
**Mīnōs, –ōis,** *m.,* Minos
**mīrābilis, –e,** remarkable
**mīrāculum, –ī,** *n.,* miracle
**mīrē,** *adv.,* wonderfully, strangely
**mīrificus, –a, –um,** singular, extraordinary
**mīror,** 1, wonder, admire
**mīrus, –a, –um,** strange, wonderful
**misceō, –ēre, –uī, mixtus,** mix, mingle
**miser, –era, –erum,** unhappy, poor, wretched
**miserābilis, –e,** pitiable, wretched
**miserātiō, –ōnis,** *f.,* pity
**miserē,** *adv.,* wretchedness, miserably
**misereor, –ērī, misertus,** pity
**miseria, –ae,** *f.,* wretchedness, trouble
**misericordia, –ae,** *f.,* pity
**misericors, –cordis,** compassionate
**miseror,** 1, pity
**Mithridātēs, –is,** *m.,* Mithridā´tes, *king of Pontus*
**Mithridāticus –a, –um,** Mithridatic

**mītis, –e,** mild, kind
**mittō, –ere, mīsī, missus,** let go, send
**mōbilitas, –tātis,** *f.,* fickleness
**moderātus, –a, –um,** self-controlled, restrained
**moderor,** 1, guide
**modestia, –ae,** *f.,* restraint
**modestus, –a, –um,** moderate, scrupulous
**modicus, –a, –um,** moderate, small
**modius, –dī,** *m.,* bushel
**modo,** *adv.,* only, merely; just now; **nōn modo... sed** (*or* **vērum) etiam,** not only . . . but also; **modo... modo,** now . . . now; *conj.,* provided (that)
**modus, –ī,** *m.,* measure; moderation; manner, method, way; **quem ad modum,** how, as; **eius** (or **huius**) **modī,** of this kind, such
**moenia, –ium,** *n. pl.,* (city) walls
**mōlēs, –is,** *f.,* mass, burden
**molestia, –ae,** *f.,* annoyance
**molestus, –a, –um,** troublesome, annoying, disagreeable
**mōlior, –īrī, –ītus,** strive, plan, undertake; plot
**molliō, –īre, –īvī, –ītus,** soften
**mollis, –e,** soft; easy, mild
**molliter,** *adv.,* softly, gently
**molō, –ere, –uī, –itus,** grind
**Molossī, –ōrum,** *m. pl.,* the Molossians, *people of Epirus*
**monastērium, –rī,** *n.,* monastery
**moneō, –ēre, –uī, –itus,** remind, warn, advise; suggest
**monitus, –ūs,** *m.,* warning
**mōns, montis,** *m.,* mountain, hill
**mōnstrō,** 1, point out, show, indicate
**montānus, –a, –um,** of the mountains
**monumentum, –ī,** *n.,* memorial, monument, remembrance
**mora, –ae,** *f.,* delay
**morbus, –ī,** *m.,* disease
**mordeō, –ēre, momordī, morsus,** bite
**moribundus, –a, –um,** dying
**morior, morī, mortuus,** die
**moror,** 1, delay, linger
**mors, mortis,** *f.,* death
**morsus, –ūs,** *m.,* biting, teeth
**mortālis, –e,** mortal, human; *as noun, m.,* a mortal
**mortuus, –a, –um,** dead
**mōs, mōris,** *m.,* custom, manner; *pl.,* customs, character
**mōtus, –ūs,** *m.,* movement, activity
**moveō, –ēre, mōvī, mōtus,** move; influence, disturb
**mox,** *adv.,* soon
**mūcrō, –ōnis,** *m.,* point, edge
**mulcō,** 1, beat, injure
**muliebris, –e,** womanly, feminine
**mulier, mulieris,** *f.,* woman
**mūliō, –ōnis,** *m.,* mule driver
**multiplex, –icis,** manifold, many
**multitūdo, –dinis,** *f.,* multitude, great number
**multō,** 1, punish
**multō,** *adv.,* much, by far
**multum,** *adv.,* much; *comp.,* **plūs,** more; *superl.,* **plūrimum,** most
**multus, –a, –um,** much; *pl.,* many; *comp.* **plūrēs, plūra,** more, several; *superl.* **plūrimus, –a, –um,** most, very many
**mūlus, –ī,** *m.,* mule
**Mulvius, –a, –um,** Mulvian
**munditia, –ae,** *f.,* neatness
**mundus, –ī,** *m.,* world
**mūniceps, –cipis,** *m.,* fellow citizen
**municipālis, –e,** of the towns
**mūnicipium, –pī,** *n.,* town
**mūnificentia, –ae,** *f.,* generosity
**mūniō, –īre, –īvī, –ītus,** fortify, defend; **viam mūniō,** build a road
**mūnus, mūneris,** *n.,* duty, office, service; gift
**mūrex, –ricis,** *m.,* (shellfish), purple
**murmur, –uris,** *n.,* whisper
**mūrus, –ī,** *m.,* wall
**mūs, mūris,** *m.,* mouse
**Mūsa, –ae,** *f.,* Muse, *one of the nine goddesses of the fine arts*
**mūsica, –ae,** *f.,* music
**mūtātiō, –ōnis,** *f.,* change
**mutātus, –a, –um,** changed
**mūtō,** 1, change
**muttiō, –īre, –īvī, —,** mutter

**mūtus, –a, –um,** mute
**mūtuus, –a, –um,** mutual

## N

**nactus,** *part. of* **nancīscor**
**Naevius, –vī,** *m.,* Naevius
**nam, namque,** *conj.,* for
**nancīscor, nancīscī, nactus (nānctus),** get, gain, obtain, find, meet with
**Nannēs, –is,** *m.,* Nannes, *brother of Pope Pius II*
**nārrō,** 1, tell, relate
**nāscor, nāscī, nātus,** be born, be found; **duōs annōs nātus,** two years old; **nātus, –ī,** *m.,* son
**Nāsō, –ōnis,** *m.,* P. Ovidius Naso, *the poet Ovid*
**nāsus, –ī,** *m.,* nose
**nātālis, –e,** of one's birth; *as noun, m.,* birthday, natural
**nātiō, –ōnis,** *f.,* nation, tribe
**natō,** 1, swim, float
**nātūra, –ae,** *f.,* nature, character
**nātūrālis, –e,** natural
**nātus, –a, –um,** born; *as noun, m. and f.,* son, daughter; *pl.,* children
**nausiābundus, –a, –um,** seasick
**nauta, –ae,** *m.,* sailor
**nāvālis, –e,** naval
**nāvicula, –ae,** *f.,* small vessel, boat
**nāvigātiō, –ōnis,** *f.,* sailing
**nāvigō,** 1, sail
**nāvis, –is,** *f.,* ship
**nē,** *adv.,* no, not; **nē... quidem** *(emphatic word between),* not even; *conj.,* that . . . not, not to, lest, for fear that
**–ne,** (*enclitic*), *introduces question;* whether
**nebula, –ae,** *f.,* mist, cloud
**nec,** *see* **neque**
**necdum,** *adv.,* not yet
**necessārius, –a, –um,** necessary; *as noun, m.,* relative, friend
**necesse,** *indecl. adj.,* necessary
**necessitās, –tātis,** *f.,* necessity
**necessitūdō, –dinis,** *f.,* necessity; relationship
**necō,** 1, kill, put to death, murder
**necopīnātus, –a, –um,** unexpected
**nectar, –aris,** *n.,* nectar, *the drink of the gods*
**nefārius, –a, –um,** impious, base
**nefās,** *indeclinable, n.,* sin
**neglegēns,** *gen.* **–entis,** careless
**neglegenter,** *adv.,* carelessly
**neglegentia, –ae,** *f.,* negligence
**neglegō, –ere, –lēxī, –lēctus,** disregard, neglect
**negō,** 1, say no, deny, say . . . not
**negōtior,** 1, carry on business, be a trader
**negōtium, –tī,** *n.,* business, affair, trouble; undertaking
**nēmo,** *dat.* **nēminī,** *acc.* **nēminem** (*no other forms*), no one
**nemus, –oris,** *n.,* grove, forest
**nepōs, –ōtis,** *m.,* grandson
**Neptūnus, –ī,** *m.,* Neptune, *god of the sea*
**nēquam,** *indecl. adj.,* worthless, wretched; *compar.* **nēquior**
**neque** (*or* **nec**), and not, nor; **neque... neque,** neither . . . nor
**nequeō, –īre, –īvī, —,** be unable
**nēquīquam,** *adv.,* in vain
**nēquitia, –ae,** *f.,* worthlessness, neglect
**nervōsus, –a, –um,** sinewy
**nervus, –ī,** *m.,* sinew, nerve; string
**nesciō, –īre, –īvī, –ītus, —,** not know, be ignorant; *w.* **an,** I know not whether, very likely
**neuter, –tra, –trum,** neither (*of two*)
**nēve (neu),** *conj.,* and not, nor, and that . . . not
**nex, necis,** *f.,* murder, (violent) death
**nexus, –ūs,** *m.,* (binding together), embrace
**nī,** *see* **nisi**
**Nicaeēnsis, –e,** Nicene
**Nīcānor, –oris,** *m.,* Nicanor
**Nīcomēdensis, –e,** of the Nicomedians; *as noun, m. pl.,* Nicomedians
**Nīcomēdia, –ae,** *f.,* Nicomedia, *capital of Bithynia*
**Nīcopolis, –is,** *f.,* Nicopolis
**nīdus, –ī,** *m.,* nest
**niger, –gra, –grum,** black
**nihil,** *adv.,* nothing; not at all; **nihildum,** nothing as yet
**nihil,** *indeclinable, n.,* nothing
**nihilō minus,** *adv.,* none the less, nevertheless
**Nīlus, –ī,** *m.,* the Nile, *a river in Egypt*

**nimbus, –ī,** *m.,* cloud; rain cloud
**nīmīrum,** *adv.,* of course
**nimis,** *adv.,* too much, too
**nimium,** *adv.,* too, too much
**Ninus, –ī** *m.,* Ninus, *an Assyrian king*
**nisi, nī,** *conj.,* unless, except, if not
**niteō, –ēre, —, —,** shine, be well fed
**nitēscō, –ere, nituī, —,** grow sleek (*of animals*)
**nītor, nītī, nīxus (nīsus),** strive, struggle
**niveus, –a, –um,** snow-white
**nix, nivis,** *f.,* snow
**nōbilis, –e,** noble
**nōbilitās, –tātis,** *f.,* fame; nobility
**nōbīscum = cum nōbīs**
**nocēns,** *gen.* **–entis,** harmful; guilty
**noceō, –ēre, nocuī, nocitus,** do harm to, injure (*w. dat.*)
**noctū,** *adv.,* at night
**nocturnus, –a, –um,** of *or* by night
**nōlō, nōlle, nōluī, —,** be unwilling, not wish
**nōmen, nōminis,** *n.,* name
**nōminātim,** *adv.,* by name, expressly
**nōminō,** 1, name, call
**nōn,** *adv.,* not; **nōn iam,** no longer
**Nōnae, –ārum,** *f. pl.,* Nones
**nōndum,** *adv.,* not yet
**Nōniānus, –ī,** *m.,* Nonianus
**nōnne,** *interrog. adv.* (*in a direct question*), not; (*in an indirect question*), if not, whether not
**nōnnullus, –a, –um,** some, several
**nōs, nostrum,** we, *pl. of* **ego**
**nōscitō, –āre, —, —,** know, recognize
**nōscō, –ere, nōvī, nōtus,** learn; *in perf. tenses,* have learned, know
**noster, –tra, –trum,** our
**nota, –ae,** *f.,* mark
**notābilis, –e,** noteworthy, remarkable
**notārius, –rī,** *m.,* secretary
**nōtitiā, –ae,** *f.,* knowledge, acquaintance
**notō,** 1, note, mark, observe
**nōtus, –a, –um,** known, familiar
**novem,** nine
**novitās, –tātis,** *f.,* newness, strangeness
**novus, –a, –um,** new, strange; last
**nox, noctis,** *f.,* night
**nūbēs, –is,** *f.,* cloud
**nūbō, –ere, nūpsī, nūptus,** veil oneself, wed
**nūdō,** 1, strip, expose
**nūdulus, –a, –um,** bare, exposed
**nūdus, –a, –um,** bare, naked, vacant
**nūgae, –ārum,** *f. pl.,* nonsense
**nūllus, –a, –um,** no, none; *as noun, m.,* no one; **nōn nūllī,** some
**num,** *adv., introduces questions expecting negative answer; conj.,* whether
**nūmen, nūminis,** *n.,* nod; divine will *or* power; divinity
**numerōsus, –a, –um,** numerous; manifold; full of rhythm
**numerus, –ī,** *m.,* number
**Numidae, –ārum,** *m. pl.,* the Numidians
**Numidicus, –ī,** *m.,* Numidicus
**nummus, –ī,** *m.,* coin, money
**numquam,** *adv.,* never
**nunc,** *adv.,* now
**nuncupō,** 1, call by name, name
**nūntiō,** 1, report, announce
**nūntius, –tī,** *m.,* messenger; message, news, report
**nūper,** *adv.,* recently
**nūptiae, –ārum,** *f. pl.,* wedding
**nūptiālis, –e,** nuptial
**nūrus, –ī,** *f.,* daughter-in-law
**nusquam,** *adv.,* nowhere
**nūtriō, –īre, –īvī, –ītus,** nourish, keep alive, foster
**nūtrīx, –īcis,** *f.,* nurse
**nūtus, –ūs,** *m.,* nod, will
**nux, nucis,** *f.,* nut
**nympha, –ae,** *f.,* nymph

## O

**ō!** *interj.,* O! oh!
**ob,** *prep. w. acc.,* because of, on account of, for
**obeō, –īre, obīvī, obitus,** go to meet, attend to, engage in; reach
**obequitō,** 1, ride toward
**obiciō, –ere, obiēcī, obiectus,** throw to *or* against, put in the way, oppose

**obiurgātiō, –ōnis,** *f.,* rebuke
**oblectātiō, –ōnis,** *f.,* delight
**oblectō,** 1, delight
**obligō,** 1, bind
**oblinō, –ere, oblēvī, oblitus,** smear, stain
**oblitterō,** 1, erase
**oblīviō, –ōnis,** *f.,* forgetting, forgetfulness
**oblīvīscor, –ī, oblītus,** forget
**obnoxius, –a, –um,** obliged, servile, weak
**oboediō, –īre, oboedīvī, oboedītus,** give heed to
**obrēpō, –ere, obrepsī, obreptus,** steal in
**obruō, –ere, obruī, obrutus,** overwhelm, bury
**obscūrō,** 1, darken, hide
**obscūrus, –a, –um,** dark, secret, obscure
**obsecrō,** 1, implore
**obsequor, –ī, obsecūtus,** yield, comply
**observō,** 1, observe, watch, heed
**obses, obsidis,** *m.,* hostage
**obsideō, –ēre, obsēdī, obsessus,** beset, besiege, blockade, hem in
**obsidiō, –ōnis,** *f.,* siege
**obsistō, –ere, obstitī, obstitus,** resist
**obstinātiō, –ōnis,** *f.,* stubbornness
**obstinātus, –a, –um,** stubborn
**obstō, –āre, obstitī, obstātus,** prevent, withstand, stand in the way
**obstrepō, –ere, obstrepuī, —,** drown out (*with noise*)
**obstringō, –ere, obstrīnxī, obstrictus,** bind
**obstruō, –ere, obstrūxī, obstrūctus,** block
**obstupēscō, –ere, obstupuī, —,** be astounded
**obsum, obesse, obfuī, —,** injure
**obtemperō,** 1, submit to, obey, consult
**obtestor,** 1, entreat, pray
**obtineō, –ēre, obtinuī, obtentus,** hold, obtain
**obtingō, –ere, obtigī, —,** happen
**obturbō,** 1, confuse, disturb
**obtūsus, –a, –um,** blunt, dull; weak
**obviam,** *adv.,* in the way; *w.* **veniō,** come to meet
**obvius, –a, –um,** meeting, encountering
**occāsiō, –ōnis,** *f.,* opportunity
**occāsus, –ūs,** *m.,* going down, downfall, setting; **occāsus sōlis,** sunset, west
**occidō, –ere, occidī, occāsus,** set, fall down; die
**occīdo, –ere, occīdi, occīsus,** kill
**occultē,** *adv.,* secretly
**occultō,** 1, conceal, hide
**occultus, –a, –um,** secret, hidden
**occupātiō, –ōnis,** *f.,* occupation, business
**occupō,** 1, seize, occupy
**occupātus, –a, –um,** busy
**occurrō, –ere, occurrī, occursus,** run against, meet, occur
**ōceanus, –ī,** *m.,* ocean (*esp. the Atlantic Ocean*)
**ōcior, ōcius,** *comp. adj.,* swifter
**Octāviānus, –ī,** *m.,* Octavian, *the emperor Augustus*
**Octāvius, –vī,** *m.,* Octavius
**octāvus, –a, –um,** eighth
**octō,** eight
**oculus, –ī,** *m.,* eye
**ōdī, ōdisse, ōsus** (*perf. translated as pres.*), hate
**odiōsus, –a, –um,** hateful, offensive
**odium, odī,** *n.,* hatred
**odōrātus, –a, –um,** fragrant
**offendō, –ere, offendī, offēnsus,** (strike against); come upon, find
**offerō, offerre, obtulī, oblātus,** bear to, offer, present, expose; **mē offerō,** rush against
**officīna, –ae,** *f.,* factory
**officiōsus, –a, –um,** obliging, dutiful
**officium, –cī,** *n.,* duty, service, allegiance, function
**ōh!** *interj.,* oh!
**olfaciō, –ere, olfēcī, olfactus,** smell
**ōlim,** *adv.,* once, formerly; hereafter, sometime
**Olympia, –ae,** *f.,* Olympia, *a Greek city*
**Olympicus, –a, –um,** Olympic
**Olympiēum, –ī,** *n.,* Olympieum, *temple of the Olympian Jupiter*
**ōmen, ōminis,** *n.,* omen, sign
**ōminor,** 1, augur, prophesy
**omittō, –ere, omīsī, omissus,** let go, pass over, drop, disregard
**omnīnō,** *adv.,* altogether, in all, entirely, at all, to be sure
**omnis, omne,** all, every, whole
**onerārius, –a, –um,** for freight; **nāvis onerāria,** transport

**onerōsus, –a, –um,** heavy
**onus, oneris,** *n.,* weight, load, burden, cargo
**onustus, –a, –um,** loaded
**opācus, –a, –um,** gloomy
**opera, –ae,** *f.,* work, service, assistance, aid, effort; w. **dare,** see to it
**operiō, –īre, operuī, opertus,** cover
**operōsus, –a, –um,** painstaking, industrious; troublesome
**opifer, –era, –erum,** helping
**opifex, –ficis,** *m.,* workman
**opīniō, –ōnis,** *f.,* belief, opinion, expectation; reputation
**opīnor,** 1, imagine, judge, think
**opitulor,** 1, bring aid, help
**oportet, –ēre, oportuit,** it is fitting *or* necessary, ought
**oppetō, –ere, –īvī, –ītus,** seek
**oppidum, –ī,** *n.,* town
**opportūnitās, –tātis,** *f.,* suitableness
**opportūnus, –a, –um,** fit, timely, opportune, convenient, advantageous
**opprimō, –ere, oppressī, oppressus;** overcome, surprise, crush, oppress
**oppugnātiō, –ōnis,** *f.,* siege, method of attack
**oppugnō,** 1, attack, besiege
**ops, opis,** *f.,* aid, might; *pl.,* wealth, resources, influence
**optimē,** *see* **bene**
**optimus,** *see* **bonus**
**optō,** 1, desire, wish
**opus, operis,** *n.,* work, labor, task, exercise; **magnō opere** *or* **magnopere,** greatly; **tantō opere,** so greatly
**opus,** *n., indeclinable,* need; necessary, necessity; **opus est,** it is necessary, there is need
**ōra, –ae,** *f.,* coast, edge
**ōrāculum, –ī,** *n.,* oracle, prophesy
**ōrārius, –a, –um,** of the coast, coastal
**ōrātiō, –ōnis,** *f.,* speech, words, eloquence; argument
**ōrātor, –ōris,** *m.,* speaker, orator
**ōrātōria, –ae,** *f.,* oratory
**orbis, –is,** *m.,* circle; *esp. w. or without* **terrae** *or* **terrārum,** the world (*i.e., the circle of lands around the Mediterranean*)
**orbō,** 1, deprive, rob; bereave
**orbus, –a, –um,** childless
**Orcus, –ī,** *m.,* Orcus, *god of Hades;* Hades; the Lower World; Pluto
**ōrdior, –īrī. ōrsus,** begin
**ōrdō, ōrdinis,** *m.,* row, order, turn, rank, company, body; class
**oriēns, –entis,** *m.,* rising sun, east
**orīgo, originis,** *f.,* origin
**Ōrīōn, –ōnis,** *m.,* Orion, *a constellation*
**orior, orīrī, ortus,** rise, arise, begin, descend, be descended from
**ōrnāmentum, –ī,** *n.,* (mark of) distinction, decoration, ornament
**ōrnātus, –ūs,** *m.,* adornment, decoration
**ōrnō,** 1, adorn, furnish, equip; honor, **ōrnātus,** fitted out
**ōrō,** 1, beg, ask, pray (for), plead, implore
**Orpheus, –ī,** *m.,* Orpheus (Or´fēŭs), *a famous musician*
**ortus, –ūs.,** *m.,* rising; east
**ōs, ōris,** *m.,* mouth, face, expression; lips
**os, ossis,** (*gen. pl.,* **ossium**) *n.,* bone
**Oscē,** *adv.,* in Oscan
**ōsculor,** 1, kiss, embrace
**ōsculum, –ī,** *n.,* kiss
**ostendō, –ere, ostendī, ostentus,** (stretch out), point out, show, display; declare
**ostentō,** 1, hold up, display
**Ōstiēnsis, –e,** to Ostia
**ōtiōsus, –a, –um,** idle, unemployed; peaceful
**ōtium, ōtī,** *n.,* leisure, quiet, peace
**Ovidius, –dī,** *m.,* Ovid
**ovis, –is,** *f.,* sheep
**ōvum, –ī,** *n.,* egg

## P

**P.,** *abbreviation for* **Pūblius**
**pābulos,** 1, forage
**pābulum, –ī,** *n.,* food (for cattle), fodder
**pacīscor, –ī, pactus,** agree, appoint
**pācō,** 1, pacify, subdue
**pactum, –ī,** *n.,* agreement; manner
**Paelignus, –a, –um,** Pelignian, *of a people of central Italy*

**paene**, *adv.*, almost

**paenitentia, –ae,** *f.*, repentence

**paenitet, –ēre, –uit,** *impers.*, it makes regret, it grieves

**Paestum, –ī,** *n.*, Paestum, *a town in southern Italy*

**pāgānus, –a, –um,** rustic, pagan

**pāgus, –ī,** *m.*, district, canton

**palam**, *adv.*, openly, publicly

**Palātīnus (mōns), –ī,** *m.*, **Palātium, –tī,** *n.*, the Palatine Hill; palace

**Palātium, –tī,** *n.*, the Palatine, *one of the seven hills of Rome*

**palātum, –ī** *n.*, palate

**palea, –ae,** *f.*, chaff, straw

**Palicānus, –ī,** *m.*, Palicanus

**palla, –ae,** *f.*, robe

**pallēscō, –ere, palluī, —,** become pale, turn yellow

**pallidus, –a, –um,** pale

**palma, –ae,** *f.*, hand, palm; date

**palūs, palūdis,** *f.*, marsh, swamp

**Pān, Pānis,** *m.*, Pan, *god of shepherds*

**pānis, –is,** *m.*, bread

**Pāniscus, –ī,** *m.*, Paniscus, *a rural deity*

**Pannonia, –ae,** *f.*, Hungary

**panthēra, –ae,** *f.*, panther

**Papa, –ae,** *m.*, the pope

**papae!** *interj.*, indeed!

**pār**, *gen.* **paris**, equal, like, fair; *as noun, n.*, pair

**parātus, –a, –um,** ready, prepared

**parcē**, *adv.*, sparingly

**parcō, –ere, pepercī, parsus,** spare, save

**parcus, –a, –um,** sparing, economical, frugal, saving

**parēns, –entis,** *m. and f.*, parent

**pāreō, –ēre, pāruī, pāritus,** (appear), obey

**pariēs, –ētis,** *m.*, wall

**parilis, –e,** equal

**pariō, –ere, peperī, partus,** give birth, produce; gain

**pariter**, *adv.*, equally, in like manner, likewise

**Parnāsis, –idis,** of Parnassus

**Parnassius, –a, –um,** Parnassian

**Parnassus, –ī,** *m.*, Parnassus, *a mountain range in central Greece*

**parō**, 1, get, get ready (for), prepare; **parātus, –a, –um,** prepared, ready

**Paros, –ī,** *f.*, Paros, *an island in the Aegean*

**parricīda, –ae,** *m.*, murderer

**parricīdium, –dī,** *n.*, parricide, murder

**pars, partis,** *f.*, part, role, side; direction; duty

**particeps, participis,** *m.*, participant, sharer

**particula, –ae,** *f.*, small part, particle

**partim**, *adv.*, partly

**partiō, –īre, –īvī, –ītus,** divide

**partītiō, –ōnis,** *f.*, division

**partus, –ūs,** *m.*, birth

**parum**, *adv.*, little, too little

**parvulus, –a, –um,** very small, little, petty

**parvus, –a, –um,** small, little, slight, low; *comp.* **minor, minus,** smaller, less, lesser, younger; *superl.* **minimus, –a, –um,** smallest, least, very little, youngest

**pāscō, –ere, pāvī, pāstus,** feed, feast

**passim**, *adv.*, everywhere

**passus, –ūs,** *m.*, step, pace (*about five feet*); **mīlle passūs,** mile

**passus**, *part. of* **patior**

**pāstor, –ōris,** *m.*, shepherd

**Patareus, –a, –um,** of Patara, *a seaport of Lycia*

**patefaciō, –ere, –fēcī, –factus,** open (up), lay open, expose

**patēns**, *gen.* **patentis,** open, extending

**pateō, –ēre, patuī, —,** stand *or* be open, be exposed; extend

**pater, patris,** *m.*, father, senator; *pl.*, **patrēs cōnscrīptī,** senators, patricians

**paternus, –a, –um,** of the father

**patienter**, *adv.*, patiently

**patientia, –ae,** *f.*, patience

**patior, patī, passus,** suffer, endure, allow, permit

**patria, –ae,** *f.*, fatherland, native land, country

**patricius, –a, –um,** patrician

**patrīmonium, –nī,** *n.*, paternal estate; inheritance

**patrius, –a, –um,** of a father, father's, ancestral

**patrōcinium, –nī,** *n.*, patronage

**patrōnus, –ī,** *m.*, patron

**patrūus, –ī,** *m.*, uncle

**patulus, –a, –um,** spreading, wide

**paucī, –ae, –a,** few, only a few

**paucitās, –tātis,** *f.,* small number, scarcity
**pauculus, –a, –um,** very few, very little
**paucus, –a, –um,** little; *pl.,* few, only a few
**paulātim,** *adv.,* gradually, little by little; a few at a time
**paulisper,** *adv.,* for a little while; for a short time
**paulō** *and* **paulum,** *adv.,* shortly, a little
**paulum, –ī,** *n.,* a little
**pauper,** *gen.* **pauperis,** poor
**paupertās, –tātis,** *f.,* poverty
**paveō, –ēre, pāvī, —,** be afraid, tremble with fear
**pavidus, –a, –um,** trembling, scared
**pāx, pācis,** *f.,* peace, truce
**peccātum, –ī,** *n.,* mistake
**peccō,** 1, sin
**pectus, pectoris,** *n.,* breast, heart
**pecūnia, –ae,** *f.,* money; *pl.,* riches
**pecūniārius, –a, –um,** pecuniary
**pecus, pecoris,** *n.,* cattle, flock
**pecus, –udis,** *f.,* beast; *pl.,* herds
**pedes, peditis,** *m.,* foot soldier; *pl.,* infantry
**pedester, –tris, –tre,** (of) infantry; on foot
**peditātus, –ūs,** *m.,* infantry
**peierō,** 1, commit perjury
**pelagus, –ī,** *n.,* sea
**pellis, –is,** *f.,* skin
**pellō, –ere, pepulī, pulsus,** beat, drive, put to flight; banish, defeat
**pendeō, –ēre, pependī, —,** hang, hover
**pendō, –ere, pependī, pēnsus,** hang, weigh, pay
**penetrō,** 1, penetrate
**Pēnēius, –a, –um,** Penē´an (*of a river in Thessaly*)
**penetrō,** 1, penetrate, enter
**penitus, –a, –um,** remote
**penitus,** *adv.,* deeply, within
**penna, –ae,** *f.,* feather, wing
**per,** *prep. w. acc.,* through, by, over, among, during, along, by means of, during; in the name of
**peragō, –ere, –ēgī, –āctus,** complete; obey
**peragrō,** 1, traverse
**peramanter,** *adv.,* very lovingly
**perantīquus, –a, –um,** very ancient
**percipiō, –ere, –cēpī, –ceptus,** seize; hear, feel, learn, appreciate, obtain
**percontor,** 1, inquire
**percrebrēscō, –ere, –crēbruī, —,** grow prevalent, be spread abroad
**percurrō, –ere, –cucurrī, –cursus,** hasten through, run over
**percutiō, –ere, –cussī, –cussus,** strike, pierce, beat
**perdiscō, –ere, –didicī, —,** learn thoroughly
**perditus, –a, –um,** lost; desperate, corrupt
**perdō, –ere, –didī, –ditus,** lose, destroy, waste
**perdūcō, –ere, –dūxī, –ductus,** lead *or* bring through, extend, win over
**perdūrō,** 1, harden, endure
**peregrīnātiō, –ōnis,** *f.,* foreign travel
**peregrīnor,** 1, go abroad
**peregrīnus, –a, –um,** strange, foreign; *as noun m.,* foreigner
**perennis, –e,** through the year, unceasing, perpetual
**pereō, –īre, –iī (–īvī), –itus,** perish, pass away, be lost, disappear
**perexcelsus, –a, –um,** exalted
**perfero, –ferre, –tulī, –lātus,** carry (through), report, bring; endure
**perficiō, –ere, –fēcī, –fectus,** do thoroughly, accomplish, make of, bring about, finish, carry out; cause
**perfidēlis, –e,** very faithful
**perfidia, –ae,** *f.,* faithlessness, treachery
**perfidus, –a, –um,** treacherous, dishonest, faithless
**perfringō, –ere, –frēgī, –frāctus,** break through *or* down, violate
**perfruor, –fruī, –frūctus,** enjoy fully
**perfuga, –ae,** *m.,* deserter
**perfugiō, –ere, –fūgī, —,** flee
**perfugium, –gī,** *n.,* refuge
**perfungor, –ī, –fūnctus,** perform
**Pergamum, –ī,** *n.,* Troy
**pergō, –ere, perrēxī, perrēctus,** proceed, continue, hasten
**perhorrēscō, –ere, –horruī,** shudder at
**perīclitor,** 1, try, risk, endanger
**perīculōsus, –a, –um,** dangerous

**perīculum, –ī,** *n.,* trial, danger
**perimō, –ere, –ēmī, –ēmptus,** destroy
**perior,** *see* **malus**
**perītus, –a, –um,** skilled, experienced, acquainted with
**periūrus, –a, –um,** oath-breaking, perjured
**perlegō, –ere, –lēgī, –lēctus,** read through, examine thoroughly
**permaneō, –ēre, –mānsī, –mānsus,** remain
**permātūrēscō, –ere, –mātūrui, —,** ripen fully
**permittō, –ere, –mīsī, –missus,** let go through, leave, allow, grant, entrust, permit
**permoveō, –ēre, –mōvī, –mōtus,** move deeply, induce, alarm
**permultus, –a, –um,** very much, very many
**permūtātiō, –ōnis,** *f.,* exchange
**permūtō,** 1, exchange
**perniciēs, –ēī,** *f.,* destruction, ruin
**perniciōsus, –a, –um,** destructive, dangerous
**pernoctō,** 1, spend the night
**perofficiōsē,** *adv.,* very attentively
**peropportūnus, –a, –um,** very seasonable *or* opportune
**perōsus, –a, –um,** loathing
**perparvulus, –a, –um,** very little, very small
**perpaucī, –ae, –a,** very few
**perpetior, –ī, perpessus,** bear steadfastly, suffer firmly, endure
**perpetuō,** *adv.,* permanently
**perpetuus, –a, –um,** constant, lasting; **in perpetuum,** forever
**perquīrō, –ere, –quīsīvī, –quīsītus,** make a diligent search for
**perrārus, –a, –um,** very rare
**perrumpō, –ere, –rūpī, –ruptus,** break through
**Persae, –ārum,** *m. pl.,* the Persians
**persaepe,** *adv.,* very often
**perscrībō, –ere, perscrīpsī, perscrīptus,** write out
**persequor, –sequī, –secūtus,** follow up, pursue, punish, avenge
**persevērō,** 1, persist, continue
**persōna, –ae,** *f.,* part, character, personage
**personō, –āre, personuī, personitus,** resound
**perspiciō, –ere, –spexī, –spectus,** see (through, clearly), perceive, examine
**perspicuus, –a, –um,** clear, manifest
**perstō, –āre, –stitī, –stātus,** persist, continue standing
**persuādeo, –ēre, –suāsī, –suāsus,** persuade
**perterreō, –ēre, –terruī, –territus,** frighten thoroughly, scare thoroughly, alarm
**pertimēscō, –ere, pertimuī, —,** become thoroughly alarmed; fear, dread
**pertinācia, –ae,** *f.,* obstinacy
**pertināciter,** *adv.,* persistently
**pertineō, –ēre, –tinuī, –tentus,** extend (to), pertain to, belong to, concern
**pertrāctō,** 1, touch, investigate
**pertrānseō, –īre, –īvī, –itus,** pass through
**perturbō,** 1, disturb, alarm, throw into confusion
**perturbātiō, –ōnis,** *f.,* confusion
**pervagor,** 1, wander through, spread through, pervade
**perveniō, –īre, –vēnī, –ventus,** come (through), arrive (at), reach, attain
**pervetus,** *gen.* **–eris,** very old, most ancient
**pēs, pedis,** *m.,* foot; **pedibus,** on foot
**pessimus,** *see* **malus**
**pestifer, –era, –erum,** destructive
**pestis, –is,** *f.,* plague, destruction, curse, ruin
**petītiō, –ōnis,** *f.,* candidacy
**petītor, –ōris,** *m.,* candidate
**petō, –ere, petīvī, petītus,** seek, ask, beg; attack
**petulantia, –ae,** *f.,* wantonness
**pexus, –a, –um,** combed
**Phaedimus, –ī,** *m.,* Phaedimus, *one of Niobe's sons*
**pharetra, –ae,** *f.,* quiver
**Pharsālus, –ī,** *f.,* Pharsalus, *a town in Thessaly*
**Philēmōn, –ōnis,** *m.,* Philemon, *husband of Baucis*
**Philippī, –ōrum,** *m. pl.,* Philippi, *a city in Macedonia*
**Philippus, –ī,** *m.,* Philip
**Philistiōn, –ōnis,** *m.,* Philistion
**philosophia, –ae,** *f.,* philosophy
**philosophus, –ī,** *m.,* philosopher
**Phoebus, –ī,** *m.,* Phoebus, Apollo
**Phrygius, –a, –um,** Phrygian
**pictūra, –ae,** *f.,* picture, painting

**pictus, –a, –um**, painted
**pietās, –tātis,** *f.*, dutiful conduct, devotion, piety
**piger, –gra, –grum**, reluctant, slow, lazy, dull
**piget, –ēre, piguit**, it grieves
**pigrē**, *adv.*, slowly, reluctantly
**pila, –ae,** *f.*, ball, ballplaying
**pilula, –ae,** *f.*, pill
**pīlum, –ī,** *n.*, spear (*for throwing*), javelin
**piscis, –is,** *m.*, fish
**piscor**, 1, fish
**Pīsistratus, –ī,** *m.*, Pisistratus, *a tyrant of Athens*
**Pīsō, –ōnis,** *m.*, Piso
**pius, –a, –um**, dutiful, righteous, pious, devoted, loyal, loving
**Pius, –ī,** *m.*, Pius
**placeō, –ēre, placuī, placitūrus**, be pleasing to, please; *impers.*, it seems best, (he) decides, it is decided by, **placet**, it pleases (him), *i.e.*, (he) decides, be decided
**placidus, –a, –um**, gentle, calm
**plācō**, 1, appease
**plāga, –ae,** *f.*, blow; disaster
**plānē**, *adv.*, plainly
**plangor, –ōris,** *m.*, beating (*of the breast*); shrieking
**plānitiēs, –iēī,** *f.*, level ground, plain
**planta, –ae,** *f.*, sprout, twig
**plānus, –a, –um**, level, plane
**Platō, –ōnis,** *m.*, Plato, *a Greek philosopher*
**plaudō, –ere, plausī, plausus**, applaud
**plausus, –ūs,** *m.*, clapping of hands, applause
**plēbs, plēbis,** *f.*, people, common people
**plēctrum, –ī,** *n.*, pick (*for striking the lyre*)
**Plēiades, –um,** *f.*, Pleiades, *the seven daughters of Atlas*
**plēnus, –a, –um**, full, abounding in
**plērīque, –aeque, –aque**, most, the majority
**plērumque**, *adv.*, usually
**plexus, –a, –um**, woven
**plōrō**, 1, cry out, wail, lament
**Plōtius, –tī,** *m.*, Plotius
**plūma, –ae,** *f.*, feather
**plumbum, –ī,** *n.*, lead
**plūrēs**, *see* **multus**
**plūrimum**, *adv.*, very much, most, especially
**plūrimus**, *see* **multus**
**plūs**, *see* **multum, multus**
**pōcillātor, –ōris,** *m.*, cupbearer
**pōculum, –ī,** *n.*, cup
**poena, –ae,** *f.*, penalty, punishment; **poenam dō,** pay the penalty
**Poenī, –ōrum,** *m. pl.*, the Carthaginians
**Poenicus**, *see* **Pūnicus**
**Poenus, –a, –um**, Punic; *as noun, m. pl.*, the Carthaginians
**poēta, –ae,** *m.*, poet
**poēticus, –a, –um**, poetic
**Poggius, –ī,** *m.*, Poggio
**pol!** *interj.*, by Pollux!
**poliō, –īre, polīvī, polītus**, polish
**pollex, –icis,** *m.*, thumb
**polliceor, pollicērī, pollicitus**, promise
**pollicitātiō, –ōnis,** *f.*, promise
**Pollux, –cis,** *m.*, Pollux
**pōmārium, –rī,** *n.*, orchard
**pōmifer, –era, –erum**, fruit-bearing
**pompa, –ae,** *f.*, parade, procession
**Pompeiānus, –a, –um**, of Pompeii
**Pompeius, –peī,** *m.*, Pompey
**Pompōnius, –nī,** *m.*, Pomponius
**Pomptīnae palūdēs**, Pontine Marshes, *south of Rome*
**Pomptīnus, –a, –um**, Pontine
**pōmum, –ī,** *n.*, fruit, apple, berry
**pondus, ponderis,** *n.*, weight
**pōnō, –ere, posuī, positus**, put, place, set, pitch, lay aside, serve, lay down; *pass.*, be situated, depend upon; *w.* **castra**, pitch
**pōns, pontis,** *m.*, bridge
**pontifex, pontificis,** *m.*, priest
**pontificātus, –ūs,** *m.*, pontificate
**pontus, –ī,** *m.*, sea
**Pontus, –ī,** *m.*, Pontus, *the region south of the Black Sea*
**poples, –litis,** *m.*, knee
**poposcī**, *see* **poscō**
**populāris, –e**, popular
**populor**, 1, destroy
**populus, –ī,** *m.*, people; *pl.*, peoples
**Porcius, –a, –um**, Porcian

**porrigō, –ere, porrēxī, porrēctus,** stretch out, extend

**porrō,** *adv.,* then

**porta, –ae,** *f.,* gate, door

**portentum, –ī,** *n.,* portent

**Porthaōn, –ōnis,** *m., a mythological character*

**porticus, –ūs,** *f.,* colonnade, gallery, porch

**portō,** 1, carry

**portus, –ūs,** *m.,* harbor, port

**poscō, –ere, poposcī, —,** demand, call for, ask

**possessiō, –ōnis,** *f.,* possession

**possideō, –ēre, possēdī, possessus,** own, possess

**possum, posse, potuī, —,** can, can do, be able; **multum (plūs, plūrimum) possum,** be very powerful

**post,** *adv. and prep. w. acc.,* behind; after, later, since; **paulō post,** a little later

**posteā,** *adv.,* afterwards, later

**posteāquam,** *conj.,* after

**posteritās, –tātis,** *f.,* the future, posterity

**posterus, –a, –um,** following, next; **in posterum,** for the future; *as noun, m. pl.,* posterity, descendants

**posthāc,** *adv.,* hereafter

**postis, –is,** *m.,* doorpost; *pl.,* door

**postpōnō, –ere, –posuī, –positus,** put after, esteem less

**postquam,** *conj.,* after

**postrēmō,** *adv.,* at last, finally; in short

**postrēmus, –a, –um,** last

**postrīdiē,** *adv.,* on the next day

**postulō,** 1, demand

**potēns,** *gen.* **potentis,** strong, powerful

**potentia, –ae,** *f.,* power

**potestās, –tātis,** *f.,* power, opportunity

**pōtiō, –ōnis,** *f.,* drink

**potior, potīrī, potītus,** get possession of, gain possession of (*w. gen. or abl.*)

**potissimum,** *adv.,* especially, above all, in preference to all others

**potius,** *adv.,* rather

**prae,** *prep. w. abl.,* before; in comparison with

**praeacūtus, –a, –um,** pointed

**praebeō, –ēre, –uī, –itus,** offer, hold forth, furnish, present, show

**praecēdō, –ere, –cessī, –cessus,** go before, precede

**praeceps,** *gen.* **praecipitis,** headlong, rash; rushing, steep; **in praeceps,** headfirst

**praeceptum, –ī,** *n.,* precept, rule; instructions

**praecipiō, –ere, –cēpī, –ceptus,** instruct, direct, lay down a rule

**praecipitō,** 1, rush headlong, sink

**praecipuē,** *adv.,* especially

**praeclārus, –a, –um,** brilliant, remarkable

**praeclūdō, –ere, –clūsī, –clūsus,** shut, close, hinder, impede

**praecō, praecōnis,** *m.,* announcer, crier, herald

**praecōnium, –nī,** *n.,* public praise

**praecordia, –ōrum,** *n.,* breast, heart

**praecurrō, –ere, –cucurrī (–currī), –cursus,** run before, precede, excel

**praeda, –ae,** *f.,* loot, prey

**praedātor, –ōris,** *m.,* robber

**praedicātiō, –ōnis,** *f.,* proclamation

**praedicō,** 1, announce, declare, say, proclaim

**praedīcō, –ere, –dīxī, –dictus,** predict, foretell

**praediolum, –ī,** *n.,* small estate

**praeditus, –a, –um,** endowed, possessing

**praedium, –dī,** *n.,* farm, estate

**praedō, –ōnis,** *m.,* pirate

**praedor,** 1, loot

**praedūcō, –ere, –dūxī, –ductus,** extend

**praefātiō, –ōnis,** *f.,* preface, prologue

**praefectūra, –ae,** *f.,* prefecture

**praefectus, –ī,** *m.,* commander, prefect

**praeferō, –ferre, –tulī, –lātus,** carry before, prefer

**praeficiō, –ere, –fēcī, –fectus,** put *or* place in charge of, set over, put in command of

**praefor,** 1, say, beforehand, preface

**praefulgeō, –ēre, —, —,** beam forth, shine greatly

**praelambō, –ere, —, —,** wash lightly

**praemittō, –ere, –mīsī, –missus,** send ahead

**praemium, –mī,** *n.,* reward, prize

**praemūniō = mūniō**

**praenōscō, –ere, –nōvī, –nōtus,** learn beforehand

**praeparō,** 1, prepare

**praepōnō, –ere, –posuī, –positus,** prefer

**praeproperus, –a, –um,** too hasty, sudden

**praerumpō, –ere, –rūpī, –ruptus,** break off

**praescius, –a, –um,** foreknowing, foreseeing

**praescrībō, –ere, –scrīpsī, –scrīptus,** direct, require of

**praescrīptum, –ī,** *n.,* order

**praesēns,** *gen.* **praesentis,** present, in person, evident; providential

**praesentia, –ae,** *f.,* presence; **in praesentiā,** for the present

**praesentiō, –īre, –sēnsī, –sēnsus,** foresee, look forward to

**praesertim,** *adv.,* especially

**praesidium, –dī,** *n.,* garrison, guard, fortification; protection, aid, help

**praestāns,** *gen.* **praestantis,** outstanding, preeminent

**praestō, –āre, –stitī, –stitus,** stand before, excel; guarantee; offer, perform, show; **praestat,** *impers.,* it is better

**praestō,** *adv.,* at hand, ready

**praestōlor,** 1, wait for

**praesum, –esse, –fuī, –futūrus,** be in charge of, be in command of

**praesūmō, –ere, –sūmpsī, –sūmptus,** undertake

**praeter,** *prep. w. acc.,* besides, contrary to, beyond; except

**praetereā,** *adv.,* besides, furthermore, moreover

**praetereō, –īre, –iī, –itus,** go by, pass by, omit; outstrip

**praeterhāc,** *adv.,* besides, moreover

**praeteritus, –a, –um,** past; *as noun, n. pl.,* the past

**praetermittō, –ere, –mīsī, –missus,** let go, omit, pass over

**praeterquam,** *adv.,* other than, *conj.,* except

**praetor, –ōris,** *m.,* praetor (*an official*), judge, *a Roman judicial magistrate*

**praetōrium, –rī,** *n.,* headquarters

**praetōrius, –a, –um,** praetorian; *as noun, m.,* ex-praetor

**praetūra, –ae,** *f.,* the praetorship

**praevaleō, –ēre, –valuī, –valitūrus,** prevail

**prandium, –dī,** *n.,* lunch

**prātum, –ī,** *n.,* meadow

**prāvus, –a, –um,** crooked, vicious, depraved

**precor,** 1, entreat, pray

**prehendō, –ere, –hendī, –hensus,** grasp, seize, catch

**premō, –ere, pressī, pressus,** press, press hard, oppress, crowd; cover

**prēndō = prehendō**

**prēndō, –ere, prēndī, prēnsus,** seize

**prēnsātiō, –ōnis,** *f.,* soliciting, canvassing

**pretiōsus, –a, –um,** costly

**pretium, –tī,** *n.,* price; reward

**prex, precis,** *f.,* prayer, entreaty

**prīdem,** *adv.,* long ago; *w.* **iam,** now for a long time

**prīdiē,** *adv.,* on the day before

**prīmō,** *adv.,* at first

**prīmum,** *adv.,* first, in the first place, at first, for the first time; *w.* **quam,** as soon as possible; *w.* **ut** *or* **cum,** as soon as

**prīmus, –a, –um,** first, foremost; **in prīmīs,** especially

**prīnceps, prīncipis,** *adj. and noun, m.,* chief, first (man), leader, emperor; **princeps,** under the direction of

**prīncipātus, –ūs,** *m.,* first place, leadership

**prīncipiō,** *adv.,* in the first place

**principium, –pī,** *n.,* beginning

**prior, prius,** former, first; **prior, –ōris,** *m.,* prior

**prīscus, –a, –um,** ancient, primitive

**Prīscus, –ī,** *m.,* Priscus

**prīstinus, –a, –um,** former

**prius,** *compar. adv.,* before, first

**priusquam (prius... quam),** *conj.,* before

**prīvātim,** *adv.,* privately

**prīvātus, –a, –um,** private; *as noun, m.,* private citizen

**prīvō,** 1, deprive

**prō,** *prep. w. abl.,* in front of, before, for, instead of, as, in accordance with, in proportion to, in behalf of, in return for, on account of, instead of, according to

**proavus, –ī,** *m.,* great-grandfather

**probitās, –tātis,** *f.,* honesty

**probō,** 1, prove; approve

**probrum, –ī,** *n.,* disgraceful conduct

**probus, –a, –um,** upright
**procācitās, –tātis,** *f.,* boldness, impudence
**prōcēdō, –ere, –cessī, –cessus,** go forward, advance, proceed
**prōcēritās, –tātis,** *f.,* height, tallness
**procul,** *adv.,* at a distance, far off
**prōcumbō, –ere, –cubuī, –cubitus,** lie down, sink down
**prōcūrō,** 1, take care of
**prōcurrō, –ere, –currī, –cursus,** run forward
**prōdeō, –īre, prōdiī, prōditus,** go *or* come forth
**prōdigiōsus, –a, –um,** unnatural, strange
**prōdō, –ere, –didī, –ditus,** give (forth), hand down, betray, transmit
**prōdūcō, –ere, –dūxī, –ductus,** lead forth *or* bring out, induce, prolong, coax (*of a fire*)
**proelior,** 1, battle
**proelium, –lī,** *n.,* battle
**profānus, –a, –um,** unholy, profane
**profectiō, –ōnis,** *f.,* departure
**profectō,** *adv.,* for a fact, certainly, doubtless
**prōferō, –ferre, –tulī, –lātus,** bring out, bring forth, produce, extend
**professor, –ōris,** *m.,* professor
**prōficiō, –ere, –fēcī, –fectus,** accomplish
**proficīscor, proficīscī, profectus,** set out, start, march, depart
**profiteor, –ērī, professus,** confess; offer, promise; register
**prōflīgātus, –a, –um,** corrupt, unprincipled
**profugiō, –ere, –fūgī, –fugitus,** flee, escape
**profugus, –ī,** *m.,* fugitive
**profundō, –ere, –fūdī, –fūsus,** waste
**prōgeniēs, –iēī,** *f.,* descendants
**prōgredior, –gredī, –gressus,** proceed, step forward, advance
**prōgnātus, –a, –um,** descended
**prohibeō, –ēre, –hibuī, –hibitus,** prevent, keep from, cut off, protect
**prōiciō, –ere, –iēcī, –iectus,** throw, thrust (forward), abandon
**proinde,** *adv.,* therefore
**prōlabor, –ī, prōlāpsus,** slip
**prōlēs, –is,** *f.,* offspring, young son
**prōloquor, –loquī, –locūtus,** say
**prōmiscuus, –a, –um,** mixed
**prōmittō, –ere, –mīsī, –missus,** let go; promise; **prōmissus, –a, –um,** long
**prōmō, –ere, prōmpsī, prōmptus,** give out, bring forth
**prōmoveō, –ēre, –mōvī, –mōtus,** move forward
**prōmptus, –a, –um,** ready
**prōnūntiō,** 1, announce, recite
**prōnus, –a, –um,** flat, headlong, steep
**prōpāgō,** 1, extend
**prope,** *adv.,* almost; *prep. w. acc.,* near
**prōpellō, –ere, –pulī, –pulsus,** drive away, dislodge
**propemodum,** *adv.,* nearly, almost
**prōpēnsus, –a, –um,** coming near; inclined, ready
**properē,** *adv.,* quickly
**properō,** 1, hasten, hurry (on)
**propinquitās, –tātis,** *f.,* nearness
**propinquus, –a, –um,** near; *as noun, m.,* relative
**propitius, –a, –um,** favorable, kind
**prōpōnō, –ere, –posuī, –positus,** explain, present, offer, raise, propose
**prōpositum, –ī,** *n.,* subject
**proprius, –a, –um,** (one's) own, characteristic of, belonging to, proper
**propter,** *prep. w. acc.,* because of, on account of, for the sake of; *adv.,* near
**propterea,** *adv.,* on this account; **propterea quod,** because
**prōpugnātiō, –ōnis,** *f.,* defense, vindication
**prōpugnō,** 1, fight on the offensive, fight for, defend
**prōra, –ae,** *f.,* prow
**prōrogō,** 1, prolong, continue
**prōrsum, prōrsus,** *adv.,* forward; certainly
**prōscrīptiō, –ōnis,** *f.,* prescription, list of condemned
**prōsequor, –sequī, –secūtus,** pursue, address, accompany, follow (after)
**Prōserpina, –ae,** *f.,* Proser´pina, *wife of Pluto*
**prōsiliō, –īre, prōsiluī, —,** leap forth
**prōspectō,** 1, look at, look for
**prōspectus, –ūs,** *m.,* view
**prosperus, –a, –um,** favorable

**prōspiciō, –ere, –spexī, –spectus,** look out for *or* over, foresee, look forward to

**prōsternō, –ere, –strāvī, –strātus,** overthrow

**prōsum, prōdesse, prōfuī, —,** benefit, help, profit

**prōtegō, –ere, –tēxī, –tēctus,** cover

**prōtinus,** *adv.,* immediately, at once

**prōvehō, –ere, –vexī, –vectus,** carry forward

**prōverbium, –bī,** *n.,* saying, proverb

**prōvidentia, –ae,** *f.,* foresight

**prōvideō, –ēre, –vīdī, –vīsus,** foresee, provide, look out for

**prōvincia, –ae,** *f.,* province

**prōvinciālis, –e,** provincial

**proximē,** *adv.,* recently

**proximus, –a, –um,** nearest, last, next, very near; *as noun, n.,* neighborhood

**prūdēns,** *gen.* **prūdentis,** sensible, wise

**prūdentia, –ae,** *f.,* foresight, good sense, discretion

**pruīna, –ae,** *f.,* frost

**pruīnōsus, –a, –um,** frosty

**prūnum, –i,** *n.,* plum

**Prūsēnsis, –e,** of Prusa, *a Bithynian town*

**Psychē, –ēs,** *f.,* Psyche

**Ptolemaeus, –a, –um,** public; Ptolemaic, Egyptian; *as noun, m.,* Ptolemy, *general name for the Egyptian kings*

**pūblicē,** *adv.,* publicly

**pūblicō,** 1, confiscate

**pūblicus, –a, –um,** public

**Pūblilia, –ae,** *f.,* Publilia

**Pūblius, –lī,** *m.,* Publius

**pudet, –ēre, puduit,** *impers.,* it makes ashamed

**pudicitia, –ae,** *f.,* virtue

**pudicus, –a, –um,** modest, chaste

**pudor, –ōris,** *m.,* (sense of) shame, modesty, sense of honor

**puella, –ae,** *f.,* girl

**puer, puerī,** *m.,* boy, child

**puerīlis, –e,** boyish, childish, youthful

**puerīliter,** *adv.,* childishly, foolishly

**pueritia, –ae,** *f.,* childhood, boyhood

**pugillārēs, –ium,** *m. pl.,* writing tablets

**pugna, –ae,** *f.,* fight, battle

**pugnō,** 1, fight

**pulcher, –chra, –chrum,** beautiful; honorable, fine

**pulchritūdō, –dinis,** *f.,* beauty

**pullus, –a, –um,** dark-colored

**pulsō,** 1, dash against, beat

**pulsus,** *part. of* **pellō**

**pulvīnārius, –a, –um,** of *or* belonging to the couches of the gods

**pulvis, –eris,** *m.,* dust

**Pūnicus, –a, –um,** Punic, Carthaginian

**pūniō, –īre, –īvī, –ītus,** punish

**puppis, –is,** *f., acc.* **–im,** *abl.* **–ī,** stern; ship

**pūrgō,** 1, cleanse

**pūritās, –tātis,** *f.,* cleanness, purity

**purpurātus, –a, –um,** purple

**purpureus, –a, –um,** purple

**purpurō,** 1, beautify, adorn

**pūrus, –a, –um,** clean, pure

**pusillus, –a, –um,** very little, petty

**putō,** 1, think, consider

**Pyramus, –ī,** *m.,* Pyramus

**Pӯthōn, –ōnis,** Python, *a mythological serpent*

**Pӯrēnaeī montēs,** Pyrenees Mountains

# Q

**Q.,** *abbreviation for* **Quīntus**

**quā,** *adv.,* where; *w.* **nē,** in any way

**quadrāgēsimus, –a, –um,** the fortieth; *as noun, f.,* a tax of one fortieth

**quadrāgintā,** forty

**quadringentī, –ae, –a,** four hundred

**quadrupēs, –pedis,** *m.,* horse, steed

**quaerō, –ere, quaesīvī, quaesītus,** seek, inquire, ask, examine

**quaesō, –ere, —, —,** beg

**quaestiō, –ōnis,** *f.,* investigation, trial; question

**quaestiuncula, –ae,** *f.,* a little question

**quaestor, –ōris,** *m.,* quaestor (*a Roman official*), treasury official

**quaestus, –ūs,** *m.,* gain, profit; business

**quālis, –e,** what kind of, what, such as, of what sort, of such a kind as; *w.* **tālis,** as

**quāliscumque, quālecumque,** of whatever sort

**quam**, *adv. and conj.*, how, as; *w. comp.*, than; *w. superl.*, as . . . possible; **quam prīmum**, as soon as possible; **quam diū**, as long as, how long

**quamlibet**, *adv.*, according to inclination; however much, to any extent

**quamobrem (quam ob rem)**, *interrog. adv.*, for what reason, why

**quamquam**, *conj.*, although; however; and yet

**quamvīs**, *adv.*, however

**quandō**, *adv. and conj.*, when; at any time, ever

**quandōquidem**, *adv.*, since

**quantuluscumque, –lacumque, –lumcumque**, however small

**quantum**, *adv.*, how much

**quantus, –a, –um**, how great, how much, what, as (great *or* much as); **quantō... tantō**, the . . . the

**quantuscumque, –tacumque, –tumcumque**, however great, however small

**quāpropter**, *adv.*, why, for what reason

**quārē**, *adv.*, why, wherefore; therefore

**quartus, –a, –um**, fourth; **quārtus decimus**, fourteenth

**quasi**, *adv. and conj.*, as if, like, as it were

**quatiō, –ere, —, quassus**, shake, flutter

**quattuor**, four

**–que**, *conj.* (*added to second word*), (*enclitic*), and

**quemadmodum**, *adv.*, in what manner

**queō, quīre, quīvī, —**, be able, can

**quercus, –ūs**, *f.*, oak; garland

**querēla, –ae**, *f.*, complaint

**querimōnia, –ae**, *f.*, complaint

**queror, querī, questus**, complain

**quī, quae, quod**, *rel. pron.*, who, which, what, that; *interrog. adj.*, what; **quī, qua, quod**, *indef. adj.*, any

**quia**, *conj.*, because

**quīcumque, quaecumque, quodcumque**, *rel. pron.*, whoever, whatever

**quid**, *adv.*, why

**quīdam, quaedam, quiddam** (*adj.* **quoddam**), *indef. pron.*, a certain one *or* thing; *adj.*, certain, some, a, one

**quidem**, *adv.* (*follows emphasized word*), at least, to be sure; **nē... quidem**, not even

**quidnam**, what in the world

**quiēs, quiētis**, *f.*, rest, sleep, quiet, repose

**quiēscō, –ere, quiēvī, quiētus**, be quiet, rest

**quiētus, –a, –um**, quiet, undisturbed; **quiētē**, *adv.*, quietly

**quīn**, *conj.*, (but) that; *adv.*, why not; *w.* **etiam**, in fact, moreover

**Quīnctīlis, –e**, (of) July

**quīngentī, –ae, –a**, five hundred

**quīnquāgintā**, fifty

**quīnque**, five

**quīnquennium, –nī**, *n.*, five-year period

**Quīntiliānus, –ī**, *m.*, Quintilian

**quīntus, –a, –um**, fifth

**Quīntus, –ī**, *m.*, Quintus

**quippe**, *adv. and conj.*, surely, indeed

**Quirīnālis (mōns), –is**, *m.*, Quirinal Hill

**Quirītēs, –ium**, *m. pl.*, fellow citizens

**quis, quid**, *interrog, pron.*, who, what; **quid**, again; **quid quod**, what of the fact that

**quis, quid**, *indef. pron.*, **quī, qua, quod**, *indef. adj.*, any, anyone, anything (*usually after* **sī, nisi, nē** *or* **num**)

**quisnam, quaenam, quidnam**, *interrog. pron.*, who *or* what in the world

**quispiam, quaepiam, quidpiam (quodpiam)**, *indef. pron.*, anyone, any; someone, something

**quisquam, quicquam**, *indef. pron.*, anyone, anything, any; **neque quisquam**, not a single one

**quisque, quidque**, *indef. pron.*, each one, each thing, each, every

**quisquis, quicquid**, *rel. pron.*, whoever, whatever

**quīvīs, quaevīs, quidvīs**, *indef. pron.*, any

**quō**, *adv.*, where, wherefore, to which; **quō usque**, how long; **quō modō**, how

**quō**, *conj.*, in order that, that; **quō minus (quōminus)**, that not

**quoad**, *conj.*, as long as

**quōcumque**, *adv.*, wherever

**quod**, *conj.*, because, that, since; **quod sī**, but if

**quōmodō**, *adv.*, how

**quōmodōnam**, *adv.*, how then

**quondam**, *adv.*, once (upon a time)

**quoniam**, *conj.*, since, because

**quoque,** *adv.,* also, even, too (*follows the word it emphasizes*)

**quot,** *indeclinable adj.,* how many; as (many as), as

**quotannīs,** *adv.,* every year

**quotiēns,** *adv.,* as often as; how often

**quotiēnscumque,** *adv.,* as often as

## R

**radiō,** 1, shine, gleam

**radius, –dī,** *m.,* rod; ray, beam; spoke

**rādīx, –dīcis,** *f.,* root, radish

**raeda, –ae,** *f.,* carriage, bus

**rāmulus, –ī,** *m.,* branch

**rāmus, –ī,** *m.,* branch

**rana, –ae,** *f.,* frog

**rapiditās, –tātis,** *f.,* swiftness

**rapidus, –a, –um,** fierce, swift

**rapīna, –ae,** *f.,* plunder, robbery

**rapiō, –ere, rapuī, raptus,** seize, carry off, hurry along

**raptor, –ōris,** *m.,* thief

**rārō,** *adv.,* rarely

**rārus, –a, –um,** rare

**ratiō, –ōnis,** *f.,* reckoning, account, plan, manner, reason, consideration, method, theory, system, judgment, means, nature

**ratis, –is,** *f.,* raft

**rebelliō, –ōnis,** *f.,* rebellion

**Rebilus, –ī,** *m.,* Rebilus

**recēdō, –ere, recessī, recessus,** withdraw, go back

**recēns,** *gen.* **recentis,** new, recent, fresh

**recēnseō, –ēre, recēnsuī, recēnsus,** count again, review

**receptāculum, –ī,** *n.,* receptacle, shelter

**receptus, –ūs,** *m.,* retreat, place of refuge

**recidō, –ere, recīdī, recāsus,** fall

**recingō, –ere, recīnxī, recīnctus,** loosen

**recipiō, –ere, recēpī, receptus,** take (back), receive, recover; **mē recipiō,** withdraw, recover, retire, retreat

**recitātiō, –ōnis,** *f.,* reading, recitation

**recitātor, –ōris,** *m.,* reader, reciter

**recitō,** 1, recite, read aloud

**reclīnō,** 1, bend back; *pass.,* lean

**reclūdō, –ere, reclūsī, reclūsus,** disclose, reveal; shut off *or* up

**recognōscō, –ere, recognōvī, recognitus,** recognize; review

**recolō, –ere, recoluī, recultus,** renew

**reconciliātiō, –ōnis,** *f.,* reconciliation

**reconciliō,** 1, reconcile

**recondō, –ere, recondidī, reconditus,** hide; close

**recordātiō, –ōnis,** *f.,* recollection

**recordor,** 1, call to mind

**recreō,** 1, recreate, restore; *w.* **mē,** recover

**rēctē,** *adv.,* rightly, correctly

**rēctus, –a, –um,** right; **rēctā,** *adv.,* straight; *see* **regō**

**recumbō, –ere, recubuī, —,** lie down; fall

**recuperō,** 1, get back, recover

**recursō,** 1, run back and forth

**recūsātiō, –ōnis,** *f.,* declining

**recūsō,** 1, refuse, reluctant to do

**reddō, –ere, reddidī, redditus,** give (back), render, return, restore, make, deliver; reflect; vomit

**redeō, –īre, rediī, reditus,** go back, return

**redigō, –ere, redēgī, redāctus,** bring (back), drive back, reduce

**redimō, –ere, redēmī, redēmptus,** buy back, ransom

**redintegrō,** 1, renew

**reditus, –ūs,** *m.,* return, revenue

**redolēns,** *gen.,* **–entis,** fragrant

**redormiō, –īre, redormīvī, redormītus,** sleep again

**redūcō, –ere, redūxī, reductus,** lead back, bring back, restore

**redundō,** 1, overflow, rodound

**referō, referre, rettulī, relātus,** bring *or* carry (back), lay *or* bring before, report, reply, reproduce; **pedem referō,** withdraw; **grātiam referō,** show gratitude

**reficiō, –ere, refēcī, refectus,** repair, renew, refresh, restore, recruit, reinforce

**refugiō, –ere, refūgī, refugitus,** flee back, flee for safety, escape

**regerō, –ere, regessī, regestus,** throw back

**rēgia, –ae,** *f.,* palace

**rēgīna, –ae,** *f.,* queen

**regiō, –ōnis,** *f.,* district, region

**rēgius, –a, –um,** royal

**rēgnō,** 1, reign, rule

**rēgnum, –ī,** *n.,* royal power, kingdom, rule

**regō, –ere, rēxī, rēctus,** guide, rule, direct, control; **rēctus,** straight

**regredior, –ī, regressus,** return

**Rēgulus, –ī,** *m.,* Regulus

**reiciō, –ere, reiēcī, reiectus,** throw, drive back, reject; vomit

**relābor, relābī, relāpsus,** slip back

**relanguēscō, –ere, –languī, —,** become weak, sink down

**relaxō,** 1, relax

**relevō,** 1, lighten, relieve, rest

**religiō, –ōnis,** *f.,* religion, superstition, scrupulousness, sacredness

**religiōsē,** *adv.,* religiously

**religiōsus, –a, –um,** sacred

**relinquō, –ere, relīquī, relictus,** leave (behind), abandon; leave unmentioned

**reliquiae, –ārum,** *f. pl.,* remains, relics

**reliquus, –a, –um,** remaining, rest (of), left, future; *w.* **tempus,** the future; **reliquum est,** it remains

**remaneō, –ēre, remānsī, remānsus,** remain (behind)

**remedium, –dī,** *n.,* remedy

**rēmigō, –āre, —, —,** row

**remigrō,** 1, go back

**remissiō, –ōnis,** *f.,* forgiveness, relaxation, recreation

**remissus, –a, –um,** gentle, mild

**remittō, –ere, remīsī, remissus,** send *or* throw back, remit, relax; drop

**remoror,** 1, hold back, delay

**removeō, –ēre, remōvī, remōtus,** move back, remove; **remōtus, –a, –um,** remote

**rēmus, –ī,** *m.,* oar

**Rēmus, –ī,** *m.,* a Rē´man

**renīdeō, –ere, —, —,** shine; smile

**renovō,** 1, renew

**renūntiō,** 1, report, declare elected

**reparō,** 1, restore

**repellō, –ere, reppulī, repulsus,** drive back, repulse

**repente,** *adv.,* suddenly

**repentīnus, –a, –um,** sudden

**reperiō, –īre, repperī, repertus,** find, discover

**repetō, –ere, –īvī, –ītus,** seek back, seek again, demand; repeat

**repleō, –ēre, replēvī, replētus,** fill again

**repōnō, –ēre, reposuī, repositus,** place

**reportō,** 1, carry *or* bring back

**reposcō, –ere, repoposcī, —,** demand in return

**repraesentō,** 1, show, represent

**reprehendō, –ere, reprehendī, reprehēnsus,** (hold back), censure, criticize

**reprimō, –ere, repressī, repressus,** stop, press back, check, thwart

**rēptō, –āre, —, —,** creep, crawl

**repudiō,** 1, divorce, reject, scorn

**repugnō,** 1, oppose, fight against, resist

**reputō,** 1, compute, ponder

**requiēs, –ētis,** *f.,* rest

**requiēscō, –ere, –ēvī, –ētus,** rest, repose

**requīrō, –ere, requīsīvī, requīsītus,** hunt up, search for, inquire; demand; miss

**rēs, reī,** *f.,* thing, fact, matter, affair, object, circumstance; **novae rēs, novārum rerum,** *f. pl.,* revolution; **rēs frūmentāria, reī frūmentāriae,** *f.,* grain supply, supplies; **rēs mīlitāris,** military affairs, art of war, warfare; **rēs pūblica,** republic, state, public interest, public affairs, government, state; **rēs gestae,** deeds

**rescindō, –ere, rescidī, rescissus,** cut down

**rescrībō, –ere, rescrīpsī, rescrīptus,** write back

**resecō, –āre, resecuī, resectus,** cut off

**reservō,** 1, reserve

**resideō, –ēre, resēdī, —,** remain, be left, sit down

**resistō, –ere, restitī, —,** stand against; resist, stop

**resolūtiō, –ōnis,** *f.,* relaxing, looseness; solution

**resolvō, –ere, resolvī, resolūtus,** loosen, solve

**respiciō, –ere, respexī, respectus,** look back (at), look at, consider

**resplendeō, –ēre, —, —,** shine brightly, gleam

**respondeō, –ēre, respondī, respōnsus,** reply, answer

**respōnsum, –ī,** *n.,* answer, reply

**respuō, –ere, respui, —,** reject

**restinguō, –ere, restīnxī, restīnctus,** extinguish

**restituō, –ere, restituī, restitūtus,** restore

**restō, –āre, restitī, —,** remain, withstand, be left

**restringō, –ere, restrīnxī, restrictus,** bind back, restrict

**resupīnus, –a, –um,** on one's back

**resūmō, –ere, resūmpsī, resūmptus,** take up again, resume

**resurgō = surgō**

**retardō,** 1, check, hinder

**reticeō, –ēre, reticuī, —,** be *or* keep silent

**retineō, –ēre, retinuī, retentus,** hold back, restrain, keep, hold to

**retorqueō, –ēre, retorsī, retortus,** turn back

**retrahō, –ere, retrāxī, retrāctus,** drag back

**retrō,** *adv.,* back, backward

**retrūdō, –ere, —, retrūsus,** thrust back

**retundō, –ere, rettudī, retūsus,** beat back

**rettulī,** *see* **referō**

**reus, –ī,** *m.,* defendant

**revellō, –ere, revellī, revulsus,** tear away

**revereor, reverērī, reveritus,** respect

**revertō, –ere, revertī, reversus,** (*sometimes deponent*), turn back, return

**revīsō, –ere, —, —,** revisit

**revocābilis, –e,** revocable

**revocō,** 1, recall, call back

**revolō,** 1, fly back

**rēx, rēgis,** *m.,* king

**Rhēnus, –ī,** *m.,* Rhine river

**rhētor, –ōris,** *m.,* rhetorician, orator

**rhētorica, –ae,** *f.,* rhetoric

**rhētoricus, –a, –um,** rhetorical

**Rhodanus, –ī,** *m.,* Rhone river

**rictus, –ūs,** *m.,* jaws

**rīdeō, –ēre, rīsī, rīsus,** laugh (at)

**rīdiculus, –a, –um,** absurd

**rigeō, –ēre, —, —,** be stiff

**rigidus, a, um,** stiff (with cold)

**rigor, –ōris,** *m.,* stiffness

**riguus, –a, –um,** well-watered

**rīma, –ae,** *f.,* crack

**rīmor,** 1, tear up; examine

**rīpa, –ae,** *f.,* bank (*of a river*)

**rīte,** *adv.,* duly, rightly

**rōborō,** 1, strengthen

**rōbur, rōboris,** *n.,* oak; strength

**rōbustus, –a, –um,** (of oak), hardy, robust

**rogātus, –ūs,** *m.,* request

**rogitō,** 1, keep on asking

**rogō,** 1, ask, beg; propose, pass

**rogus, –ī,** *m.,* funeral pile, grave

**Rōma, –ae,** *f.,* Rome

**Rōmānus, –a, –um,** Roman; *as noun,* a Roman, *m. pl.,* the Romans

**rosa, –ae,** *f.,* rose

**rostrum, –ī,** *n.,* prow (of a ship); beak, mouth, bill

**rota, –ae,** *f.,* wheel; *pl.,* chariot

**rotundus, –a, –um,** round

**rubēns,** *gen.* **–entis,** red

**ruber, rubra, rubrum,** red

**rubor, –ōris,** *m.,* redness, blush; modesty

**rudis, –e,** untrained, ignorant, rough

**Rūfus, –ī,** *m.,* Rufus

**rūgōsus, –a, –um,** wrinkled

**ruīna, –ae,** *f.,* ruin, destruction

**rūmor, –ōris,** *m.,* rumor

**rumpō, –ere, rūpī, ruptus,** break, pierce

**rūpēs, –is,** *f.,* cliff, rock

**rūrsus,** *adv.,* again

**rūs, rūris,** *n.,* country; farm; pl., fields

**rūsticānus, –a, –um,** rural

**rūsticatiō, –ōnis,** *f.,* living in the country

**rūsticor,** 1, go into the country

**rūsticus, –a, –um,** rustic

## S

**Sabella, –ae,** *f.,* Sabella

**Sabellus, –a, –um,** Sabellian, Sabine

**Sabidus, –ī,** *m.,* Sabidus

**Sabīna, –ae,** *f.,* Sabine woman

**Sabīnus, –a, –um,** Sabine; *as noun, pl.,* the Sabines, *a people of Italy*

**sacculus, –ī,** *m.,* little sack

**saccus, –ī,** *m.,* sack, bag

**sacer, sacra, sacrum,** sacred; *n. pl.,* sacred rites, ceremonies
**sacerdōs, –dōtis,** *m. and f.,* priest, priestess
**sacerdōtium, –tī,** *n.,* priesthood
**sacramentum, –ī,** *n.,* oath
**sacrārium, –rī,** *n.,* shrine
**sacrificium, –cī,** *n.,* sacrifice
**sacrificō,** 1, sacrifice
**sacrōsānctus, –a, –um,** sacred, inviolable
**saeculāris, –e,** secular
**saeculum (saeclum), –ī,** *n.,* age, generation
**saepe,** *adv.,* often
**saepēs, –is,** *f.,* hedge, fence; enclosure
**saeviō, –īre, saevīvī, saevītus,** rage, rant
**saevitia, –ae,** *f.,* fierceness
**saevus, –a, –um,** cruel, fierce
**sagāx,** *gen.* **–ācis,** keen
**sagitta, –ae,** *f.,* arrow
**sagittārius, –rī,** *m.,* bowman
**sagittifer, –fera, –ferum,** arrow-bearing
**sagulum, –ī,** *n.,* small military cloak
**sāl, salis,** *m.,* salt
**salārium, –rī,** *n.,* pension, stipend
**salignus, –a, –um,** of willow
**Saliī, –ōrum,** *m. pl.,* the Salii *or* "Jumpers" (*priests of Mars*)
**saliō, –īre, saluī, saltus,** jump, beat
**saltātor, –ōris,** *m.,* dancer
**saltō,** 1, dance
**salūbris, –e,** wholesome, healthy, healthful
**salūbritās, –tātis,** *f.,* health
**salūs, –ūtis,** *f.,* health, safety, greeting
**salūtātor, –ōris,** *m.,* greeter, visitor
**salūtō,** 1, greet, pay one's respects
**salvē, salvēte,** be well, greetings, hail
**salvus, –a, –um,** safe, well, solvent
**Samos, –ī,** *f.,* Samos, *an island in the Aegean Sea*
**sānābilis, –e,** curable
**sānciō, –īre, sānxī, sānctus,** decree
**sānctē,** *adv.,* religiously, scrupulously
**sānctus, –a, –um,** sacred, holy, venerable, upright
**sānē,** *adv.,* indeed, truly, of course
**Sanga, –ae,** *m.,* Sanga
**sanguis, sanguinis,** *m.,* blood
**sānitās, –tātis,** *f.,* sanity, soundness of mind
**sānō,** 1, make sound, cure
**sānus, –a, –um,** sound, in one's right mind, sane
**sapiēns,** *gen.* **sapientis,** wise; *as noun, m.,* philosopher
**sapienter,** *adv.,* wisely
**sapientia, –ae,** *f.,* wisdom
**sapiō, –ere, sapīvī, —,** taste, savor
**sarcina, –ae,** *f.,* burden, load
**Sardēs, –ium,** *f. pl.,* Sardis, *capital of Lydia, in Asia Minor*
**Sardinia, –ae,** *f.,* Sardinia
**satelles, –litis,** *m. and f.,* attendant; accomplice
**satietās, –tātis,** *f.,* abundance, satiety
**satiō,** 1, satisfy, sate
**satira, –ae,** *f.,* miscellany, satire
**satis,** *adv. and indeclinable adj.,* enough, rather; quite, sufficiently; *comp.,* **satius,** better
**satisfaciō, –ere, –fēcī, –factus,** satisfy
**Sāturnālia, –ium,** *n. pl.,* the Saturnalia, *a festival in honor of Saturn*
**Sāturnius, –a, –um,** of Saturn, Saturnian
**Sāturnus, –ī,** *m.,* Saturn
**saturō,** 1, fill, saturate
**Satyrus, –ī,** *m.,* Satyr, wood deity
**sauciō,** 1, wound
**saxum, –ī,** *n.,* rock, stone
**scaena, –ae,** *f.,* stage, theater
**scaenicus, –a, –um,** of the theater, of the stage; *w.* **lūdī,** stage plays
**scandō, –ere, —, —,** rise, climb
**scelerātē,** *adv.,* wickedly, impiously
**scelerātus, –a, –um,** wicked, accursed, criminal
**scelus, sceleris,** *n.,* crime, wickedness
**scēptrum, –ī,** *n.,* scepter
**schola, –ae,** *f.,* school
**scholāris, –e,** of *or* belonging to a school
**scholasticus, –a, –um,** scholastic; *as noun, m.,* student
**scientia, –ae,** *f.,* knowledge
**scīlicet,** *adv.,* of course, doubtless
**scindō, –ere, scidī, scissus,** cut, split
**sciō, scīre, scīvī, scītus,** know, know how
**Scīpiō, –ōnis,** *m.,* Scipio
**scītē,** *adv.,* skillfully, well

**scitor**, 1, inquire
**scrība, –ae**, *m.,* secretary
**scrībō, –ere, scrīpsī, scrīptus**, write
**scrīptor, –ōris**, *m.,* writer
**scrīptum, –ī**, *n.,* writing
**scrīptūra, –ae**, *f.,* writing, Scripture
**scrūtor**, 1, examine thoroughly
**sculpō, –ere, sculpsī, sculptus**, carve
**scūtum, –ī**, *n.,* shield
**Scythae, –ārum**, *m. pl.,* the Scythians, *people beyond the Black Sea*
**sē**, *acc. and abl. of* **suī**
**sēcēdō, –ere, sēcessī, sēcessus**, secede, withdraw, go away, retire
**sēcernō, –ere, sēcrēvī, sēcrētus**, separate
**sēcessus, –ūs**, *m.,* departure, retirement
**secō, secāre, secuī, sectus**, cut
**sēcrētō**, *adv.,* in private, secretly
**sectus, –a, –um**, cut off
**sēcum = cum sē**
**secundum**, *prep. w. acc.,* following, according to, behind, next to
**secundus, –a, –um**, second, favorable; successful; *w.* **rēs**, prosperity
**Secundus, –ī**, *m.,* Secundus
**secūris, –is**, *f.,* ax
**sed**, *conj.,* but
**sedeō, –ēre, sēdī, sessus**, sit, sit down, lie idle
**sēdēs, –is**, *f.,* abode, place; seat
**sedīle, –is**, *n.,* seat
**sēditiō, –ōnis**, *f.,* rebellion, sedition
**sēdō**, 1, quiet, bring to an end, stop
**sēdūcō, –ere, sēdūxī, sēductus**, set aside
**sēductor, –ōris**, *m.,* misleader, seducer
**sēductus, –a, –um**, separated
**sēdulitās, –tātis**, *f.,* diligence
**sēdulō**, *adv.,* busily, carefully, eagerly
**sēdulus, –a, –um**, diligent
**segnitiēs, –eī**, *f.,* slowness, inactivity
**sēgregō**, 1, exclude
**sēiungō, –ere, sēiūnxī, sēiūnctus**, disjoint, separate, sever
**Seleucus, –ī**, *m.,* Seleucus, *king of Syria*
**sella, –ae**, *f.,* chair, seat, stool
**semel**, *adv.,* once
**sēmen, –minis**, *n.,* seed
**sēmēsus, –a, –um**, half-eaten
**sēmibarbarus, –a, –um**, half-barbarian
**sēminārium, –rī**, *n.,* nursery
**semita, –ae**, *f.,* path, footpath
**semper**, *adv.,* always
**sempiternus, –a, –um**, everlasting, perpetual
**Semprōnius, –a, –um**, Sempronian
**senātor, –ōris**, *m.,* senator
**senātōrius, –a, –um**, senatorial
**senātus, –ūs**, *m.,* senate
**Seneca, –ae**, *m.,* Seneca
**senecta, –ae**, *f.,* old age
**senectūs, –tūtis**, *f.,* old age
**senēscō, –ere, senuī, —**, grow old
**senex, senis**, *m.,* old man; *adj.,* old; *comp.* **senior**
**senīlis, –e**, of an old man
**senior, –ius**, older; aged
**sēnsus, –ūs**, *m.,* feeling; consciousness
**sententia, –ae**, *f.,* feeling, opinion; proposal; meaning, sentiment
**sentīna, –ae**, *f.,* sewage, sewer
**sentiō, –īre, sēnsī, sēnsus**, feel, think, realize, vote, perceive, know
**sentis, –is**, *m.,* thorn, briar
**sepeliō, –īre, –īvī, sepultus**, bury
**sēpōnō, –ere, sēposuī, sēpositus**, separate, assign
**septem**, seven
**September, –bris, –bre**, (of) September
**septentriōnēs, –um**, *m. pl.,* seven plow-oxen (*the seven stars of the constellation Great Bear or Big Dipper*), north
**septimus, –a, –um**, seventh
**septingentī, –ae, –a**, seven hundred
**sepulchrum, –ī**, *n.,* tomb
**sepultūra, –ae**, *f.,* burial
**Sēquana, –ae**, *m.,* the Seine river
**Sēquanus, –a, –um**, Sequanian; *as noun, m. pl.,* the Sequanians
**sequor, sequī, secūtus**, follow, pursue, seek
**serēnō**, 1, clear up
**serēnus, –a, –um**, quiet, clear, serene
**Serēnus, –ī**, *m.,* Serenus
**Sergius, –gī**, *m.,* Sergius

**sērius, –a, –um,** grave, serious; *comp. adv.,* later
**sermō, –ōnis,** *m.,* conversation, talk, speech, report
**serō, –ere, sēvī, satus,** plant, sow, produce; **satus, –a, –um,** sprung from
**sērō,** *adv.,* late
**serpēns, –entis,** *m. and f.,* snake
**serpō, –ere, serpsī, serptus,** crawl
**sertum, –ī,** *n.,* wreath of flowers, garland
**sērus, –a, –um,** late
**serva, –ae,** *f.,* slave
**servīlis, –e,** of a slave
**serviō, –īre, servīvī, servītus,** be a slave (to), serve, have regard for, court
**servitium, –tī,** *n.,* slavery
**servitūs, –tūtis,** *f.,* slavery
**Servius Tullius,** *m.,* Servius Tullius, *a Roman king*
**servō,** 1, save, preserve, guard, keep
**servus, –ī,** *m.,* slave
**sescentī, –ae, –a,** six hundred
**sēsē,** *acc. and abl. of* **suī**
**seu,** *see* **sīve**
**sevērē,** *adv.,* severely
**sevēritās, –tātis,** *f.,* severity
**sevērus, –a, –um,** stern, severe
**sex,** six
**sexāgintā,** sixty
**Sextīlis, –e,** August
**sextus, –a, –um,** sixth
**sexus, –ūs,** *m.,* sex
**sī,** *conj.,* if
**Sibylla, –ae,** *f.,* the Sibyl, *a prophetess*
**Sibyllīnus, –a, –um,** Sibylline
**sīc,** *adv.,* so, thus, in this way
**sīca, –ae,** *f.,* dagger
**sīcārius, –rī,** *m.,* assassin
**siccō,** 1, dry up
**siccus, –a, –um,** dry
**Sicilia, –ae,** *f.,* Sicily
**Siculī, –ōrum,** *m.,* Sicilians
**sīcutī (sīcut),** *adv.,* just as, as if
**sīdus, sīderis,** *n.,* star, constellation
**sigilla, –ōrum,** *n. pl.,* small statues
**signifer, –ferī,** *m.,* standard bearer
**significātiō, –ōnis,** *f.,* signal, meaning
**significō,** 1, indicate, mean, show
**signō,** 1, seal, mark
**signum, –ī,** *n.,* sign, token, signal; standard; seal, mark
**Silānus, –ī,** *m.,* Silanus
**silentium, –tī,** *n.,* silence
**silva, –ae,** *f.,* forest, woods
**Sīlēnus, –ī,** *m.,* Silenus
**sileō, –ēre, siluī, —,** be silent, leave unmentioned
**silva, –ae,** *f.,* forest, woods
**Silvānus, –ī,** *m.,* Silvanus
**silvestris, –e,** wild
**Simeōn, –ōnis,** *m.,* Simeon
**similis, –e,** like, similar
**similitūdō, –dinis,** *f.,* likeness, resemblance
**simplex, –plicis,** simple, single
**simplicitās, –tātis,** *f.,* simplicity, frankness, naturalness
**simpliciter,** *adv.,* plainly, openly
**simul,** *adv.,* at the same time, at once, together; **simul atque (ac),** as soon as
**simulācrum, –ī,** *n.,* figure, image, likeness
**simulātor, –ōris,** *m.,* pretender
**simulō,** 1, pretend
**simultās, –tatis,** *f.,* rivalry, enmity
**sīn,** *conj.,* but if
**sincērus, –a, –um,** pure, chaste
**sine,** *prep. w. abl.,* without
**singillātim,** *adv.,* one by one, individually, singly
**singulāris, –e,** one by one, remarkable, unique, separate
**singulārius, –a, –um,** single, separate; singular
**singulī, –ae, –a,** *pl.* only, separate, each, one after another, one at a time; one each, single
**sinister, –tra, –trum,** left; *comp.,* **sinisterior,** the left
**sinō, –ere, sīvī, situs,** allow
**Sinōpēnsis, –e,** of Sinope, *a Greek colony; as noun, m. pl.,* the people of Sinope
**sinus, –ūs,** *m.,* fold; bosom; bay
**Sipylus, –ī,** *m.,* Sipylus, *a son of Niobe*
**sistō, –ere, stitī, status,** place; stop, check
**sitiō, –īre, sitīvī, —,** be thirsty

**sitis, –is,** *f.,* thirst

**situs, –a, –um,** placed; **situm est,** it lies

**situs, –ūs,** *m.,* position

**sīve (seu),** *conj.,* or if, or; **sīve (seu)... sīve (seu),** whether . . . or, either . . . or

**sōbrius, –a, –um,** sober

**socer, –erī,** *m.,* father-in-law

**societās, –tātis,** *f.,* fellowship, alliance

**socius, –cī,** *m.,* comrade, companion, associate, ally, accomplice; *pl.,* allies, provincials

**Sōcratēs, –is,** *m.,* Socrates

**sodālis, –is,** *m.,* companion

**sōl, sōlis,** *m.,* sun

**sōlācium, –cī,** *n.,* comfort

**solea, –ae,** *f.,* sandal, shoe

**soleō, –ēre, solitus,** *semideponent,* be used to, be accustomed

**solidus, –a, –um,** solid

**sōlitūdō, –dinis,** *f.,* wilderness, solitude

**solitus, –a, –um,** customary

**sollemnis, –e,** (annual), customary, appointed, solemn

**sollertia, –ae,** *f.,* skill, ingenuity, adroitness

**sollicitātiō, –ōnis,** *f.,* inciting

**sollicitō,** 1, stir up, disturb, incite to revolt, tamper with

**sollicitūdō, –dinis,** *f.,* uneasiness, anxiety

**sollicitus, –a, –um,** anxious, worried

**Solōn, –ōnis,** *m.,* Solon

**sōlor,** 1, comfort

**solum, –ī,** *n.,* soil

**sōlum,** *adv.,* only, alone; **nōn sōlum... sed (vērum) etiam,** not only . . . but also

**sōlus, –a, –um,** alone, only, lonely

**solūtiō, –ōnis,** *f.,* payment

**solvō, –ere, solvī, solūtus,** loose, break, free, release, solve; set sail; *w.* **poenam,** pay

**somnium, –nī,** *n.,* dream

**somnus, –ī,** *m.,* sleep

**sonitus, –ūs,** *m.,* sound

**sonō, –āre, sonuī, sonitus,** resound; **sonāns,** *gen.* **–antis,** clanking

**sonōrus, –a, –um,** sonorous

**sonus, –ī,** *m.,* sound, noise

**Sophia, –ae,** *f.,* Wisdom

**sophisma, –atis,** *n.,* false conclusion, sophism

**sōpiō, –īre, sōpīvī, sōpītus,** lull to sleep, stun

**sopor, –ōris,** *m.,* deep sleep, stupor; laziness

**sordidus, –a, –um,** dirty, stained, mean

**soror, –ōris,** *f.,* sister

**sors, sortis,** *f.,* lot, prophecy

**sortior, –īrī, sortītus,** cast lots, ballot

**sortītō,** *adv.,* by lot

**Spanius, –ī,** *m.,* Spanius

**spargō, –ere, sparsī, sparsus,** scatter, sprinkle, spread

**Sparta, –ae,** *f.,* Sparta, *a Greek city*

**Spartacus, –ī,** *m.,* Spartacus, *leader in a revolt of gladiators*

**Spartānus, –ī,** *m.,* a Spartan

**spatior,** 1, take a walk, walk

**spatiōsus, –a, –um,** roomy, large

**spatium, –tī,** *n.,* space, distance; time, period

**speciēs, speciēī,** *f.,* appearance, sight

**speciōsus, –a, –um,** showy, glittering

**spectābilis, –e,** conspicuous, beautiful

**spectāculum, –ī,** *n.,* spectacle, show

**spectātiō, –ōnis,** *f.,* viewing

**spectātor, –ōris,** *m.,* spectator

**spectō,** 1, look at *or* on, face, see

**speculāria, –ōrum,** *n. pl.,* windows

**speculātor, –ōris,** *m.,* spy

**speculor,** 1, watch

**speculum, –ī,** *n.,* mirror; copy

**spēlunca, –ae,** *f.,* cave, cavern, den

**spērō,** 1, hope (for)

**spēs, speī,** *f.,* hope

**spīna, –ae,** *f.,* thorn

**spīritus, –ūs,** *m.,* breath, spirit, air; pride

**spīrō,** 1, breathe

**splendidus, –a, –um,** shining, brilliant, distinguished

**spolia, –ōrum,** *n., pl.,* spoils, booty

**spoliō,** 1, rob, deprive

**spondeo, –ēre, spopondi, sponsus,** promise, engage

**sponsa, –ae,** *f.,* a betrothed woman

**sponsus, –ī,** *m.,* a betrothed man

**sponte,** *w.* **suā,** of his/her/their own accord, by his/her/their own influence, voluntarily

**spūmāns,** *gen.* **–antis,** foaming
**spūmiger, –gera, –gerum,** foaming
**squālēns,** *gen.* **squālentis,** foul
**squāleō, –ēre, squāluī, —,** be stiff, be filthy
**st!** *interj.,* hush!
**stabilitās, –tātis,** *f.,* steadfastness, firmness
**stabulum, –ī,** *n.,* stable
**Statilius, –lī,** *m.,* Statilius
**statim,** *adv.,* at once, immediately
**statiō, –ōnis,** *f.,* outpost, guard, picket, station
**statua, –ae,** *f.,* statue
**statunculum, –ī,** *n.,* a little statue
**statuō, –ere, statuī, statūtus,** decide, determine, set up, place
**statūra, –ae,** *f.,* stature
**status, –a, –um,** fixed, appointed
**status, –ūs,** *m.,* state, position, condition, status
**stēlla, –ae,** *f.,* star
**sterilis, –e,** barren, unproductive, unfruitful
**sternō, –ere, strāvī, strātus,** strew, scatter; level, cover; overthrow, raze
**stetī,** *see* **stō**
**stilus, –ī,** *m.,* stylus (*instrument used in writing on wax tablets*)
**stimulō,** 1, urge on; disturb
**stimulus, –ī,** *m.,* incentive
**stīpendiārius, –a, –um,** tributary
**stīpendium, –dī,** *n.,* pay, tribute; campaign
**stīpes, –itis,** *m.,* log, post, trunk, stake
**stipula, –ae,** *f.,* stem, straw
**stō, stāre, stetī, status,** stand, stop
**stolidus, –a, –um,** dull, stupid
**stomachus, –ī,** *m.,* stomach
**Strabō, –ōnis,** *m.,* Strabo
**stragēs, –is,** *f.,* overthrowing, confusion; destruction
**strāmen, –minis,** *n.,* straw; *pl.,* thatch
**strātum, –ī,** *n.,* cover, horse blanket
**strēnuē,** *adv.,* briskly, actively
**strēnuus, –a, –um,** energetic
**strepitus, –ūs,** *m.,* noise
**stringō, –ere, strīnxī, strictus,** draw (tight); ruffle
**studeō, –ēre, studuī, —,** be eager (for), study, desire
**studiōsē,** *adv.,* eagerly
**studiōsus, –a, –um,** fond of
**studium, –dī,** *n.,* eagerness, desire, interest, zeal, enthusiasm; study, pursuit
**stultitia, –ae,** *f.,* stupidity, folly, foolishness, silliness
**stultus, –a, –um,** foolish, stupid
**stupendus, –a, –um,** stupendous
**stupeō, –ēre, –uī, —,** be amazed, stand aghast
**suādeō, –ēre, suāsī, suāsus,** urge, advise, persuade
**suāvis, –e,** sweet, pleasant, agreeable
**suāvitās, –tātis,** *f.,* sweetness, pleasantness, agreeableness
**sub,** *prep.,* under, close to, at the foot of, just before (*w. acc. after verbs of motion; w. abl. after verbs of rest or position*)
**subdō, –ere, subdidī, subditus,** put *or* plunge under
**subdūcō, –ere, –dūxī, –ductus,** lead up; draw up
**subeō, –īre, –iī, –itus,** go under, enter, come up, undergo
**subiciō, –ere, –iēcī, –iectus,** throw under, spread beneath, throw from below, subject, conquer; **subiectus,** lying beneath
**subigō, –ere, –ēgī, –āctus,** force, subdue
**subinde,** *adv.,* suddenly
**subinvideō, –ēre, —, —,** be envious of
**subitō,** *adv.,* suddenly
**subitus, –a, –um,** sudden
**sublātus,** *part. of* **tollō**
**sublevō,** 1, lighten, help, raise; *w. reflex.,* rise
**sublīmē,** *adv.,* aloft, on high
**submergō, –ere, –mersī, –mersus,** plunge
**subministrō,** 1, furnish
**submittō, –ere, –mīsī, –missus,** send, *see* **summittō**
**submoveō, –ēre, –mōvī, –mōtus,** drive back, send away, remove
**subrēpō, –ere, –rēpsī, —,** creep *or* steal along
**subruō, –ere, –ruī, –rutus,** undermine
**subsellium, –lī,** *n.,* bench, seat
**subsequor, –sequī, –secūtus,** follow (closely)
**subsidium, –dī,** *n.,* aid, reserve
**substō, –āre, —, —,** stand firm
**subterrāneus, –a, –um,** subterranean

**subtilis, –e,** fine, slender

**subveniō, –īre, –vēnī, –ventus,** come to help

**succēdō, –ere, –cessī, –cessus,** come up, enter, follow, succeed (*w. dat.*)

**successor, –ōris,** *m,* follower, successor

**successus, –ūs,** *m.,* success

**succrēscō, –ere, –crēvī, –crētus,** grow

**succurrō, –ere, –currī, –cursus,** run to help, run to one's aid

**Suēbī, –ōrum,** *m. pl.,* the Suebans *or* Suebi

**sufferō, –ere, sustulī, sublātus,** hold up, sustain; undergo

**sufficiō, –ere, –fēcī, –fectus,** suffice

**suffrāgium, –gī,** *n.,* vote, ballot

**suffundō, –ere, suffūdī, suffūsus,** pour into, overspread, infuse

**suī,** *reflexive pron.,* of himself, herself, itself, themselves

**Sulla, –ae,** m., Sulla

**sum, esse, fuī, futūrus,** be, exist

**summa, –ae,** *f.,* sum, total, chief part, substance; leadership; **summa rērum,** general interest; **summa imperī,** supreme command; **ad summam,** in short

**summittō, –ere, –mīsī, –missus,** lower

**summus, –a, –um,** highest, most important, greatest; top of, surface of

**summum, –ī,** *n.,* top, greatest

**sūmō, –ere, sūmpsī, sūmptus,** take, assume

**sūmptuōsē,** *adv.,* extravagantly

**sūmptuōsus, –a, –um,** extravagant; very expensive; lavish

**sūmptus, –ūs,** *m.,* expense, extravagance

**super,** *prep. w. acc.,* over, upon, above

**superbē,** *adv.,* arrogantly

**superbia, –ae,** *f.,* pride, arrogance

**superbus, –a, –um,** haughty, proud

**superficiārius, –a, –um,** situated on another man's land

**superiniciō, –ere, –iniēcī, –iniectus,** cast over, scatter upon

**superior, –ius,** higher, elder, upper, superior; previous, former

**superō,** 1, overcome, conquer; surpass; beat; defeat; pass over

**superstitiō, –ōnis,** *f.,* superstition

**supersum, –esse, –fuī, –futūrus,** be left (over), remain, survive

**superus, –a, –um,** upper; *as noun, m. pl.,* gods (above)

**supīnus, –a, –um,** thrown backwards, on the back, supine; sloping

**suppeditō,** 1, supply

**suppetō, –ēre, suppetīvī, suppetītus,** be at hand, be present; be sufficient for

**suppīlō,** 1, pilfer, rob

**suppleō, –ere, supplēvī, supplētus,** fill

**supplex,** *gen.* **supplicis,** begging, suppliant

**supplicātiō, –ōnis,** *f.,* thanksgiving, public prayer

**supplicium, –cī,** *n.,* punishment, torture

**supplicō,** 1, kneel down (to), pray, worship

**suprā,** *adv. and prep. w. acc.,* above, beyond, before, previously

**suprēmus, –a, –um,** highest, last, dying

**surgō, –ere, surrēxī, surrēctus,** rise, arise

**surripiō, –ere, –ripuī, –reptus,** seize (secretly), steal

**suscēnseō, –ēre, –cēnsuī, —,** be angry with

**suscipiō, –ere, –cēpī, –ceptus,** undertake, incur, suffer

**suscitō,** 1, rekindle

**suspendō, –ere, –pendī,** hang, suspend

**suspēnsus, –a, –um,** in suspense

**suspīciō, –ōnis,** *f.,* suspicion

**suspīciō, –ere, suspexī, suspectus,** esteem, admire; suspect

**suspicor,** 1, suspect

**suspīro,** 1, sigh

**suspīrium, –rī,** *n.,* sigh

**sustentō,** 1, maintain

**sustineō, –ēre, –tinuī, –tentus,** hold up, keep up *or* back; bear, endure, withstand, hold out, check

**sustulī,** *see* **tollō**

**suus, –a, –um,** *reflexive adj.,* his, her, its, their; his own, her own, etc.; *as noun,* **suī,** his (her, their) men, friends; **sua,** *n.,* his (her, their) possessions

**syllaba, –ae,** *f.,* syllable

**Syrācūsae, –ārum,** *f. pl.,* Syracuse, *a city in Sicily*

**Syrtis, –is,** *f.,* Syrtis

## T

**T.,** *abbreviation for* **Titus**

**tabella, –ae,** *f.,* tablet; *pl.,* letter, ballot, record

**tabellārius, –rī,** *m.,* letter carrier

**taberna, –ae,** *f.,* shop, tavern

**tābēscō, –ere, tābuī, —,** melt

**tabula, –ae,** *f.,* board, painting; table, tablet (of the law); writing tablet; *pl.,* records, accounts

**taceō, –ēre, tacuī,** be silent, leave unmentioned

**taciturnitās, –tātis,** *f.,* silence

**tacitus, –a, –um,** silent, secret

**taeda, –ae,** *f.,* torch; wedding

**taeter, –tra, –trum,** foul, revolting

**tālāris, –e,** reaching the ankles

**tālis, –e,** such

**tam,** *adv.,* so, so much (*w. adj. and adv.*)

**tamen,** *adv.,* yet, still, nevertheless; however

**tametsī,** *conj.,* although

**tamquam,** *adv.,* as if, as, as it were

**Tanais, –is,** *m.,* Tanais, *a river*

**tandem,** *adv.,* at last, finally; *in questions,* I ask

**tangō, –ere, tetigī, tāctus,** touch, move, reach; partake of

**Tantalus, –ī,** *m.,* Tantalus, (1) *Niobe's father,* (2) *son of Niobe*

**tantō,** *adv.,* so much

**tantulus, –a, –um,** so small

**tantum,** *adv.,* so much, so greatly; only, merely; *w.* **modo,** only, merely

**tantus, –a, –um,** so great, so much, so large, such

**tantusdem, tantadem, tantundem,** as great *or* large

**tardē,** *adv.,* slowly, late, tardily

**tarditās, –tātis,** *f.,* slowness

**tardō,** 1, slow up, delay, check

**tardus, –a, –um,** slow, late

**Tarentīnī, –ōrum,** *m. pl.,* the people of Tarentum

**Tarpeius, –a, –um,** Tarpeian

**Tarquinius, –nī,** *m.,* Tarquinius, Tarquin

**Tarquinius Superbus, –ī,** *m.,* Tarquin the Proud, *king of Rome*

**Tartarus, –ī,** *m.,* Hades

**taurus, –ī,** *m.,* bull

**tēctum, –ī,** *n.,* roof, house, dwelling, home

**tegimentum, –ī,** *n.,* cover

**tegō, –ere, tēxī, tēctus,** cover, conceal; protect

**tellūs, –ūris,** *f.,* earth; land

**tēlum, –ī,** *n.,* weapon, missile, shaft

**temerārius, –a, –um,** rash

**temere,** *adv.,* rashly, without reason

**temeritās, –tātis,** *f.,* rashness

**temperāmentum, –ī,** *n.,* right proportion; moderation

**temperātē,** *adv.,* moderately

**temperātus, –a, –um,** temperate

**tempestās, –tātis,** *f.,* weather, storm; season

**templum, –ī,** *n.,* temple

**temptō,** 1, test, try, attempt, tempt; attack

**tempus, temporis,** *n.,* time, period, temple (*of the head*); *w.* **ex,** offhand

**tenāx,** *gen.* **tenācis,** tenacious

**tendō, –ere, tetendī, tentus,** stretch, extend, go

**tenebrae, –ārum,** *f. pl.,* darkness

**Tenedos, –ī,** *f.,* Tenedos, *an island*

**teneō, –ēre, tenuī, tentus,** hold, keep, possess; **memoriā teneō,** remember

**tener, –era, –erum,** tender; young

**tenuis, –e,** thin, little; humble

**tenuitās, –tātis,** thinness, slenderness; poverty

**tenuō,** 1, make thin *or* slender

**tenus,** *postpositive prep. w. abl.,* up to

**tepeō, –ēre, —, —,** be warm

**tepidus, –a, –um,** warm

**tepor, –ōris,** gentle warmth

**ter,** *adv.,* three times

**terebrō,** 1, pierce

**Terentius, –tī,** *m.,* Terence

**tergum, –ī,** *n.,* **tergus, –goris,** *n.,* back; side (of pork); **ā tergō,** in the rear

**terminō,** 1, bound, limit; end, close

**terminus, –ī,** *m.,* boundary

**ternī, –ae, –a,** three at a time

**terō, –ere, trīvī, trītus,** wear away, grind; exhaust

**terra, –ae,** *f.,* land, earth, ground

**terreō, –ēre, terruī, territus,** scare, frighten, terrify

**terrestris, –e,** terrestrial

**terribilis, –e,** frightful

**terror, –ōris,** *m.,* terror

**tertius, –a, –um,** third
**testa, –ae,** *f.,* brick
**testāmentum, –ī,** *n.,* will
**testimōnium, –nī,** *n.,* testimony, proof
**testis, –is,** *m.,* witness
**testor,** 1, call to witness
**testūdō, –dinis,** *f.,* shed, turtle, testudo
**Teutonī, –ōrum,** *m. pl.,* the Teutons
**thalamus, –ī,** *m.,* bedchamber; marriage bed, marriage
**theātrum, –ī,** *n.,* theater
**Thēbae, –ārum,** *f. pl.,* Thebes, *a Greek city*
**thema, –atis,** *n.,* theme
**Thermus, –ī,** *m.,* Thermus
**Thessalia, –ae,** *f.,* Thessaly, *part of Greece*
**Thisbē, –ēs,** *f.,* Thisbe
**Thrācia, –ae,** *f.,* Thrace, *a country north of Greece*
**Thrācius, –a, –um,** Thracian; of Thrace, *a country north of Greece*
**Thrāx, –ācis,** *m.,* a Thracian
**thronus, –ī** *m.,* throne
**Thynēius, –a, –um,** of Thynaeum
**tiāra, –ae,** *f.,* turban, tiara
**Tiberis, –is,** *m.,* Tiber River, the Tiber, *a river in Italy*
**Tiberius, –rī,** *m.,* Tiberius
**tībia, –ae,** *f.,* pipe, flute
**tignum, –ī,** *n.,* beam
**Tigurīnus, –ī,** *m.,* Tigurinus, *a Helvetian canton; pl.,* the Tigurini
**timeō, –ēre, timuī, —,** fear, be afraid
**timidus, –a, –um,** timid, cowardly; **timidē,** *adv.,* timidly
**timor, –ōris,** *m.,* fear
**tingō, –ere, tīnxī, tīnctus,** wet; color, stain
**tintinnābulum, –ī,** *n.,* bell
**Tīrō, –ōnis,** *m.,* Tiro
**Titius, –tī,** *m.,* Titius
**titulus, –ī,** *m.,* title, sign
**Tmōlus, –ī,** *m.,* Tmolus, *a mountain in Lydia*
**toga, –ae,** *f.,* toga (*cloak*)
**togātus, –a, –um,** in civilian garb, toga-clad
**tolerābilis, –e,** endurable, tolerable
**tolerō,** 1, bear
**tollō, –ere, sustulī, sublātus,** raise, take *or* pick up, carry, remove, destroy
**tormentum, –ī,** *n.,* torture; artillery, hurling machine
**torpor, –ōris,** *m.,* numbness, sluggishness
**torqueō, –ēre, torsī, tortus,** twist, whirl, turn; torture
**torus, –ī,** *m.,* cushion, couch
**torreō, –ēre, torruī, tostus,** roast, scorch
**tot,** *indecl. adj.,* so many
**totidem,** *indecl. adj.,* just as many, the same number
**totiēns,** *adv.,* so often
**tōtus, –a, –um,** whole, entire, all
**trabs, trabis,** *f.,* beam
**trāctātus, –ūs,** m., handling, treatment
**trāctō,** 1, handle, treat, conduct; draw into
**trāditiō, –ōnis,** *f.,* surrender
**trādō, –ere, –didī, –ditus,** give *or* hand over, transmit, relate, surrender; deliver
**trādūcō, –ere, –dūxī, –ductus,** lead across, win over
**tragicus, –a, –um,** of tragedy, tragic
**trāgula, –ae,** *f.,* javelin
**trahō, –ere, trāxī, trāctus,** draw, influence, derive, drag; take on; *w.* **ad mē,** claim
**trāiciō, –ere, –iēcī, –iectus,** strike through, hurl through, pierce
**trāmittō, –ere, –mīsī, –missus,** transmit, hand over; cross
**trānō,** 1, swim across
**tranquillitās, –tātis,** *f.,* calm, tranquility
**tranquillus, –a, –um,** peaceful, quiet
**trāns,** *prep. w. acc.,* across
**Trānsalpīnus, –a, –um,** beyond the Alps, Transalpine
**trānscendō, –ere, –cendī, —,** board, climb over
**trānscurrō, –ere, –currī, –cursus,** traverse
**trānseō, –īre, –iī, –itus,** cross, pass, go over
**trānsferō, –ferre, –tulī, –lātus,** carry over, transfer
**trānsfīgō, –ere, –fīxī, –fīxus,** pierce through
**trānsfodiō, –ere, –fōdī, –fossus,** pierce through
**trānsfuga, –ae,** *m.,* deserter
**trānsigō, –ere, –ēgī, –āctus,** carry out

**trānsiliō, –īre, –siluī, —,** jump across
**trānsitus, –ūs,** *m.,* passage
**trānsmittō, –ere, –mīsī, –missus,** pass on
**trānsportō,** 1, carry over, transport
**trānsverberō, –āre, —, —,** strike through, pierce through
**trānsversus, –a, –um,** cross
**trecentī, –ae, –a,** three hundred
**tremebundus, –a, –um,** shake, trembling
**tremō, –ere, tremuī, —,** shake, tremble
**tremor, –ōris,** *m.,* shaking
**tremulus, –a, –um,** trembling
**trepidō,** 1, tremble; rush about
**trepidus, –a, –um,** trembling
**trēs, tria,** three
**tribūnicius, –a, –um,** tribunician
**tribūnus, –ī,** *m.,* tribune
**tribuō, –ere, tribuī, tribūtus,** bestow, grant, assign
**tribūtum, –ī,** *n.,* tax, tribute
**trīclinium, –nī,** *n.,* dining room, dining couch
**trīduum, –ī,** *n.,* three days
**triennium, –nī,** *n.,* (a period of) three years
**trīgintā,** thirty
**Trimalchiō, –ōnis,** *m.,* Trimalchio
**triplex,** *gen.* **triplicis,** threefold, triple
**trīstis, –e,** sad, severe
**tristitia, –ae,** *f.,* sadness
**triumphō,** 1, triumph, celebrate a triumph
**triumphus, –ī,** *m.,* triumph, triumphal procession
**Troia, –ae,** *f.,* Troy, *a city in Asia Minor*
**Troiānus, –a, –um,** Trojan; *as noun, m. pl.,* the Trojans
**tropaeum, –ī,** *n.,* trophy
**trucīdō,** 1, butcher, murder
**trūdō, –ere, trūsī, trūsus,** thrust, shove forward
**truncō,** 1, strip
**truncus, –ī,** *m.,* trunk (*of a tree*)
**tū, tuī,** *pers. pron.* you, yourself
**tuba, –ae,** *f.,* trumpet
**Tuberō, –ōnis,** *m.,* Tubero
**tubulātus, –a, –um,** formed like a pipe, tubular
**tueor, tuērī, tūtus,** watch, look, guard, defend, maintain
**tulī,** *see* **ferō**
**Tullia, Tulliola, –ae,** *f.,* Tullia
**Tullius, –lī,** *m.,* Tullius
**tum,** *adv.,* then
**tumeō, –ēre, —, —,** swell
**tumidus, –a, –um,** swollen; enraged; haughty
**tumultus, –ūs,** *m.,* uproar, disturbance
**tumulus, –ī,** *m.,* hill, tomb
**tunc,** *adv.,* then; accordingly
**tunica, –ae,** *f.,* tunic
**turba, –ae,** *f.,* turmoil, throng
**turbō,** 1, roughen
**turbulentus, –a, –um,** muddy, disorderly, violent
**turma, –ae,** *f.,* troop (*of cavalry*)
**turpis, –e,** disgraceful, ugly
**turpiter,** *adv.,* basely
**turpitūdō, –dinis,** *f.,* disgrace, baseness
**turris, –is,** *f.,* tower
**tūs, tūris,** *n.,* incense
**Tuscia, –ae,** *f.,* Tuscany
**Tusculānī, –ōrum,** *m. pl.,* the Tusculans, people of Tusculum, *a town in Italy*
**Tusculānum, –ī,** *n.,* Tusculan estate
**Tusculānus, –a, –um,** Tusculan; *as noun, m.,* a citizen of Tusculum
**tussiō, –īre, —, —,** cough
**tutēla, –ae,** *f.,* charge, guardian
**tūtō,** *adv.,* safely
**tūtus, –a, –um,** safe
**tuūs, –a, –um,** your, yours (*referring to one person*)
**tyrannus, –ī,** *m.,* tyrant
**Tyrius, –a, –um,** Tyrian

## U

**ūber, –eris,** abounding, full
**ubi,** *adv.,* where; when; **ubi prīmum,** as soon as
**ubicumque,** *adv.,* wherever
**ubinam,** *adv.,* where
**ubīque,** *adv.,* everywhere
**ulcīscor, ulcīscī, ultus,** avenge, punish
**ūllus, –a, –um,** any, anyone
**ulterior, –ius,** farther; **ultimus, –a, –um,** farthest, last
**ultimus, –a, –um,** last, farthest

**ultrā**, *adv. and prep. w. acc.,* beyond, more
**ultrīx**, *gen.* **ultrīcis**, avenging
**ultrō**, *adv.,* voluntarily; actually
**ultus**, *part. of* **ulcīscor**
**umbra, –ae,** *f.,* shade, shadow
**Umbrēnus, –ī,** *m.,* Umbrenus
**umbrōsus, –a, –um,** shady, shading
**umerus, –ī,** *m.,* shoulder
**umidus, –a, –um,** moist, dewy
**umquam**, *adv.,* ever, at any time
**ūnā**, *adv.,* at the same time, along with, together
**ūnanimus, –a, –um,** of one mind, sympathetic
**unda, –ae,** *f.,* wave; water
**unde**, *adv.,* from which (place), by which, from where
**undecimus, –a, –um,** eleventh
**undique**, *adv.,* from *or* on all sides, everywhere
**ungō, –ere, ūnxī, ūnctus,** anoint
**unguentārius, –ī,** *m.,* ointment, perfume
**unguentum, –ī,** *n.,* ointment, perfume, salve
**unguis, –is,** *m.,* nail (*of finger or toe*); claw
**ungula, –ae,** *f.,* hoof, claw
**ūnicē**, *adv.,* singularly, devotedly
**ūnicus, –a, –um,** only
**ūniversus, –a, –um,** all (together), whole, in a body
**ūnus, –a, –um,** one, alone, single, sole
**urbānitās, –tātis,** *f.,* wit
**urbānus, –a, –um,** of *or* in the city; polished; facetious
**urbs, urbis,** *f.,* city
**urgeō, urgēre, ursī, ursus,** press hard
**urna, –ae,** *f.,* urn
**ūrō, –ere, ussī, ustus,** burn, parch
**uspiam**, *adv.,* anywhere
**usque**, *adv.,* even (to), all the time, as far as, up to, continuously, still; *w.* **adeō**, to such an extent
**usquequāque**, *adv.,* in everything, on every occasion
**ūsūra, –ae,** *f.,* use, enjoyment
**ūsūrpātiō, –ōnis,** *f.,* use
**ūsūrpō**, 1, use, employ
**ūsus, –ūs,** *m.,* use, need, advantage; practice, experience
**ut, utī,** *conj.,* (in order) that, to, so that; as (to), when; *adv.,* how as; **ut... non,** that . . . not
**uter, utra, utrum,** which (of two); whichever
**uterque, utraque, utrumque,** each (of two), either, both
**utervīs, utravīs, utrumvīs,** either
**utī = ut**
**ūtilis, –e,** useful, helpful
**ūtilitās, –tātis,** *f.,* usefulness, advantage
**utinam!** *adv.,* O that! would that!
**utique**, *adv.,* certainly
**ūtor, ūtī, ūsus,** use, employ, make use of (*w. abl.*), enjoy
**utrimque**, *adv.,* on both sides
**utrum**, *conj.,* whether; **utrum... an,** whether . . . or; *in dir. quest. it cannot be translated*
**ūva, –ae,** *f.,* grapes
**uxor, –ōris,** *f.,* wife

## V

**vacillō**, 1, stagger
**vacō**, 1, be uninhabited, have leisure, empty
**vacuēfaciō, –ere, –fēcī, –factus,** make empty, free
**vacuus, –a, –um,** empty, free, without
**vadimōnium, –nī,** *n.,* bail bond
**vādō, –ere, —, —,** go
**vadum, –ī,** *n.,* ford, shallow place
**vafer, vafra, vafrum,** sly, crafty
**vāgīna, –ae,** *f.,* sheath
**vagor**, 1, wander
**vagulus, –a, –um,** wandering
**vagus, –a, –um,** wandering, uncertain, vague
**valdē**, *adv.,* strongly, very (much)
**valeō, –ēre, valuī, valitus,** be strong, be well, be able, be powerful, prevail; have influence, excel; *imper.,* **valē, valēte,** farewell
**Valerius, –rī,** *m.,* Valerius
**valētūdō, –dinis,** *f.,* health; illness, sickness
**validus, –a, –um,** strong
**vallēs, –is,** *f.,* valley
**vāllō**, 1, defend
**vāllum, –ī,** *n.,* rampart, wall, barricade
**valvae, –ārum,** *f. pl.,* doors
**vānitās, –tātis,** *f.,* folly, vanity

**vānum, –ī,** *n.,* emptiness
**vānus, –a, –um,** empty, false, vain
**vapor, –ōris,** *m.,* steam, heat
**vāpulō,** 1, be flogged
**Vargunteius, –ī,** *m.,* Vargunteius
**varietās, –tātis,** *f.,* variety, variation
**varius, –a, –um,** changing, varying, various
**Varrō, –ōnis,** *m.,* Varro
**vas, vadis,** *m.,* bail, security
**vās, vāsis,** *n.,* kettle, pot, vessel, dish, utensil; baggage
**vāstitās, –tātis,** *f.,* devastation
**vāstō,** 1, destroy, ruin
**vāstus, –a, –um,** huge, vast, immense
**Vatīnius, –nī,** *m.,* Vatinius
**vātēs, –is,** *m.,* prophet; poet
**–ve,** *enclitic,* or
**vehemēns,** *gen.* **vehementis,** vigorous, rigorous, strong
**vehementer,** *adv.,* violently, greatly, earnestly
**vehiculum, –ī,** *n.,* carriage
**vehō, –ere, vexī, vectus,** carry, bear; *pass.,* sail, ride
**Veiī, –ōrum,** *m. pl.,* Veii, *a town in Italy*
**vel,** *conj.,* or; **vel... vel,** either . . . or; *adv.,* even, at least; very; *w. superl.,* the most . . . possible
**vēlāmen, –minis,** *n.,* veil, cloak
**Velleius Blaesus, –ī,** *m.,* Velleius Blaesus
**vellus, –eris,** *n.,* fleece, wool
**vēlō,** 1, cover, veil
**vēlōcitās, –tātis,** *f.,* swiftness
**vēlōx, –ōcis,** swift
**vēlum, –ī,** *n.,* sail; awning
**velut, velutī,** *adv.,* just as, as, like
**vēna, –ae,** *f.,* vein
**vēnābulum, –ī,** *n.,* hunting spear
**vēnālis, –e,** for sale
**vēnātiō, –ōnis,** *f.,* hunting, hunt
**vēnditō,** 1, try to sell, sell
**vēndō, –ere, –didī, –ditus,** sell
**venēnō,** 1, poison
**venēnum, –ī,** *n.,* poison
**venerābilis, –e,** reverend
**venerātiō, –ōnis,** *f.,* reverence, veneration
**veneror,** 1, worship
**venia, –ae,** *f.,* favor, pardon
**Venetī, –ōrum,** *m. pl.,* the Veneti
**veniō, –īre, vēnī, ventus,** come
**vēnor,** 1, hunt
**venter, –tris,** *m.,* belly, stomach
**ventus, –ī,** *m.,* wind
**Venus, –eris,** *f.,* Venus, *goddess of love and beauty*
**venustās, –tātis,** *f.,* charm
**venustē,** *adv.,* gracefully, beautifully
**venustus, –a, –um,** lovely, charming
**vēr, vēris,** *n.,* spring
**Verānia, –ae,** *f.,* Verania
**verber, –eris,** *n.,* blow
**verberō,** 1, beat, strike
**verbum, –ī,** *n.,* word; **verba faciō,** speak, make a speech
**Vercingetorīx, –īgis,** *m.,* Vercingetorix
**vērē,** *adv.,* truly
**verēcundia, –ae,** *f.,* modesty
**verēcundus, –a, –um,** ashamed, shy, modest
**vereor, verērī, veritus,** fear, respect
**Vergilius, –lī,** *m.,* Vergil
**Verginius, –nī,** *m.,* Verginius
**vergo, –ere, —, —,** slope, lie
**vēritās, –tātis,** *f.,* truth
**vernīliter,** *adv.,* servilely
**vernus, –a, –um,** of spring, spring
**vērō,** *adv.,* in truth, in fact; but, however
**Vērōna, –ae,** *f.,* Verona
**verrēs, –is,** *m.,* boar
**Verrēs, –is,** *m.,* Verres
**verrō, –ere, verrī, versus,** sweep
**versicolor,** *gen.* **–ōris,** of various colors
**versificātor, –ōris,** *m.,* versifier, poet
**versō,** 1, turn over, turn (often); *pass.,* live, be engaged in, be employed; remain, exist; be skilled; depend on
**versor,** 1, move about, be engaged, live, be
**versus, –ūs,** *m.,* line, verse
**vertex, –ticis,** *m.,* (whirl), head, peak
**vertō, –ere, vertī, versus,** turn; *pass.,* turn (oneself); *sometimes deponent;* **vertō,** wheel about

**vērum,** *adv.,* but

**vērus, –a, –um,** true; *as noun, n.,* truth; **rē vērā,** really

**vēscor, vēscī, —, —,** feed, eat

**Vespasiānus, –ī,** *m.,* Vespasian, *the emperor*

**vesper, –erī,** *m.,* evening; **vesperī,** in the evening

**vespera, –ae,** *f.,* the evening star, evening

**Vesta, –ae,** *f.,* Vesta, *goddess of the hearth*

**Vestālis, –e,** Vestal, of Vesta

**vester, –tra, –trum,** your, yours (*referring to two or more persons*)

**vēstibulum, –ī,** *n.,* entrance

**vēstīgium, –gī,** *n.,* footprint, foot, footstep, track, sole (*of the foot*); *pl.,* fragments

**vestīmentum, –ī,** *n.,* clothing

**vestiō, –īre, –īvī, –ītus,** clothe, dress

**vestis, –is,** *f.,* clothing, garment, robe

**vestītus, –ūs,** *m.,* clothing

**veterānus, –a, –um,** veteran, experienced

**vetō, –āre, vetuī, vetitus,** forbid

**vetus,** *gen.* **veteris,** old, former, ancient

**vetustās, –tātis,** *f.,* old age, age

**vetustus, –a, –um,** old, ancient

**vexātiō, –ōnis,** *f.,* harassment

**vexō,** 1, disturb, trouble, harass

**via, –ae,** *f.,* way, road, street; journey; **viam mūniō,** build a road

**viāticum, –ī,** *n.,* traveling money

**viātor, –ōris,** *m.,* traveler; court officer

**Vibō, –ōnis,** *f.,* Vibo

**vibrō,** 1, brandish

**vīcēnī, –ae, –a,** twenty (each)

**vīcēsimus, –a, –um,** twentieth

**vīciēs,** *adv.,* twenty times

**vīcīnia, –ae,** *f.,* neighborhood, nearness

**vīcīnitās, –tātis,** *f.,* neighborhood, vicinity

**vīcīnus, –a, –um,** neighboring; *as noun, m.,* neighbor

**(vicis), –is,** *f.,* change; **in vicem** *or* **vicēs,** in turn

**victima, –ae,** *f.,* victim

**victor, –ōris,** *m.,* victor; *adj.,* victorious

**victōria, –ae,** *f.,* victory

**victrīx, –īcis,** *f.,* victor

**vīctus, –ūs,** *m.,* living, food

**vīcus, –ī,** *m.,* village, street

**vidēlicet,** *adv.,* evidently; of course, doubtless

**videō, –ēre, vīdī, vīsus,** see; *pass.,* be seen, seem, seem best

**viduus, –a, –um,** widowed

**vigeō, –ēre, viguī, —,** be vigorous, thrive

**vigil,** *gen.* **vigilis,** wakeful, watchful

**vigilāns,** *gen.* **–antis,** watchful, active

**vigilia, –ae,** *f.,* loss of sleep, guarding; watchman, watch; sentinel (*a fourth part of the night*)

**vigilō,** 1, keep awake, watch

**vīgintī,** twenty

**vigor, –ōris,** *m.,* force, vigor

**vīlicus, –ī,** *m.,* farm manager

**vīlis, –e,** cheap, worthless

**vīlla, –ae,** *f.,* farmhouse, country home, villa

**vīllula, –ae,** *f.,* small villa

**vīllus, –ī,** *m.,* shaggy hair

**Vīminālis (mōns), –is,** *m.,* the Viminal Hill

**vinciō, –īre, vinxī, vinctus,** bind

**vincō, –ere, vīcī, victus,** conquer, defeat, overcome, win; exhaust

**vinculum, –ī,** *n.,* bond, chain, fastening

**Vindex, –dicis,** *n.,* Vindex

**vindicō,** 1, avenge, punish; claim, assert one's claim to, appropriate

**vīnea, –ae,** *f.,* grape arbor, shed, vineyard

**vīnētum, –ī,** *n.,* vineyard

**vīnum, –ī,** *n.,* wine

**violō,** 1, wrong, dishonor, injure

**vir, virī,** *m.,* man, husband

**virēns,** *gen.* **–entis,** green

**virga, –ae,** *f.,* twig, rod

**virginālis, –e,** maidenly, virgin

**virginitās, –tātis,** *f.,* virginity

**virgō, –ginis,** *f.,* virgin, maiden

**Viriāthus, –ī,** *m.,* Viriathus

**virīlis, –e,** manly

**virtūs, –tūtis,** *f.,* manliness, courage, virtue, character, ability

**vīs, —,** *f.,* force, power, violence, energy; *pl.,* **vīrēs, vīrium,** strength

**vīscera, –um,** *n. pl.,* vitals

**vīsō, –ere, vīsī, vīsus,** go to see, view

**vīta, –ae,** *f.,* life

**vītātiō, –ōnis,** *f.,* shunning, avoidance

**vīticula, –ae,** *f.,* little vine
**vitiōsus, –a, –um,** full of faults, wrong
**vītis, –is,** *f.,* vine
**vitium, –tī,** *n.,* fault, defect, vice
**vītō,** 1, avoid, escape
**vitta, –ae,** *f.,* headband
**vituperō,** 1, blame, censure
**vīvo, –ere, vīxī, victus,** live
**vīvus, –a, –um,** alive, living
**vix,** *adv.,* hardly, scarcely, with difficulty, hardly
**vōbīscum = cum vōbīs**
**vocābulum, –ī,** *n.,* word
**vocātīvus, –a, –um,** vocative
**vocō,** 1, call, summon, invite, invoke
**volātus, –ūs,** *m.,* flying, flight
**volō,** 1, fly
**volō, velle, voluī, —,** want, wish, intend, be willing
**Volscī, –ōrum,** *m. pl.,* the Volscians
**Volturcius, –cī,** *m.,* Volturcius
**volucris, –ris,** *f.,* bird
**volūmen, –minis,** *n.,* roll, volume
**voluntās, –tātis,** *f.,* will, good will, wish, purpose; consent
**voluptās, –tātis,** *f.,* pleasure
**volvō, –ere, volvī, volūtus,** roll (up); turn over, ponder; *pass.,* roll, be hurled, toss about
**vōs,** you, *pl. of* **tū**
**vōsmet,** you yourselves
**vōtum, –ī,** *n.,* vow, wish, prayer
**voveō, –ēre, vōvī, vōtus,** vow, wish for, promise
**vōx, vōcis,** *f.,* voice, cry; word, remark, talk
**Vulcānus, –ī,** *m.,* Vulcan, *god of fire*
**vulgus, –ī,** *n.,* common people, crowd
**vulnerō,** 1, wound
**vulnus, vulneris,** *n.,* wound
**vultus, –ūs,** *m.,* expression, face, features; presence

## X

**Xerxēs, –is,** *m.,* Xerxes, *king of Persia*

# English–Latin

For proper nouns and proper adjectives not given in this vocabulary, see the Latin–English Vocabulary or the text.

Verbs of the first conjugation whose parts are regular are indicated by the figure 1.

## A

**able (be),** possum, posse, potuī, —

**about,** dē, *w. abl.*

**accomplice,** socius, –cī, *m.*

**accomplish,** cōnficiō, –ere, –fēcī, –fectus

**account,** ratiō, –ōnis, *f.; **on account of,** see* **on,** ob, propter

**accustomed (be),** cōnsuēscō, –ere, –suēvī, –suētus

**achieve,** cōnsequor, cōnsequī, cōnsecūtus; efficiō, –ere, effēcī, effectus

**acknowledge,** cognōscō, –ere, cognōvī, cognitus

**across,** trāns, *w. acc.*

**action,** factum, –ī, *n.*

**add,** adiciō, –ere, adiēcī, adiectus

**admire,** admīror, 1

**adopt,** adoptō, 1

**adorn,** ōrnō, 1

**advice,** cōnsilium, –lī, *n.*

**affairs (public),** rēs pūblica, reī pūblicae, *f.*

**afraid (be),** timeō, –ēre, timuī, —

**after,** post (*conj.*), postquam; *use abl. abs.*

**again,** rūrsus, iterum

**against,** contrā, *w. acc.*

**age,** aetās, –tātis, *f.*

**agree,** cōnsentiō, –īre, –sēnsī, –sēnsus

**aid,** auxilium, –lī, *n.*

**all,** omnis, –e; tōtus, –a, –um; **all other,** cēterī, –ae, –a

**allow,** licet, –ēre, licuit *or* licitum est

**almost,** paene

**alone,** sōlus, –a, –um

**already,** iam

**also,** etiam

**although,** etsī, cum; quamquam; *use participle or abl. abs.*

**always,** semper

**among,** inter, *w. acc.*

**and,** et; –que

**another,** alius, alia, aliud

**answer,** solūtio, –ōnis, *f.*

**any,** ūllus, –a, –um; **any longer (not),** nōn iam

**anyone,** quisquam, quicquam; quis, quid (*after* sī)

**appear,** appāreō, –ēre, appāruī, appāritus

**Appian,** Appius, –a, –um

**apply,** subiciō, –ere, subiēcī, subiectus

**approach** (*noun*), adventus, –ūs, *m.;* (*verb*), accēdō, –ere, accessī, accessus (*w.* ad); adeō, adīre, adiī, aditus; appropinquō, 1 (*w. dat.*)

**approve,** probō, 1

**arena,** arēna, –ae, *f.*

**arise,** orior, orīrī, ortus

**arouse,** commoveō, –ēre, commōvī, commōtus

**arm,** armō, 1

**arms,** arma, –ōrum, *n. pl.*

**army,** exercitus, –ūs, *m.*

**arrival,** adventus, –ūs, *m.*

**arrive,** perveniō, –īre, –vēnī, –ventus

**art,** ars, artis, *f.*

**as,** quantum; **as . . . as,** quam; **as long as,** dum; **as much,** tantum; **as . . . as possible,** quam, *w. superl.;* **as soon as possible,** quam prīmum; **as to,** ut

**ask,** rogō, 1; **ask for,** petō, –ere, petīvī, petītus

**assign,** attribuō, –ere, –uī, –ūtus

**at (near),** ad, *w. acc.; abl. of time or place*

**at once,** statim

**Athens,** Athēnae, –ārum, *f. pl.*

**attack,** impetus, –ūs, *m.;* oppugnō, 1; aggredior, aggredī, aggressus

**author,** auctor, –ōris, *m.*

**await,** exspectō, 1

**away (be),** absum, –esse, āfuī, āfutūrus

**away (go),** discēdō, –ere, –cessī, –cessus

## B

**bad,** malus, –a, –um

**badly,** male

**baggage,** impedīmenta, –ōrum, *n. pl.*

**band,** manus, –ūs, *f.*

**bandit,** latrō, –ōnis, *m.*

**banish,** expellō, –ere, expulī, expulsus

**battle line,** aciēs, aciēī, *f.*

**be,** sum, esse, fuī, futūrus

**bear,** ferō, ferre, tulī, lātus

**beat,** superō, 1

**beautiful,** pulcher, –chra, –chrum

**because,** *use participle or abl. abs.;* quod, quoniam

**become,** fīō, fierī, (factus)

**before,** priusquam, (*adv. and prep.*), ante, *w. acc.*

**beg,** ōrō, 1; petō, –ere, petīvī, petītus

**begin,** incipiō, –ere, incēpī, inceptus; **began,** coepī, coeptus

**believe,** crēdō, –ere, crēdidī, crēditus (*w. dat.*)

**besiege,** obsideō, –ēre, obsēdī, obsessus

**best,** optimus, –a, –um

**betroth,** dēspondeō, –ēre, dēspondī, dēspōnsus

**better,** melior, melius

**between,** inter, *w. acc.*

**blame,** accūsō, 1

**block,** comprimō, –ere, compressī, compressus

**body,** corpus, –oris, *n.*

**book,** liber, librī, *m.*

**born (be),** nāscor, nāscī, nātus

**boy,** puer, puerī, *m.*

**brave,** fortis, –e; **bravely,** fortiter

**bridge,** pōns, pontis, *m.*

**bring,** ferō, ferre, tulī, lātus; afferō, afferre, attulī, allātus; īnferō, īnferre, intulī, illātus; **bring together,** condūcō, –ere, –dūxī, –ductus; **bring back,** reportō, 1

**Britons,** Britannī, –ōrum, *m. pl.*

**build,** exstruō, –ere, exstrūxī, exstrūctus; aedificō, 1

**building,** aedificium, –cī, *n.*

**burn,** incendō, –ere, incendī, incēnsus

**business,** negōtium, –tī, *n.*

**but,** sed; **but also,** sed etiam

**buy,** emō, –ere, –ēmī, emptus

**by,** ā, ab, *w. abl.; sometimes abl. alone*

## C

**Caesar,** Caesar, –aris, *m.*

**call,** appellō, 1

**camp,** castra, –ōrum, *n. pl.*

**can,** possum, posse, potuī, —

**capture,** expugnō, 1; capiō, –ere, cēpī, captus

**care,** eī cūra est

**careful,** dīligēns, *gen.* dīligentis; **carefully,** dīligenter

**carry,** portō, 1; ferō, ferre, tulī, lātus; **carry on war,** bellum gerō; **carry back,** referō, referre, rettulī, relātus

**carry out,** administrō, 1

**Carthage,** Carthāgō, –ginis, *f.*

**Catiline,** Catilīna, –ae, *m.*

**Cato,** Catō, –ōnis, *m.*

**cause,** efficiō, –ere, effēcī, effectus (*w.* ut *and subjunct.*)

**cavalry,** equitātus, –ūs, *m.;* equitēs, –um, *m. pl.*

**censor,** cēnsor, –ōris, *m.*

**certain, a certain (one),** quīdam, quaedam, quiddam; **certainly,** certē

**chain,** vinculum, –ī, *n.*

**chance,** occāsiō, –ōnis, *f.*

**charge,** crīmen, –minis, *n.*

**check,** sustineō, –ēre, –tinuī, –tentus

**children,** līberī, –ōrum, *m. pl.*

**choose,** dēligō, –ere, dēlēgī, dēlēctus

**Cicero,** Cicerō, –ōnis, *m.*

**circumstance,** rēs, reī, *f.*

**citadel,** arx, arcis, *f.*

**citizen,** cīvis, –is, *m. and f.*

**city,** urbs, urbis, *f.*

**civil,** cīvīlis, –e

**clearly,** clārē

**client,** cliēns, –entis, *m.*

**close,** claudō, –ere, clausī, clausus

**collect,** conferō, conferre, contulī, collātus

**come,** veniō, –īre, vēnī, ventus; **come out,** ēgredior, ēgredī, ēgressus

**command (be in),** praesum, –esse, –fuī, –futūrus (*w. dat.*)

**commit,** faciō, –ere, fēcī, factus

**common people,** plēbs, plēbis, *f.*

**compel,** cōgō, –ere, coēgī, coāctus

**complain,** queror, querī, questus
**complete,** cōnficiō, –ere, –fēcī, –fectus
**conceal,** cēlō, 1
**concern,** cūra, –ae, *f.*
**condemn,** damnō, 1
**condition,** condiciō, –ōnis, *f.*
**conference,** colloquium, –quī, *n.*
**conquer,** vincō, –ere, vīcī, victus; superō, 1
**conspiracy,** coniūrātiō, –ōnis, *f.*
**conspire,** coniūrō, 1
**consul,** cōnsul, –sulis, *m.*
**consult (for),** cōnsulō, –ere, –suluī, –sultus
**correct,** vērus, –a, –um
**country,** patria, –ae, *f.*
**courage,** virtūs, –tūtis, *f.*
**cover,** tegō, –ere, tēxī, tectus
**creditor,** crēditor, –ōris, *m.*
**crime,** scelus, sceleris, *n.*
**criticize,** accūsō, 1
**cross,** trānseō, –īre, –iī, –itus
**crow,** corvus, –ī, m.
**crowded together,** cōnfertus, –a, –um
**cruel,** crūdēlis, –e
**cruelty,** crūdēlitās, –tātis, *f.*
**custom,** mōs, mōris, *m.*
**cut off,** interclūdō, –ere, –clūsī, –clūsus

## D

**danger,** perīculum, –ī, *n.*
**dare,** audeō, –ēre, ausus
**daughter,** fīlia, –ae, *f.*
**day,** diēs, diēī, *m. and f.;* **day by day,** in diēs
**dead,** mortuus, –a, –um
**dear,** cārus, –a, –um
**debt,** aes aliēnum, aeris aliēnī, *n.*
**decide,** cōnstituō, –ere, –stituī, –stitūtus
**decided (be),** placet, –ēre, placuit
**decorated,** adōrnātus, –a, –um
**decree** (*noun*), dēcrētum, –ī, *n.;* (*verb*), dēcernō, –ere, dēcrēvī, dēcrētus
**deed,** factum, –ī, *n.*
**defeat,** superō, 1
**defeat** (*noun*), calamitās, –tātis, *f.;* (*verb*), superō, 1; pellō, –ere, pepulī, pulsus; vincō, –ere, vīcī, victus
**defend,** dēfendō, –ere, dēfendī, dēfēnsus
**defenses,** mūnītiō, –ōnis, *f.*
**definite,** certus, –a, –um
**delay,** mora, –ae, *f.*
**demand,** postulō, 1
**depart,** dēcēdō, –ere, dēcessī, dēcessus; proficīscor, proficīscī, profectus; excēdō, –ere, excessī, excessus
**departure,** exitus, –ūs, *m.;* profectiō, –ōnis, *f.*
**deserve,** mereō, –ēre, meruī, meritus
**desire,** *(noun),* cupiditās, –tātis, *f.;* (*verb*), cupiō, –īre, –īvī, –ītus
**despair (of),** dēspērō, 1
**destroy,** dēleō, –ēre, –ēvī, –ētus; ēvertō, –ere, –ēvertī, ēversus
**determine,** cōnstituō, –ere, –stituī, –stitūtus
**dictate,** dictō, 1
**die,** morior, –īrī, mortuus
**differ,** differō, differre, distulī, dīlātus
**difficult,** difficilis, –e
**dinner,** cēna, –ae, *f.;* convīvium, –vī, *n.*
**divide,** dīvidō, –ere, dīvīsī, dīvīsus
**disagree,** dissentiō, –īre, dissēnsī, dissēnsus
**disaster,** calamitās, –tātis, *f.*
**disgrace (in),** turpiter
**do,** faciō, –ere, fēcī, factus; agō, –ere, ēgī, āctus
**Domitian,** Domitiānus, –ī, *m.*
**draw up,** īnstruō, –ere, īnstrūxī, īnstrūctus
**drive out,** ēiciō, –ere, ēiēcī, ēiectus; expellō, –ere, expulī, expulsus
**during,** per, *w. acc.*
**dutiful,** pius, –a, –um
**duty,** officium, –cī, *n.*

## E

**each one,** quisque, quidque
**eager,** cupidus, –a, –um
**eager for (be),** studeō, –ēre, studuī, — (*w. dat.*)
**eagerness,** studium, –dī, *n.*
**earn,** mereō, –ēre, meruī, meritus
**earth,** terra, –ae, *f.*
**easy,** facilis, –e; **easily,** facile
**eat,** edō, –ere, –ēdī, ēsus
**elect,** creō, 1
**elevated,** ēditus, –a, –um

**eloquence,** ēloquentia, –ae, *f.*
**embassy,** lēgātiō, –ōnis, *f.*
**empire,** imperium, –rī, *n.*
**encourage,** cōnfirmō, 1
**endure,** ferō, ferre, tulī, lātus
**enemy** (*personal*), inimīcus, –ī, *m.;* (*national*), hostis, –is, *m.*
**enjoy,** fruor, fruī, frūctus; ūtor, ūtī, ūsus (*w. abl.*)
**enmity,** inimīcitia, –ae, *f.*
**enter,** introeō, –īre, –iī, –itus; ingredior, ingredī, ingressus
**entire,** tōtus, –a, –um
**entrust,** mandō, 1
**envoy,** lēgātus, –ī, *m.*
**envy,** invideō, –ēre, invīdī, invīsus (*w. dat.*)
**equal,** aequālis, –e
**erect,** exstruō, –ere, exstrūxī, exstrūctus
**escape,** fugiō, –ere, fūgī, fugitus
**establish,** cōnstituō, –ere, –stituī, –stitūtus
**ever,** umquam
**everybody,** omnēs
**everyone,** omnis, –is, *m. and f.*
**everything,** omne *or* omnia, omnium, *n. pl.*
**examine,** excutiō, –ere, excussī, excussus
**example,** exemplum, –ī, *n.*
**excel,** praestō, –āre, –stitī, –stitus (*w. dat.*)
**excellent,** bonus, –a, –um; optimus, –a, –um
**exclaim,** (ex)clāmō, 1
**exile,** exsilium, –lī, *n.*
**expel,** expellō, –ere, expulī, expulsus
**explain,** expōnō, –ere, –posuī, –positus

## F

**facility,** facultās, –tātis, *f.*
**fact that,** quod
**Faesulae,** Faesulae, –ārum, *f. pl.*
**fall,** incidō, –ere, incidī, —
**fame,** fāma, –ae, *f.*,
**family,** familia, –ae, *f.*
**famous,** clārus, –a, –um
**farm,** ager, agrī, *m.*,
**farmer,** agricola, –ae, *m.*
**farthest,** extrēmus, –a, –um; ultimus, –a, –um
**fate,** fātum, –ī, *n.*
**father,** pater, patris, *m.*
**fault,** culpa, –ae, *f.*
**favor,** faveō, –ēre, fāvī, fautus
**fear,** timeō, –ēre, timuī, —; vereor, verērī, veritus
**feel,** sentiō, –īre, sēnsī, sēnsus
**few,** paucī, –ae, –a
**fierce,** ferus, –a, –um
**fiercely,** ferōciter
**fight,** pugnō, 1
**find, find out,** inveniō, –īre, invēnī, inventus
**fine,** pulcher, pulchra, pulchrum
**finish,** cōnficiō, –ere, –fēcī, –fectus
**fire,** incendium, –dī, *n.*
**firm,** firmus, –a, –um
**first,** prīmus, –a, –um; (*adv.*), prīmum; **at first,** prīmō
**flame,** flamma, –ae, *f.*
**flee,** fugiō, –ere, fūgī, fugitus
**food,** cibus, –ī, *m.*
**foot,** pēs, pedis, *m.*
**for** (*conj.*), nam; (*prep.*), ad, ob, *w. acc.;* prō, *w. abl.;* **for the purpose** *or* **sake of,** causā *or* grātiā (*preceded by gen.*); *sometimes not expressed*
**force,** cōgō, –ere, coēgī, coāctus
**forest,** silva, –ae, *f.*
**forget,** oblivīscor, –ī, oblītus
**former,** ille, illa, illud; **the former . . . the latter,** ille... hic
**fortify,** mūniō, –īre, –īvī, –ītus
**fortune,** fortūna, –ae, *f.*
**Forum,** Forum, –ī, *n.*
**found,** condō, –ere, condidī, conditus
**four,** quattuor
**free** (*adj.*), līber, –era, –erum; (*verb*), līberō, 1; **be free,** careō, –ēre, caruī, caritus
**freedom,** lībertās, –tātis, *f.*
**fresh,** integer, –gra, –grum
**friend,** amīcus, –ī; *m.;* **(female) friend,** amīca, –ae, *f.*
**friendly,** amīcus, –a, –um
**frighten,** terreō, –ēre, terruī, territus
**frog,** rāna, –ae, *f.*
**from,** ē, ex, ā, ab, dē, *w. abl.*; **from one another,** inter sē
**furnish,** praebeō, –ēre, –uī, –itus

## G

**game,** lūdus, –ī, *m.*

**garden,** hortus, –ī, *m.*

**gate,** porta, –ae, *f.*

**Gaul,** Gallus, –ī, *m.;* Gallia, –ae, *f.;* **Gauls,** Gallī, –ōrum, *m. pl.*

**general,** dux, ducis, *m.;* lēgātus, –ī, *m.*

**get,** accipiō, –ere, accēpī, acceptus; parō, 1; **get (possession of),** potior, potīrī, potītus (*w. abl.*)

**girl,** puella, –ae, *f.*

**give,** dō, dare, dedī, datus; **give up,** dēdō, –ere, dēdidī, dēditus

**gladiator,** gladiātor, –ōris, *m.;* **gladiatorial,** gladiātōrius, –a, –um

**glory,** glōria, –ae, *f.*

**go,** eō, īre, iī, itus; **go out,** ēgredior, ēgredī, ēgressus; exeō, exīre, exiī, exitus; **go away,** discēdō, –ere, discessī, discessus; **go from,** abeō, abīre, abiī, abitus

**god,** deus, –ī, *m.*

**goddess,** dea, –ae, *f.*

**gold,** aurum, –ī, *n.*

**good,** bonus, –a, –um

**government,** rēs pūblica, reī pūblicae, *f.*

**grain,** frūmentum, –ī, *n.*

**grammarian,** grammaticus, –ī, *m.*

**grandfather,** avus, –ī, *m.*

**great,** magnus, –a, –um; **greater,** maior, maius; **greatest,** maximus, –a, –um; summus, –a, –um; **great deal,** plūrimum; **so great,** tantus, –a, –um

**Greece,** Graecia, –ae, *f.*

**Greek,** Graecus, –a, –um

**grow,** crēscō, –ere, crēvī, crētus

**guard,** praesidium, –dī, *n.*

**guest-friend,** hospes, –itis, *m.*

## H

**happen,** ēveniō, –īre, ēvēnī, ēventus; accidō, –ere, accidī, —

**harbor,** portus, –ūs, *m.*

**hardly,** vix

**harm,** damnum, –ī, *n.;* dētrīmentum, –ī, *n.*

**harsh,** dūrus, –a, –um

**hasten,** properō, 1; contendō, –ere, –tendī, –tentus

**hate,** ōdī, ōsus

**have,** habeō, –ēre, habuī, habitus; **have to,** *use fut. pass. part.*

**he,** is; hic; ille; *often not expressed*

**head,** caput, capitis, *n.*

**hear,** audiō, –īre, –īvī, –ītus

**heat,** aestus, –ūs, *m.*

**height,** altitūdō, –dinis, *f.*

**heir,** hērēs, –ēdis, *m.*

**help,** auxilium, –lī, *n.*

**her** (*poss.*), eius; (*reflex.*), suus, –a, –um; **herself** (*reflex.*), suī

**hesitate,** dubitō, 1

**high,** altus, –a, –um

**hill,** mōns, montis, *m.;* collis, –is, *m.*

**himself** (*reflex.*), suī; (*intens.*), ipse

**hinder,** impediō, –īre, –īvī, –ītus

**his** (*poss.*), eius; **his own** (*reflex.*), suus, –a, –um

**history,** historia, –ae, *f.*

**holiday,** fēriae, –ārum, *f. pl.*

**home,** domus, –ūs, *f.*

**honor,** honor, –ōris, *m.*

**Horace,** Horātius, –tī, *m.*

**horse,** equus, –ī, *m.*

**horseman,** eques, equitis, *m.*

**host,** dominus, –ī, *m.*

**hostage,** obses, obsidis, *m.*

**hour,** hōra, –ae, *f.*

**house,** domus, –ūs, *f.*

**how,** quōmodō; **how much,** quantus, –a, –um

**however,** autem (*never first word*)

**humble,** humilis, –e

**hurry (on),** properō, 1

## I

**I,** ego, meī; *often not expressed*

**if,** sī

**ill,** aeger, aegra, aegrum

**immediately,** statim

**impel,** impellō, –ere, impulī, impulsus

**in,** in, *w. abl.;* **in order to** *or* **that,** ut (*w. subjunctive*); **in order not to,** nē

**inferior,** īnferior, –ius

**influence** (*verb*) addūcō, –ere, addūxī, adductus; (*noun*), auctōritās, –tātis, *f.*

**inform,** (eum) certiōrem faciō, –ere, fēcī, factus; *pass.,* certior fīō, fierī

**inhabit,** incolō, –ere, incoluī, —
**injure,** noceō, –ēre, nocuī, nocitus
**inspire,** iniciō, –ere, iniēcī, iniectus
**into,** in, *w. acc.*
**investigate,** explōrō, 1
**invite,** vocō, 1
**it,** is, ea, id; hic, haec, hoc; ille, illa, illud; *often not expressed*
**Italy,** Italia, –ae, *f.*

## J

**journey,** iter, itineris, *n.*
**Jupiter,** Iuppiter, Iovis, *m.*

## K

**keep,** retineō, –ēre, retinuī, retentus; **keep from,** prohibeō, –ēre, –hibuī, –hibitus
**kill,** interficiō, –ere, –fēcī, –fectus; caedō, –ere, cecīdī, caesus; occīdo, –ere, occīdi, occīsus
**kind,** genus, generis, *n.*
**kindness,** beneficium, –cī, *n.*
**king,** rēx, rēgis, *m.*
**knight,** eques, equitis, *m.*
**know,** sciō, scīre, scīvī, scītus; *perf. of* nōscō, –ere, nōvī, nōtus, *or of* cognōscō, –ere, –nōvī, –nitus; **not know,** nesciō, –īre, nescīvī, —

## L

**lack,** careō, –ēre, caruī, caritus; **be lacking,** dēsum, deesse, dēfuī, dēfutūrus
**large,** magnus, –a, –um; **so large,** tantus, –a, –um
**last** (*adj.*), proximus, –a, –um; (*verb*), maneō, –ēre, mānsī, mānsus
**later,** posteā, post
**latter,** hic, haec, hoc
**law,** lēx, lēgis, *f.*
**lay aside,** dēpōnō, –ere, dēposuī, dēpositus
**lead,** dūcō, –ere, dūxī, ductus; **lead a life,** vītam agō
**leader,** dux, ducis, *m.;* prīnceps, prīncipis, *m.*
**learn,** discō, –ere, didicī, —; cognōscō, –ere, –nōvī, –nitus
**leave (behind),** relinquō, –ere, relīquī, relīctus; **leave bare,** vacuēfaciō, –ere, –fēcī, –factus
**legion,** legiō, –ōnis, *f.*
**let,** permittō, –ere, –mīsī, –missus
**let go,** mittō, –ere, –mīsī, –missus
**letter** (*epistle*), litterae, –ārum, *f. pl.*
**liberty,** lībertās, –tātis, *f.*
**life,** vīta, –ae, *f.*
**like,** (*adj,*), similis, –e; (*verb*), amō, 1; (*adv.*), tamquam
**little,** paulum, –ī, *n.*
**little later,** paulō post
**live (a life),** agō, –ere, ēgī, āctus; (*dwell*), habitō, 1; vīvō, –ere, vīxī, vīctus
**long,** longus, –a, –um; **long** (*adv.*), **(for) a long time,** diū; **as long as,** dum; **not any longer,** nōn iam
**look at** *or* **on,** spectō, 1
**lose,** āmittō, –ere, āmīsī, āmissus; perdō, –ere, –didī, –ditus
**loss,** dētrīmentum, –ī, *n.*
**love,** (*noun*) amor, amōris, *m.;* (*verb*), amō, 1
**luxurious,** lautus, –a, –um
**luxury,** lūxuria, –ae, *f.*

## M

**make,** faciō, –ere, fēcī, factus; **make war upon,** bellum īnferō (*w. dat.*)
**man,** vir, virī, *m.;* homō, hominis, *m.*
**manage,** gerō, –ere, gessī, gestus
**manner,** modus, –ī, *m.*
**many,** multī, –ae, –a; **so many,** tot; **very many,** plūrimī, –ae, –a
**march,** iter, itineris, *n.*
**master,** dominus, –ī, *m.*
**matter,** rēs, reī, *f.*
**may,** licet, –ēre, licuit *or* licitum est
**meanwhile,** intereā, interim
**meet (in battle),** congredior, congredī, congressus
**memory,** memoria, –ae, *f.*
**merciful,** misericors, *gen.* –cordis
**mercy,** clēmentia, –ae, *f.*
**messenger,** nūntius, –tī, *m.*
**method,** modus, –ī, *m.*
**mile,** mīlle passūs; *pl.* mīlia passuum
**mind,** animus, –ī, *m.*
**miracle,** mīrāculum, –ī, *n.*
**molest,** noceō, –ēre, nocuī, nocitus (*w. dat.*)

**money**, pecūnia, –ae, *f.*

**month**, mēnsis, –is *m.*

**monument**, monumentum, –ī, *n.*

**more**, magis, plūs, amplius; *use comparative*

**most**, maximē

**mother**, māter, mātris, *f.*

**mountain**, mōns, montis, *m.*

**move**, moveō, –ēre, mōvī, mōtus; afficiō, –ere, affēcī, affectus

**much**, multus, –a, –um

**murder**, caedēs, –is, *f.*

**must**, *use fut. pass. part.*

**my**, meus, –a, –um

## N

**name**, nōmen, nōminis, *n.*

**narrow**, angustus, –a, –um

**nature**, nātūra, –ae, *f.*

**near**, ad *w. acc.; (adj.)*, propinquus, –a, –um

**necessary (it is)**, oportet, –ēre, oportuit; necesse est

**need (is)**, opus est

**neglect**, neglegō, –ere, –lēxī, –lectus

**neighbors**, fīnitimī, –ōrum, *m.*

**never**, numquam

**nevertheless**, tamen

**new**, novus, –a, –um

**next**, proximus, –a, –um

**night**, nox, noctis, *f.*

**no**, nōn, nūllus, –a, –um; **no longer**, nōn iam

**noble**, nōbilis, –e

**no one**, nēmō, *dat.* nēminī, *acc.* nēminem

**none**, nūllus, –a, –um

**not**, nōn, nē (*w. negative volitive and purpose clauses*); **not only**, nōn sōlum

**noted**, īnsignis, –e; nōtus, –a, –um

**nothing**, nihil

**now**, nunc

**notice**, animadvertō, –ere, –vertī, –versus

**number**, numerus, –ī, *m.*

**numerous**, multus, –a, –um

## O

**obey**, pāreō, –ēre, pāruī, pāritus (*w. dat.*)

**obstruct**, impediō, –īre, –īvī, –ītus

**obtain (one's request)**, impetrō, 1

**occupy**, occupō, 1

**occur**, intercēdō, –ere, –cessī, –cessus

**often**, saepe

**Oh!** utinam!

**old man**, senex, senis, *m.*

**omen**, ōmen, ōminis, *n.*

**on**, in, *w. abl.;* **on account of**, ob *or* propter, *w. acc.*

**once (at)**, statim

**one**, ūnus, –a, –um; **one (the) . . . the other**, alius... alius

**only**, sōlum

**open**, aperiō, –īre, aperuī, apertus

**opinion**, sententia, –ae, *f.*

**opportunity**, occāsiō, –ōnis, *f.*

**oppress**, opprimō, –ere, oppressī, oppressus

**or**, vel, aut; an

**oracle**, ōrāculum, –ī, *n.*

**oratory**, ēloquentia, –ae, *f.*

**order** (*noun*), imperium, –rī, *n.; (verb)*, iubeō, –ēre, iussī, iussus; imperō, 1, (*w. dat.); in* **order to** *or* **that**, ut; **in order not to** *or* **that**, nē

**other**, alius, alia, alium; **the other**, alter, –a, –um; **others**, *see* **some; all other**, *see* **all**

**ought**, dēbeō, –ēre, dēbuī, dēbitus; oportet, –ēre, oportuit; *use fut. pass. part.*

**our**, noster, –tra, –trum

**ourselves**, nōs, nostrī

**overcome**, superō, 1; vincō, –ere, vīcī, victus

## P

**part**, pars, partis, *f.*

**pass over**, praetereō, –īre, –iī, –itus

**pay**, solvō, –ere, solvī, solūtus; pendō, –ere, pependī, pēnsus; **pay the penalty**, poenam dō

**peace**, pāx, pācis, *f.*

**peacefully**, tranquillē

**people**, populus, –ī, *m.;* hominēs, –um, *m. pl.*

**perform**, fungor, fungī, functus

**Pergamum**, Pergamum, –ī, *n.*

**permit**, licet, –ēre, licuit *or* licitum est; permittō, –ere, –mīsī, –missus

**persuade**, persuādeō, –ēre, –suāsī, –suāsus (*w. dat.*)

**philosopher**, philosophus, –ī, *m.*

**pity,** misericordia, –ae, *f.*

**place** (*noun*), locus, –ī, *m.; pl.* loca, –ōrum, *n.;* (*verb*), pōnō, –ere, posuī, positus; **place in charge,** praeficiō, –ere, –fēcī, –fectus

**plainly,** simpliciter

**plan** (*noun*), cōnsilium, –lī, *n.;* (*verb*), in animō habeō; cōgitō, 1

**please, be pleasing to,** placeō, –ēre, placuī, placitus (*w. dat.*)

**pleasure to me,** mihi placet

**Pliny,** Plīnius, –nī, *m.*

**plot,** coniūrō, 1

**poem,** carmen, carminis, *n.*

**poet,** poēta, –ae, *m.*

**Pompey,** Pompeius, –peī, *m.*

**poor,** pauper, *gen.* –eris

**possession of (get),** potior, potīrī, potītus (*w. gen. or abl.*)

**possible (as soon as),** quam prīmum

**power,** potestās, –tātis, *f.;* imperium, –rī, *n.*

**praetor,** praetor, –ōris, *m.*

**praise,** laudō, 1

**prefer,** mālō, mālle, māluī, —

**prepare,** parō, 1

**present (be),** adsum, adesse, adfuī, adfutūrus

**preserve,** cōnservō, 1

**prevent,** prohibeō, –ēre, –hibuī, –hibitus

**prison,** carcer, –eris, *m.*

**prisoner,** captīvus, –ī, *m.*

**prize,** praemium, –mī, *n.*

**proceed,** prōcēdō, –ere, –cessī, –cessus

**procession,** pompa, –ae, *f.*

**produce,** pariō, –ere, peperī, partus

**promise,** polliceor, pollicērī, pollicitus

**property,** bona, –ōrum, *n. pl.*

**protect,** tegō, –ere, tēxī, tēctus

**protection,** praesidium, –dī, *n.*

**provided that,** dum

**public affairs,** rēs pūblica, reī pūblicae, *f.*

**punish,** pūniō, –īre, –īvī, –ītus

**punishment,** supplicium, –cī, *n.*

**purpose (for the),** causā, grātiā

**pursue,** īnsequor, īnsequī, īnsecūtus

**put in charge of,** praeficiō, –ere, –fēcī, –fectus

## Q

**queen,** rēgīna, –ae, *f.*

**question,** quaestiō, –ōnis, *f.*

**quickly,** celeriter

## R

**reach,** perveniō, –īre, –vēnī, –ventus

**read,** legō, –ere, lēgī, lēctus

**ready,** parātus, –a, –um

**realize,** intellegō, –ere, –lēxī, –lēctus

**reason,** causa, –ae, *f.*

**recall,** recordor, 1; revocō, 1

**receive,** accipiō, –ere, accēpī, acceptus; excipiō, –ere, excēpī, exceptus

**recitation,** recitātiō, –ōnis, *f.*

**recite,** recitō, 1

**recognize,** cognōscō, –ere, –nōvī, –nitus

**reconnoiter,** explōrō, 1

**refrain,** abstineō, –ēre, –tinuī, –tentus

**region,** regiō, –ōnis, *f.*

**rejoice,** gaudeō, –ēre, gāvīsus

**remain,** maneō, –ēre, mānsī, mānsus

**remember,** memoriā teneō

**repair,** reficiō, –ere, refēcī, refectus

**reply,** respondeō, –ēre, respondī, respōnsus

**report** (*noun*), nūntius, –tī, *m.;* (*verb*), nūntiō, 1

**republic,** rēs pūblica, reī pūblicae, *f.*

**reputation,** fāma, –ae, *f.*

**reserve,** reservō, 1

**resist,** resistō, –ere, restitī, — (*w. dat.*)

**resources,** opēs, –um, *f. pl.*

**respond,** respondeō, –ēre, respondī, respōnsus

**rest (of),** reliquus, –a, –um; cēterī, –ae, –a

**retire,** mē recipiō

**return** (*verb*), redeō, –īre, rediī, reditus; (*noun*), reditus, –ūs, *m.*

**revolution,** novae rēs, novārum rērum, *f. pl.*

**reward,** praemium dō, dare, dedī, datus

**rich,** beātus, –a, –um; dīves, *gen.* dīvitis

**right,** rēctus, –a, –um

**river,** flūmen, flūminis, *n.*

**road,** via, –ae, *f.;* iter, itineris, *n.*

**Roman,** Rōmānus, –a, –um

**Rome,** Rōma, –ae, *f.*

**rule,** regō, –ere, rēxī, rēctus; imperō, 1 (*w. dat.*)

## S

**sacrifice,** sacrificium, –cī, *n.*

**safe,** tūtus, –a, –um

**safety,** salūs, –ūtis, *f.*

**sail,** vēlum, –ī, *n.;* nāvigō, 1

**sailor,** nauta, –ae, *m.*

**sake of (for the),** causā *or* grātiā (*w. gen. preceding*)

**sally,** ēruptiō, –ōnis, *f.*

**same,** īdem, eadem, idem

**save,** servō, 1

**say,** dīcō, –ere, dīxī, dictus; inquit (*w. direct quotations*)

**scare,** terreō, –ēre, terruī, territus

**school,** lūdus, –ī, *m.*

**Scipio,** Scīpiō, –ōnis, *m.*

**scout,** explōrātor, –ōris, *m.*

**sea,** mare, maris, *n.*

**seal,** signum, –ī, *n.*

**seats,** subsellia, –ōrum, *n. pl.*

**section,** pars, partis, *f.*

**see,** videō, –ēre, vīdī, vīsus; **see to it,** prōvideō, –ēre, –vīdī, –vīsus

**seek,** petō, –ere, petīvī, petītus

**seem, seem best,** videor, vidērī, vīsus

**seize,** capiō, –ere, cēpī, captus; occupō, 1; comprehendō, –ere, –hendī, –hēnsus

**select,** legō, –ere, lēgī, lēctus; dēligō, 1

**senate,** senātus, –ūs, *m.*

**senator,** senātor, –ōris, *m.*

**send,** mittō, –ere, mīsī, missus; **send out,** dīmittō, –ere, –mīsī, –missus; **send ahead,** praemittō, –ere, –mīsī, –missus; **send for,** arcessō, –ere, –īvī, –ītus

**set out,** proficīscor, proficīscī, profectus; **set on fire,** incendō, –ere, incendī, incensus

**severe,** acerbus, –a, –um

**she,** ea; haec; illa; *often not expressed*

**shield,** scūtum, –ī, *n.*

**ship,** nāvis, –is, *f.*

**short,** brevis, –e

**show** (*noun*), mūnus, –eris, *n.;* (*verb*), ostendō, –ere, ostendī, ostentus; dēmōnstrō, 1; monstro, 1

**sign, signal,** signum, –ī, *n.*

**sight,** cōnspectus, –ūs, *m.*

**since,** quod, cum, quoniam; *use abl. abs.*

**sing,** cantō, 1

**singing teacher,** cantandī magister, –trī, *m.*

**single one (not a),** neque quisquam

**sister,** soror, –ōris, *f.*

**sit,** sedeō, –ēre, sēdī, sessus

**six,** sex

**sixty,** sexāgintā

**size,** magnitūdō, –dinis, *f.*

**slave,** servus, –ī, *m.*

**slavery,** servitūs, servitūtis, *f.*

**small,** parvus, –a, –um

**snow,** nix, nivis, *f.*

**so,** ita, tam; **so great, so much** *or* **so large,** tantus, –a, –um; (*adv.*), tantopere; **so that,** ut; **so as not to, so that not,** nē

**soldier,** mīles, mīlitis, *m.*

**some,** nōn nūllī, –ae, –a; quīdam, quaedam, quiddam; **some . . . others,** aliī... aliī; **some (one),** aliquis

**son,** fīlius, –lī, *m.*

**soon as possible (as),** quam prīmum

**speak,** dīcō, –ere, dīxī, dictus; loquor, loquī, locūtus; verba faciō

**speaker,** ōrātor, –ōris, *m.*

**spear,** pīlum, –ī, *n.*

**spectacle,** spectāculum, –ī, *n.*

**speech,** ōrātiō, –ōnis, *f.*

**spend,** cōnsūmō, –ere, –sūmpsī, –sūmptus; (*of time*), agō, –ere, ēgī, āctus; **spend the winter,** hiemō, 1

**stand,** stō, stāre, stetī, stātus

**start,** proficīscor, proficīscī, profectus

**state,** rēs pūblica, reī pūblicae, *f.;* (*noun*), cīvitās, –tātis, *f.;* (*verb*), dīcō, –ere, dīxī, dictus

**station,** collocō, 1

**statue,** statua, –ae, *f.*

**stay,** maneō, –ēre, mānsī, mānsus

**sternness,** sevēritās, –tātis, *f.*

**stop,** subsistō, –ere, substitī, —; cōnsistō, –ere, –stitī, –stitus

**storm,** tempestās, –tātis, *f.*

**story,** fābula, –ae, *f.*

**strange,** novus, –a, –um

**strive,** contendō, –ere, –tendī, –tentus

**struggle,** labōrō, 1

**stupid,** stultus, –a, –um

**succeed,** succēdō, –ere, –cessī, –cessus
**such,** tālis, –e; tantus, –a, –um
**suffer,** patior, patī, passus
**suffice,** sufficiō, –ere, –fēcī, –fectus
**summer,** aestās, –tātis, *f.*
**summon,** vocō, 1; convocō, 1
**supplies,** commeātus, –ūs, *m.*
**surpass,** superō, 1
**surrender,** mē dēdō, dēdere, dēdidī; trādō, –ere, –didī, –ditus
**surround,** circumsistō, –ere, –stetī, —
**survive,** supersum, –esse, –fuī, –futūrus
**suspect,** suspicor, 1
**swear,** iūrō, 1
**swiftly,** celeriter
**swim,** natō, 1

## T

**tablet (of the law),** tabula, –ae, *f.*
**take away,** adimō, –ere, adēmī, adēmptus
**talk,** loquor, loquī, locūtus
**tall,** altus, –a, –um
**task,** opus, operis, *n.*
**teach,** doceō, –ēre, docuī, doctus
**teacher,** magister, –trī, *m.*
**tell,** dīcō, –ere, dīxī, dictus
**temple,** templum, –ī, *n.*
**tempt,** temptō, 1
**tenant,** colōnus, –ī, *m.*
**terrible,** terribilis, –e
**terrify,** terreō, –ēre, terruī, territus
**territory,** fīnēs, –ium, *m. pl.*
**terror,** terror, –ōris, *m.*
**than,** quam
**thank,** grātiās agō, agere, ēgī, āctus
**that** (*dem. pron.*), ille, illa, illud; is, ea, id; (*conj.*), quod, ut; **so that,** ut; **that not,** nē;
**that, in order that, so that** (*conj.*), ut(ī); **that . . . not** (*purpose*), nē; (*result*), ut... nōn
**their** (*poss.*), eōrum, eārum, eōrum; (*reflex.*), suus, –a, –um
**themselves** (*reflex.*), suī; (*intens.*), ipsī, –ae, –a
**then,** tum
**they,** eī, eae, ea; illī, illae, illa; *often not expressed*
**thing,** rēs, reī, *f.; often not expressed*
**think,** putō, 1; existimō, 1; arbitror, 1
**third,** tertius, –a, –um
**this,** hic, haec, hoc; is, ea, id
**thousand,** mīlle; *pl.* mīlia
**threaten,** minitor, 1
**throw,** iaciō, –ere, iēcī, iactus; coniciō, –ere, –iēcī, –iectus; **throw down,** dēiciō, –ere, dēiēcī, deiectus; proiciō, –ere, –iēcī, –iectus
**thus,** ita
**time,** tempus, temporis, *n.*
**to,** ad, in, *w. acc.;* (*purpose*), ut
**toga,** toga, –ae, *f.*
**too,** quoque; *use comparative*
**too much,** nimius, –a, –um
**top (of),** summus, –a, –um
**torture,** cruciātus, –ūs, *m.*
**toward,** ad, *w. acc.*
**tower,** turris, –is, *f.*
**town,** oppidum, –ī, *n.*
**train,** instituō, –ere, instituī, institūtus
**Trajan,** Traiānus, –ī, *m.*
**travel,** iter faciō
**traveler,** viātor, –ōris, *m.*
**tribe,** gēns, gentis, *f.*
**troops,** cōpiae, –ārum, *f. pl.*
**trouble,** labor, –ōris, *m.*
**trust,** crēdō, –ere, crēdidī, crēditus
**truth,** vērum, –ī, *n.*
**try,** cōnor, 1
**tunic,** tunica, –ae, *f.*
**twenty,** vīgintī
**two,** duo, duae, duo

## U

**under,** sub, *w. abl.;* **under the direction of,** dux *or* prīnceps *in abl. abs.*
**understand,** intellegō, –ere, –lēxī, –lēctus
**unfriendly,** inimīcus, –a, –um
**unharmed,** incolumis, –e
**unless,** nisi
**unlike,** dissimilis, –e
**until,** dum
**unwilling (be),** nōlō, nōlle, nōluī, —
**unworthy,** indignus, –a, –um

**urge,** hortor, 1; impellō, –ere, impulī, impulsus
**use,** ūtor, ūtī, ūsus (*w. abl.*)

## V

**various,** varius, –a, –um
**verse,** versus, –ūs, *m.*
**very,** *use superlative;* **very many,** plūrimī, –ae, –a
**victory,** victōria, –ae, *f.*
**villa,** vīlla, –ae, *f.*
**village,** vīcus, –ī, *m.*
**Vergil,** Vergilius, –lī, *m.*

## W

**wage war,** bellum gerō, –ere, gessī, gestus
**wait,** exspectō, 1
**walk,** ambulō, 1
**want,** volō, velle, voluī, —
**war,** bellum, –ī, *n.*
**warn,** moneō, –ēre, monuī, monitus
**waste,** cōnsūmō, –ere, –sūmpsī, –sūmptus
**water,** aqua, –ae, *f.*
**wave,** unda, –ae, *f.*
**way,** via, –ae, *f.*
**we,** nōs, nostrī; *often not expressed*
**wealth,** opēs, opum, *f. pl.*
**weapon,** tēlum, –ī, *n.;* **weapons,** tēlā, –ōrum, *n. pl.*
**wear,** gerō, –ere, gessī, gestus
**wearied,** dēfessus, –a, –um
**wedding,** nūptiae, –ārum, *f. pl.*
**weep,** fleō, flēre, flēvī, flētus
**well,** bene
**well (be),** valeō –ēre, valuī, validus
**what** (*pron*), quis, quid; (*adj.*), quī, quae, quod
**when,** ubi; cum; *expressed by participle or abl. abs.*
**where in the world,** ubinam gentium
**whether,** utrum
**which** (*rel. pron.*), quī, quae, quod; **which (of two),** uter, utra, utrum
**while,** dum
**who** (*rel. pron.*), quī, quae, quod; (*interrog. pron.*), quis, quid
**whole,** tōtus, –a, –um
**wholesome,** salūbris, –e
**why,** cūr
**wicked,** nefārius, –a, –um
**wife,** uxor, –ōris, *f.*
**will,** testāmentum, –ī, *n.*
**willing (be),** volō, velle, voluī, —; **be unwilling,** nōlō, nōlle, nōluī, —
**win,** capiō, –ere, cēpī, captus; vincō, –ere, vīcī, victus; mereō, –ēre, meruī, meritus
**window,** fenestra, –ae, *f.*
**winter,** hiems, hiemis, *f.*
**wisely,** sapienter
**wish,** (*noun*), voluntās, –tātis, *f.,* cupiō, –ere, –īvī, –ītus; (*verb*), volō, velle, voluī, —; **wish not,** nōlō, nōlle, nōluī, —
**with,** cum, *w. abl.; sometimes abl. alone*
**withdraw,** concēdō, –ere, –cessī, –cessus; discēdō, –ere, –cessī, –cessus
**without,** sine, *w. abl.*
**woe,** dolor, –ōris, *m.*
**woman,** mulier, –eris, *f.;* fēmina, –ae, *f.*
**wonder,** mīror, 1
**word,** verbum, –ī, *n.*
**work** (*noun*), labor, –ōris, *m.;* opus, operis, *n.;* (*verb*), labōrō, 1
**worship,** colō, –ere, coluī, cultus
**world,** mundus, –ī, *m.;* **where in the world,** ubinam gentium
**worthwhile,** operae pretium
**worthy,** dignus, –a, –um
**write,** scrībō, –ere, scrīpsī, scrīptus
**writing,** scrīptum, –ī, *n.*

## Y

**year,** annus, –ī, *m.*
**yield,** cēdō, –ere, cessī, cessus; concēdō, –ere, –cessī, –cessus
**you,** tū (*sing.*); tuī, vōs (*pl.*); *often not expressed*
**young man,** adulēscēns, –entis; iuvenis, –is, *m.*
**your,** tuus, –a, –um; **yourself** (*reflex.*), tuī
**youth,** adulēscēns, –entis, *m.*

# SUBJECT INDEX

## C



## D

# GRAMMAR/VOCABULARY INDEX